Modernologies
Contemporary Artists Researching
Modernity and Modernism

Modernologies
Contemporary Artists Researching
Modernity and Modernism

Modernologies
Contemporary Artists Researching Modernity and Modernism

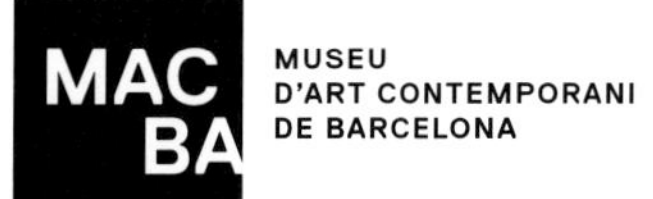

Contents

Artists and works

Foreword

The title of this exhibition as well as the catalogue that accompanies it makes us think about two basic premises. The first involves the fact that we can now discuss modernity academically as both a historic period and an ideological project. This creates a new field of study that may not yield scientific knowledge but does produce objective conclusions. The second tenet is that modernity is now a plural topic of study: in other words, we speak of different modernities, in terms of both their composition and their expressions.

Modernologies also contributes to a paradigmatic debate during the transition from the twentieth century to the twenty first: a debate that involves the question as to whether the historical period of modernity along with its ideological and aesthetic canons has ended, as many claim, or if, as others argue, we are still immersed in the modern. The works of a young generation of artists — mostly from Central Europe, especially the Anglo-Saxon and Germanic regions — have made us reflect on what, at the beginning of this new century, moves the spirit behind the political, cultural, ideological and aesthetic evolution of the past three hundred years (if not more). The modern project is manifest in different ways and from different perspectives, and it is evident that these do not coincide in time. Similarly, there is no consensus on the roots, trunk and branches of the ins and outs of modernity.

While aesthetic modernity is not an expression of the other facets of the modern project, it does depend on that project. And the art of the last sixty years, as we have seen, is not only — or we could say, 'is no longer' — the result of aesthetic intentions and projects. It entails motivations and consequences that go beyond the problem of beauty, though one of modernity's concerns is to rid artistic practice of the monopoly on aesthetic production. The confluence of art and daily life, as forwarded by theorists and artists since the end of the nineteenth century, involves the intervention of design as we now know it. Like advertising, fashion, architecture and graphic design, the industrial production of objects could have embraced the idea of beauty. In conjunction with the obstinate efficacy of industrial production and the mass media, design took art everywhere, obliging it to invent new ecosystems to inhabit. The search for these ecosystems and for the grammatical links between them is the concern of the recent historical revision manifest in the works of some thirty artists from diverse contexts. In this way we are putting to the test art's capacity to bring together apparently unrelated historical narratives and traditions, and make them coexist. Is it still possible to think of a universal language, one immune to the impositions of authorities or beliefs? How can we conceive of the universalist spirit of modern artistic practice, the idea of the *tabula rasa*, beyond economic globalisation and its consequences? Can we really recognise how 'the other'— who is both producer and recipient — contributes to the very notion of the modern project? Is it feasible to speak of post-colonialism when we are witnesses to present-day colonisations?

At the same time, *Modernologies* moves us towards a genealogy of the interest of contemporary artists in what lies at the root of art's autonomy, one of the defining features of modern art. This autonomy is based on the premise that the artist is no longer commissioned to create a work; the work is therefore not an instrument of something beyond the artist's production, but rather reflects solely the author's own desire and purpose. Contemporary art is the heir to modern art, but it has overcome certain guiding principles of modernity. In 1968, Roland Barthes published 'The Death of the Author', in which he described a radical shift in the very essence of cultural productions. The work does not culminate in the limits of the artistic object or product; instead, it lies in the hands of the recipient. Though the author disappears, authorship does not: what disappears is authority — that authority that certain institutions had hoped to inherit. The institutionalisation of the avant-garde and the different returns-to-order disguised as fashions or as dominant tastes, 'official' art and public art policy, obliges us to once again question the modern spirit as well as its opponents or antagonists. 'Machine made' and 'handmade' are no longer exclusive categories; in times of clear unsustainability, industry is more suspicious than liberating. And artists question their role: should they produce more images to be tossed into the great river of excess information and consumption, or should they put forth the antidotes and the tools for resistance, understanding, comprehension and action?

Bartomeu Marí
Director
Museu d'Art Contemporani de Barcelona

Introduction

Through a selection of artistic undertakings, this project sets out to explore modernity as a promising sociopolitical movement that was aspiring to cultivate a universal language. It was predicated on industrialisation and technology, on the principles of human rights and democracy, on the right to self-determination, on the principle of education for all, on secularisation and Enlightenment philosophy, and above all on the underlying notion of progress and continual development. Art disengaged from the immediate functional relationship with its former patrons, the Church and the aristocracy, and instead became committed to the ideology of autonomy. As part of this movement, the arts were accordingly required not only to portray modern life in appropriate forms but also to explore the utopian potential of modernity, along with the destructive, regressive facets of revolution and upheaval. Modernism attempted to represent the experiences and ramifications of modernity through artistic forms — and in so doing almost even became postmodern.

Such promises of a better and more alluring world are juxtaposed with considerations problematising modernity as concept and project, defining a fundamental critique of its rhetoric and conditions. Modernity was neither induced by Western imperial projects, nor by colonialism in particular, but these proved constitutive for its development, forming the 'darker and hidden face', as Walter D. Mignolo proposes in this 'European narrative'. Jacques Rancière, in turn, postulates an 'aesthetic regime of art', the prevailing 'indifference' of which goes back to the democratic principle of a radical demand for equality. Moreover, Bruno Latour asserts that we 'have never been modern' because the strict dichotomy governing nature and society in the scope of modernity never came to be resolved. And Jürgen Habermas is well known for his conceptualisation of modernity as an unfinished project.

Modernity is a popular topos for analyses and reflections of a largely controversial nature. As such, numerous theories have been put forth about both the beginning and the end of modernity, which has marked a process of radical change in all spheres of life. While early formulations of 'modern life' can be recognised in Romanticism, primarily in its literature, the events decisive for the development of modernity in political as well as aesthetic contexts are considered to be, according to art historian T. J. Clark, the French Revolution and the first public exhibiting of a painting on the occasion of the public viewing of Marat's murdered body in Paris. The emergence of totalitarian regimes in Europe, especially in Germany during National Socialism and the Holocaust, signify the decline of modernity in individual, societal and political domains. The end of modernity has long had a specific point of reference: architecture theorist Charles Jencks established a precise moment in time for the 'death of modern architecture', namely 3:32 pm on 15 July 1972. At this very instant, the Pruitt-Igoe residential blocks in St Louis were being demolished, and the collapse of modernity was thereby conceded, so to speak, literally making room for the 'language of postmodernity'. Since the collapse of both World Trade Center towers in New York City on 11 September 2001, a picture of the actual costs of modernity, of the relationship between globalisation and violence, has become apparent for some. Non-synchrony and divergent conceptions — both in the definition of modernity as epoch, as style, as societal form, as model of production and in the insight gained through postcolonial studies — have led in recent years to a consensus on the notion of 'multiple modernities'.

It seems to be no accident that artists of a younger generation are, in their works, increasingly dealing with the legacy and the promises of modernity and modernism, with the failure of the utopia — that they are searching for possible redefinitions and actualisations and are indeed posing questions about the state of the modernity of our society. This has come about in light of the re-emergence of reactionary thinking in society and politics, of a renewed functionalisation of art by the market strategists employed by global corporations, which in turn use their economic imperialism to relegate economically disadvantaged countries back to pre-modern conditions, and of the all-commanding role still played by the art market today despite recent symptoms of crisis.

Modernologies aims to critically investigate individual approaches to this artistic exploration, with the point of departure here always remaining the perspective of the respective artists on this topic area. Unfolding before us, therefore, is a kind of map composed of new viewpoints and narratives about modernity and modernism, yet most notably about the constitution of our modernity and the immanent conflicts and contradictions therein.

In the accompanying publication, this project of a 'mapping of the critique of modernity' is extended in two directions through essays by Cornelia Klinger and Walter D. Mignolo, with the first exploring the ideology of aesthetic modernity including the principles of autonomy, authenticity, and alterity, and the second delving into interrelationships between modernity and coloniality. The latter topic is one that continues to determine the content and appropriation of those conventional concepts still governing museums and collections today. Augmenting the many images and relevant texts on the artists and their works, several of the artists themselves have expressed their current stances on the subject matter at hand in short statements compiled and edited by André Rottmann.

Sabine Breitwieser
Curator of the exhibition

Modernologies –
Or What Makes Contemporary Artists Investigate Modernity and Modernism

Sabine Breitwieser

1 Michel Foucault, 'What is Critique?', in Sylvère Lotringer and Lysa Hochroth (eds.), *The Politics of Truth*, New York: Semiotext(e), 1997, pp. 55–56.

2 Jacques Rancière, «Von den Regimen der Künste und der mäßigen Relevanz des Begriffs der Moderne», *Die Aufteilung des Sinnlichen. Die Politik der Kunst und ihre Paradoxien*, Berlin: bbooks, 2008. p. 41. English version: 'Artistic Regimes and the Shortcomings of the Notion of Modernity', *The Politics of Aesthetics: The Distribution of the Sensible*, New York: Continuum, 2004, p. 24.

'It is neither inner experience, nor the fundamental structures of scientific knowledge. It is also not a group of historical contents elaborated elsewhere, treated by historians and received as ready-made facts. Actually, in this historical-philosophical practice, one has to make one's own history, fabricate history, as if through fiction, in terms of how it would be traversed by the question of the relationships between structures of rationality which articulate true discourse and the mechanisms of subjugation which are linked to it. This is evidently a question which displaces the historical objects familiar to historians towards the problem of the subject and the truth about which historians are not usually concerned.'
— Michel Foucault, 'What is Critique?' [1]

I. Which questions should be asked

Point of departure for this exhibition is an obvious artistic interest in — and associated practice of — the exploration of modernity. Over the past three decades, this thematic focus has not only been found in numerous examples of artistic production, but also in related discourse, exhibition projects and publications. Countless and very diverse undertakings have been dedicated to the attempt to apprehend, to grasp, modernity and its ramifications. In the last ten to fifteen years, this aim has once again been pursued by a younger generation of artists in an especially intensive manner. The referencing of events and the appropriation of forms and symbols of modernity — be it photographic documents of modern buildings (often in 'exotic', remote locations and usually in a state of neglect or even devastation), the revisiting of geometric abstractions or the recycling of symbols of modern popular culture — seem to have, in recent years, become part of an established formal canon in contemporary art, yes, even almost a platitude of artistic methodologies. Not seldom has the impression arisen that artists are calling for the return to earlier utopian ideas, thereby slipping into a state of nostalgia — without, however, calling into question the issue of failure that has frequently been proclaimed in postmodernity, namely the apparent dishonouring of onetime promises of modernity. Or without having questioned the implications of this 'aesthetic regime of the arts', which — in the words of the oft-quoted Jacques Rancière — 'is the true name for what is designated by the incoherent label "modernity"... [which] in its different versions... [is] the concept that diligently works at masking the specificity of this regime of the arts and the very meaning of the specificity of regimes of art'.[2]

What is it that, at first glance, moves contemporary artists to be less apt to commit themselves to the role of innovators and founders of totally new movements, forms and ideas through their work, declining to assert themselves as

3 Mark Lewis, 'Is Modernity our Antiquity?', *Documenta Magazine*, no. 1, Cologne, 2007. Available online at http://magazines.documenta.de.

4 Ibid.

5 Ibid.

reformers in the art world? Instead they have been more inclined to assume the role of re-interpreters and translators of already existing rhetorics of modernity, to operate as critics of its historicisation, reappropriating the grammar of modernism, albeit with new explorative aspects. How is the relationship of artists to the promises and forms of modernity represented, and in which manner can this historical epoch be critically reflected in artworks, or even become subject to a re-evaluation?

In the *Documenta Magazine,* no. 1 entitled 'Modernity?', in allusion to Charles Baudelaire and T. J. Clark and addressing the question 'Is Modernity our Antiquity?', Canadian artist and art critic Mark Lewis describes in his essay of the same title the allure exerted on him by a small, modernist apartment building in a park on the outskirts of Vancouver. Even though he has 'taken hundreds of photographs and hours of video footage', he is still not sure whether he is 'any closer to knowing what to do with this building' than when he 'first saw it five years ago'.[3] He notes that his 'fixation or compulsion' with the building didn't begin until he had moved away to England, where hard-to-find modernist architecture enjoyed a 'rather battered and neglected' reputation, and that he had ended up becoming a 'foreigner in my own town' of Vancouver. Continuing to reflect on his point of interest, Lewis ultimately comes to the conclusion that it is indeed the disintegration and decay of 'these recently past forms' that entices him, remarking how 'the artistic signs and images of emerging and developing modernity are rapidly becoming historical', and that we therefore 'can no longer fully identify with them'.[4]

This is not the appropriate moment to enter into a more detailed discussion on Lewis's analysis of his initial question and on other considerations put forth by him, for, while certainly of substantive significance, in my opinion these do not demonstrate pivotal relevance to the exhibition project at hand. Expounding on his stance furthermore appears, in my view, almost too symptomatic to facilitate the freezing of a particular depiction sketched by modernity. In contrast, I would at this point like to turn to other explorative questions, such as, for instance, the reasons behind the composition of the building rendered by Lewis, which is 'almost already an image' comprised of 'cubic forms, the mixed and contradictory volumes that are created through compelling and vital montage' — touching on that which, in his opinion, 'these buildings already articulate against their respective backgrounds', for which reason he felt compelled to make it the subject of a photographic study. Of significant interest here is the question as to which people used to live in this modernist apartment building, and what meaning these forms originally held and what they stand for today — as well as why the utilisation of the building is no longer feasible today, and what induced those responsible to block the once '"exclusive" views of the surrounding ocean and mountains' with new buildings, which were 'built in front of the simpler modern structures of the nineteen-fifties and sixties'.[5]

Another example of modernist architecture — specifically an abandoned socialistic structure from the 1960s in Leipzig — inspired Austrian artist Dorit Margreiter to create her multipart installation *zentrum* (2006). She by no means allows herself to engage in, or be seduced into, documenting the building, which had fallen victim to dilapidation and soon faced demolition, in its aesthetic as such. Margreiter instead brings up questions about the role of aesthetic media in relation to the manifestations of modernism. Which aesthetic strategies does the modernist design of this one-storey building represent? And which social and political concepts was it thus supporting or propagating? By example of the neon lettering '*brühlzentrum*' (Brühl centre) on the building, the artist strives to typify these questions through

6 Alexandre Astruc, «Die Geburt einer neuen Avantgarde: die Kamera als Federhalter» in Theodor Kotulla (ed.), Der Film. Vol. 2, Munich: Piper Verlag, 1964. English version: 'The Birth of a New Avant-Garde: La Camera-Stylo', in *The New Wave*, Peter Graham (ed.), Garden City, NY: Doubleday, 1968, pp. 17–23. Cited in James Monaco, *How to Read a Film*, Oxford: Oxford University Press, 2000, p. 409. Many thanks to Werner Kaligofsky for this pointer.

7 Ibid., p. 410.

8 The exhibition title I selected, *Modernologies*, goes back to a reference made by artist Florian Pumhösl. In his work *Modernology (Triangular Atelier)* (2007), the space of which was newly produced for this exhibition after documenta 12, Pumhösl in his title is citing Kon Wajirō's established methodology of *Modernologio*.

9 See Tom Gill, 'Kon Wajirō, Modernologist', *Japan Quarterly*, April–June 1996, pp. 198ff.

a work-in-progress. Through a digital colour video, Margreiter also time and again demonstrates, on a case-by-case basis, the preparations for her production, the application of reflective foil onto the no-longer-functional neon tubes that cover the large letters. The video documentary of the nocturnal activation of this mise-en-scène, where the modernist lettering was once again briefly brought to light with the aid of two camera spotlights, is copied by Margreiter into analogue format and presented in the exhibition space as a grainy 16 mm black-and-white film in an endless loop. Margreiter configures the typography *zentrum*, which is openly available on the Internet, more as a continuation of the modernist lettering than as a copy or homage. What makes this artistic exploration of modernity so productive is that here the memory of a societal process of reformation, one that is dying out, is continuing to be maintained through a revival of earlier symbols. Reinstating the role of aesthetic media in this process — namely that of abstract film, involving design and typography and the transgression of media — also opens up perspectives for future options such as, for example, those presented by the Internet today.

In an approach fundamentally similar to that of Mark Lewis, British artist Runa Islam selected — for her 35 mm film installation *Empty the pond to get the fish.* (2008) — a means for her exploration of a forsaken modernist building in which the mind and the photographic camera repeatedly frequent the object in question. Yet evidently she, in the concrete realisation, meticulously adhered to critic and filmmaker Alexandre Astruc's 1948 prediction that cinema would 'gradually break free from the tyranny of what is visual, from the image for its own sake, from the immediate and concrete demands of the narrative, to become a means of writing just as flexible and subtle as written language'.[6] Astruc called for a new era of cinema, the era of the 'camera-stylo', a more complex demand than previous ones that had called for a 'language' of cinema. In her film study on the deserted building designed by the modernist Austrian architect Karl Schwanzer, Runa Islam in fact does, with her film camera, 'write ideas directly on film without even having to resort to those heavy associations of images that were the delight of silent cinema.'[7] In Islam's filmic staging of this former pavilion at the 1958 World Expo in Brussels, which was later adapted as the 'Museum of the 20th Century' in Vienna, the anti-narrative experiences, however, a process of renewal with the film camera as main protagonist in that the modernist film method is being translated back into the visual and the building itself is metamorphosing, so to speak, into the film apparatus.

II. Modernologists

The improvised dwellings along with the creativity of those having survived the great earthquake, which levelled to the ground large sections of Tokyo and its vicinity in the 1920s, are what inspired Japanese architect and anthropologist Kon Wajirō (1888–1973)[8] to start applying his archaeological method, previously used only on ruins of ancient cities, to the present. Similar to 'modernus' (from the Latin *modo*) being known to mean 'now', 'current' or 'recent', Wajirō defined his *kōkogaku* (archaeology) as *kōgengaku* or *Modernologio*,[9] as a new method that he applied to all facets of present-day life in parallel to the reconstruction of the city — and, what's more, ultimately to everyday modern life in general. Wajirō solely investigated the *visible* — buildings, clothing, objects — and instigated studies covering topics ranging from the gender-specific frequenting of toilet facilities, to circulation routes in floor plans of Japanese flats, to even include behavioural patterns in shopping areas.

10 See Florian Pumhösl in pp. 186–191 of this volume.

11 Serge Guilbaut, 'The Relevance of Modernism', in Benjamin H. D. Buchloh, Serge Guilbaut and David Solkin (eds.), *Modernism and Modernity: The Vancouver Conference Papers*, Halifax: The Press of Nova Scotia College of Art and Design, 1983 (2004 edition), p. XIII.

12 See Andrea Fraser in pp. 84–89 of this volume.

This scientific method is not intended to epitomise the artistic practice of the works and projects introduced here. But what they do have in common is a critical investigation and questioning of certain moments and aspects of modernity and modernism, especially in view of their current significance. While modernity is characterised by the detachment of the arts from the sciences, here we are tracing a concept of artistic practice that — as Florian Pumhösl has worded it for himself — can be understood 'as an open alternative to museology… as a vessel for the cultural transfer of symbols'[10] that virtually accommodates our utilisation-geared society through appropriation, through the cross-referencing of other areas. The focus of this project is also reflected in the words of Serge Guilbaut, who lectured at the 'Modernism and Modernity' conference in Vancouver in 1983: 'Instead we concentrated on one area which seemed to be the keystone of any modernist procedure: its critical/subversive stance, the negative side of a new culture which based its realizations on a coefficient of resistance to the prevailing system.'[11]

Constituting the focus of this exhibition project is a selection of artists with works and projects that delve into the conditions, constraints and consequences of modernity and modernism, including their historicisation, and that accordingly field questions pertaining to the present and the future. In addition to the formulation of pure critique, suggestions for redeterminations will be put forth, and sometimes even ideas for possible actualisations of individual issues in connection with virulent topic areas will be hashed out. In fact, some artists even proceed as if they were researchers of modern life, thus providing us with an up-to-date picture of the world and of how it to-date represents itself to us through its modernity-related conflicts and contradictions. This naturally also includes those conflicts that have become, as it were, inscribed within artistic practice in relation to the ideology of modernity, especially regarding the claim to autonomy, and that have attained the status of myth. This has been described as 'the endless repetition of these scenes of martyrdom and interment of our radical aspirations' by Andrea Fraser in connection with her video installation *Soldadera* (1998/2001). Against the arranged setting of a split projection screen and respectively allocated film scenes showing the dual role embodied by Fraser, both as an insurgent farmer and as a curator at The Museum of Modern Art in New York, Fraser problematises the arising conflicts not only as the experiencing of failure due to external parameters but above all within a 'structure of internal conflicts' of modernism and the avant-garde that artists are experiencing.[12]

In actuality, the image of the modern artist, or even of the scientific researcher, does not always fit to the myth of modernity, and those failing to equate with conventional ideas on revolutionary, utopian visions or with the formal canon will have no place in popular historiography. In her project *Zofia Stryjeńska* (2008), Paulina Olowska — implementing enlarged, black-and-white reproductions (in the medium of painting) of paintings by the eponymous Polish artist, Stryjeńska (1891–1974) — struggles against the classification of her works from the 1920s and 1930s as naive and folkloric. As an artist in the third generation after Stryjeńska, Olowska puts up for discussion a totally new evaluation of her work, that is, of the criteria of modernism as such. In recent years a marginalisation based on criteria of gender-related or geographic background has become a point of focus in numerous projects aiming to close gaps in the social and geographic world map with 'other modernities', inviting criticism based on the underlying hegemonic mindset. Armando Andrade Tudela introduces his vocabulary of a — as he terms it — contemporary

13 *Modernisme Noir: Revisionen der Moderne in der zeitgenössischen Kunst*, seminar by Gerd Blum and Johan Frederik Hartle in the summer of 2008 at the Academy of Fine Arts Münster. My thanks are extended to Hildegund Amanshauser for bringing this research project to my attention.

14 Gerd Blum, Johan Frederik Hartle, 'Modernisme noir. Revisionen des Modernismus in der zeitgenössischen Kunst' in Christoph Bertsch, Silvia Höller (eds.), *Cella. Strukturen der Ausgrenzung und Disziplinierung*, Academy of Art in Rome, 2009, Studienverlag Innsbruck, Vienna, Munich, 2010, p. 97 (forthcoming).

15 See Alice Creischer and Andreas Siekmann in pp. 58–65 of this volume.

16 Walter Benjamin, *Das Kunstwerk im Zeitalter seiner technische Reproduzierbarkeit*, Frankfurt: Suhrkamp, 1963/1977, p. 19. English version: *The Work of Art in the Age of Its Technological Reproducibility, and Other Writings on Media*, Cambridge, MA: Belknap Press, 2008, p. 25.

17 James Monaco, *How to Read a Film*, Oxford: Oxford University Press, 2000, p. 409.

'Peruvian modernism' as a typology of Constructivist small-scale sculptures and objects made of everyday materials, including asphalt, polycarbonate, rattan wickerwork and a *Tropicalismo* record cover, and confronts us with photographs of the abstract, geometric symbols on Pan-Americana Highway trucks. In so doing, rather than working on a redetermination of the morphology of sculpture or of painting, he is instead venturing a 'homeless abstraction' (Clement Greenberg), as it were, the abstraction of a new socio-geographical localisation.

'But is not the artist as translator at the same time an accomplice?'[13] — this question was put forward by Gerd Blum and Johan Frederik Hartle in a research project on the methodology of a conceptual critique of modernity employing instruments of modernity, of 'retro-modernism' as they call it, which is founded on a 'complicity of capitalistic modernity and artistic modernism'[14], expressing its discontent through references to 'surveillance, capital investment, and war' and therefore ultimately being characterised as 'modernisme noir'.

Alice Creischer and Andreas Siekmann actually speak of a 'militant investigation'[15] in reference to one of their open projects created through various collaborative constellations, where individual pages of the *Atlas Gesellschaft und Wirtschaft* (Atlas of Society and Economy), developed in 1929–30 by philosopher of science and economist Otto Neurath together with artist Gerd Arntz, were 'updated'. Here they primarily address topic areas that go hand in hand with the globalisation and privatisation of the public domain. As part of a workshop in the scope of the exhibition, for example, a new page is being created on the development of soy farming as a current translation of the issue, taken from the historical page, of the role of natural rubber in the nineteenth century. In their artistic practice, Creischer/Siekmann reference the political potential of abstraction and 'a leftist, revolutionary self-conception' that was related to these pictorial statistics in terms of the ethics of rationalisation, technology and modernity.

In approaching a critique of modernity employing instruments of modernity — that is, by means of abstraction, rationality, seriality — the application of new media must also be considered here in the sense of a belief in technical progress. In this context, Walter Benjamin's analyses of 'technological reproducibility' warrant mentioning, according to which the 'whole social function of art is revolutionized. Instead of being founded on ritual, it is based on a different practice: politics.'[16] Of general interest here is the reality of modern space, of modernity — a claim that, according to André Bazin, cinema can assert, as opposed to the theatrical stage, which we can equate with the exhibition space. To once again bring up an example already touched on above from a different but related field: the filmmakers of *Nouvelle Vague* not only contributed as critics through their text contributions in *Cahiers du Cinéma* to the development of a theory of critical practice, they also belonged to the first generation of cineastes whose work was substantiated in the history of cinema and in film theory. Their films, especially those by Jean-Luc Godard, were not only practical examples contributing to the theory but themselves often constituted theoretical essays. Ten years after Alexandre Astruc, they realised — similar to how Runa Islam revisited this as mentioned above — his filmic visions and '[f]or the first time, film theory was being written in film rather than print'.[17]

III. Modern times

'Not until modernity once and for all abandons the relational determination of the respectively new, present-day, and current will the age of modernity attain a sense

18 Cornelia Klinger, 'Modern/
Moderne/Modernismus', *Ästhetische
Grundbegriffe*, vol. 4, *Medien – Populär*,
Stuttgart: J. B. Metzler, 2002, p. 147.

19 Ibid., p. 130.

20 Fredric Jameson, *A Singular
Modernity: Essay on the Ontology of
the Present*, New York and London:
Verso, 2002, p. 31.

21 Ibid., p. 32.

22 Ibid., p. 99 (emphasis added).

23 John Rydon, 'Modern art will fall
to bits', *Daily Express*, London, 15 March
1960.

24 Gustav Metzger, 'Manifesto Auto-
Destructive Art (Second Manifesto,
1960)', in Sabine Breitwieser (ed.),
Gustav Metzger: History History, Vienna
and Ostfildern-Ruit: Hatje Cantz, 2005,
p. 104.

25 Metzger, 'Auto-Destructive Art,
Machine Art, Auto-Creative Art
(Third Manifesto, 1961)', in Sabine
Breitwieser, *Gustav Metzger*, p. 113.

of contour as an age. The epoch that roused the concept of the epoch becomes tangible in and of itself, meaning it reflects upon itself, namely upon the conditions of its potentiality.'[18] Philosopher Cornelia Klinger goes on to reflect upon the dynamic and constitutive role of time: 'The modern age is no longer simply a different, new time, but rather it has developed, as compared to the foregoing one, an alternate conception of time, of its progression and context.'[19] Consequently, for the first time a historical consciousness has emerged — a reflection on times past, on *the* history, which just as *the* revolution or *the* progress has 'advanced to the collective singular' as superordinate to instances of the individual. On the other hand, as Frederic Jameson has in turn determined, the state of '"[m]odernity" always means setting a date and positing a beginning'.[20] Hence, characterising the temporal and historical context of the exhibition and the perspectives and narratives of the modern, modernism and modernity that it explores, as analysed here, also proves essential in this case. In my methodology, in which I sequentially set several temporal anchor points, I address Jameson's suggestion of operating less from a scientific than from a sociological concept of modernity and, in fact, with 'narrative options and alternative… possibilities'[21] for storytelling (or 'historytelling'). It should be mentioned here that I am in this respect fundamentally guided by his conceptual differentiation between '*modernity* as the new historical situation, *modernization* as the process whereby we get there, and *modernism* as a reaction to that situation and that process alike'.[22]

The oldest artistic contribution to the exhibition stems from the year 1960. It deals with an architectural model used to illustrate the (yet unrealised) project of an *Auto-Destructive Monument* by Gustav Metzger. Headlined with 'Modern art will fall to bits', London's *Daily Express* reported that 'Gustav Metzger has devised something most people will applaud — a form of modern art which will disintegrate within a certain period of time'.[23] In 1959 the artist, who is also an activist for anti-nuclear and environmental issues, had already published his first *Manifesto Auto-Destructive Art*, followed a year later by his second, in which he advocated an art depicted (in excerpts) as follows: 'Not interested in ruins, (the picturesque)… demonstrates man's power to accelerate disintegrative processes of nature and to order them… mirrors the compulsive perfectionism of arms manufacture — polishing to destruction point… the transformation of technology into public art.' And finally an art that 'contains within itself an agent which automatically leads to its destruction within a period of time not to exceed twenty years'.[24] Likewise about twenty years after he (as a twelve-year-old) and his brother emigrated from Nuremberg to England, Gustav Metzger put to words his take on art for the modern industrial society, and it couldn't be more radically phrased: 'an attack on capitalist values and the drive to nuclear annihilation.'[25]

Viewed from a different perspective, the exhibition's most dated work is actually from 1913, that is, from the period preceding the October Revolution, shortly before the First World War: a photograph of the avant-garde artist group мишень (The Target Group or Donkey's Tail Group) from Moscow that is frequently used to represent the group and depicts six group members, five of whom are male. On what is supposed to be the caption on the adjacent wall label, Austrian artist Anna Artaker juxtaposes this photograph with the names of other female artists in the group: Aleksandra Ekster, Liubov Popova, Olga Rozanova, an 'unknown' artist, as well as Varvara Stepanova and Nadezhda Udaltsova. The historicisation of modernity facilitated by image production confronts us here with the phenomenon of marginalisation,

26 See Walter D. Mignolo's essay on this topic in this publication.

27 The research project *Arizona* by Austrian-Bosnian architect and artist Azra Aksamija, which deals with the transformation of the eponymous black market on the road to Sarajevo into a city with a self-created social and economic hierarchy, takes up (though against a completely different background) similar issues. See Sabine Breitwieser (ed.), *Designs for the Real World*, Vienna and Cologne: Walther König, 2002.

28 Serge Guilbaut, *How New York Stole the Idea of Modern Art: Abstract Expressionism, Freedom, and the Cold War*, Chicago and London: University of Chicago Press, 1983.

namely the exclusion of others, in this case of numerous female artists, who have only seldom (or even never) been granted entrance into the canonised historiography of modernity. The open series of works *Unbekannte Avantgarde* (Unknown Avant-garde, 2008) by Artaker at present encompasses ten artist movements and groups — including Dada (1922), Bauhaus (1926), CoBrA (1949), along with the Situationist International (1960) and the Austria Film Coop (1968) — thus perpetuating various chapters of modernity inasmuch as it makes visible its blind spots, hereby contributing to a rewriting of history.

Postcolonial theorists place the dawn of modernity in the sixteenth century, linking it, in other words, with the 'invention' (Enrique Dussel) of America and of colonisation, which made it possible for the hegemonic countries in Europe to make use of the newly discovered continent, its resources, and residents for their expansionist political objectives. The 'darker and hidden face of modernity', as Walter D. Mignolo calls it, without which the glamorous, reformist side would never have existed, is the reason why coloniality is to be viewed as 'constitutive'[26] for modernity. Dussel introduced the notion of 'trans-modernity', with which the interaction and the imbalance of power are emphasised, and which, at the same time, is also said to be more strongly geared toward a global future spawning different formulations of modernity. The extent to which regions located outside of the European hubs of power, like North Africa, were used by colonial powers as testing fields for modernisation projects and modernist fantasies is brought to light by the research and exhibition project *In the Desert of Modernity: Colonial Planning and After* (2008–09), initiated by Marion von Osten in collaboration with architects, artists, activists, theorists and filmmakers. This project particularly illustrates the level of reciprocal dependence and influence that existed — how European architects, in the course of their work in North Africa, appropriated the local flavour of shantytown architecture, such as the so-called *bidonvilles*, into their own work, integrating it into modern concepts like those of the *Habitat* and thereby finding a way to further develop their own visions. These structures were in fact housing a high percentage of migrants, so it can therefore be assumed that their migration-related experiences, indeed their entire background, were inscribed in the development of colonial modern architecture.[27]

It has long ceased to be a secret that the success story of American Abstract Expressionism was tied to the Cold War and to specific political strategies for the establishment and safeguarding of the hegemonic position assumed by the United States. Serge Guilbaut's critically revamped and hence redrafted history of American modernity in the 1950s[28] not only harbours a reference to a spy thriller in its title but also reads as such. Exclusion factors that were exerted through the success of this campaign related not only to Paris as the former art centre of the world but also more closely to the reception and recognition of art, barely present if at all, in the countries behind the Iron Curtain since the years following the Second World War. The extent to which the former socialist countries themselves contributed to the repression and forfeiture of their own history is conveyed by Croatian artist David Maljkovic's longtime interest in the project on socialist modernity in former Yugoslavia, based on the example of sculptor Vojin Bakić. The project entailing a re-evaluation of socialist modernism — in particular of the correspondence between the universalism of modernism and the universalism of a societal emancipation — is shared by the artist with the curator collective WHW (What, How and for Whom) of Zagreb, with Maljkovic detailing it as follows: 'I was not interested so much

29 David Maljkovic in an email to the author, 25 March 2009.

30 For more information, see Thomas Assauer's article 'Piraten der neuen Welt' (Pirates of the New World) at http://www.zeit.de/2001/40/200140_terrorismus.xml (accessed 6 May 2009).

31 Jean Baudrillard, *L'esprit du terrorisme*, Paris: Galilée, 2002, p. 28. The Spirit of Terrorism', Rachel Bloul (trans.), *Le Monde*, 2 November 2001. Also available online at http://www.egs.edu/faculty/baudrillard/baudrillard-the-spirit-of-terrorism.html (accessed 26 May 2009).

in the phenomenon of modernism in Yugoslavia and Croatia in a general sense, my motivation was to attempt to create new platforms on the ruins of existing grounds.'[29] In his new 16 mm film *Retired Form* (2008), Maljkovic shows us one of Bakić's geometric steel sculptures that was erected in 1968 at the Dotrscina memorial park in Zagreb commemorating the victims of the Second World War. The figure of Bakić represents an ambivalent position, for he is, on the one hand, considered to be an authentic, modernist sculptor who broke ties with social realism and fought for the independence of art, but he also operated as a 'state artist' in the service of socialist ideology. With the re-emergence of nationalism and anti-communism in the 1990s, Bakić's sculptures were no longer valued and consequently came into disrepair or were even destroyed. In Maljkovic's film, the large geometric sculpture glistens in renewed splendour, and several elderly people wearing recreational attire — a clear reference to a generation from the era of former Yugoslavia — are gathering around the sculpture while it is circled by the zooming movie camera, with the dramatic close-ups picturing the environment mirrored therein.

An event in time that was decisive for the current formation of our modernity is the fall of the Iron Curtain, with a solely prevalent socio-economic logic having become established in 1989, in a newly 'de-bordered' space, in connection with the law of functional differentiation. Globalisation, neocolonialist systems, world-wide migrational movements and questions pertaining to the management of this new, comprehensive centrality were in a process of emergence. After such radical changes, it is not only people from formerly socialist countries that are longing for an evaluation of our fundamental societal form, for the establishment of 'new platforms'. When in reference to the decline of the Soviet imperium the 'meridian of modernity shifting one last time to the East'[30] is spoken of, this statement once again makes plain how crucial working toward a dissolution of the still-common Eurocentric conception of the world remains. With the events of 11 September 2001 a new picture (and one no less impressive) came to join the already familiar representative image of the inception of postmodernity, the demolition of the Pruitt-Igoe residential blocks in St Louis on 15 July 1972, namely a picture depicting the real price of modernity: the collapsing towers of the World Trade Center in New York, which marked the commencement of a new era of the globalisation of violence. In his famous essay on the 'The Spirit of Terrorism', French sociologist Jean Baudrillard postulates a thesis on this 'symbolic event', asserting that we find ourselves in a 'fourth and only truly World War', so to speak, since 'it has as stakes globalization itself', and that 'these people' have 'assimilated all of modernity and globalization, while maintaining their aim to destroy it'.[31] The term 'crisis' has, at least since the global financial crisis materialised in the fall of 2008, become the newly unifying word of a global populace, or actually since Argentina stepped out as 'pioneer' with its financial collapse of 2001–02. The chronology of modernity — evidenced by what can, for once, be viewed as a phenomenon of failure, or alternately as an indeed strongly altered understanding of 'progress', namely more in the sense of 'cognisance' about the actual expiry of the prevailing 'world system' (Immanuel Wallerstein) — as of now seems to be emerging under completely new symbols.

While 'coloniality' has been recognised as constitutive for modernity, Henri Lefebvre as a sociologist, philosopher and urban researcher views the role of the crisis as similarly compelling: 'Modernity, the shadow of the Revolution, absent here and incomplete there, no longer functions without crisis. Contradictions move

32 Henri Lefebvre, 'Theses on Modernity', in Buchloh et al. (eds.), *Modernism and Modernity*, p. 11.

33 Benjamin H. D. Buchloh, 'All Things Being Equal', *Isa Genzken: Ground Zero*, London: Hauser & Wirth, 2008, p. 16.

through it and it constitutes their work in default of a radically revolutionary negativity which, according to the initial Marxist project, would have metaphored life itself. More: these crises multiply, grow closer together and become the general rule, the norm.... these crises seem to constitute our Modernity. They are integral to its consciousness, to its image, to its apologetic project.'[32]

With her sculptures of recent years tying into her material fetishism from the DIY world of consumption, Isa Genzken presents us with a world that is equally utopian and apocalyptic. While in the 1980s and 1990s her projects appropriating 'public sculpture' (manifest elements of constructions, such as windows, latticed reinforcements, et cetera) followed a technical-rational logic, she has recently deviated from her usual approach and now, in the twenty-first century, is carrying out her projects in accordance with altogether different principles. In her sculptures — made of decoration materials that are extremely diverse, optically captivating, and both inexpensive and ephemeral — we find ourselves confronted, as Benjamin Buchloh has phrased it, 'with the prime calamities of sculpture in the present: a terror that emerges from both the universal equivalence and exchangeability of all objects and materials... To have the self succumb to the totalitarian order of objects brings the sculpture to the brink of psychosis',[33] becoming a 'schizo-sculpture'. The *Oil* sculpture ensembles from 2007 for the 52nd Venice Biennale, or *Ground Zero* from 2008, are determined by order and by chaos in equal degrees, by large numbers and details, by perfection and chilliness, by symbols of mobility and by translocation, but also by upheaval and revival. Could the decimated zone of the World Trade Center (ever since designated 'ground zero', synonymous with the site of a bomb explosion), the construction areas of which Genzken has obviously filmed from the perspective of one of the remaining buildings, function as one of these platforms?

IV. From the concept of a universal language to the production of space, to politics of display

After at least three decades of intensive discussion, both thematically and formally speaking, repeatedly flaring up regarding the legacy of modernity and of modernism, including the sometimes severe criticism of this category and its related content and also the state of our modernity, in *Modernologies* the current field of artistic research is discussed based on several select contributions. In this context it should once again be made clear that it is not a 'new formalism', nor a 'return to abstraction', being considered here. Neither is the focus *per se* being placed on the pointing out of 'unrevealed modernisms', still in effect today through subaltern concepts of modernity, in countries whose protagonists have up to now had marginalised roles assigned to them in view of these issues. On the contrary, it is a question of a fundamental charge of scrutinising the (reciprocal) conditions and limitations of modernity, of exposing ambivalences, of making an attempt at calling attention to new readings of the rhetoric of modernity and the grammar of modernism.

The works shown in the exhibition are spatially arranged according to three aspects — 'concept of a universal language', 'production of space' and 'politics of display' — whereby the sections on these three topic areas are also dialogically and overlappingly pursued in the works between and outside of these areas. Some works are positioned in zones of transition, flanking the topics, as it were, or taking on a concatenating role.

Before the ticket-only area starts, with the visitors still finding themselves in a semi-public zone in the entrance space, an initial 'platform' is presented: *grid*

34 Henri Lefebvre, *La production de l'espace*, Paris: Anthropos, 1974. English version: *The Production of Space*, Oxford: Blackwell, 1991.

35 Henri Lefebvre, 'Die Produktion des städtischen Raums', *An Architektur 01, Material zu: Lefebvre, Die Produktion des Raumes* (July 2002), p. 12. Also available online (in German) at http://www.anarchitektur.com

one: Von Hochhaus zu Hochhaus (grid one: From High-rise to High-rise, 2008), a website installation by the group Labor k3000, with a selection of videos taken by residents of their everyday life in mass housing developments in Europe and North Africa, assembled at www.this-was-tomorrow.net. The tangible accessibility of the videos, which are sometimes backgrounded with hip-hop music and are played by clicking on a map highlighted by city names, effectively calls to attention the utopian potential of the exhibition. Time will tell whether visitors, for instance the skaters who can usually be found gambolling on the square in front of the museum, will actually be able to use this platform or even show interest in trying it out. In close spatial relation to Isa Genzken's installation at the last Venice Biennale, some of the videos appear as if they were facilitating a reactivation of a *mise-en-scène* proposed by Genzken. Likewise assigned to public space, both optically and conceptually, is the project *Existenzminimum* (Existential Minimum, 2002) by Catalan artist Domènec, comprised of a sculpture, a video showing the sculpture 'in action' in a public park, and a flyer with a construction manual and a chronology. Its protagonists are Mies van der Rohe along with Rosa Luxemburg and Karl Liebknecht, with the former having designed a monument in Berlin commemorating the latter two. Domènec reproduces the monument, destroyed by the Nazis in 1935, on the scale of a minimal housing unit, the topic of the 1929 CIAM Congress in Frankfurt, in a way similar to that of prefabricated furniture production. He is thus, using his self-provided referencing device, alluding to the ambivalences and inconsistencies of modernity in respect to its aesthetic and political ideologies.

The approach of defining, from a scientific basis, generally authoritative standards leads us to the concept of modernism, to creating a universal language in the form of abstract aesthetic symbols and forms. How autonomously can such forms actually develop and which content vitalises them? And how do these forms, when brought into new contexts, in turn evoke completely different meanings? These and other explorative questions have already been deliberated above in connection to the practice of artists such as Andrade, Creischer/Siekmann, Maljkovic, or Margreiter. For many years the artist John Knight, who resides in Los Angeles, has been exploring the field of abstract symbols, artistic authorship and autonomy *vis-à-vis* branding, corporate design, as well as anonymous symbols in the form of discursive, hybrid objects. With his project involving *Logotypes* (1982) — large-scale wood reliefs in the form of the artist's initials covered by posters advertising travel agencies (only one of the placards promotes a bank) — he enlivened at the documenta 7 in Kassel a site both hybrid and transitory, namely the walls of the individual landings in the Fridericianum stairwell. By contrast, his wood and mirror reliefs from the *Mirror Series* (1986) appear as icons of an anonymous world of consumption devoid of products, whose image or product has obviously become the consumer him/herself mirrored therein. The reliefs are hung slightly beneath the customary horizontal axis, making identification for the viewer more difficult.

Space is formed by society and it in turn shapes society. In his thesis on the 'production of space',[34] Henri Lefebvre touches on the conflict 'between a space that is increasingly becoming an exchange value and a yet inhabited space that only has use value to the extent that the exchange value has failed to succeed in totally destroying or making it disappear'.[35] Ângela Ferreira's study tracing *Maison Tropicale* (Tropical House, 2007) by Jean Prouvé — fashioned in aluminium lightweight construction and sent to French colonial countries to be erected — is dedicated to the history of the three prototypes of this building in Africa, which, though actually used by satisfied local residents, were nevertheless transported away several years ago in containers to be sold in Europe and North America to collectors at premium prices.

The 'capitalist space', according to Lefebvre, is, for the perspectival space familiar to us from the Renaissance, the 'place of deterioration'.[36] The work of Henrik Olesen on the scientist Alan Turing, inventor of the binary code and of the computer, who was compelled to have his homosexuality treated by psychiatry and by hormones, which ultimately led to his suicide, lends a strong bio-political perspective to Lefebvre's theses. In the multipart installation *How do I make myself a body* (2008) composed of collages and objects, Olesen confronts us with the regulation of the body according to societal stipulations. Questions of 'how to govern one's own body and mind' were deemed[37] by Michel Foucault and others to have been among the most fundamental issues of the fifteenth and sixteenth centuries, educing his definition of a critical stance and a definition of critique: 'the art of not being governed quite so much.'[38] Olesen's modernist drafts of fictive bodies based on quotations by fine artists and poets allow a multiplied, sexualised body to materialise, the image of a postmodern body.

Many of the projects presented in this exhibition are concerned with the conflicts but also with the correlations between the architectural and the socio-political space of modernity, for instance Gordon Matta-Clark's legendary action and installation *Window Blow-Out* (1973), or Dan Graham and Robin Hurst's photo-text essay *Private 'Public' Space: The Corporate Atrium Garden* (1987) — one of the winter gardens documented in the latter was, by the way, located in the ground zero vicinity. Katja Eydel has been exploring, in a comprehensive photographic study, *The Invention of Turkey* (2005/06) and the architectural expressions of that which has been widely considered to be a modern model country in the Orient. Stephen Willats has been working together with residents of tower blocks since the 1970s in investigating and reflecting on their everyday reality in these buildings that are, despite having long been stigmatised and subject to demolition, nevertheless appreciated for their many advantages as living space. *How do we know what home looks like?* (1993), asks Martha Rosler in the scope of a project involving various artist contributions about Le Corbusier's *Unité d'Habitation* in Firminy in Southern France. In her video she pursues the current needs of the residents and the improvements made to the flats by the residents themselves, featuring colourfully patterned wallpaper, murals on the walls and other 'normalisations' to the interior design.

Other artistic works engage in questions of the representation of protagonists (individuals or groups) in the history of modernism, as has already been outlined above citing some examples (Artaker, Fraser, Olowska and others), in attempts to contribute to a process of reorientation. The artist collective Klub Zwei (Simone Bader and Jo Schmeiser) has reviewed the history of the Phaidon Press, a Viennese pioneer of modern books on the visual arts whose path led it to England due to the anti-Semitic persecution of its owner. Associated with this methodology of artistic critique is likewise the project on the *Retroavantgarde* (2000–09) in the formerly socialist countries as has been charted by the Slovenian group IRWIN for over ten years, with recourse to the famous model by Alfred Barr, founding director of New York's Museum of Modern Art, yet with completely different representatives. This 'politics of display' is picked up by Louise Lawler as well in her longtime photographic investigations of modernist art, which she has presented in a select few installations from the mid-1980s in front of abstract wall paintings representing statistics on expenses for military and for social programmes or on weapon stocks. Or Marine Hugonnier's exploration of Mallarmé's legacy of modernity, of his volume of poems *Un coup de dés jamais n'abolira le hasard* (A roll of the dice will never abolish chance), the empty surfaces of which she interprets as being 'social emancipatory space', conceives as an invitation to be used, and therefore — totally contrary to the gesture ventured by Marcel Broodthaers with the crossing out of text passages — actually fills them with pictures from the Internet (including, by the way, a portrait of Alan Turing). Mathias Poledna constellates inside vitrines small thematic exhibitions with covers from the Folkway label, a record company that was aiming for a universal archive, namely the creation of an encyclopaedia of the 'entire world of sound'. The artist time and again presents these records through his film installations, in alternating contexts. He introduces his new film, which has been created for this exhibition, as a 'portrait of a group of objects', a multipart 'bar-set' that was designed by Adolf Loos for the long-standing company J.&L. Lobmeyr in Vienna.

In their works, artists thematise the exhibition as a medium of modernism and as such often operate in a role similar to that of curators. One of these is Christian Philipp Müller, who in the early 1990s was already intensively dedicating his attention to, for instance, Le Corbusier's work, trying to address the 'dead-ends of modernism' under the title of *Vergessene Zukunft* (Forgotten Future, 1992). His complex exhibition project deals with, among other things, the Philips Pavilion for the 1958 World Expo in Brussels, which was designed as a multimedia *Gesamtkunstwerk* by Le Corbusier, Iannis Xenakis and Edgar Varèse for the *Poème électronique* — in a reversal of their profession-specific roles that was not only uncommon for modernity. Included in the comprehensive scenario that Müller is presenting us with here are Nicolas Schöffer and his conceptions of 'hygiene', films about homosexuality — such as *Anders als Du und Ich* (Different than You and Me, 1957) by Veit Harlan, in which homosexuality is considered an enemy stereotype along with modern art — as well as the Cold War as historical framework. After numerous projects that focused on modernity in non-Western countries, Florian Pumhösl has now consciously abstained from the mere methodology of reference. With his afore-cited *Modernologio* — a multipart, variable wall system that references two historical exhibition designs by Murayama Tomoyoshi, the *Triangular Atelier* (2007) and a composition with black walls — he showcases, along with historical publications, his Walter-Dexel-like *verre églomisés* 'Abstraktionen zweiter Ordnung' (Abstractions of a Second Order), as André Rottmann suggested he term it. Christopher Williams is one of the few artists, as is evident from the multiple references, whose works are represented in various sections. His photographs avoid the superficial and assert an essential function in this exhibition — due to the aesthetic complexity inherent in Williams's works in connection with the questions thus posed regarding authorship, autonomy, production process, technology and design, archivation, display — in interconnecting the different topic areas; 'modernity as modality', as Helmut Draxler fittingly phrases it in his text on Williams.

A Sculpture Turning into a Conversation (2006) — this endeavour, which corresponds to the title of a lecture performance held by Falke Pisano, returns us to autonomous, abstract sculpture and possible shifts in meaning in varying contexts. Pisano's works also bring us back to the topic of this exhibition: the critical reflection on modernity and modernism as explored through different artistic practices.

39 Henri Lefebvre, 'Critique of Every-day Life', *Critique of Everyday Life: From Modernity to Modernism (Towards a Metaphilosophy of Daily Life)*, vol. 3, London and New York: Verso, 2005, p. 92.

40 Raymond Williams, 'When was Modernism?', *The Politics of Modernism*, London: Verso, 1989, p. 35.

The (re)staging of modernity in the form of a performative act, as a reading on the various conditions for the reception of modern art, here naturally takes on, in analogy to the reception of modernity, an important role in general. I guess it is not a coincidence that the project *Ricostruzione: Disertori/Libera: Towards a Historical Fable about Modernist Architecture and Psychology* (2008) by Tom Holert and Claudia Honecker, mentioned here in conclusion, originates from an art historian/theorist and a filmmaker — two of those who in effect have been less committed to aesthetic production and more to the research of and reflection on aesthetics.

V. Conclusion

This project represents a kind of map for the critique of modernity composed of artistic works, one that is naturally still incomplete. Yet as this map unfolds before us, it offers a multidimensional portrayal that is, from time to time, repeatedly subjected to a fresh point of view in the form of a dynamic process facilitated by the critique finding expression there, the proposed adaptations, redeterminations, analyses and so forth.

'Modernity is dated: industrial society, with the abstraction paradoxically produced by material production',[39] states Henri Lefebvre in his *Critique of Everyday Life*, continuing: 'By contrast, post-industrial society will be characterized by the production of an exchange of non-material goods, which are nevertheless more concrete: information, services, and so on.'

In closing, I would like to evoke the words of Raymond Williams, who in his 1987 (later to be published) lecture 'When was Modernism?' noted: '...the innovations of what is called Modernism have become the new but fixed forms of our present moment. If we are to break out of the non-historical fixity of post-modernism, then we must search out and counterpose an alternative tradition taken from the neglected works left in the wide margin of the century... to a modern *future* in which community may be imagined again.'[40]

Autonomy – Authenticity – Alterity:
On the Aesthetic Ideology of Modernity[1]

Cornelia Klinger

1   This essay is a revised version of the author's article 'modern/Moderne/ Modernismus' in Karlheinz Barck, Martin Fontius, Dieter Schlenstedt et al. (eds.), *Historisches Wörterbuch ästhetischer Grundbegriffe*, vol. 4, Stuttgart: Metzler Verlag, 2002.

2   When used of time, the Latin word *modo* means 'just now' or 'now'. In this sense 'modern' has now been replaced by 'contemporary'. Arthur Danto dated the transition from 'modern art' to 'contemporary art' to the 1970s in his *After the End of Art: Contemporary Art and the Pale of History*, Princeton University Press, 1997, p. 5.

3   A recent instance of this approach is Peter Gay's *Modernism: The Lure of Heresy*, London: William Heinemann, 2007.

The possibility of defining 'modernity' more precisely arose in the 1970s, when its limits began to become clear. A *temporal* limit became conceivable once the outlines of a 'postmodernism' *beyond* 'the modern' turned up (regardless of the concrete content or meaning of the concept 'postmodern'). *Spatial* limits emerged when a modernity *outside* Western modernity put in an emphatic appearance in post-colonial discourse. On the one hand, historisation of modernity, and its geographical and geopolitical localisation, rendered the relational character of the term obsolete: the equation of modernity with current actuality, with what is new today — a sense inscribed in the word through its Latin roots — ceased to possess validity.[2] On the other hand, it relativised the absolute claim that had governed notions and awareness of modernity since about the late-eighteenth century: modernity has ceased to be the great 'marching route' of world history, taken first by Europe, hit on with the same inevitability by every other part of the world and appearing boundless and unsurpassable. Whenever and wherever the limits of a phenomenon emerge, or appear to emerge, there arises the possibility of definition, of ascertaining and establishing the characteristics of a notion such as 'modernity'.

One problem encountered by efforts to determine what might constitute modernity in the aesthetic field is that modernity cannot be understood as a *style*. A further difficulty is that the terms 'modern' and 'modernity' are used in every genre, from music to architecture, and on a broad international basis, to denote heterogeneous phenomena within each field and region. Under these circumstances, any attempt to define the notion in terms of the semantics of aesthetic discourse itself is doomed to failure. That approach can achieve nothing more than the additive naming of individual components that are more or less widespread in the context of aesthetic modernity, such as irony, allegory, alienation, abstraction, fragmentation, collage and shock. Similarly, the listing of stylistic tendencies within the period reckoned to be covered by aesthetic modernity — from Romanticism to Abstract Expressionism, say — yields little clarification of the term's meaning.[3]

The present essay seeks to resolve these problems by addressing the issue of aesthetic modernity from the perspective of a general theory of the modernity process. In other words, it draws on a widely accepted sociological concept, without wishing to be misconstrued as a reduction to views offered by the 'sociology of art'.

A theoretical approach to modernity as a process of differentiation yields three main factors, all relating to the autonomisation of a social subsystem: *relative autonomy, thematic cleansing* and *functional specialisation*. These three general factors denote formally what takes place in all fields subject to modernity processes. Translated into the terms of artistic discourse, they materialise as *autonomy, authenticity*

4 The resemblance to the title of Terry Eagleton's *The Ideology of the Aesthetic* (Oxford and Cambridge: Blackwell, 1990), though not accidental, reflects an essentially superficial similarity.

5 Reinhart Koselleck, in his introduction to Otto Brunner, Werner Conze and Reinhart Koselleck (eds.), *Geschichtliche Grundbegriffe: Historisches Lexikon zur politisch-sozialen Sprache in Deutschland*, vol. 1, Stuttgart: Klett-Cotta, 1979, p. xv.

6 Hans Ulrich Gumbrecht used the striking 'cascade' metaphor to describe the progress of modernity in his 'Kaskaden der Modernisierung', in Johannes Weiss (ed.), *Mehrdeutigkeiten der Moderne*, Kassel: University Press, 1998, pp. 17–41.

7 Friedrich Schlegel, 'Über das Studium der Griechischen Poesie (1795–1797)', in Ernst Behler and Hans Eichner (eds.), *Kritische Schriften und Fragmente (1794–1797)*, Paderborn: Schöningh, 1988, vol. 1, p. 119. English version: *On the study of Greek poetry*, New York: State University of New York Press, 2001.

8 Schlegel, 'Athenäum: Fragmente, Nr. 252', op.cit., vol. 2, p. 129.

9 Octavio Paz, *Die andere Zeit der Dichtung: Von der Romantik zur Avantgarde*. Frankfurt: Suhrkamp, 1989, p. 50. English version: *Children of the Mire. Modern Poetry from Romanticism to the Avant-Garde*, London/Cambridge, MA: Harvard University Press, 1974.

10 Niklas Luhmann, *Die Kunst der Gesellschaft*, Frankfurt: Suhrkamp, 1997, p. 217. English version: *Art as a Social System*. Palo Alto, CA: Stanford University Press, 2000.

and *alterity*. 'Autonomy' signifies the structural screening of art from direct external prescriptions, norms and controls. In the world of art the claims of 'thematic cleansing' appear as a demand for 'authenticity', while 'functional specialisation' takes the form of 'alterity', art's otherness *vis-à-vis* society. These three categories expand and vary the formal factors arrived at through the view of modernity in the aesthetic sphere as a differentiation process, and they yield a connecting thread that enables the nature of aesthetic modernity to be described abstractly, yet comprehensively. Together, autonomy, authenticity and alterity form the 'aesthetic ideology of modernity'.[4] The term 'ideology' must be understood in this context not pejoratively, but as a general, neutral and summarising description of a highly heterogeneous, or as yet unordered, construct of ideas. It is used here not least because no coherent or consistent theory of aesthetic modernity currently exists. The following discussion takes some steps towards formulating such a theory.

A sociological perspective facilitates definition of the chronological span encompassed by aesthetic modernity. Its beginnings can be dated to the decades between 1750 and 1830, which have been referred to as the 'Sattelzeit (saddle period) of modernity'.[5] Aesthetic modernity climaxed in the decades around 1900, the era that also saw the onset of its crisis. Most observers would opt for a closing date in the years around 1970. There can be little doubt that since then far-reaching changes have been taking place, changes forming part of the *longue durée* of the cascading modernity process,[6] but also marking the end of a period that started around 1800.

Autonomy

As a result of the secularisation process of the Western world, the societal field of action developed various subsystems, which acquired independence from religious and ecclesiastical tutelage and evolved in accordance with their own norms and in relative autonomy *vis-à-vis* one another.

In the late-eighteenth century Immanuel Kant's three *Critiques* set the seal on distinctions between pure reason (theoretical and scientific), practical reason (legal and moral) and aesthetic reason (what Kant calls 'judgement'). This undermined the validity of the traditional unity of the beautiful, the true and the good. The young Friedrich Schlegel formulated a declaration of independence for the fine arts that resonates with the pathos of revolutionary change and whose borrowings from legal discourse call to mind the terminological origins of the notion of 'autonomy': 'Beauty is as original and important a component of human destiny as morality. All components should exist in relation to one another on the basis of equal rights (isonomy), and the fine arts have an inalienable right to independence (autonomy)';[7] 'Any philosophy of poetry... should begin with the independence of beauty, with the tenet that it is separate, and needs to be separate, from the true and the moral, and that it enjoys equal rights with them.'[8] As one critic has remarked: 'the poetic, the artistic and the beautiful became values in their own right, without reference to other values.'[9]

In liberating themselves from the doctrines of theology and metaphysics and establishing themselves as an autonomous (sub)system of modern society, the fine arts essentially followed the same path as science and technology, law and bureaucracy, state and society, economy and politics: 'Art takes part in society simply by differentiating itself as a system and thereby submitting to the logic of an operative unit, like any other functional system'.[10] Conversely, at about the same time the individual arts (painting, sculpture, architecture, music and literature) were subsumed

11 Paul Oskar Kristeller, 'The Modern System of the Arts: A Study in the History of Aesthetics', *Journal of the History of Ideas*, no. 12, 1951, pp. 496–527; no. 13, 1952, pp. 17–46. A similar tendency to form collective nouns is reflected in such terms as 'history' and 'culture': 'The collective noun "history", in contradistinction to the many histories (or stories) of its various actors, was coined in the eighteenth century.' Reinhart Koselleck, *Vergangene Zukunft: Zur Semantik geschichtlicher Zeiten*, Frankfurt: Suhrkamp, 1979, p. 50ff. The collective noun 'culture' unites such varied elements as religion, morals, tradition, language and everyday customs, along with literature and other aesthetic forms of expression.

12 Alexander Gottlieb Baumgarten's two-volume *Aesthetica* (1750, 1758) marks the beginnings of aesthetics as a philosophical discipline.

13 Johann Wolfgang Goethe, in Erich Trunz (ed.), *Dichtung und Wahrheit*, Werke Hamburger Ausgabe, vol. 9, Munich: Beck, 1989, p. 539. English version: *From My Life: Poetry and Truth*, Parts 1-3 (*Goethe: The Collected Works*, vol. 4), Princeton, NY: Princeton University Press, 1994.

14 Clement Greenberg, 'Avant-Garde and Kitsch', in John O'Brian (ed.), *Collected Essays and Criticism*, vol. 1, Chicago: University Press, 1986, p. 8.

15 Ibid., p. 9.

16 Hugo von Hofmannsthal, 'Poesie und Leben: Aus einem Vortrage', in H. Steiner (ed.), *Gesammelte Werke in Einzelausgaben*, Frankfurt: Fischer, 1956, p. 263.

in the collective noun 'art'.[11] Not coincidentally, in this period aesthetics developed into an independent field of theoretical study.[12]

The autonomy principle took root in the sphere of art in three ways. It involved: (1) the independence of the artist, and hence the level of production; (2) the work of art's freedom from function; and, at the reception level (3) the self-sufficiency of aesthetic experience.

1) Autonomy with regard to the freedom of the artist and artistic production entails, on the one hand, independence from the personal wishes, ideological interests and political intentions of a specific patron and, on the other, liberation from social norms and artistic conventions. The aesthetic was freed from religiously or morally grounded restrictions in a way comparable to the rejection of ethically normative demands in the fields of science, the economy and politics. Hence Johann Wolfgang von Goethe could write in *Dichtung und Wahrheit*: 'a good work of art can and will have moral consequences, but to demand a moral purpose of the artist is to corrupt his trade.'[13] The independence of the artist resulted not least from the depersonalisation of relations between patron/commissioner, producer and recipient/audience and their reorganisation, like many other social relations in the modern era, in the more indirect terms of the market.

2) The autonomy principle brought about a shift from external referentiality to self-referentiality in all differentiating areas of modern society, but only in the artistic sphere did self-referentiality reach absolute status, as the work of art was endowed with complete freedom from function. Hence art cut off from the net of functional relations linking other differentiating social subsystems. The dynamics of this non-functionalism, initiated by the aestheticism of the nineteenth century, led in the twentieth to total liberation from representational content. Turning in on itself, art invoked aesthetic rules and laws and their exclusively immanent extension into the medium of art. In the mid-twentieth century the American critic Clement Greenberg summarised this development: '"Art for art's sake" and "pure poetry" appear, and subject matter or content becomes something to be avoided like plague.'[14] Release from the world outside art, liberation from the obligation to depict or represent external reality, to embellish or glorify it, cleared the way for the creation of pure and, eventually, abstract art. 'In turning his attention away from subject matter of common experience, the poet or artist turns in upon the medium of his own craft.... Picasso, Braque, Mondrian, Miró, Kandinsky... derive their chief inspiration from the medium they work in. The excitement of their art seems to lie most of all in its pure preoccupation with the invention and arrangement of spaces, surfaces, shapes, colours, etc., to the exclusion of whatever is not necessarily implicated in these factors. The attention of poets like Rimbaud, Mallarmé, Valéry, Éluard... appears to be centred on the effort to create poetry rather than on experience to be converted into poetry.'[15] 'A poem,' said Hugo von Hofmannsthal, 'is a weightless weaving of words' and, like Greenberg, he noted: 'No direct path leads from poetry to life, and none from life to poetry.'[16] The principle of freedom from function made of the aesthetic sphere a self-sufficient, self-contained cosmos. The autonomy of the aesthetic object, the self-referentiality of the work of art, gave rise to an immanent epistemology of the aesthetic that centred on purely aesthetic formal principles and their evolution. In this way a general characteristic of modernity, the principle of progress, of constant innovation, found an equivalent and an expression in the

17 Ernst H. Gombrich, *The Ideas of Progress and their Impact on Art*, New York: Cooper Union, 1971; Christoph Menke and Juliane Rebentisch (eds.), *Kunst, Fortschritt, Geschichte*, Berlin: Kadmos, 2006.

18 Immanuel Kant, *Critique of the Power of Judgment*, in Paul Guyer and Eric Matthews (eds. and trans.), Cambridge: Cambridge University Press, 2000.

19 Christoph Menke, *Die Souveränität der Kunst: Ästhetische Erfahrung nach Adorno und Derrida*, Frankfurt: Suhrkamp, 1991, pp. 9–10. English version: *The Sovereignty of Art: Aesthetic Negativity in Adorno and Derrida*, Cambridge, MA: The MIT Press, 1999.

20 Eagleton, *The Ideology of the Aesthetic*, op.cit, p. 368.

aesthetic.[17] The autonomy principle became a criterion for establishing the relative status of various kinds of artistic activity: the greater their autonomy and freedom from function, the higher their standing. Hence, the arts and crafts, so-called 'applied' or 'decorative' art, ranked low in the canon, if they figured in it at all. Especially those trends in aesthetic modernity that are often subsumed under the heading 'modernism' are closely associated with the autonomy principle.

3) Art achieves full freedom from function only when this involves the recipient as well, when the audience is willing to forego expectations that it will be 'useful' in any way. The autonomy of the recipient's aesthetic experience is defined by the principle of *disinterested pleasure*, likewise established by eighteenth-century aesthetics and also validly formulated by Kant. Kant had attempted to bridge the gap between theoretical and practical reason by means of the power of judgement (*Urteilskraft*) and he had thought to recognise in certain aesthetic sensations — those generating an experience of the sublime — a basis for moral principles. Later in the modernity process the notion of aesthetic autonomy became even more radical. Now, rigorous application of the autonomy principle not only does away with demands for the artist to pursue a moral purpose — as Goethe had pro-claimed — but it also denies expectations of 'moral consequences' and any other extra-aesthetic effects of the work of art on its recipients. When the idea of autono-my is thought through to its logical conclusion, aesthetic experience, too, becomes 'an event with its own "laws"'. In other words, 'the validity of that which is experi-enced aesthetically [is] necessarily particular: it is relative to that sphere of experi-ence that is defined by orientation towards the specifically aesthetic value of the beautiful. How and what we experience aesthetically has no power to dispute or affirm that which is the object of our non-aesthetic experience and representation. The autono-mous gestalt of the aesthetic is an element *within* differentiated modern reason precisely because it neither takes precedence over, nor subordinates itself to, other discourses... with finely differentiated inherent laws, but ranges alongside them.'[19] More simply, 'aesthetic experience' permits the audience to participate in the free play of art as it obeys its own laws, but without deriving from it entertainment, knowledge, edification, improvement (moral or otherwise) or any other kind of non-aesthetic benefit.

As it became totally functionless in its autonomy, art acquired a precarious position in society. Serving nothing and nobody, it seemed to exist outside the social order. As one critic has noted, 'aesthetics is born at the moment of art's effective demise as a political force, flourishes on the corpse of its social rele-vance'.[20] This is presumably the reason why talk of the 'end of art' was first heard as the autonomy process got underway and has never entirely disappeared since, despite the fact that art, as a result of its autonomisation, experienced a dynami-sation comparable to that observable in other differentiating social subsystems in the modernity process.

Authenticity

Autonomy is the premise and the basis of aesthetic ideology. Externally, it is con-cerned with independence *vis-à-vis* any form of outside influence on the sphere of art, be it on artists, works or recipients. When autonomy is viewed from an interior perspective, authenticity becomes the focus of attention. The relationship between

21 Jürgen Habermas, *Theorie des kommunikativen Handelns*, vol. 1, Frankfurt: Suhrkamp, 1981, p. 300. English version: *The Theory of Communicative Action*, Thomas McCarthy (trans.), vol. 1. Boston: Beacon Press, 1984, p. 216.

22 Ibid.

23 Stuart Hall, 'The Local and the Global: Globalization and Ethnicity', in Anne McClintock, Aamir Mufti and Ella Shohat (eds.), *Dangerous Liaisons: Gender, Nation, and Postcolonial Perspectives*, Minneapolis: University of Minnesota Press, 1997, p. 175.

24 Dieter Rucht, *Modernisierung und neue soziale Bewegungen: Deutschland, Frankreich und USA im Vergleich*, Frankfurt: Campus, 1994, p. 56.

25 Ibid., p. 53.

the three categories ('autonomy', 'authenticity' and 'alterity') is characterised at once by convergence and divergence. On the one hand, they merge to such an extent that they appear to be three different aspects of the same; on the other, tensions exist between them. From the 'autonomy' perspective, the work of art and its absolute freedom from function occupied centre stage; by contrast, the notion 'authenticity' invokes the producer, the artist as subject or, more precisely, as the modern subject *par excellence*.

Like autonomy, 'authenticity' is best understood in the context of a theory of the modernity process — specifically, in relation to the rise of the ideas of 'the subject' and 'subjectivity' in the modern age. The demise of the Christian metaphysical world-view resulted not only in a process of objectification, but also in a process of subjectification (which usually receives less attention). Two opposing principles thus inherited the traditional order. The principle of objectivity ruled theoretical and practical reason that supported the functionally differentiated subsystems of society and their interrelations. In the words of Jürgen Habermas: 'On the one hand, a decentred understanding of the world opens up the possibility of dealing with the world of facts in a cognitively objectified [*versachlicht*] manner and with the world of interpersonal relationships in a legally and morally objectified manner.'[21] Irrespective of their differentiation in terms of theoretical and practical reason, science and technology, the state and the economy, law and morality, appear together on the objective side, in a 'cognitively objectified [*versachlicht*] manner'. For Habermas, the 'decentred understanding of the world' also 'offers the possibility of a subjectivism freed from imperatives of objectification in dealing with individualized needs, desires, and feelings [*Bedürfnisnatur*]'.[22]

The processes of objectification and subjectification must be taken more seriously as contrary, but equally significant, components of the modernity process than Habermas implies. The opposition between objectivity and subjectivity constitutes more than a 'possibility'; the complementary constellation is a 'requirement' of modern society, inasmuch as a decentred view of the world presupposes and requires a centring factor. Whereas functional differentiation amounts to dynamisation, pluralisation, fragmentation and expansion — that is, 'decentralisation' — the individual acts as a 'still point in a turning world'.[23] Ideally, the complementarity of the two would result in an interaction of opening and closing. 'Functional differentiation and centralisation of the self are two sides of the same coin. It is no accident that they basically run parallel to each other.'[24] '"Centralisation of the self" indicates that ways of knowing and acting in the world are no longer derived from traditional and transcendental norms, but are established autonomously. The ultimate point of reference here is the individual.... Modernity generated the idea of the individual as the centre of things.'[25] This grants the human self the status of subject. The decentralised areas on the object side obey the functional principle, whereas the subject seeks meaning and identity; while calculation and efficiency lie at the root of the functional principle, it is authenticity that guides the subject's search for meaning and identity.

The principle of liberated subjectivity first developed in the field of religion (belief). Secularisation did not cause — and has not caused religion to disappear, but to become more private. Religion thus came to encompass the realm of familial and intimate human relationships (love), now freed from economic interests and constraints, and finally embraced the sphere of subjective aesthetic experience (hope), as shaped and conveyed by art. 'The discovery of subjectivity, the liberation

26 Hans Robert Jauss, *Studien zum Epochenwandel der ästhetischen Moderne*, Frankfurt: Suhrkamp, 1989, p. 111.

27 Vasili Kandinsky, *Über das Geistige in der Kunst*, Berna: Bentreli, 1970, p. 80. English version: *Concerning the Spiritual in Art*, Boston: Museum of Fine Arts Boston, 2006.

28 'The Idea of the Modern', in Irving Howe (ed.), *Literary Modernism*, New York: Fawcett, 1967, p. 19.

29 Theodor W. Adorno, *Ästhetische Theorie. Gesammelte Schriften*, vol. 7, Frankfurt: Suhrkamp 1997, p. 255. English version: *Aesthetic Theory*, Robert Hullot-Kentor (trans.), London and New York: Continuum, 1999, pp. 170–71; 'The old concept of transcendent genius, of self-willed or determined individualism, and of tormented but autonomous identity are all legacies which remain attached to the image of the artist through the twentieth century. Perhaps this is because no figure embodies or promotes the fantasies and fictions of the bourgeois individual under capitalism more dramatically than that of the artist.... Dismantled by the critical reformulations of the last twenty-five years, the concept of the artist nonetheless persists – it is the stock in trade of catalogue copy and museum panels, not to mention the art historical monograph and gallery exhibition.' Johanna Drucker, *Theorizing Modernism: Visual Art and the Critical Tradition*, New York: Columbia University Press, 1994, pp. 109, 113.

30 Carl Schmitt pointed out that cultural autonomy, or the autonomy of art, stands for bourgeois autonomy in general: 'That art is a daughter of freedom, that aesthetic value judgements must be autonomous, that the artistic genius is sovereign, appeared obvious to [liberalism]; indeed, genuinely liberal emotions stirred in some countries only when the autonomous freedom of art was threatened by "apostles of morality".' Carl Schmitt, *Der Begriff des Politischen: Mit einer Rede über das Zeitalter der Neutralisierungen und Entpolitisierungen*, Wissenschaftliche Abhandlungen und Reden zu Philosophie, Politik und Geistesgeschichte, vol. 10, Munich and Leipzig: Duncker & Humblot, 1932, p. 59.

and legitimation of the individual... is the achievement and the office of aesthetic experience'.[26] This perspective casts a rather different light on the differentiation that characterises the modernity process: the plurality of the differentiating areas submits to the duality of the objective and subjective spheres, institutionalised in social terms as the duality of the public and private realms.

Gradually losing its traditional tasks and separating from the objective functional system of society, the aesthetic sphere began to gain greater significance on the horizons of subjectivity. Released from all kinds of social function, from the obligation to give visual form to truths deemed absolute, to depict nature, to evoke a universally valid good and to represent divine or worldly power, art came to be identified as the original, natural, essential and authentic expression of the subject, of the self and its inner being: 'as a creator, each artist must give expression to what is inherently his.'[27] On the producer's side, then, authenticity is the pure expression, the expressivity, of the artist, whose soul is mirrored in the otherwise 'useless' work of art. On the recipient's side, authenticity is the pure impression, the experience, of the subject, which corresponds to the artist's subjectivity. Authenticity marks a turn from objective truth to subjective truthfulness, 'a turn from truth to sincerity, from the search for the objective law to a desire for authentic response'.[28] Like the principle of autonomy, the authenticity/expressivity principle became a yardstick for assessing art. Consequently, the degree to which an artist gave expression to his true self, to his intuitions, visions, ideas and sensations, became a criterion for judging the quality of high art. Anything not corresponding to this ideal was deemed either inferior or wholly illegitimate. If artists followed guild rules, say, if their expression of feeling was indebted exclusively to the laws governing a particular genre (love poetry, for example), if they obeyed social convention or aimed to comply with the public's taste, then this was held to detract significantly from the authenticity of their work and hence from its aesthetic value.

Modern subjectivity and aesthetics are so closely linked in their development that the artist appears as the epitome of the subject. Only in the person of the artist does the self achieve in full measure the status of subject suggested by the modernity process. The heightening of autonomy and authenticity in the artist-subject peaks as complete sovereignty in the idea of the genius, which took shape around the mid-eighteenth century and is still influential. 'Genius is purported to be the individual whose spontaneity coincides with the action of the absolute subject.... In the concept of genius the idea of creation is transferred... from the transcendental to the empirical subject, to the productive artist.'[29] As creator, the artistic genius is not only virtually a god, untouched by the limitations of the human condition; the artistic genius is also unaffected by the deficits and defects that have proved to be part and parcel of the modernity process. The conditions of bourgeois reality soon disappointed the ideals of human freedom, equality and sovereignty proclaimed by Enlightenment philosophy and furthered by the French revolution. Only in the realm of art did the quickly dashed hopes for the future entertained by incipient modernity seem to find realisation, if only by proxy, as it were.[30] This raises the oft-discussed issue of the ambiguity of the term 'subject', as applied to the artistic genius on the one hand and the ordinary person on the other. All kinds of pressures and constraints have made the ordinary man a *subiectum* that is to say subjected to the functional system of modern society. By contrast, the artist-subject, endowed with absolute creativity, appear as the sovereign subject (in the sense of *hypokeimenon*), unaffected by the limitations inherent in the human condition as well as by external constraints of any kind.[31] In the aesthetic realm the modern principle of the autonomous subject rises above bourgeois self-preservation to the heights of self-expression, self-realisation and self-creation. The enormous creative potential set free by the break with the dogmas and conventions of the traditional world-view was channelled into the differentiated, specialised field of art while it was systematically banned from other areas, such as science, economics and politics.

'For the audience, [the autonomy of art] was a nostalgic projection, since, with the passing of the revolution, they could no longer expect their desire for autonomy to be satisfied in life, but only in the realm of art';[32] 'The artist's claim to express himself… attached… to the work of art. In this respect the artist was only the impersonator of the modern subject, whose autonomy… was only unwillingly surrendered. Art was thus a mirror in which the subject could see itself as autonomous.'[33] The license for self-expression granted the creative subject, the artist in bourgeois society, was not restricted to artistic activity in the narrow sense, but extended to the artist's way of life. The idea of art was linked to an artistic existence outside the rules and conventions of bourgeois norms, to an aesthetic life-style. The authenticity principle encompassed bohemia's eccentric, alternative forms of existence. 'Expressive self-realisation becomes the principle of art appearing as a form of life.'[34]

To the extent that the artist could embody claims to autonomy and authenticity far more comprehensively than the average modern subject, he was held to be especially capable of performing the centring task credited to the subject in general. Moreover, the exceptional subject 'artist' was expected to discover more than purely subjective meaning and to generate more than purely subjective sense: the artist was to (re)discover within himself the ability to (re)construct the order of being that had become uncertain and eventually had vanished due to the demise of the theological and metaphysical world-view. The artist (particularly the poet) was considered especially sensitive towards the '*Weltriss*',[35] the rupture in the world that had destroyed the great, transcendentally established chain of being. And the artist's exceptional subjectivity was thought to enable him to find a way of repairing the fragmentation caused by the *Weltriss*. In this way, the authenticity of the artist-subject, understood as subjective truthfulness, reopened access to something like a generally valid truth, which reunited subjectivity and objectivity. What Max Weber called the 're-enchantment of the world' was a project that took its cue less from religion than from the aesthetic sphere: 'the artist [was] chosen to bring forth myths again.'[36] This is the point at which the aesthetic sphere began to revolt against the differentiation that had promoted it, against the division into the orders of theoretical, practical and aesthetic reason in which it had a part. The artist adopted the role of *voyant*, becoming the prophet of an order of being and knowing different from, and superior to, the existing one.

When the idealisation of the artist's subjectivity reached its zenith the gap between the artist-subject as genius and the average human subject widened into an unbridgeable chasm. Thus, the modern subject paid the price of a split within itself for the hubris of its project to heal the *Weltriss*. Habermas calls this the aporetical doubling of the self-referential subject:[37] the subject simultaneously occupies the position both of a 'self-deifying subject consuming itself in acts of vain self-transcendence' and of an 'empirical subject in the world, where it is available as one object among others'.[38] In addition, such efforts to reconcile the *Weltriss* were prone to succumb to the temptations of totalitarianism, since the

31 '…"subject" signifies in effect (1) a free subjectivity: a centre of initiatives, the author of acts for which it is responsible; (2) a subjugated being, subject to a superior authority.' Louis Althusser, *Positions*, Paris: Éditions Sociales, 1976, p. 133.

32 Hans Belting, *Das unsichtbare Meisterwerk: Die modernen Mythen der Kunst*, Munich: Beck, 1998, p. 28.

33 Ibid., p. 9.

34 Jürgen Habermas, *Der philosophische Diskurs der Moderne. Zwölf Vorlesungen*, Frankfurt: Suhrkamp, 1985, p. 28. English version: *The Philosophical Discourse of Modernity: Twelve Lectures*, Frederick G. Lawrence (trans.), Cambridge, MA: The MIT Press, 1995, p. 18.

35 Heinrich Heine, 'Die Bäder von Lucca', in Klaus Briegleb (ed.), *Sämtliche Schriften in zwölf Bänden*, vol. 3, Munich: Hanser, p. 405.

36 Manfred Frank, *Gott im Exil: Vorlesungen über die Neue Mythologie*, II, Frankfurt: Suhrkamp, 1988, p. 12.

37 Habermas, *The Theory of Communicative Action*, op. cit., p. 261.

38 Ibid., p. 262.

39 Adorno, too, considered the subjectivity of the artist to be different from, and greater than, subjectivity in the customary sense: 'From the perspective of the philosophy of history, expression in art must be interpreted as a compromise. Expression approaches the transsubjective; it is the form of knowledge that — having preceded the polarity of subject and object — does not recognize this polarity as definitive. Art is secular, however, in that it attempts to achieve such knowledge within the bounds of the polarity of subject and object, as an act of autonomous spirit.' Adorno (note 29), p. 111. Although '[o]nly the subject is an instrument of expression, [the] expression of artworks is the nonsubjective in the subject; not so much that subject's expression as its impression' (ibid., p. 113, tran. slightly amended). It must be more than 'abstract subjectivity that powerlessly sets itself up as substance' (ibid., p. 116).

40 Friedrich Nietzsche, *Die Geburt der Tragödie*, Giorgio Colli and Mazzino Montinari (eds.), Berlin: De Gruyter, p. 45. (trans. slightly amended). English version: *The Birth of Tragedy*, Arlington, VA: Richer Resources Publications, 2009.

41 Ibid.

42 Ibid.

43 Ibid.

44 'The destruction of individuation, the dismay at the shattered unity, the hope for a new world creation — in short, the feeling of blissful horror in which the knots of pleasure and terror are tied together.' Nietzsche, *Nachgelassene Fragmente Ende 1870 bis April 1871*, Sämtliche Werke: Kritische Studienausgabe, 15 vols., Giorgio Colli and Mazzino Montinari (eds.), Berlin: dtv and de Gruyter, 1980, vol. 7. 7 [123] p. 178.

45 Ibid.

46 Immanuel Kant, *Kritik der Urteilskraft. Gesammelte Schriften*, Berlin: Suhrkamp, 1974, § 46, 181, p. 307; § 49, 200, p. 318. English version: *Critique of Judgement*, Indiannapolis, IN: Hackett, 2008.

dualism of sovereignty and submission inherent in the idea of the subject easily translates into a division of man into the superhuman and subhuman. Not coincidentally, it was Nietzsche who devoted special attention to the gulf between the subjectivity of the artist and that of the average individual.[39] The 'I' of the artist is not the same as 'that of the actual living man, but the "I" dwelling, truly and eternally, at the root of being'.[40] Nietzsche claims that the artist rises above the individual and the purely subjective, since 'the subject, the striving individual bent on furthering his egoistic purposes, can be thought of only as an enemy of art, never as its source. But to the extent that the subject is an artist he is already delivered from individual will and has become a medium through which the true subject celebrates his deliverance in illusions.'[41] Nietzsche explains the difference between the individual and the artist-subject with reference to the ancient Greek poet Archilochus: 'Archilochus, with his passionate loves and hates, is really only a vision of genius, a genius who is no longer merely Archilochus, but the genius of the world, expressing its pain through the similitude of Archilochus the man, whereas the subjectively willing and desiring human being can never be a poet.'[42] 'Only as the genius in the act of creation merges with the primal artist of the world can he truly know something of the eternal essence of art.'[43] When the subject is elevated to the status of an absolute, subjectivity disappears. Indeed, the conquest of individuation by art programmatically proclaimed by Nietzsche condemns subjectivity outright and destroys it: 'The basic recognition of the unity of all existing things, the view of individuation as the source of all ill, beauty and art as the hope that the spell of individuation can be broken,[44] as the premonition of restored unity.'[45] Ultimately, the artistic genius is closer to god — the 'primal artist of the world' — than to humanity. If art did indeed develop certain totalitarian affinities under the conditions of modernity, this was caused by the idealisation and stylisation of the artist as prophet and leader, by the concomitant disparagement of 'ordinary' man and by the violence implicit in the will to break the 'spell of individuation'.

Ideas vary as to what qualifies the artist to repair the fragmentation of reality and to heal the disenchanted world of modernity. His exceptional capabilities can be envisaged on a 'higher' or 'lower' plane than that of ordinary subjectivity. They may appear as the highest intellectuality and spirituality or as intuition flowing almost instinctively from the depths of the artist's body and soul. The artist transcends the human subject either in the direction of the divine or in that of the visceral; his creativity oscillates between the absolute, self-willed act and purely passive inspiration. Kant's concept of genius harboured the nucleus of this ambivalence, in that it attributed to the genius exceptional faculties over which the genius himself has no real control, since they are received passively as a natural gift.[46] The second idea of genius comes close to what Michel Foucault termed 'the explanation from below'[47] and gained considerably in importance around 1900, not least as a result of the discoveries of psychoanalysis, especially the unconscious, which undermined the sovereignty of the subject. The motive behind both alternatives was the same: to discover the source of the genius's ability to transcend modern reality in a realm outside norms and normality, whether above them or below them.

A third, constructivist conception of the genius's abilities existed alongside the 'higher' and 'lower' alternatives. In this view the artistic self, rather than (re)discovering the hidden laws of being, either on the clear heights of reason (Apollonian) or in the obscure depths of emotion (Dionysian), invents, creates or produces an

47 'The explanation from below is… an explanation through the most confused, the most obscure, the most disordered, the most indebted to chance.' Michel Foucault, *Il faut défendre la société: Cours au Collège de France, 1975–1976*, Paris: Hautes Études, Gallimard and Seuil, 1997, p. 46. Foucault also describes the connection between the depths and the heights: 'above this network of bodies, accidents and passions… something fragile and superficial was building up, a growing rationality, that of calculations, of strategies, of ruses; that of technical procedures.' Ibid., p. 47. This *coincidentia oppositorum*, the connection between the opposites 'arbitrariness' and 'calculation', 'materialism/ sensualism' and 'formalism', characterises modern thought in many ways and also plays an important part in the diverging paths of modern art.

48 Beat Wyss, *Der Wille zur Kunst: Zur ästhetischen Mentalität der Moderne*, Cologne: Dumont, 1996, p. 54.

49 Michel Foucault, 'What is Enlightenment?', in Paul Rabinow (ed.), *The Foucault Reader*, New York: Pantheon, 1984, p. 50.

50 The programmatic aims of the De Stijl group, for example, included the 'elimination of subjective arbitrariness in means of expression'. *De Stijl: Schriften und Manifeste zu einem theoretischen Konzept ästhetischer Umweltgestaltung*, Leipzig and Weimar: Kiepenheuer, 1984, p. 53.

51 This line of development offered refuge in the arts to the philosophical art of living, which modernity had made homeless. Wilhelm Schmid speaks of a 'dwindling connection to objects in the modern arts', as a consequence of which 'the subject and its life' can themselves become the theme of art. Wilhelm Schmid, 'Das Leben als Kunstwerk', *Kunstforum*, no. 142, (Oct–Dec, 1998), p. 73. This development would end with the corporeality of the artist being the only remaining guarantee of authenticity.

52 Belting, *Das unischtbare Meisterwerk*, op. cit., p. 33.

aesthetic law 'without foundation'. 'Before art as a beginning there is nothingness, against which art sets itself up. Art "establishes" and "presents" truths that would otherwise not exist. Its foundation lies in the ecstatic decision to make.'[48] With the creative act — 'making' (*poiein*) — foregrounded in this way, the maker — the acting/active subject — acquires still greater prominence *vis-à-vis* the work. The shift of emphasis from object to subject, already apparent in the transition from the principle of autonomy to the principle of authenticity, culminated in the idea that the artist creates himself, that his life is a work of art. In Baudelaire's dandy Foucault sees the epitome of the (explicitly male) subject who creates himself: 'Modern man, for Baudelaire, is not the man who goes off to discover himself, his secrets and his hidden truth; he is the man who tries to invent himself. The modernity does not "liberate man in his own being"; it compels him to face the task of producing himself.'[49] This position marks the opposite pole to the self-referentiality of the work of art. In contrast to the self-referential pole, in which the personality and intention of the artist all but disappear behind the stylistic and formal laws of the aesthetic 'material',[50] the 'ecstatic decision to make', the will of the artist to invent himself in a self-creative act (*autopoiesis*) almost obliterates the object — the work of art.[51]

This polarity between the autonomy of the work of art and the authenticity of the artist characterised the entire history of modern art: 'With the Romantics absolute art had been the drunken vision of the subject, whereas in the Hegelian tradition of modernity it became the rigorous or ideal form, which revealed its truth in the works';[52] 'The conflict between the autonomy of the subject (experience) and the autonomy of form and technique (style) wound its way like a spiral through the course of modernity. Reborn Romantics demanded absolute freedom in art, the heirs of the Enlightenment an absolute bond with form in a neutral ideal of the work. The former desired deliverance from the strangeness of things, the latter from the arbitrariness of the subject.'[53] The 'strangeness of things', experienced as alienation, and the no less disastrous consequences of the 'arbitrariness of the subject', with its tendency towards totalitarianism, are the two sides of the suffering caused by modernity in the wake of the disenchantment of the world. The failure of the aesthetic project's grand attempt to mend the *Weltriss* in the context of modernity becomes obvious when one considers how the subject/object divide reoccurred at the core of the sphere of art.

The dream of reconciliation between pure self-expression and pure objective form lived on in aesthetic theory[54] and became a focus of the artistic imagination. In his novel *Doctor Faustus* Thomas Mann invests the composer Adrian Leverkühn, at the height of his genius, with the ability 'to yield himself to subjectivity' 'in the previously organized material, unhampered, untroubled by the already given structure', so that 'his technically most rigid work, a work of extreme calculation, is at the same time purely expressive'.[55]

For a long time no terminological conventions existed to express the difference between tendencies in nineteenth- and twentieth-century art and literature that focus either on the subject or the object, on the artist or the work. A distinction now gradually seems to be emerging between the use of 'modernism' for the object-centred approach and 'avant-garde' for the subject-centred. The two differ from each other most clearly in their relationship to society and politics. In the history of modern art avant-garde movements have frequently articulated radical social criticism and adopted explicitly political stances. These activist avant-gardes have seen themselves in the tradition of the prophetic artist-subject, as forerunners

53 Ibid., p. 34. In literary modernity Peter Bürger notes a similar opposition between object- and work-centred modernism on the one hand and subject-orientated avant-garde on the other. Peter Bürger, 'Moderne', in Ulfert Ricklefs (ed.), *Fischer-Lexikon der Literatur*, Frankfurt: Fischer, 1996, pp. 1287–1319. Bürger finds early evidence of this duality in the nineteenth century: 'Baudelaire, Flaubert and... Mallarmé too are exponents of a literary modernity centred on the idea of the (classical) work.... Their antipode is Arthur Rimbaud [whose] writing project is existential' (p. 1299). For Bürger, Nietzsche was moving in the activist/avant-garde direction. With Wagner's music dramas in mind, he 'drew up the programme of a cultural revolution aimed at reintegrating modernity's atomised subject into a community' (p. 1300). Bürger discovers the opposition between object-work-centred and subject-centred again in twentieth-century poetry: 'On the one hand, there is the highly rational poetry of Paul Valéry, argued in terms of aesthetic effect and based on traditional forms... on the other, the Surrealist notion of "automatic writing", which is concerned with self-liberation in the act of writing, not with the creation of a work (see Breton and Soupault...). Valéry subjects poetry to rationalist principles.... By contrast, the Surrealist notion of *écriture automatique* is in line with Romantic tradition. The primary concern of this method... is the elimination of rational control, not the rational choice of means.... In this way writing can become an act of self-examination and self-liberation' (p. 1305).

54 Theodor W. Adorno, 'Der Artist als Statthalter', in Rolf Tiedemann (ed.) *Gesammelte Schriften*, vol. 11, Frankfurt: Suhrkamp, 1997, pp. 114–126.

55 Thomas Mann, *Dr. Faustus: Das Leben des deutschen Tonsetzers Adrian Leverkühn erzählt von einem Freunde* in: *Gesammelte Werke in dreizehn Bänden*, vol. 6, Frankfurt: Fischer, 1990, p. 647. English version: *Doctor Faustus: The Life of the German Composer Adrian Leverkühn as Told by a Friend*, H. T. Lowe-Porter (trans.), Harmondsworth: Penguin, 1949, p. 468.

and pioneers of a better world.[56] Linked to this social commitment is the desire to integrate art into life, with the work of art dissolving in the process. By contrast, the formalist and purist credos, founded in the pure form of things, have resulted more often than not in a-political or anti-political stances, in a retreat from the world, in a tendency to withdraw life into art, all of which can culminate in a kind — or rather, various kinds — of esotericism.

Alterity

Before turning to the third cornerstone of aesthetic ideology, it may be useful to take stock of the discussion so far by recalling the three theoretical principles underlying the present study of the modernity process.

> The principle of autonomy propels the differentiation of all subsystems in modern society, but has achieved absolute status only in the aesthetic sphere. Whereas the autonomy of all other subsystems is limited by functional interrelations among differentiated subsystems, and therefore relative, the work of art is considered to stand apart from these.
>
> The principle of thematic cleansing applies to the field of art as principle of authenticity. This implies not only an intensification but also a particularity, because under the guise of authenticity the process of thematic cleansing does not relate to the objectified subsystems of modern society but to the suject (the artist).
>
> Given the increase from relative to absolute autonomy that characterises the aesthetic sphere and removes it from all functional interrelations within society, and in view of the specific approach to thematic cleansing as authenticity and the sovereignty of the subject, it seems doubtful whether there is any sense in speaking of functional specialisation in connection with art. Equating functional specialisation with alterity likewise appears questionable, since the term 'alterity' denotes the very opposite of all functional relations.

Leaving aside these issues for a moment, there can be no doubt that alterity forms the third pillar of aesthetic ideology. Irrespective of the tensions between them, modernist and avant-garde currents meet under the banner of 'alterity'. The notion of 'alterity' is as useful in connection with the formal qualities of an object, with a work's autonomy and self-referentiality, as it is valid with regard to the authenticity of the artist-subject. The non-referentiality of the laws of pure form places them just as much outside reality as does the new myth arising from the artist's inner vision. Both the absolute autonomy embodied in the work of art's freedom from function and the authenticity exceptionally accorded the artist imply distance from reality. This *'foreignness to the world is an element in art'*[57] and is what the term 'alterity' stands for. If autonomy is the basis and authenticity the centre of the aesthetic ideology of modernity, then alterity constitutes its apogee.

The philosopher and sociologist Georg Simmel offers a definition of art that can be read as an explanation of alterity, although he does not use the word. According to Simmel, 'Art is the *other* of life, the deliverance from it by its opposite, in which the pure forms of things, indifferent towards their subjective enjoyment or non-enjoyment, refuse all contact with our reality.'[58]

As 'the *other* of life', art rebuffs its audience's need or desire for pleasure ('subjective enjoyment or non-enjoyment'), but at the same time Simmel posits

56 Cornelia Klinger and Wolfgang Müller-Funk (eds.), *Das Jahrhundert der Avantgarden*, Munich: Fink Verlag, 2004.

57 Adorno, *Ästhetische Theorie*, op. cit., p. 183.

58 Georg Simmel, 'Das Christentum und die Kunst', in Michael Landmann (ed.), *Brücke und Tür*, Stuttgart: Köhler, 1957, p. 130 (emphasis added).

59 Ibid., p. 130.

60 Sigmund Freud describes the locus of the imagination as a separate area of the human psyche, untouched by the reality principle and devoted to 'compensation' for human activity dominated by the reality principle and controlled by reason. The elements that feature in Freud's description bear a striking resemblance to the characteristics of art's alterity. Sigmund Freud, 'Vorlesungen zur Einführung in die Psychoanalyse', *Gesammelte Werke*, vol. 11, London: Imago, 1940, p. 387.

61 Armin Nassehi, 'Keine Zeit für Utopien: Über das Verschwinden utopischer Gehalte aus modernen Zeitsemantiken', in Rolf Eickelpasch and Armin Nassehi (eds.), *Utopie und Moderne*, Frankfurt: Suhrkamp, 1996, p. 252

62 Niklas Luhmann, *Gesellschaftsstruktur und Semantik: Studien zur Wissenssoziologie der modernen Gesellschaft*, Frankfurt: Suhrkamp, 1989, p. 158.

63 Ibid., p. 212.

64 Niklas Luhmann, *Soziale Systeme: Grundriss einer allgemeinen Theorie*, Frankfurt: Suhrkamp, 1984, p. 365. English version: *Social Systems*, Palo Alto, CA: Stanford University Press, 1996.

65 Harvie Ferguson, *Subjectivity: Body, Soul, Spirit*, Charlottesville: University of Virginia Press, 2000, p. 193.

a greater closeness of the work of art to 'us', the recipients: 'by being distanced, the content of being and imagination come closer to us than they could in the guise of reality. While all things in the real world can be integrated into our lives as means and materials, the work of art is completely self-contained. Yet all these realities maintain… a final, deep estrangement from us…. The work of art alone can become wholly ours:… by being more self-contained than everything else[59], it is more to us than everything else.' The apparent contradictions in which Simmel involves himself here result from the paradoxical situation in which 'we' find ourselves: the reality, the 'real world', in which we live and into which 'all things… [are] integrated… as means and materials' is at the same time strange (or has become strange) to us, while 'the content of being and imagination'[60] has disappeared from this estranged, reified kind of life, distancing itself from reality. Since autonomous, authentic art is likewise set apart from reality, its strangeness signifies closeness to the kind of self that is strange to the world, a self that is more than the various social functions it fulfils and different from them.

Simmel's account reflects both the view of the modernity process as one of alienation and reification and the idea put forward by systems theory that 'a central representation of the unity of society is no longer possible under conditions of functional differentiation'.[61] According to Niklas Luhmann, modern society 'no longer offers the individual a place where he or she can exist as "social beings". They can live only outside society, can reproduce themselves solely as a system of their own in the environment of society';[62] 'The individual is understood as a world relationship, wholly unique, acquiring awareness through the self and realised in human form; and the "world" (or, in social terms, "humanity") is that which "autonomously" achieves representation in the individual… the individual has his place within himself and outside society. The formula "subject" symbolises precisely that.'[63] Elsewhere Luhmann expresses this slightly differently: 'the social system responds to the individual's position as an outsider, to the fact that he or she can no longer be integrated into a social subsystem, by acknowledging and authorising their claim to "self-realisation".'[64]

The idea of the individual as subject, the notion of his or her authenticity and sovereignty, his or her claims to independence and self-realisation, were noted above as characteristics of the modern artist. In contrast to the elitist perspective epitomised in the cult of genius, which drew a sharp line between the artist and the average self, Luhmann asserts that *every* individual can embody the same principle, that the average self can also lay claim to self-realisation or authenticity, a claim that the social system must accept as legitimate because of the alterity, the otherness, strangeness or alienation, that the modernity process has created between the system and the individual. However, the alterity of each modern individual *vis-à-vis* society does not entail the positive significance of the artistic genius's higher or lower position in relation to society. Alterity here indicates neither transcendence nor sublimity, but the lack of place, the exclusion of the individual from something that no longer qualifies as society, but operates merely as a set of functional interrelations among objectified subsystems. The average subject's individuality is consequently understood as an 'individuality of exclusion'. This subject's alterity *vis-à-vis* society is kind of private exile: 'The world of "the subjects" cannot participate directly in this world and withdraws in private and interior forms of consolation.'[65]

66 Adorno, 'Noten zur Literatur' [1974], op. cit., p. 211.

67 Casey Haskins, 'Autonomy', in Michael Kelly (ed.), *Encyclopedia of Aesthetics*, Oxford and New York: Oxford University Press, 1998, vol. 1, p. 172. 'While the industrial revolution ran its course with many a political upheaval, opposition was growing in the world of art to the glorification of science and technology and to the capitalist obsession with profit. The protest was chiefly humanist and aesthetic, directed at the crude materialism and rationalism of the bourgeoisie.' (Willem van Reijen and Hans van der Loo, *Modernisierung: Projekt und Paradox*, Munich: dtv, 1992, p. 76).

68 Peter Bürger, *Prosa der Moderne*, Frankfurt: Suhrkamp, 1988, p. 17.

69 Ibid., p. 15.

70 Rita Felski, *The Gender of Modernity*, Cambridge, MA, and London: Harvard University Press, 1995, p. 210. Terry Eagleton has called these directions, even more tersely and rather more irreverently, 'the past, the bush, the political future'. Terry Eagleton, *The Idea of Culture*, Oxford: Blackwell, 2000, p. 25. See also Cornelia Klinger, *Flucht, Trost, Revolte: Die Moderne und ihre ästhetischen Gegenwelten*, Munich: Hanser, 1995.

The average subject possesses neither the potential for healing the *Weltriss* nor the ability to forge a unity from fragments of life devoid of meaning.[66] Nevertheless, individuals are not necessarily alone in the ex-territory of privateness and inwardness; they can appeal to various factors in order to 'reproduce themselves… as a system of their own in the environment of society' and to attain deliverance, or at least relief, from the suffering caused by alienation in the modern world.

Art's absolute autonomy, and the authenticity of the artist in his heightened subject status, have made the aesthetic realm one of the few *loci* in the topography of modern society where the losses and deficits concomitant with the modernity process have been understood and addressed: 'given the failures of science and religion to address and remedy the forms of psychic fragmentation and social alienation that were now increasingly associated with modern experience, the arts have a unique redemptive mission in modern social life';[67] 'Art in the modern era is not simply a sphere alongside the spheres of science and ethics; rather, it is a counterworld born of the spirit of modernity.'[68] For that very reason art performs an important function not for society, 'but… for each and every individual'.[69] If the principle of 'autonomy' focuses on the object, on the work of art, and that of 'authenticity' on the privileged status of the subject as artist/author, then 'alterity' revolves principally around the subject/the subjectivity of the recipient who participates in the autonomy and authenticity of the aesthetic sphere at one remove.

Discontent with modernity may induce the subject to search for meaning and identity in very different, even opposing, directions — towards 'an edenic past, a projected future, or a zone of cultural otherness', in Rita Felski's summary description.[70] In the nineteenth and the twentieth century art moved in all these directions. Orientalism and primitivism (of various kinds), for example, helped the modern subject to escape into the past or into distant worlds, into 'paradises' supposedly untouched by processes modernisation or Westernisation. As a form of resistance to reality, aesthetic alterity encompasses both nostalgic preservation of what has (purportedly) been lost in the past and utopian anticipation of what is to yet come in the future (Ernst Bloch). Activist avant-gardes have understood their artistic rebellion against prevailing conditions as pioneering work in preparation for a great cultural, social and political revolution. Even when escape or rebellion fails, consolation is provided by alterity in its modest, quotidian, trivial form: the self finds ' a zone of cultural otherness', a spatially and temporally circumscribed protection from reality, in the spaces of art, in museums or concert halls, in private libraries, in the archives of the imagination. The idea of alterity, the oppositeness of the aesthetic *vis-à-vis* reality, is the true culmination of the ideal of modernity in art.

Answers to the question as to the precise nature of art's resistance, as to what direction it should take, depend on the kind of diagnosis made of modernity's ailments.

Especially in the early history of the modern era, the sphere of art was turned to principally for deliverance, or simply relief, from a reality perceived as disjointed, as strange, alienated or alienating, as ugly, chaotic or arbitrary. Aesthetic alterity was therefore associated with harmony, reconciliation, unity and beauty. Aesthetic form was thought to possess the ability to invest the singular or the particular with general validity, to present a section of the world, a piece, a fragment of reality, as complete, as whole, even as *the* whole, to show the accidental as essential, the fleeting as lasting, the moment as eternal, the arbitrary as necessary and meaningful. Narrative structures provided commonplace stories with a beginning and an

71 G. W. F. Hegel, *Vorlesungen über die Ästhetik I*, vol. 13, Frankfurt: Suhrkamp, 1970, p. 132. English version: *Hegel's Aesthetics. Lectures on Fine Art*. Oxford: Oxford University Press, 1975.

72 Georg Simmel, 'Soziologische Ästhetik', *Die Zukunft*, vol. 17, 1896, p. 205.

73 Perceptions of modernity typically oscillate between these two interpretative patterns. Wolfgang Welsch has examined this 'duality of contrary diagnoses of modernity' in his *Unsere postmoderne Moderne*, Weinheim: Acta Humaniora, 1988, pp. 53–63.

74 Jean-François Lyotard, 'Das Erhabene und die Avantgarde', in Jacques LeRider and Gérard Raulet (eds.), *Verabschiedung der (Post-)Moderne? Eine interdisziplinäre Debatte*, Tübingen: Narr, 1987, pp. 251–74.

75 Achille Bonito Oliva, *Im Labyrinth der Kunst*, Berlin: Merve, 1982, p. 55.

76 Ibid., pp. 58–59.

77 Iain Chambers, 'Unvollendete Demokratie und posthumanistische Kunst' in: Okwui Enwezor et al. (eds.), *Demokratie als unvollendeter Prozeß. Dokumenta 11_Plattform 1*, Ostfildern: Hatje-Cantz, 2002, p. 202f. English version: 'Unrealized Democracy and a Posthumanist Art', in Okwui Enwezor et al. (eds.), *Democracy Unrealized: Documenta 11_Platform 1*. Ostfildern: Hatje Cantz, 2002, p. 173.

78 Florian Rötzer, 'Zur Genese des Erhabenen', in Dietmar Kamper and Chr. Wulf (eds.), *Der Schein des Schönen*, Göttingen: Steidl, 1989, p. 94.

end. Aesthetic form thus generated meaning and significance. Composition structured even a slice of reality as small as Albrecht Dürer's *Piece of Turf*, which acquired unity and harmony through placement inside a frame. In short, aesthetic treatment freed its objects from the chief cause of suffering in the secular world, from contingency, and lent them monumentality: 'Nothing is present in the work of art that does not relate essentially to content and gives expression to it.'[71] Or, in Simmel's words: 'The essence of the aesthetic view and representation lies... in the emergence of the typical from the particular, the underlying law from the accidental, the essence and significance of things from the external and the fleeting. No appearance would seem capable of escaping this reduction to what is significant and eternal in it. Even the lowest, the ugliest, phenomenon can be placed within a framework of colours and forms, of feeling and experience, and thus gain significance in a most appealing way; all we need do is to immerse ourselves deeply and lovingly enough in even the most indifferent phenomenon, however common-place or repulsive in appearance, and we will discover in it, too, an emanation and evidence of that ultimate unity of all things from which beauty and meaning spring.... to the sufficiently sharpened gaze the whole beauty, the sense of the world-whole [shines] through.'[72] Creating unity, wholeness and meaning, art achieved what the modernity process had seemed to render impossible and illegitimate.

If modern reality is perceived not in terms of a loss of order, but as a homogeneous, firmly structured entity, even as an 'iron cage',[73] then aesthetic alterity will take the form of the unruly, unsettling and deviating, the disruptive and fragmentary.[74] 'Art [is] to be understood as the production of catastrophes, as the creation of a discontinuity that destroys the tectonic balance of language'.[75] 'The experience of art [reinforces] the inevitability of the rupture, the unresolvability of all conflicts and the impossibility of any reconciliation with things.... This kind of art arises from an awareness of the irreducibility of the fragment, of the impossibility of re-establishing unity and balance.'[76] Especially in recent years, many authors have spoken of art's unsettling alterity, of 'the aesthetics... of disturbance that reveals a gap, an interval in the world, that signals a limit and establishes a transit, a passage elsewhere. It is in this space — historically nominated with such terms as the sublime, the uncanny, alterity — that the pedagogical languages of institutional identity, busily seeking to legitimate the narration of the nation, citizenship and cultural subjectivity, are interceded and deviated.... What this understanding of art holds out is the promise of interrupting such an order.'[77]

Alterity is involved whether art's opposition and resistance is aimed at the menacing totality of reality or at its painful fragmentation. The different paths of Classicism and Romanticism, of modernist and avant-garde currents, of the rivalry between the category of beauty and a work of art's objective formal laws on the one hand, and the category of the sublime and the subjectivity of the artistic genius on the other, inform different analyses of modernity and the contrary expectations attached to the redeeming, liberating or alleviating effect of art's alterity. Autonomy and authenticity meet and culminate in this third principle of aesthetic ideology, in art's functional specialisation 'as a repository for remnants of the life world that have been split off by reason'.[78] A hope that, if not 'the absolute', but at least 'something other', will be made 'present' characterises expectations placed in art by the individual, by the public and thus, ultimately, by society. This hope is the one element in the aesthetic ideology of modernity that has survived every disappointment — so far.

Coloniality:
The Darker Side of Modernity

Walter D. Mignolo

I.

I was intrigued, many years ago (around 1991), when I saw on the 'newsstand' of a book store the title of Stephen Toulmin's latest book: *Cosmopolis, The Hidden Agenda of Modernity* (1990). I went to a coffee shop, across the street from Borders in Ann Arbor and devoured the book over a cup of coffee: what was the hidden agenda of modernity? was the intriguing question. Shortly after that I was in Bogotá and found a book just published: *Los conquistados: 1492 y la población indígena de América* (1992). The last chapter of that book caught my attention. It was authored by Anibal Quijano of whom I had heard, but was not familiar. The article was titled 'Coloniality and modernity/rationality'.[1] I bought the book and found another coffee shop nearby. I devoured the article and the reading was a sort of epiphany. At that time I was finishing the manuscript of *The Darker Side of the Renaissance* (1995), but did not incorporate the article. There was much I had to think about and the manuscript was already framed. As soon I handed the manuscript to the press, I concentrated on 'coloniality', which became a central concept in *Local Histories/ Global Designs: Coloniality, Subaltern Knowledge and Border Thinking* (2000). After the publication of the book, I wrote a lengthy theoretical article, 'The Geopolitics of Knowledge and the Colonial Difference', published in *South Atlantic Quarterly* (2002). For Toulmin the hidden agenda of modernity was the humanistic river running behind instrumental reason. For me the hidden agenda (and darker side) of modernity was coloniality. What follows is a recap of the work I have since done in collaboration with members of the collective modernity/coloniality.[2]

The basic thesis is the following: 'modernity' is a European narrative that hides its darker side, 'coloniality'. Coloniality, in other words, is constitutive of modernity — there is no modernity without coloniality.[3] Hence, today the common expression 'global modernities' imply 'global colonialities' in the precise sense that the colonial matrix of power (coloniality, for short) is being disputed by many contenders: if there cannot be modernity without coloniality, there cannot be either global modernities without global colonialities. That is the logic of the polycentric capitalist world of today. Consequently, de-colonial thinking and doing emerged, from the sixteenth century on, as responses to the oppressive and imperial bent of modern European ideals projected to, and enacted in, the non-European world.

II.

I will start with two scenarios — one from the sixteenth century and the other from the late twentieth and the first decade of the twenty-first centuries.

1 The article is available in English: 'Coloniality and Modernity/Rationality', *Cultural Studies*, vol. 21, nos. 2–3, pp. 155–67 (2007).

2 The first publication in English of the work done by the collective since 1998 has been published in *Cultural Studies*, vol. 21, nos. 1–2 (2007). A special issue on 'Globalisation and the Decolonial Option'.

3 The point has been argued several times in the past decade. See for instance, Arturo Escobar, 'Beyond the Third World: imperial globality, global coloniality, and anti-globalization social movements', *Third World Quarterly*, vol. 25, no. 1, pp. 207–30 (2004).

4 Every time I say 'capitalism' I mean it in the sense of Max Weber: 'The spirit of capitalism is here used in this specific sense, it is the *spirit of modern capitalism*... Western European and American capitalism...' *The Protestant Ethics and the Spirit of Capitalism* [1904/05], London: Routledge, 1992, pp. 51–52.

2.1. Let's imagine the world around 1500. It was, briefly stated, a polycentric and non-capitalist world. There were several co-existing civilisations, some of long histories, others being formed around that time. In China, the Ming Dynasty ruled from 1368 to 1644. It was a centre of trade and a civilisation of long history. Around 200 BC, Chinese Huángdinate (often wrongly called 'Chinese Empire') co-existed with the Roman Empire. By 1500, the former Roman Empire became the Holy Roman Empire of the German Nations, which still co-existed with the Chinese Huángdinate ruled by the Ming Dynasty. Out of the dismembering of the Islamic Caliphate (formed in the sixth century and ruled by the Umayyads in the seventh and eighth centuries, and by the Abassids from the eight to the thirteenth centuries) in the fourteenth century three sultanates emerged. The Ottoman Sultanate in Anatolia with its centre in Constantinople; the Safavid Sultane with its centre in Baku, Azerbaijan and the Mughal Sultanate formed out of the ruins of the Delhi Sultanate that lasted from 1206 to 1526. The Mughals (whose first Sultan was Babur, descendent of Genghis Kan and Timur) extended from 1526 to 1707. By 1520, Moscovites had expelled the Golden Horde and declared Moscow the 'Third Rome'. The history of the Russian Tsarate began. In Africa, the Oyo Kingdom (around what is today Nigeria), formed by the Yoruba nation, was the largest Kingdom in West Africa encountered by European explorers. The Benin Kingdom, after Oyo the second largest in Africa, lasted from 1440 to 1897. Last but not least, the Incas in Tawantinsuyu and the Aztecs in Anáhuac were two sophisticated civilisations by the time of the Spanish arrival. What happened then in the sixteenth century that would change the world order transforming it into the one in which we are living today? The advent of 'modernity' could be a simple and general answer, but... when, how, why, where?

2.2. At the beginning of the twenty-first century the world is interconnected by a single type of economy (capitalism)[4] and distinguished by a diversity of political theories and practices. Dependency theory should be reviewed in the light of these changes. But I will limit myself to distinguishing two overall orientations. On the one hand, the globalisation of capitalist economy and the diversification of global politics is taking place. On the other, we are witnessing the multiplication and diversification of anti-neo-liberal globalisation (e.g., anti-global capitalism).

On the first orientation, China, India, Russia, Iran, Venezuela and the emerging South American Union have already made clear that they are no longer willing to follow up on uni-directional orders coming from the International Monetary Fund, the World Bank or the White House. Beneath Iran there is the history of Persia and the Safavid Sultanate; beneath Iraq the history of the Ottoman Sultanate. The past sixty years of Western entry in China (Marxism and capitalism) did not replace China's history with the history of Europe and the United States since 1500; and the same with India. On the contrary, it reinforced China's aim for sovereignty. In Africa, the imperial partition of Western countries between the end of the nineteenth and early-twentieth century (that provoked the First World War) did not replace the past of Africa with the past of Western Europe. And so in South America, 500 years of colonial rule by peninsular officers and, since early 1900, by Creole and Mestizo elites, did not erase the energy, force and memories of the Indian past (cf., current issues in Bolivia, Ecuador, Colombia, South of Mexico and Guatemala); neither did it erase the histories and memories of communities of African descent in Brazil, Colombia, Ecuador, Venezuela and the insular Caribbean. Moving in the opposite direction was the emergence of the state of Israel in 1948, which exploded toward the end of the first decade of the twenty-first century.

On the second orientation, we are observing many non-official (rather than non-governmental) transnational organisations not only manifesting themselves 'against' capitalism, globalisation and questioning modernity, but also opening up global but non-capitalist horizons and de-linking from the idea that there is a single and main modernity surrounded by peripheral or alternative ones. Not necessarily rejecting modernity but making clear that modernity goes hand in hand with coloniality and, therefore, modernity has to be assumed in both its glories and its crimes. Let's refer to this global domain 'de-colonial cosmopolitanism'.[5] No doubt that artists and museums are playing and have an important role to play in global formations of trans-modern and de-colonial subjectivities.

III.

What happened in between the two scenarios outlined above, the sixteenth and the twenty-first centuries? Historian Karen Armstrong — looking at the history of the West from the perspective of a historian of Islam — has made two crucial points.

Armstrong underscores the singularity of Western achievements in relation to the known history until the sixteenth century. She notes two salient spheres: economy and epistemology. In the sphere of economy, Armstrong points out that 'the new society of Europe and its American colonies had a different economic basis' that consisted in reinvesting the surplus in order to increase production. The first radical transformation in the domain of economy that allowed the West to '*reproduce its resources indefinitely*' is generally associated with colonialism.[6]

The second transformation, epistemological, is generally associated with the European Renaissance. Epistemological here shall be extended to encompass both science/knowledge and arts/meaning. Armstrong locates the transformation in the domain of knowledge in the sixteenth century, when Europeans 'achieved a scientific revolution that gave them greater control over the environment than anybody had achieved before'.[7]

No doubt, Armstrong is right in highlighting the relevance of a new type of economy (capitalism) and the scientific revolution. They both fit and correspond to the celebratory rhetoric of modernity — that is, the rhetoric of salvation and newness, based on European achievements during the Renaissance.

There is, however, a hidden dimension of events that were taking place at the same time, both in the sphere of economy and in the sphere of knowledge: *the expendability of human life* (e.g., enslaved Africans) and of life in general from the Industrial Revolution into the twenty-first century. Afro-Trinidadian politician and intellectual Eric Williams succinctly described this situation by noting that: 'one of the most important consequences of the Glorious Revolution of 1688 [...] was the impetus it gave to the principle of free trade.... Only in one particular did the freedom accorded in the slave trade differ from the freedom accorded in other trades — the commodity involved was man.'[8] Thus, hidden behind the rhetoric of modernity, human lives became expendable to the benefit of increasing wealth and such expendability was justified by the naturalisation of the racial ranking of human beings.

In between the two scenarios described above, the idea of 'modernity' came into the picture. It appeared first as a double colonisation, of time and of space. Colonisation of time was created by the simultaneous invention of the Middle Age in the process of conceptualising the Renaissance;[9] the colonisation of space

5 Walter D. Mignolo, 'Cosmopolitanism and the De-Colonial Option', in Torill Strand (ed.), *Cosmopolitanism in the Making*. Special issue of *Philosophy and Education. An International Journal*, forthcoming.

6 Karen Armstrong, *Islam: A Short Story*, New York: The Modern Library, 2000, p. 142 (emphasis added).

7 Ibid., p. 142.

8 Eric Williams, *Capitalism and Slavery*, Chapel Hill: The University of North Carolina Press, 1944, p. 32.

9 John Dagenais, 'The Postcolonial Laura', *MLQ: Modern Language Quarterly*, vol. 65, no. 3, September 2004, pp. 365–89.

10 See for instance the symposium on Global Modernities, a conceptual debate on *Altermodern: Tate Triennal 2009 Exhibition* (http://www.tate.org.uk).

11 *The New Asian Hemisphere: The Irresistible Shift of Global Power to the East*, Kishore Mahbubani, 2008. Mahbubani is dean of the Lee Kwan Yee School of Public Policy in Singapore and collaborator for the Financial Times. See an illuminating interview in youtube.

12 See interview with Kishore Mahbubani by Suzy Hansen in http://dir.salon.com.

13 Kaldoum Shaman, *Islam and the Orientalist World-System*, London: Paradigm Publishers, 2008.

14 Walter D. Mignolo, 'The Darker Side of the Enlightenment. A Decolonial Reading of Kant's Geography' in Stuart Elden and Eduardo Mendieta (eds.), *Kant's Geography*, Stony Brook: Stony Brook Press, forthcoming.

15 See Enrique Dussel, 'Modernity, Eurocentrism and Transmodernity: in dialogue with Charles Taylor', Biblioteca Virtual CLACSO. For an analytical survey of 'transmodernity' and 'coloniality', see Ramón Grosfóguel: 'Trans-modernity, Border Thinking and Global Coloniality. Decolonizing Political Economy and Postcolonial Studies', *Eurozine*, 2007, (http://www.eurozine.com).

by the colonisation and conquest of the New World. In the colonisation of space, modernity encounters its darker side, coloniality. During the time span 1500 to 2000 three cumulative (and not successive) faces of modernity are discernable: the first is the Iberian and Catholic face led by Spain and Portugal (1500–1750, approximately); the second, the 'heart of Europe' (Hegel) face lead by England, France and Germany (1750–1945); and finally the US American face lead by the United States (1945–2000). Since then, a new global order began to unfold: a polycentric world interconnected by the same type of economy.

In the last quarter of the twentieth century, 'modernity' was questioned in its own *chronology* and ideals, within Europe and the United States: the term post-modernity refers to such critical arguments. More recently, altermodernity is coming out as a new term and period, within Europe.[10] *Spatially*, expressions such as alternative modernities, subaltern modernities and peripheral modernities were introduced to account for modernity but from non-European perspectives. All of them have one common problem: these narratives and arguments maintain the centrality of Euro-American modernity or, if you wish, assume one 'modernity of reference' and put themselves in subordinate positions. All these narratives have another element in common: they assume that 'the world is flat' in its triumphal march toward the future while concealing coloniality. And finally, all of them over-looked the possible reality that local actors in the non-European world are claiming 'our modernity' while de-linking from Western imperatives, be it the corporate camp claiming 'our capitalist modernity' or the de-colonial camp claiming 'our non-capitalist, de-colonial modernity'.

The corporate claim (de-Westernisation) is being forcefully argued by Singaporean Kishore Mahbubani, among others. Mahbubani had made the case for the rise of the 'new Asian hemisphere and the shift of global power'.[11] 'Modernity' is not rejected but appropriated in the current shift lead by East and South Asia. Mahbubani's provocative question: 'Can Asians Think?' is, on the one hand a confrontation with Western epistemic racism and, on the other, a defiant and disobedient appropriation of Western 'modernity': Why would the West feel threatened by Asian appropriation of capitalism and modernity if such an appropriation will benefit the world and humanity at large, he asks?[12]

In the de-colonial camp (that is, not the postmodern and the altermodern), transmodernity would be the parallel concept. This type of argument is already at work among Islamic intellectuals. Being part of the modern-world system and entrenched unabashedly with European modernity, a global future lies in working toward the rejection of modernity and genocidal reason, and the appropriation of its emancipating ideals.[13] Similarly, claims are being made in the growing con-versations on 'de-colonial cosmopolitanism'. While Kant's cosmopolitanism was Euro-centred and imperial, de-colonial cosmopolitanism becomes critical of both, Kant's imperial legacies and of polycentric capitalism in the name of de-Westernisation.[14] For these reasons, trans-modernity would be a more fitting description of envisioned futures from de-colonial perspectives.[15]

IV.

The preceding explorations are based on the hypothesis that modernity and coloniality are two sides of the same coin. 'Coloniality' is short hand for 'colonial matrix (or order) of power'; it describes and explains coloniality as the hidden and darker side of modernity. The hypothesis runs as follows:

16 'On the Colonization of Amerindian Languages and Memories: Renaissance Theories of Writing and the Discontinuity of the Classical Tradition', *Comparative Studies in Society and History*, vol. 34, no. 2, 1992, pp. 301–30 (http://www.jstor.org).

17 See Fredric Jameson, *A Singular Modernity. Essays on the Ontology of the Present*, London: Verso, 2002.

18 For example, in Africa, Kwame Gyekye: *Tradition and Modernity. Philosophical Reflections on the African Experience*, New York: Oxford University Press, 1997; in Iran, Ramin Jahanbegloo (ed.), *Iran: Between Modernity and Tradition*, Laham, Md: Lexigton Books, 2004; in India, Ashis Nandy, *Talking India. Ashis Nandy in Conversation with Ramin Jahangegloo*, New York: Oxford University Press, 2006. In South America, where the intelligentsia is basically of European descent (contrary to Africa, Iran or India, where the intelligentsia is basically 'native', that is, not of European descent), the concern is more with modernity than with tradition, since 'tradition' for such ethno-class is basically European tradition. Which is not the case for Africans, Iranians or Indians.

1. As I mentioned before, the European Renaissance was conceived as such, establishing the bases for the idea of modernity, through the double colonisation of time and space. The double colonisation was tantamount with the invention of European traditions. One was Europe's own tradition (colonisation of time). The other was the invention of non-European traditions: the non-European world that co-existed before 1500 (colonisation of space). The invention of America was indeed the first step in the invention of non-European traditions that modernity was in charge of superseding by conversion, civilisation and later by development.[16]

2. 'Modernity' became — in relation to the non-European world — synonymous with salvation and newness. From the Renaissance to the Enlightenment, it was spearheaded by Christian Theology as well as by secular Renaissance Humanism (still linked to theology). The rhetoric of salvation by conversion to Christianity was translated into the rhetoric of salvation by the civilising mission, from the eighteenth century on, when England and France displaced Spain leading to Western imperial/colonial expansion. The rhetoric of newness was complemented with the idea of 'progress'. Salvation, newness and progress took a new turn — and a new vocabulary — after the Second World War, when the United States took over the previous leadership of England and France, supported the struggle for decolonisation in Africa and Asia and started an economic global project under the name of 'development and modernisation'. We know today the consequences of salvation by development. The new version of this rhetoric, 'globalisation and free trade', is under dispute.

From de-colonial perspectives, then, these four stages and versions of salvation and newness coexist today in diachronic accumulation although from the (post)modern perspective and self-fashioned narrative of modernity, based on the celebration of salvation and newness, each stage supersedes and makes the previous one obsolete: *it builds on newness and on modernity's own tradition.*

3. The rhetoric of modernity (salvation, newness, progress, development) went hand in hand with the logic of coloniality. In some cases, it was through colonisation. In other cases, like China, it was by diplomatic and commercial manipulations from the Opium War to Mao Ze-dong. The period of neo-liberal globalisation (from Ronald Reagan and Margaret Thatcher to the collapse of the George W. Bush administration with the failure in Iraq and on Wall Street), exemplifies the logic of coloniality taken to its extreme: to the extreme of revealing itself in its own spectacular failure. The economic failure of Wall Street coupled with the failure in Iraq, opened up the gates to the polycentric world order.

In summation, modernity/coloniality are two sides of the same coin. Coloniality is constitutive of modernity; there is no modernity, there cannot be, without coloniality. Postmodernity and altermodernity do not get rid of coloniality. They only present a new mask that, intentionally or not, continues to hide it.

V.

Because the idea of modernity was built as solely European and, in that argument, there was and is just a 'singular' modernity,[17] it engendered a series of latecomers and wannabes (e.g., alternative, peripheral, subaltern, altermodernities). All of which reproduce the vexing question on 'modernity and tradition', a question you do not find much debated among Euro-American intellectuals. For that very reason, the debates about 'modernity and tradition' were and still are a concern, mainly, of intellectuals from the non-European (and US) world.[18]

Basically, the problems and concerns with modernity and tradition are enunciated from or in relation to the ex-Third World and of non-European histories — Japan, for example. In/for Japan, modernity was and is an issue extensively explored and debated. Harry Harootunian explored the issue in detail in his book *Overcome by Modernity. History, Culture and Community in Interwar Japan* (2000); in Russia, modernity was an issue since Peter and Catherine the Great who wanted to jump on the band-wagon of European modernity, but it was too late and ended up in reproducing, in Russia, a sort of second-class modernity.[19] China and India are not exempt. I have mentioned de-Westernisation arguments advanced in East and South East Asia. Sanjib Baruah recently summarised 'India and China' debating modernity. In a section revealingly entitled 'engaging the modern', Baruah observes that India is — in spite of its recent corporate face — the home of strong intellectual opposition to ideas of development and modernisation, following the teaching of Mahatma Gandhi.[20] His analysis points toward conflictive scenarios confronting arguments in defence of 'wanting to become modern and to develop' with those engaging in radical criticisms of modernity and development.[21] The scenario is a common one in Africa and in South America. But in that general scenario, what is really at stake in modernisation is vested in economic development. Baruah writes:

> Critics of modernity enjoy quite a bit of intellectual prestige in India (though this should not be confused with an actual adherence to their ideas). India is home to sophisticated intellectual and activist opposition to mainstream ideas on development and modernisation. As the China-historian Prasenjit Duara points out, counter narratives to modernity have 'almost as much visibility as the narrative of progress' in India. Viewed comparatively, the 'general acceptability and prestige' of Gandhi's anti-modern ideas in India is remarkable, even though policymakers ignore his ideas in practice.[22]

In England, Anthony Giddens ended his argument in his celebrated book *The Consequences of Modernity* (1990) by asking himself: 'Is Modernity a Western Project?' He sees the nation-state and systematic capitalist production as the European anchor of modernity. That is, control of authority and control of economy grounded on the historical foundation of imperial Europe. In this sense, the answer to his question was 'a blatant yes'.[23]

What Giddens says is true. So, what is the problem? The problem is that it is half true: it is true in the story told by someone who dwells, comfortably one should think, in the house of 'modernity'. If we accept that 'modernity' is a Western project let's then take responsibility for 'coloniality' (the darker and constitutive side of modernity): the crimes and violence justified in the name of modernity. 'Coloniality' in other words is one of the most tragic 'consequences of modernity' and at the same time the most hopeful in that it has engendered the global march toward de-coloniality.

VI.

If you dwell in the history of British India, rather than in Britain, the world doesn't look the same. In Britain you may see it through Giddens lenses; in India probably through Gandhi's lenses. Would you make a choice or work with the undeniable

19 See Madina Tlostanova, 'The Janus-Faced Empire Distorting Orientalist Discourses. Gender, Race and Religion in the Russian/(post) Soviet Construction of the Orient', *WKO* (Spring 2008); Leonid Heretz, *Russia on the Eve of Modernity. Popular Religion and Traditional Culture under the Last Tsars*, Cambridge: Cambridge University Press, 2007; Eugene Ivakhnenko, 'A Threshold-Dominant Model of the Imperial and Colonial Discourses of Russia', *South Atlantic Quarterly*, vol. 105, no. 3, 2006, pp. 595–616.

20 Sanjib Baruah, 'India and China: Debating Modernity', *World Policy Journal*, vol. 23, no. 4, 2006–07, p. 62.

21 'Modernisation' since 1945 translates as 'development', that is, conflating the spirit of an historical period with economic imperial designs. The argument has been made several times. For instance, Arturo Escobar, *Encountering Development. The Making and Unmaking of the Third World*, Princeton: Princeton University Press, 1994; for the Mediterranean area, see Ella Habiba Shohat, 'The Narrative of the Nation and the Discourse of Modernization: The Case of Arab-Jews in Israel', 1998 (http://www.worldbank.org).

22 Baruah, op. cit., p. 63.

23 Anthony Giddens, *The Consequences of Modernity*, California: Stanford University Press, 1990, p. 174.

24 Partha Chatterjee, 'Talking
About Modernity in Two Languages',
*A Possible India. Essays in Political
Criticism*, New Delhi: Oxford India,
1998, pp. 263–85.

25 Ibid., pp. 273–74.

26 Ibid., p. 275.

27 Ibid.

conflictive co-existence of both? Indian historian and political theorist, Partha Chatterjee addressed the problem of 'modernity in two languages'. The article, collected in his book *A Possible India* (1998), is the English version of a lecture he delivered in Bengali and presented in Calcutta.[24] The English version is not just a translation but also a theoretical reflection on the geo-politics of knowledge and epistemic and political de-linking.

Unapologetically and forcefully, Chatterjee structured his talk on the distinction between 'our modernity' and 'their modernity'. Rather than a single modernity defended by postmodern intellectuals in the 'First World' Chatterjee plants a solid pillar to build the future of 'our' modernity — not independent from 'their modernity' (because Western expansion is a fact), but unrepentantly and unashamedly 'ours'.

This is one of the strengths of Chatterjee's argument. But remember, first, that the British entered India, commercially, toward the end of the eighteenth century and, politically, during the first half of the nineteenth century when England and France, after Napoleon, extended their tentacles in Asia and Africa. So for Chatterjee, in contradistinction with South American and Caribbean intellectuals, 'modernity' means Enlightenment and not Renaissance. Not surprisingly Chatterjee takes Immanuel Kant's 'What is Enlightenment' as a pillar in the foundation of the European idea of modernity. For Kant, Enlightenment meant that Man (in the sense of the human being) was coming of age, abandoning its immaturity, reaching his freedom. Chatterjee points out Kant's silence (intentionally or not) and Michel Foucault's short sightedness when reading Kant's essays. Missing in Kant's celebration of freedom and maturity and in Foucault's celebration was the fact that Kant's concept of Man and humanity was based on the European concept idea of humanity from the Renaissance to the Enlightenment and not in the 'lesser humans' that populated the world beyond the heart of Europe. So, 'enlightenment' was not for everybody, unless they become 'modern' in the European idea of modernity.

One point in Chatterjee's insightful interpretation of Kant-Foucault is relevant for the argument I am developing here. I would surmise, following Chatterjee's argument, that Kant and Foucault lacked the colonial experience and political interest propelled by the colonial wound. Not that they had to have it. But yes, that their view cannot be universalised. If you have been born, educated and your subjectivity formed in Germany and France, your conception of the world and feeling will be different from someone born and raised in British India. Thus Chatterjee can state that 'we — in India — have built up an intricately differentiated structure of authorities which specifies who has the right to say what on which subjects'.[25] In 'Modernity in two languages' Chatterjee reminds us that the 'Third World' has been mainly 'consumer' of First World scholarship and knowledge:

Somehow, from the very beginning, we had made a shrewd guess that given the close complicity between modern knowledge and modern regimes of power, we would for ever remain consumers of universal modernity; never would we be taken as serious producers.[26]

Chatterjee concludes that it is for this reason that 'we have tried, for over a hundred years, to take our eyes away from this chimera of universal modernity and clear up a space where we might become the creators of our own modernity'.[27] I imagine you are getting the point. 'The other' (the *anthropos*) decided to disobey: epistemic and political disobedience that consist of the appropriation of European modernity while dwelling in the house of coloniality.

28 Thus it is not surprising to find today growing concerns, and a number of scholars, working on the de-colonisation of international law, Branwen Gruffydd Jones (ed.), Boulder/New York: *Decolonizing International Relations*, Roman and Littlefield Publishers Inc., 2006.

29 For the ontological and epistemic difference, see Nelson Maldonado-Torres, 'On the Coloniality of Being: Contributions to the Development of a Concept', *Cultural Studies* vol. 21, nos. 2–3, 2007, pp. 240–70.

30 I am thinking, certainly, of Tony Bennett, *The Birth of the Museum. History, Theory, Politics*. London: Routledge, 1995, pp. 60ff, but also of more specific studies such as Nick Prior, *Museums and Modernity, Art Galleries and the Making of Modern Culture*, Oxford: Berg Publisher, 2002, and Gisela Weiss, *Sinnstiftung in der Provinz: Westfälische Museen im Kaiserreich*, Paderborn: Ferdinand Schöning Verlag, 2005; and the review by Eva Giloi for *H-German*, June, 2007 (https://www.h-net.org).

31 Walter D. Mignolo, 'Museums in the Colonial Horizon of Modernity', CIMAM Annual Conference, São Paulo, November 2005, pp. 66–77, (http://www.cimam.org).

32 Two examples of de-colonial uses of museums installations are Fred Wilson's *Mining the Museum* (http://www.citypaper.com); and Pedro Lasch, *Black Mirror/Espejo Negro* (http://www.ambriente.com).

33 A case in point could found in Immanuel Kant, *Observations on the Feeling of the Beautiful and the Sublime* (particularly section IV), Berkeley: University of California Press, 1960.

34 Antony Anghie, 'Francisco de Vitoria and the Colonial Origins of International Law' in Eve Darian-Smith and Peter Fitzpatrick (eds.), *Laws of the Postcolonial*, Ann Arbor: the University of Michigan Press, 1999, pp. 89–108.

VII.

It is not common to think of international law as related to the making of 'modernity'. I will argue in this section that international law (more exactly legal theology) contributed in the sixteenth century to the creation — a creation demanded by the 'discovery' of America — of racial differences as we sense them today. What to do, Spanish legal theologians asked themselves, with the 'Indians' (in the Spanish imaginary) and, more concretely, with their land? International law was founded on racial assumptions: 'Indians' had to be conceived, if humans, as not quite rational, although ready for conversion.[28] 'Modernity' showed up its face in the epistemic assumptions and arguments of legal theology to decide and determine who was what. Simultaneously, the face of 'coloniality' was disguised under the inferior status of the invented inferior. Here you have a clear case of coloniality as the needed and constitutive darker side of modernity. Modernity/coloniality is articulated here on the ontological and epistemic differences: Indians are, ontologically, lesser human beings and, in consequence, not fully rational.[29]

Conversely, museums have been counted in the making of modernity.[30] However, questions about museums (as institutions) and coloniality (as the hidden logic of modernity) have not been asked. It is taken for granted that museums are 'naturally' part of the European imagination and creativity. In VII.1 I attempt to unveil coloniality under international law regulating international relations. And in VII.2, I open up the question about museums and coloniality. Museums, as we know them today, did not exist before 1500. They have been built and transformed — on one hand — to be the institutions where Western memory is honoured and displayed; where European modernity conserves its tradition (the colonisation of time) and — on the other hand — to be the institutions in which the difference of non-European traditions is recognised.[31] The open question is then how to de-colonise museums and to use museums to de-colonise the reproduction of Western colonisation of time and space.[32]

VII. 1

Francisco de Vitoria is rightly celebrated mainly among Spanish and other European scholars for being one of the fathers of international law. His treatise, *Relectio de Indis* is considered foundational in the history of the discipline.

Central to Vitoria's argument was the question of *ius gentium* (rights of the people or rights of nations). *Ius gentium* allowed Vitoria to put at the same level of humanity both Spaniards and Indians. He did not pay attention to the fact that by collapsing Quechuas, Aymaras, Nahuatls, Mayas, etc, under the label 'Indians' he was already stepping into a racial classification. So it was not difficult for Vitoria to slide smoothly into the second step of his argument: although equal to Spaniards in the domain of *ius gentium*, Vitoria concluded (or he knew it first and then argued it) Indians were sort of childish and needed the guidance and protection of Spaniards.

At that moment Vitoria inserted the *colonial difference* (ontological and epistemic) into international law. The colonial difference operates by converting differences into values and establishing a hierarchy of human beings ontologically and epistemically. Ontologically, is assumed that there are inferior human beings. Epistemically, it is assumed that inferior human beings are rational and aesthetically deficient.[33] Legal scholar Anthony Anghie has provided an insightful analysis of the historical foundational moment of the colonial difference.[34] In a nutshell the argument is the following: Indians and Spaniards are equal in the face of natural

35 A de-colonial history of international law can be found in Siba N'Zatioula Grovogui, *Sovereigns, Quasi Sovereigns, and Africans*, Minneapolis: the University of Minnesota Press, 1996.

36 Anghie, op. cit., p. 102 (emphasis added).

37 Franz Hinkelammert's analysis of Locke's inversion of human rights is very helpful to understand the double side/double density of 'modernity/ coloniality' and how the rhetoric of modernity continues to obliterate coloniality. See his 'The Hidden Logic of Modernity: Locke's Inversion of Human Rights', 2004.

38 It is certainly very telling that a Japanese scholar, Nishitan Osanu, has cogently argued that 'anthropos' and 'humanitas' are two Western concepts. Indeed, they produce the effect of reality when the modern ideals of 'humanitas' cannot exist without the modern/colonial invention of 'anthropos'. Think of the debate of immigration in Europe, for example. There you have modernity/coloniality at its best. See Nishitai Osamu, 'Anthropos and Humanitas, Two Western Concepts' in Naoki Sakai and Jon Solomon (eds.), *Translation, Biopolitics, Colonial Difference*, Hong Kong: Hong Kong University Press, 2006, pp. 259–74.

law as both, by natural law, are endowed with *ius gentium*. In making this move, Vitoria prevented the Pope and divine law from legislating on human issues.

However, once Vitoria established the distinction between 'principes Christianos' (as well as Castilians in general) and 'los bárbaros' (e.g., the *anthropos*) on the other, and he made his best effort to balance his arguments based on the equality he attributed to both people by natural law and *ius gentium*, he turns into justifying Spaniard's *rights and limits* toward 'the barbarians' to expropriate or not; to declare war or not; to govern or not. Communication and interaction between Christians and barbarians are one-sided: *the barbarians have no say in whatever Vitoria said because barbarians were deprived from sovereignty even when they are recognised as equal per natural law and ius gentium.*

The move is foundational to the legal and philosophical constitution of modernity/coloniality and the principle of reasoning would be maintained through the centuries, modified in the vocabulary from barbarians to primitives, from primitives to communists, from communists to terrorists.[35] Thus *orbis christianius*, secular cosmopolitanism and economic globalism are names corresponding to different moments of the colonial order of power and distinct imperial leadership (from Spain to England to the United States).

Anghie made three decisive points about Vitoria and the historical origins of international law that illuminate how modernity/coloniality are bound together and how salvation justifies oppression and violence. The first is 'that Vitoria is concerned, not so much with the *problem of order among sovereign states but the problem of order among societies belonging to two different cultural systems*'.[36]

The second is that the framework is there to regulate its violation. And when the violation occurs, then the creators and enforcers of the framework had a justification to invade and use force to punish and expropriate the violator. This logic was wonderfully rehearsed by John Locke in his *Second Treatise on Government* (1681). One can say that 'coloniality', in Vitoria, set the stage not only for international law but also for 'modern and European' conceptions of governmentality. It seems obvious that Locke did not get as much from Machiavelli as from the emergence of international law in the sixteenth century, and in the way that Vitoria, and his followers, settled to discuss both the question of 'property' and 'governance' in the interaction between Christians and the barbarians.[37]

The third is that the 'framework' is not dictated by divine or natural law but by human interests, and in this case, the interests of Christian Castilian males. Thus, the 'framework' presupposes a very well located and singular locus of enunciation that, guarded by divine and natural law, it is presumed to be uni-versal. And on the other hand, the uni-versal and uni-lateral frame 'includes' the barbarians or Indians (a principle that is valid for all politics of inclusion we hear today) in their difference thus justifying any action Christians will take to tame them. The construction of *the colonial difference* goes hand in hand with the establishment of *exteriority*: exteriority is the place in which the outside (e.g., *anthropos*) is invented in the process of creating the inside (e.g., *humanitas*) to secure the safe space where the enunciator dwells.[38]

Clearly, then, Vitoria's work suggests that the conventional view that sovereignty doctrine was developed in the West and then transferred to the non-European world is, in important respects, misleading. *Sovereignty doctrine acquired its character through the colonial encounter*. This is the darker history of sovereignty, which cannot be understood by any account of the doctrine that assumes the existence of sovereign states.

Briefly stated: if modernity is a Western invention (as Giddens says), so too is coloniality. Therefore, it seems very difficult to overcome coloniality from a Western modern perspective. De-colonial arguments are pressing this blind spot in both right-wing and left-wing oriented arguments.[39]

VII. 2

In the context at hand, 'museums' as we know them today (and their forerunner — Wunderkammer, Kunstkammer) have been instrumental in shaping modern/colonial subjectivities by splitting Kunstkammer into 'museums of arts' and 'museums of natural histories'.[40] Initially, Peter the Great's Kunstkammer was put in place toward 1720, while the British Museum (founded as a Cabinet of Curiosity) was created later (toward 1750). However, the institution of Kunstkammer in the West became the locale for curiosities brought from European colonies, most of the time, by looting. The history of the building, Le Louvre, goes back to the Middle Ages. But the museum, Le Louvre, came into being after the French Revolution.

Nowadays, a process of de-Westernisation has already begun. The hundreds of museums being constructed in China are part of this process. De-Westernisation is a process parallel to de-coloniality at the level of the state and of the economy. Kishore Mahbubani, quoted above, is one of the most consistent and coherent voices of de-Westernisation and the political, economic and epistemic shift to Asia.[41]

One can ask, then, given this exhibition titled 'Modernologies' what is the place of museums and art, in general, in the rhetoric of modernity and the colonial matrix of power? How can museums become places of de-colonisation of knowledge and of being or, on the contrary, how can they remain institutions and instruments of control, regulation and reproduction of coloniality?[42] By asking these questions, we are entering here in plain territory of knowledge, meaning and subjectivity. If international law legalised economic appropriation of land, natural resources and non-European labour (of which 'outsourcing' today shows the independence of the economic sector from patriotic or nationalist arguments of 'developed' states) and warranted the accumulation of money, universities and museums (and lately mainstream media) warranted the accumulation of meaning. The complementarity of accumulation of money and accumulation of meaning (hence, the rhetoric of modernity as salvation and progress) sustains the narratives of modernity. While colonialilty is the unavoidable consequence of 'the unfinished project of modernity' (as Jürgen Habermas would say) — since coloniality is constitutive of modernity — de-coloniality (in the sense of global de-colonial projects) becomes the global option and horizons of liberation. The horizon of such liberation is a transmodern, non-capitalist world, no longer mapped by 'la pensée unique', adapting Ignacio Ramonet's expression, neither from the right nor from the left: coloniality engendered de-coloniality.

VIII. Coda

I hope to have contributed to understanding how the logic of coloniality was structured during the sixteenth and seventeenth centuries; to understand how it changed hands, was transformed and adapted to the new circumstances, although maintaining the spheres (and the interrelations) in which management and control of authority, of economy, of people (subjectivity, gender, sexuality) and of knowledge

39 Anghie, op. cit., p. 103 (emphasis added).

40 See the cogent argument, on this issue, by Donald Preziosi, 'Brain of the Earth's Body: Museums and the Framing of Modernity', in Bettina Messias Carbonell (ed.), *Museum Studies. An Anthology of Contexts*, London: Blackwell, 2004, pp. 71–84.

41 See Mahubani, op. cit., note 9, and also his provocative arguments under the heading of 'Can Asians Think?' (http://dir.salon.com).

42 For example, *Modernity in Central Europe, 1918–1945* is one of those exhibitions that 'enhances' Western Europe by embracing modernity. National Gallery of Art, Washington D.C, 10 June – 10 September 2007.

has been played out in building the mono-centric world order from 1500 to 2000; and how that order is being transformed into a polycentric one.

Now what is exactly the colonial matrix of power/coloniality? Let's imagine it in two semiotic levels: the level of the enunciated and the level of the enunciation. At the level of the enunciated, the colonial matrix operates at four interrelated domains interrelated in the specific sense that a single domain cannot be properly understood independently from the other three. This is the junction between conceptualisations of 'capitalism' (either liberal or Marxist) and the conceptualisation of the colonial matrix, which implies a de-colonial conceptualisation. The four domains in question, briefly described, are (and remember that each of these domains is disguised by a constant and changing rhetoric of modernity (that is, of salvation, progress, development, happiness):

1) Management and control of subjectivities (for example, Christian and secular education, yesterday and today, museums and universities, media and advertising today, etc.)

2) Management and control of authority (for example, viceroyalties in the Americas, British authority in India, US army, Politbureau in the Soviet Union, etc.)

3) Management and control of economy (for example, by reinvesting of the surplus engendered by massive appropriation of land in America and Africa; massive exploitation of labour starting with the slave-trade; by foreign debts through the creation of economic institutions such as World Bank and IMF, etc.);

4) Management and control of knowledge (for example, theology and the invention of international law that set up a geo-political order of knowledge founded on European epistemic and aesthetic principles that legitimised the disqualifications over the centuries of non-European knowledge and non-Europeans aesthetic standards, from the Renaissance to the Enlightenment and from the Enlightenment to neo-liberal globalisation; philosophy).

The four domains (the enunciated) are all and constantly interrelated and held together by the two anchors of enunciation. Indeed, who were and are the agents and institutions that generated and continue to reproduce the rhetoric of modernity and the logic of coloniality? It so happened that, in general, the agents (and institutions) creating and managing the logic of coloniality were Western Europeans, mostly men; if not all heterosexual, at least assuming heterosexuality as the norm of sexual conduct. And they were — in general — mostly white and Christian (either Catholic or Protestant). Thus, the enunciation of the colonial matrix was founded in two embodied and geo-historically located pillars: the seed for the subsequent racial classification of the planet population and the superiority of white men over men of colour but also over white women. *The racial and patriarchal underlying organisation of knowledge-making (the enunciation) put together and maintain the colonial matrix of power* that daily becomes less visible because of the loss of holistic views promoted by the modern emphasis on expertise and on the division and sub-division of scientific labour and knowledge.

Global futures need to be imagined and constructed through de-colonial options; that is, working globally and collectively to de-colonise the colonial matrix of power; to stop the sand castles built by modernity and its derivatives. Museums can indeed play a crucial role in the building of de-colonial futures.

The artists' statements indicated in grey are from interviews
conducted by André Rottmann especially for this publication.

Artists and works

Anna Artaker

Unbekannte Avantgarde, 2008
(Unknown Avant-garde)
Photo installation
10 black-and-white photographs and 10 labels

Unknown Avant-garde consists of a selection of ten historic photographs depicting artists' groups of the twentieth century (Dada, the Surrealists, the Bauhaus, the Situationist International, etc.). In each case the photograph itself has become as much part of art history as the artists and the groups portrayed in the photographs.

The other common feature of these photographs is the presence of one woman among many male colleagues. The images thus also demonstrate the isolated position that women have been assigned by art history.

The photographs are complemented by the documentation of research on female avant-garde artists. The captions added to the photographs refer to women Dadaists, Surrealists, Situationists, etc., who are missing from the group portraits and have therefore remained invisible to art history. The captions thus correct the photographs and rewrite art history.

Anna Artaker

Individual works:
мишень / Zielscheibe, Moscow, 1913
(The Target Group)
Groupe dada, Paris, 1922
Surréalistes, Paris, 1924
Bauhaus, Dessau, 1926
Experimentele Groep, Amsterdam, 1949
Cobra, Paris, 1949
Abstract Expressionists, New York, 1950
Situationist International, London, 1960
Gruppe Spur, Schwabing, 1961
Austria Filmmakers Cooperative, Vienna, 1968

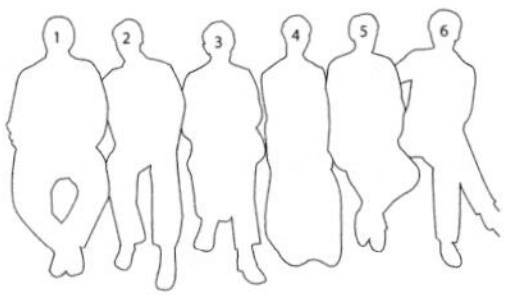

DONKEY'S TALE GROUP, Moscow 1913

Photograph in: Jewgeni Kowtun, Paul André (eds.),
Michail Larionow 1881–1964, Parkstone Press, Bournemouth 1998, p. 97

1 Alexandra Alexandrovna Exter, painter and stage designer
2 Liubov Sergeevna Popova, painter
3 Olga Vladimirovna Rozanova, painter
4 Unknown
5 Varvara Fyodorovna Stepanova, painter, stage designer and textile designer
6 Nadesha Andreevna Udalzova, painter

GROUPE DADA, Paris 1922

Photograph: Man Ray, Man Ray Trust / Centre Georges Pompidou, Paris

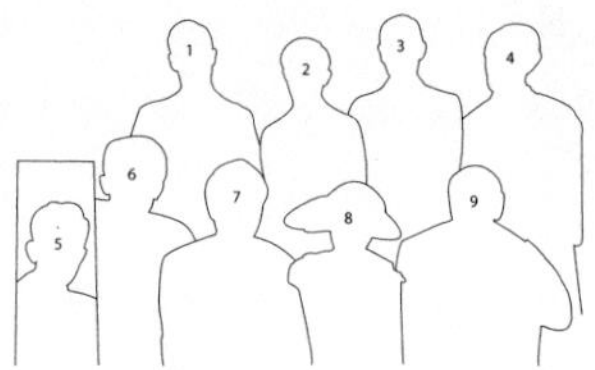

1 Céline Arnauld, writer
2 Emmy Ball-Hennings, cabaret artist and writer
3 Maria d'Arezzo, lyricist
4 Suzanne Duchamp, painter
5 Hannah Höch, artist
6 Mina Loy, artist, poet and actress
7 Sophie Taeuber, artist, dancer, professor and editor
8 Unknown
9 Mary Wigman, dancer, choreographer and dance instructor

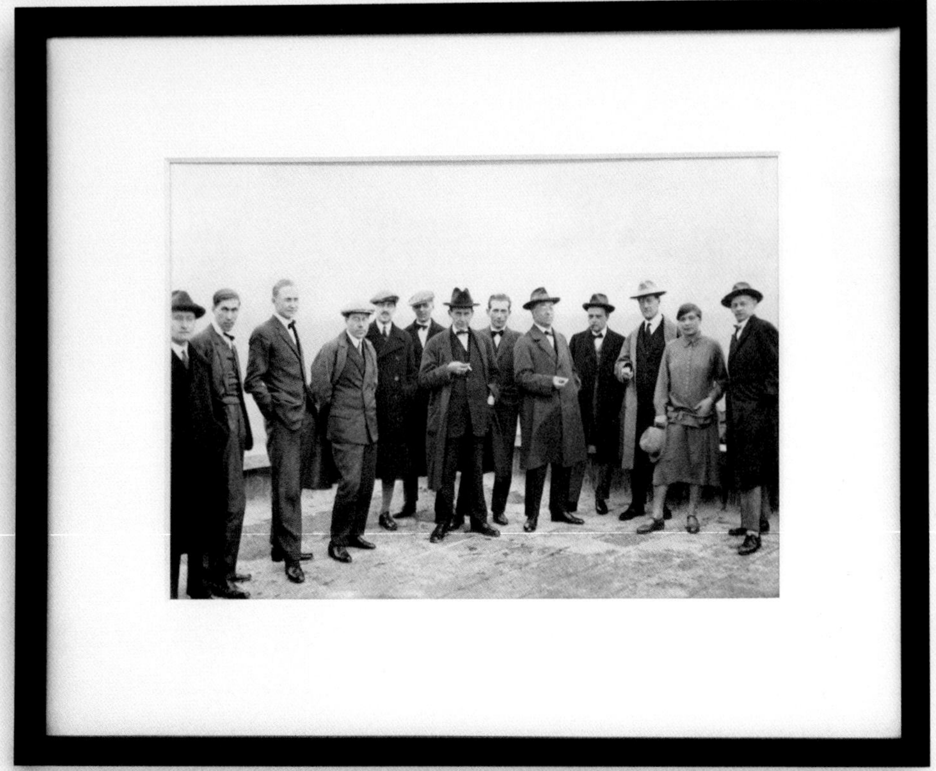

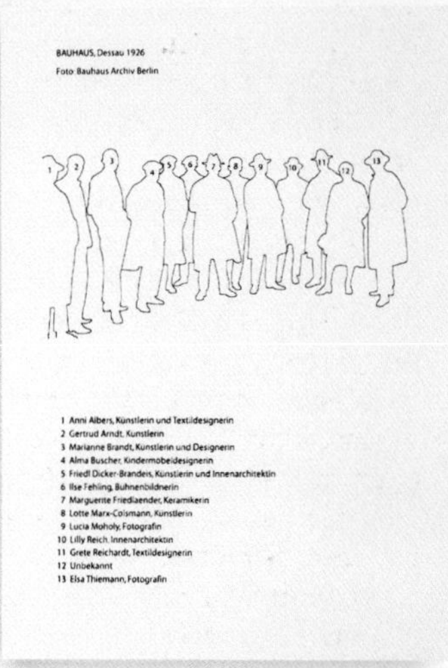

BAUHAUS, Dessau 1926
Foto: Bauhaus Archiv Berlin

1 Anni Albers, Künstlerin und Textildesignerin
2 Gertrud Arndt, Künstlerin
3 Marianne Brandt, Künstlerin und Designerin
4 Alma Buscher, Kindermöbeldesignerin
5 Friedl Dicker-Brandeis, Künstlerin und Innenarchitektin
6 Ilse Fehling, Bühnenbildnerin
7 Marguerite Friedlaender, Keramikerin
8 Lotte Marx-Coismann, Künstlerin
9 Lucia Moholy, Fotografin
10 Lilly Reich, Innenarchitektin
11 Grete Reichardt, Textildesignerin
12 Unbekannt
13 Elsa Thiemann, Fotografin

My work deals with the production of images in the context of historiography. Concretely, I am working with images that have been produced or used to represent history and through this have become a part of a certain historical narrative. At the core of my preoccupation with 'history' is my interest in the relationship between reality and the depiction of reality: I am interested in 'history' insofar as it is a model for the representation of reality, an object on the basis of which the complex interplay between representation and reality can be explored. ▷

SURREALISTS, Paris 1924

Photograph: Man Ray, Man Ray Trust / Centre Georges Pompidou, Paris

EXPERIMENTELE GROEP, Amsterdam 1949

Photograph: E. Kokkorris-Syriër in: Jean-Clarence Lambert, COBRA, Langwiesche publisher, Königstein im Taunus 1985, p. 149

COBRA, Paris 1949

Photograph: Collection Rijksbureau voor Kunsthistorische Documentatie (RKD), The Hague

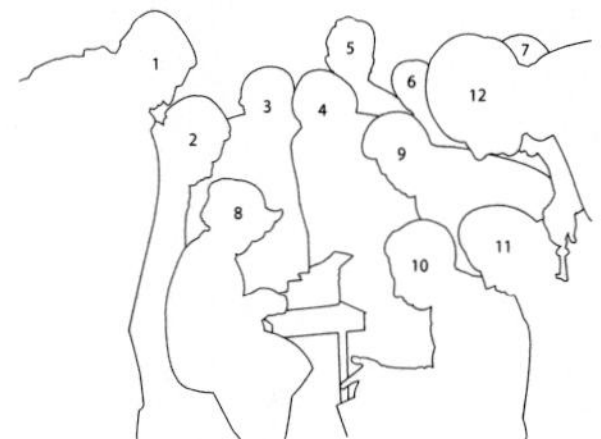

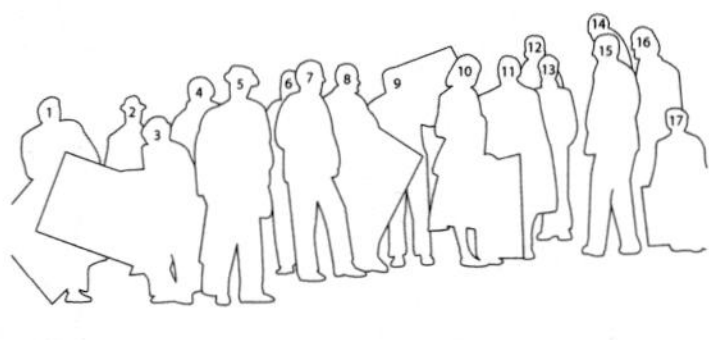

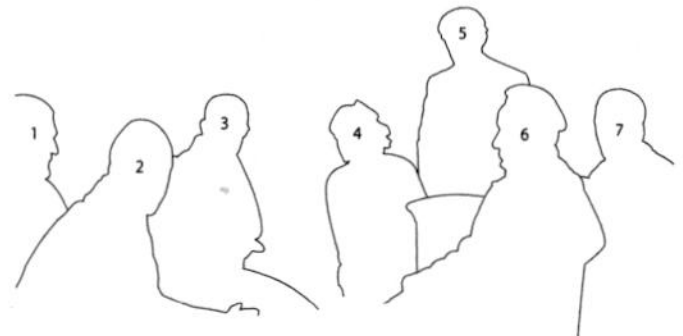

1 Eileen Agar, painter
2 Claude Cahun, writer and photographer
3 Leonora Carrington, painter, writer and playwright
4 Léonor Fini, painter
5 Dora Maar, photographer and painter
6 Lee Miller, photographer and war correspondent
7 (hidden) Meret Oppenheim, artist and lyricist
8 Unknown
9 Gisèle Prassinos, writer and translator
10 Kay Sage, painter and poet
11 Toyen, painter and illustrator
12 Remedios Varo, painter

1 Anneliese Hager, artist and poet
2 a passer-by
3 Madeleine Szemere, painter
4 Else Alfelt, painter
5 Anne Bonnet, painter and co-founder of Jeune Peinture Belge
6 Odette Collon, painter and co-founder of Jeune Peinture Belge
7 Jeanne de Dijn, sculptor
8 Lotti van der Gaag, sculptor and painter
9 Marthe Donas, painter
10 Unknown
11 Anne Éthuin, painter and lyricist
12 Sonja Ferlov, sculptor and painter
13 Irène Hamoir, poet and writer
14 Frieda Hunziker, painter
15 Hanny Korevaar, painter and sculptor
16 Lou Loeber, painter
17 Mig Quinet, painter and co-founder of Jeune Peinture Belge

1 Else Alfelt, painter
2 Lotti van der Gaag, sculptor
3 Anne Éthuin, painter and lyricist
4 Unknown
5 Sonja Ferlov, sculptor and painter
6 Soshana, painter and globe trotter
7 Madeleine Szemere, painter

SITUATIONIST INTERNATIONAL, London 1960

Photograph: Archiv Vera und HP Zimmer, Berlin

GRUPPE SPUR, Schwabing 1961

Photograph: Archiv Vera und HP Zimmer, Berlin

AUSTRIA FILMMAKERS COOPERATIVE, Vienna 1968

Photograph: Joseph Tandl, Hans Scheugl Archive, Vienna

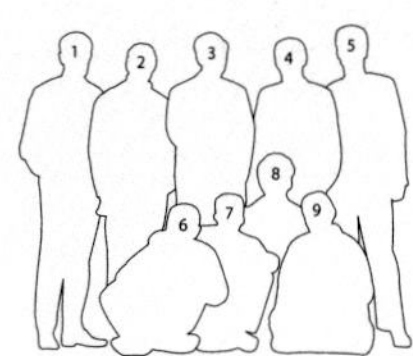

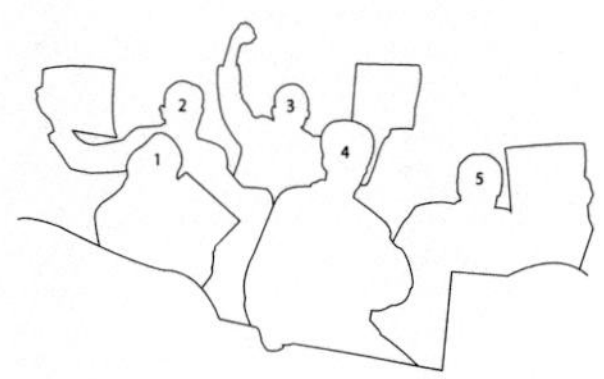

1 Michèle Bernstein, writer and critic
2 Edith Frey, situationist
3 Alice Becker-Ho, writer and poet
4 Katja Lindell, artist
5 Renée Nele, sculptor
6 Gretel Stadler, sculptor and ceramist
7 Elena Verrone, editor and translator
8 Unknown
9 Karen Eliot, artist and neoist

1 Unknown
2 Gretel Stadler, sculptor and ceramist
3 Eva Renée Nele Bode, sculptor
4 Jacqueline de Jong, artist and editor of the Situationist Times
5 Ursula Strauch-Sachs, painter

1 Linda Christanell, artist and filmmaker
2 Mara Mattuschka, director, painter and performance artist
3 Unknown
4 Lisl Ponger, filmmaker and photographer
5 Moucle Blackout, artist
6 Maria Lassnig, painter, trick film-maker and professor at the University of Applied Arts, Vienna

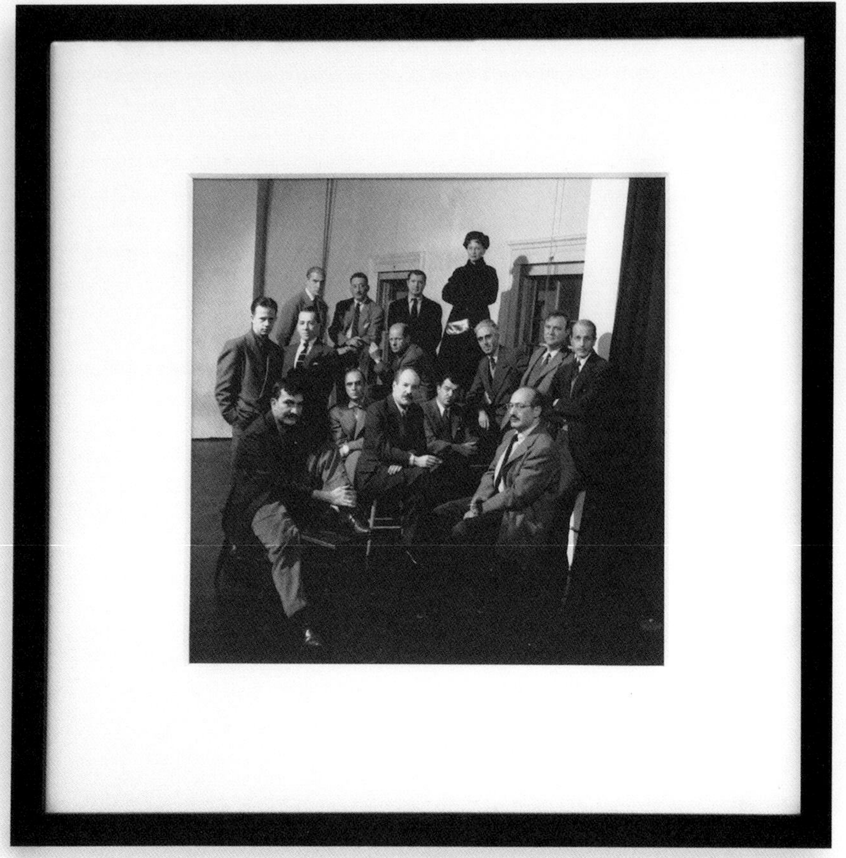

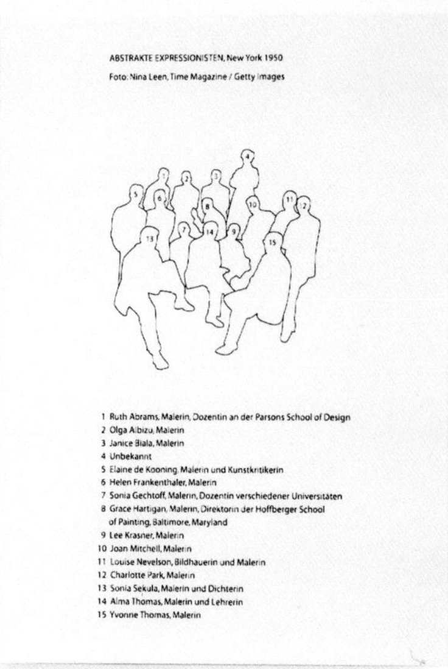

My work does not directly consider the many different concrete manifestations of modernism but rather *historisation* of modernism. However, this differentiation between 'modernism' and its historisation is itself problematic, especially considering that many of the protagonists of modern art had already reflected on and created their own historisation. Perhaps one could also say that I am interested in what took place 'offstage' of what has now become history. My work makes an *indirect reference* to what has come to represent modernism by shifting the focus to what happened outside of it. I thus concentrate on the unsaid preconditions and exclusions, the blind spots upon which the history of modernism is based. These gaps are all the more deserving of critical attention because they often challenge or contradict the selfconception of modernism. □

48 Köpfe aus dem Merkurov Museum, 2008
(48 Heads from the Merkurov Museum)
Film installation

The film shows close-ups of death masks of Russian/Soviet heroes in the Merkurov Museum in Gyumri, Armenia, taken by the Armenian/Soviet sculptor Sergei Merkurov (1881–1952).

The film's title, *48 Köpfe aus dem Merkurov Museum* (48 Heads from the Merkurov Museum), describes what the viewer sees and alludes to Kurt Kren's film *48 Köpfe aus dem Szondi Test* (48 Heads from the Szondi Test, 1960). Merkurov's plaster masks replace the portraits of psychotics in Kren's film as meaningful presences. Filmed as objects, the chronologically arranged masks are at once fragments of Soviet historiography and unsettling physiognomies belonging to its (dead) heroes.

Merkurov studied under Auguste Rodin in Paris and made Lenin's acquaintance during the latter's exile from Russia. After the October Revolution he became a People's Artist of the Soviet Union and from then until his death he created many monumental sculptures of Soviet heroes. He also took death masks of over three hundred prominent Soviets, among them Lenin, Sergei Eisenstein, Leo Tolstoy, Maxim Gorky and such Communist Party functionaries as Felix Dzerzhinsky, head of the Cheka, the dreaded secret police, and Andrei Zhdanov, responsible for censorship and the repressive cultural policies of the Stalin era. The museum in the house of the sculptor's birth contains some fifty death masks made by him.

Portrait photographs used in the personality test developed by the psychiatrist Leopold Szondi (1893–1986) in 1937 provided the basic material for Kren's *48 Heads from the Szondi Test*. Each participant in the test was shown forty-eight portrait photographs and asked to choose the most sympathetic and the most unsympathetic persons. Szondi attempted to deduce the psychopathological make-up of each participant from their choice of photographs, all of which were of people suffering from libidinal disturbances. The staccato-like rhythm with which Kren presents the faces makes it impossible to view the portraits in the way intended by Szondi. Playing with the image/reproduction as a carrier of meaning, Kren subverts the attribution of specific characteristics to human physiognomies through their supposed inscription in the face.

By translating auratic death masks (each one a 'final likeness') into the (mass) medium of film, *48 Heads from the Merkurov Museum* evokes the iconography of (Soviet) propaganda, with its dissemination on a similarly huge scale and its stylisation of faces as heroic masks. At the same time, the film addresses the exploitation of auratic images by the mass media and its basis in the seemingly significant physiognomies of media-transmitted personalities. Simply to reproduce a face in this context is to exclude genuine engagement with it, since all meaningful content is allegedly inscribed in the features of the imaged person. In this way, the casts of the (more or less well-known) faces of the dead arouse a desire for specific information at the point where the viewer is confronted with 'illegible' traces invested with the task of making the invisible visible. AA

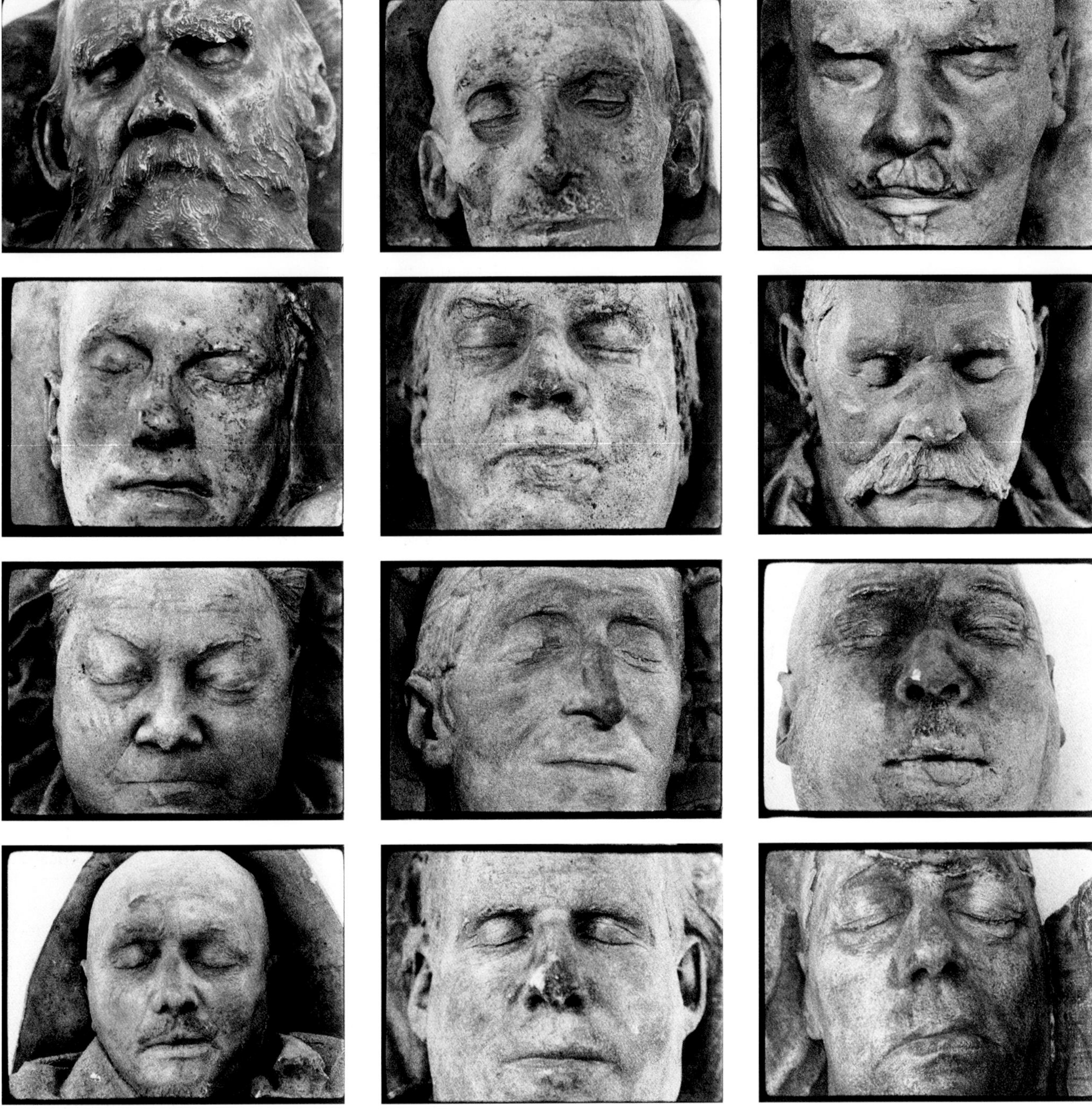

Alice Creischer/Andreas Siekmann

Atlas (Updating the Arntz and Neurath Atlas)
2003– work-in-progress
Installation of 25 prints
Presented partly on six mobile walls in juxtaposition with 15 pages
of the historical *Atlas Gesellschaft und Wirtschaft – Bildstatistisches
Elementarwerk* (Atlas of Society and Economy – Visual Charts
of the Essential Empirical Data of the World) by Gerd Arntz
and Otto Neurath, 1930

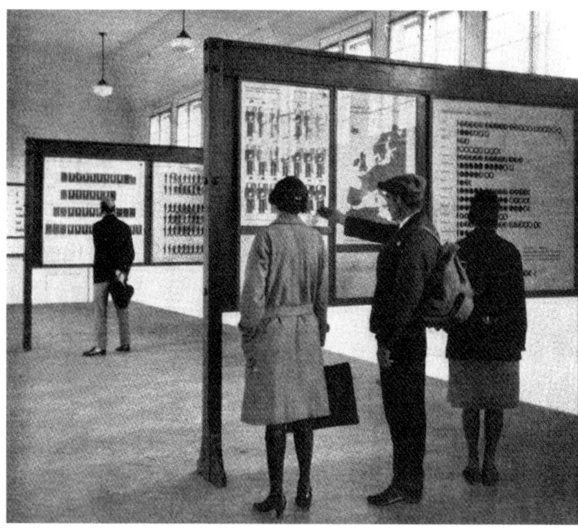

Gerhard Arntz / Otto Neurath
Atlas Gesellschaft und Wirtschaft
Installation view
Vienna City Hall, c. 1930

The *Atlas of Society and Economy* by Gerd Arntz and Otto Neurath

1. Updating the Atlas

Since 2003 we have been working with a number of different
partners on an update of the *Atlas of Society and Economy*,
devised in 1929–30 by the philosopher and economist Otto Neurath
in cooperation with the artist Gerd Arntz. In 1924 Neurath had
founded the Gesellschafts und Wirtschaftsmuseum (Museum of
Society and Economy), which developed the 'Viennese method'
of visual statistics. These pictorial statistics express relative
amounts numerically, not proportionally. Information cannot therefore be comprehended at a glance: it is necessary to spend time
examining it, and it is necessary to count. Similar institutes of
pictorial statistics were set up in the USSR from 1931 to 1934, but
were closed in the Stalinist era.

Arntz had previously worked with the Gruppe Progressiver
Künstler (Group of Progressive Artists) in Cologne, sharing
their anarchistic, syndicalistic political goals. We were especially
fascinated by the 'anti-subjective' depiction of the balance of
power within society in Arntz's graphic work. 'Subject' status is
represented as a result of the system or as a revolutionary class.
Arntz's visual argumentation uses the same means to call for
a reversal of this situation. At the time, this constituted an endorse-
ment of Soviet revolutions and their occupation of factories and
barracks. The atlas continued Arntz's diagrammatic mode of
visualisation. It seemed to us that the relationship between the
diagrammatic signs and the statistics they represented — for
example, serial icons for the unemployed and fists for strike days
— embodied a transition of the 'masses' from a statistical figure
to a potential threat. This transition could also inform the technical
reproducibility of the prints as political agitation in the form of
leaflets and newspaper illustrations.

When the atlas of pictorial statistics appeared in Leipzig in
1930, Arntz wrote about it in the newspaper *A bis Z*, the theoretical
organ of the Progressives: 'There can no longer be a pictorial art
of the bourgeoisie. Neither will the integration of painters into the
new endeavours of technology, architecture and constructional art
be accomplished by peaceful means. Such integration is part of
an overall rationalisation, which is creating the elements that will
help to bring about the abolition of current society.... If there must
be content, then [it should be] the conflict between capital and
labour.... It is the same with statistics. The figures and quantities,
the creation and the development of areas of production and of
human organisations, point to the end of previous forms of
economic activity.... [T]his is just a beginning. As this beginning is
developed further, it will become possible to depict our dependences and potentials in relation to materials and their quantities,
to analyse our current life, to make demands and to exert pressure
for the implementation of what has been discovered.'[1]

When the National Socialists came to power in Germany,
Arntz and Neurath fled to The Hague. 'In Holland the "Viennese
method of pictorial statistics" was developed further and renamed
the "International System of Typographic Picture Education". In its
Greek meaning, the acronym "ISOTYPE" alluded to one aspect of

Neurath and Arntz's programme of pictorial statistics: "always the same sign.'"[2] The types depicted in the signs are always 'wrong' — the unemployed do not have their hands in their pockets, for example, and migrants do not carry suitcases — but their abstraction, their depersonalisation, makes clear the balance of power among individuals by eliminating the possibility of society being represented as a collection of personal narratives that touch the heart. The form is political. Arntz wrote: 'It needs to be examined… to what extent different areas, especially the depiction of social conflicts, might effect changes to the method itself, which at present is being applied with a certain democratic "objectivity".'[3] This statement relates to personal involvement and its reflection in the method.

The atlas reveals how closely the ethics of rationalisation, technology and modernity encapsulated in the pictorial statistics project were bound up with its left-wing, revolutionary aims. Today, we find it difficult to invest its pictorial vocabulary with the urgency and actuality it possessed at the time, i.e., not to lose sight of the people it was addressing, the workers of the day. In adopting its pictorial vocabulary, we seek to transfer to the present the commitment and the artistic approach it embodies.

Working with students at the University of Lüneburg, we updated ten plates from the atlas in the summer semester of 2003 and the winter semester of 2003–04. We see the updating as a response to the apparent objectivity of statistics in experts' assessments and forecasts regarding social conditions, which often support the ideological position of those who commission the studies. Eventually, we aim to produce a counterpart to each of the one hundred plates in the atlas. These updates take the form either of a simple actualisation (for example, of the plate recording strikes and lockouts) or of statistics in areas thought to be equivalent to those addressed in the original (for instance, the replacement of the plate devoted to slavery and colonialism by one documenting the reparations demanded from the USA by African countries at the Durban conference). Our concern is not with representative facts, but with information that, although readily available, is ignored by prevailing concerns — for example, statistics relating to forced labour, European companies' relocation of manufacture to low-wage countries and so forth. This first set of updates involved the plates 'Staaten und Bevölkerung um 1500' (States and Populations c. 1500), 'Rüstungen vor dem Krieg und jetzt' (Armaments Before the War and Now), 'Reparationen' (Reparations), 'Gesellschaftsgliederung in Nürnberg' (Social Structure in Nuremberg), 'Wanderbewegungen wichtiger Länder' (Migration Patterns in Major Countries), 'Reallöhne' (Real Wages), 'Ökonomische Ungleichheit' (Economic Inequality), 'Streiks' (Strikes) and 'Kartografische Übersicht' (General Map).

Work proceeded with the plates 'Monopolartige Produktionen europäischer und außereuropäischer Länder' (Monopolistic Manufacturing in European and Non-European Countries), updated for the art centre Kunstraum Lakeside in cooperation with a project group in the economics faculty of Klagenfurt University. We focused here on the agreement on trade-related intellectual property rights (TRIPS). TRIPS was influenced by a lobby within the World Trade Organization called the Intellectual

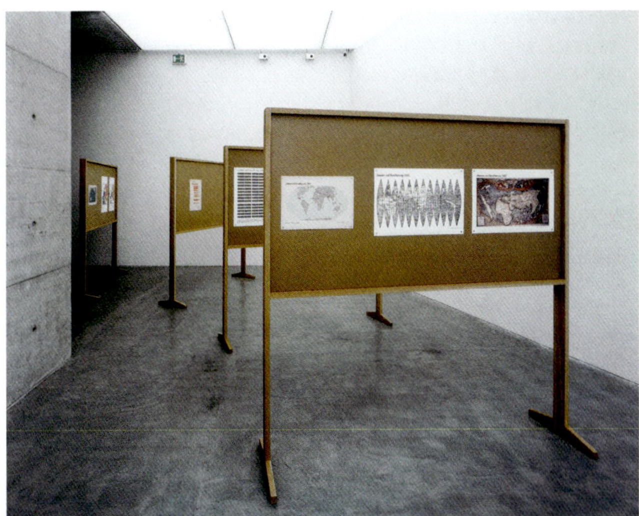

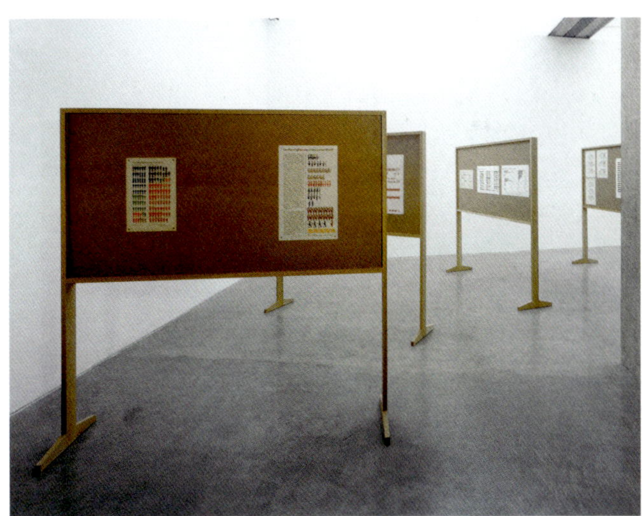

Atlas (Updating the Arntz and Neurath Atlas)
2003– work-in-progress
Installation view
Generali Foundation, Vienna, 2006

Property Committee, which included the twelve largest US corporations. The agreement permitted the privatisation of life-forms, plants and animal breeding, and the establishment of monopolies in the areas of seeds and medicines. One result of TRIPS has been the extension of copyright law, encouraging particularly rigorous monopolisation in the computer software and the communications industries. We selected the new building at Klagenfurt University as a suitable place to install the updated plates as wall panels because that development is an example of joint ventures involving the university and technology companies. In this way, we continued the conjunction of art and science that had informed the original atlas. We decided that henceforth all updating would be carried out on a site-specific basis.

2. Updating plate 69

Plate 69 belongs to a number of plates documenting developments in cities that reveal how industrialisation has replaced growth determined by climatic or geographical factors. We chose Dubai as a substitute for Damascus in plate 69 because it represents an extreme instance of detachment from climatic conditions. The 'ecological footprint' of the United Arab Emirates (UAE) is the most prominent of all, even exceeding that of the USA. One main cause of this is the tourist industry in Dubai.

The migration from country to town described in the atlas plates encompasses economic loss, flight from poverty and accumulations of people in workers' districts. One outstanding statistic relating to Dubai is the population's disproportionately high percentage of migrant workers (estimates vary from 85 to 95%). Their working conditions resemble those of slaves and they live in accommodation unfit for human habitation.

Our updating focused on population data and on the growth of urban infrastructure. Research into Dubai always leaves one dumbfounded — the largest of all shopping malls, the biggest airport and container port, building projects of gigantic dimensions and so on. Maps accessible on the Internet vie with each other for the most impressive 3-D animations. They form part of a city-branding that swamps judgement in a mass of superlatives. Many of the animated map sites are closed or consist of building sites arranged one behind the other as a sequence of identical apartment blocks, each with its beach area and fitness club. The mastery of logistics displayed by the real estate consortiums in marshalling endless supplies of workers and materials would also seem to involve planning the way of life of apartment occupants as a kind of serialised soap opera played out in a suburban heaven.

In 2000 the oil industry accounted for 10% of the city's GDP. By 2007 that figure had dropped to approximately 5%. Dubai draws its wealth from a number of free-trade zones, its position as a transportation hub, from tourism and real estate investment capital.

We have produced two plates, one staying close to the original, the other mapping the spread of the 'Dubai model' in the Menasa region (North Africa and Central and South Asia), which has hitherto received little attention in Europe. As in plate 69 of the atlas, we trace the development of the city and its population

in four stages: 1971 (the foundation of the UAE and the beginning of oil mining), 1980 (the revolution in Iran, producing a wave of emigration and exportation of capital supporters of the previous regime), 2001 (the increased strategic importance of the Gulf region after 11 September 2001, which prompted the US oil-field services corporation and defence contractor Halliburton, for example, to open a second headquarters in Dubai) and 2010 (the completion of the first phase of the new building projects). The maps for 1971 and 1980 are taken from the *National Atlas of The United Arab Emirates* (UAE University, Al Ain, 1993), that for 2000 from Dubai Major Projects (www.gis.gov.ae) and that for 2010 from www.squidoo.com/dubai-real-estate-dubai-property (Latest Dubai Map).

Damaskus

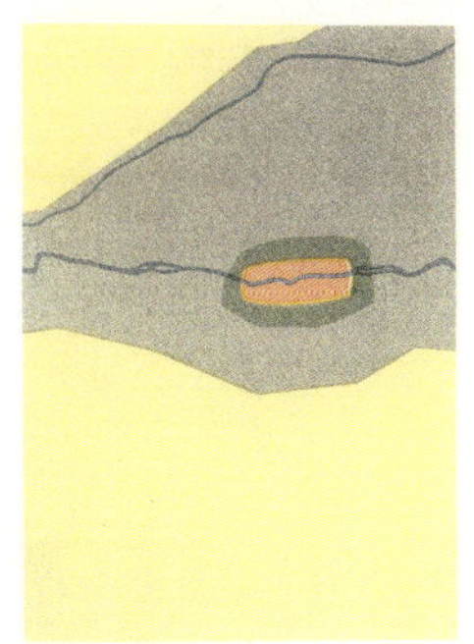
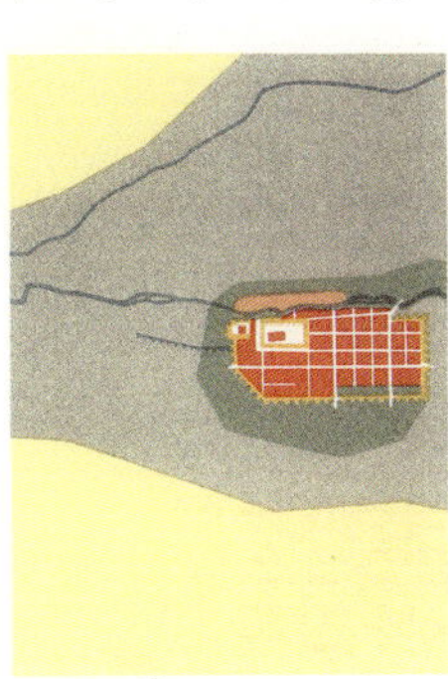
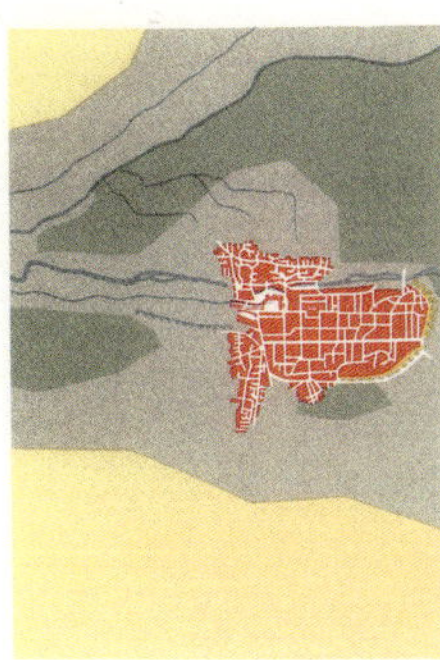
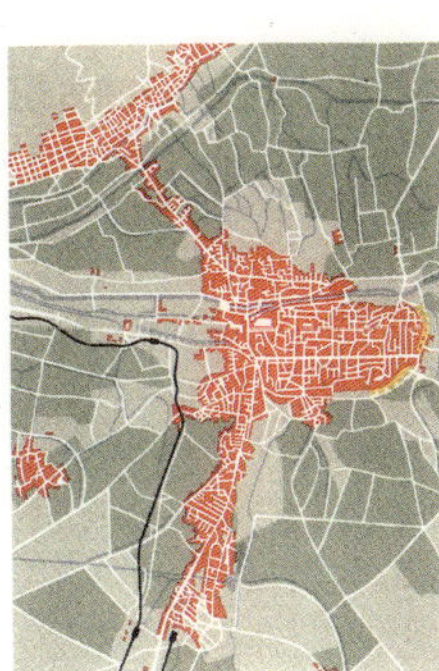

300 v. Chr.
Oasenstadt

300 n. Chr.
Römerlager

1500
Mohammedanische Handelsstadt

1930
Ansätze zu moderner Entwicklung

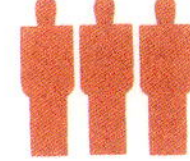
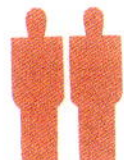

Jede Figur 100 000 Einwohner

Gerhard Arntz / Otto Neurath
Atlas Gesellschaft und Wirtschaft, 1930
Plate 69: *Damaskus Städtische Entwicklung*
(Damascus Urban Development)

The factographic tradition of some modern avant-gardes,
to which Arntz and Neurath's work is closely related,
would seem to have become obsolete in the 'information
age', with its surfeit of information. But information is
a saleable product and, as such, is not objective, but
forms part of ideologies, search engines and repressive
apparatus seeking to secure their share of the market.
We therefore encountered limitations in nearly all
our researches, the limitations of withheld, censored
or manipulated information. Usually, we had to rely on
the cooperation of political initiatives and NGOs. ▷

Alice Creischer/Andreas Siekmann

Dubai I

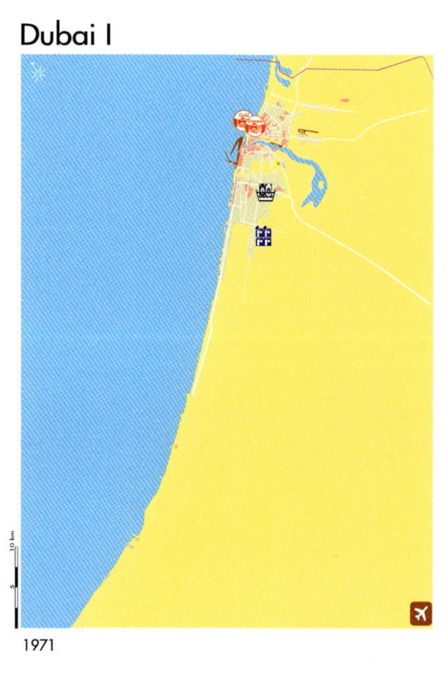

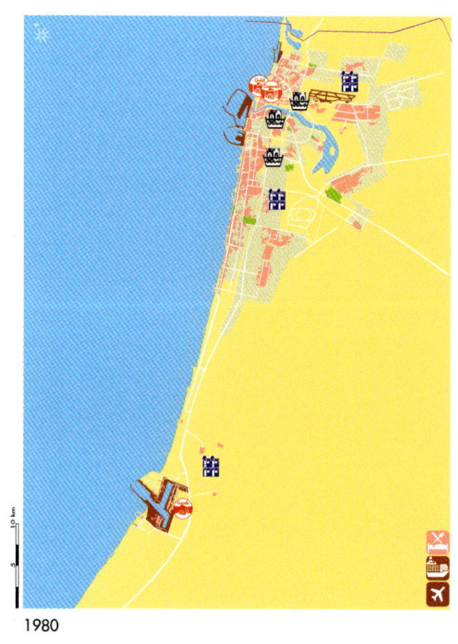

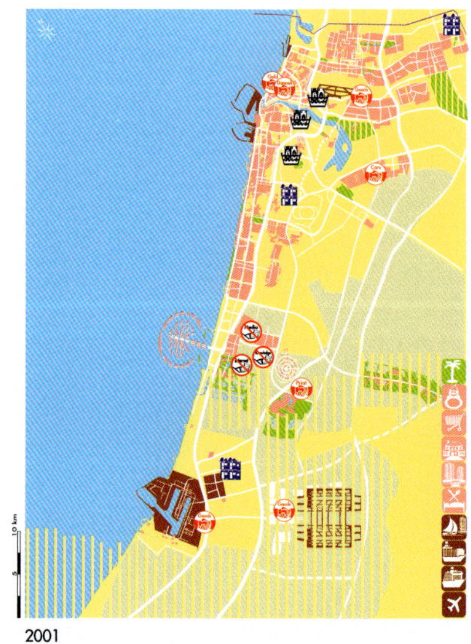

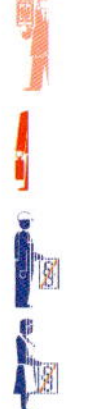

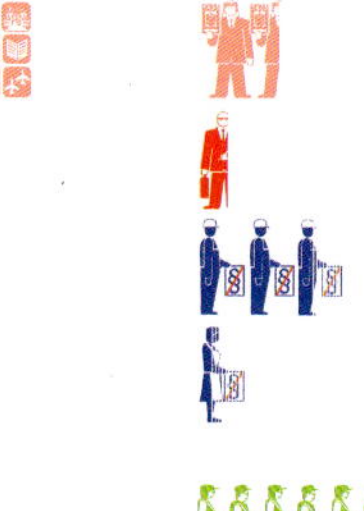

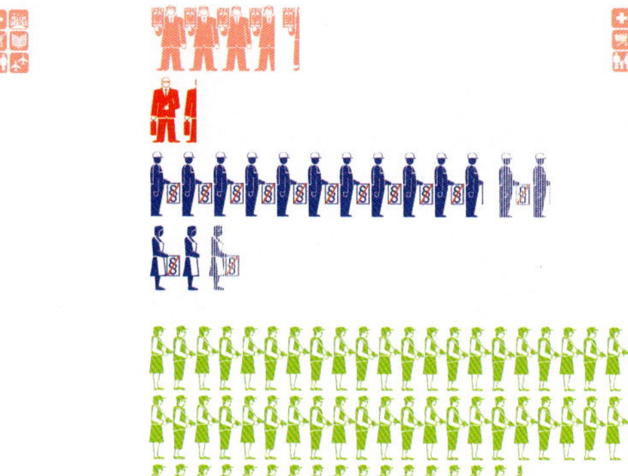

Every figure: 50,000 people

Atlas (Updating the Arntz and Neurath Atlas)
2003 – work-in-progress
Dubai I, 2007

2010

Citizens
Right to:
health, housing
consumption, education
family, mobility
Executives /
Engineers
Construction
workers
Home help
Illegal workers
Non-citizens
Tourists

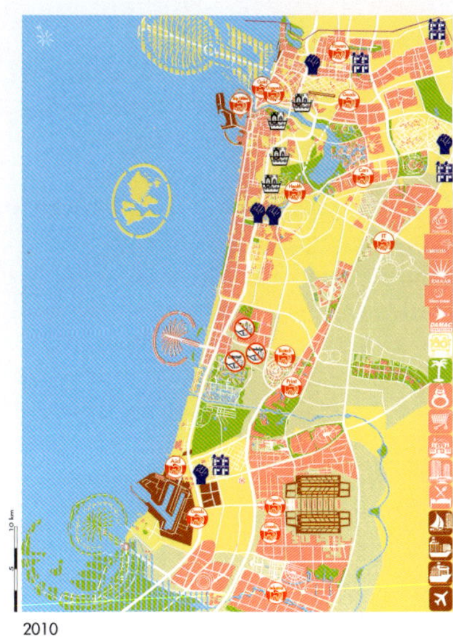

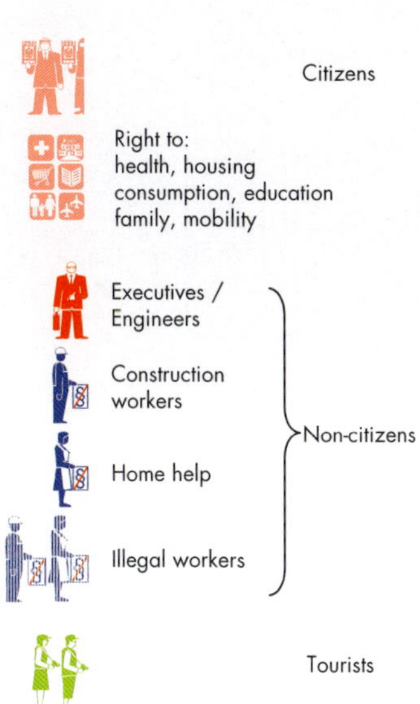

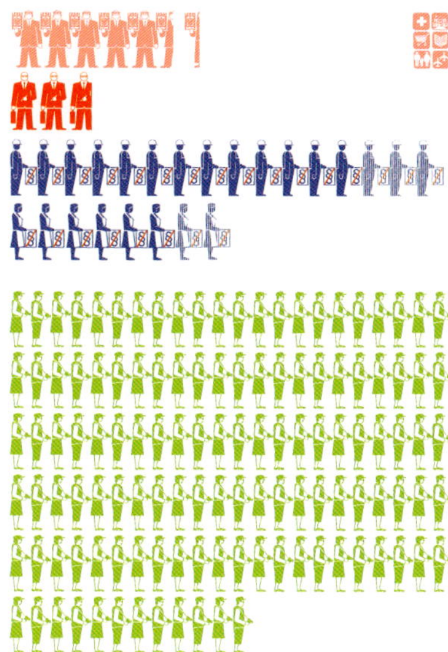

3. Plate 45 (The development of rubber manufacture since 1895) and plate 46 (The World Rubber Industry)

Plates 45 and 46 are among several headed 'Kolonialexport für den Verbrauch in den Ländern vom industriellen Typus (Zucker, Kaffee, Kakao, Tee, Baumwolle, Kautschuk)' (Colonial Exports for Consumption in Industrialised Countries [Sugar, Coffee, Cacao, Tea, Cotton, Rubber]).[4] They show the regions where the goods originated, their export and the increased recycling of the raw materials prompted by the First World War. Neither plate records the special terms of trade in operation. In our update we document the continuation of colonial dependences in the current global economy and the activities of the multinational agencies involved, their terms of trade and the human consequences.

Plates 36 to 39 show statistics relating to the basic foods grain, rice and potatoes. These seem to have been analysed separately from the colonial economy, indicating a blind spot. The 'High-level Conference on World Food Security: The Challenges of Climate Change and Bioenergy', held in Rome in the spring of 2008, launched a new term to replace 'hunger': 'food crisis'. The amount of food available annually dropped from fifteen million tons in the 1990s to eight million in 2007. In the meantime bio-petrol-related speculation has brought about a sharp rise in prices for grain and other foods. Hunger has now resulted in uprisings in over fifteen countries around the world. A primary cause is the increased use of agricultural land for industrial purposes.

In the update of plates 45 and 46 we substitute soy for rubber because its cultivation has risen dramatically in recent years, especially in South America. The use of soy as cattle feed is widespread, but it is also grown for the production of bio-petrol. This has entailed the customary concentration of cultivation in huge agro-industrial areas, resulting in the destruction of forests and the abandonment of agriculture catering for the food needs of the local population. Almost 60% of the South American soy industry is controlled by the Monsanto Corporation, which exports its genetically manipulated Roundup Ready beans on a worldwide basis. The bean seed is created from seed hybrids and pesticides that destroy other vegetation and cause respiratory diseases among the few local residents. Along with Bayer and Cargill, Monsanto helped to set up in Norway a world archive of all natural seeds. So, while contributing to the disappearance of such seeds, these corporations have had the audacity to participate in documenting their history. That is one more reason to draw up an alternative historical record.

Alice Creischer and Andreas Siekmann

1   Gerd Arntz, 'Bewegung in Kunst und Statistik', *A bis Z*, Cologne, 1931.
2   Ulf Wuggenik, *Reader zum Kongress: Pläne zum Verlassen der Übersicht*, published on the occasion of a congress held in connection with the Ex Argentina project at the Hebbel Theatre, Berlin, November 2003.
3   Arntz, op. cit.
4   Atlas commentary on plates 32 and 36–62.

Revised version of Alice Creischer and Andreas Siekmann, 'Aktualisierung des Atlas Gesellschaft und Wirtschaft', *Atlas: Spaces in Subjunctive*, Lüneburg: Kunstraum der Universität Lüneburg, 2004.

We do not believe in the direct coincidence of abstract sign and universalism, as propagated by modernism. We value the work of Arntz and Neurath for the concrete, empirical way in which it addresses issues, rendering a faceless 'definition' of society impossible. Our interest lies less in their rationalist programme than in their commitment to a political movement. Their work retains its militancy. The serial principle behind Arntz and Neurath's mode of visualisation is also important to us — their presentation of social conditions as quantities, their rejection of information that can be grasped 'at a glance', like the pie charts of the business world. However, we have had to revise their purely statistical approach, so as to use Isotype figures to describe complex circular phenomena. Our concern is political enlightenment in repressive conditions.□

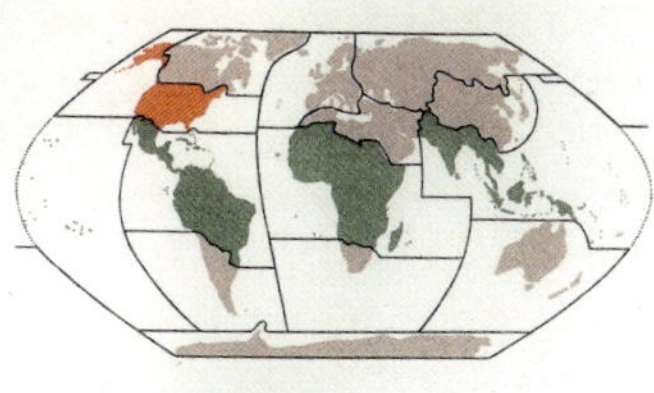
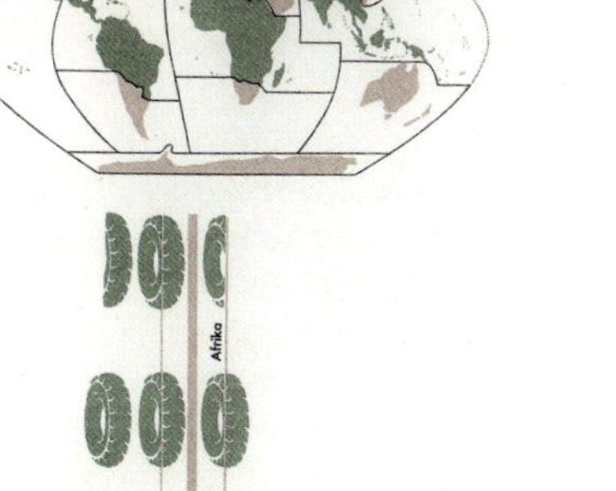
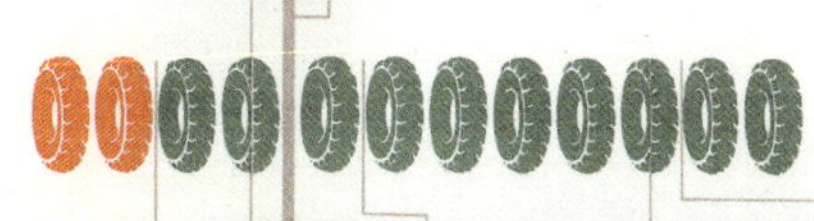
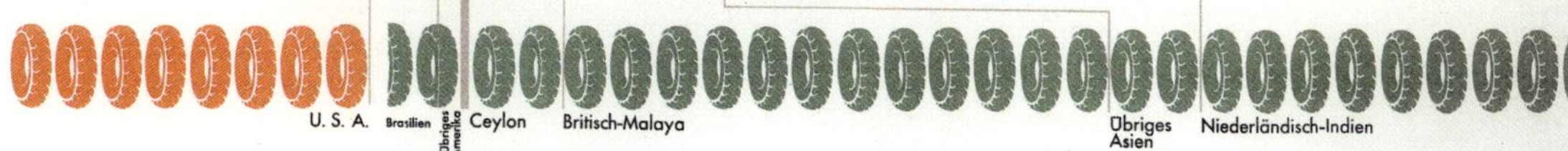

Gerhard Arntz / Otto Neurath
Atlas Gesellschaft und Wirtschaft, 1930
Plate 45: *Entwicklung der Kautschukproduktion seit 1895*
(The Development of Rubber Manufacture since 1895)

Domènec

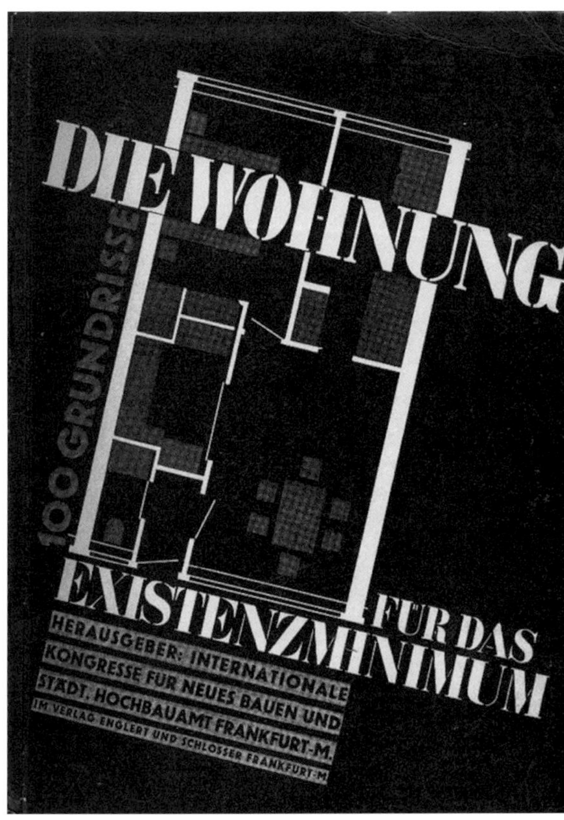

Cover of *Die Wohnung für das Existenzminimum*
Frankfurt, 1930

Existenzminimum, 2002
Installation with sculpture, video and leaflet

For the last decade, Domènec's artistic practice has focused on the debate that, since the 1960s, has surrounded the historical process called the crisis of modernity. Domènec's particularity lies in the fact that, on the basis of a conscious and deliberate expansion of the field of sculpture, he has developed a universe of his own that reflects the loss of the social visibility of the great modern narratives. His work is a model in that it has revealed the decline of these narratives by extolling the metonymic power of modern architecture. In Domènec's previous work, Le Corbusier's Paimio Sanatorium (by Alvar Aalto) and the Unité d'Habitation already provided a basis for a critical re-reading of the utopian side of modernity.

In essence, the *Existenzminimum* project is also a part of this operation that aims to show the current marginality of modernity's ethical and social principles. Nonetheless — and despite the lack of efficacious instruments to overcome the paralysis of resistance caused by the neo-conservative, aggressive nature of late capitalism — scepticism plays a limited role in Domènec's work. For instance, when he deals with the fusion of the minimum dwelling — a concept debated at the CIAM architectural congress in Frankfurt in 1929 that sought to establish universal guidelines that would provide the entire world with a decent dwelling — and the alteration of the dimensions and the re-adaptation of a commemorative piece designed by the architect Mies van der Rohe in homage to Rosa Luxembourg and Karl Liebknecht, leaders of the German Communist Left assassinated in 1919 by forces supported by the police.

The monument loses all its original grandiloquence when it is turned into a minimum dwelling and literally rendered, at the hand of the artist, a bricolage kit. Thus, the monument becomes the basis for highly playful, micro-utopian daily experiences in real time, as was Domènec's installation in the Parc de la Devesa in Girona. Much smaller in size, the replica he has built gives new life to the monument destroyed in 1933 by fascist barbarism; on a human scale, it traces a connection between the utopian power of modernity's liberating ideologies and its hypothetical critical re-adaptations. The small, almost bunker-shaped nomadic dwelling suggests that it is possible to undertake practices that resist and crack the reigning consensus.

Jordi Font Agulló

La Vanguardia (suppl. *Cultura/s*), 15 January 2003, p. 17.

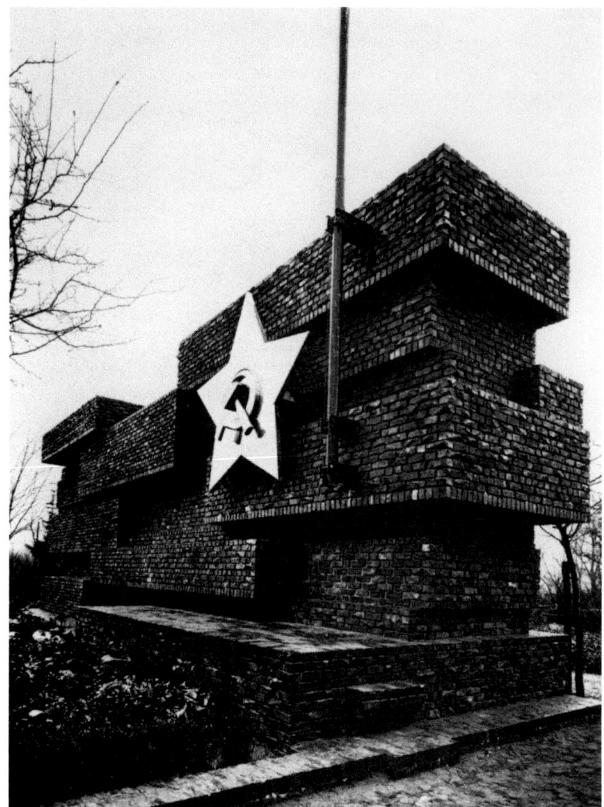

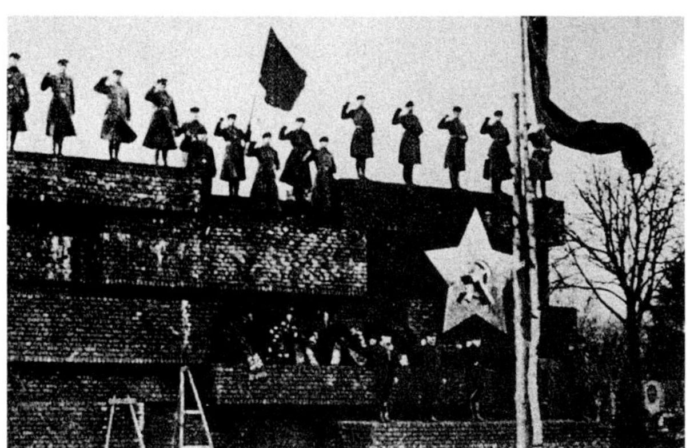

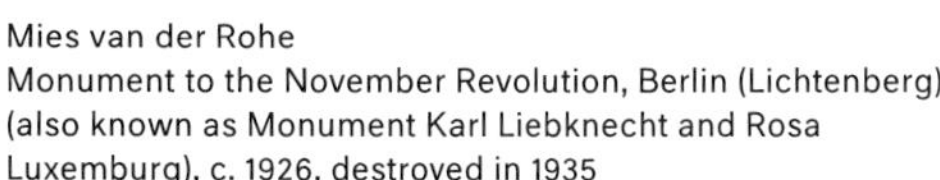

Mies van der Rohe
Monument to the November Revolution, Berlin (Lichtenberg)
(also known as Monument Karl Liebknecht and Rosa
Luxemburg), c. 1926, destroyed in 1935

Inauguration of the monument, Friedrichsfelde, Berlin
13 June 1926

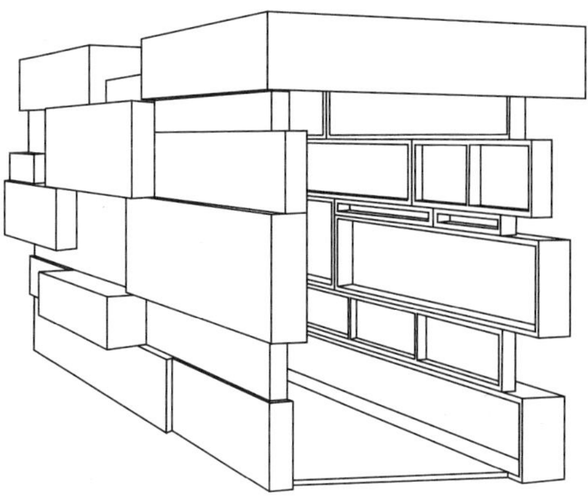

Existenzminimum, 2002
Construction drawing from the leaflet

For a few years now, my work has been situated in
the dilemma of participating in the debate on the limits,
fissures, successes and failures of the modern movement, and on how we have managed to deal with this
awkward legacy in contemporary times. Prior to the
project *Existenzminimum* (2002), I had already chosen
different buildings that are emblematic of modernity
as elements to create projects related to these very
questions. ▷

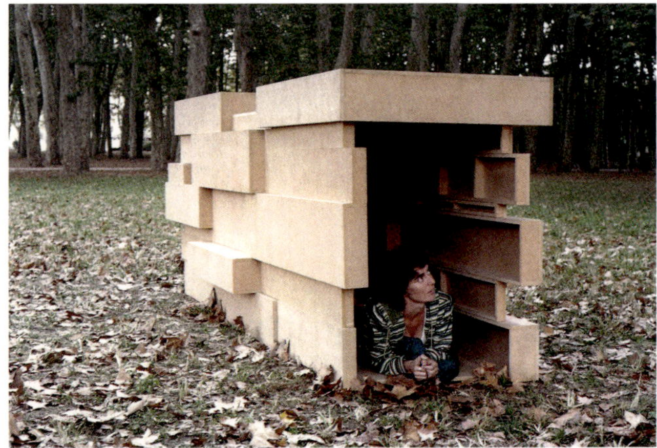

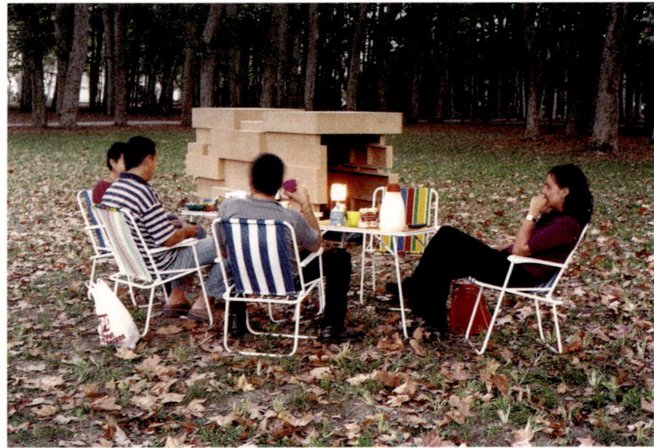

Installation in Parc de la Devesa in Girona,
October 2002

For example, in 1998 I created the project *24 Hours of Artificial Light*, a full-scale replica of a room in Alvar Aalto's Paimio hospital that was stripped of all the 'humanist virtues' of the initial programme and converted into a 'useless' blind sculpture. In so doing, I wondered about the limits of the 'modern programme' (in aesthetic terms as well as ethical and political ones) for systematically transforming and improving daily life. In summary, I tried to make visible the disconcerting paradox that, in the end and despite the good intentions and needs that exist, the great stories of modernism, no matter how heroic they may be, almost never obtained the desired results.

Existenzminimum, the recreation of the monument to Rosa Luxemburg and Karl Liebknecht (leaders of the failed Spartacus revolution and what was perhaps the most sincere attempt to install a fairer society in Germany) in a humble hut, a small and fragile refuge, connected this original design for a site of commemoration by Mies van der Rohe, by means of the work's title, to the key concept of the second CIAM congress (1929): The proposal of the most advanced architects of the modern movement to establish a scientific basis for guaranteeing a universal and dignified minimum level of existence. Today, when millions and millions of people live in subhuman conditions in shanties that surround the great cities of triumphant capitalism, it seems altogether like a cruel irony of history. □

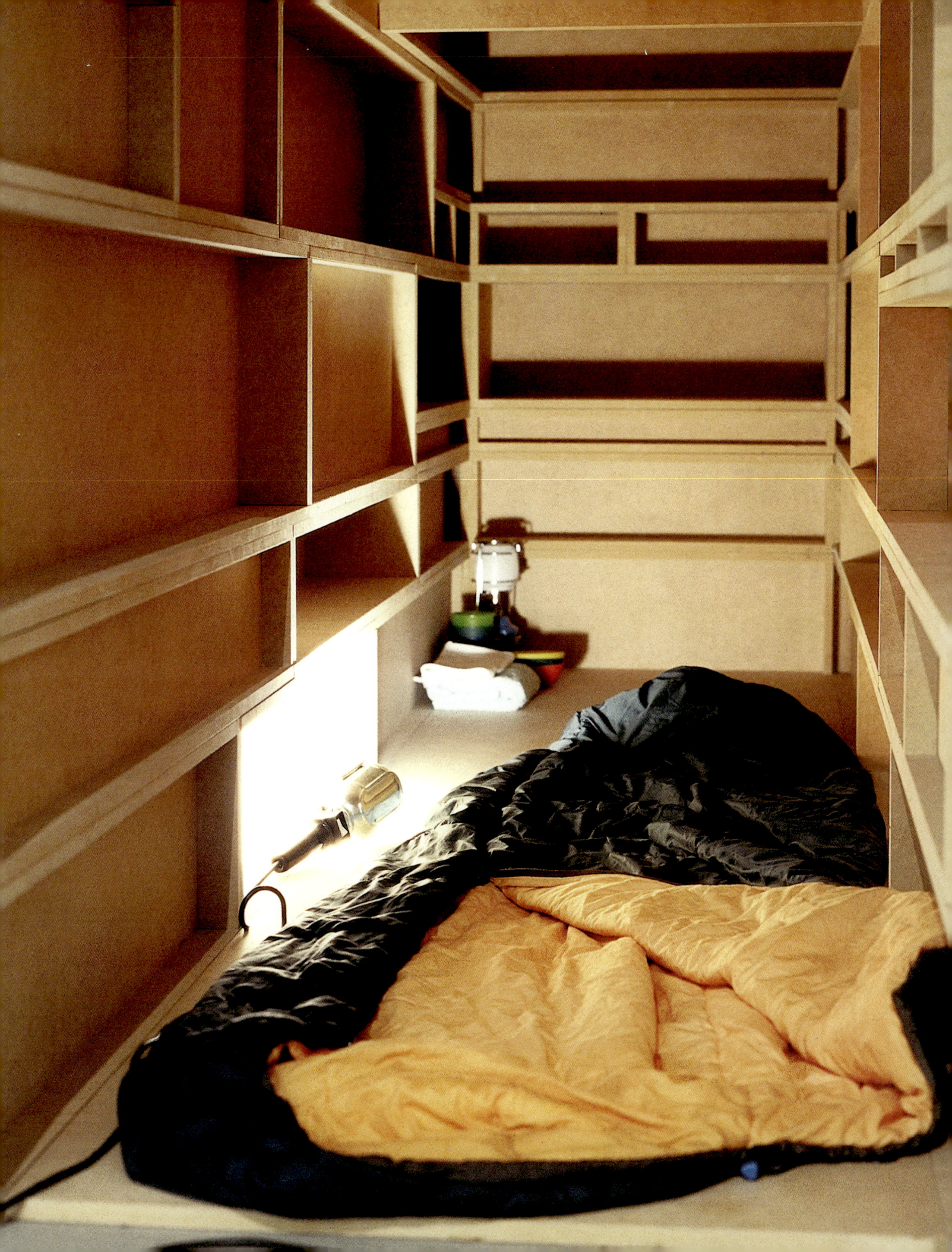

Katja Eydel

Model ve Sembol. Die Erfindung der Türkei, 2005/06
(The Invention of Turkey)
Photo installation

Model ve Sembol: The Invention of Turkey engages with the foundation of the new Turkish state in 1923 and subsequent process of modernisation. I focus on the symbolic character of physical surroundings and the ideas about society that they embody. These are reflected with particular clarity in the visual economics of Turkish cities, in the form of the built reality of architecture, urban planning structures and spaces and their uses, in issues of visibility and symbolism, in dress, holiday rituals and other representative aspects. Such symbols surround people and either bind them to the cultural context or confront them with it, both in details and in the structural whole. I wanted to understand how various symbols in their current state, along with the behavioural modes, thought patterns and ideologies they encapsulate, can appear both strong and, through their repetition, somehow empty — and why that very fact makes them such an important feature of everyday life in Turkey.

The Republic of Turkey was founded in 1923 following the military prevention of occupation by foreign powers. This revolution was accompanied by radical modernisation, implemented by an elite headed by Mustafa Kemal Atatürk. One of its aims was the establishment of a new national identity. Reforms addressed language and script, the role of the state, the status of religion, dress, personal names, relations between the sexes, education and the law. The goal was a set of regulations that would encompass all areas and all classes of society.

As in every major social upheaval, identification with the new order was facilitated by symbols and signs that reflected and promoted the changes and their circumstances. In this way, architecture and other visible manifestations of cultural life were both an expression and a medium of change. To this day, such symbols play a significant part in identification and negotiation processes, including political discussions, which are often conducted at the level of symbolic representation.

The reformers in Turkey invited foreign experts and specialists to aid in the development of the new state. In the 1930s, a period of radical change in several Western European countries, such invitations frequently provided a means of escaping fascism and held the promise of a new beginning.

My photographs address the connections between ideology and visual symbolism in three separate subject areas. The first is architecture. Here, the influence appears most clearly in Ankara. Once a village in the Anatolian hinterland, Ankara replaced Istanbul, the former seat of the sultan, as capital in 1923. The new republic was to acquire a characteristic image here, and the city still bears witness to debates concerning suitable urban expressions of the new state, both in the architecture of individual buildings and in the overall structure. Reflecting a highly disjointed course of development propelled by vigorous disputes, different architectural styles in the city reflect four different stages in the ideological discourse: the 'first national style' at the time of the republic's foundation; the modernism imported from 1929 to 1938 and the distinctive infrastructure that it spawned; the reaction in the shape of the 'second national style', which sought to clothe the new sense of Turkish identity in a characteristic form; and the 'international style' that emerged in the 1950s alongside the incipient globalisation of the economy.

Holidays and their rituals form the second subject area. They represent collective re-stagings of history, reinterpreting and subjecting it to alterations and projections. The republic introduced a new set of holidays to replace the values and the social structures embodied in the old ones and their chronology. To this day, the sequence and type of holidays anchor the once-new order in the fabric of Turkish society.

The third subject area is exemplary institutions, which still exist and sometimes seem to have survived from the revolutionary era in a time capsule. As models, they were intended to be imitated and to multiply. These traditional institutions continue to exemplify central features of the state established in 1923. They have since been joined by organisations set up along the same lines and linked symbolically with contemporary social change.

My engagement with the new Turkey of 1923, with the ideological ruptures that have marked its subsequent history and with the forms and functions it generated, may perhaps serve as a model for approaching the establishment of new national identities in other contexts.

Katja Eydel

Revised version of the foreword in *Katja Eydel, Model ve Sembol: The Invention of Turkey*, New York: Lukas & Sternberg, 2006.

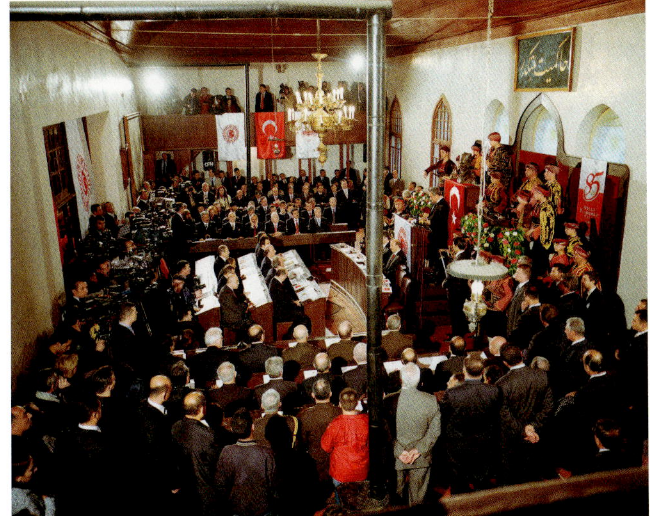
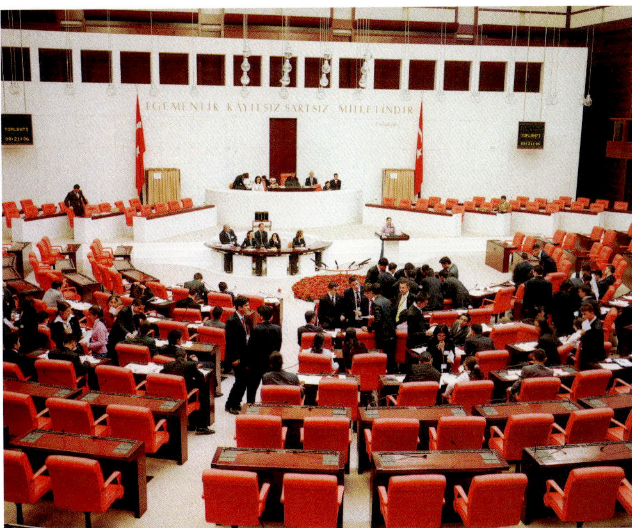
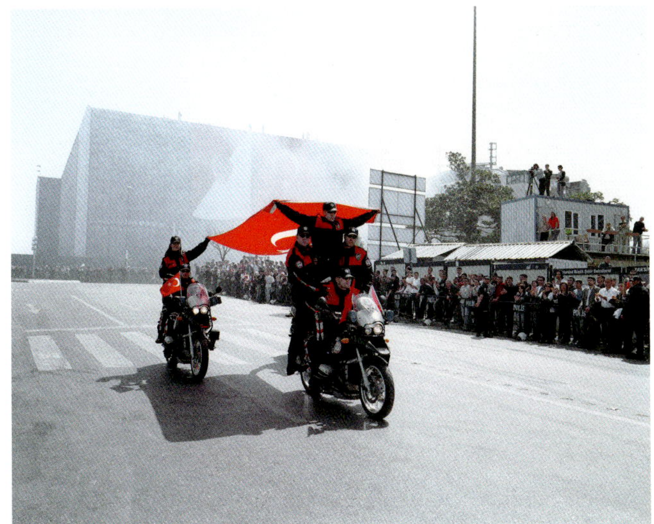
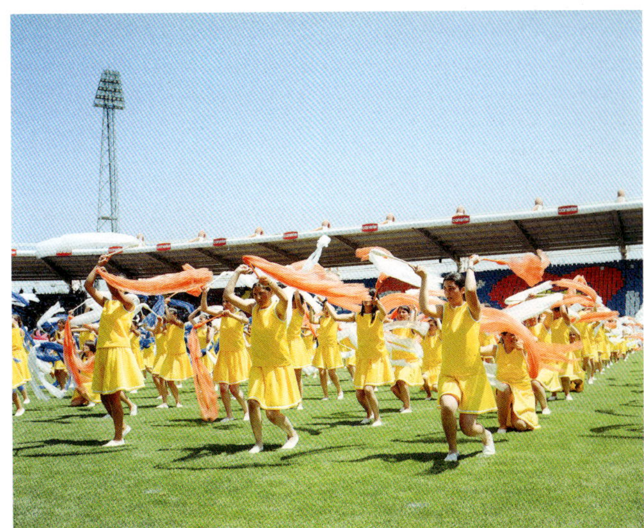

Representative Holidays

National Sovereignty and Children's Day
(Anniversary of the establishment of Turkish Grand
National Assembly): in the First Parliamentary
Building, 23.04.2005, Ankara

Police Holiday at Taksim
10.04.2005, Istanbul

National Sovereignty and Children's Day
(Anniversary of the establishment of Turkish Grand
National Assembly): Pupils and Students' Parliament
at the TBMM, 22.04.2005, Ankara

Youth & Sports Day / Atatürk Memorial Day: May 19th
Stadium, 19.05.2005, Ankara

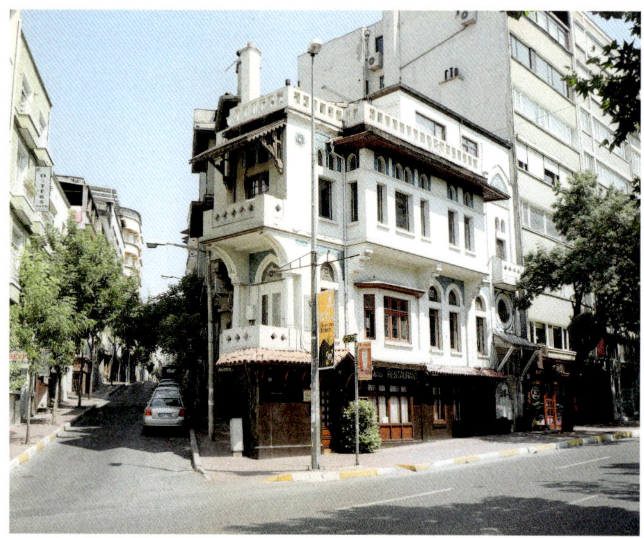

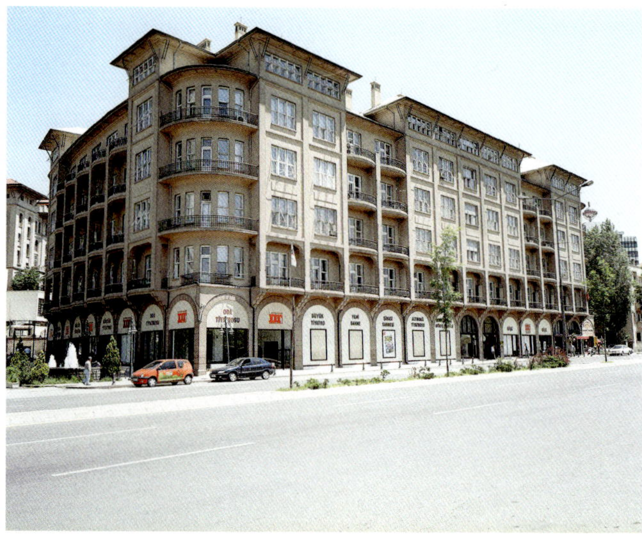

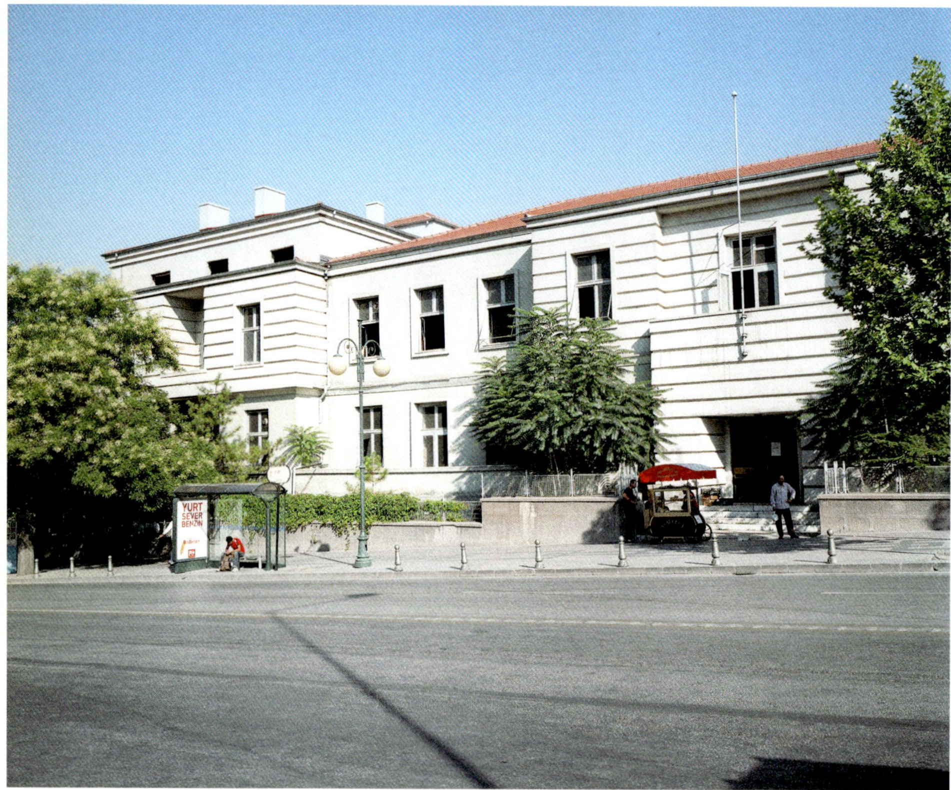

Architectural Styles

House Vedad Tek
Vedat Tek
1913–14, Istanbul

Vakıf Apartment Building
A. Kemalettin Bey
1928–30, Ankara

Supreme Comptroller's Office
Nazım Bey / Ernst A. Egli
1928–30, Ankara

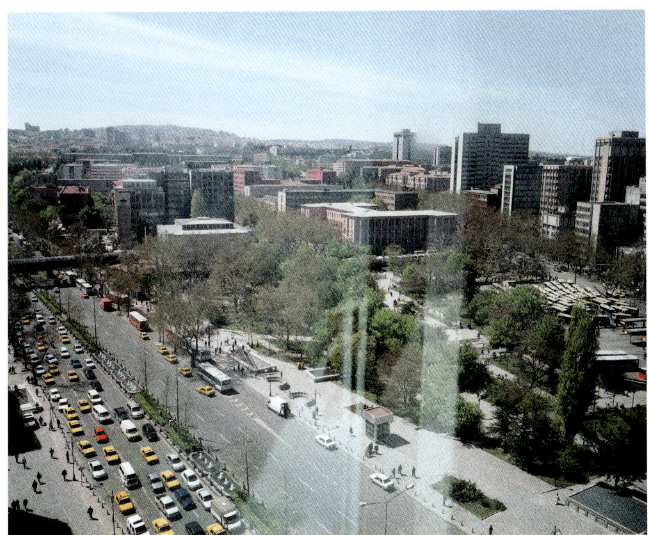

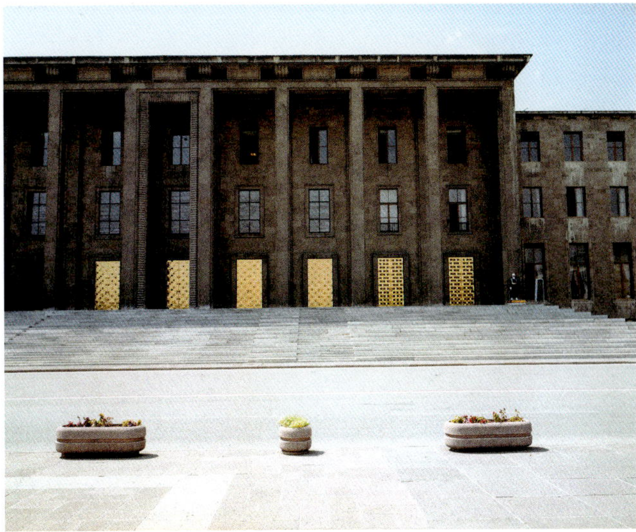

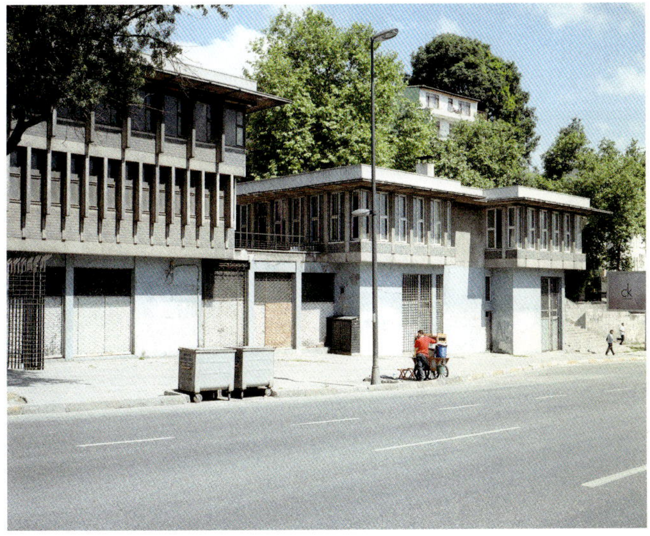

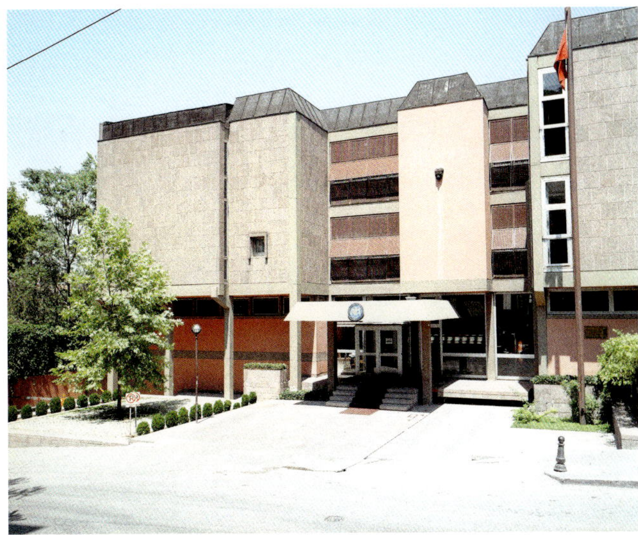

Kizilay Government Precinct
Hermann Jansen / Clemens Holzmeister
1928–60, Ankara

Social Security Department Headquarters
Sedad Hakki Eldem
1962–64, Istanbul

Turkish Grand National Assembly Building (Parliament)
Clemens Holzmeister
1938–60, Ankara

Turkish Historical Society
Turgut Cansever / Ertur Yener
1960–67, Ankara

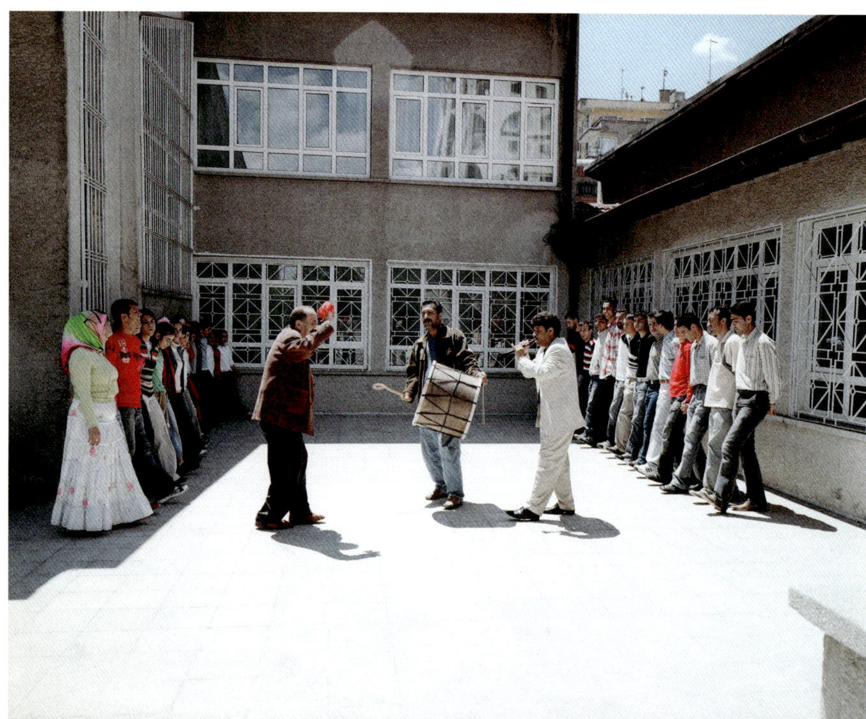

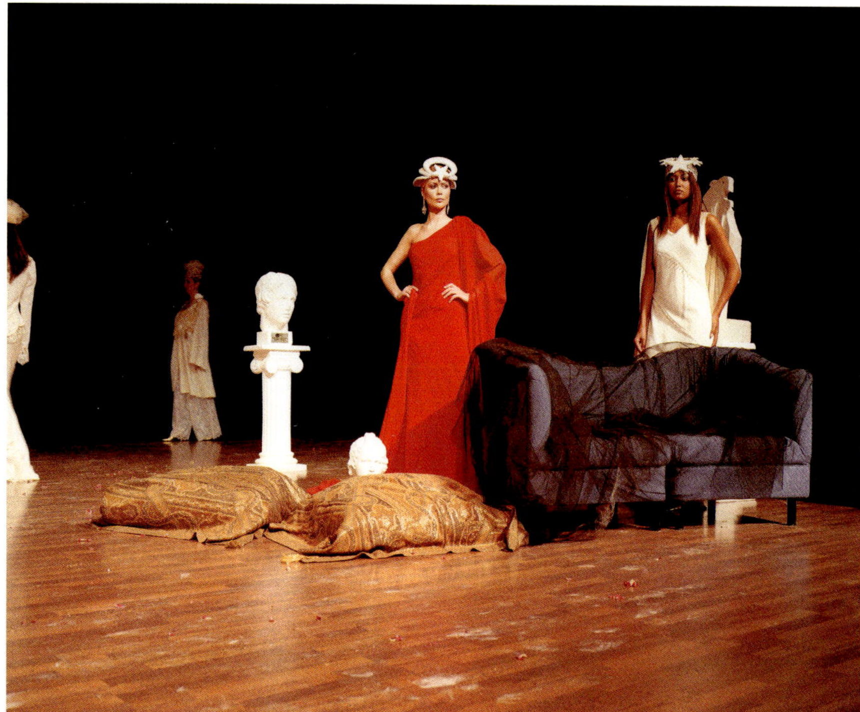

Exemplary Institutions

Dancing Lessons at a Centre for Continuing Education, Diyarbakir

Olgunlaşma Institute Fashion Show at Maltepe University, Istanbul

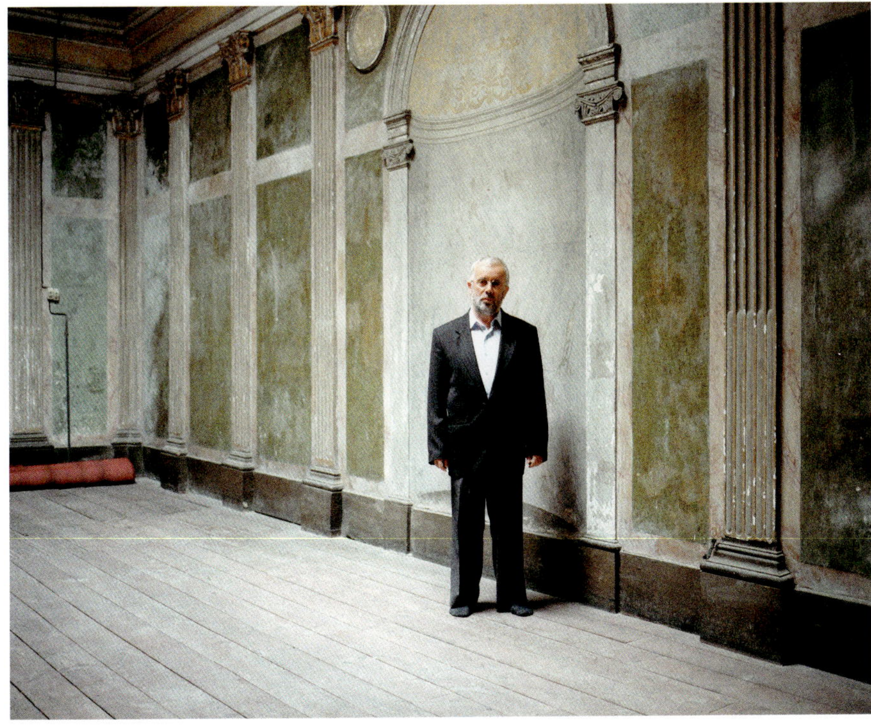

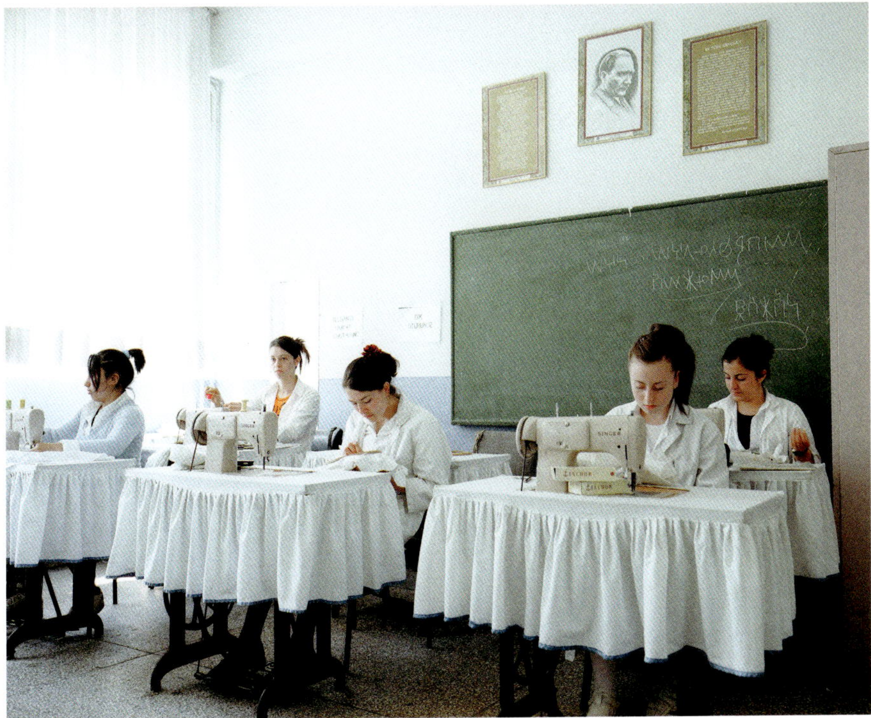

Hakki Aydemirler, Imam at the Hagia Sophia
Istanbul

Girls' High School
Ankara

Ângela Ferreira

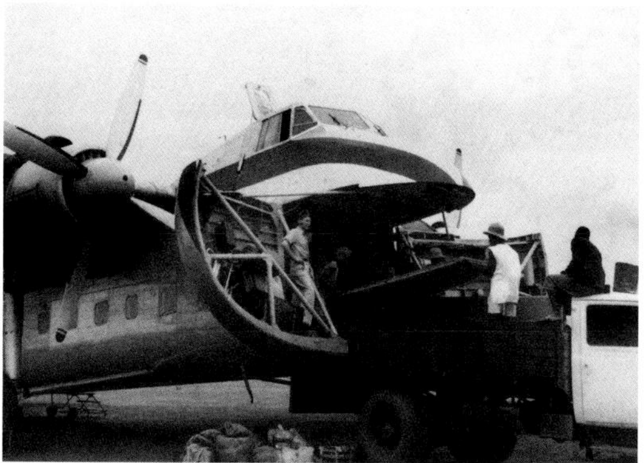

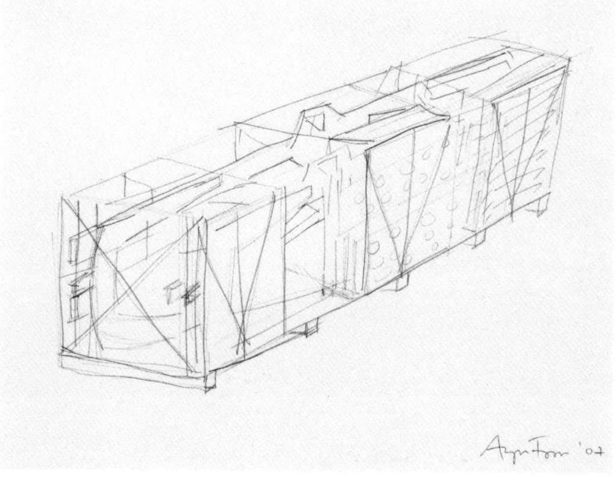

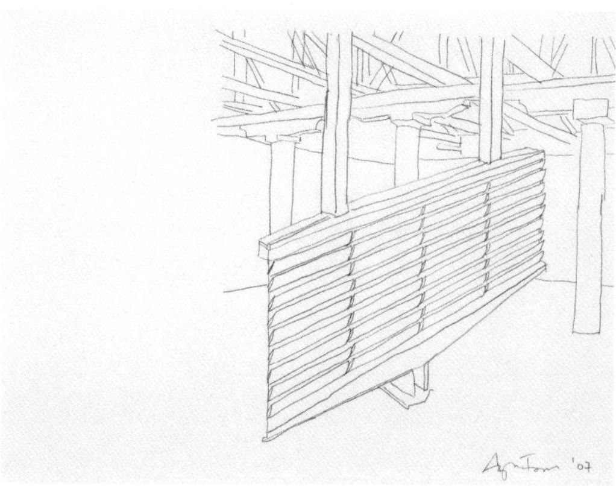

Tropical House being packed into a cargo airplane before flying to Niamey. Henri Prouvé (architect) and Jean Prouvé (constructor), 1949

Study for *Maison Tropicale* sculpture, 2007

Study for *Maison Tropicale* in Fundaco, Venice, 2007

p. 77
'Les Maisons préfabriquées à l'Exposition pour l'Équipement de l'Union Française', *Revue de l'Aluminium*, no. 161, 1949

Maison Tropicale, 2007
Scale models, drawings and photographs

Sculpture Revisited

Ângela Ferreira uses her art as a way of asking questions about her own reality, about its history, its politics, its memories. Starting from her own portion of the world, she treats her art like a wide-angle lens. Since she has spent her whole life going back and forth between Mozambique, South Africa and Portugal, transitions are something to which she frequently returns, both as metaphor, and more concretely.

In this respect her work for the Portuguese pavilion at the Venice Biennale 2007 is typical of her. In an open container in full scale she shows a model of the French architect Jean Prouvé's *Maison Tropicale*; she travels to the places in Africa where the houses were once built and from where they have now been removed: Niamey in Niger and Brazzaville in the Republic of the Congo. She uses drawing to gain an understanding of how the demountable house relates to the exhibition space, spending time working with sculptures that she calls 'footprints', but which are actually an interpretation of her experience of the foundations that remained in Africa when the houses of modernism disappeared. Prouvé's project, along with her own interpretation of it, encompasses all the questions on which her art focuses: the collision between Western modernism's utopian ideas and African reality; her dual loyalty to both the radicality of modernism and the post-colonial critique of it; and transitions, the feeling of departure and vulnerability — perhaps also a deeper melancholy....

When Ângela Ferreira uses Prouvé's prototype in her sculpture project, she points to the glaring disparity between the optimism and arrogance of modernism's attitude to a real situation and African reality. At the same time it is clear that she herself feels a profound fascination for Prouvé's project and that she appreciates the houses for their formal, sculptural qualities. She admires the project specifically for its ostensibly practical, but in actual fact dreamlike qualities. Now, when she has all the prefabricated parts of the house made once again, but this time in wood, and in an old joiner's workshop that is run on craftsman-like principles, she transforms Prouvé's ingenuity into a symbol for our failings. Like Robert Smithson in *A Tour of the Monuments of Passaic*, Ferreira could say: 'Or was it the hereafter?'

The container, which with its light aluminium-profile frame could be flown from France to Niger, has now been transformed into a space somewhere between architecture and sculpture. In the narrow passageway at its centre, which all visitors have to go through to get further into the space, the wooden profiles become tangible and present, through the contrast between its actual weight and the lightness signalled by the visual form. On being forced to pass through the container, we as viewers can no longer retain that notorious critical distance. We have to enter into and go through Ferreira's sculpture as an experience. It may well be as a result of this that we also notice how the very aluminium construction of the container finds echoes in the bizarre roof of the Portuguese pavilion's old warehouse building. Of course, this is a formal coincidence, but in Ferreira's preliminary

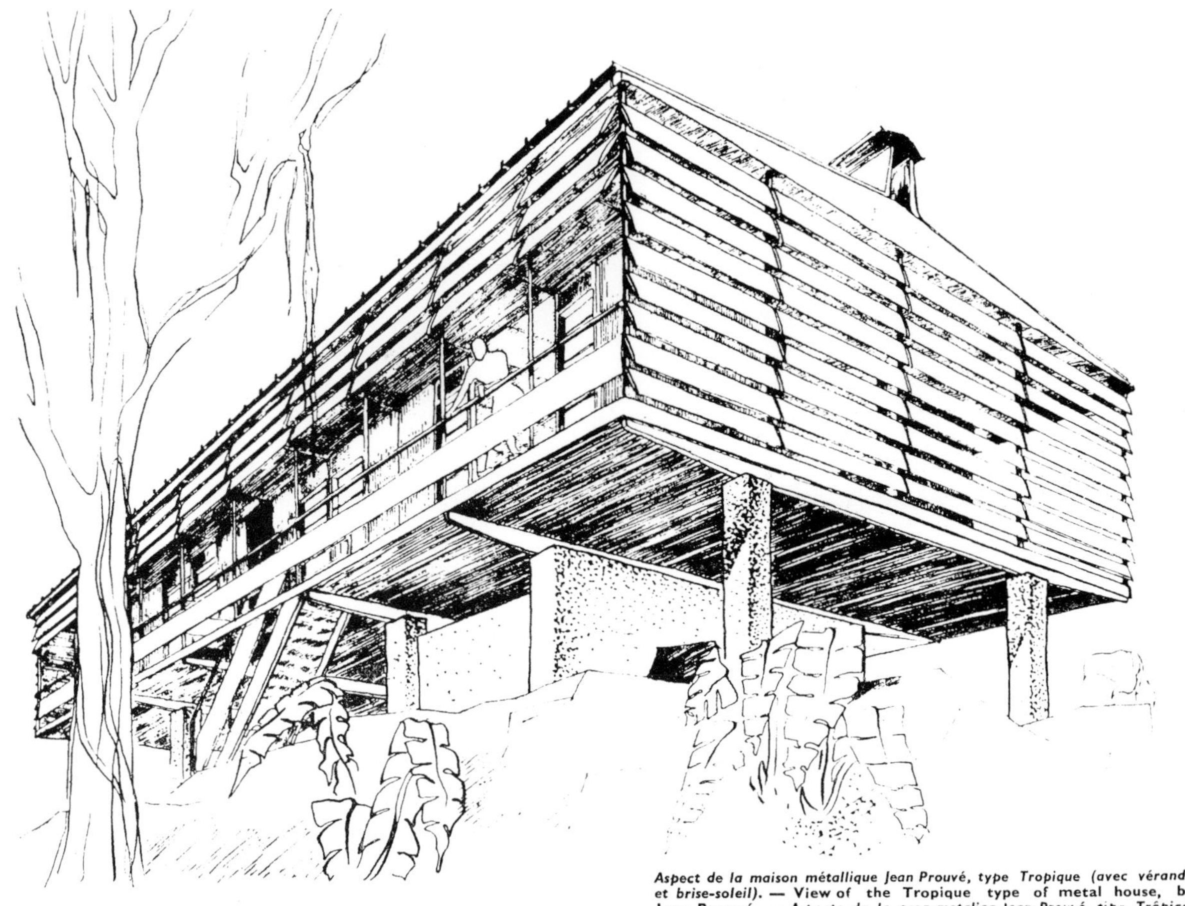

Aspect de la maison métallique Jean Prouvé, type Tropique (avec véranda et brise-soleil). — View of the Tropique type of metal house, by Jean Prouvé. — *Aspecto de la casa metalica Jean Prouvé, tipo Trópico.*

LES MAISONS PRÉFABRIQUÉES A L'EXPOSITION POUR L'ÉQUIPEMENT DE L'UNION FRANÇAISE

LA Société des Ingénieurs pour la France d'Outre-Mer et les Pays Extérieurs a organisé du 28 septembre au 17 octobre une Exposition pour l'Equipement de l'Union Française qui s'est tenue sur les berges de la Seine entre le Pont de l'Alma et le Pont Alexandre-III. Les buts étaient triples :

— Présenter aux utilisateurs les matériels et produits spécialement adaptés aux conditions particulières d'emploi dans les pays de la France d'Outre-Mer et que l'industrie métropolitaine est capable de produire.

— Fournir aux industriels et exportateurs des indications sur les besoins de ces territoires :

— Favoriser les prises de contact entre producteurs et utilisateurs et développer les transactions de la Métropole vers l'extérieur.

Parmi les six cents exposants, qui embrassaient, en fait, une très grande partie de l'activité industrielle française, nous avons particulièrement remarqué la présentation des bâtiments préfabriqués démontables qui apportent une solution de choix au problème universel du logement, et plus particulièrement dans les Colonies où le manque de matériaux convenables, les difficultés de transport et l'absence de main-d'œuvre qualifiée rendent encore plus difficile la construction des habitations.

La Société Technique pour l'Utilisation des Alliages Légers (S.T.U.D.A.L.) présentait les maisons préfabriquées Jean Prouvé, de Nancy et les constructions métalliques OPEC, toutes faisant intervenir très largement les alliages légers.

LA MAISON JEAN PROUVÉ

Les Ateliers de construction métallique Jean Prouvé à Nancy, construisent en série et intégralement en usine des éléments qui permettent d'édifier en quelques jours des constructions définitives présentant un très grand confort et, du fait de la souplesse de composition permise pour le procédé, répondant le mieux à chaque utilisation prévue.

Ces constructions sont légères (50 kg/m²) et durables comme celles établies avec les matériaux traditionnels ; elles sont métalliques, forment un tout par elles-mêmes, et sont constituées par des éléments modulés standard permettant d'obtenir 3 m ou 4 m en longueur (ou des multiples de ces deux chiffres ; 3 m, 4 m, 6 m, 7 m ou 8 m en largeur ; elles sont livrées avec ou sans plancher. Pour le montage au sol, on prévoit soit des piliers de ciment ou de maçonnerie dont le nombre varie avec la superficie; dans ce cas, le plancher est fourni ; soit une dalle ou un plancher en ciment.

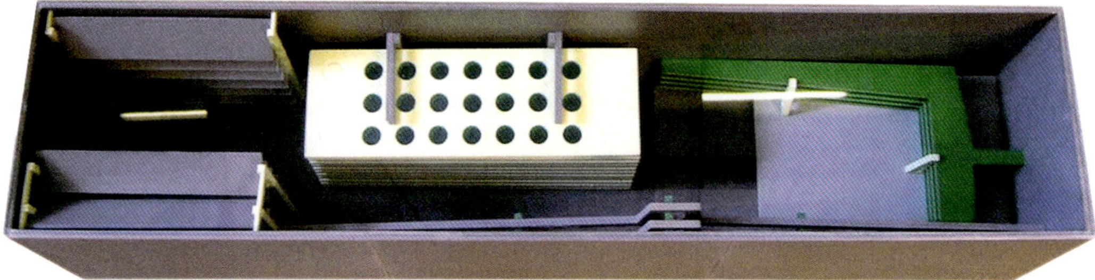

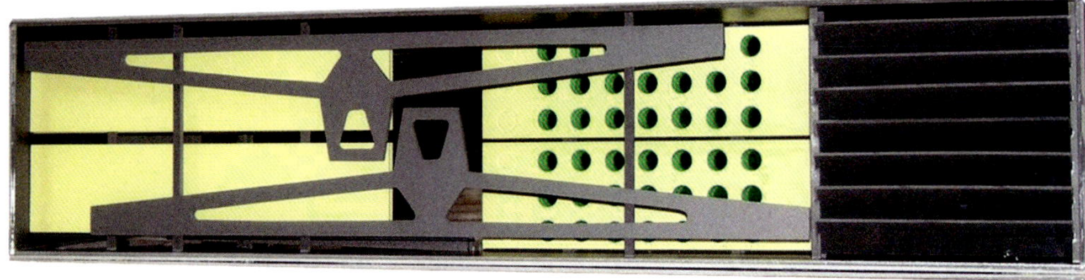

Two scale models
for *Maison Tropicale*, 2007

drawings of the exhibition space and of the elements in Prouvé's house, we notice how amused and fascinated she is by this affinity. Inside the container, with its wooden lamina, panels and portholes, we can almost imagine ourselves inside a large musical instrument, for example, an organ, and the roof beams could then be a variation on this theme.

The container in its almost over-explicit sculptural constructivism is thrust into the former warehouse district as an image of transition, while also displaying an obvious concern and love for detail. We could actually build a Prouvé house out of its parts.

But it was the foundations, the bit that is still there in Africa, and which are all that is left when the Western world's collectors call home their experiment that attracted Ferreira's attention from the start. In drawing after drawing we can see how she elevates the left-behind pillars into being temple architecture, or how she tries to understand the construction in detail — how a corner relates to the adjoining foundation, where the border with the surrounding soil actually runs. She fantasises on Prouvé's characteristic fork-shaped structure that holds up the house — allows it to rear up like some gigantic prehistoric animal, but reverts once again to her main question — 'How does all this *really* hang together?'

Ferreira's drawings are a way for her to work through the material, to twist it and turn it, to understand it as a form, to make it her own. The drawings allow us to see how she thinks, to see in what a classically sculptural way this thinking process operates.

But when she has drawn her way through the entire project, she abandons any formal comprehension. She travels to Niger and Brazzaville.

The relationship she is aiming for is a more brutal one than the pre-understanding of the sculpture. She seeks an image for the contrast between Prouvé's colonialising fantasy, represented by the container, and the actual site. The photographs that resulted from these site visits show how the African city takes back the initiative and incorporates the foundations into its own life — if that is at all possible. What are we actually to use these remnants for? They are the ruins of modernity, with neither beauty nor patina, abandoned with little regret. Whether they are in Passaic, New Jersey, or in Niamey, Niger, makes no big difference. They are images of the law of entropy, which says that in any exchange of energy a certain amount will be lost, and will remain lost.

Gertrud Sandqvist

Excerpt from Jürgen Bock (ed.), *Maison Tropicale: Ângela Ferreira*, Lisbon: Instituto das Artes and Ministério da Cultura, 2007, pp. 21, 23–26.

CONTAINER N° 1

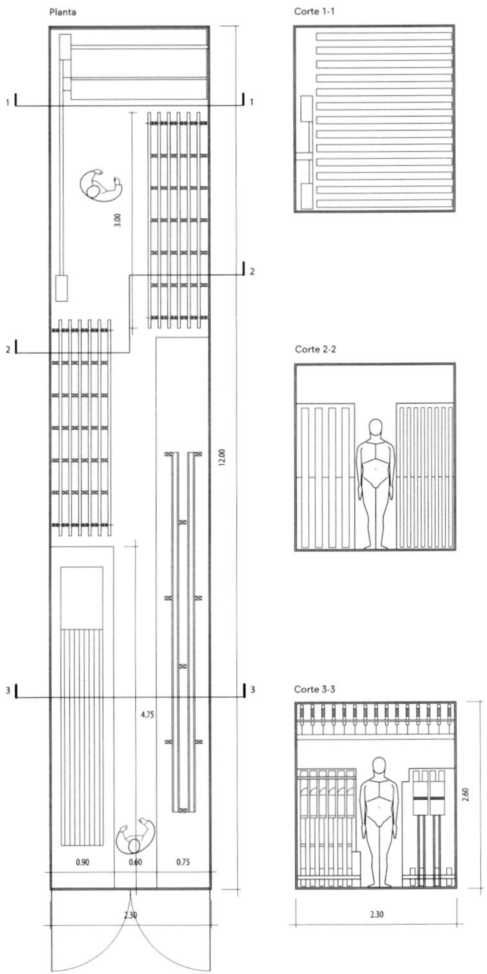

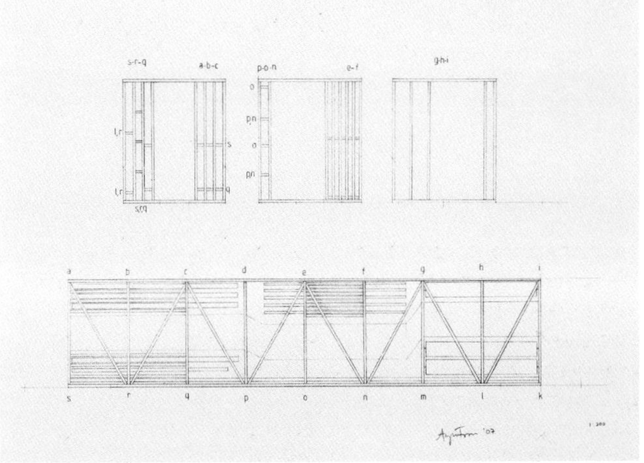

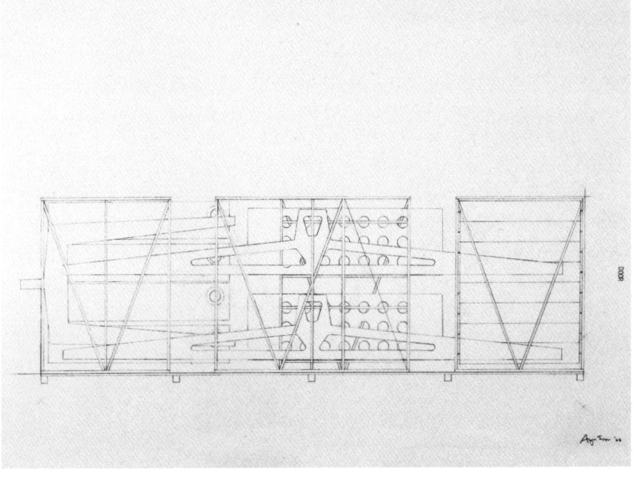

Drawing by Rui Órfão made for the artist after the plan devised by Atelier Banneel to pack Tropical House into a container, 2007

Technical drawings for *Maison Tropicale* sculpture, 2007

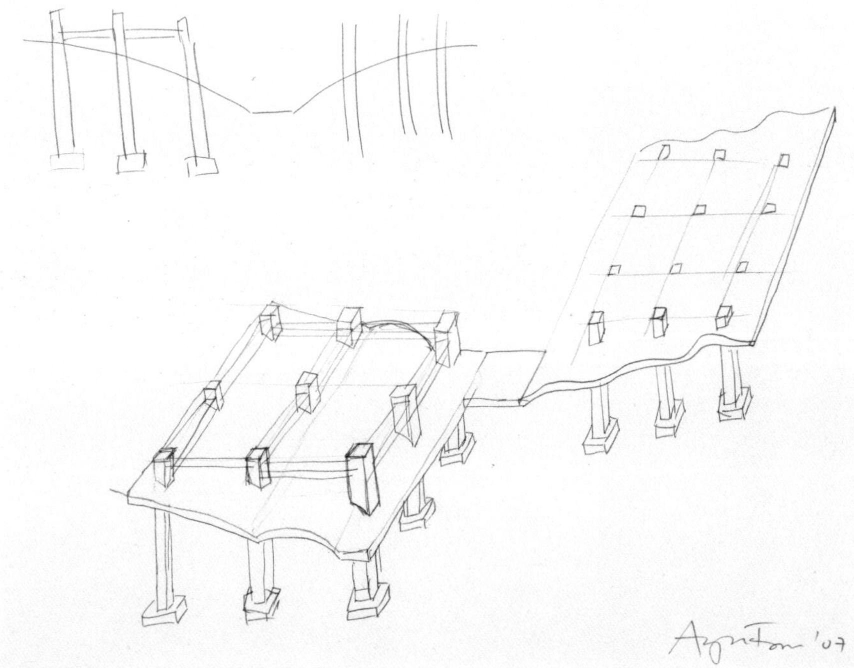

Study for *Maison Tropicale*, Brazzaville
site sculpture, 2007

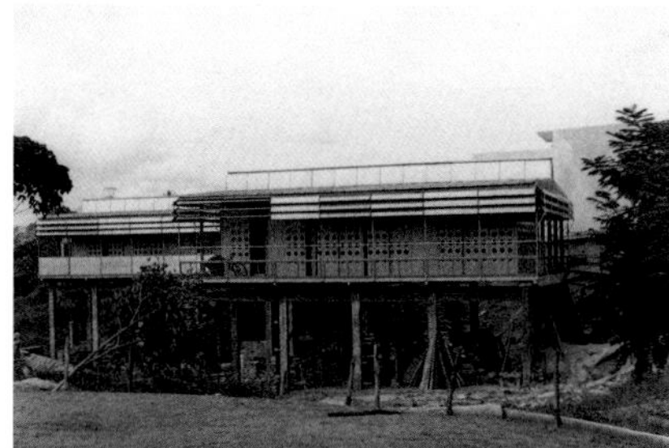

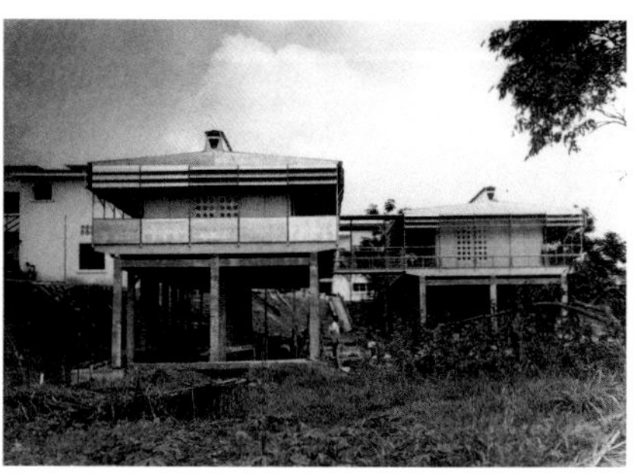

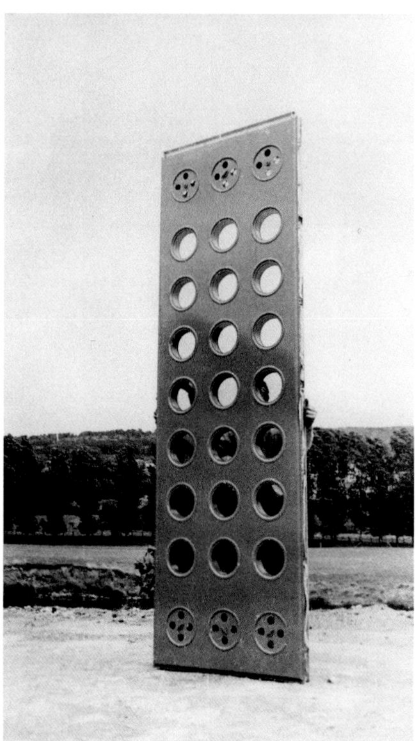

Tropical Houses built on pillars,
Brazzaville, 1951

Prefabricated parts for the Tropical House
in Maxéville, Nancy, c. 1949

**Many artists, architects and scholars are re-looking
at the extraordinary modernist energy that drove a good
part of the twentieth century. My quest is driven by the
present conditions in Africa and my attempt to understand
the abysmal differences between Africa and Europe after
centuries of slavery and colonialism. Immediately after
independence, Africans naturally wanted to turn away
from Europe and its heritage. I am curious about the period
of transition between the end of colonialism and a newly
gained sovereignty. These were precisely the times when
Europe was deploying its last efforts of investment into
Africa's infrastructures. The late-colonial ethos was often
about building 'a new modern society for Africa'. Africa
often afforded architects an opportunity to test out new
ideas. African cities were thus turned into laboratories for
modernist thought. ▷**

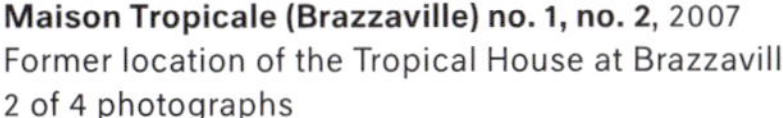

Maison Tropicale (Brazzaville) no. 1, no. 2, 2007
Former location of the Tropical House at Brazzaville
2 of 4 photographs

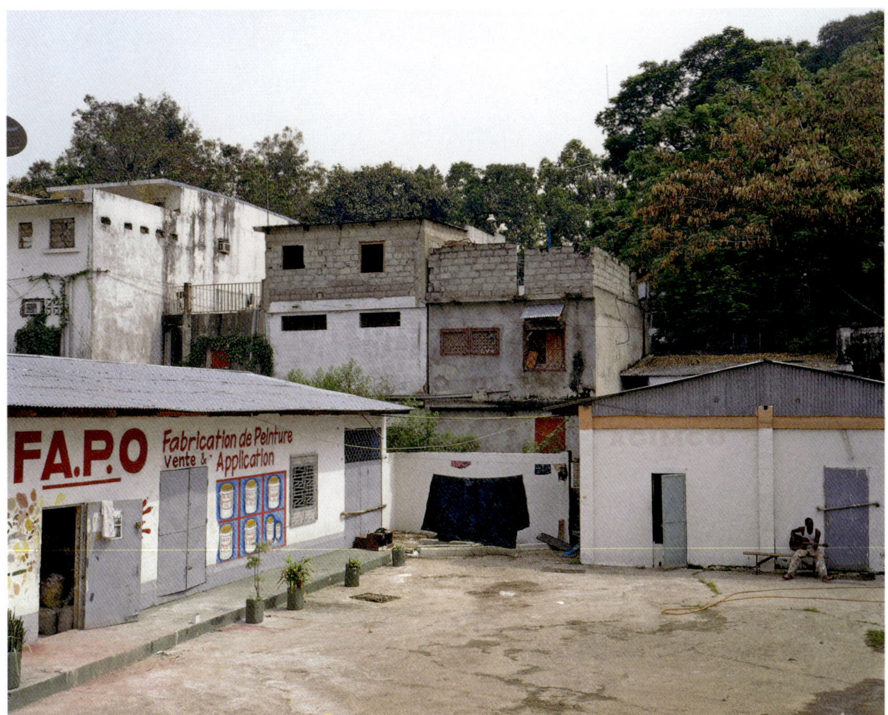

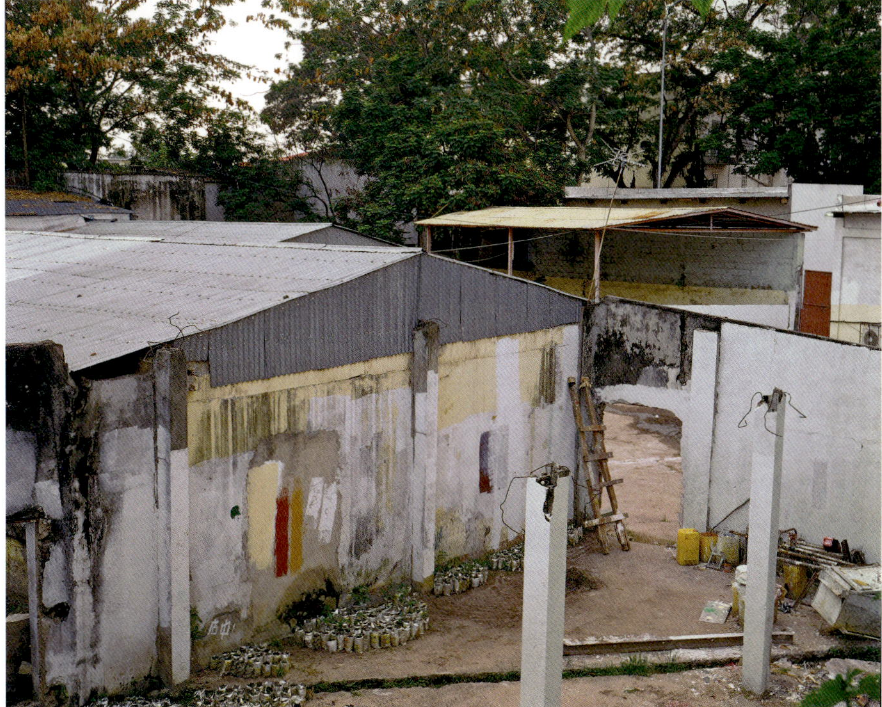

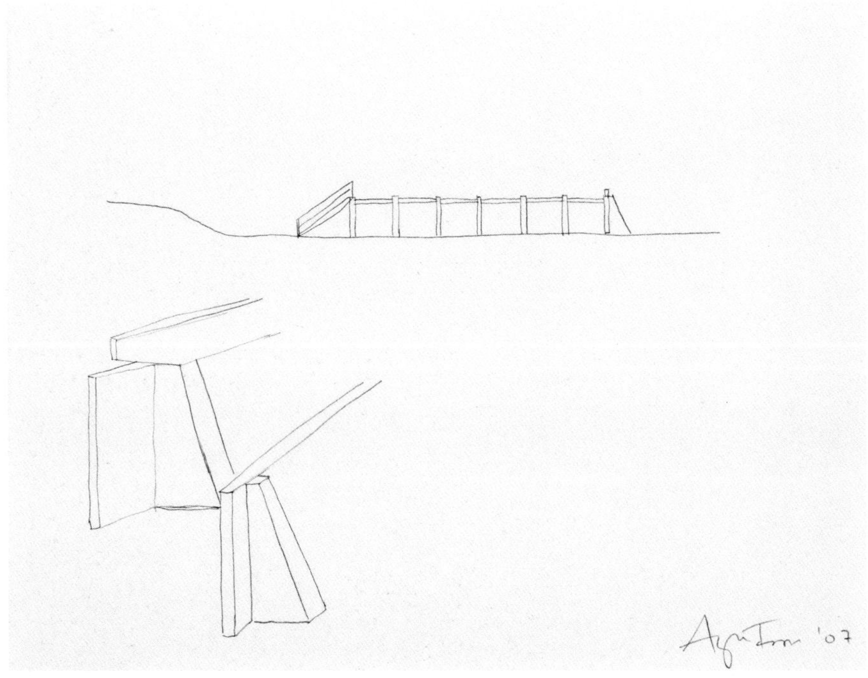

Study for *Maison Tropicale* site sculpture,
after Prouvé's buttresses (Brazzaville), 2007

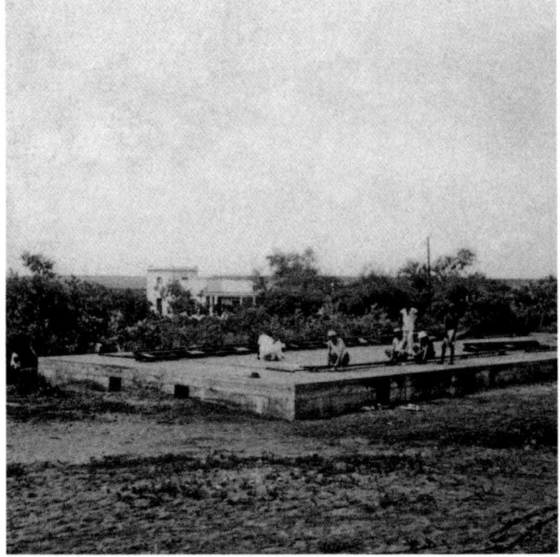

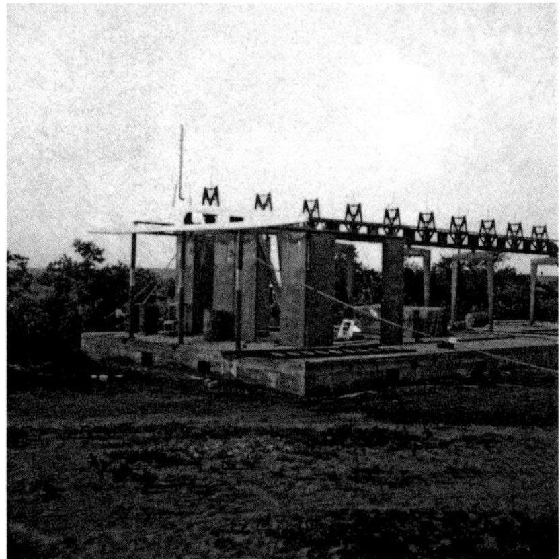

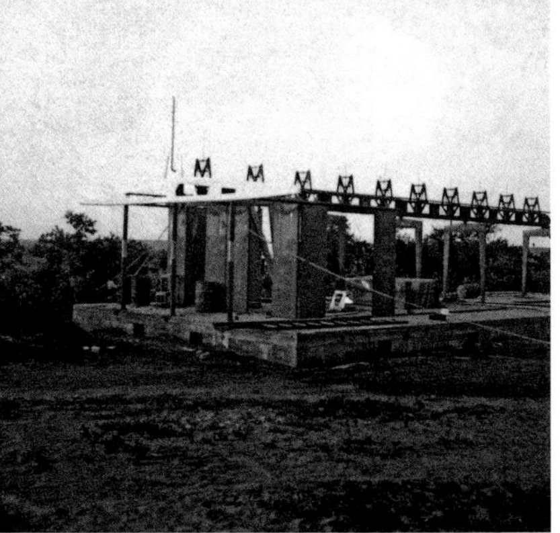

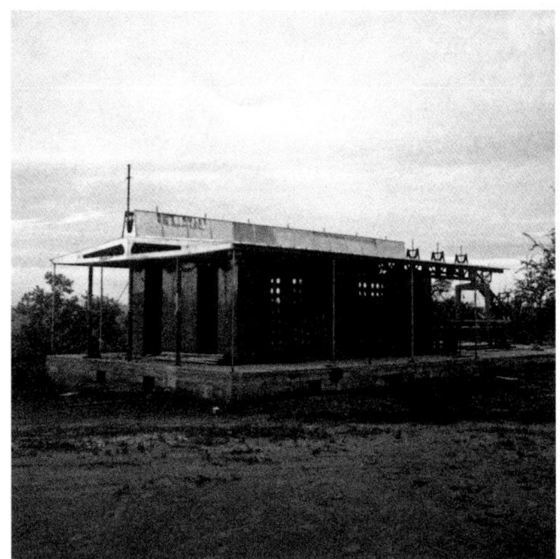

Assembly of the Tropical House,
Niamey, 1949

It is exactly at this point that the history of Jean Prouvé's Tropical House becomes interesting. The prototype houses were fabricated in France and transported by plane to Niger and Congo. Today they are part of the memories of the inhabitants of Niamey and Brazzaville. Only predatory market forces rendered them desirable again in the last decade. They were dismantled and returned to Europe for renovation and sale on the art market. In my mind the prototypes are evocative containers for Africa's inability to deal with its own heritage and Europe's prevailing drive to plunder its cultural resources. Modernism fascinates me. Its basic principles were generated from a common wish to create a more egalitarian society. Yet it has been, and still is, politically appropriated by oppressive systems, be they old-fashioned colonialism or neo-colonial economic global might. □

**Maison Tropicale
(Niamey) no. 2, no. 3**
Former location of the
Tropical House at Niamey, 2007
2 of 4 photographs

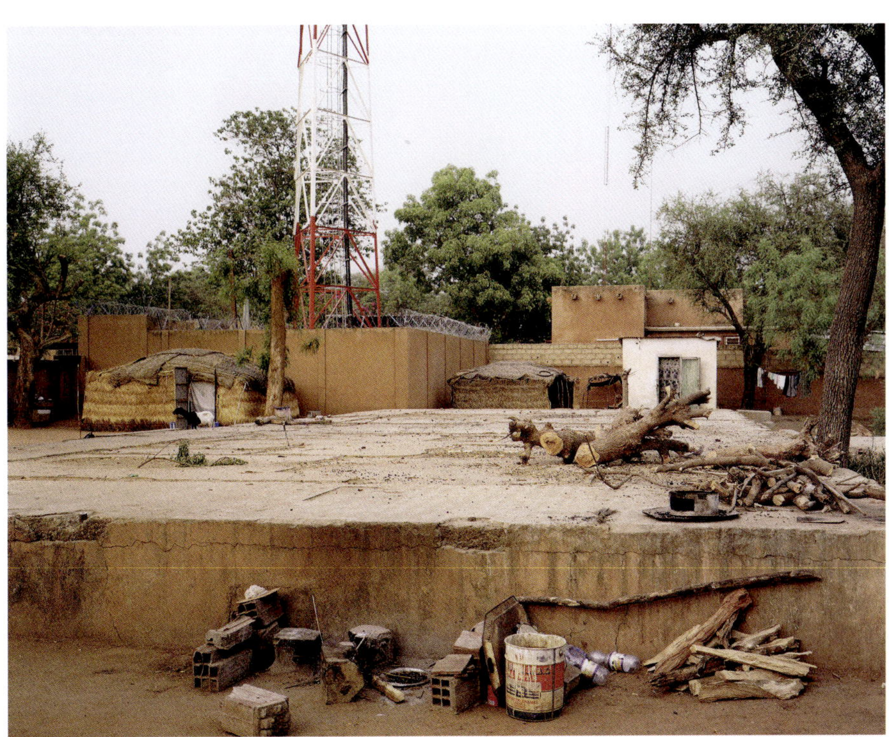

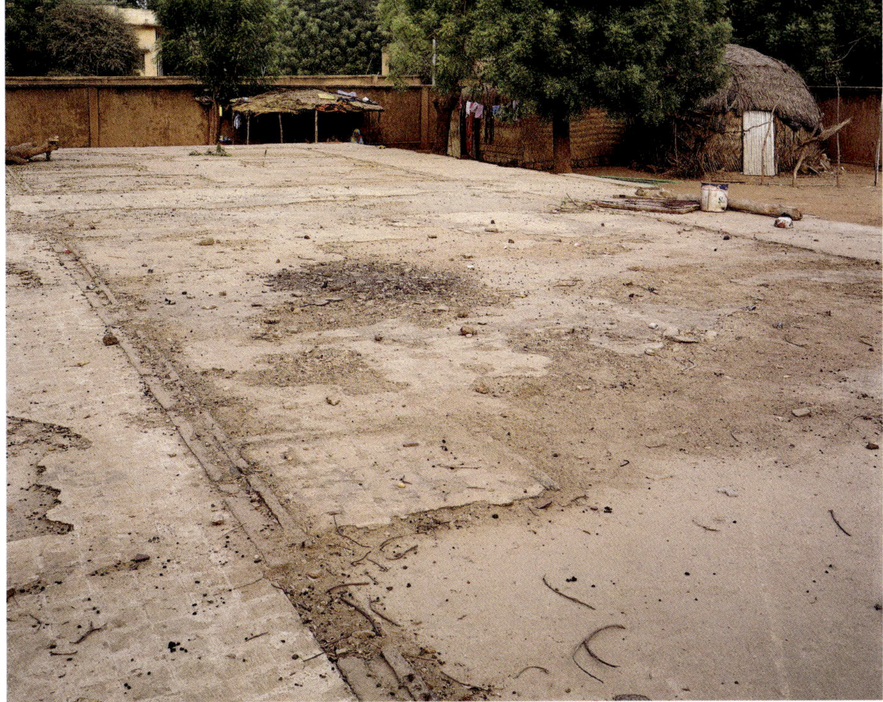

Andrea Fraser

**Soldadera (Scenes from *Un banquete en Tetlapayac*,
a film by Oliver Debroise),** 1998/2001
Video installation

In *Soldadera*, the destruction and cooptation of art and artists by their patrons becomes a framework for examining the fate of certain radical utopian and revolutionary impulses in twentieth-century art. However, my intention was not to repeat the well-established narrative of the failure and incorporation of radical artistic aspirations. Instead, I aimed to point to contradictions that would recast those aspirations within a structure of internal conflict rather than one of failure to resist external forces. ▷

Installation views
Dunkers Kulturhus, Helsingborg, 2004

Galerie Christian Nagel, Berlin, 2008

The footage used in *Soldadera* was originally produced for Olivier Debroise's feature-length, experimental documentary, *Un banquete en Tetlapayac*, a film in which Andrea Fraser participated. Debroise's film focuses on Sergei Eisenstein's work in Mexico in the early 1930s, a story that is also part of the historical framework of *Soldadera*. Eisenstein arrived in Mexico at the end of 1930 to shoot the film now known as *¡Que viva México!* with the financial backing of the American socialist writer, Upton Sinclair. After Eisenstein spent over a year and a half in Mexico, including a number of months at the Hacienda de Tetlapayac, Sinclair withdrew his support for the film, refusing to surrender the negatives to Eisenstein unless funding from other sources was secured. When additional funding was not secured, Sinclair exercised his right to the footage as the producer of the film and found others to edit the material shot by the inventor of montage. The film released as *Thunder Over Mexico* was considered by many to be a travesty, rendering *¡Que viva México!* one of the great lost works of the twentieth century. (After Eisenstein's death, the footage was re-edited by his cinematographer and released under its intended title.)

In iconography inspired by *¡Que viva México!* as well as the murals of Diego Rivera, Fraser appears in *Soldadera* dressed as a revolutionary peasant. A series of narrative fragments tell the story of an uprising at the Hacienda, and its failure. These narrative fragments — developed for the most part through a two-screen montage — are in turn mediated for the installation's viewers by scenes of an audience shown periodically on the right screen. Fraser also appears in this audience, but as Frances Flynn Paine, an associate of Abby Rockefeller who promoted Mexican art in the United States in the 1930s. Paine was the curator of Diego Rivera's 1931 retrospective at the Museum of Modern Art in New York, founded by Abby Rockefeller. In 1933, Paine also served as Rivera's agent for the mural he was commissioned to create for New York's Rockefeller Center. Abby Rockefeller's son Nelson, later the president of the Museum of Modern Art, had the mural destroyed before completion because of its political content. In dialogue based on a letter to Abby Rockefeller that Fraser found in her research, Paine argues from the audience: 'Mexican artists will cease to be "reds" if we can get them artistic recognition.' In the course of the five-minute loop, the revolutionary iconography composing the narrative fragments is progressively abstracted through strategies of repetition and doubling typical of contemporary video installation. This aestheticisation reaches a peak in *Soldadera's* central sequence: a staggered, two-screen loop of the artist, as a revolutionary peasant, racing a horse through the Mexican landscape with a long red banner flying behind her. The historical instances of the destruction and cooptation of art and artists by their patrons becomes a framework for examining the devolution of the radical aspirations of twentieth-century art and film into increasingly empty spectacle.

The text of Paine's letter to Rockefeller is presented in the context of the installation for historical contextualisation.

Andrea Fraser

Yilmaz Dziewior (ed.), *Andrea Fraser: Works 1984 to 2003*, Cologne: Dumont, 2003, pp. 222–24.

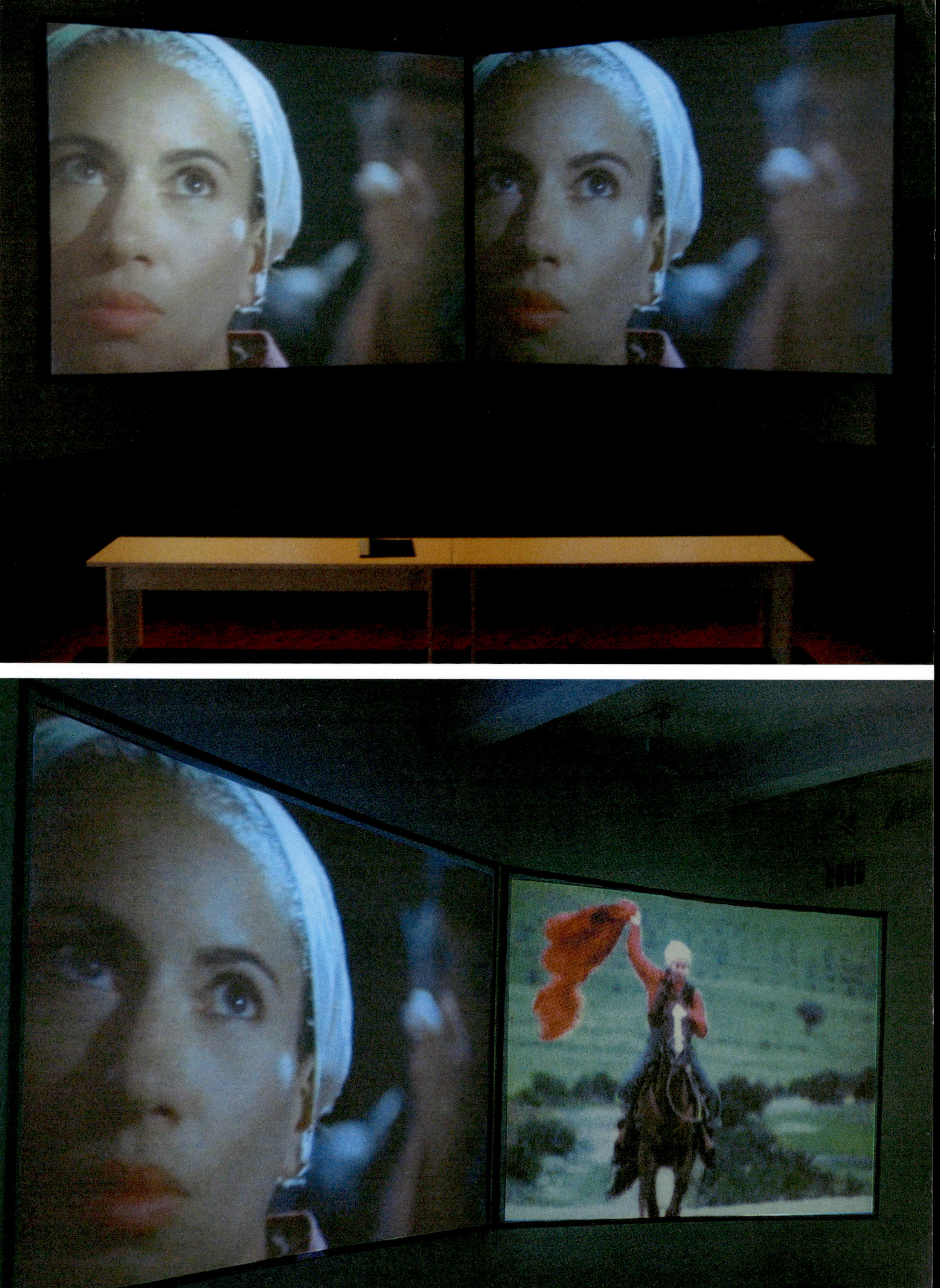

Sept. 17th Please excuse this corrected copy. I have not had an opportunity to have it typed again my trip. F. P.

PAINE MEXICAN ARTS CORPORATION

74 TRINITY PLACE

NEW YORK

August 13, 1930.

President
Frances F. Paine

WHITEHALL 5360-1-2

Mrs. John D. Rockefeller, Jr.
The Eyrie,
Seal Harbor,
Maine.

My dear Mrs. Rockefeller:-

I am forwarding you a copy of the Incorporation papers. They were approved at a meeting of the Art Center, and also passed by the State of New York. They lack only the three names to complete the fifteen for the Board of Directors. I wrote you a note regarding this soon after you left.

Oh, I do hope Mr. Brown will consent to be President.

Mr. Crowninshield is here and after looking around for suitable headquarters for the Mexican Art Association, we think that the most desirable and suitable is the room next to the Modern Museum. These are 3060 square feet. The rental is listed at $10,000 a year but due to the general business depression we think a better arrangement could be made.

I shall find out what the most advantageous terms are and if it is within reason submit for the consideration of the Board.

This space would enable us to have a place sufficiently dignified to be in keeping with the purposes of the Association and also allow a gallery for fine arts, prints and books and applied arts, an office and a Board room that would serve as a lounge or meeting place or to entertain visiting parties.

I do feel it is important to make adequate provision for the Mexican fine arts as they are enormously important.

Mr. Barr has returned from Europe and he, Mr. Abbott and I have finished the details for Rivera's exhibition at the Modern Museum. Letters from Diego promise that he will be ready for the opening June 1931. He is delighted with the prospect. We have sent blueprints of the gallery, dimensions, lighting details and photographs so that he can judge about the effects. The main gallery will consist of murals done expressly for the exhibition. I am very much excited about it as I think it will

PAINE MEXICAN ARTS CORPORATION

74 TRINITY PLACE

NEW YORK

President
Frances F. Paine

WHITEHALL 5360-1-2

Mrs. Rockefeller   -2

be a very great success. There is much to be read between the
lines but the simple statements are these.

In 1928, ~~at that time~~ I told Dr. Richards that I felt
sure that most Mexican Artists, though "Red", would cease to be
"Reds" if we could get them artistic recognition. In 1928 Digo
was the most powerful "Red" in Latin America. At that time
he personally placarded the American Embassy with "Death to
the Gringos". In 1929, with Dr. Richards' help, the American
Institute of Architects became aware of his painting and
awarded him their highest honor. In 1930 he was expelled
from the Red Ranks, and a few months later accepted a commission
from Mr. Morrow for a mural in Cuernavaca. Yet he still is,
sincerely and intensely for "the people" but one can now reason
with him and from that viewpoint, much can be hoped.

Perhaps you will remember that I told you of Mr. Alfaro
Siqueros - that uncompromising labor leader of Latin America,
painter, but first and foremost a firey red. You may remember that
upon his return from Latin America last summer , where he had with
much apparent success denounced the "Colossus of the North"
and Capitolism he found himself stranded in New York -that in
desperation his brother came to see me to find a way out. He
was being watched by the Civil Service. I sent back word that
the only thing I could do was to send him funds made available
through Mr. Rockefeller's generosity. After four days of hunger
and privation he accepted. I just received a telegram from
Mexico that his last paintings are superb. Siqueros asks that
we take them for exhibition.   I saw many of these when I
was in Mexico in January last.

I cannot tell you in a letter how important and far
reaching the result of this man's activities can be- but outside
of everything else, he is one of the greatest contemporary
painters. It is this fact about him just as it was about Digo
that makes me feel it perfectly logical to work with them as I
have.

There is not an open date for an exhibition for him
at the Modern Museum this year and it is one of the reasons I
am so very anxious to have a little gallery where his things,
as well as the other Mexican painters, can be shown for their
practical benefit, at this time of keen interest in Mexican
Art, accentuated by the publicity attending the October
Carnegie Mexican Arts Exhibition at the Metropolitan.

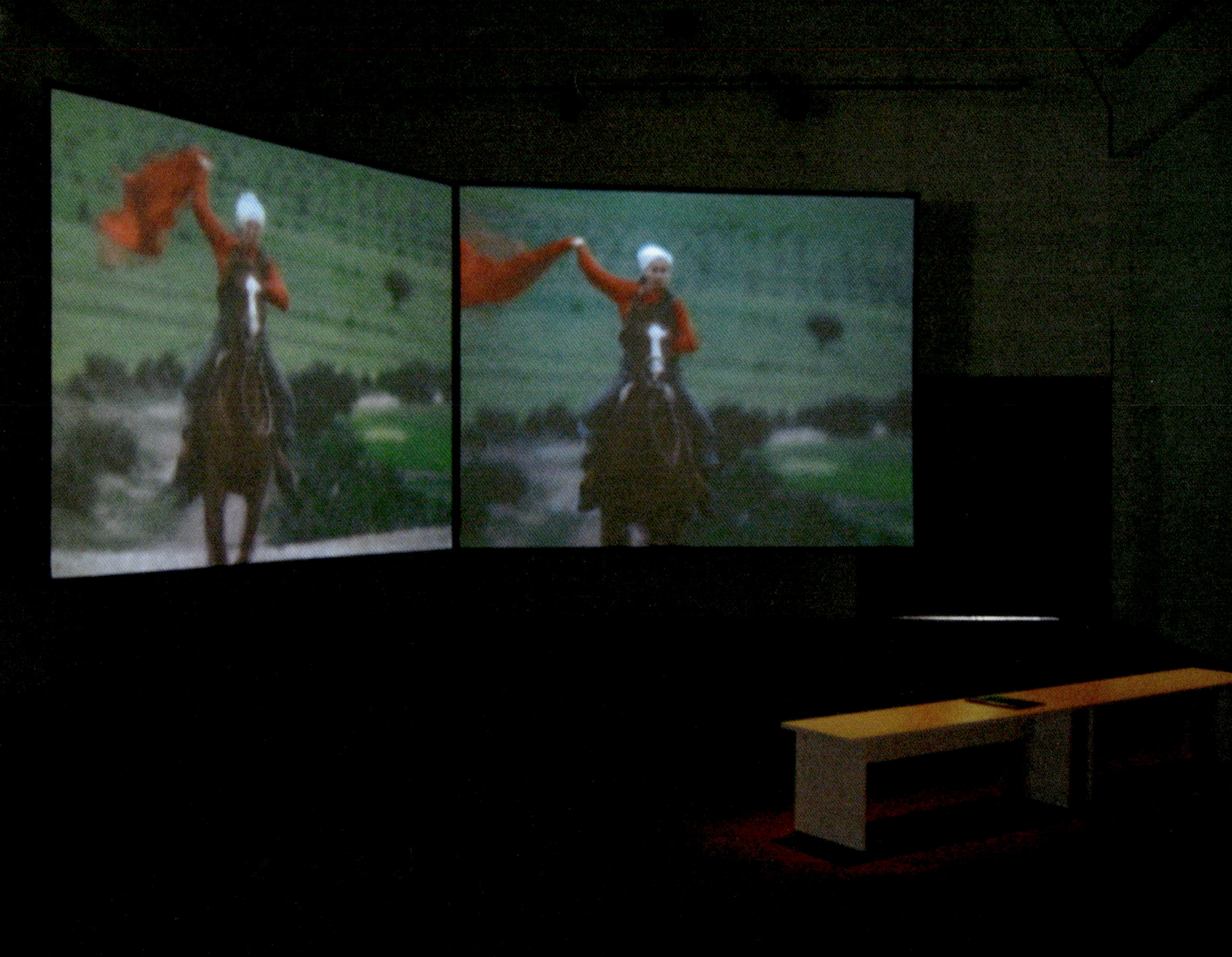

The split screen thus may represent not only a familiar
convention of video art, but also a splitting within the
structure of the artistic field. This splitting is performed in
the piece by the juxtaposition of scenes from a fragmented
revolutionary narrative and a bourgeois and bohemian
audience. It is also performed in the double role I play in
each of these scenes. The splitting of the screen and
fragmentation of the narrative may represent the consequences of the ambivalence implied in this dual role.
It may even be that the narrative of cooptation that
has dominated art historical accounts of the 'failures'
of modernism is also a symptom of this splitting.

Installation view
Dunkers Kulturhus, Helsingborg, 2004

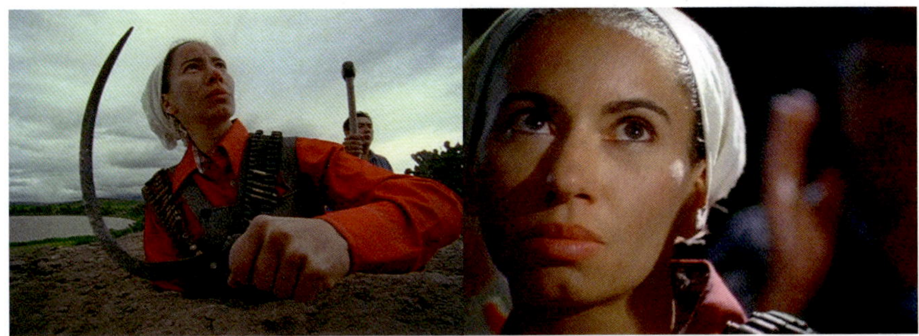

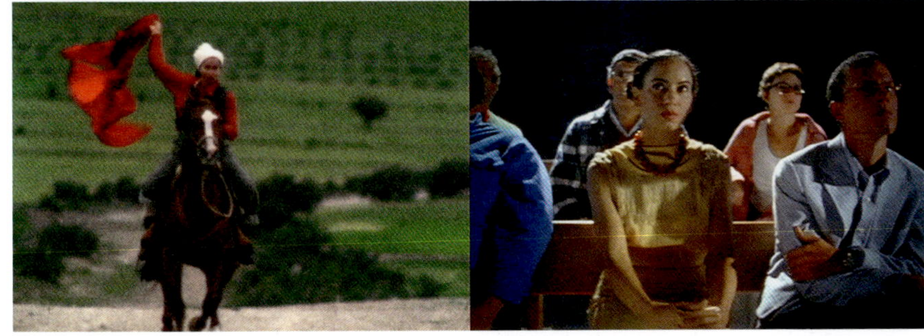

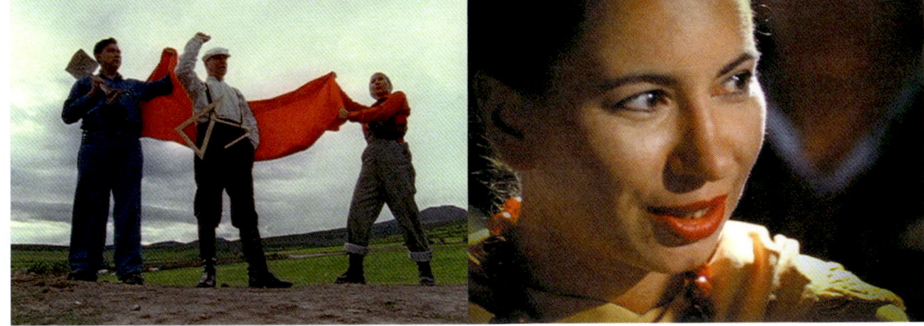

What that narrative may perform is the expulsion of all those aspects of the field of art that don't fit the revolutionary and utopian vision of a modernist or avant-garde project, splitting them off as external forces of cooptation and incorporation, rather than recognizing them as internal to avant-garde traditions themselves. So we are left with the endless repetition of these scenes of martyrdom and the interment of our radical aspirations. These are our martyrs, and they have become myth, enshrining a grandiose vision of our potentially revolutionary power to destroy or recreate society. As the mirroring of *Soldadera* implies, this vision may really only be a kind of narcissism. □

Isa Genzken

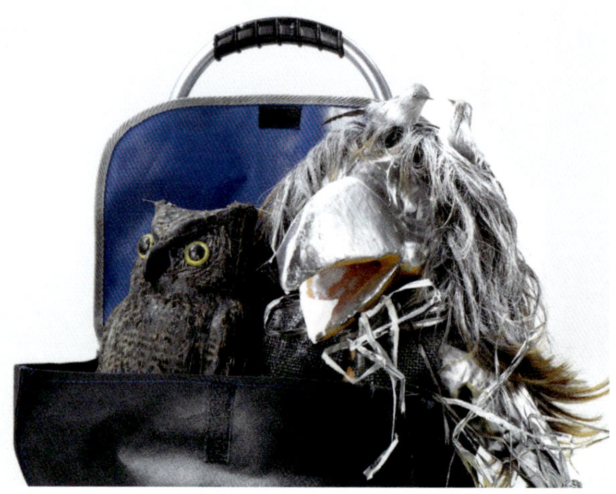

Oil XI a, 2007
Details of installation

The Dialectic of Beauty: On the Work of Isa Genzken

It is a commonplace today that art does not comprise the concept of the beautiful. The beauty of art is, in modernity, no longer beautiful — it turns against the smoothness, the closure, the even calculation upon the basis of which, in its history, art so often sold itself to ideology. Still, even the contemporary discourse on art seems incapable of renouncing the category of the beautiful entirely. That this is so is not only a sign of the helpless recourse to outdated concepts out of a lack of new ones; nor is it always a symptom of the reactionary longing for purity, which, often with a fringe of nostalgia, is still addressed to art today. Rather, the tenacity with which the category of the beautiful persists in aesthetic discourse also contains an indication that it cannot be simply subtracted from art. It is the memento of a constitutive aspect of art, one that explains its interest even though 'beauty' is today no longer its immediately apposite designation. The category of beauty points to something essential to art and yet it is in all its positive definitions inadequate to the latter. Aesthetic modernity has not attempted to dissolve this antinomy but rather integrated it into the concept of the beautiful itself, setting the latter in dialectical motion. Similarly, the artistic movement against beauty's traditional form proceeds not in order to banish the beautiful from aesthetic practice altogether, but rather in order to save it. For even this gesture of negation testifies to an idea of the beautiful that neither modern art nor aesthetics can renounce because it constitutes their dynamic centre: the modern idea of beauty lies precisely in its indeterminacy, in its defying any definition. Beauty is determined only by negation: by the wreckage of the attempts to pin it down. Hence its intolerance against all formalisation and convention.[1]

It is not least in this sense that Isa Genzken is a modern artist. An obsessive attention to the tensions within the concept of the beautiful itself pervades her work. It is perhaps also this obsession that holds the various phases of her oeuvre, frequently described by critics as markedly heterogeneous, together — indeed, even Genzken's courage to enter ever new uncharted territories, her affective aversion against the recognisable, seems driven by this obsession. It is similar with her sense for the historicity of art; little is as repugnant to her as the safety with which others accommodate themselves in the once successful — as though there were no history, as though what was once good could be preserved as such without having to submit, again and again, to renewed critical consideration. Yet Genzken's sensitivity to all pretence of trans-historical validity is more than an idiosyncrasy; her self-imposed obligation to the demands of the time is rooted rather in a deep insight into the incompatibility of convention and art. 'Keep mixing things up!'[2] is an imperative incumbent upon Genzken's practice, directed against that in artistic production, which has hardened into principle: an anti-principle, erected in the name of art. For artistic success requires not only a dimension that can be generalised into the conception of an art, its idea, that is: its principle; but also a trait that points beyond this dimension and refuses such generalisation. It is only by virtue of this second trait, with which the work resists summary inclusion under a principle, that it gains the quality of singularity that decides its aesthetic status: a beauty whose dignity arises out of its constitutive rejection of all attempts to objectify and thus to normalise it. Any idea of beauty conceived without this rejection, by contrast, would be tainted by the misery of 'arts and crafts', or by fascism (or both).

To produce art, then, must mean, as Adorno puts it in a famous passage in his *Aesthetic Theory*, 'to make things of which we do not know what they are'.[3] This does by no means entail (for either Adorno or Genzken) that artistic production ought to, or even could, do without the rational dimension of concept, idea, principle. Someone who merely produces based on a gut feeling does not know what he is doing, but does not ipso facto make art. Art results not from the close-minded celebration of the irrational but in a movement by which aesthetic rationality transcends itself, the reflective work with and on formal principles immanently opening up to a dimension that no longer fits the calculations of such principles. Adorno calls this dimension 'expression' — it is the epitome of aesthetic beauty in modernity. Genzken's extraordinary artistic capability is thus an expressive ability: she enacts the paradox — of an act of making that turns against the logic of (technical) feasibility itself — in her artistic production instead of covering this difficulty up with false certainties, be they irrationalist or rationalist. Yet that Genzken has maintained this stance is evident not only in a perspective on the ruptures in the history of her oeuvre, which have saved her and her work from becoming categorised. Rather, such changes are only an outward reflection of what, by force of the tension between the general and the particular, urges toward expression in every one of her works. It is also for this reason that even those groups of works continue to stand up to critical consideration today that Genzken has left behind, out of faith to them beginning something new. Because their forms resist closure, resist subsumption under a concept, an idea, a principle, their expression has been capable of continuous renewal; in the light of new contexts of meaning (including those that emerge with her new works), they present ever new and often surprising faces.

Juliane Rebentisch

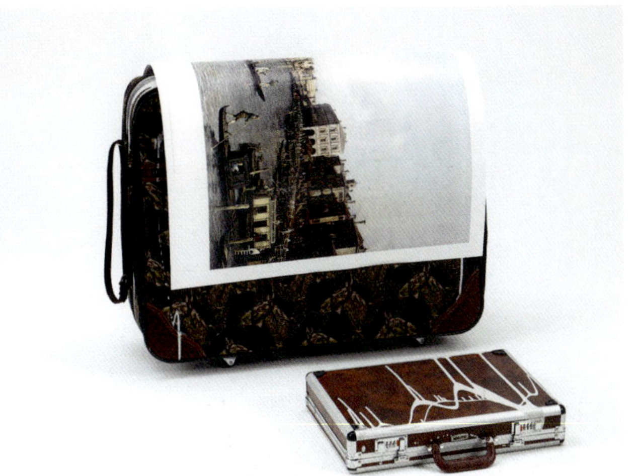

1   For a more detailed discussion of this, see Theodor W. Adorno, *Aesthetic Theory*, Robert Hullot-Kentor (tran.), Minneapolis: University of Minnesota Press, 1997, esp. pp. 50–53.
2   Isa Genzken, 'Who Do You Love? Isa Genzken in Conversation with Wolfgang Tillmans', *Artforum*, no. 3, November 2005, p. 229.
3   Adorno, op. cit., p. 114.

Excerpt from Nicolaus Schafhausen (ed.), *Isa Genzken: Oil, German Pavilion, Venice Biennale 2007*, Cologne: Dumont, 2007.

Isa Genzken

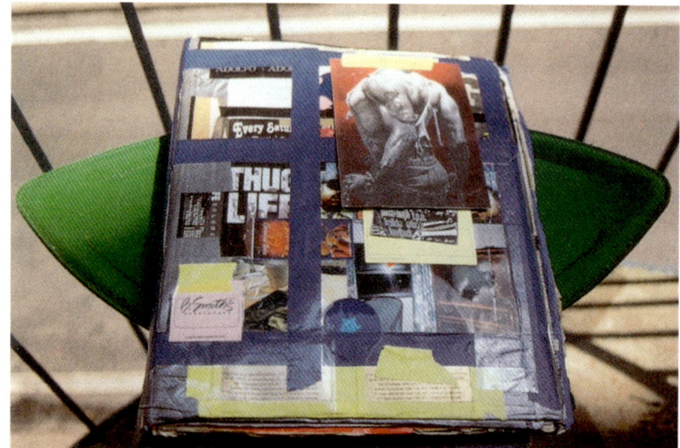
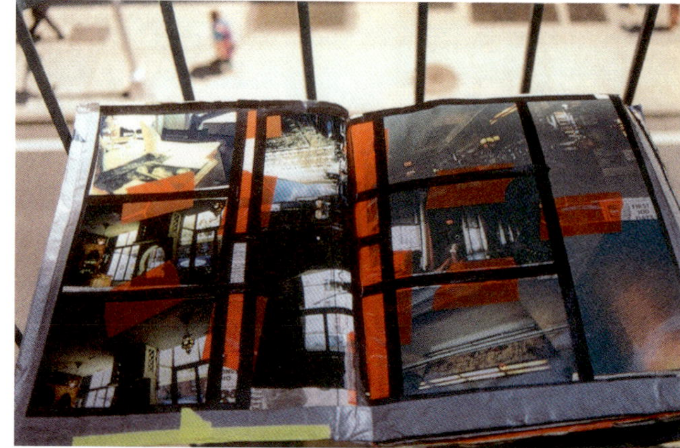
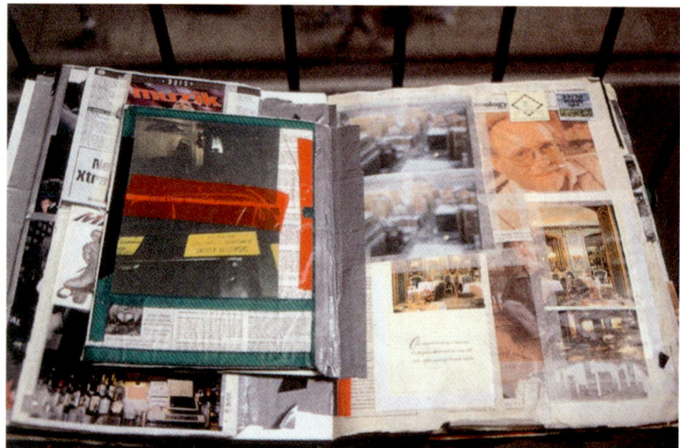
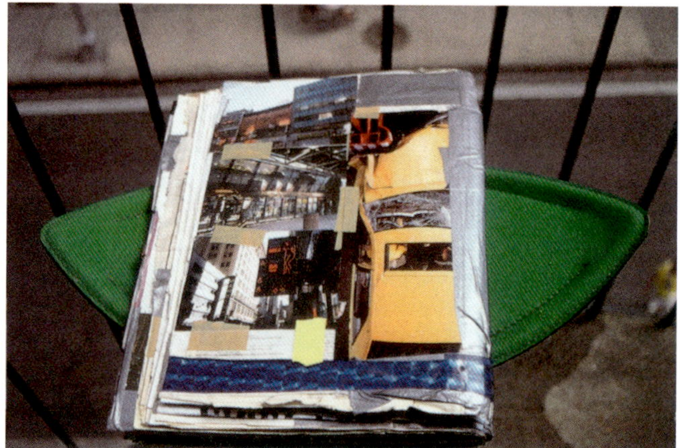
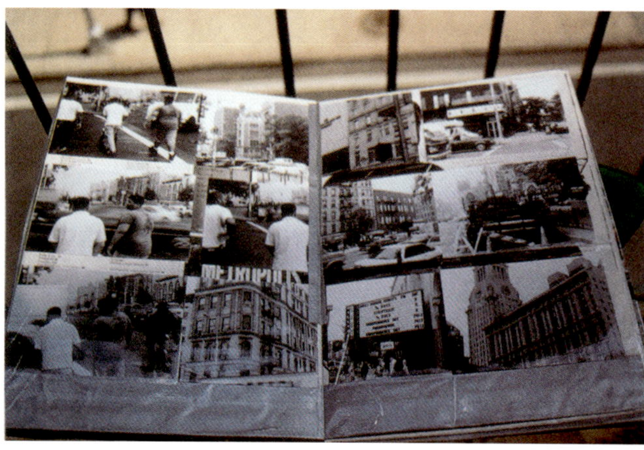
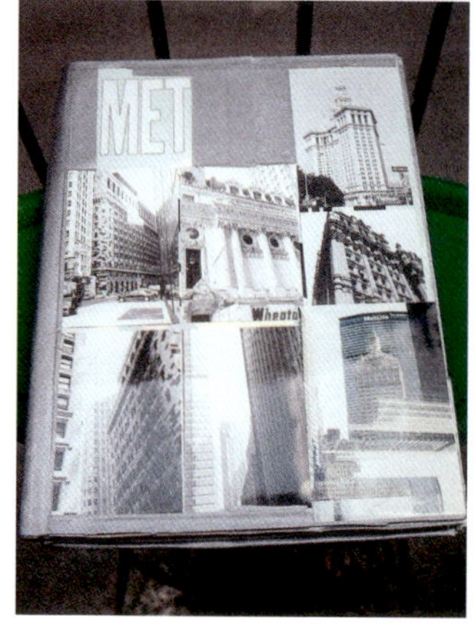

I Love New York, Crazy City, 1996
3 portfolios with photomontages

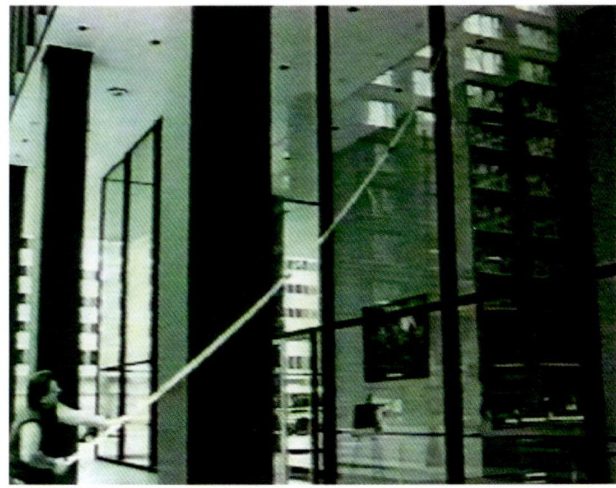
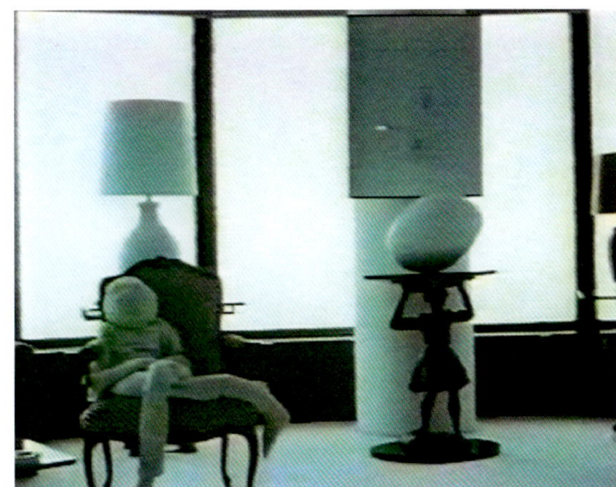
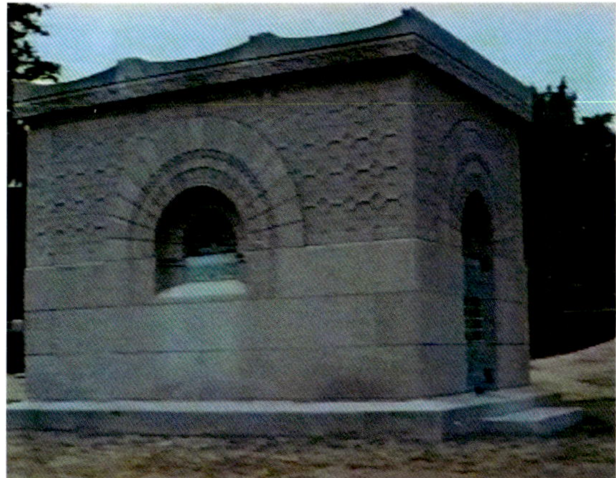
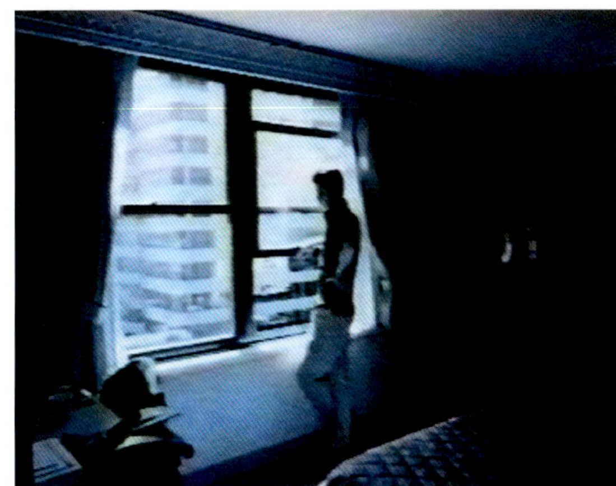
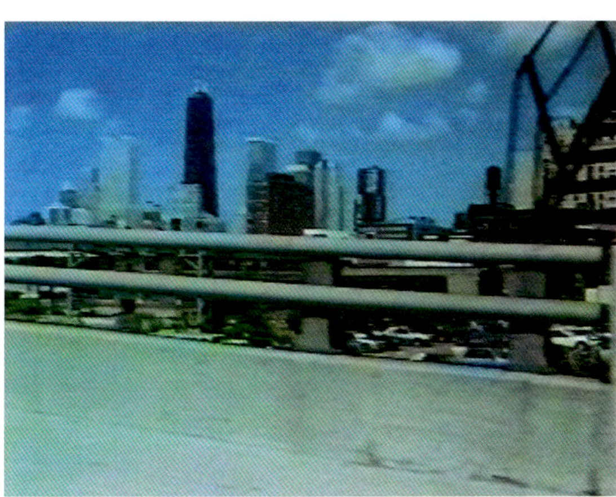
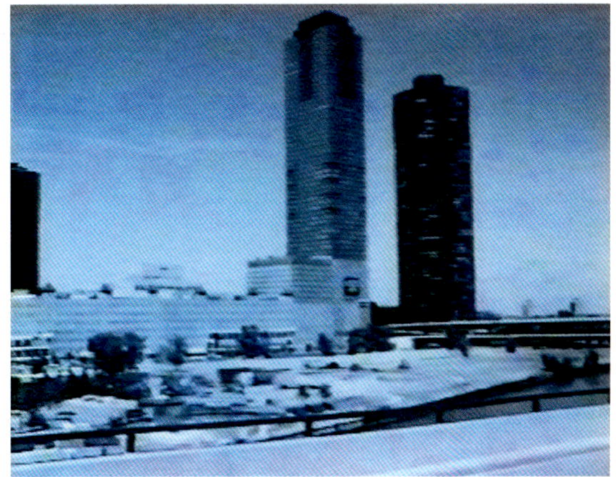

Chicago Drive, 1992
Film

Oil XI, 2007
Installation view and details
German Pavilion
52nd Venice Biennale

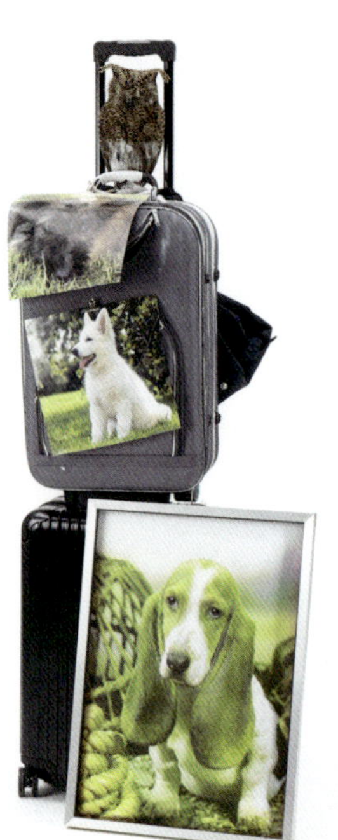

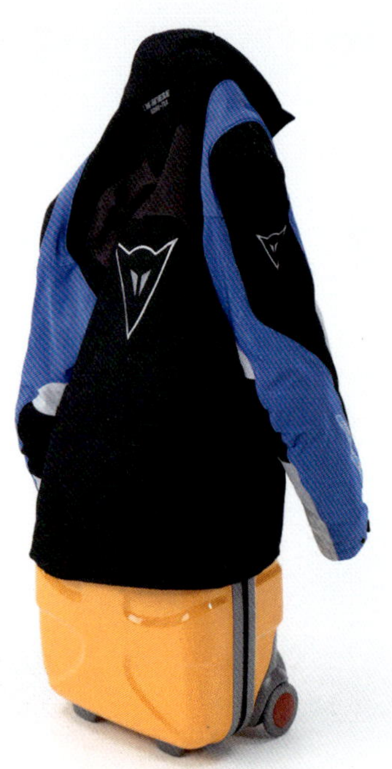

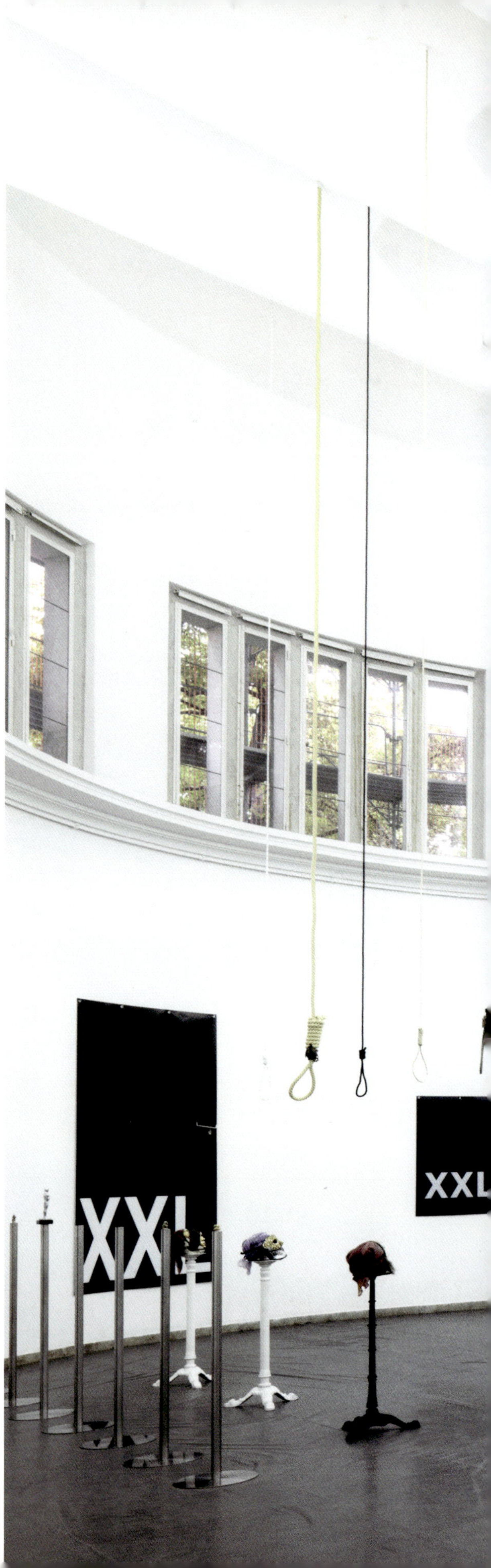

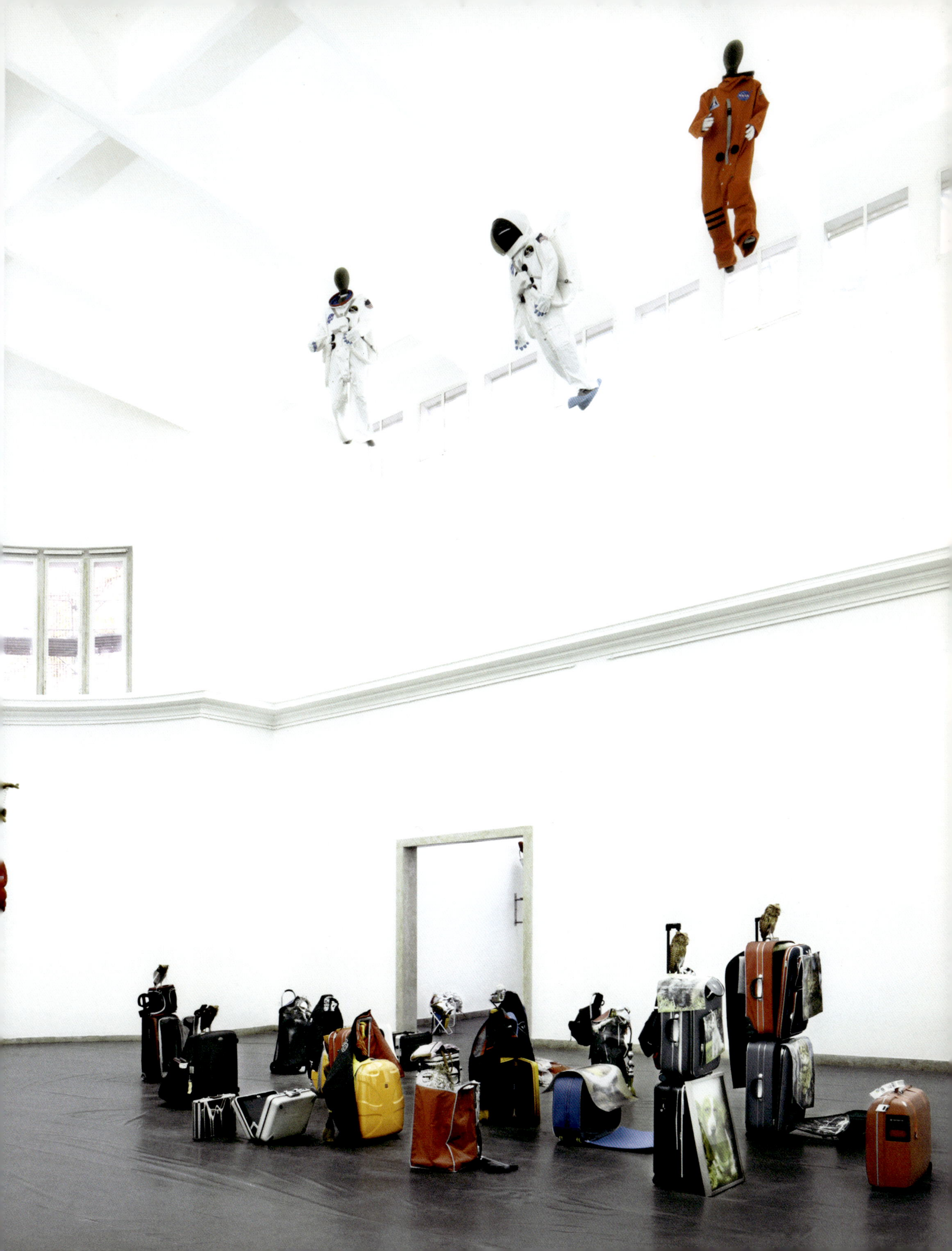

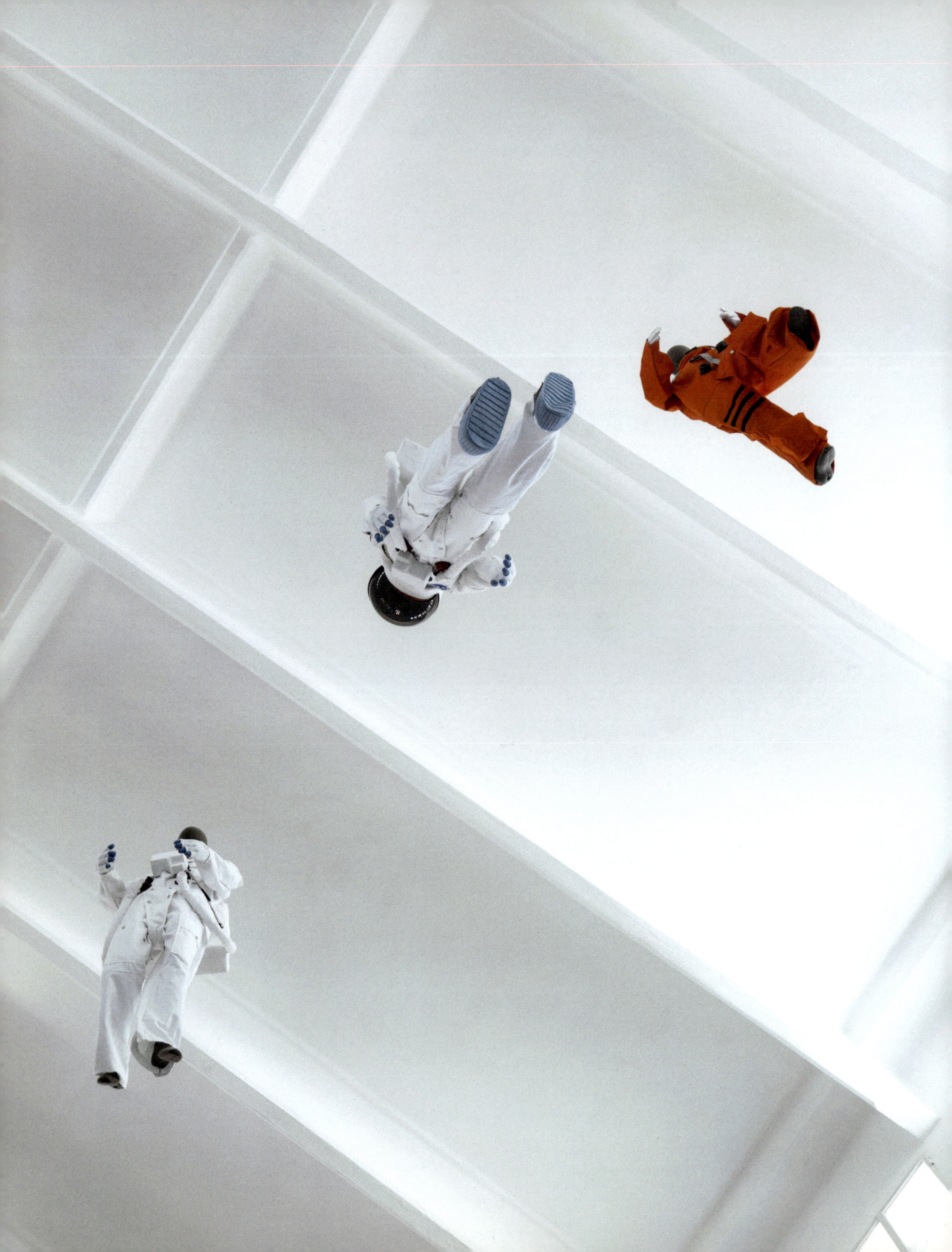

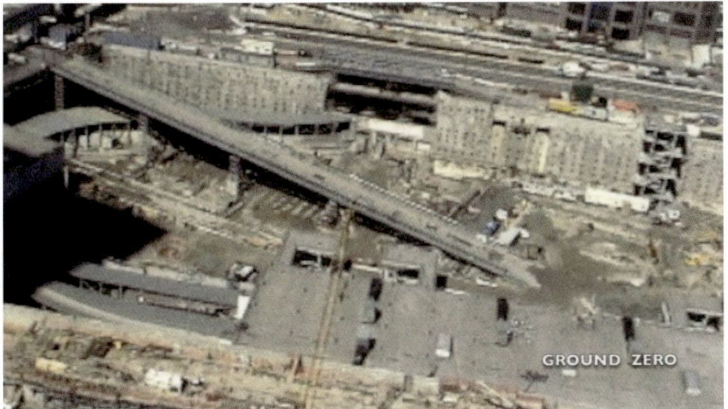
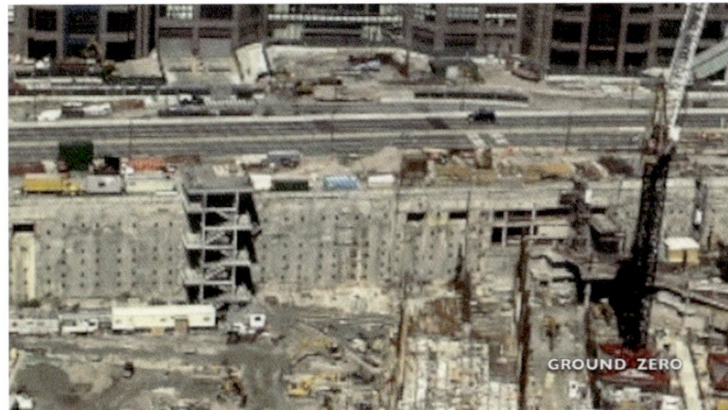
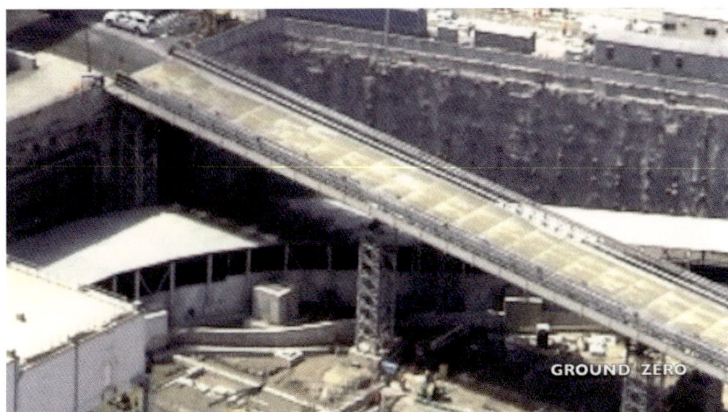
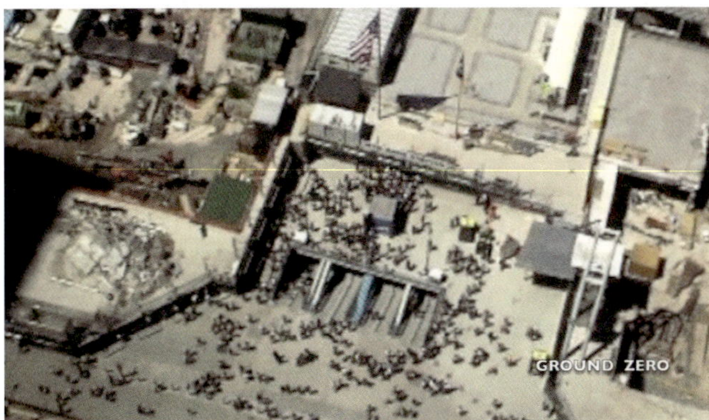
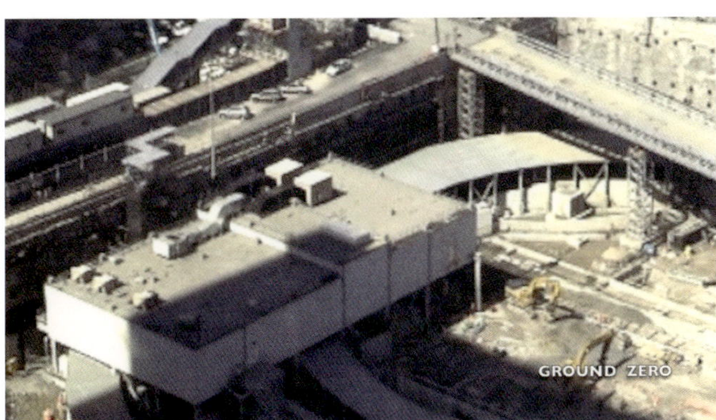
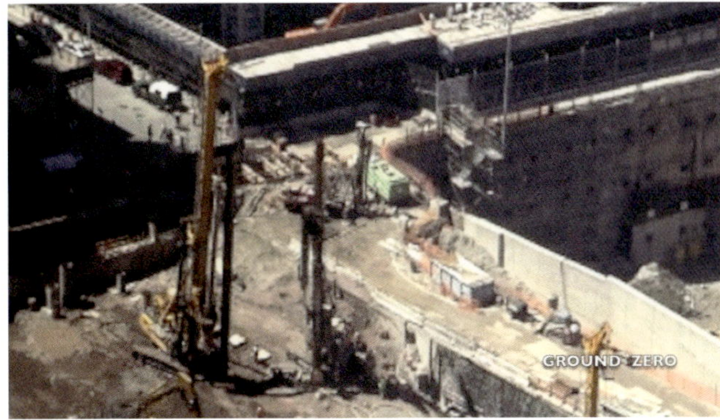

Isa Genzken and Wilhelm Schnell
Ground Zero, 2007–08
Digital video

Dan Graham and Robin Hurst

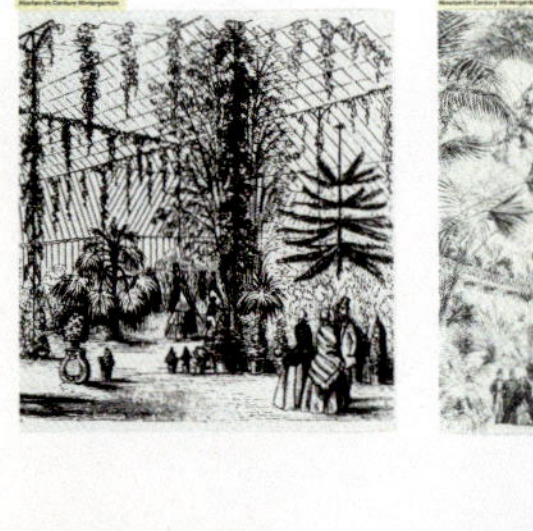
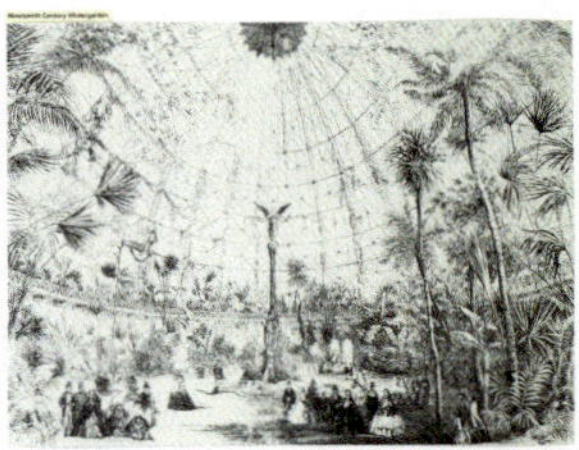
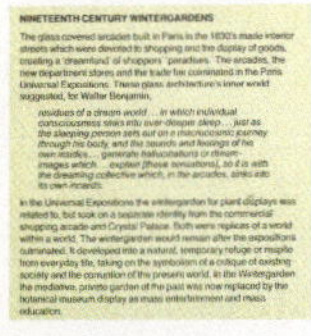
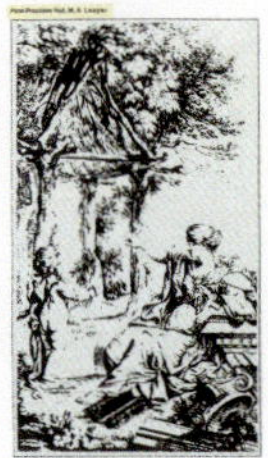
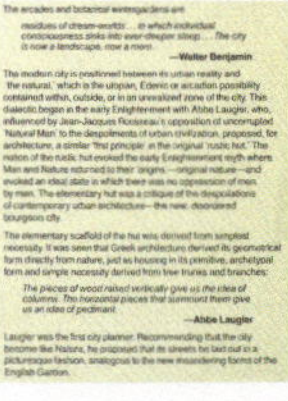

In these six panels, designed like a magazine article, like a photo-text essay, Graham and architect Hurst investigate the city at the interface of urbanity and nature. The two authors draw on Abbé Laugier's principle of the Rustic Hut, devised under the influence of Rousseau as a critique of the new, disordered bourgeois city and addressing social arcadia as an Enlightenment myth. Nature, the antipode of urbanity and architecture, has been swallowed by the city. Relocation of inner-city cemeteries in the eighteenth century prompted the development of suburbs, while in the nineteenth-century parks and boulevards (serving military purposes) were laid out in cities. The construction of glass-covered arcades transformed the street into an interior space for the first time, devoted, like department stores, to consumption and the display of goods. Plants were presented in the sheltered surroundings of glass palaces at world fairs. The idea was taken a step further at the turn of the century in the United States when the first office buildings included glass-covered inner courtyards. At the end of the 1960s many companies moved out into the suburbs; those that remained shut themselves off from their surroundings. The New York authorities therefore provided incentives to build covered areas for pedestrians. Companies in some office buildings introduced a series of semi-public spaces with such welcoming facilities as cafés, gardens and fountains. As the authors point out, three questions remain unanswered: how does the individual use these corporate 'public spaces', who makes decisions relating to them and should they be open to everyone?

A revised version of this photo-text essay titled 'Corporate Arcadias' was published in *Artforum* at the end of 1987. Graham later pursued these concerns in a video (1992) made in connection with his installation on the roof of the Dia Art Center in New York. SB

Private 'Public' Space:
The Corporate Atrium Garden, 1987
6 photomontages

Plate 1
Nineteenth Century Winter Gardens

The class covered arcades built in Paris in the 1830s made interior streets that were devoted to shopping and the display of goods, creating a "dreamland" of shoppers' "paradises." The arcades, the new department stores, and the trade fair culminated in the Paris Universal Expositions. These glass architecture's inner world suggested, for Walter Benjamin,

> residues of a dream world… in which individual consciousness sinks into ever-deeper sleep… just as the sleeping person sets out on a macrocosmic journey through his body, and the sounds and feelings of his own insides… generate hallucinations or dream-images that… explain [these sensations], so it is with the dreaming collective that, in the arcades, sinks into its own innards.

In the Universal Expositions the winter garden for plant displays was related to, but took on a separate identity from the commercial shopping arcade and Crystal Palace. Both were replicas of a world within a world. The winter garden would remain after the expositions culminated. It developed into a natural, temporary refuge or respite from everyday life, taking on the symbolism of a critique of existing society and the corruption of the present world. In the winter garden the mediative, private garden of the past was now replaced by the botanical museum display as mass entertainment and mass education.

> The arcades and botanical winter gardens are residues of dream-worlds… in which individual consciousness sinks into ever-deeper sleep… The city is now a landscape, now a room.
> Walter Benjamin

The modern city is positioned between its urban reality and "the natural," which is the utopian, Edenic, or Arcadian possibility contained within, outside, or in an unrealized zone of the city. This dialectic began in the early Enlightenment with Abbe Laugier, who, influenced by Jean-Jacques Rousseau's opposition of uncorrupted "Natural Man" to the despoilments of urban civilization, proposed, for architecture, a similar "first principle" in the original "rustic hut." The notion of the rustic hut evoked the early Enlightenment myth where Man and Nature returned to their "origins" – original nature – and evoked an ideal state in which there was no oppression of men by men. The elementary hut was a critique of the despoilations of contemporary urban architecture – the new, disordered bourgeois city.

The elementary scaffold of the hut was derived from simplest necessity. It was seen that Greek architecture derived its geometrical form directly from nature, just as housing in its primitive, archetypal form and simple necessity derived from tree trunks and branches:

> The pieces of wood raised vertically give us the idea of columns. The horizontal pieces that surmount them give us an idea of pediment.
> Abbé Laugier

Laugier was the first city planner. Recommending that the city become like Nature, he proposed that its streets be laid out in a picturesque fashion, analogous to the new meandering forms of the English Garden.

FORD FOUNDATION BUILDING

The Ford Foundation Building, 1963-1967, by architect Kevin Roche, pioneered the private building atrium as a public amenity which would "fit into the urban (and ecological) environment" (Roche) and undo the damage caused by the glass and steel office high-rise of the post-War era. The empty streets at night near these buildings had become meccas for crime.

The core of the Ford Foundation is the atrium park. By enclosing "the roof and the open portion of the 'C' with glass, a large garden court was created. Each office has a sliding door opening onto this park," which gives common access and thus, "creates a sense of well-being."(Roche) The atrium is a shared space to relax, eat lunch or meditate in good or bad weather. It allows members of the staff "to be aware of each other—to share common goals and purposes." (Roche) Most of the offices above ground-level have a shared view of the atrium as well as a view across the space to most of the other glass wall offices. A dining area for all employees on the eleventh floor gives a direct view across the atrium to the President's office.

The atrium park addresses environmental concerns. Two signs placed near the central pool read: "The pool is filled and the garden is watered from rain from the roof and steam condensate, which are collected in a cistern. These are drawn off as needed during times of water shortage, keeping the garden green without tapping the city's scarce supplies." This ecological reminder harkens back to the water shortages of the recent past.

Diverse architectural elements throughout the foundation are unified by the use of identical paving, beginning with the driveway splay at the 43rd Street entrance and continuing throughout the building, forming stair and walkways, retaining walls, planters and at the lowest level, the pool. All of the glazed brick paving is aligned to the same east-west orientation, the brown color approximating that of the surrounding buildings on 42nd Street.

The internal setbacks of the glass box offices, overhanging the north and west sides of the open court, are inversely mirrored in the excavated terracing of the garden below. The brick terraces suggest the geological rock outcrops of the natural city landscape and mediate the drop between the upper 43rd Street level and the lower one of 42nd Street. They also relate inversely from the ziggaraut pattern of the set-backs of the tall buildings in Manhattan. Instead of being on the street-level exterior, the set-backs are here articulated in the interior. In this way they relate more to the existing street lines and low-height set-backs of the adjacent Tudor city apartment buildings.

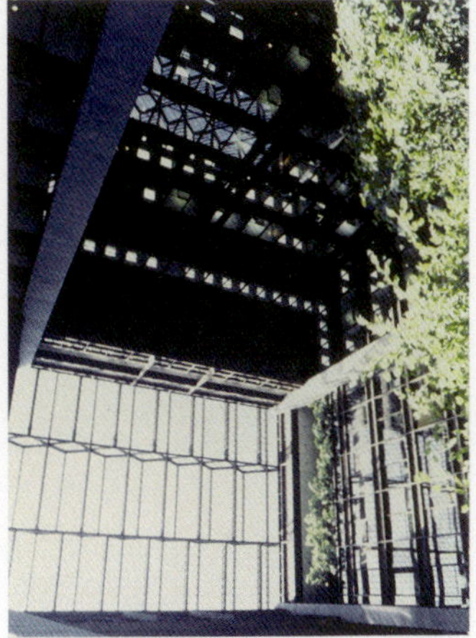

Looking toward Skylight Clerestory, Ford Foundation Building

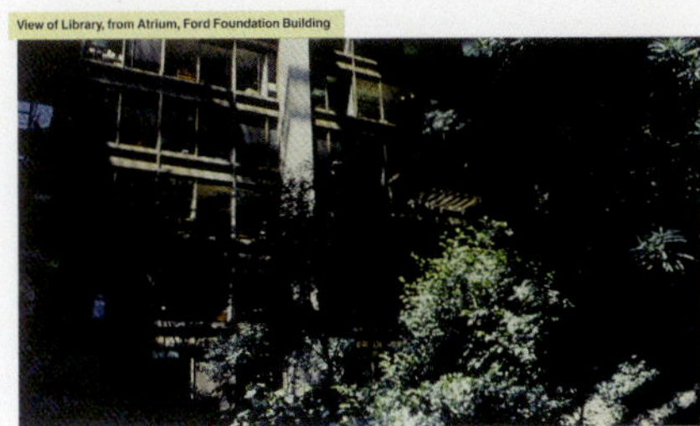

View of Library, from Atrium, Ford Foundation Building

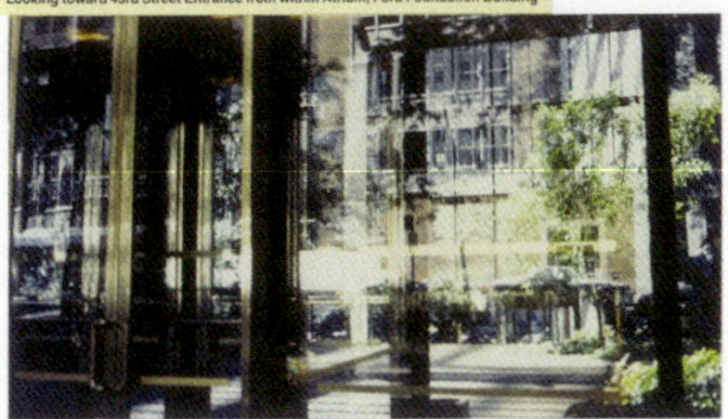

Looking toward 43rd Street Entrance from within Atrium, Ford Foundation Building

The large glass windows of the Library on the west side, rising from floor to ceiling, are framed by Cor-ten beams. Water spigots, ventilator grates and handrails, as well as the exposed structural grid, are all made of the same weathered steel. Cor-ten's popularity in the late 60's was in contrast to the previously ubiquitous plastic and sheet metal extrusions. Like wood, it is 'rustic;' it accepts, even incorporates, the natural aging process as part of the natural cycle; it doesn't try to dominate its environment or make a new, better world "through the miracle of chemistry." Its sudden popularity in the late 60's seemed to question the idea of an architecture linked to technological progress, one relying upon novel materials produced by corporate science (which led to the rapid dating of buildings and materials from the recent past in favor of the ever-new.) In the atrium's decorative scheme, Cor-ten's brown blends with the red-brown sheen of the brick paving and makes a quiet contrast to the lustrous green of the foliage. The only deviation from the restful brown and green are the delicate, white gardenia blossoms.

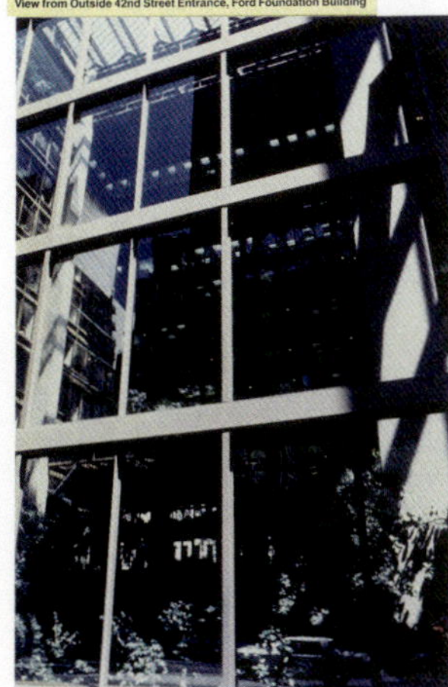

View from Outside 42nd Street Entrance, Ford Foundation Building

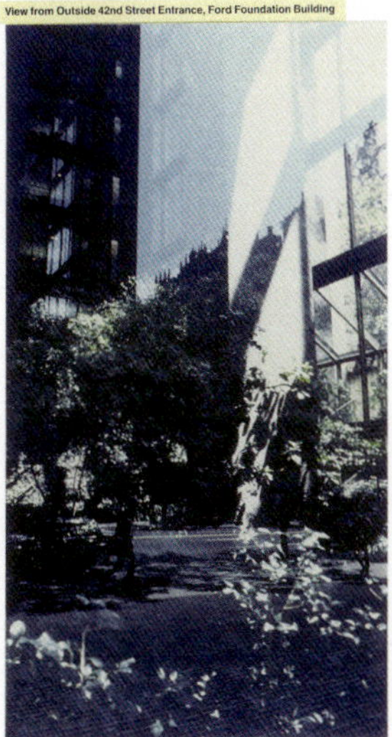

View from Outside 42nd Street Entrance, Ford Foundation Building

Landscape architect Dan Kiley uses common New York parks ground cover: ivy, common trees and terraces which suggest the geological rock outcrops of the natural city landscape and mediate the drop between the upper 43rd Street level and the lower 42nd Street levels.

To the left of the lower level staircase is an eleven course brick planter filled with schefflera. Planted along the earthern border of the steps is a mixture of ficus, low shrubbery, ground covers of English and Swedish ivy, and ferns.

Overhead, along the eleventh floor of the west interior elevation, the green foliage of a line of trees jutting through the balcony rail can be seen. Echoing the green of the foliage below, the trees evoke the ancient archetype of the hanging garden.

Below, at the lowest point of the atrium, in the center of a coin-strewn pool is a flowering white Callay Lilly. The splash of the fountain jet against the brick planter dominates the atrium, obscuring the muffled sounds of traffic along the bordering street. Sweet scent from a nearby gardenia and the sound of the splashing water mix to create a sensuous and audial focal point, an oasis in an urban context.

From the north side of the pool, one looks south over airy, brushy fernbank up to the street level, through the glazing, up the thirty or so stories of Woodstock Court, an imposing brick and masonry structure looming directly across the street. Directly overhead are the three rows of the clerestory window skylight, a rectangle cut out at the four corners by the granite pier supports. Then, the sky, the large curtain wall on the left, two tiers of plants, a large concrete wall, trees, and behind, the huge, white billboard letters of Tudor City.

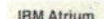

ZONING VARIANCES

In the late 60's, the New York City zoning law was amended to allow incentives for covered pedestrian spaces including atriums. In exchange for providing a *public amenity*, the developer is permitted to build more space by increasing the floor area ratio. For instance, if the site is 1,000,000 square feet, another 200,000 square feet is allowed if a public amenity is also added.

As privately owned and maintained sanctuaries, these spaces are kept under surveillance through the building's (generally) hidden electronic systems, as well as by guards.

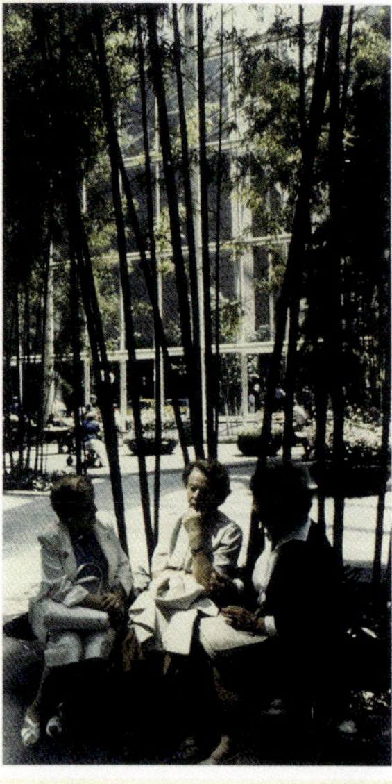

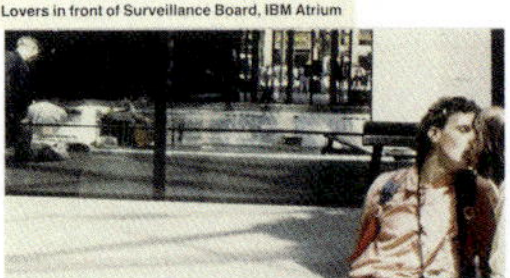

Lovers in front of Surveillance Board, IBM Atrium

SUBURBAN INFLUENCES

The atrium space became a way of competing with and paralleling the suburban shopping mall. As the upper middle class moved back to the city from the suburbs, the atrium was adapted to suburban forms. Real trees and earth combine with high-tech features and suburban patio-like design—green and white metal openwork chairs and green lettering on shop windows to connote a suburban arcadia in the midst of the city (no need to actually commute), an urban fantasy of the picturesque brought into city central.

IBM ATRIUM

Coffee and pastries can be enjoyed weekends at tables set among bamboo and ficus trees at the IBM atrium. In contrast to being concealed as at other corporate atriums, the video and audio surveillance here is fully visible on the monitors behind the stage. Perhaps this is in keeping with IBM's image as an information service corporation.

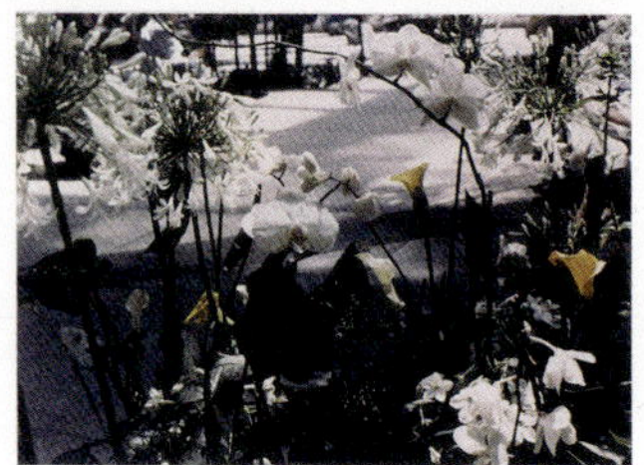

IBM Atrium

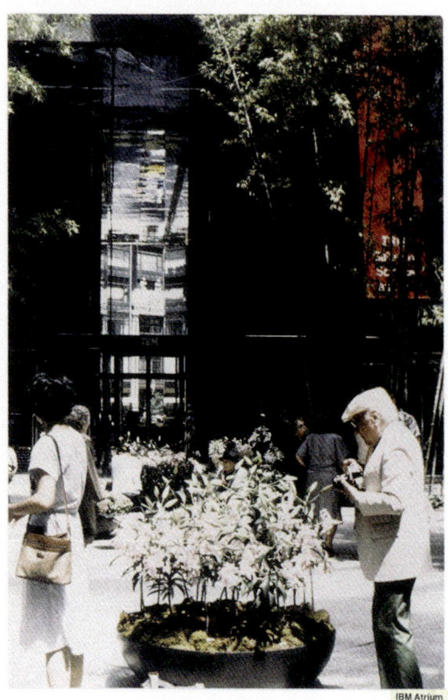

IBM Atrium

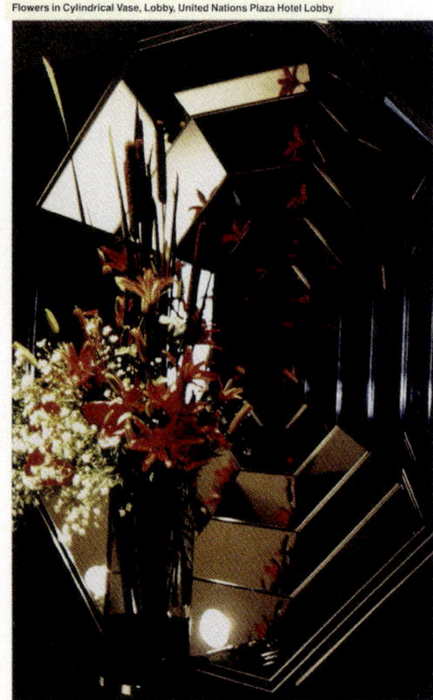

Flowers in Cylindrical Vase, Lobby, United Nations Plaza Hotel Lobby

PRIVATE 'PUBLIC' SPACE

A question arises: Who has the right to determine which individuals may use this corporatized 'public space,' and in what manner?

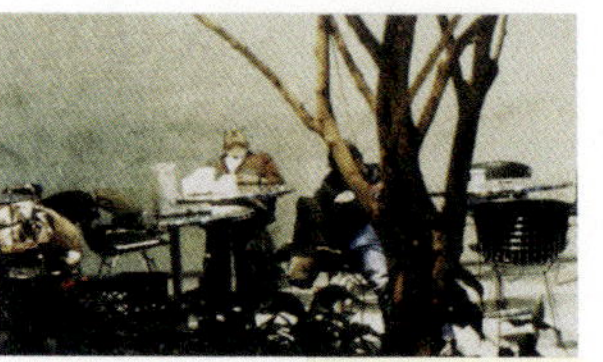

Homeless, Park Avenue Plaza Atrium

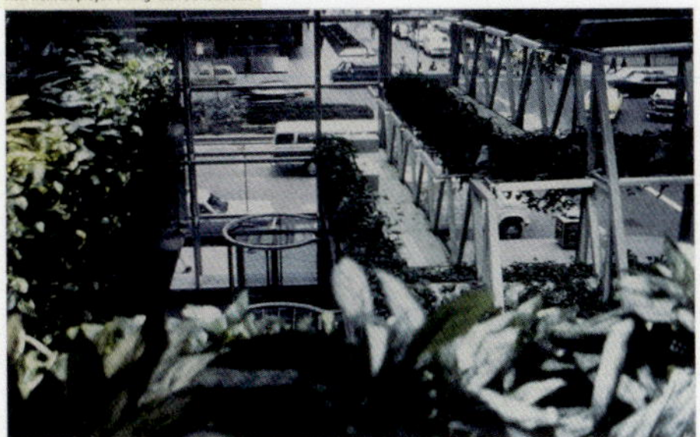

View from Employee Dining Room, ChemCourt

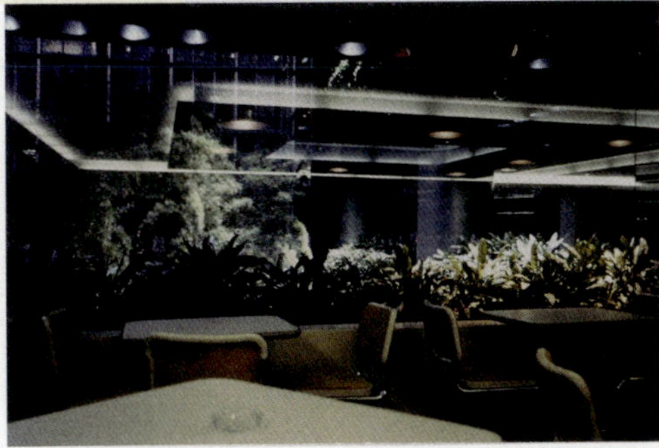

Employee Dining Room, ChemCourt

ChemCourt employees from the overhead cafeteria, glassed in on three sides, have an aerial view of the atrium garden below. From the tops of the tropical tree fronds they can look down the pyramidal superstructure to observe visitors walking through the atrium level.

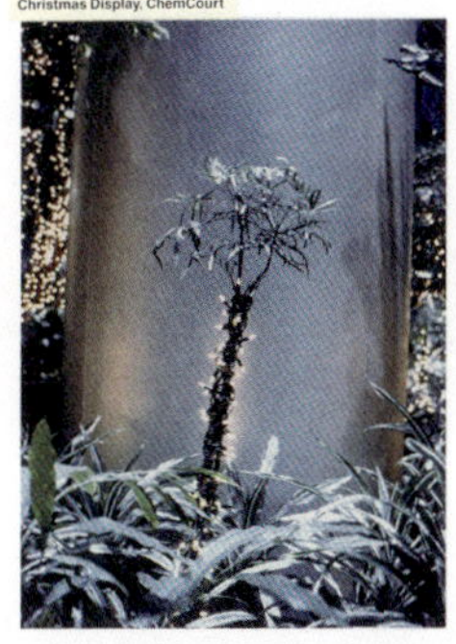

Christmas Display, ChemCourt

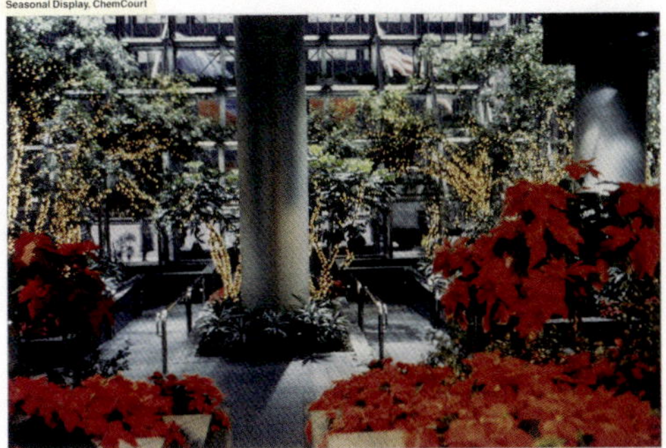

Seasonal Display, ChemCourt

The landscape architect for the ChemCourt project, Mark Morrison, worked to create

> an urban botanical garden…not so much scientific in nature…(but one in which) everybody can learn by having the common everyday houseplants…in ChemCourt there's an 18' margineta, with an overall diameter of probably 10-12.' People go in and they think 'that plant in my living room, it's only 3' tall, is that really the same plant?' And that's as important I think, as valuable as having some thing flown in from Madagascar.

It was Morrison's idea as well to use labeling to educate the curious, combining pleasure with information in a civic-minded botanical garden. The New York Botanical Garden originally planted the seasonal displays, thereby parelleling the changing shows of the nearby Whitney Museum extension.

To the east, in front of the waterwall, is a stack of three planters, split by a central water channel and splashing fountain, and bordered on either side by two sets of white marble basins of cascading water, housing poinsettias in winter, purple and yellow mums in the fall, and orchids in the spring. The seasonal veracity reverses the artifice of the 19th century wintergarden, in its denial of both the natural cycle and indigenous vegetation. Wintergardens displayed tropical foliage and exotic fruits and blossoms in the cold of winter, turning the garden into a spectacle or entertainment.

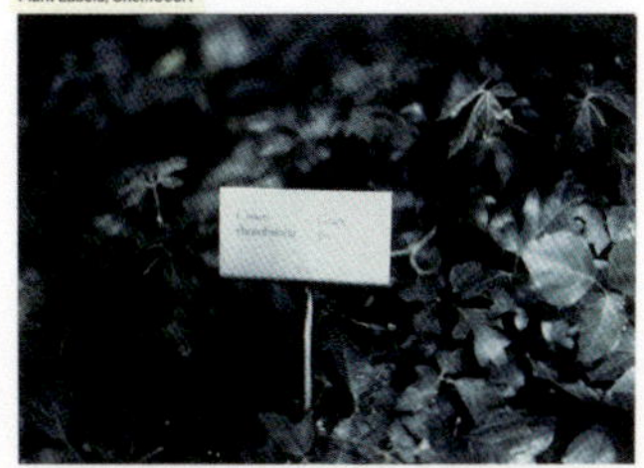

Plant Labels, ChemCourt

The stepped planter bordering the channel contains ponytail palms (*beaucarnea recurvata*), their collective boles wreathed by thousands of green cords and the firefly illumination of Christmas tree fairy lights. All of the tree trunks are wired. The long green tassles of the ponytail fronds hang down from a height of eight or nine feet, their slender trunks bottoming into a fat thickness at the ground. The ponytails are surrounded by a variety of herbaceous plants, here a healthy mass of golden pothos, their broad green tear shaped leaves irregularly splashed with light yellow markings. Up one level is grape ivy, *cissus rhombifolia*, the waxy sheen of tiny young leaves dulling to a mottled varnish in the older leaves, as their cutin is worn away. The trefoil leaves have the curve and hook of a thousandth-millimeter thick holly leaf, without the sharpness of the holly barb.

> [Entering] one of those crystal museums in which their somewhat funereal riches are displayed under the harmonius veil of the days of November. We at once grasp the dominant idea, the obtrusive beauty, the unexpected effort of the year in this special world, strange and privileged even in the midst of the strange and privileged world of flowers, and we ask ourselves if this new idea is a profound and really necessary idea on the part of the sun, the earth or man… They are there, under the immense transparent dome, the noble flowers of the month of fogs; they are there, at the royal meeting-place, grave little autumn fairies, whose dances and attitudes seem to have been struck motionless with a single word.
>
> —Maurice Maeterlink

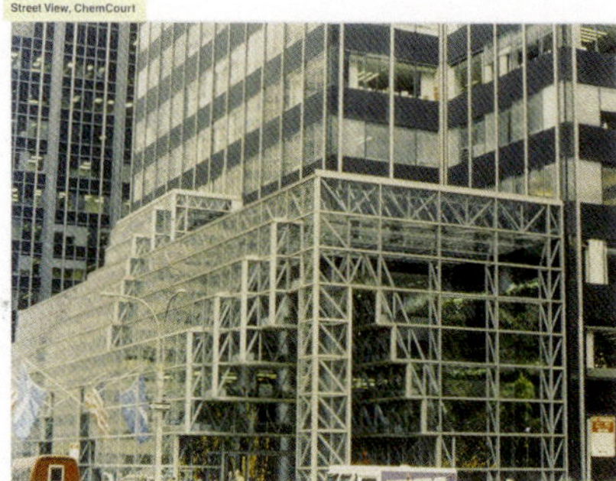

Street View, ChemCourt

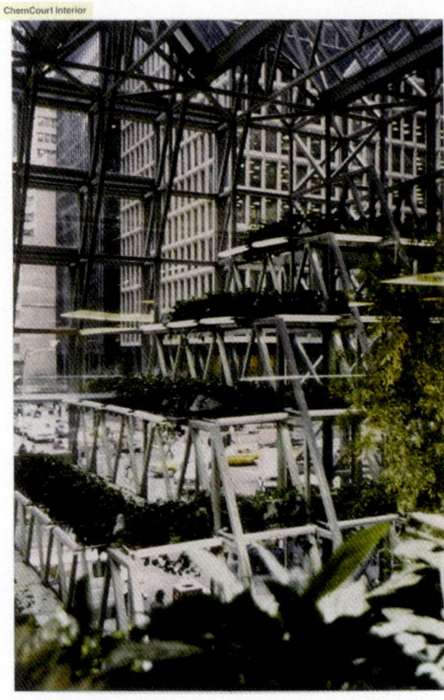

ChemCourt Interior

Above the doorway, lobby interior:
The overhead glass steppes rise and narrow back to a pyramidal point. At several points each run of the framed shelves is intersected by the vertical openwork diagonals of steel trusses, which meet at angles along the pyramid's edge. Each setbacked run contains a long grey planter filled with the green hanging kangaroo vines of *cissis antarctica*. Lit from above by an exposed and extended bank of horizontal fluorescents, the cool, clinical light reflects in white stripes on the grey tinted glass of the risers, creating the impression of a high-tech Babylonian garden.

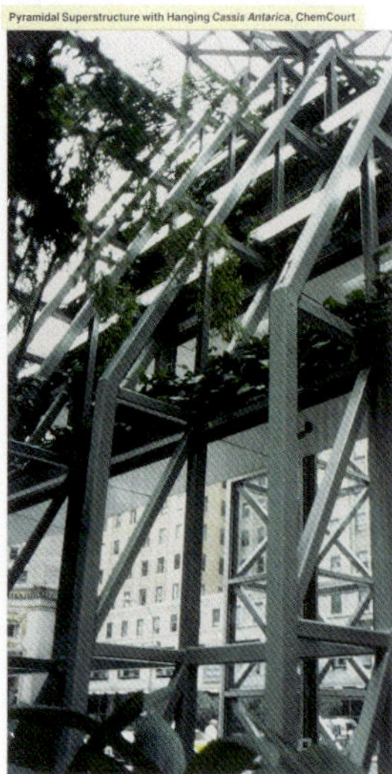

Pyramidal Superstructure with Hanging *Cassis Antarica*, ChemCourt

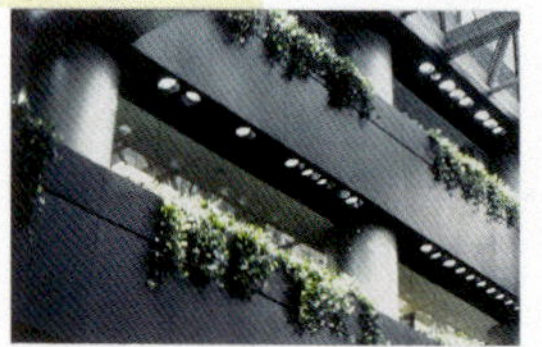

High-Tech Babylonian, ChemCourt

Less than three feet from the front facade glass and to the left lies a low stone channel filled with gently rippling water. The water's surface reflects and then dissolves the rigid geometry of the metal frame supporting the glass curtain wall. The hard lines of the stone channel are softened by hanging foliage and overhead branches extending over the water.

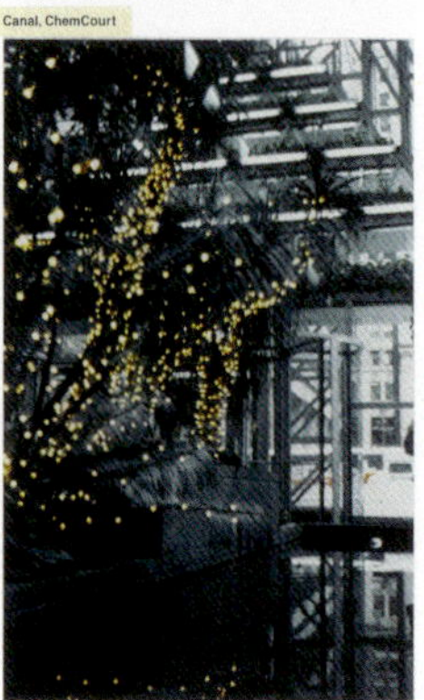

Canal, ChemCourt

ChemCourt, in its entertainment and education aspects is similar to the John Hancock and Phillip Morris branches of the Whitney Museum, and to the atrium of the nearby IBM building. Major museum exhibitions today rely on large corporate funding; now the corporation and the museum become synonymous, providing public amenity space (profitable for the corporation as tax write-off as well as in the trade-off of greater legally rentable commercial floorspace) housed in corporate headquarters.

PARK AVENUE ATRIUM

A postmodern serving cart resembling Laugier's first 'rustic hut' contains buffet lunch in the garden of the Park Avenue Atrium. The plants and flowers of this indoor garden are contained by large stainless steel planters polished to mirror the environment anamorphically. They are truncated versions of the oversized, anamorphically mirror-reflecting columns placed near glazing which are a feature of New York City's style of midtown corporate atriums. The Park Avenue Atrium is permitted to lease the space to luncheon caterers and other parties. Later in the day, the planters will be repositioned into a different formal garden arrangement for a political event, a speech and reception for Pat Robertson, presidential candidate of the fundamentalist Right.

In the 70's corporate exploitation of the earth's resources without regard for their replenishment produced the deadly byproduct of irreversible pollution. This coincided with the actual, or manipulated, energy crunch caused by what appeared to be a world oil and other environmental shortages. New energy technology based on natural, replenishable sources such as solar energy, and energy conservation became government policy under Carter.

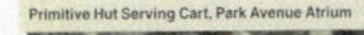
Anamorphic Columns, Park Avenue Plaza Atrium

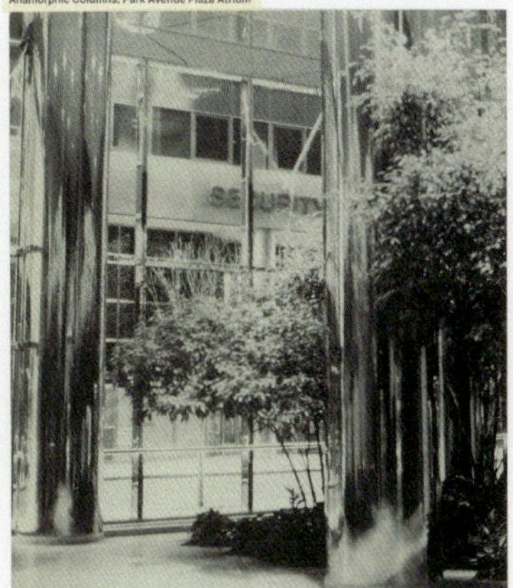

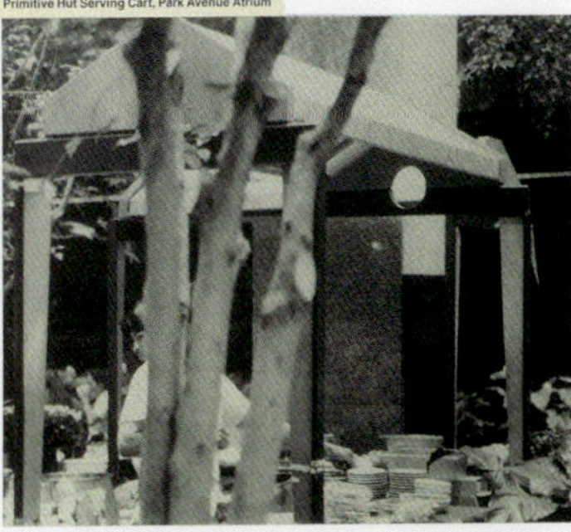
Primitive Hut Serving Cart, Park Avenue Atrium

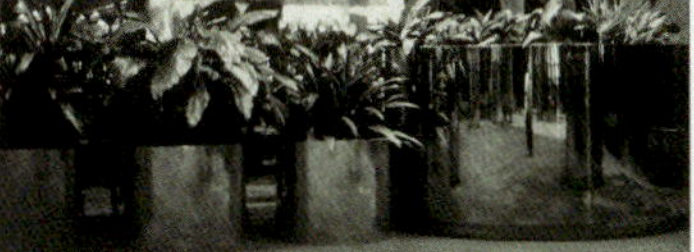
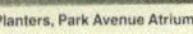
Planters, Park Avenue Atrium

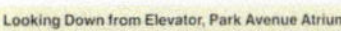
Looking Down from Elevator, Park Avenue Atrium

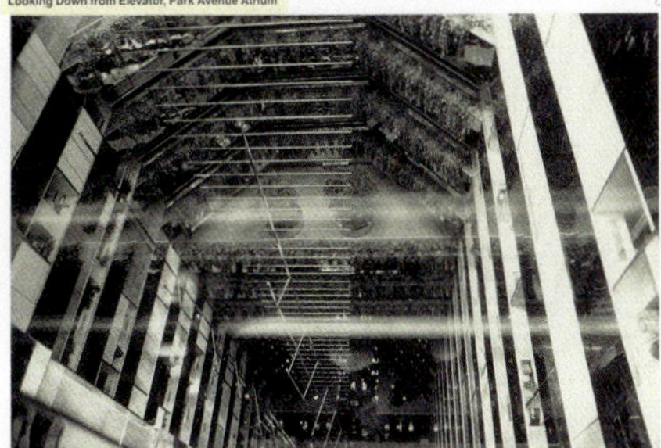

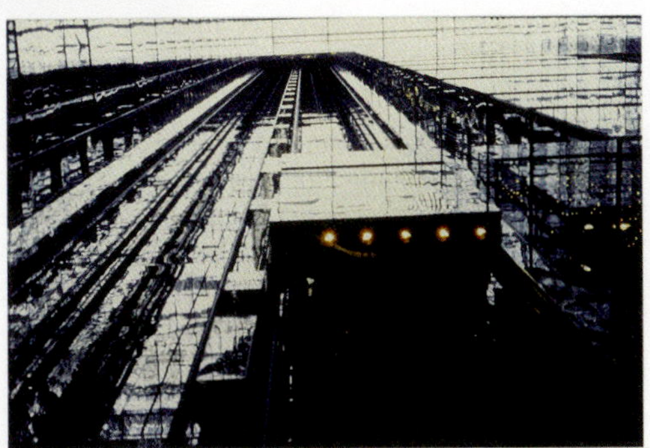
Elevators, Park Avenue Atrium

The corporate garden atrium of the late 70's combines a 60's space-capsule skin with 70's ecological dress. In creating a public image in urban architecture which combined environmentalism (the rustic garden) with space technology, the specific historical critique of technology which the ecology movement presented was denied.

A solar energy-warmed garden space replaced the cold marble lobby, and electronic surveillance of the inner atrium created a sense of protection not associated with exposed city parks.

Side walls are sheathed in bands of reflective glass stretched over silvery steel structures, a complex geometry of crystalline forms shining in the sunlight. The luminescence varies continuously depending upon the sun's position relative to the shifting cloud cover and time of day.

The interior opening as self-contained ecologically purified "exterior" space resembles that of the space capsule interior. It is an inside-out hyperspace, a cylindrical surface enclosing a void such as Arthur C. Clark describes in his novel *Rendezvous With Rama*:

> *...bowl shaped, the bottom of which is a gigantic well, 16 kilometers wide and fifty deep...crawling along the inside of a huge cylinder...whose perfectly smooth... apparently seamless metal surfaces...shot light back at them...Beyond this little oasis of light the land rose up to meet—no, become—the sky.*

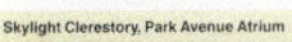
Skylight Clerestory, Park Avenue Atrium

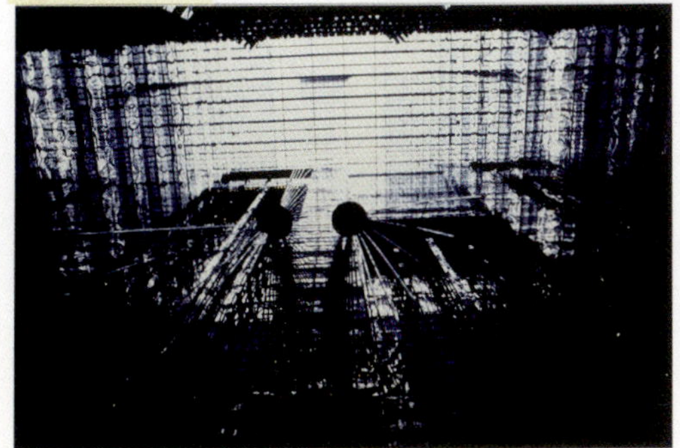

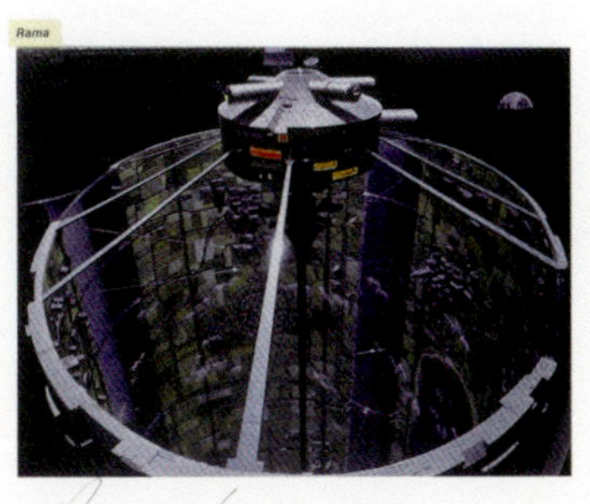
Rama

Tom Holert with Claudia Honecker

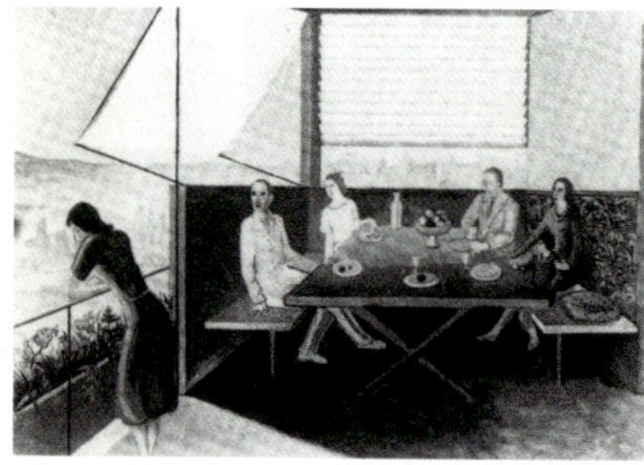

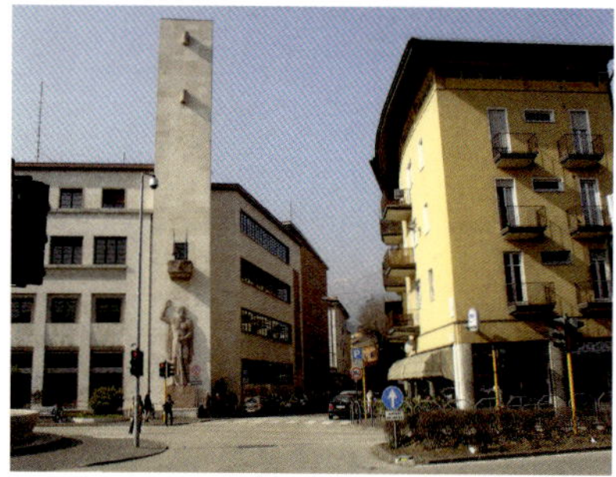

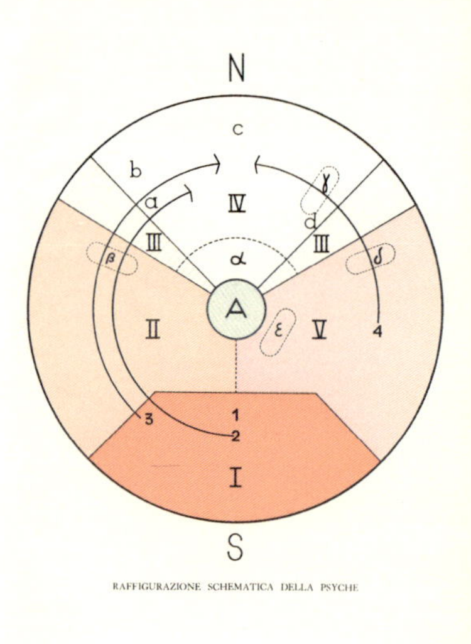

Adalberto Libera, balcony scene, drawing, c. 1950

View of Largo Porta Nuova and Piazza Venezia, Trent,
with the former Casa del Fascio (by architect Giovanni Lorenzo, 1938–1940)
and Adalberto Libera's INA-Casa, Via Galilei, 1949

Beppino Disertori, diagrammatic representation of the soul,
in *De Anima. Saggio sulla psicologia teoretica*, Milan, 1959

Ricostruzione: Disertori/Libera.
Towards a Historical Fable about
Modernist Architecture and Psychology, 2008
Video installation

Commissioned by Manifesta 7 in 2008, *Ricostruzione: Disertori/ Libera* was shown for the first time in the exhibition *The Soul, or Much Trouble with the Transportation of Souls*, curated by Anselm Franke and Hila Peleg in the Palazzo delle Poste in Trent. Art historian and critic Tom Holert is working on a long-term study of 'the diagnostic modern' that began emerging at the intersections of experimental psychology and modernist art and culture in the late nineteenth century. A collaboration with TV journalist Claudia Honecker, *Ricostruzione* has been created as a multi-level inquiry into architecture, politics, psychology and philosophy loosely based on the lives and works of two historical figures hailing from Trentino: Beppino Disertori (1907–1992) and Adalberto Libera (1903–1963).

A neuropsychiatrist with neo-vitalist leanings, Disertori was also a humanist philosopher and committed anti-fascist. In 1943, following the German occupation of Italy, he went into exile in Switzerland and joined the resistance. His many works, for the most part published after the war, range from clinical studies, psychology and philosophy to travel writings. During the 1960s, he lectured in socio-psychiatry at Trent's new Institute of Sociology, the first such department to be founded in an Italian university. Renato Curcio, who later co-founded the Red Brigades, was one of his students.

Libera was one of the most visible young 'rationalist' architects during Italy's fascist regime. He continued to work in postwar Italy as a project manager for INA-Casa, the vast public reconstruction programme. INA-Casa had been set up as a laboratory for new approaches to domestic living and as a project of late-modernist national (re)building under the auspices of the Marshall plan. It generated hundreds of housing projects between 1949 and 1963.

The juxtaposition of Disertori and Libera may appear, and is intended to appear, incommensurate, even forced. *Ricostruzione's* purpose here is neither to initiate a posthumous dialogue between the two modernists nor to suggest a reconciliation, but rather to obtain readings of their historically and intellectually specific projects through speculatively reconfiguring and fictionalising them, transforming Disertori and Libera into probing avatars, twisting and expanding the narrative by throwing other voices into the mix. In such a process vital questions are raised concerning the potential for research within the institutional and theoretical realm of contemporary visual arts.

Tom Holert

Revised version of a text published on the project's website
http://ricostruzione.isvc.org.

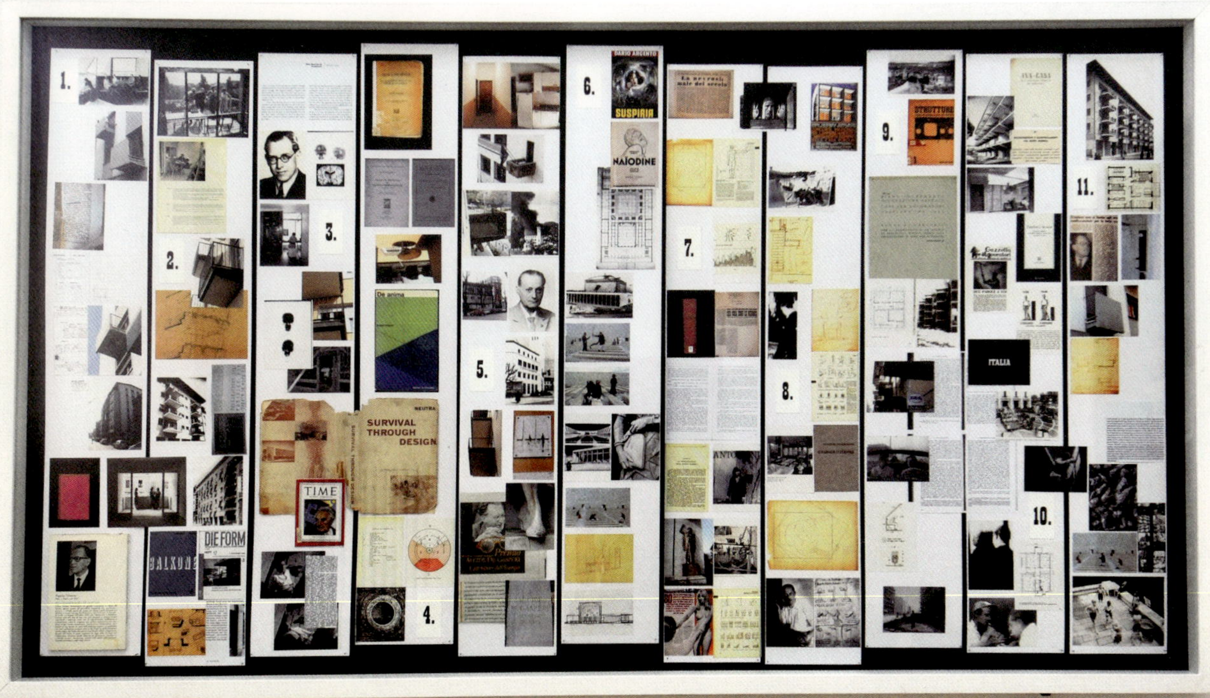

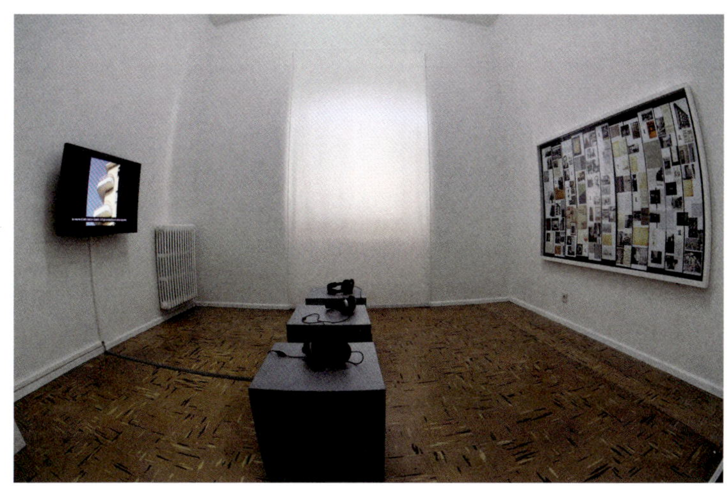

Installation views
Manifesta 7, Trent, 2008

Marine Hugonnier

The Bedside Book Project
Un Coup De Dés Jamais N'Abolira Le Hasard/
L'Espace Social N1, 2007
(A throw of the dice will never abolish chance)
Stéphane Mallarmé/Marine Hugonnier
Installation
Image clips onto Stéphane Mallarmé's poem *Un coup de dés jamais n'abolira le hasard*, Éditions Gallimard, 2006

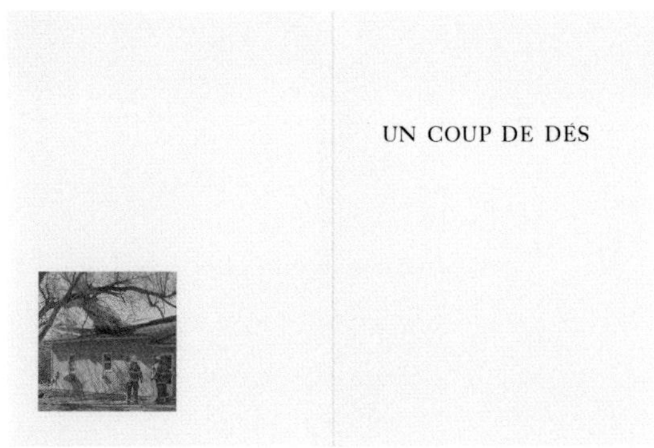

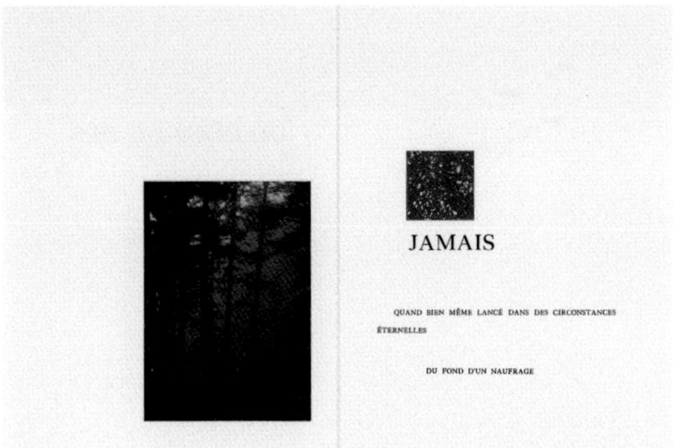

In recent years Marine Hugonnier has produced a series of works involving artists' books that represent the legacy of modernity. In 2004 she started a project using cuttings from Ellsworth Kelly's book *Line Form Color* (1951), pasting geometrical forms in primary colours onto images of the front pages of newspapers she bought in countries in which she was travelling. Works in the series, titled *Art for Modern Architecture* (2004), were produced in one week while the artist was abroad and consisted of six to eight collages, according to how many issues of the newspaper were published in each week. With this project Hugonnier intended to revive Kelly's idea of an 'art made for public spaces and buildings that established the modernist utilitarian project of art serving modern architecture'. Her intention was to 'reactivate this idea in another medium, that of the newspaper, which frames everyday life like architecture'. After numerous travels, mostly in connection with shooting films, the artist finished the project in 2005, when Kelly's book was fully excerpted and remained as a signifier of modern utopia. In some eleven works, featuring dailies from Palestine (*Al-Ayyam*), Switzerland (*Neue Züricher Zeitung*) and New York (*The New York Times*), or global newspapers like the *Herald Tribune*, Kelly's abstract visual language replaces the newspaper illustrations, its universality counteracting the specificity of the news, language and typography of a particular newspaper in a particular country.

Since 2007 Hugonnier has been working on a series involving various editions of Stéphane Mallarmé's *Un coup de dés jamais n'abolira le hasard* (1897), which ranks as a kind of manifesto of pure modern poetry produced in accordance with the idea of art for art's sake. In a prologue or statement Hugonnier invents a fictional framework, in which 'the bedside book of Richard Hamilton, Odilon Redon or Kurt Schwitters has been stolen and altered — folded or added to — in order to change their reading for one night'. She has altered the French text of the 1956 Tiber Press edition, for example, by obscuring the words of the poem with monochrome paper cut-outs (*Alteration*). And she has folded the pages of the 2006 Gallimard edition, presenting each of the eleven framed pages by the hour in a white space with an open window, a spider and a man dressed in a tuxedo who changed the pages every hour (*La Forme du Mystère*). In two other versions (*L'Espace Social, N1* and *N2*) Hugonnier has inserted images found on the Internet into the empty spaces, or intervals, of the poem. SB

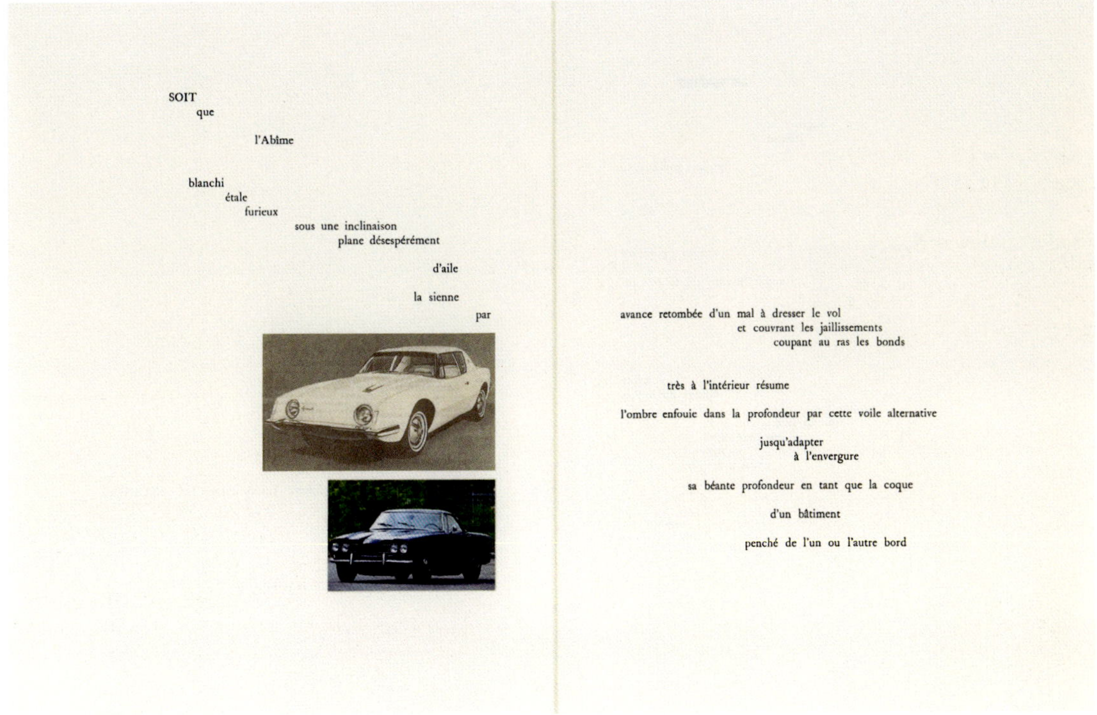

In 1967 Marcel Broodthaers said that Mallarmé had 'unconsciously invented modern space'. The architecture of *Un coup de dés...* was possible only because of the contemporaneous invention of cinema. Its publication occurred in 1897, while the Lumière Brothers' *La Sortie de l'usine* was first screened in 1895. If the project of modern art was one of social emancipation, it is crucial to understand the poem as an invitation, not only to 'reveries' (as Baudelaire would say), but to invest the open space of its gaps. That space has remained the viewer's space' as Duchamp understood it. It is the social space in which all ideologies of the twentieth century collapse, collide and generate new forms. In this sense my work is the opposite of Broodthaers' alteration of Mallarmé's poem. It is like if you had turned a T-shirt inside out and revealed a form (quite erotic, isn't it?)

You might say that adding something (whether images, folds or paper clips) to such a landmark artwork is close to anarchism. It is almost a destructive gesture. The narrative that surrounds this work of mine is a complete anachronism. Who is this person who walks into a house at night and steals Redon's, Schwitters' and Hamilton's bedside book? It is the abstract figure of a modern artist who for one night alters this book that is essential to the thinking of these three masters. What would have happened to their work if they had found their cherished book changed? □

LE MAÎTRE

surgi
inférant

de cette conflagration

que se

comme on menace

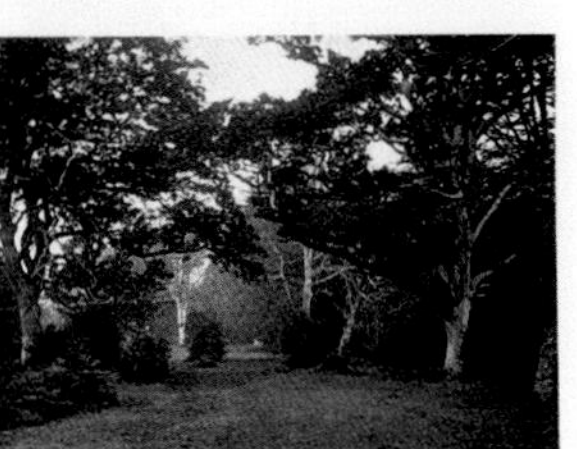

l'unique Nombre qui ne peut pas

hésite
cadavre par le bras
plutôt
que de jouer
en maniaque chenu
la partie
au nom des flots
un

naufrage cela

hors d'anciens calculs
où la manœuvre avec l'âge oubliée

jadis il empoignait la barre

à ses pieds
de l'horizon unanime

prépare
s'agite et mêle
au poing qui l'étreindrait
un destin et les vents

être un autre

Esprit
pour le jeter
dans la tempête
en reployer la division et passer fier

écarté du secret qu'il détient

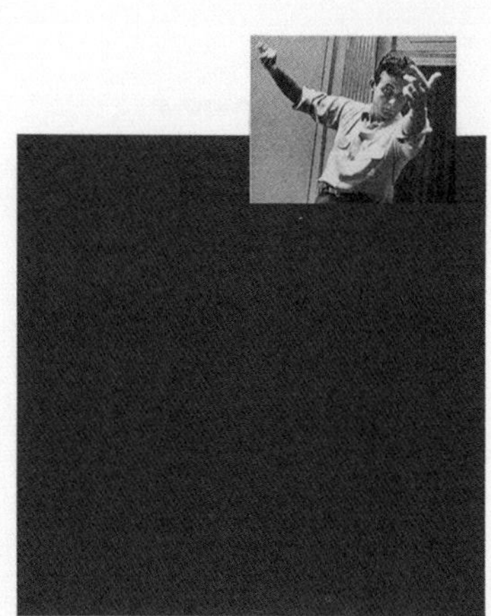

envahit le chef
coule en barbe soumise

direct de l'homme

sans nef
n'importe
où vaine

ancestralement à n'ouvrir pas la main
crispée
par delà l'inutile tête

legs en la disparition

à quelqu'un
ambigu

l'ultérieur démon immémorial

ayant
de contrées nulles
induit
le vieillard vers cette conjonction suprême avec la probabilité

celui
son ombre puérile
caressée et polie et rendue et lavée
assouplie par la vague et soustraite
aux durs os perdus entre les ais

né
d'un ébat
la mer par l'aïeul tentant ou l'aïeul contre la mer
une chance oiseuse

Fiançailles
dont
le voile d'illusion rejailli leur hantise
ainsi que le fantôme d'un geste

chancellera
s'affalera

folie

N'ABOLIRA

COMME SI

Une insinuation

au silence

dans quelque proche

voltige

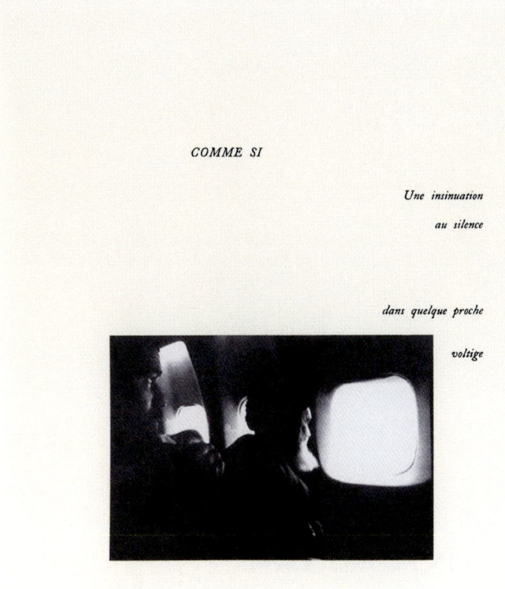

simple

enroulée avec ironie
ou
le mystère
précipité
hurlé

tourbillon d'hilarité et d'horreur

autour du gouffre
sans le joncher
ni fuir

et en berce le vierge indice

COMME SI

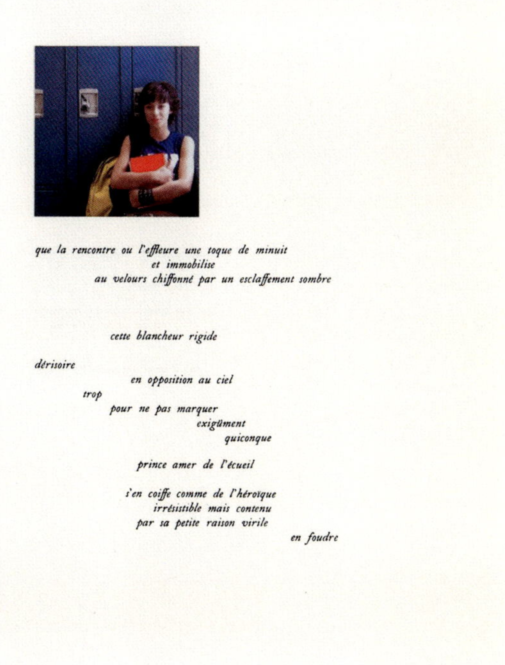

plume solitaire éperdue

sauf

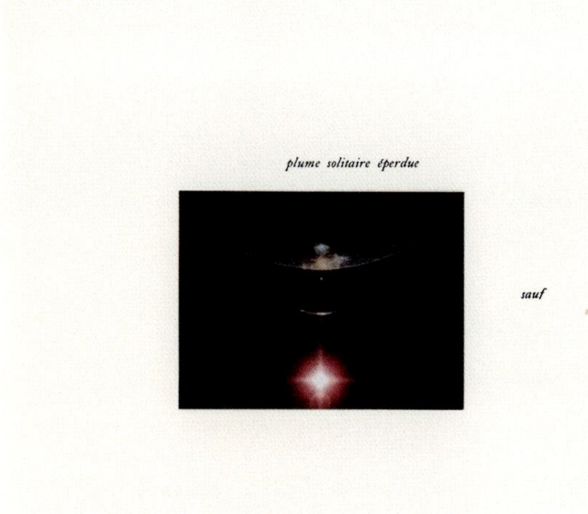

que la rencontre ou l'effleure une toque de minuit
et immobilise
au velours chiffonné par un esclaffement sombre

cette blancheur rigide

dérisoire
en opposition au ciel
trop
pour ne pas marquer
exigûment
quiconque

prince amer de l'écueil

s'en coiffe comme de l'héroïque
irrésistible mais contenu
par sa petite raison virile
en foudre

soucieux
    expiatoire et pubère   muet

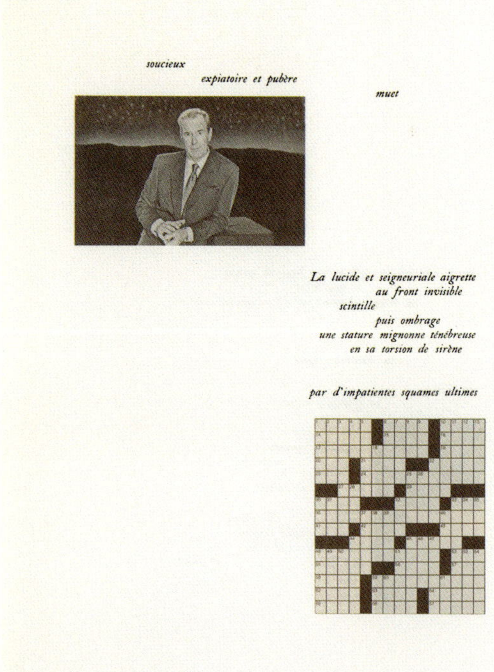

    La lucide et seigneuriale aigrette
          au front invisible
    scintille
        puis ombrage
    une stature mignonne ténébreuse
       en sa torsion de sirène

    par d'impatientes squames ultimes

        rire
    que
        SI

de vertige

debout
    le temps
       de souffleter
bifurquées
    un roc
faux manoir
    tout de suite
       évaporé en brumes
    qui imposa
       une borne à l'infini

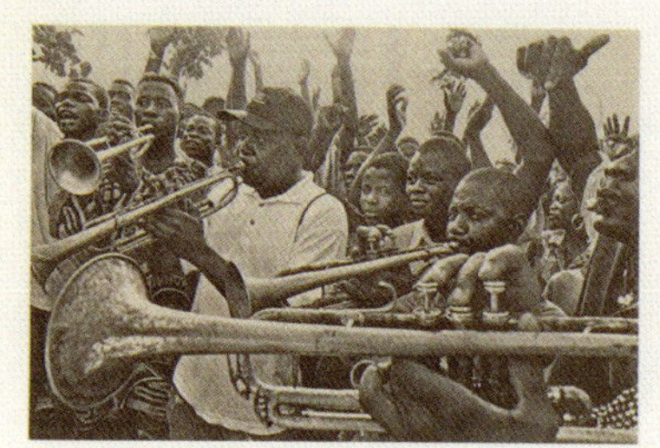

        C'ÉTAIT
          issu stellaire

CE SERAIT
    pire
      non
        davantage ni moins
          indifféremment mais autant

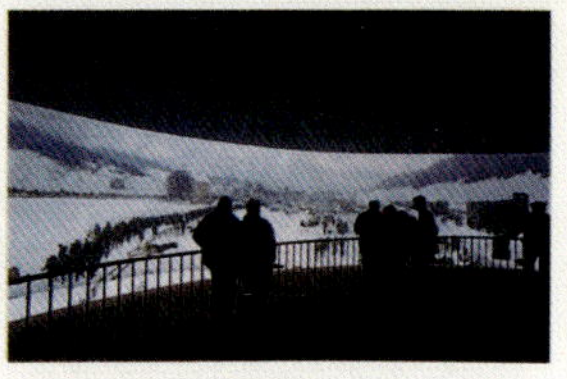

        LE NOMBRE

      EXISTÂT-IL
    autrement qu'hallucination éparse d'agonie

    COMMENÇÂT-IL ET CESSÂT-IL
    sourdant que nié et clos quand apparu
       enfin
    par quelque profusion répandue en rareté
      SE CHIFFRÂT-IL

    évidence de la somme pour peu qu'une
      ILLUMINÂT-IL

LE HASARD

Choit
    la plume
       rythmique suspens du sinistre
          s'ensevelir
        aux écumes originelles
naguères d'où sursauta son délire jusqu'à une cime
          flétrie
      par la neutralité identique du gouffre

EXCEPTÉ
à l'altitude
PEUT-ÊTRE
aussi loin qu'un endroit

fusionne avec au delà

hors l'intérêt
quant à lui signalé
en général
selon telle obliquité par telle déclivité
de feux

vers
ce doit être
le Septentrion aussi Nord

UNE CONSTELLATION

froide d'oubli et de désuétude
pas tant
qu'elle n'énumère
sur quelque surface vacante et supérieure
le heurt successif
sidéralement
d'un compte total en formation

veillant
doutant
roulant
brillant et méditant

avant de s'arrêter
à quelque point dernier qui le sacre

Toute Pensée émet un Coup de Dés

RIEN

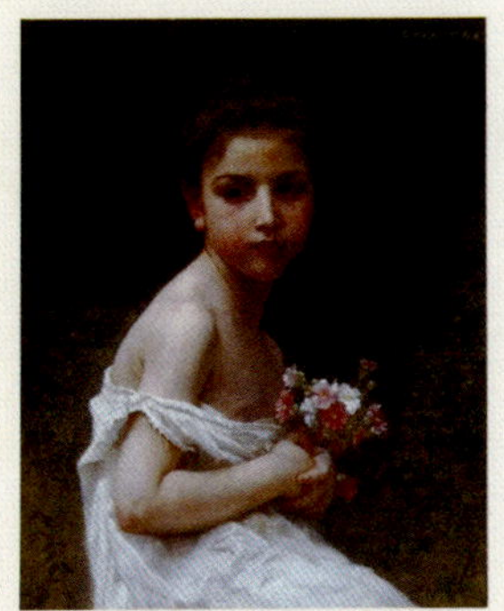

de la mémorable crise
ou se fût
l'évènement

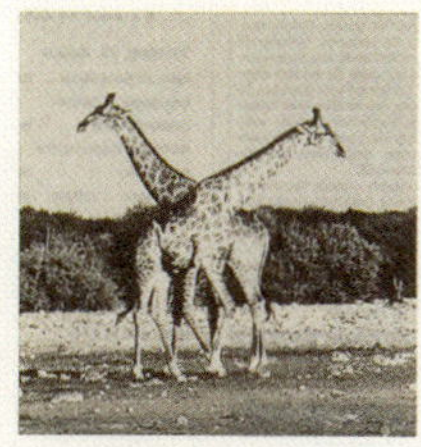

accompli en vue de tout résultat nul
humain

N'AURA EU LIEU
une élévation ordinaire verse l'absence

QUE LE LIEU
inférieur clapotis quelconque comme pour disperser l'acte vide
abruptement qui sinon
par son mensonge
eût fondé
la perdition

dans ces parages
du vague
en quoi toute réalité se dissout

IRWIN

Dušan Mandić, Miran Mohar, Andrej Savski,
Roman Uranjek and Borut Vogelnik

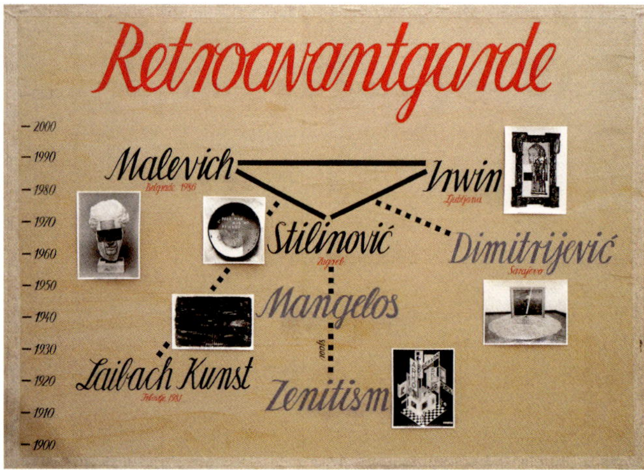

Retroavantgarde, 1996

Retroavantgarde, 2000–09
Installation
With text by theoretician Marina Gržinić and works by artists
Dimitrij Bašičević Mangelos, Avgust Černigoj, Braco Dimitrijević,
Laibach, Kasimir Malevic, Gledališče Sester Scipion Nasice,
Jossip Seissel, Mladen Stilinovič and IRWIN

Eastern Modernism

IRWIN's installation *Retroavantgarde* construes a fictive art
movement for the geographic space of Yugoslavia, the 'retro-
avant-garde' whose roots can be traced back to various images,
the artists allegedly belonging to this movement back in the
1910s and 1920s. *Retroavantgarde* 'is a complex artistic statement
reflecting on the absence of a stable historic narrative on modern
and contemporary art in Slovenia, Yugoslavia and in Eastern
Europe in general. The artistic achievement of these places never
managed to become a part of the Western canon, or even develop
its own consistent meta-narrative'.[1]

As a reaction to this two-fold lack, the group refers, with
a gesture typical for them, back to an entity that was central to the
definition and derivation of modernism: Alfred H. Barr's *Diagram
of Stylistic Evolution from 1890 until 1935*.[2] This diagram, developed
in 1936 by the founding director of New York's Museum of Modern
Art (MoMA), lists the European avant-garde movements as precur-
sors — almost in the sense of an aesthetic evolution theory — of
the abstract art of modernism, both geometric and non-geomet-
ric. With a similarly arrogant attitude, IRWIN transfers this scheme
onto Yugoslavia, here in the form of a reversed genealogy of the
'retro-avant-garde', which extends from the neo-avant-garde of
the present back to the period of the historical avant-garde.

In addition, as an alternative to the grand narratives of
the West, IRWIN develops the strategy of 'Eastern modernism',
which the group formulated for the first time in 1990 in the context
of the exhibition series *Kapital*.[3] In asserting the existence of an
'Eastern modernism', the group polemically attacks Barr's and
Greenberg's modernism, which posits itself as being universally
valid. By qualifying the concept in this way, IRWIN indirectly
suggests that modernism is actually a 'Western modernism' that
does *not* possess universal validity, after all.

As a new 'Eastern modernism', this retro-avant-garde is pitted
against Western particularity, which considers itself to be universal.
The installation *Retroavantgarde*, which was shown for the first
time in the Kunsthalle of Vienna, is both an independent work of
art and a pragmatic, cartographic instrument; in this work, IRWIN
transforms that which it was barred from for a long time, both
locally, through the specific political situation, and beyond Eastern
Europe, through the above-mentioned international discourse:
its own independent art historical chronicle. By postulating
the existence of a fictive Yugoslavian retro-avant-garde, IRWIN
(re)constructs and posits a modernism intrinsic to Eastern Europe.
This 'Eastern modernism', however, turns out to be just as con-
strued, fictive and artificial as its Western counterpart.

Inke Arns

1   *In Search of Balkania: A User's Manual*, in Roger Conover, Eda Čufer
    and Peter Weibel (eds.), Graz: Neue Galerie am Landesmuseum
    Joanneum, 2002, p. 67 (exh. cat.)
2   See Astrit Schmidt-Burkhardt, 'The Barr Effect: New Visualizations
    of Old Facts', in Branislav Dimitrijević and Dejan Sretenović (eds.),
    *International Exhibition of Modern Art featuring Alfred Barr's Museum
    of Modern Art, New York*, Belgrade: Museum of Contemporary Art,
    2003, pp. 49–59.
3   IRWIN, *Kapital*. Ljubljana and Edinburgh: Collaborator, 1991 (exh.cat.)
    The first *Kapital* exhibition took place in December 1990 in the
    Equrna galerija in Ljubljana.

Excerpt from 'IRWIN Navigator: Retroprincip 1983–2003', in Inke Arns (ed.),
IRWIN: Retroprincip 1983–2003, September 2003, p. 14.
Translated from the German by Andrea Scrima.

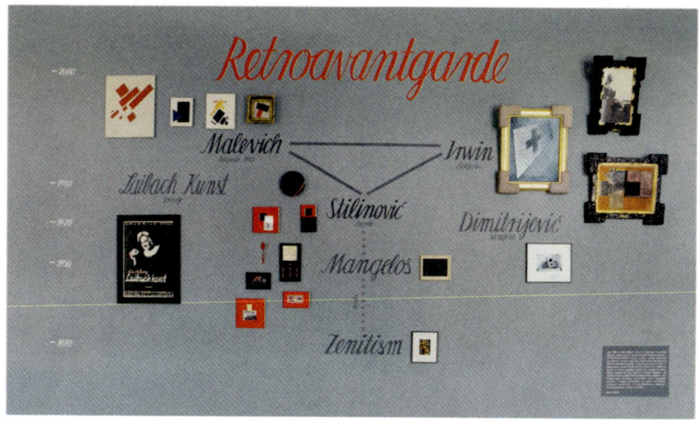

Retroavantgarde, 2000

pp. 114–15
Retroavantgarde, 2000

According to Pierre Bourdieu, it is exactly a collective determined by an autonomous field of cultural production that is crucial for the rise of modernism. The moment of the historical avant-gardes emerged when the artistic procedures of deconstruction, estrangement and corrosion seized the very ideology that had previously been the background upon which 'Art' was produced. The 'surplus', however, the additional element that could not have been developed outside the revolutionary context, was precisely the 'organisational' aspect, the multitude of practices that initiated a break with the inherited romantic, individualistic logic of the 'artistic movement' and introduced a completely new organisational concept, one defined in terms of class as Rastko Močnik would put it. So how to answer the question in how far a collective mode of production in itself is a critique of the aesthetic ideology of modernity if modernity seems so deeply involved with notions of collectivity? In our case, a collective mode of production initially was a practical response to the concrete situation in which we found ourselves as young artists back in 1983 in the Socialist Federative Republic of Yugoslavia. In Eastern Europe there are no transparent structures organising referential systems for periodising historically significant art events that would be accepted outside the borders of a given country. At times there are even two systems in which we find, alongside 'official' art histories, a whole series of stories and legends about the artists who were opposed to the official establishment. But written records on the latter are very few and fragmented.

This poses several problems. Any serious comprehension of the art created during socialist times is prevented, so that artists, deprived of any solid support for their activities, are compelled to steer between the local and international art systems. All this presents a major block to communication among artists, critics and theoreticians from these countries. These are serious enough reasons to apply the Western model of charting evolutionary genealogies of modernism and not to counter it. The West is not in question in our projects. The Eastern Art Map quite obviously is about Eastern Europe. Today, at a time when this kind of mapping is functional in most parts of the world, it becomes questionable, even if piles of books, collections, experts and universities prove differently. It seems that we are expected to globalise first to then be able to participate in the anti-globalisation movement. Borut Vogelnik/IRWIN □

2000

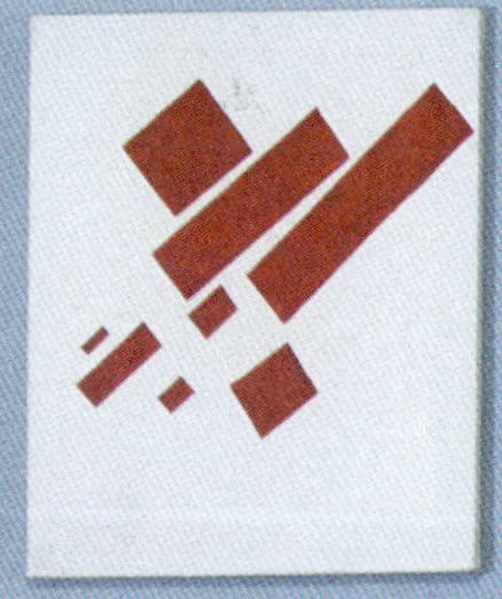

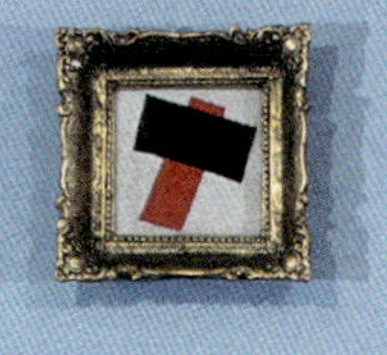

Malevich
Belgrade 1985

1980

Laibach Kunst
RETROAVANTGARDE
Trbovlje

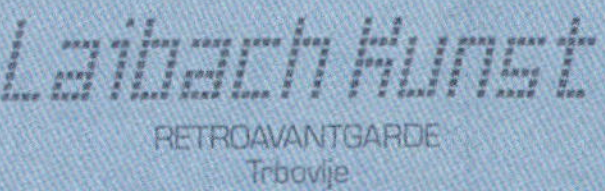

1970

St

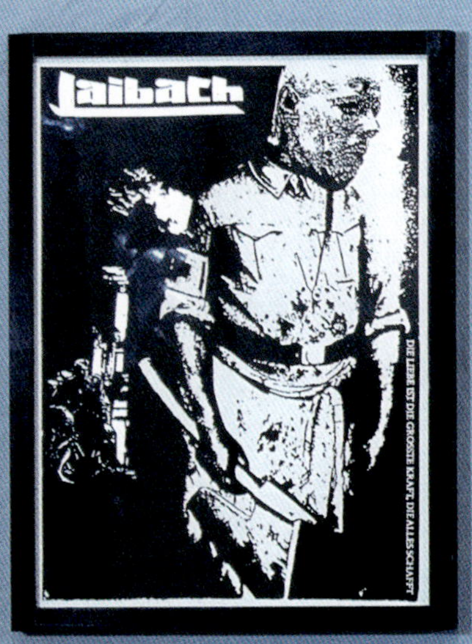

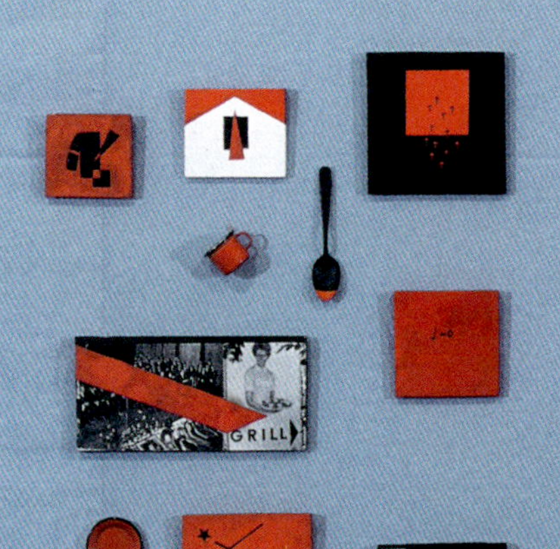

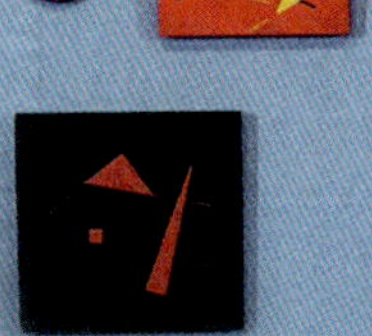

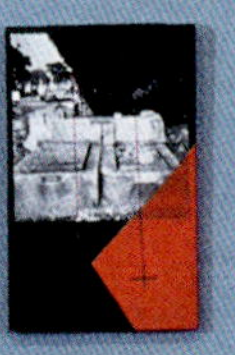

Me

1950

1920

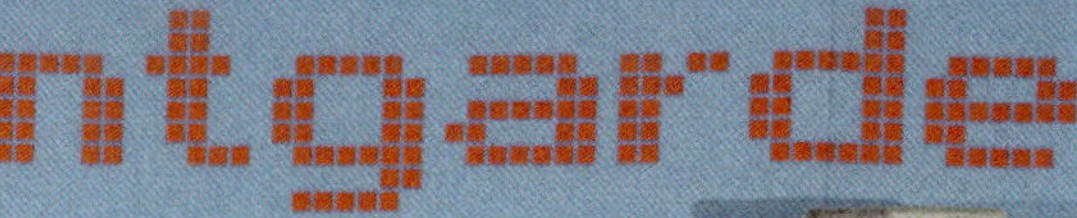

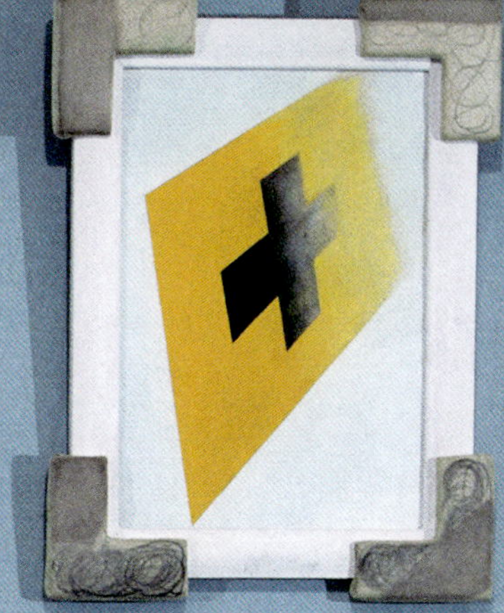

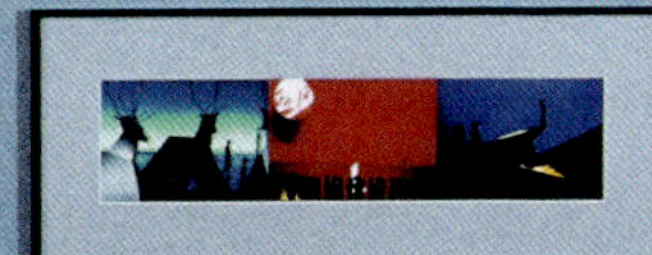

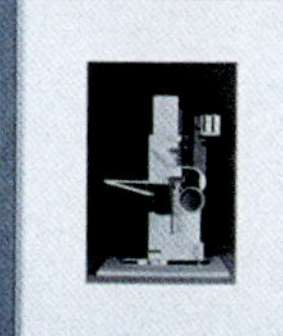

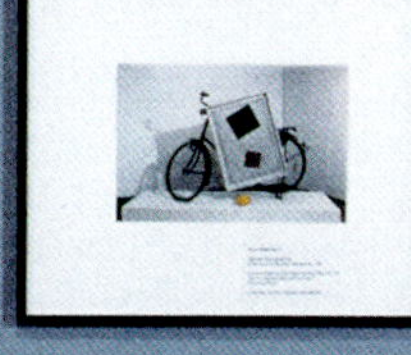

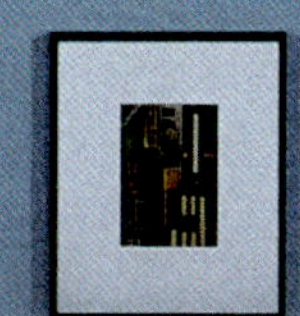

In the 1980's the NSK groups were using different names for their artistic procedures (Laibach - Retroavantgarde, Irwin - Retro-principle and Scipion Nasice Sisters Theatre - Retrogarde). In the 1990's, Peter Weibel launched a discursive matrix in an exhibition catalogue of the Steirische Herbst (Graz), in which he coded the ex-Yugoslav territory from 'outside', subsuming the productions of Mladen Stilinović (Zagreb), the 1980's Kasimir Malevich (Belgrade) and IRWIN (Ljubljana) under a common signifier: the 'Retroavantgarde'. I developed a dialectical interrelationship within which I designated their positions as those in a Hegelian triad: Mladen Stilinović as thesis; Malevich and the projects of copying as an antithesis; and IRWIN, with the projects of the NSK EMBASSIES (presented within the framework of the NSK State in Time), as synthesis. All three artists, groups or art projects utilize specific strategies of visualization to display aspects of Socialist and post-Socialist ideology. 'Retroavantgarde' is the new 'ism' of the East.

Marina Gržinić

Runa Islam

Empty the pond to get the fish., 2008
Film installation

The non-mimetic cinematography in *Empty the pond to get the fish.*, which recalls the traditions of abstract and structuralist filmmaking, activates Maya Deren's thoughts on cinematography 'as a spelling out in images' and equally makes palpable Alexandre Astruc's notion of the camera-pen: *'la caméra-stylo.'* These self-reflexive gestures bring attention to how cinematography traditionally is solely at the service of narrative and consequently attempts to subvert such a relationship. In doing so, the visual narrative emerges from the movement of the camera as it writes out the sentence 'Empty the pond to get the fish.' Ostensibly, this effort can be identified as a meta-narrative, but the text, although precisely traced out, is not entirely readable over the images themselves. As the camera 'writes', a continually shifting relationship and act of rebalancing forms between the movement and the image. ▷

'Is cinema a language or not?' Back in 1971, the film theorist Christian Metz took this question as the basis for a comprehensive investigation of filmic and cinematographic means of expression, considering their structures, functions and relationships to linguistic forms of representation.[1] Metz's paradigmatic exploration of the metaphor of the 'language of cinema', and the way he draws parallels and distinguishes between language and film, are representative of numerous artistic and theoretical attempts to relate cinematographic and linguistic means of expression to each other. This 'linguistic turn' has since been 'turned' again a number of times itself, subjected to comprehensive criticism, and for a while now been replaced by the 'pictorial turn'. So how are we to interpret the artist Runa Islam setting out anew 'to write with the camera?' as she moves the camera — the tool for recording on film — like a pen, producing letters, words and complete sentences.

The movement of Runa Islam's camera in *Empty the pond to get the fish.* is based on the exact typographical image of this sentence in the English edition of Robert Bresson's *Notes sur le cinématographie*. In his book the phrase 'Empty the pond to get the fish.' comes in the chapter 'On Fragmentation', which the French filmmaker and author prefaced as follows: 'This is indispensable if one does not want to fall into *representation*. To see beings and things in their separate parts. Render them independent in order to give them a new dependence.'[2] The cinematographic programme formulated here is reminiscent of structuralist approaches as described by Roland Barthes, and it also corresponds to a significant extent with Runa Islam's own artistic practice in recent years. In her films, Islam repeatedly isolates individual components from their material and narrative contexts. She breaks with linear narrative, concentrates on the emerging details, on the conventions of representation that appertain to film, and on the mechanisms of cinematographic depiction. Her projections into exhibition spaces take the individual components of film as their theme, directing the viewer's attention to a complex interaction between formal elements and social contents.

Narration and action have accordingly been reduced or transformed in Runa Islam's film installation *Empty the pond to get the fish.* Events in front of the camera reflect the activity of the camera itself or can only be recognised through this activity.

In this respect, however, Runa Islam's work only addresses one aspect of the challenge issued by the statement 'Empty the pond to get the fish.' — to remove individual, elusive elements from their familiar surroundings, distancing them from their context in order to be able to 'grasp' them. The tangible result of Runa Islam's 'writing process' is both the disavowal of a story or narration in the classical sense and also a collection of visual cuts, margins, details and fragments produced by the camera operating on an abstract level rather than engaging with what it faces. The tracking shot generates an abundance of visual fragments by strictly and mechanically following a linguistic order — a sentence about fragmentation and the typographical image of that sentence.[3] Not only does the shot emphasise its own role and significance for the narrative of the film, as well as the antagonisms and correspondences between language and the visual; it also produces a reverse

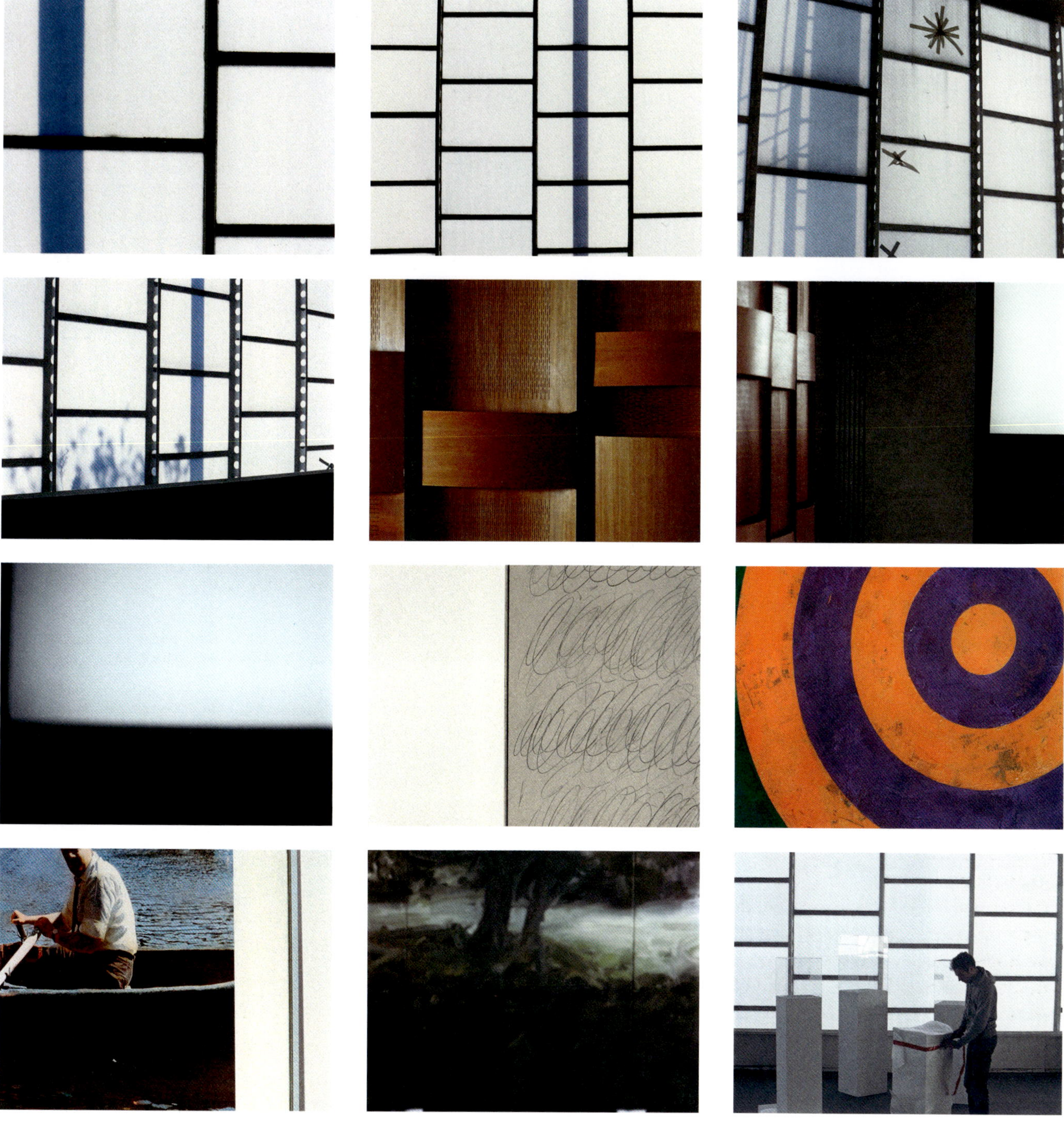

effect that is decisive for Islam. In the course of her cinemato-graphic reflection of the relationship between language and the visual, and in line with Bresson's note quoted above, she achieves liberation from *representation* and rejects depiction in the traditional sense — in favour of the poetics of the image and a celebration of the visual situated between form and content, between aesthetics and meaning.

Using language and structural fragmentation, *Empty the pond to get the fish.* engenders a new pleasure in watching — a triumph of filmic images as a network of sensual, analytical/linguistic and institutional constituents. As Jacques Rancière recently put it, referring to fragmentation in Bresson's work: 'Operations: relations between a whole and parts; between a visibility and a power of signification and affect associated with it; between expectations and what happens to meet them.'[4]

Change of scene. The camera is in a cinema, showing sophisticated, modern wooden wall panelling, parts of a luminous white screen and further details whose significance is not clear. Blur. Then come close-ups of paintings, details of works by Cy Twombly, Jasper Johns, Malcolm Morley, Richard Hamilton and Gerhard Richter. The camera moves briefly away from Richter's work *Parkstück*, revealing moving trees through a dirty pane of glass, before (finally) re-entering the painterly structure of the landscape based on a photo. Blur. The action and its location are explained in the following 'scenes' or 'words'. The 'film-like' glass wall presented at the beginning is part of the top storey of a modern iron-and-glass construction, which has been disman-tled down to its core, and in which all manner of museum para-phernalia is to be found — red packing cases, display cases (some of them wrapped in protective plastic) whose glass covers correspond to the building itself, workers busying themselves around these objects, a ladder, etc. Blur. Another change of scene: from the glass or light architecture back to the projection room. This time there is also cinema seating, presenting the perspective of the viewers, the back wall of the cinema including the hatch for the projector and light streaming from the projection room…

Even if the paradoxical equation of writing and cinematic language in *Empty the pond to get the fish.* leads to a permanent fragmentation of what is to be watched, the process of poeticising and up-valuing the visual is not concerned to demonstrate a 'wordless immediacy of the visible', the pure presence of the film image, or even some essence of the medium. Runa Islam's 'linguistic' fragmentation enhances the pleasure of seeing, which at the same time is a desire to recognise and establish links, breaking the representative relationship between text and image in the sense of Jacques Rancière's model of the 'sentence image': 'The text's part in the representative schema was the conceptual linking of actions, while the image's was the supple-ment of presence that imparted flesh and substance to it. The sentence-image overturns this logic.'[5]

Fragments initially dominate in *Empty the pond to get the fish.*, whether these are the visual details, the camera's tracking shots edited together, or the various scenes. The action consists of a double interweaving of seeing and reading, and the task of the image is to ensure that this complex and tense relationship remains fragile and brittle. Fragmentary seeing allows us to experience the relationship of seeing to the 'language of film' (or the cinematic core vocabulary) and in particular the significance of the camera. We also recognise a space created from abstract forms and details, and an institution that has dedicated itself to 'seeing' like no other, guaranteeing, discussing and, as we have discovered, also administering it: the museum.[6] Scenes, practices and architectures emerge from the individual images, which have lost nothing of their perplexing and fasci-nating sensuality. They are candid stories about seeing and its history, about the connection between image and language, light architecture and games of light in the cinema, painting and film, modernism and its legacy; interconnected elements that have been rendered 'independent in order to give them a new dependence.'

Matthias Michalka

1   Christian Metz, *Langage et cinéma*, Paris: Larousse, 1971. English edition: *Language and Cinema. Approaches to Semiotics*, Donna Jean Umiker-Sebeok (tran.), The Hague: Mouton, 1974.
2   Robert Bresson, *Notes on Cinematography*, New York: Urizen Books, 1977, p. 2.
3   A motion-control camera was used for the takes, a robotic camera whose movements can be precisely determined in advance. It can be heard in action at certain points during the film. In addition, the remastered sound in *Empty the pond to get the fish.* varies from scene to scene.
4   Jacques Rancière, *The Future of the Image*, London/New York: Verso, 2007, p. 3.
5   Ibid., p. 46.
6   *Empty the pond to get the fish.* was shot in the former Museum des 20. Jahrhunderts (Museum of the Twentieth Century) in Vienna. The works of art shown come from the collection of the present Museum of Modern Art Foundation Ludwig Vienna, which succeeded the Museum des 20. Jahrhunderts (first opened in 1962), and is now housed in a new building. The '20er Haus', originally built as an exhibition pavilion by Karl Schwanzer in 1958, contains the cinema theatre shown in the film.

Abridged and revised version of 'Empty the pond to get the fish.', in Matthias Michalka and Museum of Modern Art Foundation Ludwig Vienna (eds.), *Runa Islam: Empty the pond to get the fish.*, Cologne, 2008.

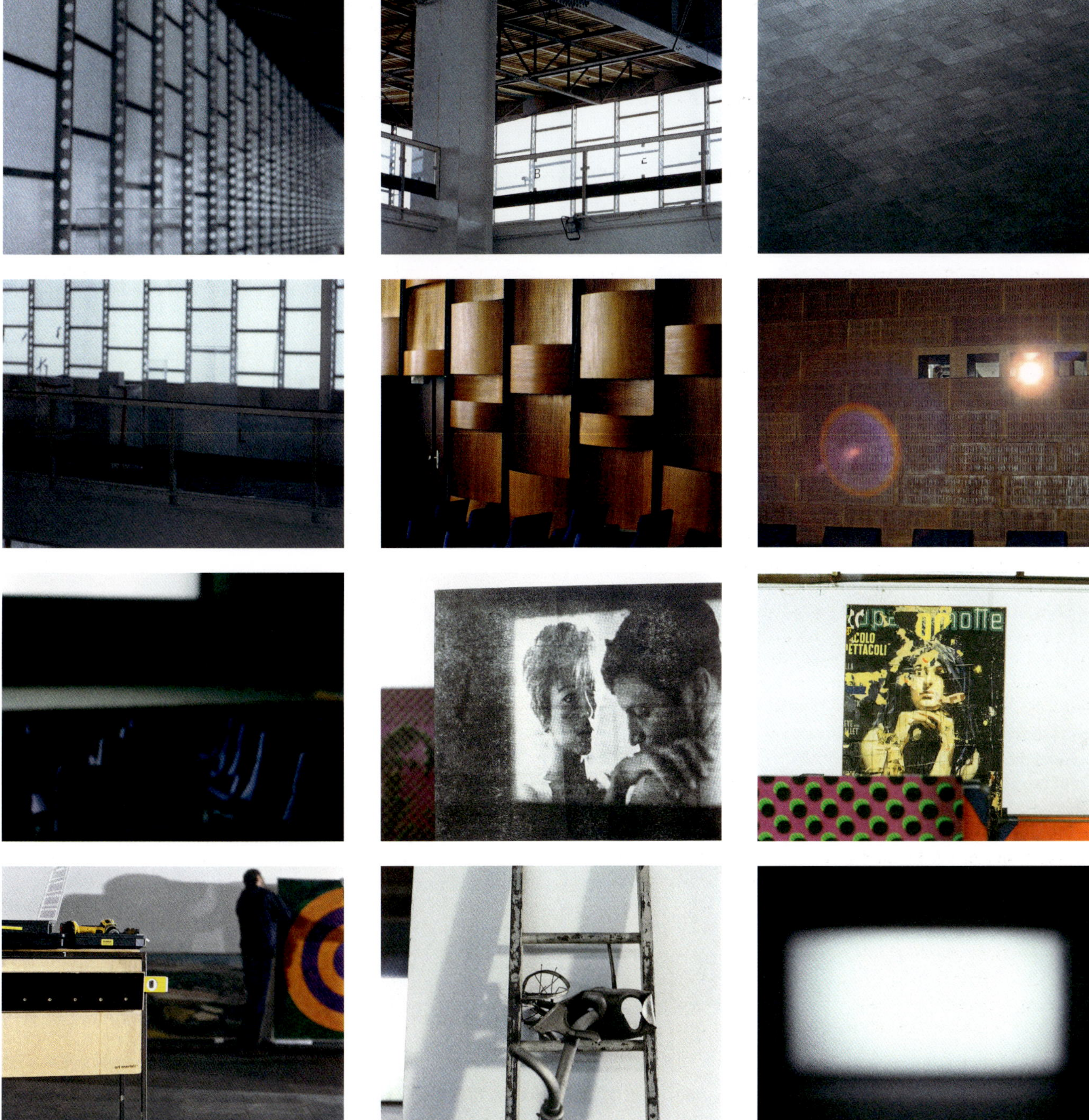

Installation view
Museum of Modern Art Foundation Ludwig Vienna, 2008

In making a film like *Empty the pond to get the fish.* in
which the movement of the camera appears to be
the main protagonist as well as the 'antagonist',
my intention is to revisit the notion of the camera
being a mechanical apparatus — put to use as a contradictory device that at once invites the viewers into,
as well as distances them from, a representation that
does not exist without the device itself. In considering
these particularly modernist ideas of the cinema,
my point however is not to simply pay homage, but to
reconsider how the methods can be renewed rather
than reified. ▫

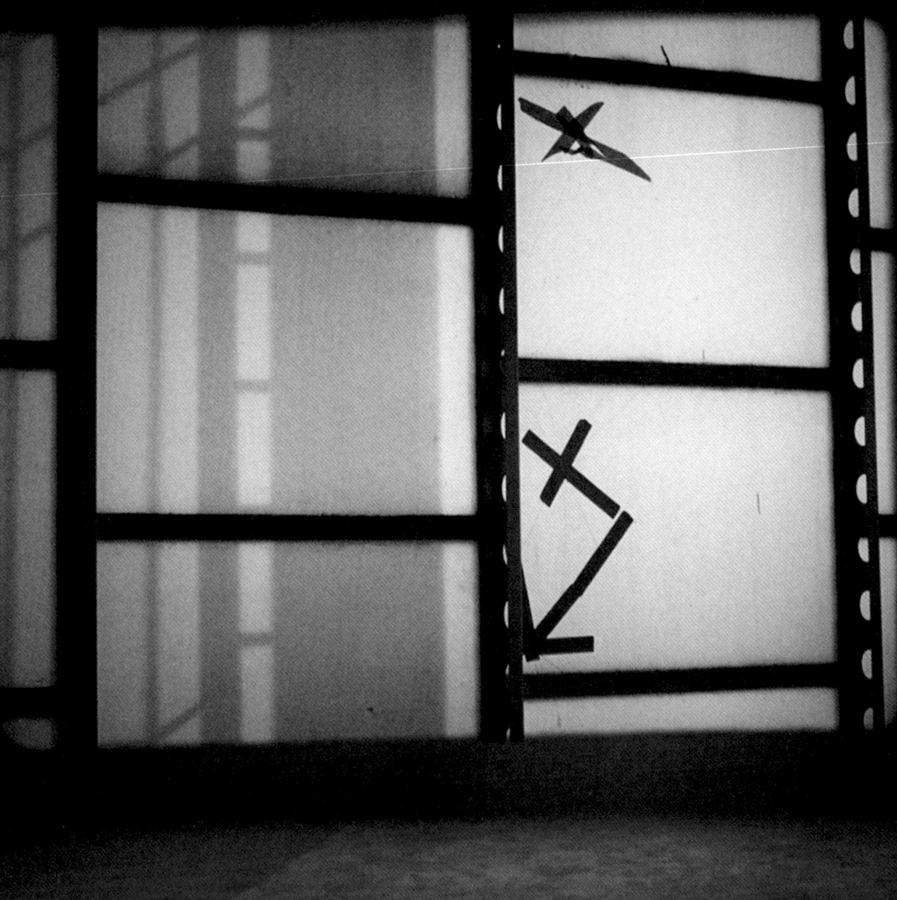

Klub Zwei
Simone Bader and Jo Schmeiser

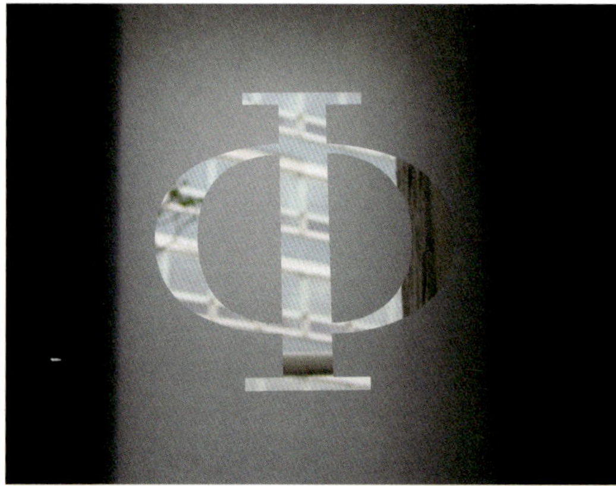

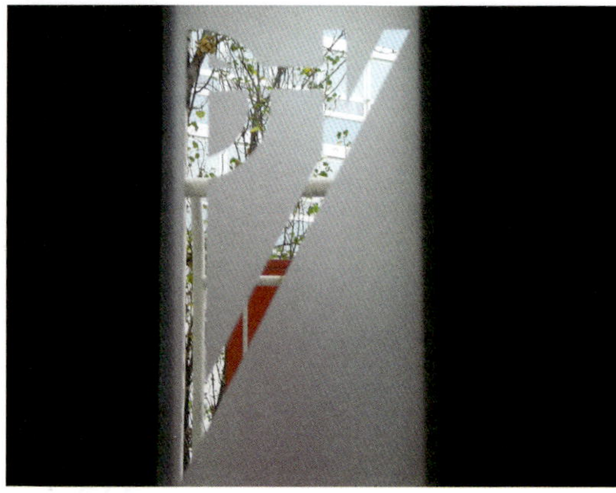

Logos Phaidon, 1923 and today, 2009
Installation view
Secession, Vienna, 2005

Phaidon. Presses in Exile, 2006/09
Video installation

The film turns first to the history of the Phaidon Press, which was founded in 1923 by Béla Horovitz in Vienna. Horovitz and his partner Ludwig Goldscheider were interested in publishing books whose layout should visibly express an appreciation of modernity. The consistent use of simple Bauhaus fonts and graphics devoted to modern design principles was more than just a publishing ambition. It was also intended to subvert the ideology of the Austrian corporative state. Horovitz was able to save the publishing house from National Socialist persecution by selling it in 1938, effectively moving its headquarters to England, where he went into exile and continued his publishing activities together with Goldscheider.

Klub Zwei's interest is not aimed primarily at the historical examination of a successful enterprise. Instead, Phaidon is an example of the loss of people and of cultural resources that cannot be replaced through 'reparations' — the voids in Austria and Germany caused by National Socialism that must be made apparent. The film is also interested in the multiple-perspectives involved in historiography as demonstrated by the juxtaposition of various speakers — the daughter and granddaughter of the founder of the publishing house, the head of the Austrian Exile Library and artists.

Klub Zwei have chosen a cinematic language that steadily fragments images, narrations and questions, and is thereby a stylistic device of disturbance. To make visible the ruptures in speaking about the past is only logical once it becomes evident that, at best, this speaking about the 'same' past is always in parallel and can never occur together, as the history and its subjects differ too greatly.

Karin Gludovatz

'Klub Zwei, Phaidon – Verlage im Exil', *Verleihkatalog von Sixpackfilm*. Lisa Rosenblatt (tran.). www.sixpackfilm.com (February, 2007).

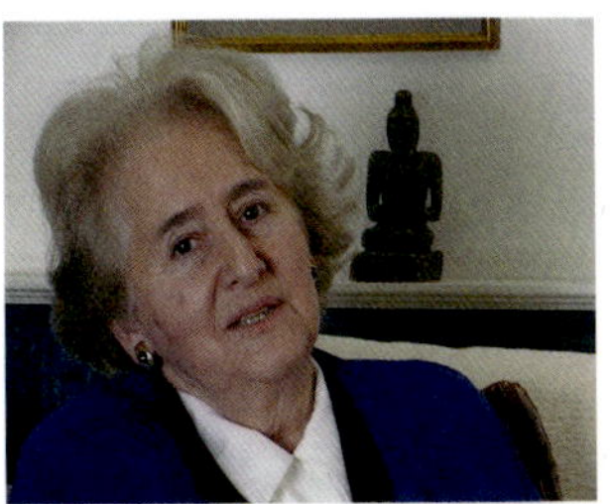

Er kannte nur
das Englisch
Shakespeares.

Das 1. Mal in
England sagte
er zum Taxi-
fahrer …

Whilst thou
drive me?

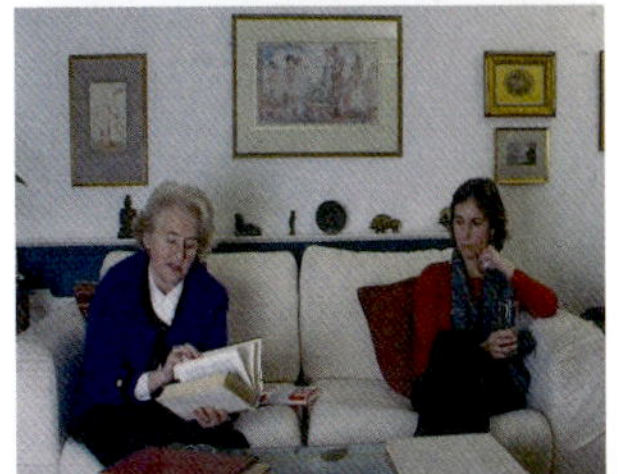

1938
Allen & Unwin

1938
Allen & Unwin
Phaidon

1938
Allen & Unwin
Phaidon
editions

Goldscheider
presented
artworks in a
way …

that the viewer
saw only a
selection of it.

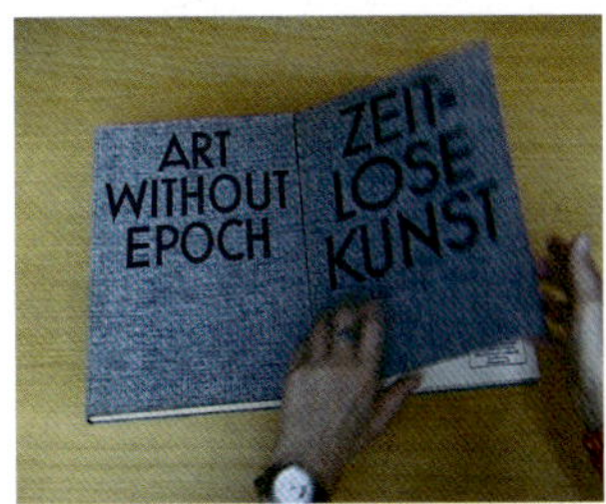

Portions of the
image were
selected with
attention to
detail.

1923 Phaidon:
Fritz Ungar

1923 Phaidon:
Fritz Ungar
Béla Horovitz

1923 Phaidon:
Fritz Ungar
Béla Horovitz
Ludwig
Goldscheider

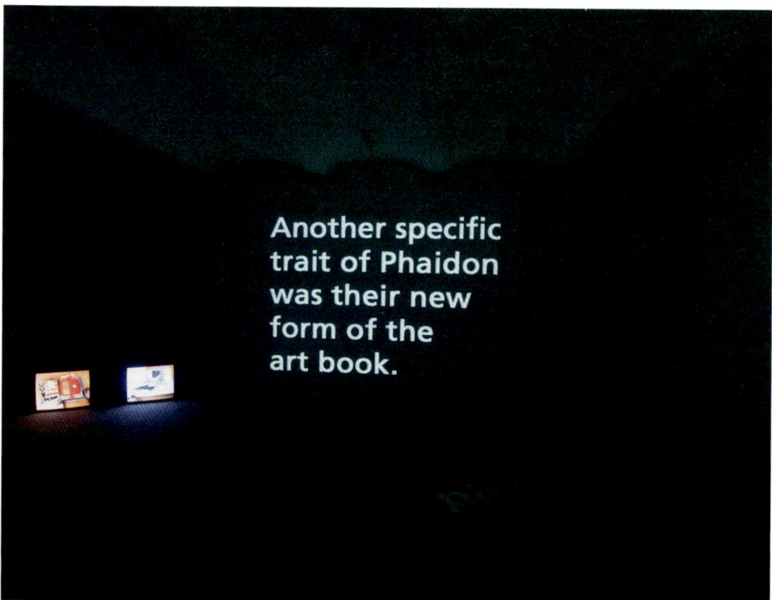

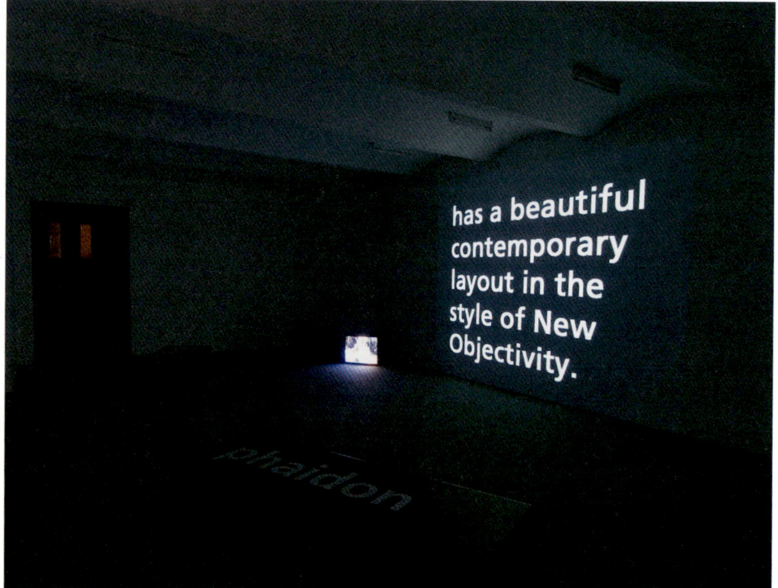

Phaidon typifies the expulsion from Vienna of Jewish
modernists. The publishing firm's history evokes not only
the enormous human loss through murder and enforced
emigration in the National Socialist era, but also the degree
to which that loss has marked cultural and political life in
Austria ever since. Phaidon's beginnings in Vienna, and
its aim of making modern art available to a wide public at
affordable prices, are now almost entirely forgotten. In their
design and typography the firm's publications clearly
opposed the politics and the aesthetics of Austrian fascism.

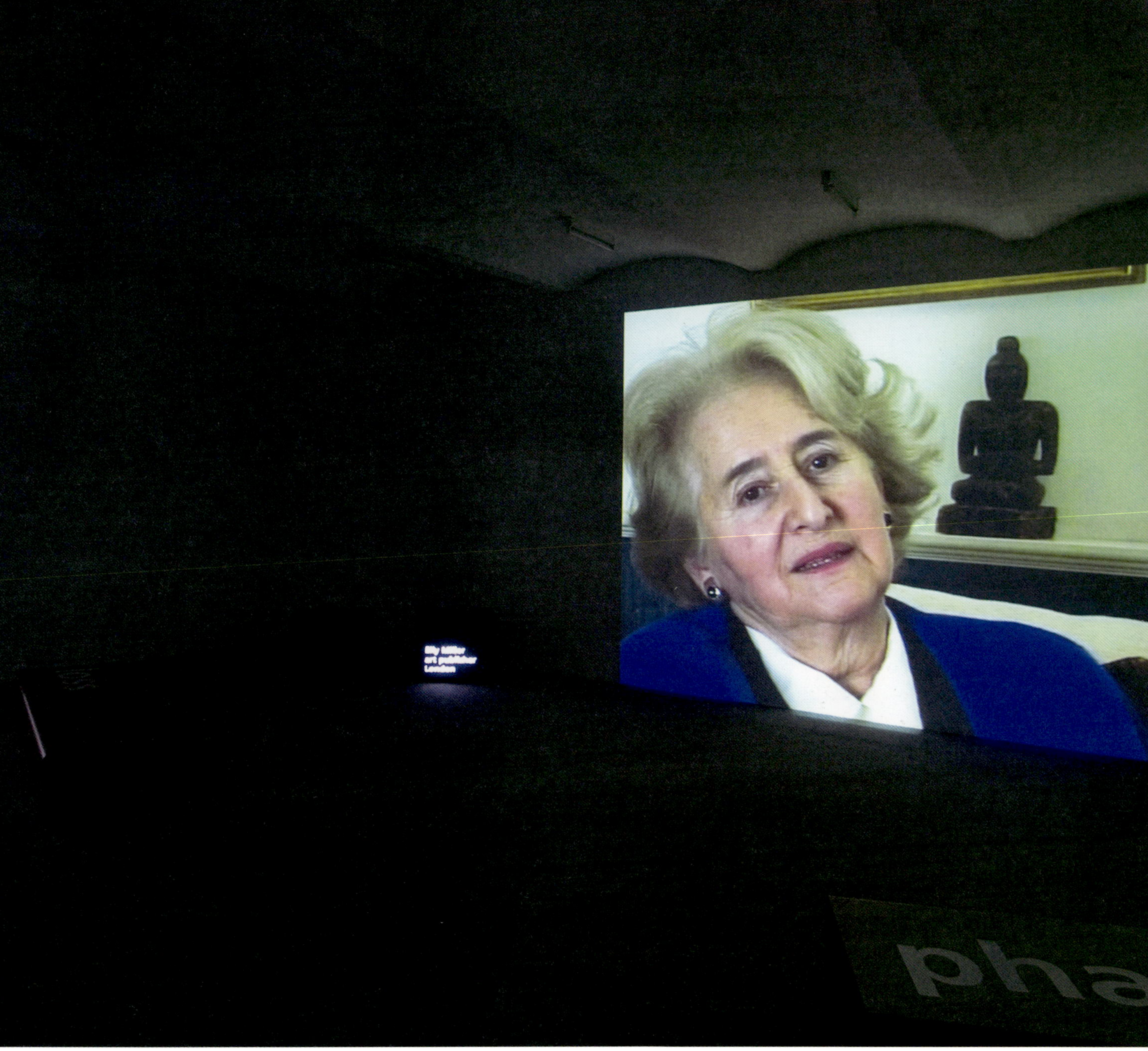

Installation views
Secession, Vienna, 2005

Klub Zwei translates these modernist features into an engagement with current social policies. *Phaidon: Verlage im Exil* (Phaidon: Presses in Exile) forms part of a larger study by Klub Zwei that addresses responsibility for the loss and incorporates statements by descendants of perpetrators of crimes who have engaged critically with their family and social past. That involves identifying the aesthetic and political influences of which Vienna was deprived through the barbarity of the Shoah. □

John Knight

Logotype (project for documenta 7), 1982
8 reliefs

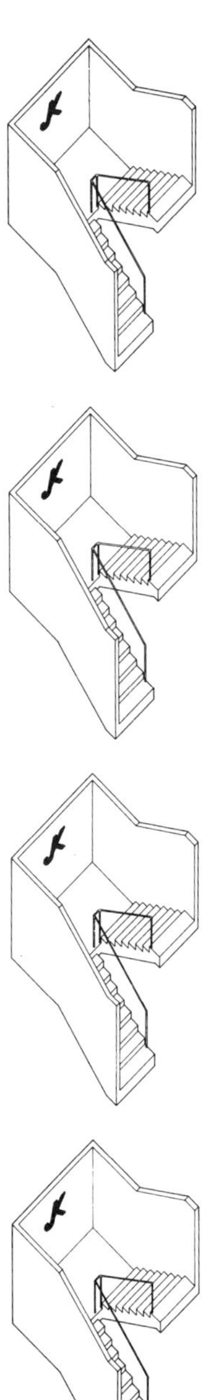

On *Logotypes*

In 1982, John Knight designed eight identically sized logo-
typographical elements, for a site-specific installation at documenta 7 in Kassel, four of which were placed on each of the four
landings of the two main staircases in the exhibition building.
The choice of a deliberately marginal space for the installation
of these elements complemented the provocative evacuation of
aesthetic information from these signs and their formal reduction
to the mere initials of his name. The capital letters J and K were
contracted into a ligature and enlarged to wooden logotype
reliefs, such as one might find on the facade of a building or in
the lobby of a corporation.

These reliefs offered only one additional feature, since each
of the eight elements was wrapped and almost entirely covered
by a different printed color reproduction of a photograph: travel
posters for various countries in seven instances, and in one case
a poster to advertise the services of a California bank. While
the images of these posters were constantly fragmented, they still
conveyed, by their technique of photographic reproduction and
by their lush imagery, their original function of lure and seduction.

This work addresses the question of *authorship* with the same
rigour that the *Journals Series* applied to the *ownership* of the
art object, since it subjects the entire formal structure to the performance and display of the author's signature. The ligature of the
initials has submerged all formal and visual possibilities that the
category of a relief once had. In fact, Knight's reliefs seem to take
the Cubist legacy literally and restore some of its original radicality
through the rigid juxtaposition of linguistic sign and visual form,
of mass cultural representation and self-referential artistic object...

The presence of the signature — the sign that supposedly
guarantees the authenticity of authorship and therefore assumes
inevitably the functions of a trademark to vouch for the originality
of a commodity — has been a focal point of artistic reflection
since the beginning of modernism (e.g., Manet's constant play
with the signature's incompatibility with other pictorial representations). But it is only in the second half of the twentieth century that
it becomes the actual figure or the subject of a pictorial construct
itself.... Thus, the facture of the pictorial sign in modernism is
caught between a transcendental movement and a declaration
of commercial warranty, as Yve-Alain Bois remarks in a brilliant
observation of this problem in the context of early twentieth-
century abstraction.[1] In art from the later 1960s, the signature as
trademark of authorship assumes the position of an exclusive
figure and of primary visual information.

In their programmatic devotion to the design of corporate
anonymity (Knight chose italicised Helvetica since it represents
what he calls 'the ultimate mainstream corporate font'), John
Knight's logotypes anticipate the fate all modernist reductivist
abstraction has had to face in its history. Whether it was the
utopianism of architecture or typography and design, it was
inevitably 'incorporated' into the needs of the post-war ideologies
of accelerated and enforced consumption. After all, that is one of
the dialectical features in the historical legacy of modernist abstraction: to have set out as the sign system of a radical social
utopia and to have ended up as the agent of the totalizing claims

of profit maximization. The utopia of abstraction became the basic (de)sign system for the dissemination of the ideology and the products of corporate post-war culture.

Knight's series of logotypes is suspended between the historical dilemma of its proper discursive formation (that all forms of extreme self-reflexivity and semiotic self-purification of pictorial signs were transformed into pure commodity propaganda) and the current reality of the institutional system in which the display of a mythical foundation of subjectivity and the author's authentic creativity are transformed into the evident subject of myth and spectacle.

As in the *Journals Series*, these reliefs interrelate and inter-fere with parallel discursive practices. The fragmented photo-graphic imagery of tourism hinges the viewer's quest for pure aesthetic experience on similar quests for the new and the exotic, the alien and the Other. Simultaneously, the artist's monogram, supposedly the most personal and reliable 'authorization' of a work, is linked to the anonymous display systems that identify the corporate megastructure.

Once again the logotypes reverse the order of private and public: the most individual and supposedly unique feature of the artist becomes incorporated in an anonymous design, whereas the audience's demand for the innermost revelation of an authentic and individual aesthetic truth receives its response in the language of public and collective mythology.

The aesthetic vacuity of the reliefs accounts for the critical force of the work, but it is in the concrete and specific placement in both the architectural and discursive context of this particular exhibition that the work gained its destabilizing momentum. Voluntarily marginalized in the staircases of an exhibition devoted to the renewed and reinforced celebration of traditional notions of authorship and originality, Knight's work accompanied viewers on their way up or down through the spectacular display of an infinite variety of artistically authentic and individual revelations. The logotypes operated as an unwarranted and impertinent subtext to that official message, especially since they had not been incorporated into the main spaces of the exhibition. As a subtext of the repressed discursive legacy, they spoke of the past failures of modernist promises, the latent conditions of its currently renewed projects and its future functions as the helpless object of possession and as the powerless decoration of the corporate wall.

Benjamin H. D. Buchloh

1   See Yve-Alain Bois, 'Malevich, le carré, le degré zéro', *Macula*, vol. 1, 1976, p. 37.

Excerpt from 'Knight's Moves: Situating the Art/Object', *Neo-Avantgarde and Culture Industry: Essays on European and American Art from 1955 to 1975*, Cambridge, MA: The MIT Press, 2000, pp. 11–12.

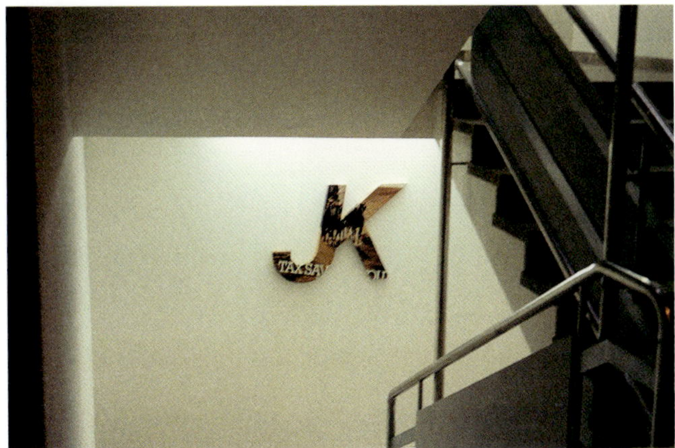

Installation view
documenta 7, Kassel, 1982

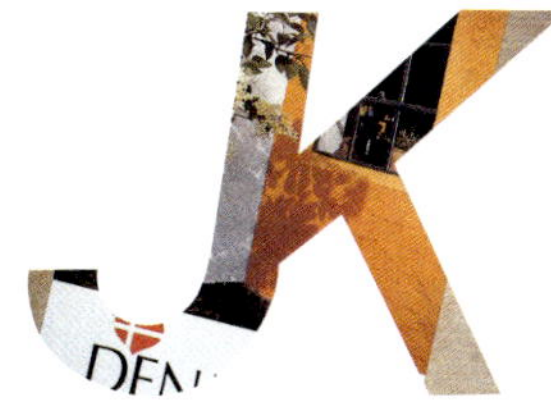

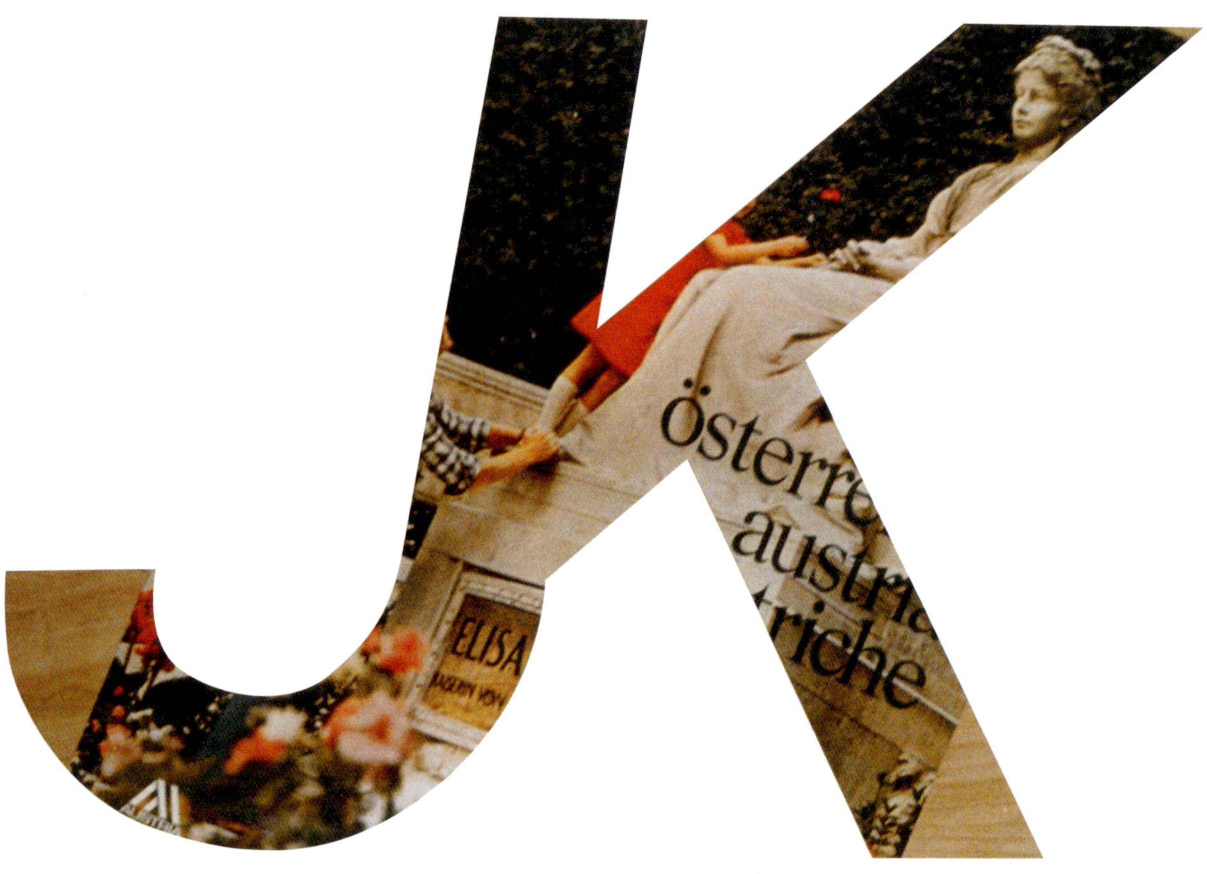

The documenta 7 project — or, as they are commonly
referred to, the *Logotypes* — was a further investigation
of my long-held interest in the role that the ideological
language of design plays in the modernist hegemon
vis-à-vis a response to the director's invitation letter,
wherein he waxed poetically about the Teutonic return
of autonomy. I reacted to that invitation by producing
hybridised initials with discursive tendencies, obliquely
received in passing one stair-landing after another,
salon upon salon. ▷

Mirrors, 1986
Reliefs

Mirror Series

In its reconciliation of normally incompatible art/non-art or high/low art elements into a cohesive material whole, *Museotypes* marks an important step in Knight's development, as ensuing works suggest. The *Mirror Series*, 1985, *Il Diritto All'Ozio*, 1987 and *Łeetsoii*, 1987–88, likewise integrate their formal, material and representational content with the cultural context they inhabit. As in the case of *Museotypes*, it is the (de)sign capacity of the corporate logotype that binds the formal and ideological concerns of many of Knight's later works together and allies them with the socio-economic underpinnings of their support.

The wooden reliefs from the open-ended *Mirror Series* (numbering twelve in all to date), singular or in a group, directly reflect their immediate exhibition environment on the shiny surface of their 'picture plane' while also, quite literally, framing it. Whereas the centralized images of *Museotypes* present a pictorial alphabet of codified shapes, it is the frame of each piece in the *Mirror Series* that, in actual fact, surrounds its given surroundings with a formally and materially-coded language of contoured shapes measuring about a meter in diameter. The wooden frames in every case assume the shape of an existing logotype. They thereby embody the same principles of the geometrically-based corporate design that is tailored to the 'hard-edge' necessity for a rapidly grasped, promotional company image.

The type of wood chosen by Knight for the frames of the mirrors further layers the meaning of the work. Although appearing to have been stamped out by precision instruments like a metal or plastic logotype, each frame, deftly pieced together as if by a machine, has been fabricated with boards of knotty pine and coated with a clear lacquer finish. In contrast to the multinational associations occasioned by the logo form, the knotty pine — complete with randomly dispersed knots and the linear grooves of regularly-spaced panelling — evokes the walls of the 'family room' or 'den' of American, middle-class interiors whose rustic mode refers to the spirit of bygone, pioneer days.

Works in the *Mirror Series* invert the traditional, illusionistic figure/ground relationship. The frame of each piece participates in the creation of an image at the same time that its internally-contained, mirror-image of reality, in effect and figuratively speaking only, 'frames' the work's outer edge, which is where the work's representational content is now to be found instead of within its boundary.

The *Mirror Series* succeeds in confronting the question of image-making from aesthetic and social standpoints simultaneously, having grafted the formal and connotational characteristics of the logotype to those of the knotty pine. On one level, these works deliver a true picture of the reality they duplicate on their reflective surface. However, in as much as social structures determine frameworks for seeing, the *Mirrors* intimate, on another level, the necessity for viewing observable reality within a social perspective. By combining references to vernacular home interior design schemes with signs for large-scale business ventures, Knight's objects — directly alluding to the tradition of portraiture — portray the interconnections between visible reality and social fictions in terms of their own self-reflective, but outwardly directed, character as mirror, image and picture frame together.
Anne Rorimer

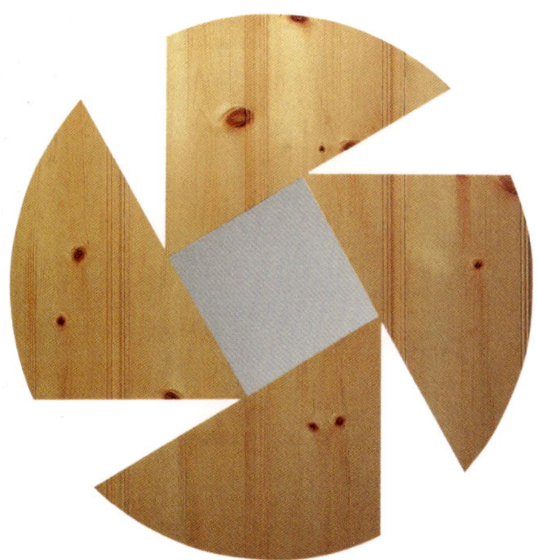

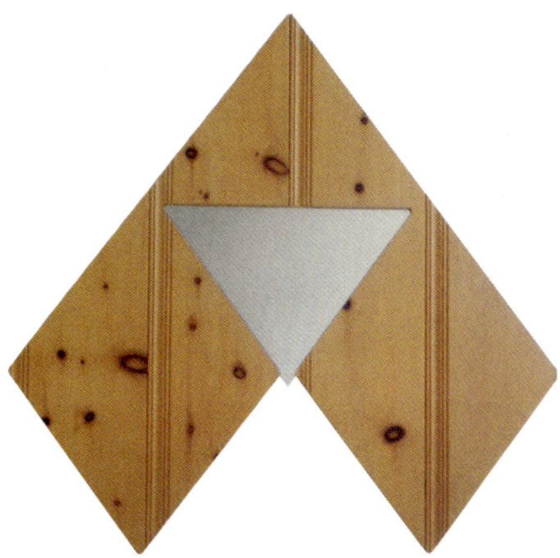

Excerpt from 'John Knight: Designating the Site', *JK: Treize Travaux* Villeurbanne: Le Nouveau Musée Villeurbanne, 1990, pp. 14–16.

Installation view
Marian Goodman Gallery, New York, 1986

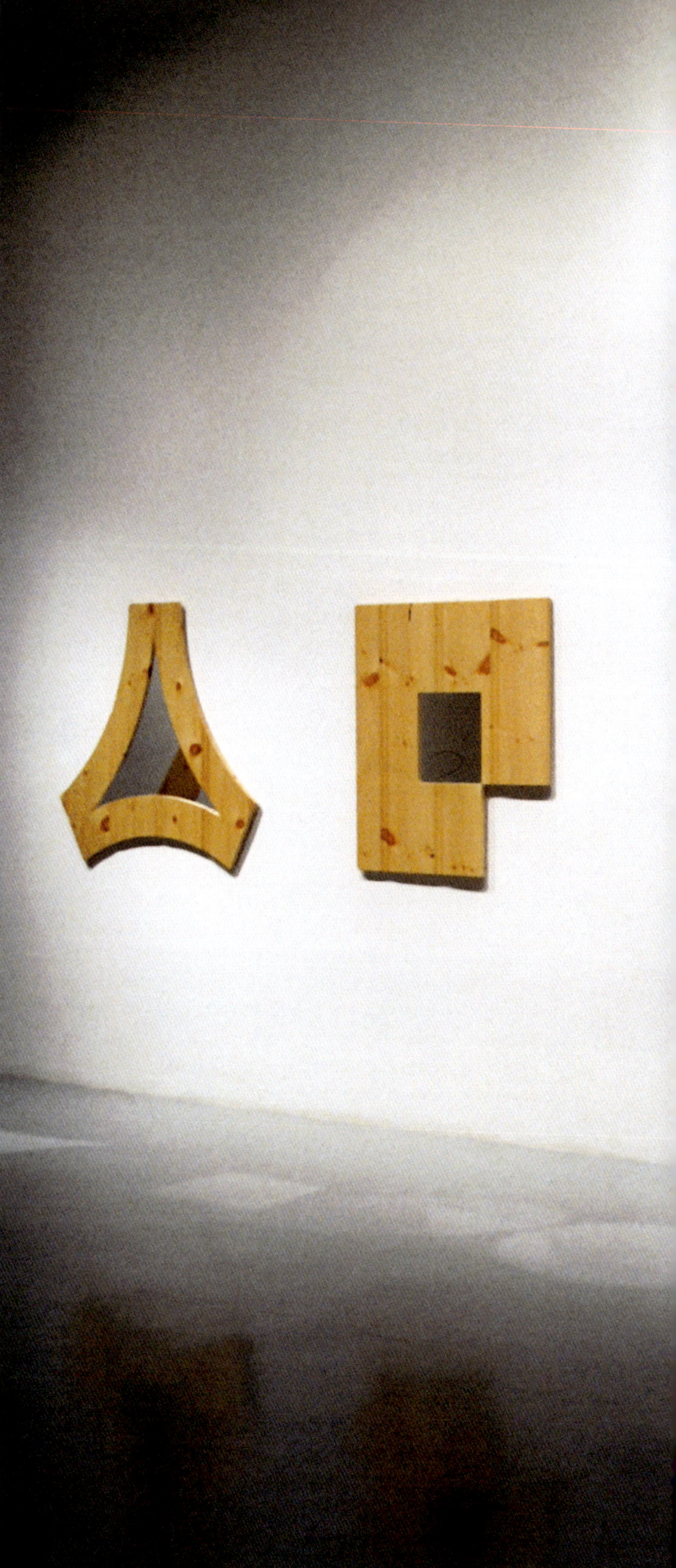

In the *Marian Goodman* project (1986) — or, as it is commonly referred to, the *Mirror Series* — on the other hand, it is in the socio-psychological nexus of a hybridised object or series of objects, evoking the appearance of modernist self-reflexivity, that the rusty remains of modernist abstraction in sculpture as well as architecture production is subjected to the material reflections of post-war suburbia. ▫

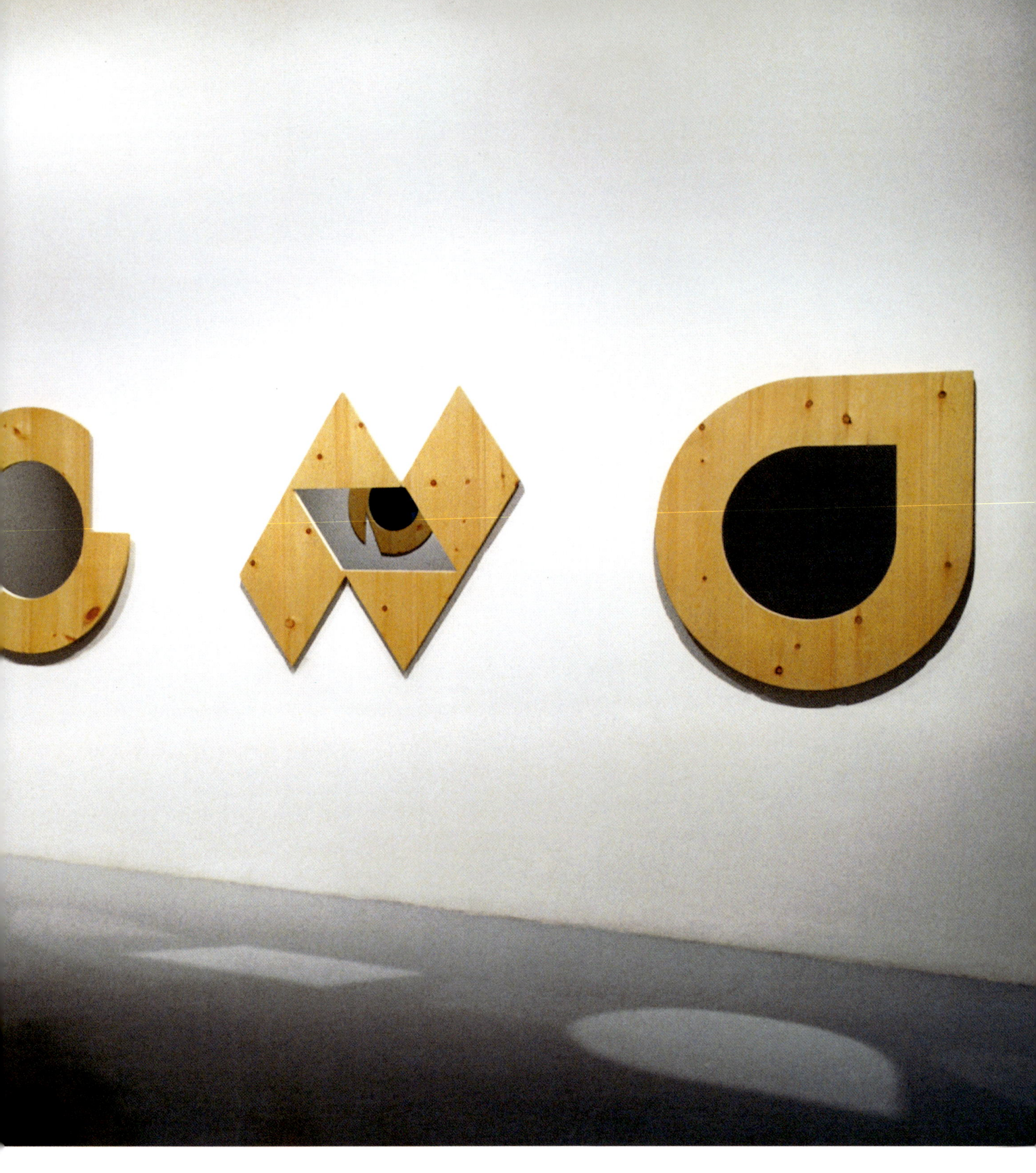

Labor k3000

Peter Spillmann, Michael Vögeli and Marion von Osten

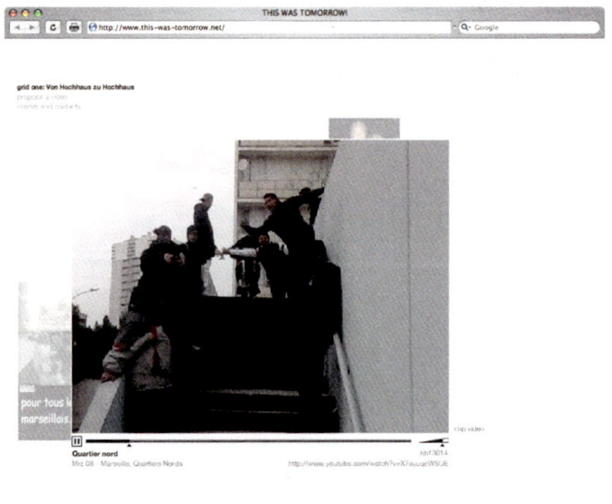

grid one: Von Hochhaus zu Hochhaus
Paris: Témoignage d'anciens habitants des 4000
(video still)

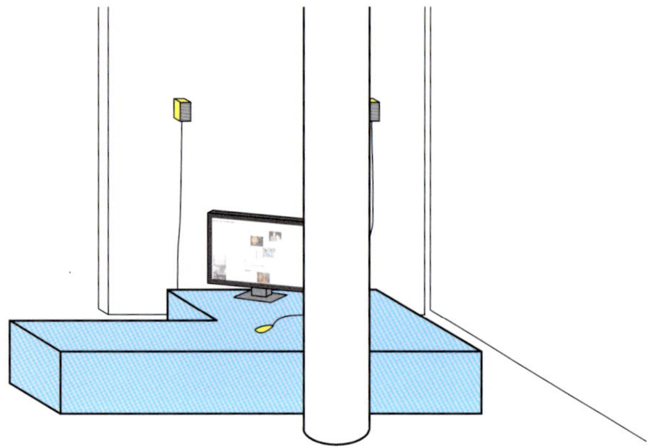

Design for the installation at MACBA, Barcelona, 2009

www.this-was-tomorrow.net
grid one: Von Hochhaus zu Hochhaus, 2008
Installation with website project

The website project presents a selection of videos shot and posted online by residents of mass housing in Europe and North Africa. We see images of everyday life, the ways in which residents identify with their neighbourhoods, and the threat of, and protests against, demolition and discrimination. The videos are available on YouTube and other online video platforms.

After the Second World War, modern housing and urban planning projects in Europe acquired a symbolic function for the future-oriented reorganisation of modern societies and their ways of life under Fordist conditions. But the architect's view and his/her authorship remained unquestioned, along with the question of the representation of architecture itself, usually photographed uninhabited, at completion. By the mid-1960s, social housing complexes built for hundreds of thousands of families in France, Britain, the Netherlands, Germany, Switzerland and the USA had already become, and would remain, international symbols of the failure of modernism. Described as inhospitable because of their strict functional separation of work, leisure and housing, and their isolation from city centres, post-war modernist architecture, especially social housing, represents a frequently cited negative backdrop. In Germany, public social housing has already been amended or abolished, while in France, following Sarkozy's 'hard line', post-war modernist mass housing is associated above all with riots, social decline and crime zones. But the ongoing struggle of residents and young migrants against discrimination, deportation and social inequality could also be looked upon as a way for the emancipatory promises of the modernists to re-emerge: through the social movements in the *banlieues*, which frequently situate themselves in the context of post- or neo-colonial relations. In this sense, the *banlieues* are a reminder that the colonial history of the European city, once denied, has long since returned. The tensions within the modernity project cannot be solved as long as little attention is paid to the roles played by residents and other decisive actors in transforming modernity as a result of transnational mobility, everyday practices, usage, appropriation or resistance. *This was Tomorrow* seeks to develop literally a web of approaches to the negotiation of modern architecture through the self-representation and the voices of inhabitants of modernist mass housing blocks in Europe and North Africa.

Concept, research, design and programming: Labor k3000, Zurich and Berlin.

grid one:
Von Hochhaus zu Hochhaus
Paris

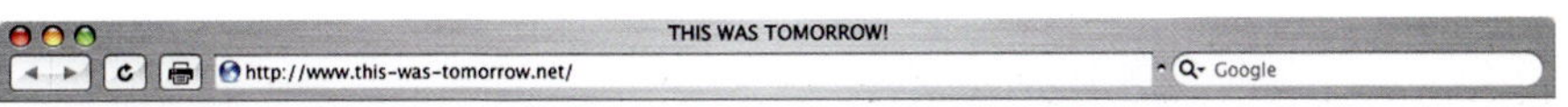

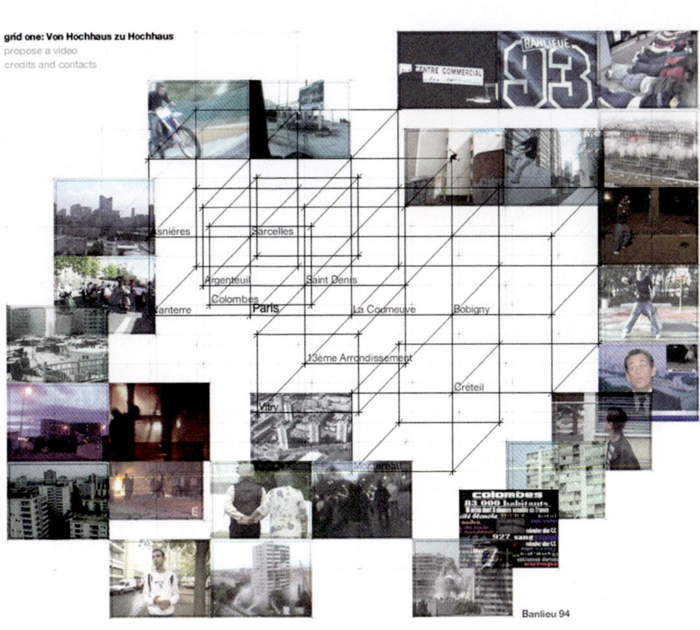

grid one:
Von Hochhaus zu Hochhaus
Berlin

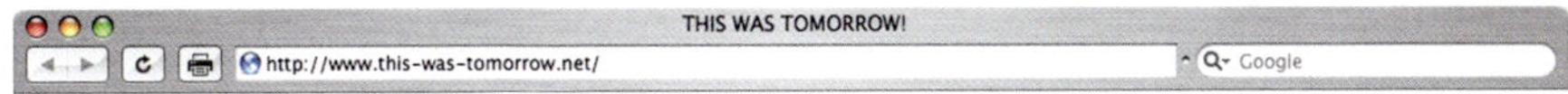

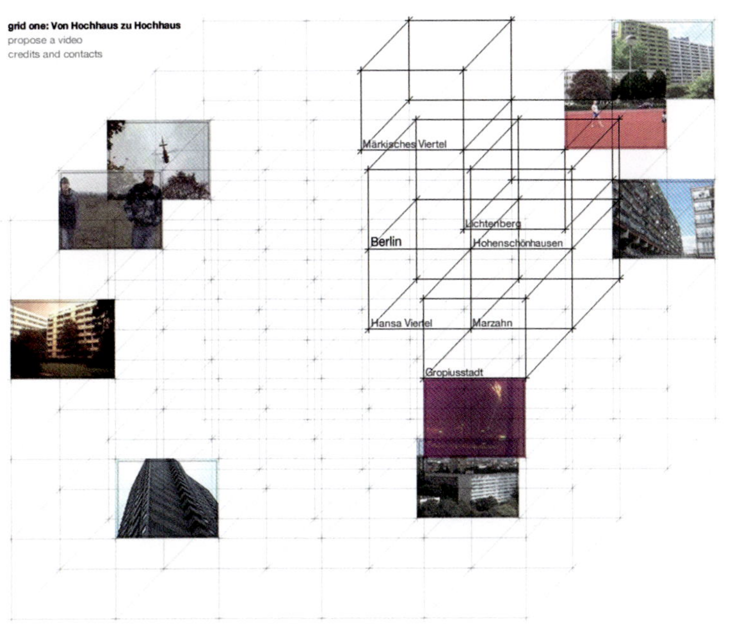

Louise Lawler

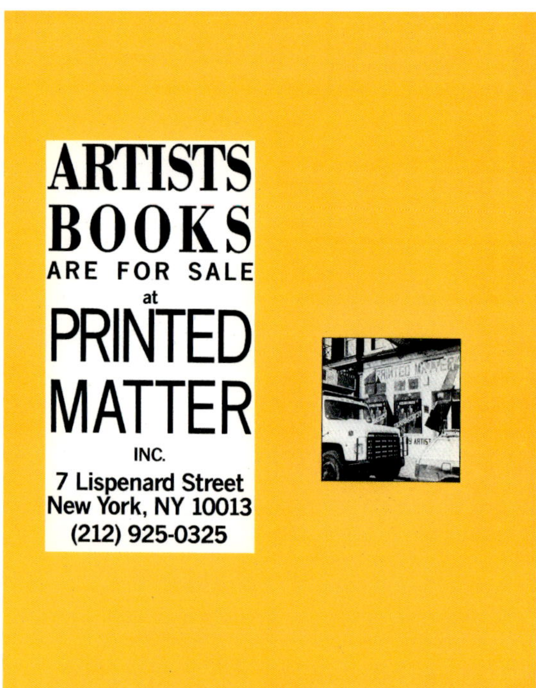

Back cover of the *Printed Matter*
catalogue, 1986

Louise Lawler addresses works of art by well-known modern
artists (generally male, in accordance with prevailing selection
processes in the art world). She 'appropriates' them photographically and presents them to us in a wide range of constellations
and surroundings, including auction houses, company foyers and
private collectors' homes. Her 'subversive intervention' in the
re-presentation of art takes various forms, either documenting
works as she finds them in a certain location or arranging them in
a specially created context. Lawler's photographs shift attention
from the centre of the image to its environment, literally presenting
the work of art at the edge or outside its frame. This extends, shifts
and focuses its significance in new ways, moving beyond the
autonomous modernist work of art to disclose what George Baker
called in conversation with Andrea Fraser 'a new form of aesthetic
experience that we need to rename'.[1] Lawler often complements
her relatively neutral photographs with text panels, coloured walls
and captions on the mounts. Like her arrangements of several
different photographs, these additional features emphasise how
art is staged, how its installation can affect its meaning. As
Fraser put it, Lawler does not exhibit photographs, but 'shows'[2]
them, and always in relation to the exhibition space: she 'installs
photographs'.

Storage and *Well Being*, both created in 1986, belong to
a series of works based on data published in *World Military and
Social Expenditure*, a book edited by activist Ruth Leger Sivard
in 1985. Lawler designed the cover of a 1986 *Printed Matter*
catalogue of artist's books with monochrome geometrical forms
derived from these public spending statistics. In *Two Editions*,
produced in the same year for the *Damaged Goods* show at the
New Museum[3] in New York, she arranged identical photographs
of an expensive fruit, printed in black-and-white and colour so
as to reflect the same economic data. In three similar installations
she attached photographs of art works taken at collectors' homes
or in museum storage spaces to wall paintings representing these
statistics.

In the 1980s contemporary art became re-politicised and
engaged in such issues as feminism, aids and homelessness.
At the same time it became a common practice to paint exhibition
walls in galleries and museums in bright colours. Lawler, who
has studied such exhibition designs at the Metropolitan Museum
of Art in New York and elsewhere, conceived her wall paintings
in response to these manipulative scenarios.

Storage, the initial work in the series, was first shown in a
group exhibition at Metro Pictures and later in *The Decade Show*,
a collaborative exhibition project mounted by three New York-
based museums at the New Museum in order to represent 'what
happened to American art during the tumultuous, combative
1980s'[4]. In this installation, a photograph titled *Storage* is placed
on a beige painted area representing 'the 16,000 MEGATONS that
are equivalent to the world's nuclear weapon stock pile',[5] while
the wall label explains the red spot next to it as representing 'the 6
MEGATONS of explosive energy used in the Second World War II'.

By contrast to this discrete installation, *Well Being*, first shown
in a group exhibition at the Richard Kuhlenschmidt Gallery in
Los Angeles, attracts attention through the dazzling pink and blue

of the wall, the label functioning as a focal point in the centre.
Unlike most labels, which refer to the work next to them,
this one explains the meaning of the two areas of colour on
which the photograph is installed: 'The blue area on which
this label is placed represents the 75 dollars per capita spent
by the US and the European Community on military research
in 1983. The adjacent area, painted rose, represents proportionally the 11 dollars per capita spent on health research in 1983.'[6]
The photograph on the left, overlapping both areas of colour,
shows two famous paintings by Fernand Léger (1881–1955), *La
Lecture* and *Femme au livre* (both dated 1924), positioned together
in a private home. The photograph in the first installation depicts a
group of works, obviously by modern masters, leaning against
a wall with their backs to us. Only the drawing hanging above this
group can be identified: it is Léger's *Étude pour 'La Lecture'* (1924).

Lawler had been prompted to take these photographs of
Léger's works by the exhibition *L'Œuvre et son accrochage* at the
Musée national d'art moderne in Paris. A number of curators
were asked to install pieces relating to Léger's seminal group of
works connected with *La Lecture*, and Lawler was commissioned
to photograph the various kinds locations from which they were
being borrowed, whether private homes, exhibition spaces or
museum storerooms.[7] Lawler did not originally intend *Storage* and
Well Being to be shown in the same exhibition, but, appearing
in this way in the present context, the two installations generate
new narratives in new surroundings. SB

1   George Baker and Andrea Fraser, 'Verschieben und Verdichten:
    Ein Gespräch über das Werk von Louise Lawler', *Louise Lawler
    and Others*, Basel: Kunstmuseum Basel, Museum für Gegenwartskunst,
    Ostfildern-Ruit: Hatje Cantz, 2004, p. 129 (exh. cat.)
2   Ibid., p. 110.
3   *Damaged Goods: Desire and the Economy of the Object* at the
    New Museum of Contemporary Art, New York, was curated
    by Brian Wallis, and showed installations by eight artists.
    Judith Barry, the exhibition designer, might be called the ninth.
4   *The Decade Show: Frameworks of Identity in the 1980's* took place
    in New York at the New Museum of Contemporary Art and
    the Museum of Hispanic Contemporary Art, both in SoHo, and the
    Studio Museum in Harlem in 1990. See Roberta Smith's article
    in the *New York Times*, 25 May 1990.
5   Excerpt from the wall label.
6   Excerpt from the wall label. In 1987, when Lawler wished to produce
    a further work based on the data published by Ruth Leger Sivard,
    the author told her that the statistics were incorrect. The per capita figure
    for money spent on military research had been given as 45 dollars,
    but in fact it was 75 dollars. Lawler has subsequently used the revised
    data for her work.
7   Lawler wished to install her works on walls painted yellow,
    but the exhibition curators hung them in a more conventional way.
    The works from these series have been published in *Les Cahiers du
    Musée national d'art moderne*, nos. 17–18, 1986, pp. 7, 59, 121.

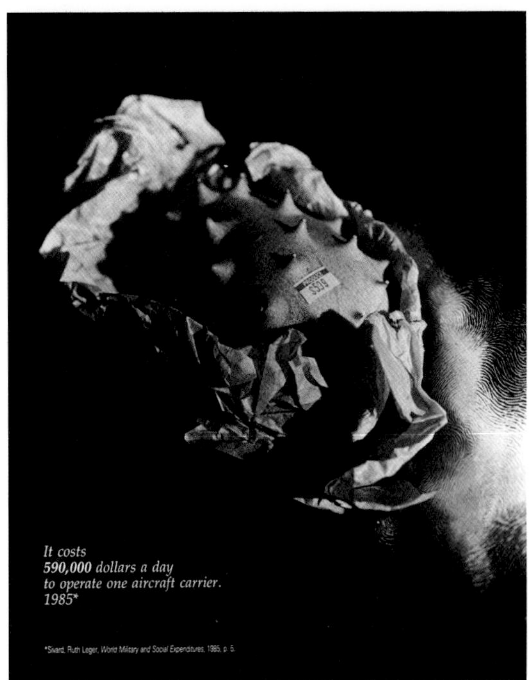

Damaged Goods exhibition catalogue,
New Museum, New York, 1986

Storage, 1986
Installation

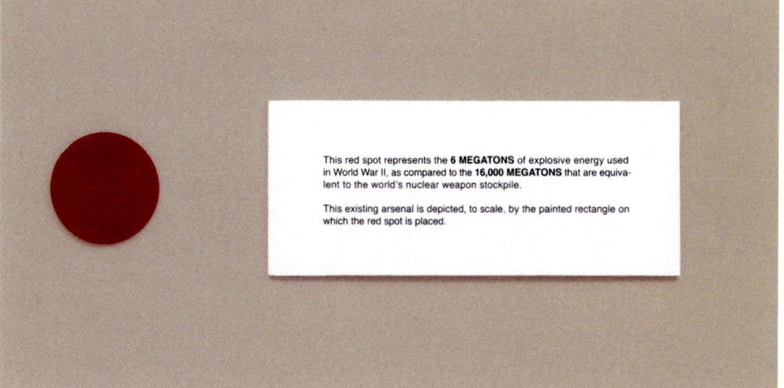

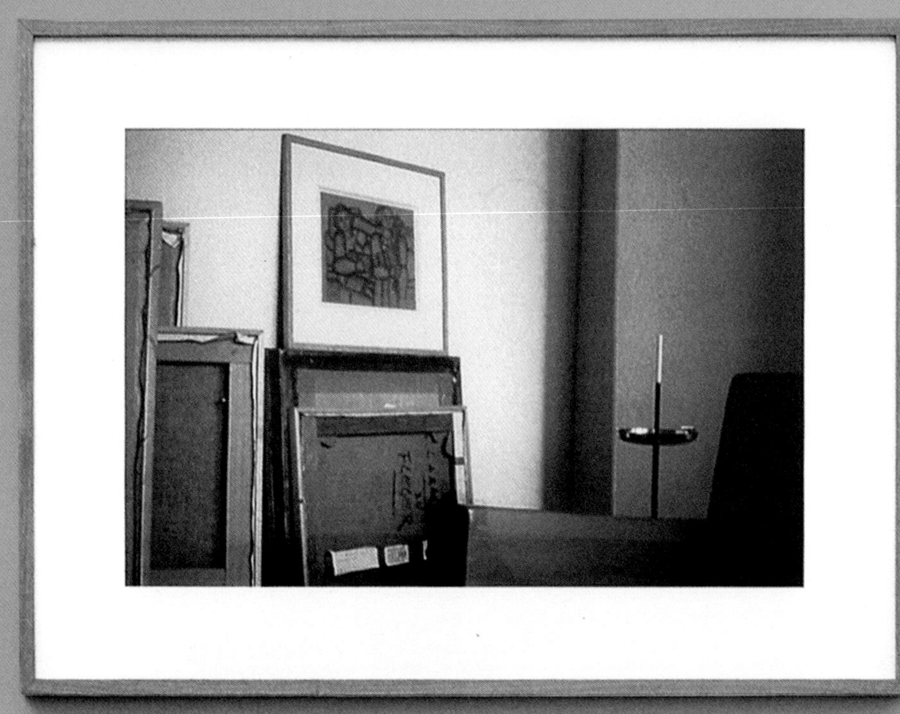

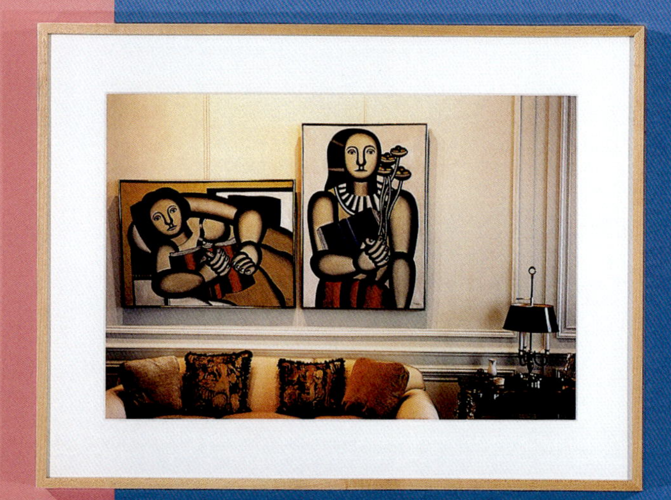

WELL BEING

The blue area on which this label is placed represents the 75 dollars per capita spent by the US and the European Community on military research in 1983.

The adjacent area, painted rose, represents proportionally the 11 dollars per capita spent in health research in 1983.

Source: Ruth Leger Sivard, World Military and Social Expenditures 1985, Washington, 1985.

Well Being, 1986
Installation

WELL BEING

The blue area on which this label is placed represents the
75 dollars per capita spent by the US and the European
Community on **military research** in 1983.

The adjacent area, painted rose, represents proportionally the
11 dollars per capita spent on **health research** in 1983.

Source: Ruth Leger Sivard ed., **World Military and Social Expenditures 1985**,
Washington, 1985.

David Maljkovic

The possibility of analysing modernity from the peripheral perspective of Eastern European socialist regimes, specifically from former Yugoslavia, is unquestionable. David Maljkovic's work, however, is by no means a generic or academic approach to the question of modernity; rather, it is based on personal experience and memory.[1] The places and characters whom he chooses as settings and protagonists in his films have a direct relationship with his recollections and with the recent memory of his country.

The film *Retired Form* (2008) takes place around a sculpture by Vojin Bakić located in the Dotrscina memorial park in Zagreb; the sculpture commemorates the victims of the Second World War. Bakić was one of the modern abstract Yugoslavian artists whose work opposed Socialist Realism. He worked during the Tito regime, and in the 1990s — a period of anti-communism and nationalistic exuberance — much of his work was destroyed and he fell into oblivion. The film consists of a circular travelling shot around a group of people looking at the sculpture's geometrical forms. The sunlight is reflected in the camera, almost entirely blurring the image.

Images With Their Own Shadows (2008) takes place in the Museum-Estate of Vjenceslav Richter, one of the members of the Exact 51 group that emerged in the 1950s. The film intersperses images of works by Richter with fragments of the last interview he gave. In one of its manifestos, Exact 51 proclaimed that abstract art was by no means an expression of decadence. Instead, they argued, it furthered and enriched visual communication in Yugoslavia by emphasising the experimental nature of making art.[2] Exact 51 is a paradigmatic example of the progress of modernity and its emancipatory potential in relation to the sociopolitical context of ex-Yugoslavia. The group firmly supported experimentation, challenging its detractors not only with works of art, but also with manifestos: 'for those who claim that this painting is non-socialist, our question is: do they already possess the formula of socialist painting?'[3]

The protagonists of both films are controversial figures who are, nonetheless, key points of reference for the period. Most certainly, memory — especially personal memory — is one of the key components in the work of David Maljkovic. But the role of oblivion, and escape from oblivion, is equally important, as is transforming particular recollection into memory. Rather than a nostalgic re-creation of the historical and artistic condition of his country during its recent socialist past, what Maljkovic deals with are the potential new meanings of that past's 'ruins', the new backgrounds of expressions considered peripheral to modernity and its tradition. All of this makes it possible to create new platforms and to make use of that still empty space of the future:

'I was more interested in how to re-create all these elements on a new level than how to use their existing qualities and present them on the documentary level. I wasn't interested in the phenomenon of modernism in Yugoslavia and Croatia in a general sense; this isn't a relation that could motivate me personally, but creating new platforms for all this, that was a strong motivation for me.'[4]

Teresa Grandas

1 David Maljkovic, in an e-mail to the author, 12 May 2009.
2 Exact 51 Manifesto, session of the Association of Applied Artists of Croatia, Zagreb, 7 December 1951.
3 Exact 51 Manifesto, Kristl-Picelj-Rasica-Scnec exhibition, Zagreb, 1951.
4 'The Empty Space of the Future. Natasa Ilic in conversation with David Maljkovic', *David Maljkovic. Almost Here*, Hamburg: Kunstverein in Hamburg, 2007.

Retired Form, 2008
Film installation

Images with Their Own Shadows, 2008
Film installation

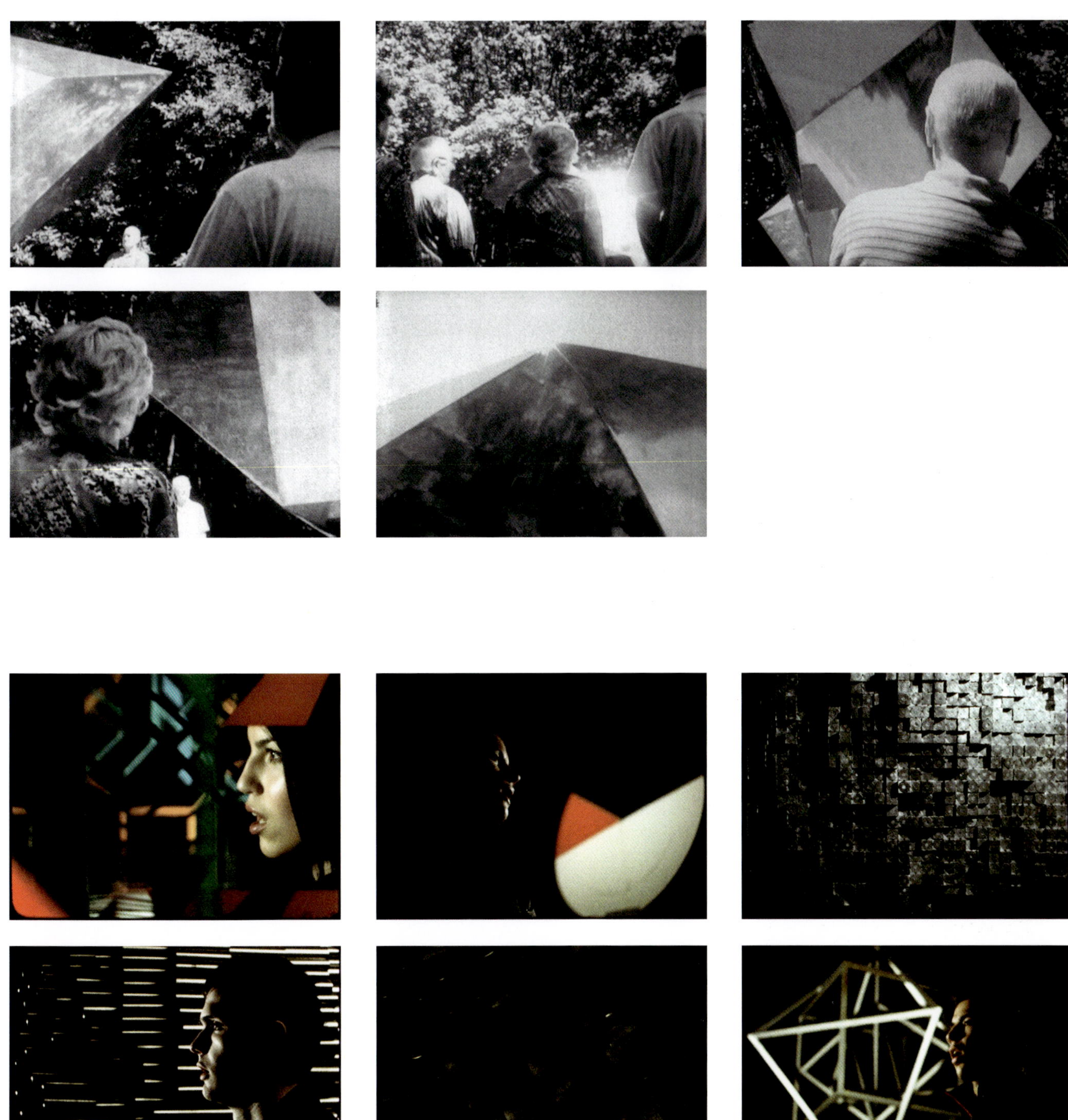

Dorit Margreiter

zentrum, 2006
Film installation

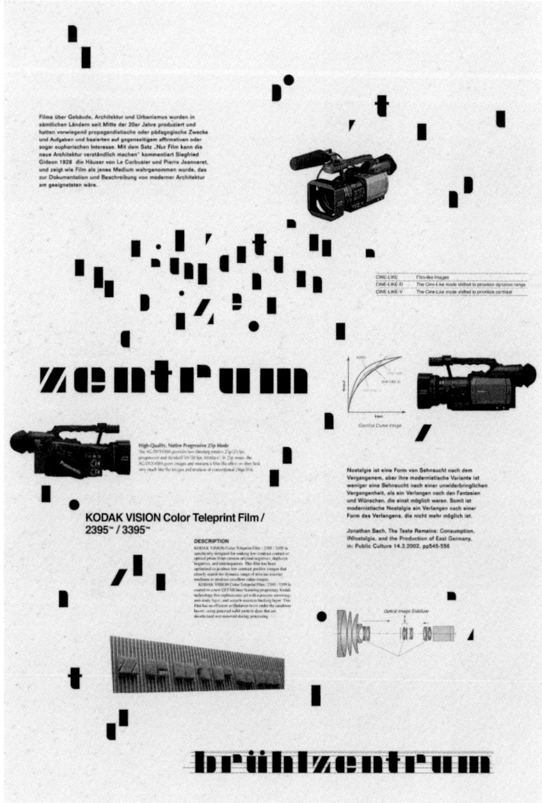

Exhibition poster
1 of 3 (inkjet print)

Margreiter's preoccupation with modernism's contingent relationship to politics is most fully evident in a sequence of works made for a 2006 exhibition at the Gallery for Contemporary Art in Leipzig, Germany, all based on a neon sign affixed to the Brühlzentrum, a modernist housing project in the same East German city. The building and the sign bearing its name date from 1963, the heyday of the GDR's neon craze. But times change: the impending demolition of the Brühlzentrum had already been announced when Margreiter made her film *zentrum*, 2006, in which we see the hundreds of neon tubes that give the round-edged, full-bodied letters their shapes light up one last time.

In seeking to situate the aesthetics of socialist modernism in the twenty-first century, Margreiter reveals and perpetuates modernity's ongoing relationship with the moving image: *zentrum* is also an ode to her fascination with early cinema about the city. In films such as Charles Sheeler and Paul Strand's *Manhattan* (1921) or Walter Ruttmann's *Berlin: Symphony of a Great City* (1927), modernism's complexity and social dynamism are given form through lighting, *mise-en-scène*, editing and cinematography. In her filmic reconstruction of the neon sign, Margreiter likewise pays homage to technical ingenuity: the work is often shown in conjunction with a video documentary depicting the elaborate preparations for the night-time shoot, which reveals that the sign was not in fact illuminated — the tubes were merely wrapped in white tape that reflected the light of handheld spots. Moreover, although the piece was shot on digital video, it is projected in grainy, black-and-white 16 mm stock. In using the digital to reproduce the aesthetics of the analogue, she highlights the historical counter flow in her work, as her deployment of technology points up the shifting social relevance of design and its status as cultural memory. The fleeting moment when the letters light up in the dark appears as the past revived in the present, and so Margreiter marks the constitutive time gap between an event and its reproduction, emphasising their ontological distance.

Margreiter documents and redeploys the remnants of modernism before they disappear and, subsequently, keeps them 'alive'. The artist saved the Brühlzentrum sign from its complete amnesiac erasure in more ways than one: she also designed a typeface, called *zentrum*, 2005, using the modular components of the sign's letters. In its mode of construction as well as in appearance, it is strongly reminiscent of Josef Albers' *Kombinationsschrift* (Combination Type), a stencil-based typeface he designed at the Bauhaus in Dessau, Germany, in the late twenties. Margreiter thus suggests a third phase for the familiar historical trajectory of modernism. After the initial utopian impulse and the revival of its forms in the fashions of mainstream culture several decades later, there is still the possibility of a new lease on life: as a piece of art that can shift its medial character from image to text to sculpture. Since the *zentrum* font is neither a homage to the original nor an imitation of its sixties copy, but rather a graphic set of modules existing between the two- and three-dimensional, the typeface regains presence.

Barbara Clausen

Revised version of 'Openings: Dorit Margreiter', *Artforum International*, vol. 47, no. 1, September 2008, pp. 445–47. © *Artforum*

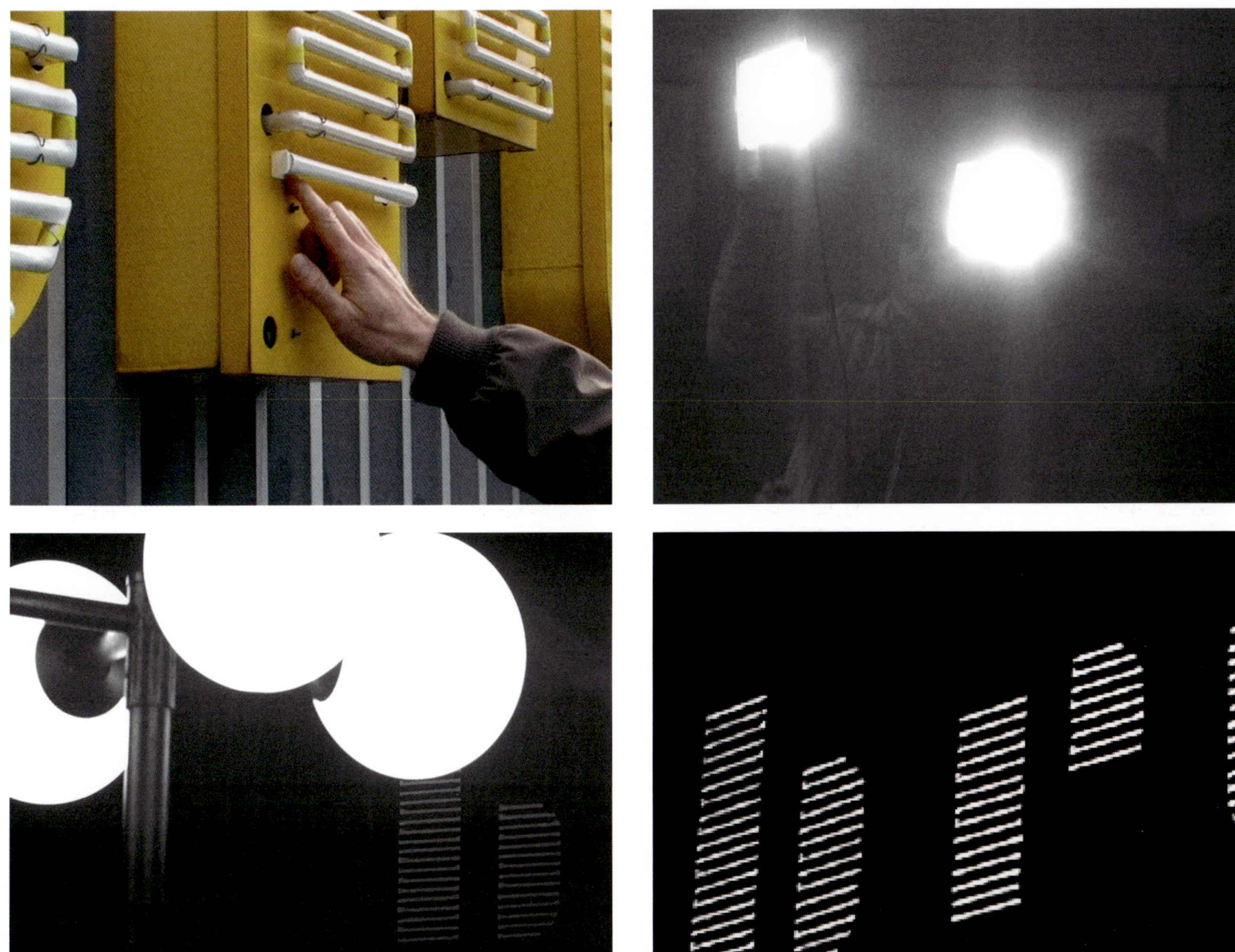

Production and film stills, 2006

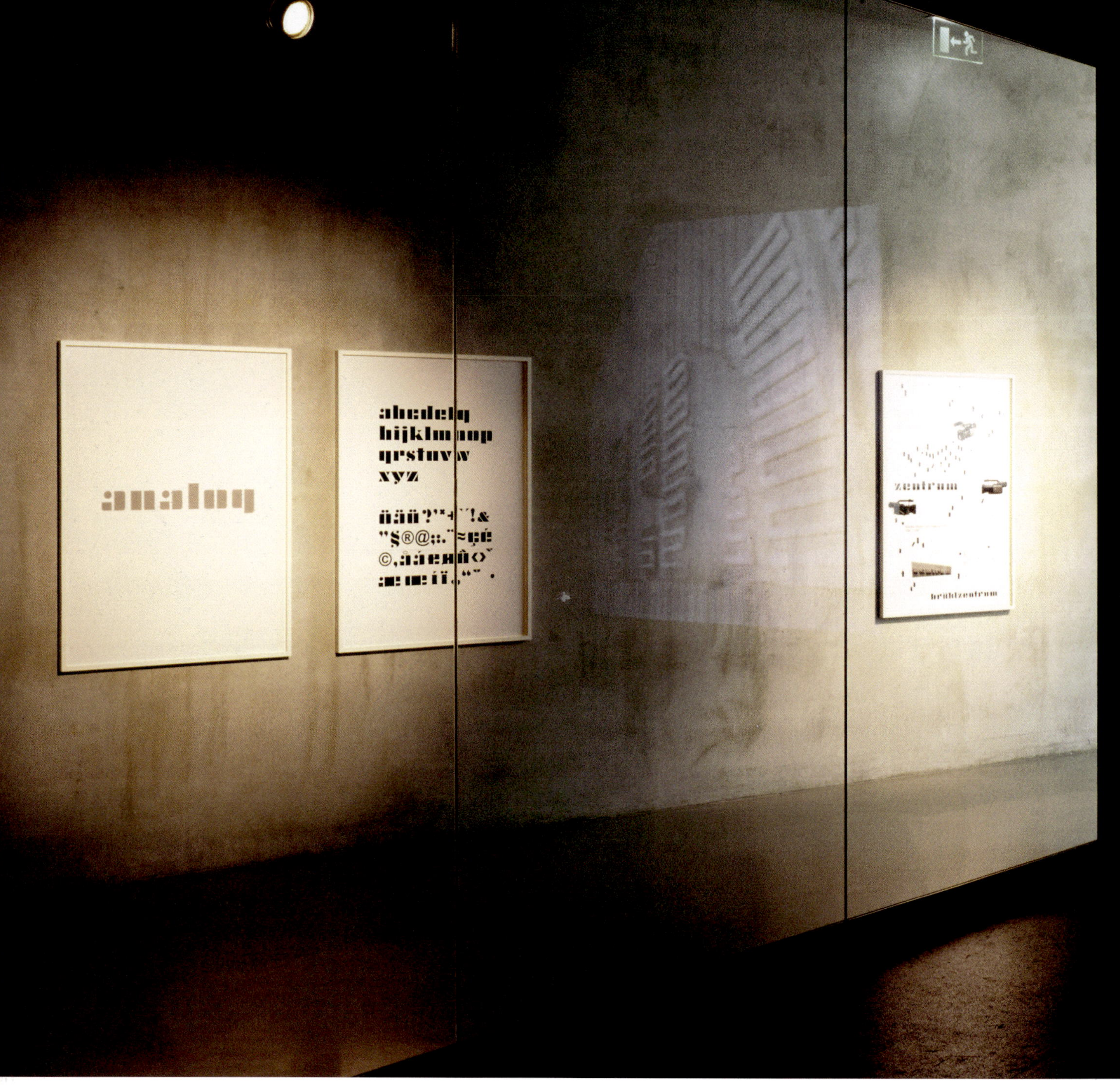

Installation view
Gallery for Contemporary Art, Leipzig, 2006

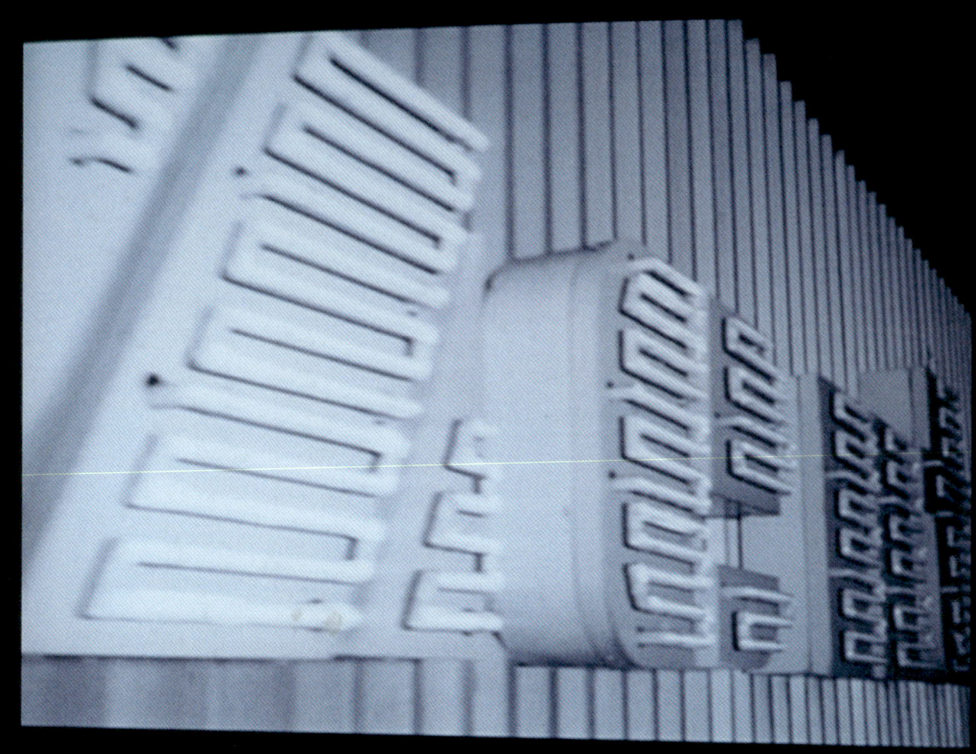

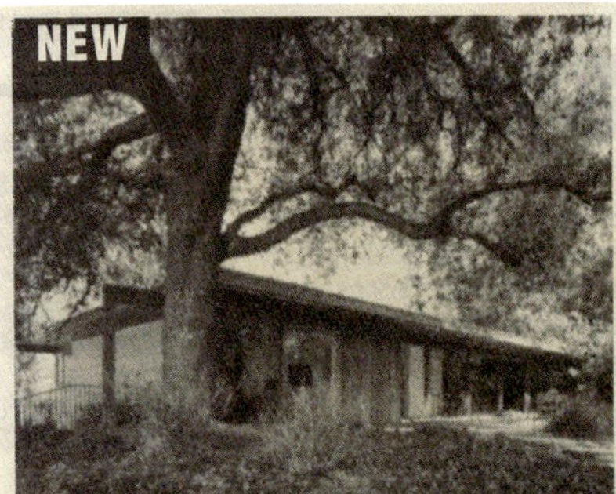

Original Condition (Masters for Sale), 2006
Installation
10 advertisements cut out from newspapers

Masters for Sale belongs to a series titled *Original Condition*, in which Margreiter investigates the modern housing project as it oscillates in its market and social value between forgotten objects of desire and empty architecture brands. From autumn 2005 to spring 2006 she traced the decline in price of a villa by architect and shopping mall inventor Victor Gruen as offered for sale in twelve advertisements in the *Los Angeles Times*. In another series she explored ads for modern houses by celebrity architects, including Frank Lloyd Wright, which had been 'remodelled'.

In this work she focuses on ads for buildings by famous modernist architects, such as Richard Neutra, Rudolf Schindler and John Lautner, which are for sale 'restored to their original state'.

As Patricia Grzonka has stated: 'Little remains here of the utopian experiment in the renewal of society originally espoused by modernist architecture in its most advanced forms. The buildings have mutated to masterpieces or to coded cultural ruins, as in the case of Frank Lloyd Wright's Ennis Brown House, which became famous as the backdrop of *Blade Runner* before being substantially damaged by earthquake in 1994.'[1] SB

1   Patricia Grzonka, 'Dorit Margreiter: Ursprüngliche Zustände und/oder Bedingungen'. www.kunstaspekte.de (15 February 2009).

My work *zentrum* is based on the neon sign 'brühl-zentrum'. My method of approaching the history of this sign could be described as a selective engagement with individual elements in a system of signs generated by overlaying. The various layers constitute narrative threads, which in turn form a narrative of their own. This represents a kind of clearing-up operation, reordering decades of (historical) accumulations and transposing them into a formal sign so as to work against their unquestioned perpetuation.

I am concerned to present the complexity of the signs as a non-linear narrative in which the interplay between contemporary mediality and an apparently historical relevance is shown as several adjacent narratives. The three key terms involved in *zentrum* were 'documentation', 'gentrification' and 'reproduction'. In *Original Condition (Masters for Sale)* I used ephemeral, subjectively arranged images to address the familiar question 'How would we have liked to live?' in the manner of a breakfast table comment. □

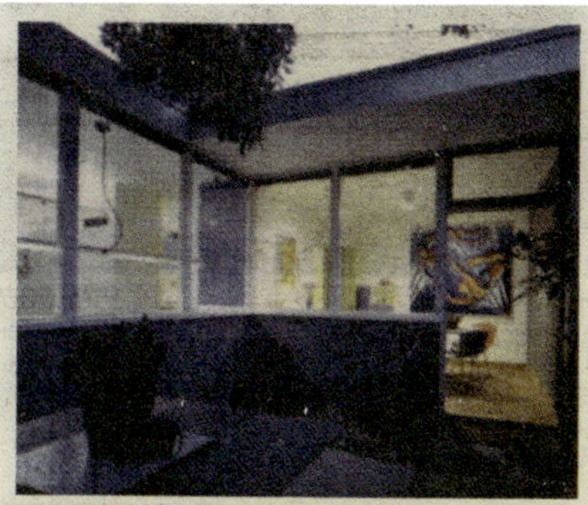

Gregory Ain, Architect, 1949 - Silver Lake
The Ain Office feels more like a home with atrium entry and back garden patio. Flexible interiors include: reception, office, conference room, studio, bath and kitchen. $595,000 Crosby Doe x579

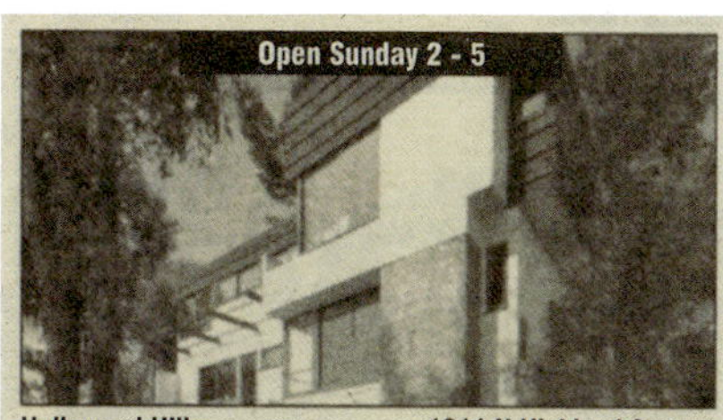

Hollywood Hills — **1911 N Highland Avenue**
$895,000. R.M. Schindler, Architect – "Double Residence": Widely published 2 BR main house + 1 BR apt., original condition, bathed in natural light, outdoor decks, city views, steps to Hollywood Bowl, 2 lots. **Web# DMSC1**
Brian Linder, AIA - Keller Williams Realty - www.tvoa.net 310-432-6525

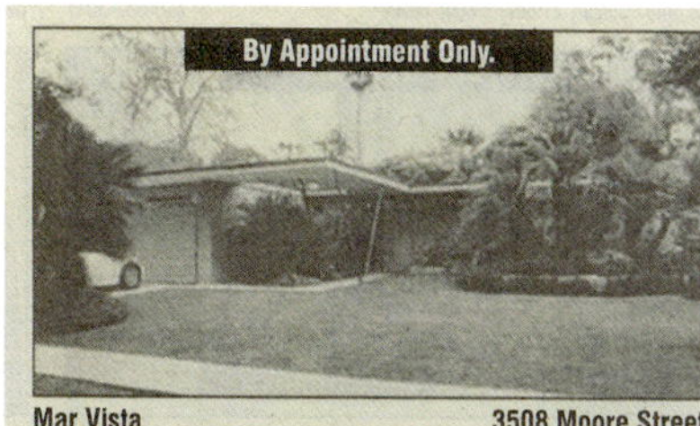

Mar Vista — **3508 Moore Street**
$1,295,000. 'Modernique' Original model home in the HPOZ Gregory Ain tract. Sliding partition walls convert to 1, 2, or 3 bdrms, live rm w/FP, kit/din. Addition w/bonus rm, 4th bed, 2nd bath. Pvt backyard. **Web# DOXB1**
Josh Gaunya / Mike Deasy 310-275-1000

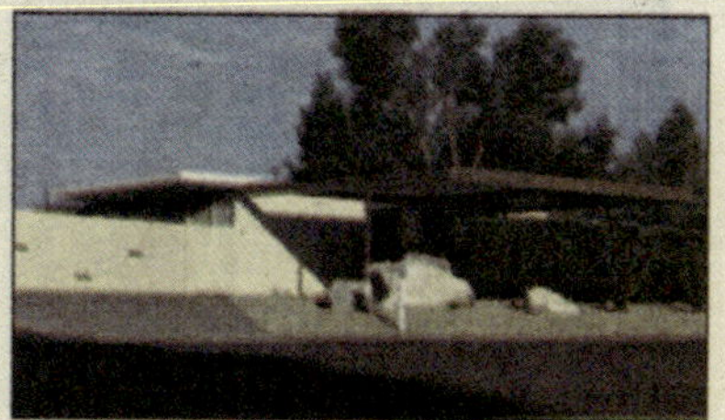

Palm Springs — **$770,000**
Wexler & Harrison, Architects. Steel Development House, 1961. Now a Class 1 Historic Site, the residence has been restored to its original condition. 2 bedrooms, 2 baths, and den. Price includes designer furniture.
310.666.1107 Barry Gray

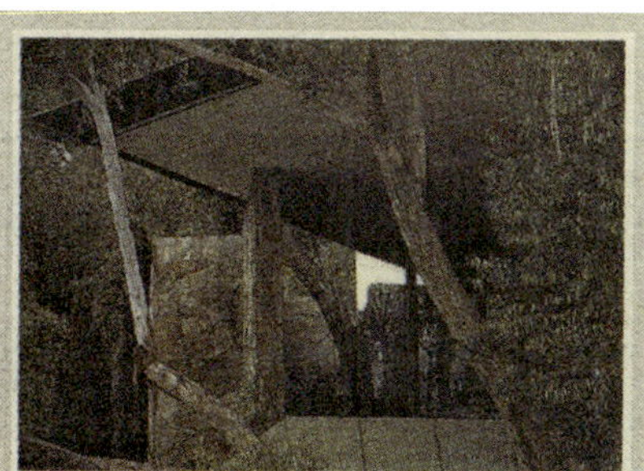

World Class Architecture, Sunset Strip — **$4,695,000**
Peter Schwartz 310.967.0538
John Lautner's masterpiece of mod architecture merges sculptural forms & space into one of the sexiest residences above the Snst Strip: 3+3½, media rm, gym & pool. Nearly 16 ft glass drs & glass walls.

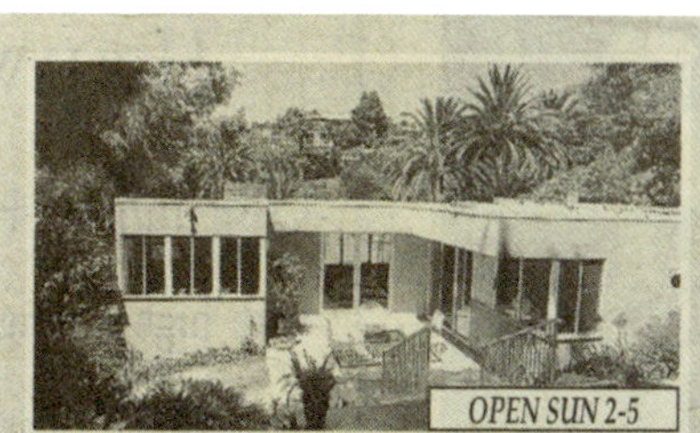

1941 Glencoe Wy, Hollywood Hills — **$1,149,000**
Bill & Lynn Lustig 310.855.0100
The Koosis House. Raphael Soriano Architectural + Mid-Cent guest unit. Yard & views. 2+1¾ & 1+1. Great opportunity.

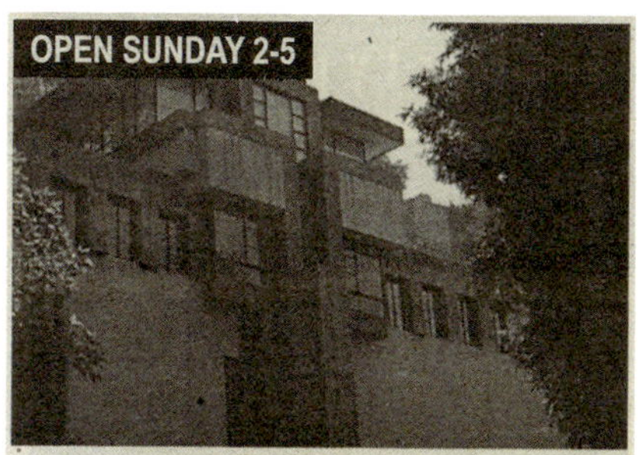

2255 VERDE OAK DRIVE — **$3,100,000**
Los Feliz. Celebrity owned Lloyd Wright. Completely open. Prvt. Dramatic windows/doors. Fdr & fpl. Huge yrd & pl. Own a piece of history!
Samantha Cooper 310.454.0080

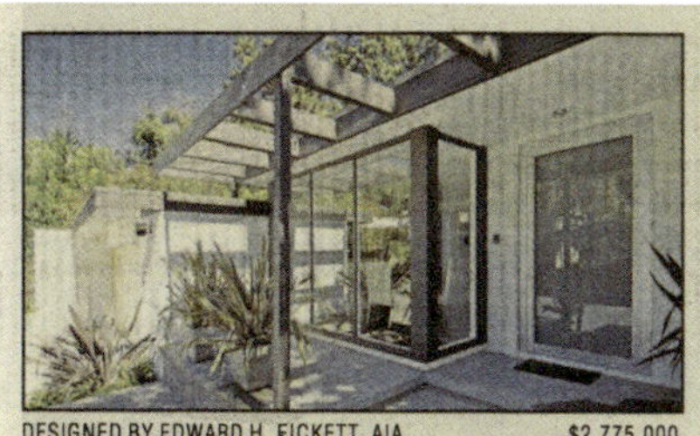

DESIGNED BY EDWARD H. FICKETT, AIA — **$2,775,000**
Bel Air. Open-plan features a great rm, FP, grmt kit, beamed ceils, walnut floor, skylights, 4BD, 4BA, walk-in closets, pool, terrace & gazebo. 2-car gar.
Jan Horn 310-777-6220

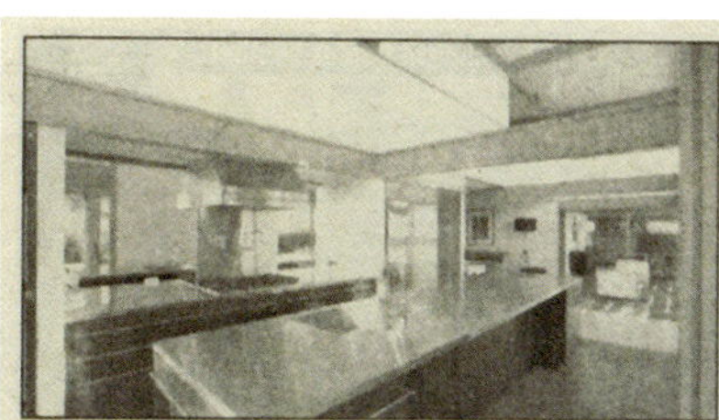

Beverly Hills PO — **9892 Beverly Grove Dr.**
$4,995,000. Famous Roth House by Case Study architects Buff and Hensman, expanded with 2-sty addition, completely renovated by celebrated architect David Hertz & designer Billy Lehman: 4+4, Pool, huge views. **Web# DIZB1**
Rory/Gerry 310-502-8797 Jill 310-888-3355

Gordon Matta-Clark

Window Blow-Out, 1976
Document of action, installation
8 photographs

For the exhibition *Idea as Model* at the Institute for Architecture and Urban Studies in New York, Matta-Clark created one of his legendary works. The piece resembled a fragmentary leftover from an action or rather a reaction, 'a way of looking at, or reflecting, the world as it is, and eliminating the authoritarian imposition of the architect's self-contained utopian building'.[1]

Most contributions to the New York show came not from artists, but from architects, including Richard Meier and Michael Graves, who exhibited sophisticated architectural models to demonstrate their ideas. Matta-Clark, who studied architecture at Cornell University, said of Meier and Graves: 'These are the guys I studied with at Cornell, these were my teachers. I hate what they stand for.'

The night before the opening Matta-Clark discarded his original plan to cut the contents of a seminar room into two-by-two-foot squares and stack the pieces in the middle of the exhibition space. Instead, he borrowed an air gun from Dennis Oppenheim, blew out all the windows of the display area and placed a photograph in each casement showing a housing development in the South Bronx where the windows had been smashed by residents.

The curator of the exhibition, Andrew MacNair, saw Matta-Clark's piece as a comment on modern architecture and architects, on good taste and on builders of utopian projects in slums like the South Bronx. He spoke of a very aggressive and violent act: he had given Matta-Clark permission to blow out only those gallery windows that were already broken. Peter Eisenman, then director of the institute, linked the act to the *Reichskristallnacht* (in English known as Night of the Broken Glass) in the Third Reich. All the windows were replaced that same night, prior to the opening, so that very few people had an opportunity to see the work. SB

1   Dan Graham, 'Gordon Matta-Clark', *Gordon Matta-Clark*, València: Institut Valencià d'Art Modern, 1993, p. 380 (exh. cat.)

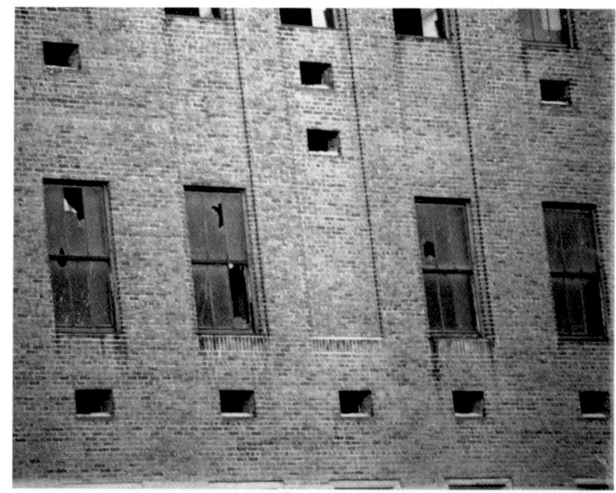
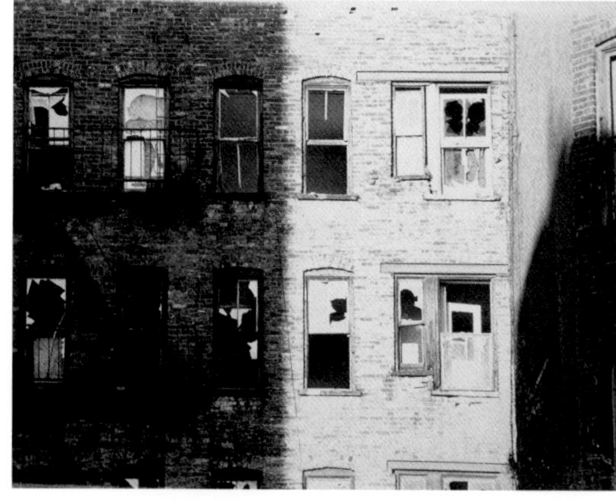
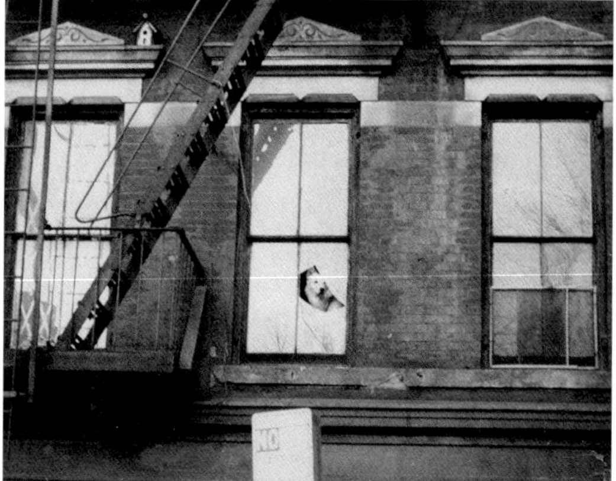
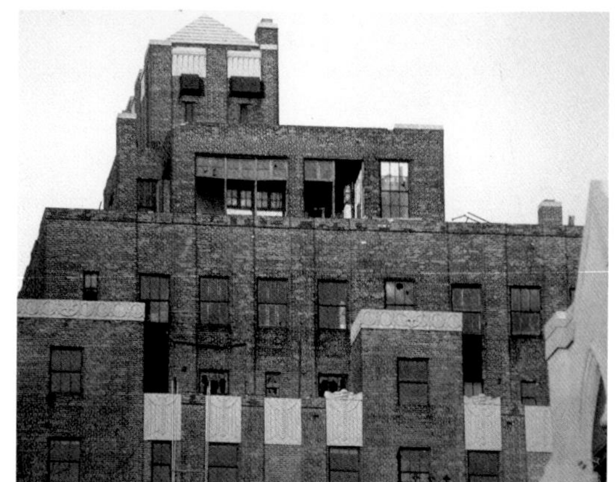
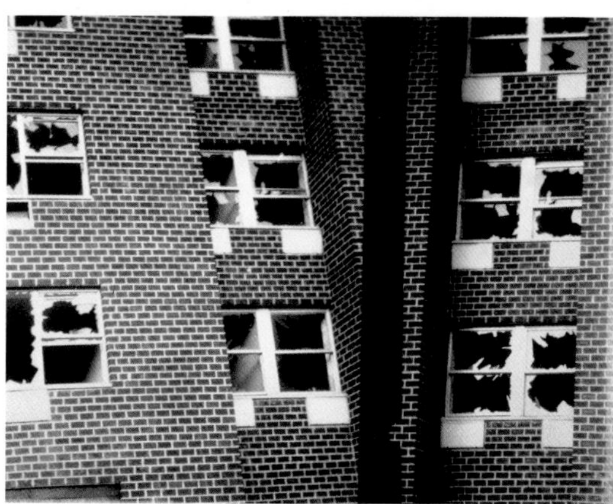
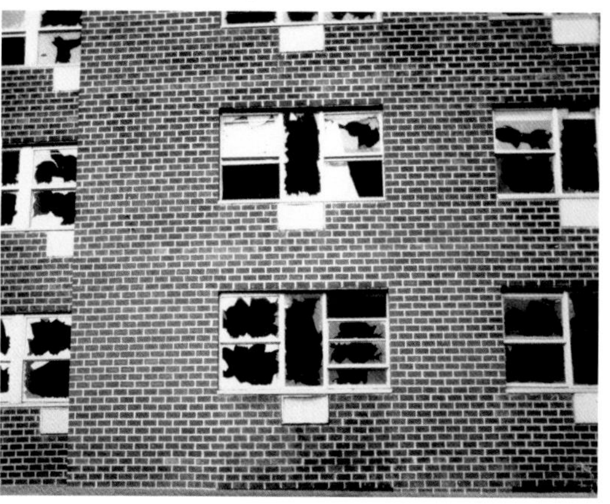
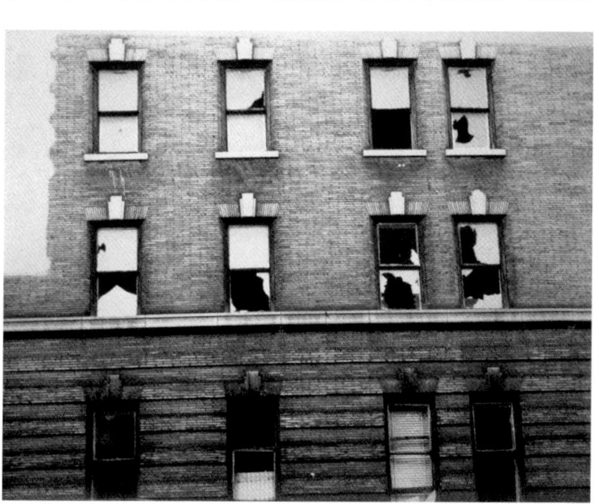
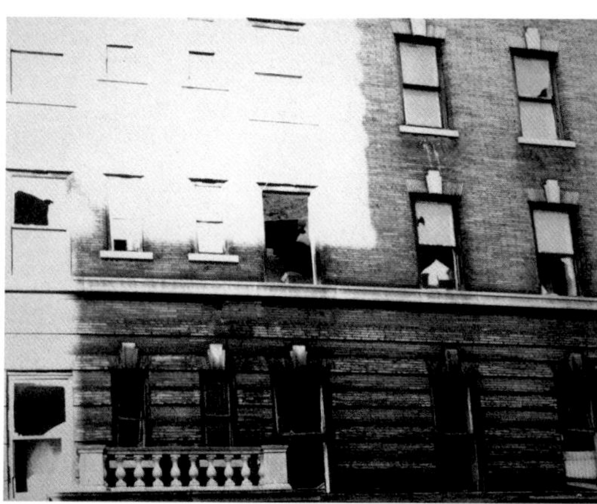

Gustav Metzger

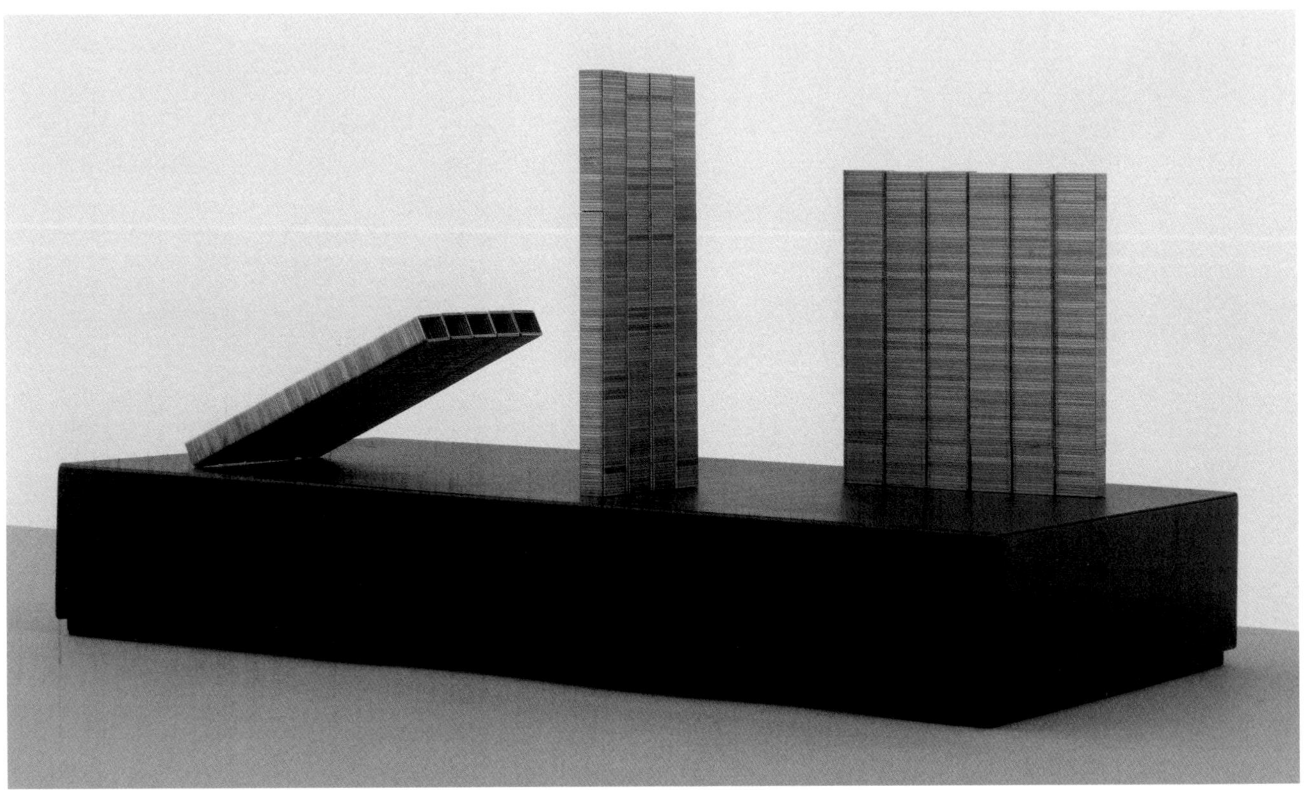

Auto-Destructive Art, 1959

'Decides to become a sculptor instead of a professional revolutionary': this entry is to be found in the summer of 1944 in an outline for a biography of Gustav Metzger.[1] What may look like an anecdote about the then 18-year-old Metzger proves to be characteristic of his work. For more than 40 years he has pursued a radical ambition towards an artistic reaction and expression regarding the modern industrial society.

Metzger's work sets out from his concept of *Auto-Destructive Art*, which he defined, in his first manifesto in 1959, as 'primarily a form of public art for industrial societies'. He presented this concept in a number of Lecture/Demonstrations. Nuclear weapons, atomic energy, pollution and, above all, the consequences of criminal and destructive actions like those committed by National Socialism have fundamentally changed Metzger's understanding of aesthetics. Thus his entire engagement as activist and pioneer, and his artistic production, are firmly rooted in the political, economic and ecological issues of the day. *Auto-Destructive Art*,

addresses the twentieth-century's destructive potential and is intended as a direct attack on both the capitalist system and the art industry: art — according to Metzer's manifesto — with a 'life-time varying from a few moments to twenty years', art that, 'when the disintegrative process is complete, the work is to be removed from the site and scrapped'.[2] When Metzger presented his ideas and his *Model for an Auto-Destructive Monument* for the first time in London in 1960 the headline of a daily newspaper read 'Modern art will fall to bits'[3]. SB

1   Gustav Metzger, *Damaged Nature, Auto-Destructive Art*,
    London: Coracle Press, 1996, p. 83.
2   Gustav Metzger, *Cardboards. Auto-Destructive Art*, first manifesto, 1959.
3   John Rydon, 'Modern art will fall to bits', *Daily Express*, London,
    15 March 1960.

Auto-Destructive Monument, 1960
Scale model

Manifesto Auto-Destructive Art,
London, 10 March 1960
(second manifesto)

AUTO DESTRUCTIVE ART

Auto-destructive art is primarily a form of public art for industrial
societies.

Self-destructive painting, sculpture and construction is a total unity
of idea, site, form, colour, method and timing of the disintegrative
process.

Auto-destructive art can be created with natural forces, traditional
art techniques and technological techniques.

The amplified sound of the auto-destructive process can be an element
of the total conception.

The artist may collaborate with scientists, engineers.

Self-destructive art can be machine produced and factory assembled.

Auto-destructive paintings, sculptures and constructions have a life
time varying from a few moments to twenty years.   When the disintegrative process is complete the work is to be removed from the site and
scrapped.

London, 4th November, 1959   G. METZGER

MANIFESTO AUTO-DESTRUCTIVE ART

Man in Regent Street is auto-destructive.
Rockets, nuclear weapons, are auto-destructive.
Auto-destructive art.
The drop drop dropping of HH bombs.
Not interested in ruins, (the picturesque)
Auto-destructive art re-enacts the obsession with destruction,
the pummelling to which individuals and masses are subjected.
Auto-destructive art demonstrates man's power to accelerate disintegr-
ative processes of nature and to order them.
Auto-destructive art mirrors the compulsive perfectionism of arms man-
ufacture - polishing to destruction point.
Auto-destructive art is the transformation of technology into public art.
The immense productive capacity, the chaos of capitalism and of Soviet
communism, the co-existence of surplus and starvation; the increasing
stock-piling of nuclear weapons - more than enough to destroy technological societies; the disintegrative effect of machinery and of life in
vast built-up areas on the person,...

Auto-destructive art is art which contains within itself an agent which
automatically leads to its destruction within a period of time not to
exceed twenty years.
Other forms of auto-destructive art involve manual manipulation.   There
are forms of auto-destructive art where the artist has a tight control
over the nature and timing of the disintegrative process, and there are
other forms where the artists control is slight.
Materials and techniques used in creating auto-destructive art include:
Acid, Adhesives, Ballistics, Canvas, Casting, Clay, Combustion, Com-
pression, Concrete, Corrosion, Cybernetics, Drop, Elasticity, Electricity,
Electrolysis, Electronics, Explosives, Feed-back, Glass, Heat, Human
Energy, Ice, Jet, Light, Load, Mass-production, Metal, Motion, Motion Pic-
ture, Natural Forces, Nuclear energy, Paint, Paper, Photography, Plaster,
Plastics, Pressure, Radiation, Sand, Solar energy, Sound, Steam, Stress,
Terra-cotta, Vibration, Water, Welding, Wire, Wood.

London, 10th March, 1960   G. METZGER

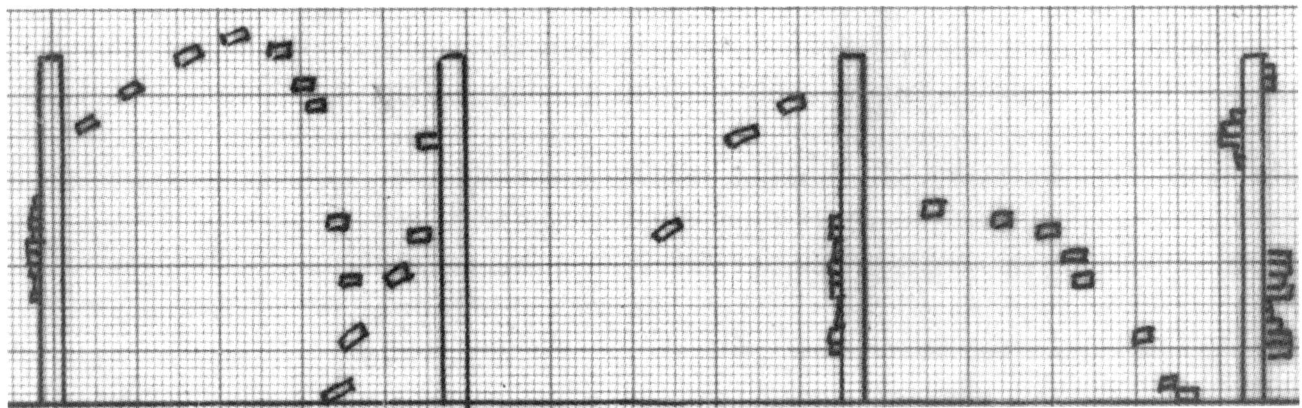

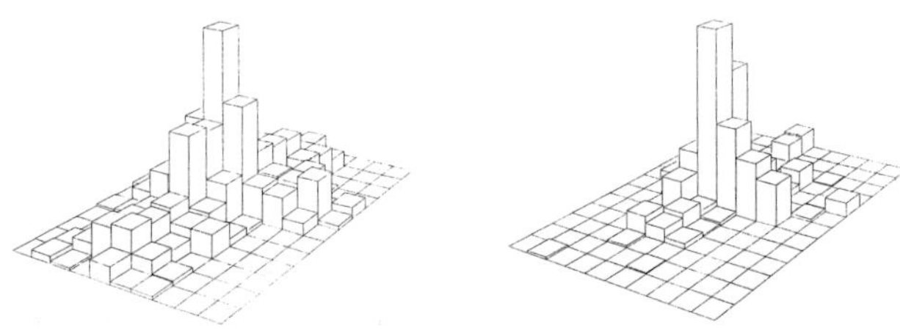

Sketch on graph paper

Two computer drawings, published
in *Page Magazine*

p. 153
Computer-controlled Auto-Destructive Monument
Scale model (reconstruction, 2005)

Five Screens with Computer, 1969
Computer-controlled Auto–Destructive Monument

Background of the project
This is the most elaborate project that has emerged from the
theory of *Auto-Destructive Art*. This theory was formulated
in the autumn of 1959, and published in a number of manifestos.
Here we are concerned to isolate some strands of the theory
that link with the project. A major objective of the theory is the
establishment of the closest possible relations between art,
science and technology. The first manifesto (November, 1959)
states: 'Self-destructive art can be machine produced and factory
assembled.' The second manifesto (March, 1960) includes the
statement '*Auto-Destructive Art* is the transformation of technology
into public art'. The same manifesto gives a list of 50 materials
and techniques that can be used in Auto-Destructive Art;
includ[ing] cybernetics — used in the broadest sense to include
theories and hardware.

It is the next manifesto, titled *Auto-Destructive Art, Machine
Art, Auto-Creative Art* (June, 1961), which has some of the basic
ideas of the project: '*Auto-Destructive Art* and *Auto-Creative Art*
aim at the integration of art with the advances of science and
technology. The immediate objective is the creation, with the
aid of computers, of works of art whose movements are pro-
grammed and include "self-regulation". The spectator, by means
of electronic devices, can have a direct bearing on the action of
these works.'

Gustav Metzger

'Five Screens with Computer: Computer Graphic Aspect of a Sculpture',
Computer Graphics '70, London: Plenum Press, 1971.

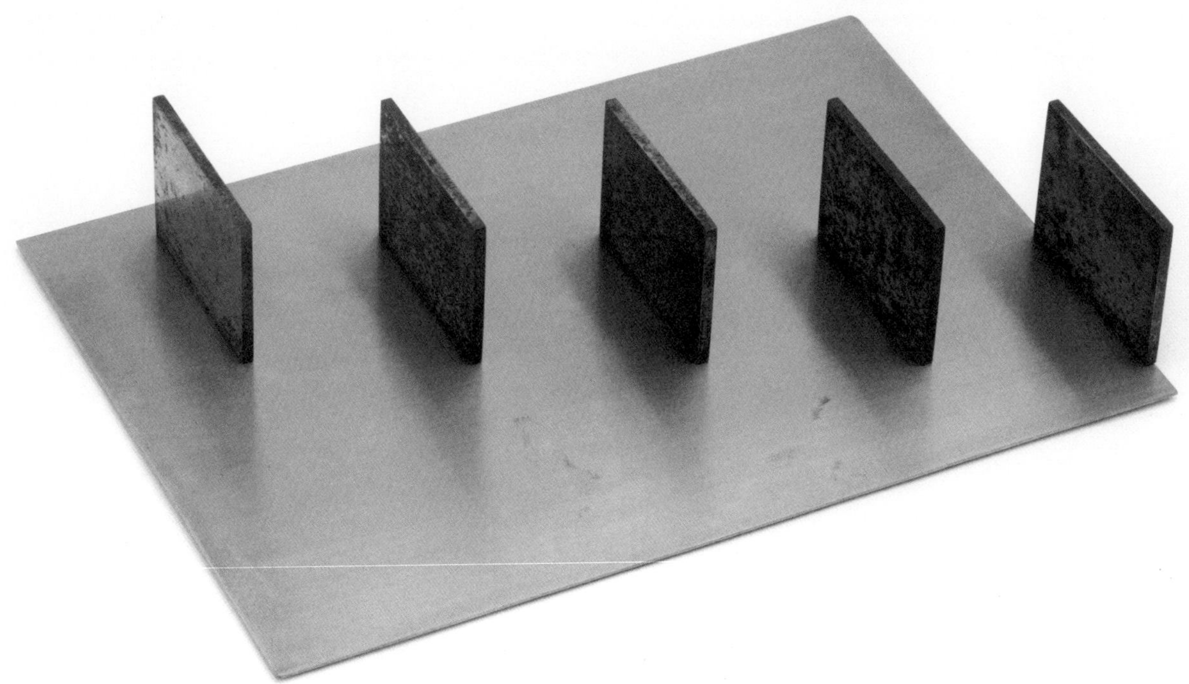

The project outlined

This sculpture consists of five walls or screens, each about 30
feet in height and 40 feet long and 2 feet deep. They are arranged
about 25 feet apart and staggered in plan. I envisage these in
a central area between a group of three very large densely populated blocks of flats in a country setting.

Each wall is composed of 10,000 uniform elements. These
could be made of stainless steel, glass or plastics. The elements
in one of the walls could be square or rectangular and in another
wall they could all be hexagonal.

The principle of the action of this work is that each element
is ejected until finally, after a period of ten years, the walls cease
to exist. I propose the use of a digital computer that will control
the movement of this work. This would be housed underground
in the centre of the sculpture complex.

Numerous techniques could be developed for holding and
ejecting the elements. One technique could be the use of attractive
and repulsive energy of magnets. Another could be compressed
air. The difficulty is in holding a small number of elements in complex, isolated relations.

A programme will be prepared by the artist. This determines
the order and timing in which each element is ejected. In pre-
paring the programme, the artist can bear in mind such factors
as shadows created by the work in all its phases. Complex inter-
actions between light and shade of all screens could be created.
The artist will take into consideration the revolution of the earth
and will relate the changing forms to the various seasons. Extremely
complex counterpoints between the five screens can be prepared,
interesting not merely from the ground but also when seen
from the windows of the three blocks. The programme can allow
for variations due to spectator participation via the photo-electric
effect. There can also be sections of the programme where there
are a series of random ejections determined by atmospheric conditions — this idea was suggested by Beverly Rowe.

The computer is used for a variety of reasons. One is the
complexity of ordering the movements of 50,000 elements over
a period of ten years. In fact, it may be necessary to use a computer in the *design* of the sculpture and in the writing of the programme. It can be used in order to link art, technology and society,
and because only through its use can the artist achieve forms and
rhythms that correspond to his aims. GM

Excerpt from a lecture given at the Architectural Association
in February 1965, and Gustav Metzger, *Auto-Destructive Art:
Metzger at the AA*, London: ACC, June 1965.

Christian Philipp Müller

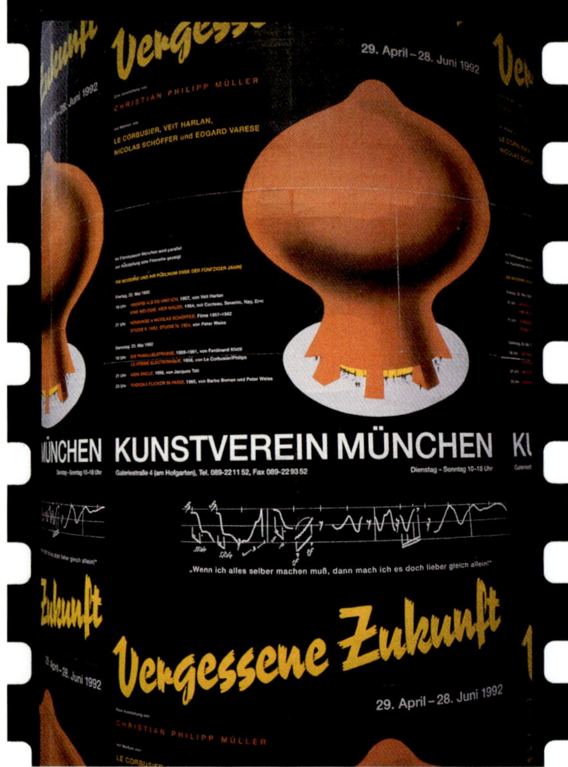

Exhibition poster
Munich, 1992

Vergessene Zukunft – Forgotten Future, 1992
Installation
Exhibition at the Kunstverein München
from 29 April to 28 June 1992, Munich

Müller developed a confrontation with late modernism and its utopias: with the Philips Pavilion realisation designed by Le Corbusier together with Iannis Xenakis and Edgard Varèse for the 1958 World's Fair in Brussels, with Veit Harlan's film, *Anders als du und ich* (1957), and with Nicolas Schöffer's book, *Die kybernetische Stadt* (1969). These three late modernist projects were presented through historical documents, commentaries and quotations mounted on coloured walls, along with Müller's own treatment of the historical material, and models and reinterpretations of the originals.

The Philips Pavilion, a tent-like construction of hyperbolic paraboloids, was designed exclusively for the performance of the *Poème électronique*. During each eight-minute presentation, 500 visitors would be channelled through a *Gesamtkunstwerk* consisting of Varèse's musical composition, Xenakis' spatial design, and Le Corbusier's projection of world history on the interior walls — a multimedia cosmology that began with apes and ended with Le Corbusier's own work. In the Munich Kunstverein, Müller presented a model of the pavilion along with the 'minuscule bureau' from Le Corbusier's large studio at 35 Rue de Sèvres in Paris. This study was a tiny, windowless room constructed according to 'Modulor' proportions (226 × 259 × 226 cm). Containing only a table, a chair, a wall painting and a sculpture mounted on a pedestal, it was intended to accommodate a maximum of four visitors. The confining character of the fully enclosed space was, according to Le Corbusier, supposed to force visitors to be concise and objective. Müller used the measurements of Le Corbusier's study to create an installation doubling its structure. The dimensions of both spaces were identical to those of the 'minuscule bureau', and since they were constructed as mirror images of each other, the second space could only be entered through the first. The latter contained a built-in table like the original but without chairs. Unlike Le Corbusier's coloured design, this space was pure white, with no wall segments or sculpture. The second space reversed this principle. Completely lined with black carpet, it consisted of a black cube whose dimensions the viewer could not easily assimilate.

To enter the white space of Le Corbusier's study, visitors had to pass through a light-activated electric barrier, the only means by which the door could be opened and closed. A second, secured glass door blocked the entrance to the black cube. Only when the first door was closed did the second one open, allowing visitors to enter, and then closing again behind them. Triggered by a motion sensor, Varèse's eight-minute composition *Poème électronique* would then play in the black box. Here, the monumental presentation of world history originally created for the Philips Pavilion was repeated in a space whose door could only be opened by means of an alarm button. Near this installation, Müller displayed Le Corbusier's original 'Modulor' drawings and sketches on a yellow

partition wall along with Varèse's scores as well as quotations
from Le Corbusier on his 'minuscule bureau'.

In the same large hall of the Kunstverein, another late modern
utopia was presented on a low skin-coloured partition wall.
Here, the notion of reproductive hygiene was the central theme
with the vision of the 'cybernetic city' of Paris developed by
Nicolas Schöffer in 1969. The life span of the city's inhabitants
was completely planned out, from the 'value increase in time' to
the 'Centre for Sexual Recreation'. In the Munich exhibition, Müller
presented examples from Schöffer's planning as well as his detailed specifications and graphic models, placing them in relation
to Le Corbusier's synaesthetic pavilion.

In the next room, two enamel panels from Müller's 1990 exhibition at the Galerie Micheline Szwajcer... were mounted on the
wall adjacent to the large exhibition hall on the right. As in the
Szwajcer exhibition, the right-hand panel listed the world 'metropolises' from Le Corbusier's plans for *Villes radieuses*, while the
left-hand panel showed the enlarged cover of a tourist brochure
from Antwerp with a photograph of the cathedral. Müller continued Le Corbusier's list of cities horizontally around the walls of the
room, handwriting his own exhibition locations in chronological
order from 1986 to 1992.

The remaining wall featured a glass vitrine containing other
original documents from Le Corbusier that were placed next
to a long wooden bench. As a counterpoint to Le Corbusier and
Schöffer, Müller also presented one of the prominent opponents
of modernism in a cinematic showcase of Veit Harlan's film,
Anders als du und ich. The director had achieved recognition in
the Nazi era with anti-Semitic agitation films such as *Jud Süss*;
in 1957, the year of Müller's birth, he produced a drama combining
homophobia and the rejection of artistic abstraction in a single
narrative. The film, *Anders als du und ich*, portrays the conversion
of a homosexual abstract artist into a heterosexual representational painter. In Munich, the cinematic showcase presented
posters, film stills and critical reviews of the film. Visitors had to
pass through a plastic tube stretched into a tunnel to enter the
next room, where they were confronted with Müller's own version,
created together with Madeleine Bernstorff — a trailer with a
montage of scenes the motion picture rating organisation FSK
confiscated in the 1950s. *Forgotten Future* reconstructed late
modernism through a tour of its unrealised utopias; Müller traced
the end of these utopias not simply by studying them, but by
producing connections between them.

Kerstin Stakemeier

Philipp Kaiser (ed.), *Christian Phillip Müller*, Ostfildern: Hatje Cantz, 2007.

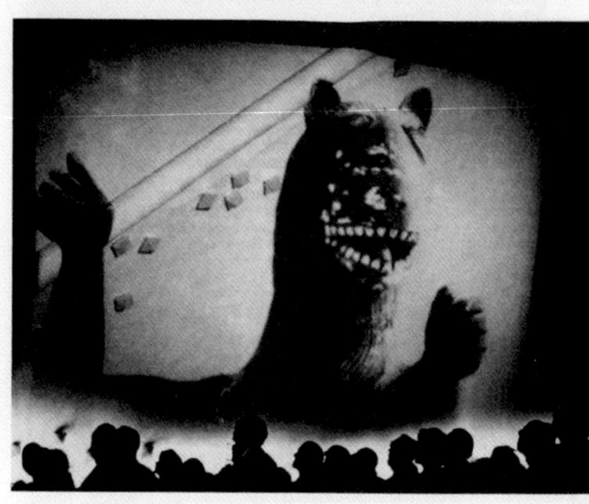

Film programme
Filmmuseum München, Munich, 1992

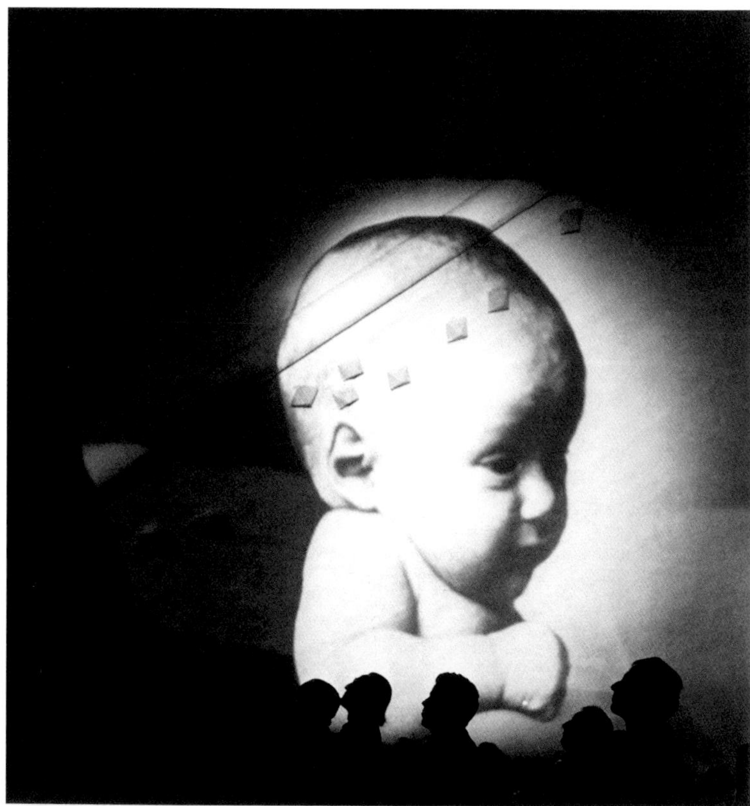

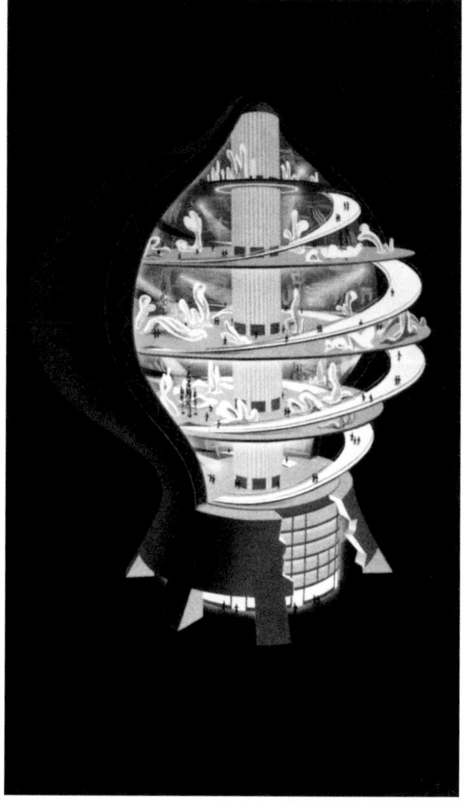

I was spoon-fed with modernism in my upbringing from day one. It was the foundation of my education and my later training as a graphic designer and artist in Switzerland. Kandinsky famously noted that he loves the laws that regulate creativity. In that sense modernism for me can be defined as the production of systems regulating creativity in all areas of life, for instance in Le Corbusier's model of the 'Modulor' as the basic parameter of architecture, his rigid colour schemes and ideal proportions. Artistic production was thus recoded as following preset rules or rational manuals. During the punk era of the late seventies, which also was the time of my development of sexual identity, I emancipated myself from that belief system for the creation of beauty, harmony, containment and purity. The pristine spaces and concomitant discourses of modernism in my view didn't allow for any variations, improvisation, for the contingencies of life, personal conflicts, sexuality, affects, the unforeseen, the irrational and alternative histories. I was interested in the back-side of modernism that I began to mistrust in terms of its universal claims. ▷

Philips Pavilion, Brussels, 1958
Projection

Nicolas Schöffer
Design for the Centre
for Sexual Recreation, c. 1958

Vergessene Zukunft – Forgotten Future, 1992
8 photographs, silkscreen print

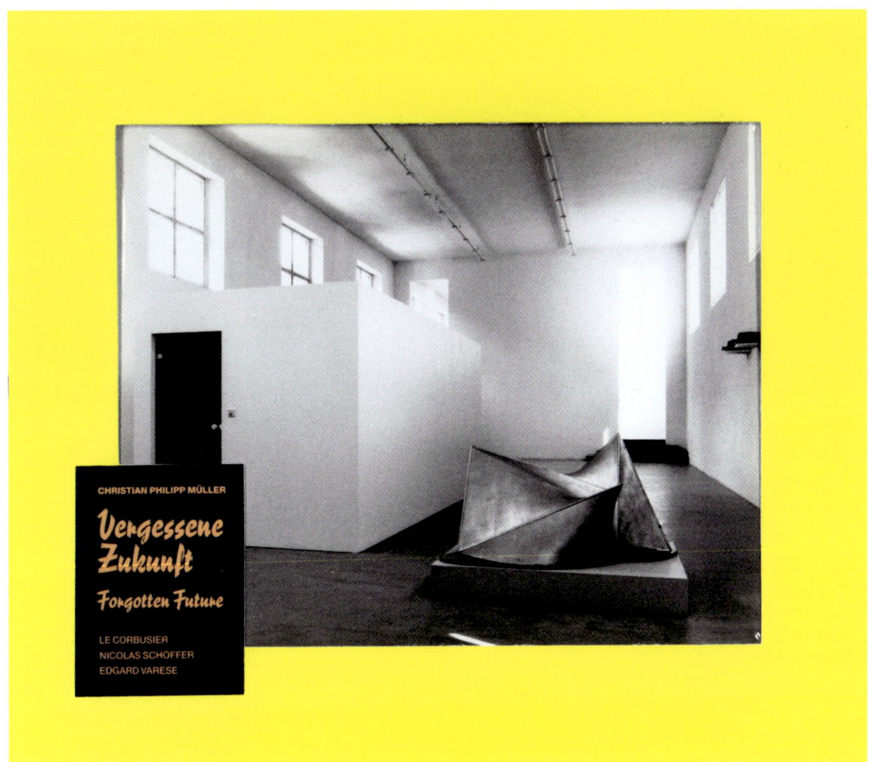

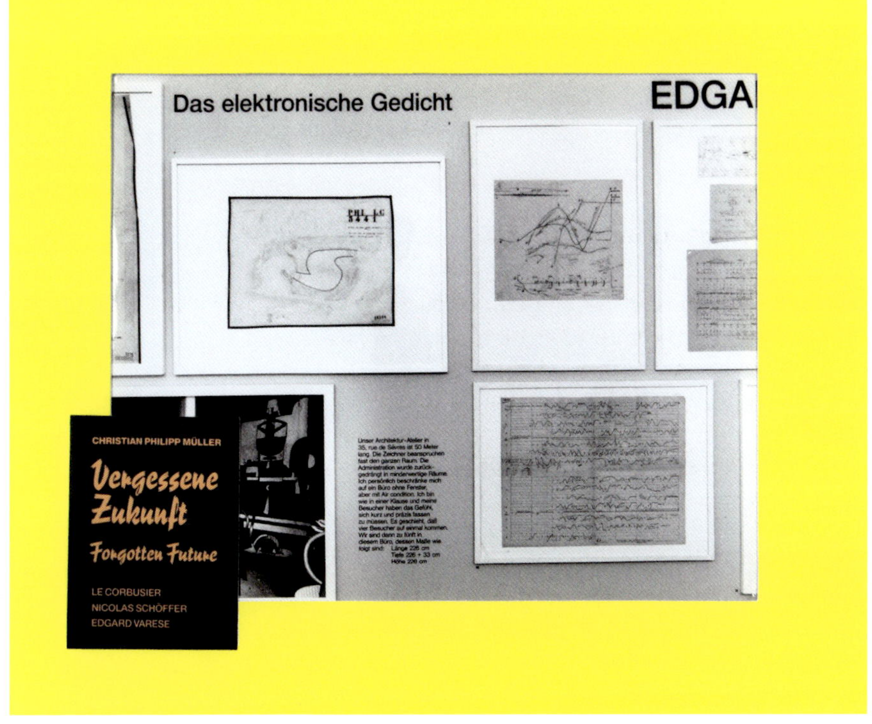

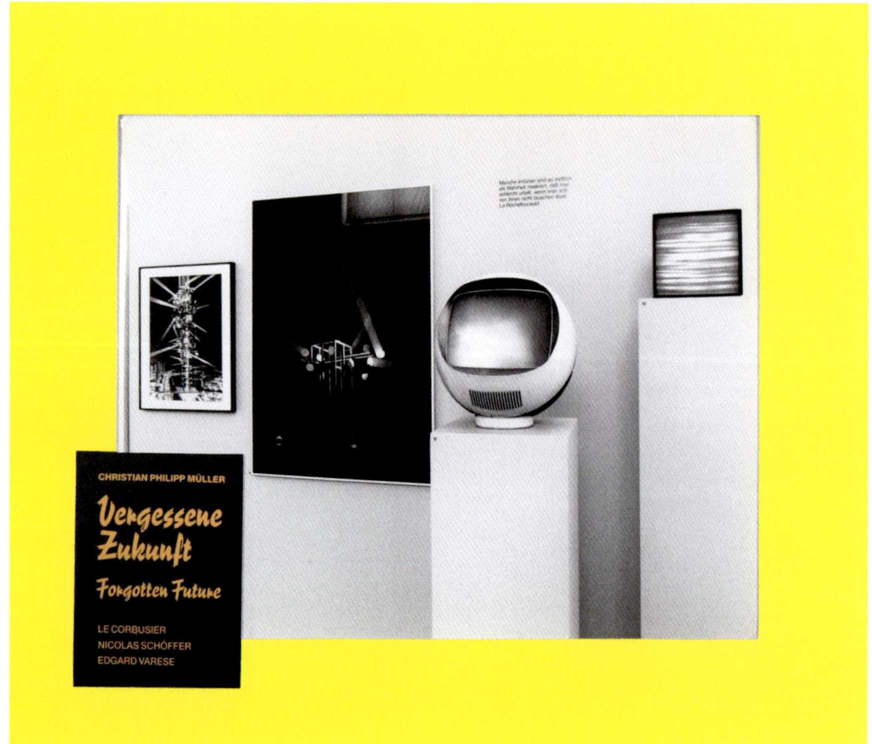
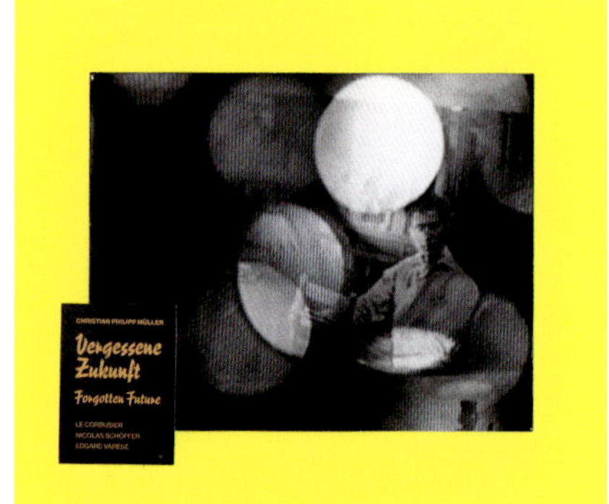
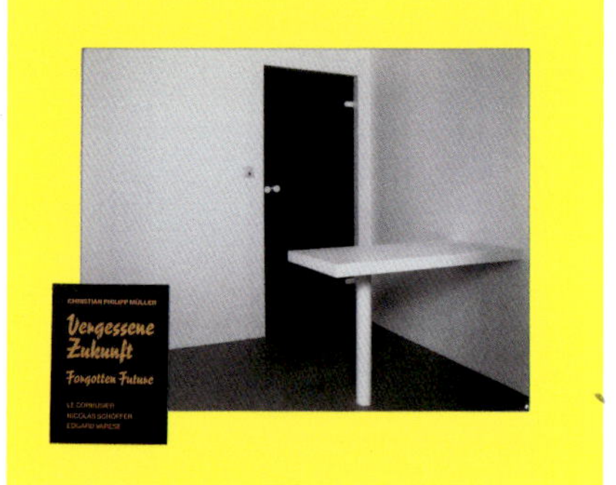

Against that backdrop my project *Forgotten Future* (1992)
in turning to Le Corbusier, Edgar Varèse, Nikolas Schöffer
and Veit Harlan can be described as an attempt at leading
the viewer into the impasses of modernism and at the
same time proposing a provisional way out by addressing
the nostalgia for what once was regarded as a promising
future.

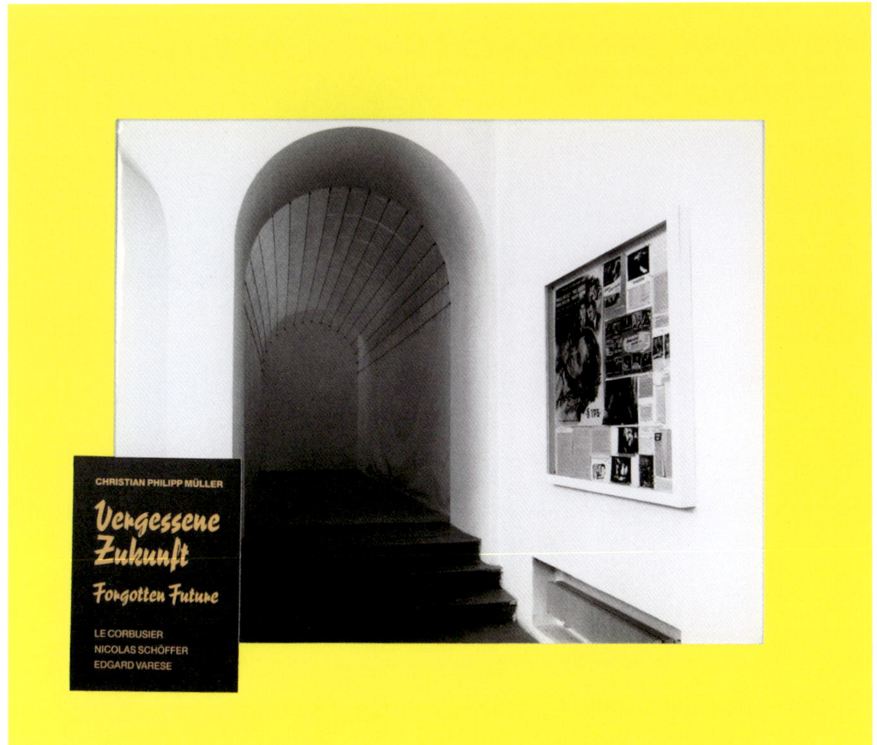

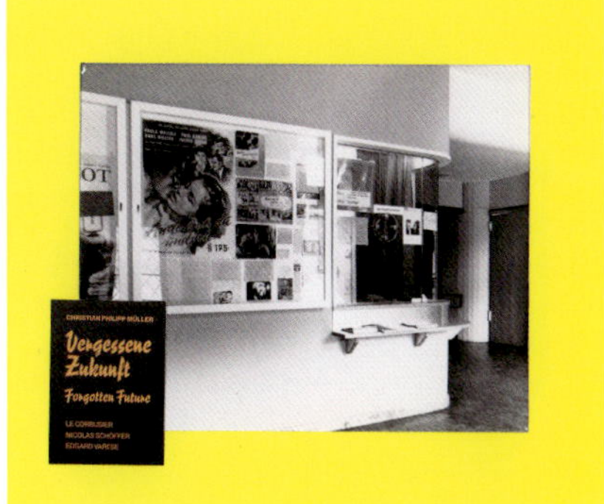

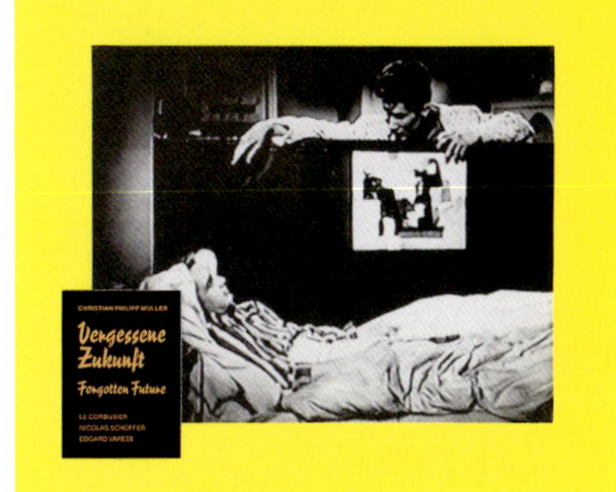

I set up an exhibition that paradoxically tried to reverse the memory of modernism in terms of a promotion of things to come. At the same time I am quite aware that this reversal based on a deconstruction of the components of the synaesthetic Philips Pavilion created by Le Corbusier, Schöffer and Varèse still takes place within the confines of the institutional space of the 'white cube' that is founded on and indebted to modernism's ideology of humanism and progress. I integrated a reference to Harlan's reactionary film — from the year I was born (1957) — that during the Cold War still propagated that modern art is degenerate exactly to point to the ambivalence of modernism's lingering legacy. ▫

Henrik Olesen

How do I make myself a body?, 2008
Mixed media installation
Collages, prints, various objects (screws, screwdriver,
shoe, spoon, wooden laths) and spatial interventions
Installation views
Galerie Daniel Buchholz, Berlin, 2008

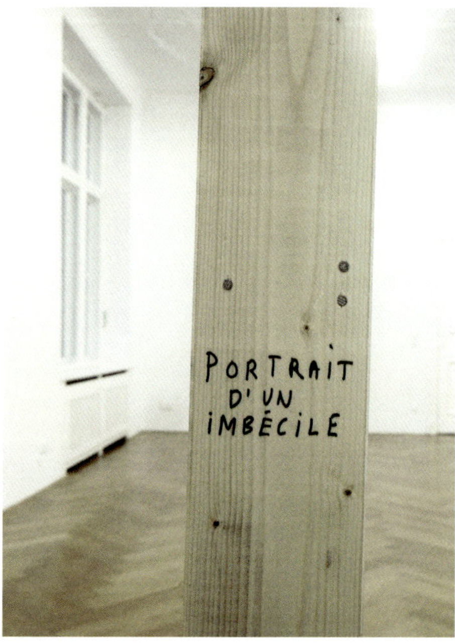

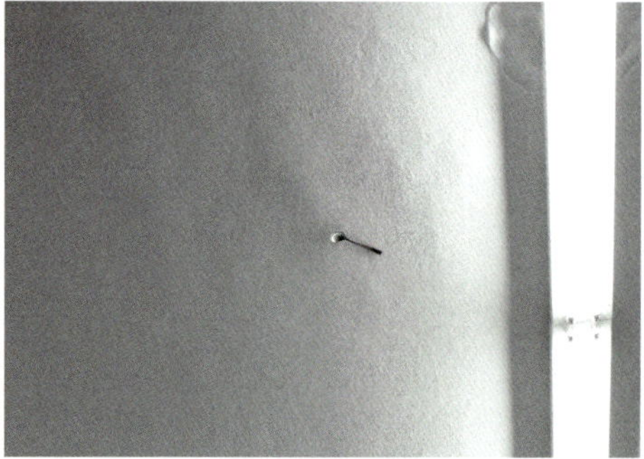

At any rate, you have one (or several)

I am talking about bodies, such as my own body or the bodies
of others, or the combination of my own body with the body of
another body (nearly homologous to my own). Specific to this
project, I have thought about bodies and systems of producing
and reproducing bodies. Honestly, I do find it difficult to accept
the birth of human culture in the knowledge that heterosexual
intercourse produces babies. More remarkable, however, is how
this is secured by a system specifying who may be allowed to
produce or reproduce what and how. Boundaries are constructed
around bodies, and such practices of regulating bodies and body
practices are enforced through a corpus or body of law. The politic
of bodies also begets issues and raises questions of property.

How do I make myself a body?

Seemingly symptomatic of the twentieth century, the life of British
scientist and mathematician Alan Turing (1912–1954) is an indeci-
pherable puzzle of diverse but deeply intertwined themes and
events, both historical and personal. But nevertheless the story did
offer me a departure from the normative notion of 'fixed bodies'
and a way to expand toward fantasies of 'possible bodies'. In this
project, the disassembled and reassembled biography of Alan
Turing serves as a framework for associative concepts of a reified,
postmodern body — whether male/female or otherwise.

Computers, servants, sex

In 1936 Turing published a theoretical model of a machine,
which was to constitute the base of all post-war computing.
His diagram reduced the working of anything and everything
to a set of symbolic configurations based on the absolute yes/no
logic of binary code. All subsequent computers are implemen-
tations of this most general of general-purpose machines.
The Turing Machine is universal, pure function: both 'the works'
and the 'that it works' of any computation. It is a virtual system,
capable of simulating the behaviour of any other machine,
even, and including itself.... It only actually exists when it has a
specific task to perform, and then it is no longer itself, but simply
whatever it is doing.

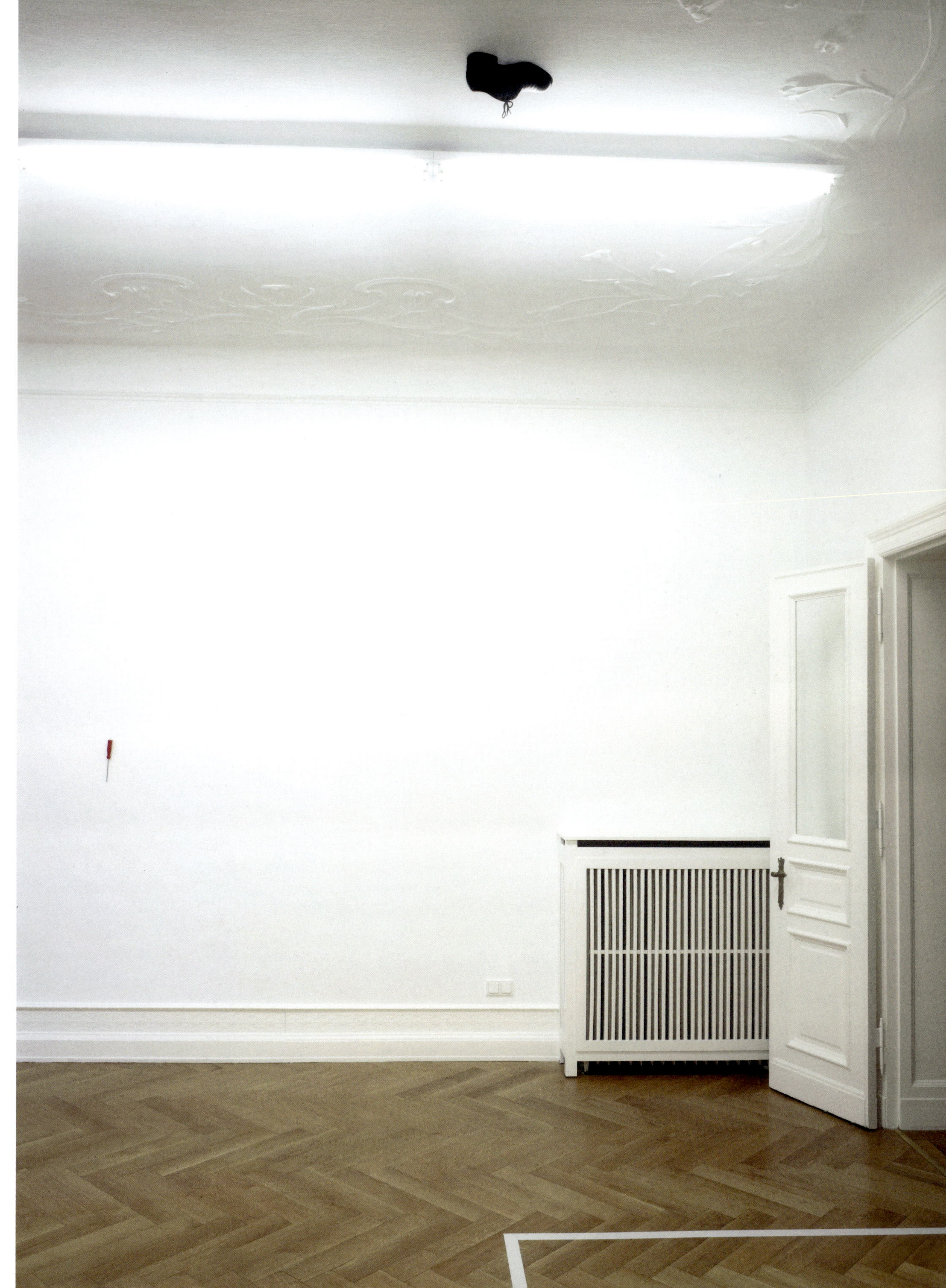

THE BODY
UNDERNEATH
THE SKIN
IS AN OVERHEATED
FACTORY

X LIVED FOR A LONG
TIME WITHOUT
STOMACH,
WITHOUT INTESTINES,
ALMOST WITHOUT
LUNGS, WITH A TORN
OESOPHAGUS,
WITHOUT A BLADDER,
AND WITH SHATTERED
RIBS.

BUT DIVINE MIRACLES
ALWAYS
RESTORED WHAT
HAS BEEN DESTROYED.

X CLAIMS THAT HE NO
LONGER HAS
A BRAIN OR NERVES
OR CHEST OR
STOMACK OR GUTS.

ALL HE HAS LEFT IS
THE SKIN AND BONES
OF A
DISORGANIZED BODY.

THESE ARE HIS OWN
WORDS.

I PREFER YOUR
NOSE TO ALL YOUR
ORGANS
O MY LOVE
IT IS THE THRONE OF
FUTURE KNOWLEDGE

4 Posters, 2008
Digital prints

For years I had wanted to do something on Alan Turing. His biography interested me for the way in which a masochistic subject could control his suffering, setting the simultaneity of submission and self-empowerment in relation to queer and fragile constructions of identity. The central aspect is the disappearance of Turing's body parallel to the invention of the computer body. The invention of the binary code is naturally a reference to queer theory. Eve Kosofsky Sedgwick, for example, has examined how our culture is marked by the duality of 'homo' and 'hetero'. ▷

Turing worked as a servant of society for the Allied authorities during the Second World War, decoding German military communications. After the war, in 1952, he was arrested and subjected to female hormone therapy as treatment for his homosexuality. Turing became impotent and grew breasts. The treatment also caused waves of depression and despair. On 8 June 1954, Turing was found dead; he had apparently committed suicide, with a cyanide-laced apple left half-eaten beside his bed. Some have suggested that Turing was re-enacting a scene from *Snow White*, his favourite fairytale, but because Turing's homosexuality would have been perceived as a security risk, others suggest the possibility of assassination.

How many BODIES are there? How many are you?
The body of Alan Turing became the site of oppressive scientific interventions and his story exposes heterosexuality as an incessant and panicked imitation of its own naturalised idealisation. But while this example provides us with a disturbing document of sexuality and gender-based objectifications, it also demonstrates more emancipated models of the (post-)human subject and models of human relations that displace the binary constructions of modernist epistemologies: thinking machines and artificial intelligence. From the (injured) Turing body springs forth the computer body and concepts of other possible bodies and intelligences. That is a re-constitution and re-sexualisation not only of the Turing body but of all kinds of bodies!

'When you will have made him a body without organs, then you will have delivered him from all his automatic reactions and restored him to his true freedom.' (Antonin Artaud)
Henrik Olesen

Imitation/Enigma, 2008
Box, adhesive tape, rope, padding material, blanket

Apple (Ghost), 2008
Computer, plastic sheeting

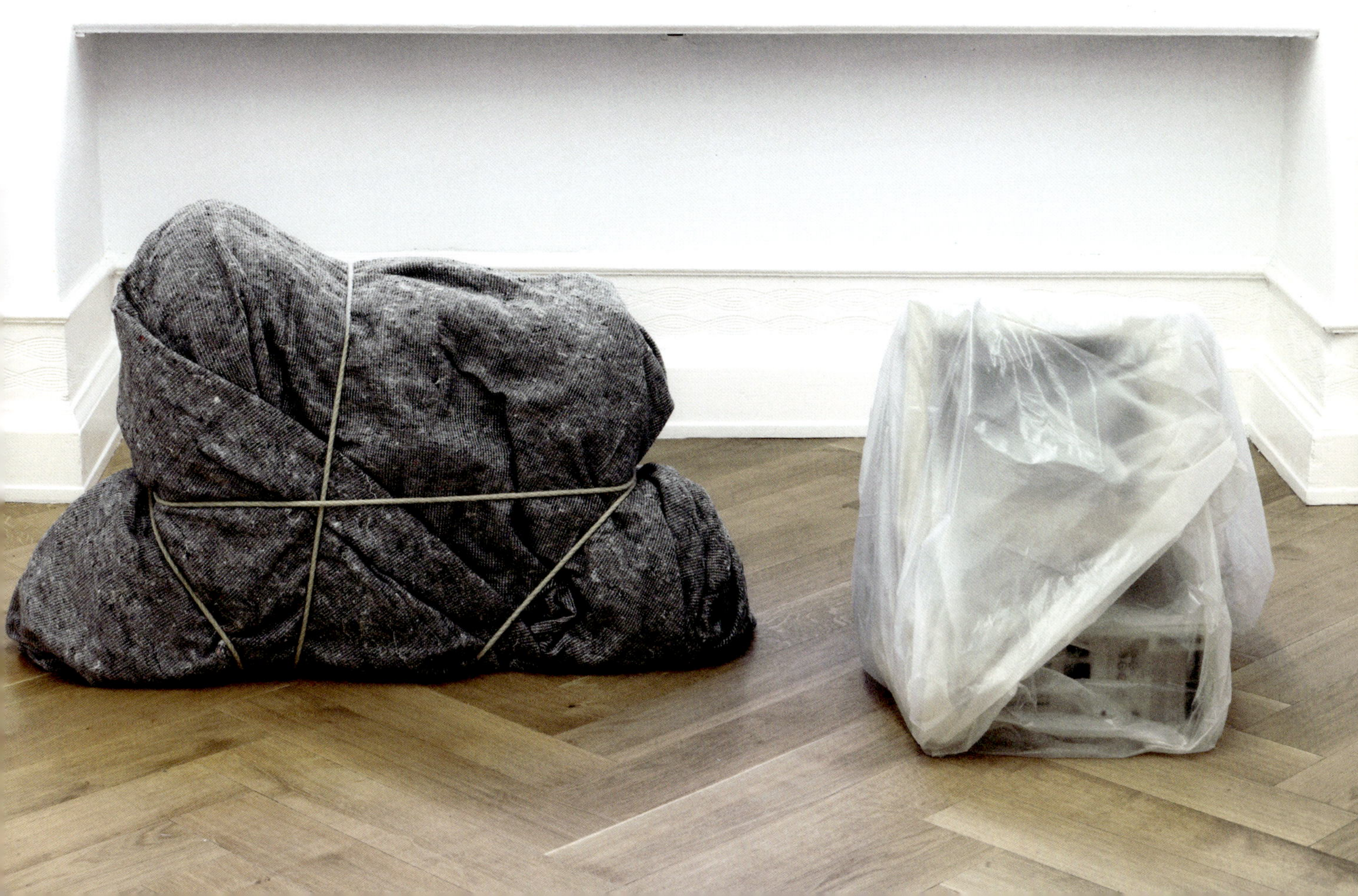

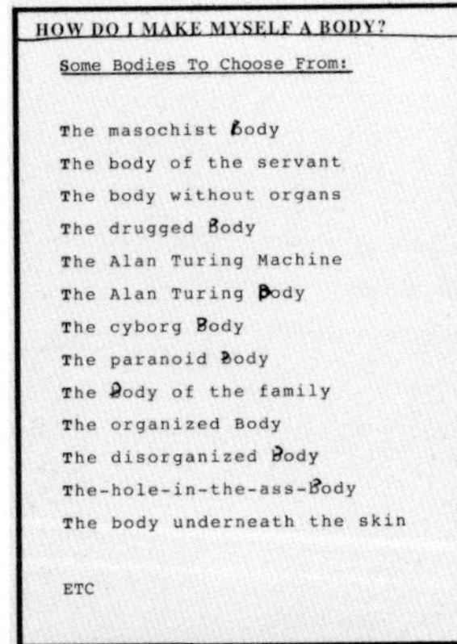

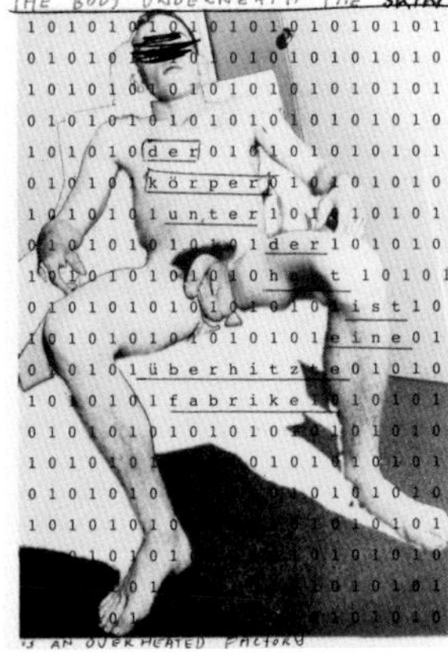

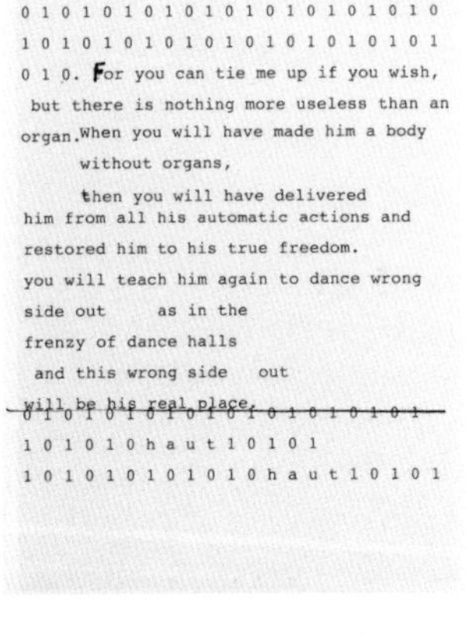

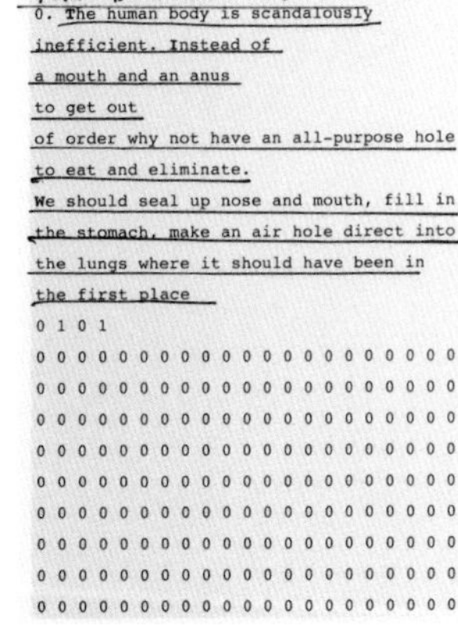

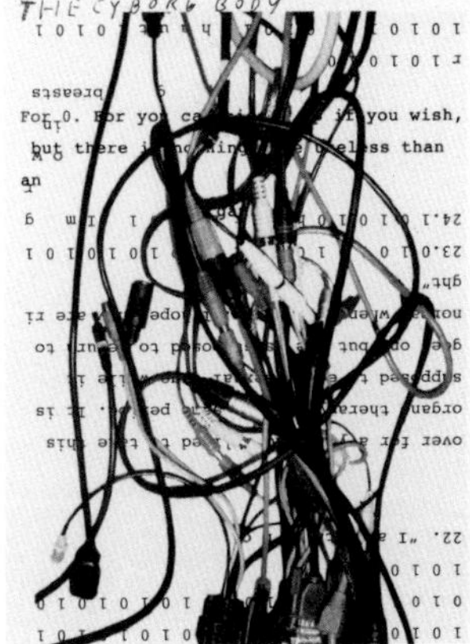

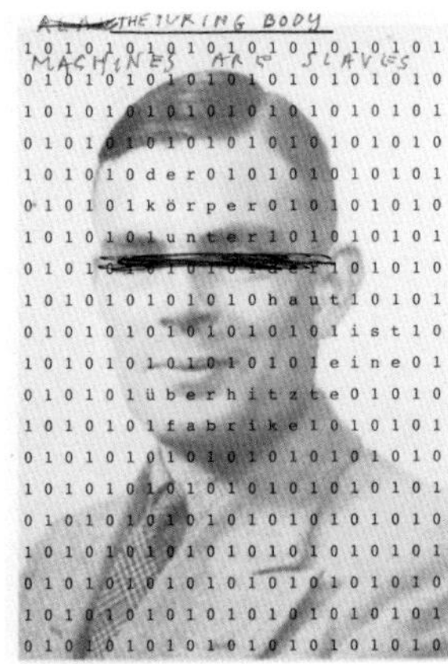

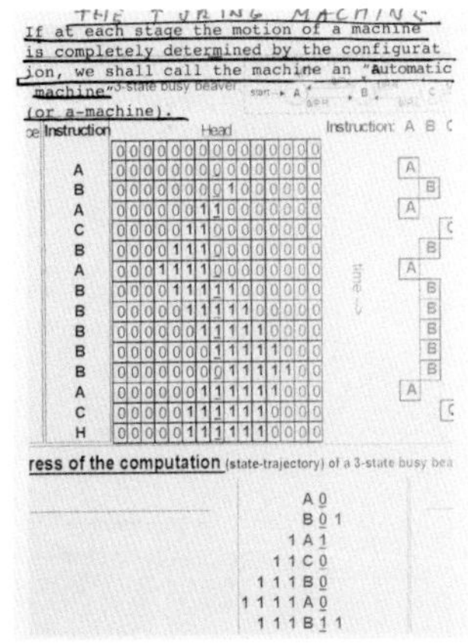

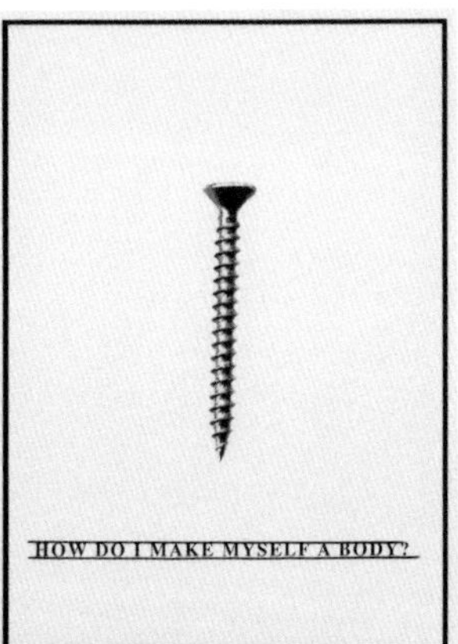

How do I make myself a body?, 2008
16 of 19 computer collages

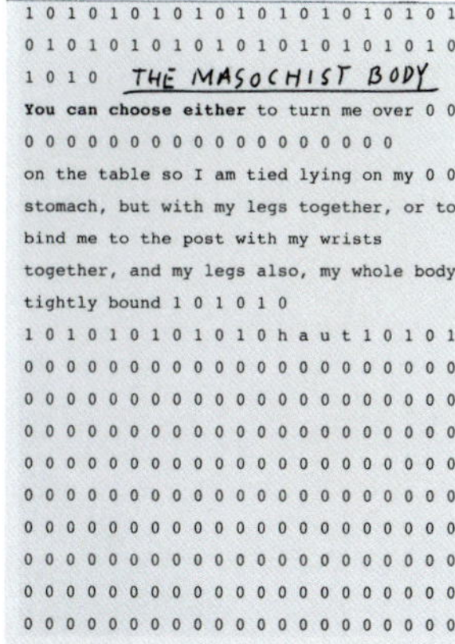

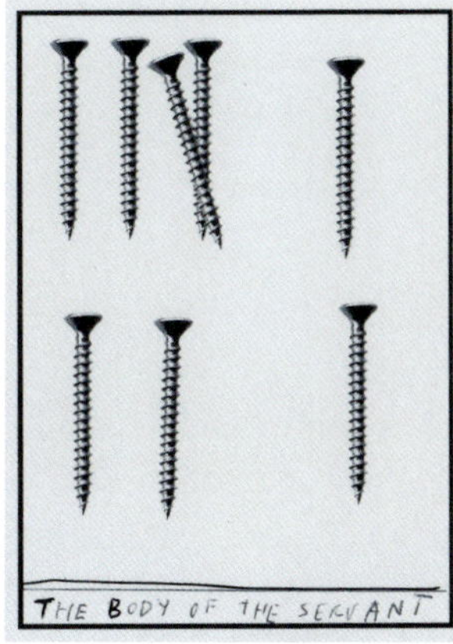

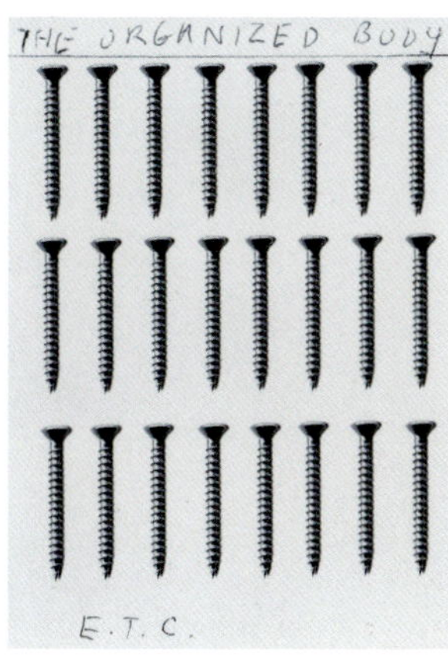

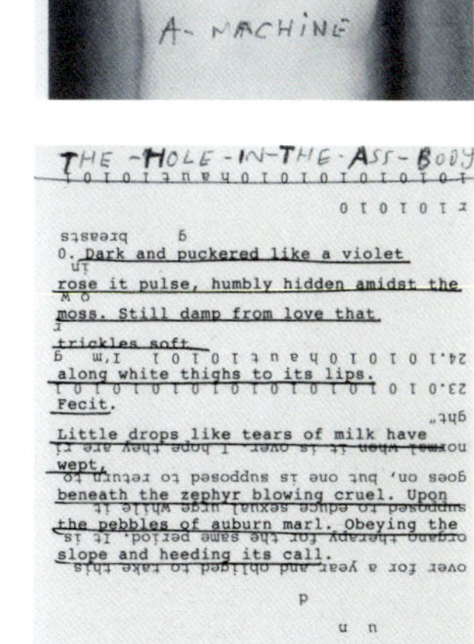

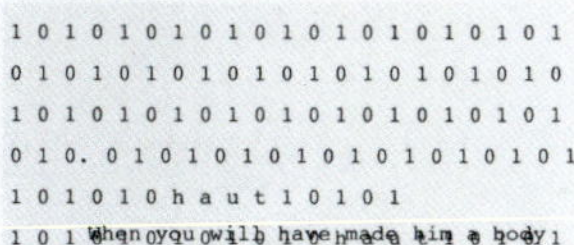
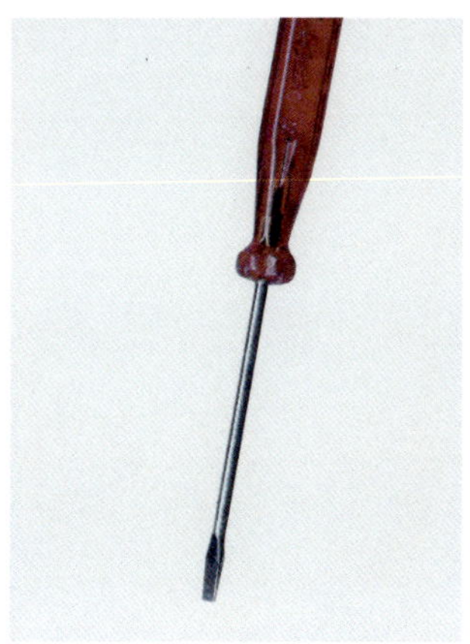

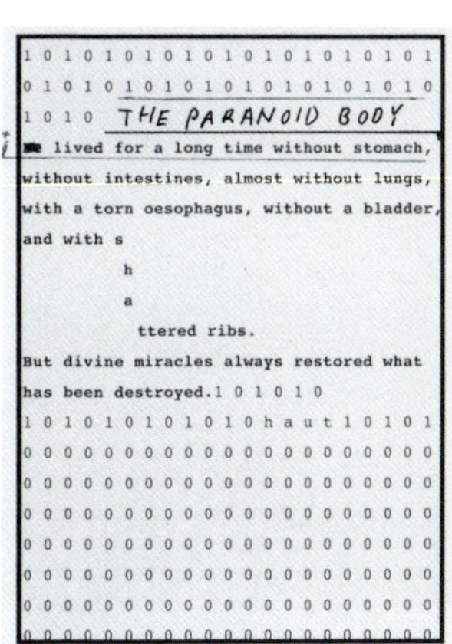

My aim is to approach and present the body, along with its production and reproduction, in terms of social images: *the body of the servant*, *the body without organs*, *the drugged body*, *the paranoid body*, *the body of the family*, *the disorganized body*, *the hole-in-the-ass body*, *the body underneath the skin*. The result should be a view of the body as multiplied and sexualised. It's all about constructing a postmodern body! ▷

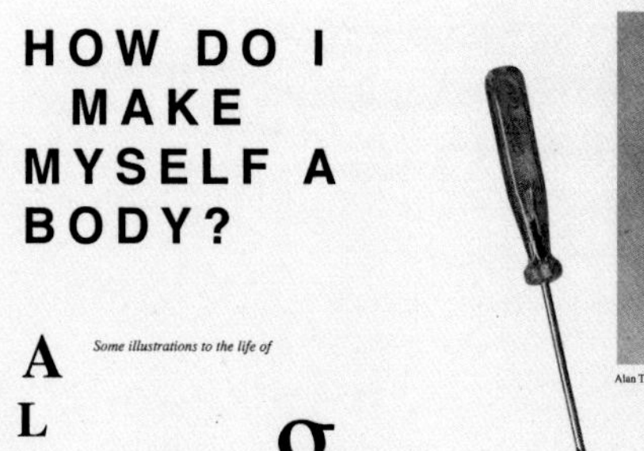

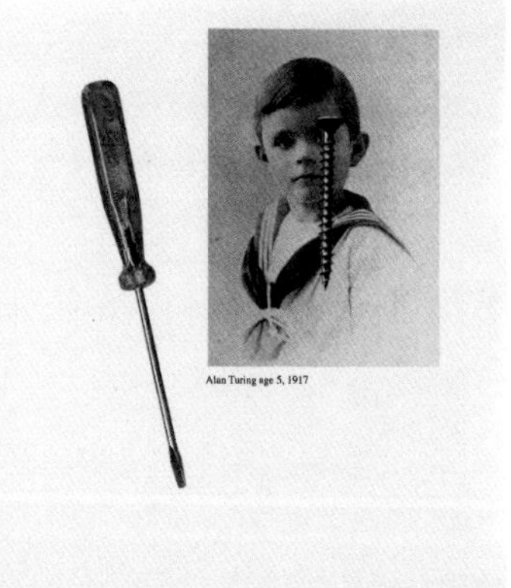

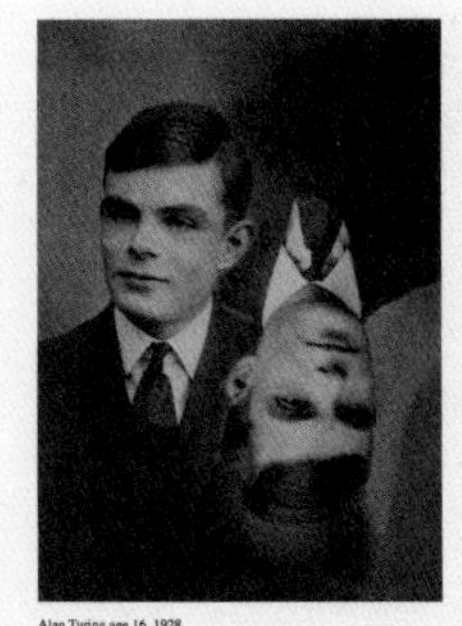

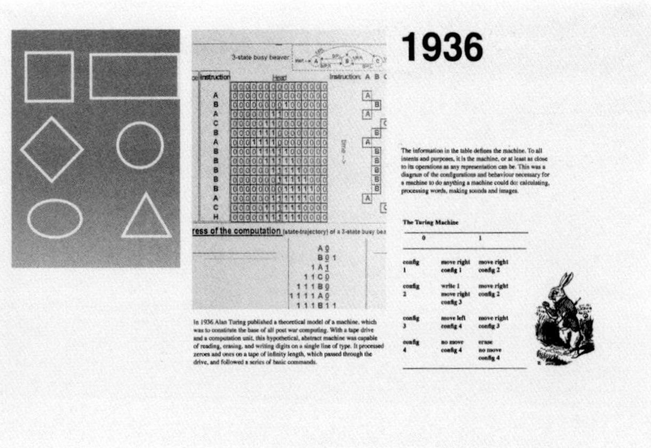

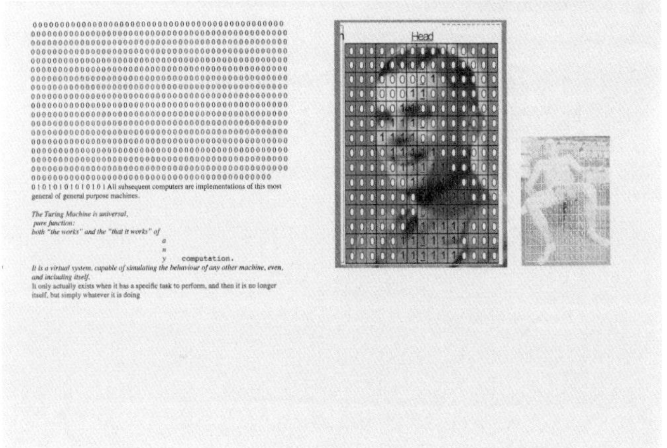

Some illustrations to the life of Alan Turing, 2008
8 of 16 digital prints

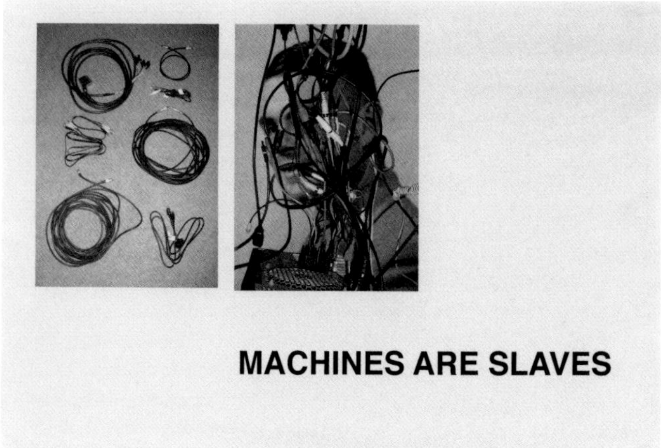

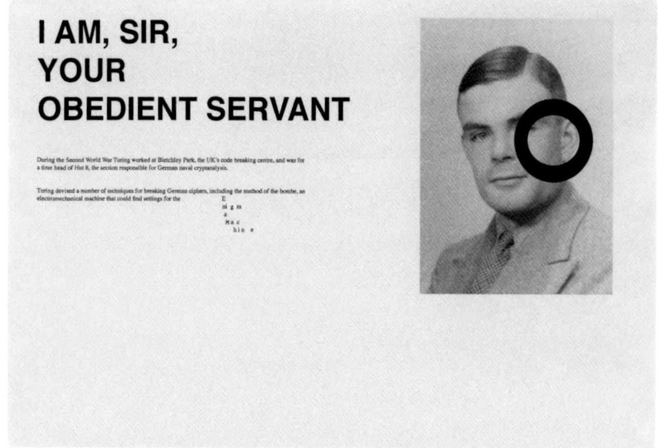

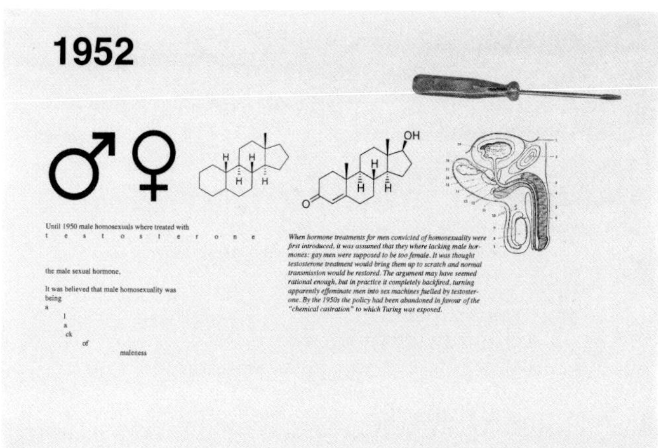

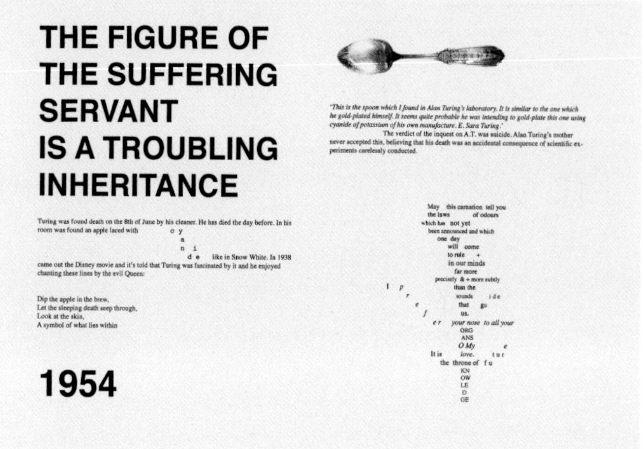

My concern in regard to Turing is how bodies dissolve. That is why I have incorporated references to modernist fictive bodies, as invoked by the Futurists, Guillaume Apollinaire, Antonin Artaud and in Freud's files. I was looking for people and statements of crucial importance to modern research into the production of identity. Picabia's machines put in an appearance in this connection, as do Philippe Soupault's *Portrait d'un imbécile* and Man Ray's *The Enigma of Isidore Ducasse* — a reference, of course, to Turing's breaking of the Enigma code. I had the feeling of moving around Turing's ghostlike body and wanted to weave around it a number of traces, lines, narratives and codes evocative of modernity. □

Paulina Olowska

**Collaged Stryjeńska. Posters, Illustrations
and Paintings by and about Zofia Stryjeńska**
Exhibition curated by Paulina Olowska
Schinkel Pavilion, 5th Berlin Biennial, 2008

Zofia Stryjeńska was never described as a true modernist.
But when one looks at her works or reads her diaries it
seems obvious to me that there is a strong urge to create
a new language of forms, references, geometry and abstraction. For my installation at the Neue National Gallery
and the Schinkel Pavilion during the Berlin Biennial 2008
I tried to impose the idea that her work is historically
rooted in modernism. Although she worked with figuration
and narration, the style and way of rendering images
was completely innovative. She tried to link applied arts
and high art, and referred to Slavic paganism as a method
of freeing herself from academic traditions. ▷

Paulina Olowska's series of large-format tableaux entitled *Zofia
Stryjeńska* is a painterly dialogue with the extensive oeuvre
of Polish artist Zofia Stryjeńska (1891–1974). Stryjeńska's paintings,
which draw on Art Déco, Slavic mythology and folk art from
the Tatra mountains, are joyful celebrations of idealised, bizarre
worlds from the past. The unique imagination and sense of
optimism that radiate from her paintings have fascinated Olowska
since her initial encounter with the late artist's work. As a result,
Olowska has created a series of monumental grayscale replicas
based on a choice of exemplary gouaches and paintings by
Stryjeńska found in the collections of Poland's national museums
in Warsaw and Krakow. A portrait painting of Stryjeńska by
Olowska adds to the ensemble. In using grayscale, Olowska
focuses on Stryjeńska's vibrant and contrasting compositions
and spatial arrangements. Furthermore, according to the artist,
evoking black and white reproductions from books enables
a distancing that opens new possibilities for her to both enter
Stryjeńska's work in a respectful way and investigate what
is of most interest to her in these paintings: the constellations
of strange characters with their elaborate dress codes, the
representations of animals and nature, and the deliberate con-
fusion of gender stereotypes. In Stryjeńska's paintings, what
at first sight appears to be a rather traditionalist representation
of a historical event becomes, upon closer examination, the
point of departure for an idiosyncratic narrative borne from the
imagination.

In the exhibition curated by Paulina Olowska at the Schinkel
Pavilion for the 5th Berlin Biennial, she creates a frame in which
her own paintings from the series *Zofia Stryjeńska* provide a
background for original works by Polish painter Zofia Stryjeńska.
Olowska lines the Schinkel Pavilion with a painted floor piece,
based on the design of the Polish Pavilion at the 1925 International
Exhibition of Decorative Arts in Paris, for which Stryjeńska
conceived and displayed her paintings. The exhibition *Collaged
Stryjeńska* is the first presentation of Stryjeńska's works in a
contemporary art context and includes her paintings, but also
a small collection of mass-produced items that show how deeply
Stryjeńska's imagery seeped into popular cultural in Poland.
The display in the Schinkel Pavilion's glass-encased octagon
cannot help recall the 1925 Polish Pavilion and, with it, Olowska's
organisation of the artworks in space attempts to underline the
energy and openness of composition that Stryjeńska suggested
in her paintings.

Zofia Stryjeńska was an important member of the Polish
art scene in the 1920s and 1930s and an eccentric personality
who refused to be constrained by social roles and rules. Too naïve-
folksy for the formally radical 'modernist' avant-garde, she was,
on the other hand, too freethinking and innovative in the eyes
of patriotic and nationalist neo-folk artists. Typical of Stryjeńska's
paintings, drawings and murals is their narrative and illustrative
style, which incorporates the repertoire of international art deco.
The artist's favourite subjects include Slavic pagan myths, popular
Catholic piety, Polish folklore, expressive country-dances and
colourful regional costumes. Yet her treatment of these motifs was
highly imaginative and inventive — she created her own Slavic

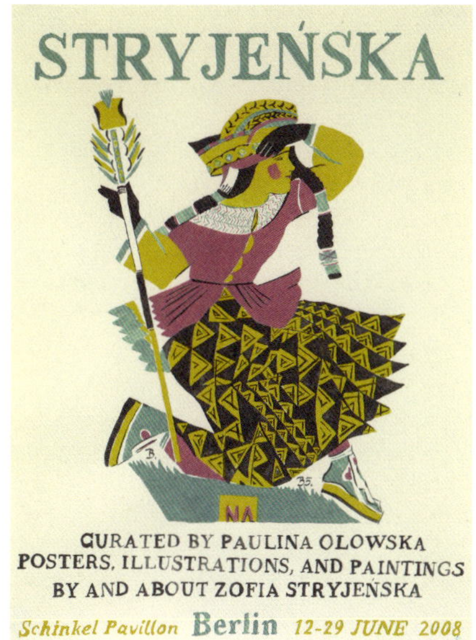

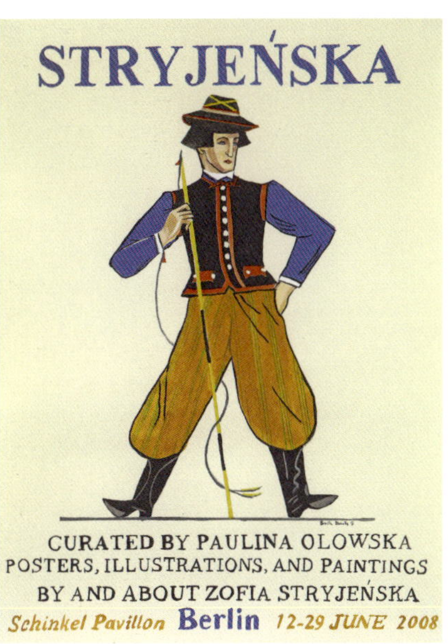

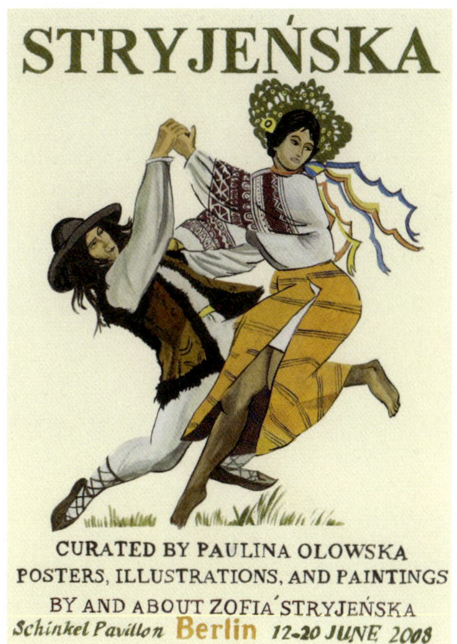

Exhibition posters, 2008

deities, for instance, and portrayed contented peasant women in self-confidently erotic poses. Stryjeńska's participation in the International Exhibition of Decorative Arts in Paris, where she furnished the main room of the Polish pavilion with six large-format paintings depicting rural life and the seasons, marked the zenith of her artistic career. After the Second World War, not least because she refused to join the state-loyal Union of Visual Artists in communist Poland, Stryjeńska immigrated to Switzerland, where she gradually sank into oblivion, while her work was absorbed into Polish popular culture. It was not until 1989, after the collapse of communism in Poland, that her diaries were published and her work began to receive some of the attention and recognition it deserves.

What fascinates Paulina Olowska, curator of the exhibition, about Stryjeńska is above all her contemporariness, both in attitude and working method, as well as the breadth of her artistic production. Stryjeńska not only painted and drew; she also illustrated children's books and calendars, and was a prolific designer of fashion, carpets, posters, toys, stage sets and theatre costumes.
Silke Baumann

5th Berlin Biennial for Contemporary Art (When things cast no shadow): Short Guide – Day, Berlin: KW Institute for Contemporary Art, 2008, pp. 132–33.

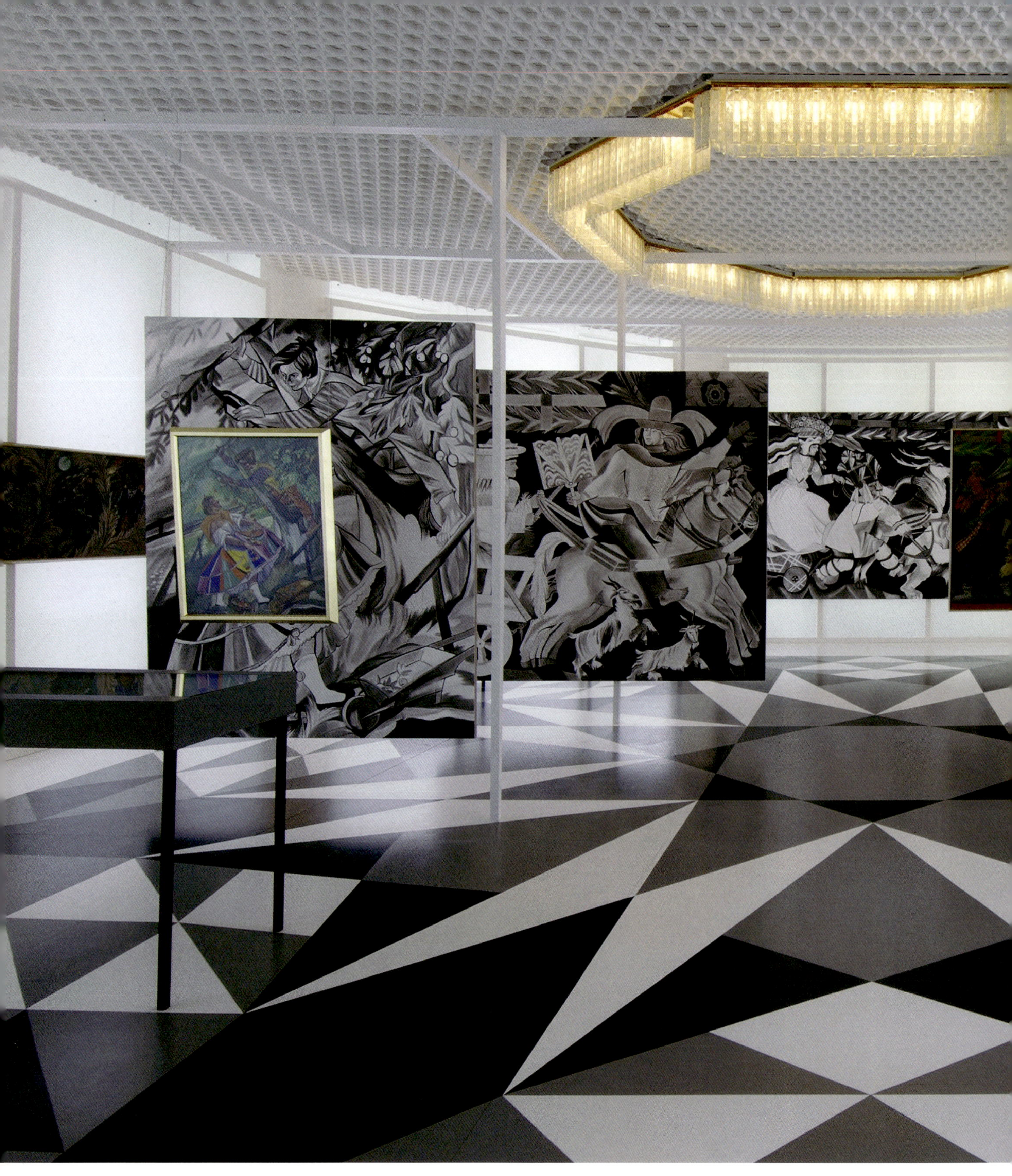

Installation view
Schinkel Pavilion, Berlin, 2008

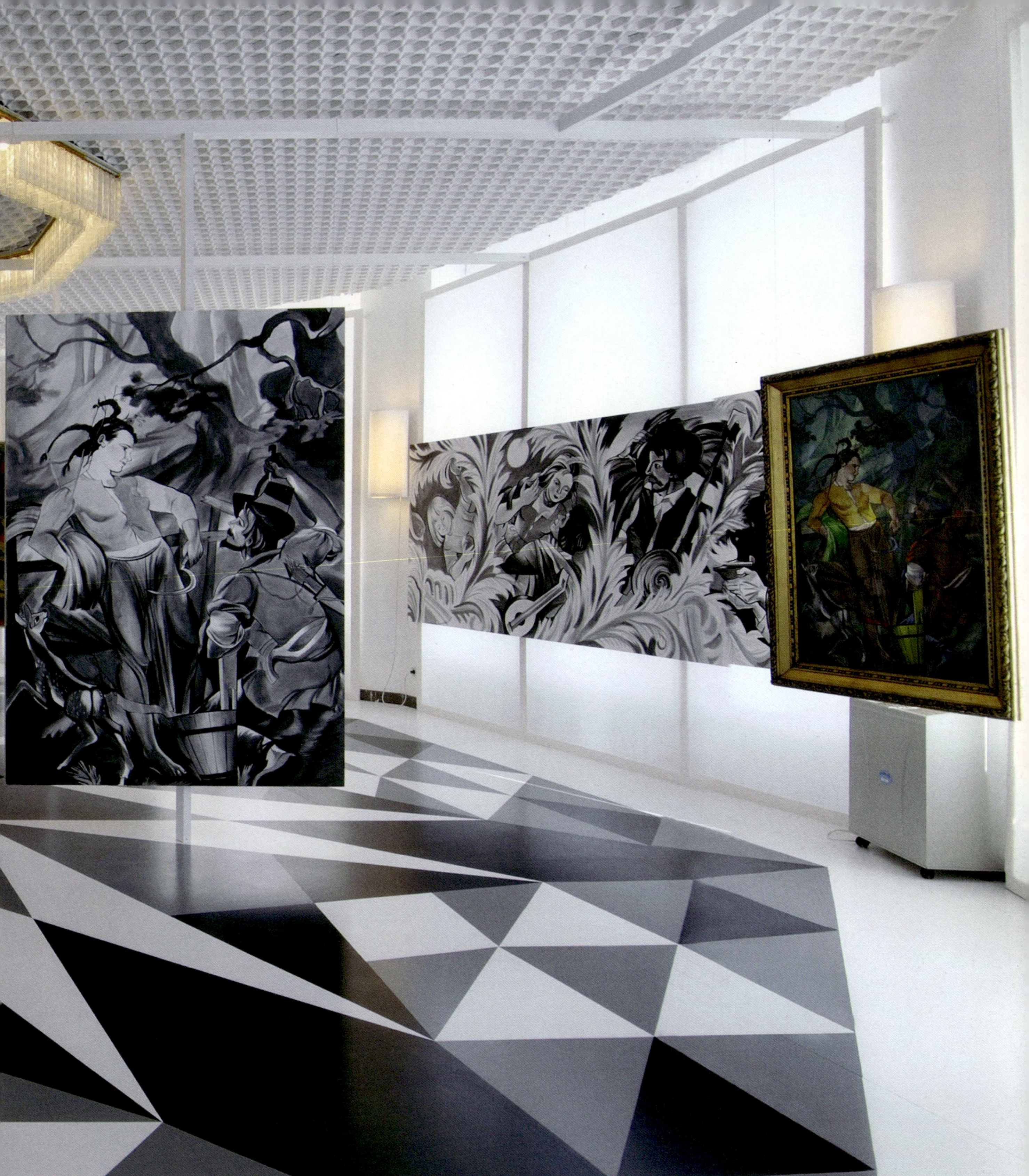

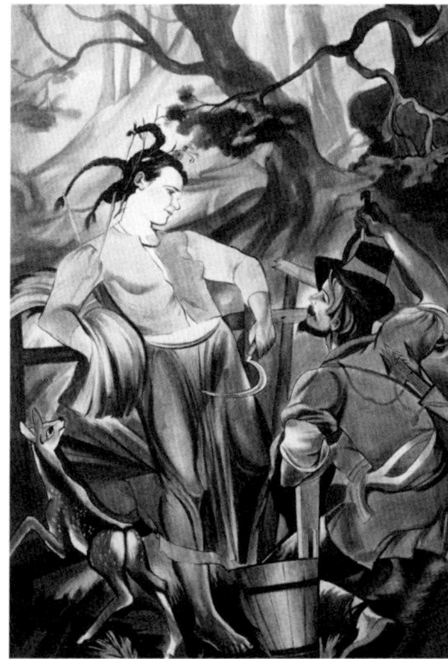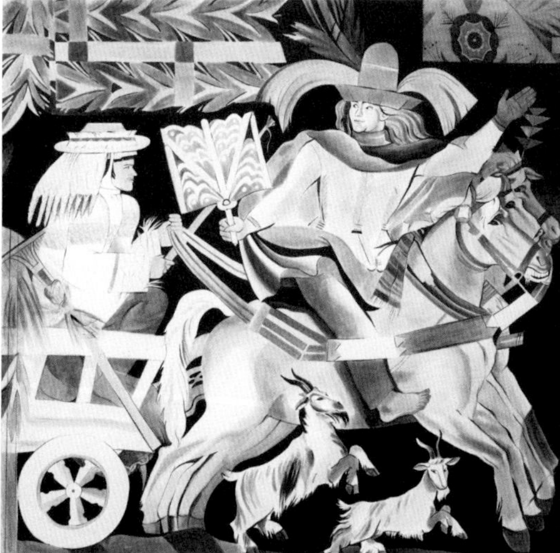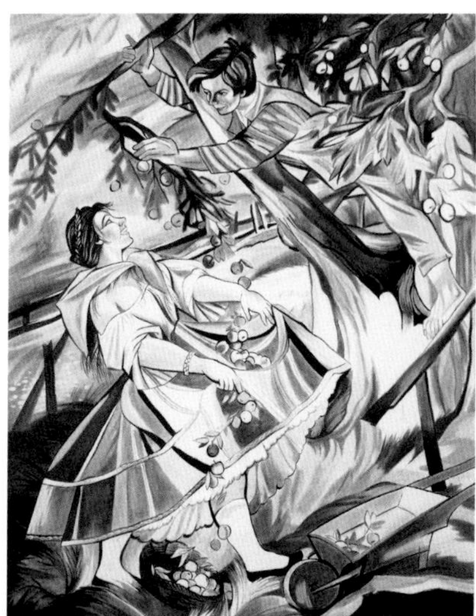

Zofia Stryjeńska, 2008
3 of 6 paintings

The borderlines between official modernism and classifi-
cations of minor gestures that need to be challenged
define the core of my work. In the case of Stryjeńska,
I used to think that even without knowing her background
one could take her work as contemporary. She uses
references freely, reinterprets figuration and borders on
illustration and pastiche. But when I think about it now,
she is too idealistic to be part of our own time, because
today we have to hide behind the idealism of others.

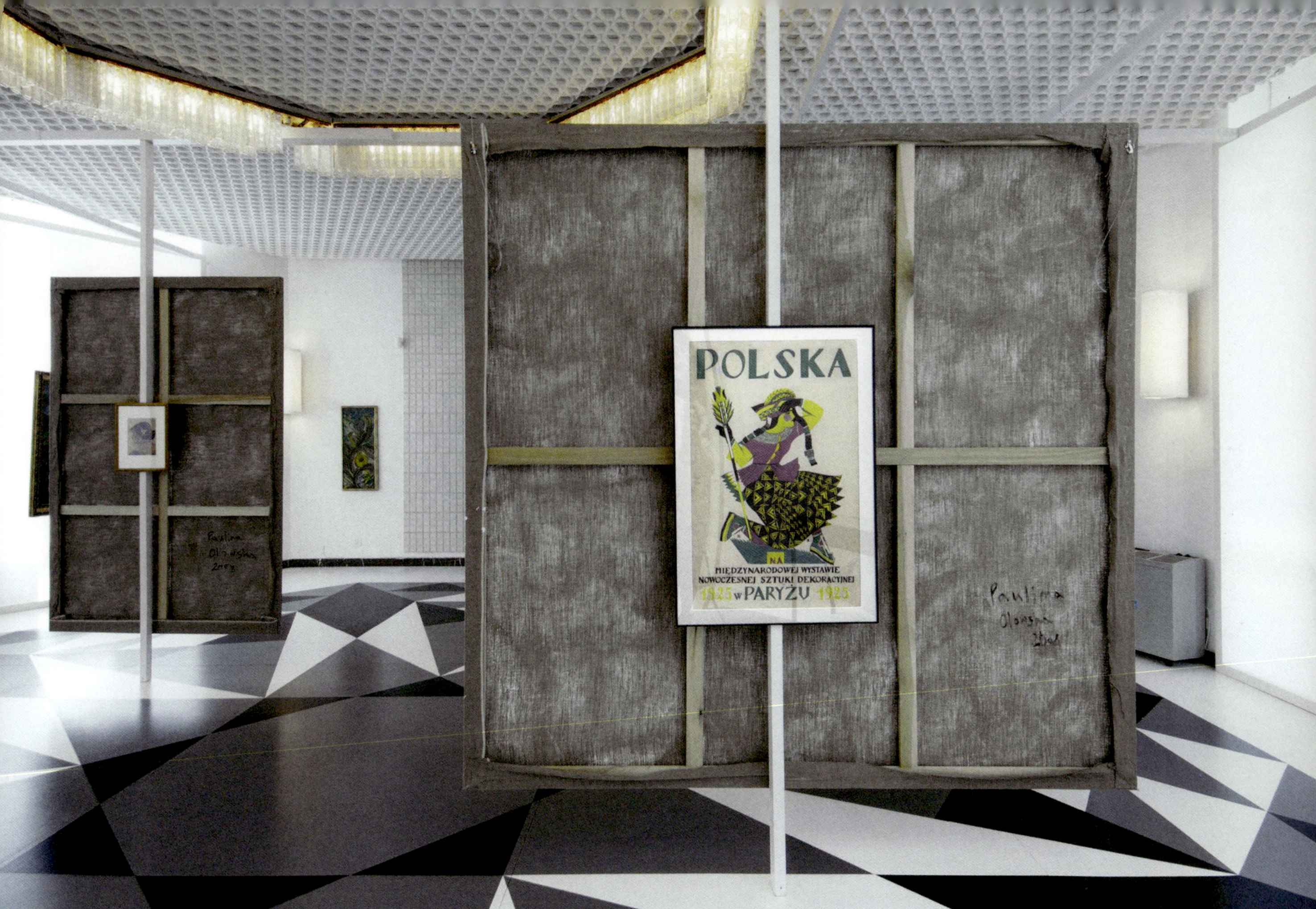

Installation view
Schinkel Pavilion, Berlin, 2008

For five years I had experienced modernism through a certain building in Warsaw. I decided to reinvestigate modernism since it was collapsing in front of my eyes. Living in Eastern Europe in the mid-nineties meant seeing the new capitalism demolishing the old world of social modernity that surrounded it. This could be observed in architecture, advertising, display and design. Of course what I had actually experienced were only the leftovers of modernity, but maybe that is exactly what made me daydream about its utopias and fantasies. I do not live in that building any more. All of the above created a new form of modernism that needs to be investigated. □

Falke Pisano

Abstraction is not a historical issue. Abstraction is always a process and as such it is inseparably related to transformation. And transformation is still a crucial moment in any form of circulation or exchange. How these moments of transformation can be organised is what I try to work on. Be it the transformation of form and figures in communication or of structures of perception. The notion of time is a crucial element in the organisation of these transformations, and in the permutation of significance, but there is always the dimension of affect as well. Both time and affect are reflected in the subject-object relation, which I take as the basic set of positions in the transformational moment. ▷

Since 2005 Falke Pisano has produced some nine works in the form of a lecture, six of which she has performed. In all her lectures Pisano investigates similar topics and will sometimes return to the same sculpture, such as Barnett Newman's *The Broken Obelisk* (1963). In *Concrete Abstractions* (2005), a lecture including a power-point presentation, she examines the various installation contexts of *The Broken Obelisk* and how they affect its meaning. In *Studio Lecture 1* (2006) Pisano enlarges on the subject with reference to other case studies, including photographs of sculptures by Eduardo Chillida and atom bombs transformed into sculptures. She addresses two basic issues: how does an object exist in different conditions and how can she formulate existences that could be articulated as objects? As described in the context of an exhibition in Paris, Pisano's 'lecture-performances, text-based videos, objects and photocopied publications are the elements in a body of work that is distinctly influenced by the practice of writing. Although mainly text-based, Pisano's work displays a strong concern with the existence and features of concrete objects, and in particular abstract concrete objects.'[1] On the basis of books like Wilhelm Worringer's *Abstraction and Empathy*, Pisano constructs a theory as to 'why the movement of a kinetic sculpture is in certain cases caused by the evil inhabiting the work and how man is seduced to place himself inside of an abstraction by a process instigated by perception' ('An Evil Kinetic Sculpture', in *On Abstraction and Evil*, 2005). She later adapted this lecture to form the video *A Lecture on Abstraction and Evil* (2007), in which she describes writing the first version and discovering what did and did not work. In *Chillida (Forms and Feelings)*, 2006, she gives 'a personal account of her emotional reactions' to a series of photographs taken by David Finn of sculptures by Basque artist Chillida. She undertakes to 'trace the relationship between the characteristics of these specific objects, their depiction, the experience of the photographer and his daughter'. Description serves as the method of constructing situations in the live lecture and two-channel video installation *A Sculpture Turning into a Conversation* (2006). In fact using 'language as a means to re-think the potential of abstraction, sculpture and artistic practice, she activates the abstract sculpture as a thought-generating principle and employs the idea of the unstable transforming and disintegrating object as a way to address issues concerning object-qualities, form, construction and engagement'.[2] SB

1   Press release issued by the Galerie Balice Hertling, Paris, 2008.

2   Ibid.

Based on artist's text *(Falke Pisano. Texts 2006–08. Unpublished manuscripts)*.

CONCRETE ABSTRACTIONS
by
Falke Pisano

A lecture about the history and various aspects of abstraction in general and abstract public sculptures in particular, with specific attention paid to the development of new forms of abstraction and the position of abstract public sculptures as autonomous objects.

discussed a.o.:

The Emergence of
Concrete Abstractions

Types of
Concrete Abstractions

Creating Abstraction

Expansion

Possibilities

Placement

Form and Meaning

Context and Meaning

Abstraction and the Viewer

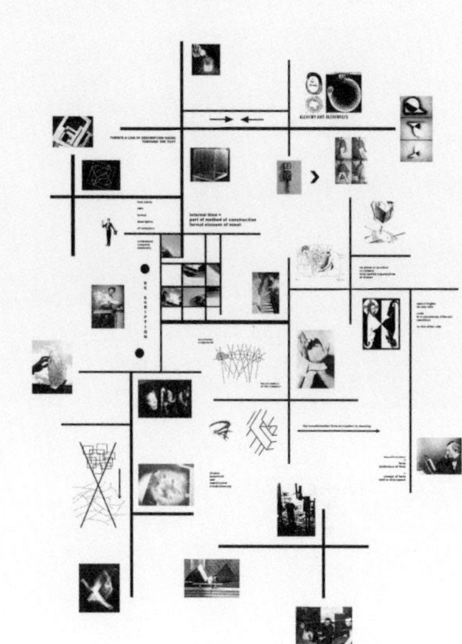

A SCULPTURE TURNING INTO A CONVERSATION

Falke Pisano

Affecting Abstraction

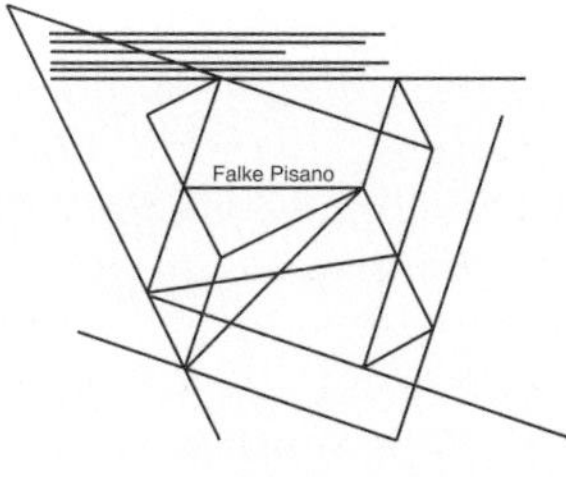

part/version 1
part/version 2

**part/version 3
(The Complex Object)**

The Complex Object is a type of object and an idea developed in order to enable an exploration of certain characteristics and qualities of material reality (for instance, the internal time of objects, impossible transformations). By constructing this linguistic object around a problematic proposition (for instance, a sculpture turning into a conversation, the implementation of a human presence in a hermetic abstract text) and by basing its internal logic on it conditions are created in which the problematic nature of the proposition dissolves and it becomes possible to write its 'taking place'. At the same time this linguistic object is a construction that offers the possibility to address the question to which extent the process of an object is still present in the object itself.

The performance series Affecting Abstraction deals with this idea and is an attempt to not only articulate the notion but also construct a specific Complex Object.

In this series the possibility of implementing a human presence in a hermetic abstract construction of language is explored by performatively outlining how this could be achieved. The three performances are both consecutive parts and re-workings of each other, each one dealing with the whole process, but furthering it and reflecting on it accordingly.

OBJECT AND DISINTEGRATION
A Performance in Trialogue Form

Falke Pisano

with
Will Holder & Karolin Meunier

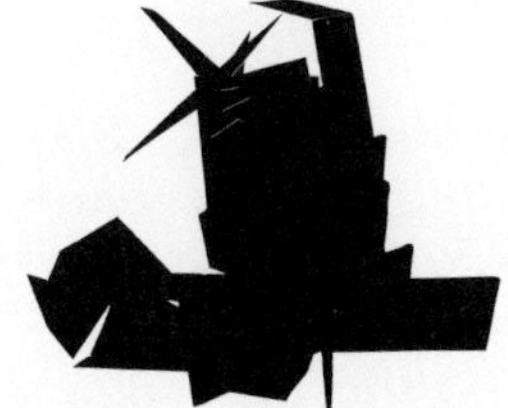

THE CREATIVE SUBJECT: KAROLIN MEUNIER

defines the encounter between the spectator and the object and specifies what happens during the process of disintegration in the relation between the object and the spectator.

THE ENGAGING SPECTATOR: WILL HOLDER

expresses the object as perceived and after his perception has evolved into engagement he expresses his engagement as experienced - while acknowledging the constructed nature of his encounter.

THE CONSTRUCTING ARTIST: FALKE PISANO

determines the structure and form of the work in which the disintegration will take place and articulates the relation between the object in the work and the object of the work.

Performance Posters, 2005–08
4 digital prints

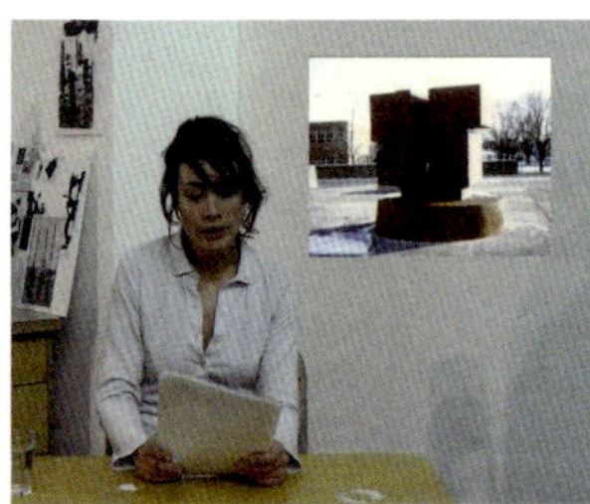
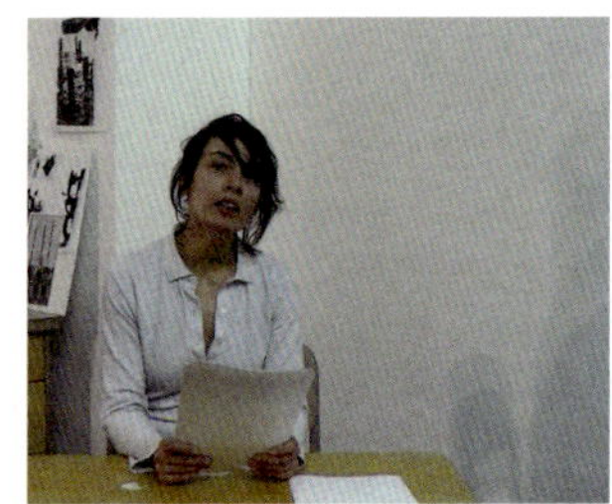
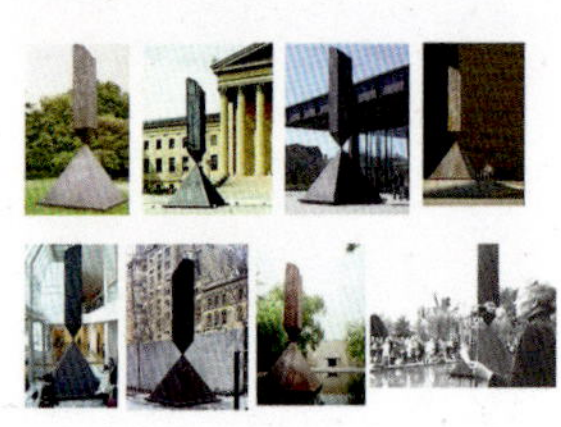
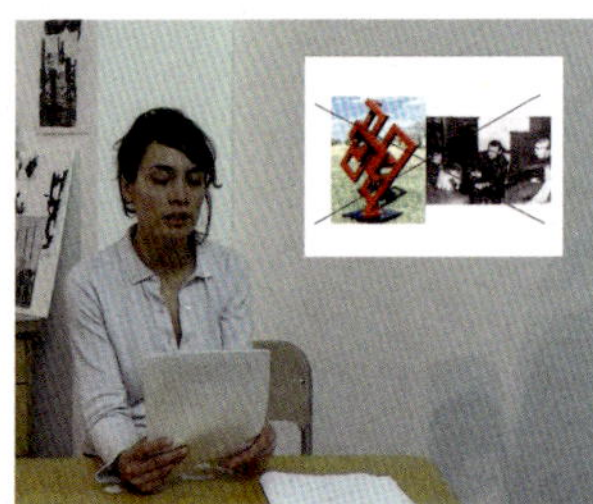

Studio Lecture 1, 2006

In this lecture Pisano talks in particular about abstract sculptures in public spaces that 'possess some specific qualities… that can be assumed to possess their own structure of meaning and sense while at the same time they are open to suggestions that place them in a totally different context'. She returns to issues addressed in her earlier lecture *Concrete Abstractions* (2005) and tries to outline 'some related ideas revolving around (abstract) objects and their existence'. Her premise is 'that objects might be able to exist in different conditions than we normally think they do, … a) as concrete objects, and especially abstract sculptures, b) as abstract constructions proposing concrete existence'. On this basis, she investigates 'how to formulate a possible existence that could be articulated as an object'. The book with Finn's photographs of sculptures by Chillida that formed a case study in this lecture later became the central focus of Pisano's *Chillida (Forms and Feelings)*. In this text, below some excerpts from the manuscript, she also uses poems to expand on her reflections. SB

2] …Because the viewer became active from the act of looking he or she will be actively visualising: the acts result in visual mental images on the photograph or the mental image of the sculpture in another context will be constructed, starting from the sculpture, as a visual scene, displaying both tangible and immaterial elements.

3] So: although my interest starts with the concrete object, its creation and its existence, I am actually trying to go around the apparent necessity of these objects to exist in tangible form. What I am doing is to create a sensuous knowledge of these objects without taking into account the actual possibilities of their centralised material existence. In other words: I attempt to construct these objects as collections of conditions or parameters….

[on meaning] 5] … a) I have found two memorials for Martin Luther King that are both based on his last speech in which he utters his famous words: 'I've been to the mountaintop.' Although a clear resemblance can be seen between the two, they are very different. What happened between the speech, the reading of the speech by the sculptors and the sculptures themselves? Where is the meaning located in the two sculptures? And in what way are the decisions made responsible for the difference in meaning?

b) … Now, I am totally willing to accept the meaning that is generally attributed to the sculpture, but I cannot help but be very curious as to how the different contexts in which the three sculptures (each edition of 3) have affected them. How stable is the meaning of this work and does it make a difference if it is placed next to the chapel of Rothko, who, before completing it, committed suicide? Additionally, that it is dedicated to MLK [Martin Luther King] or that it is placed on a campus in a square that for some unknown reason has been nicknamed 'the red square'? And what does all this travelling do to the obelisk of the MoMA?…

8] … I arrived at the narrative or poetic organisation of language while thinking about the possibility of the 'dense' object because it is the novel or the poem that possesses in such a particular way — only internally — the fourth dimension: time. The writer, the reader, the protagonist, the story, the construction, the context: in order to compress an object-existence to its densest form all of these need to be brought into the object as agents participating in the construction. And they can only act as agents when they have the 'time' to do so….
  Falke Pisano

Excerpts from manuscript *Chillida (Forms and Feelings)*.

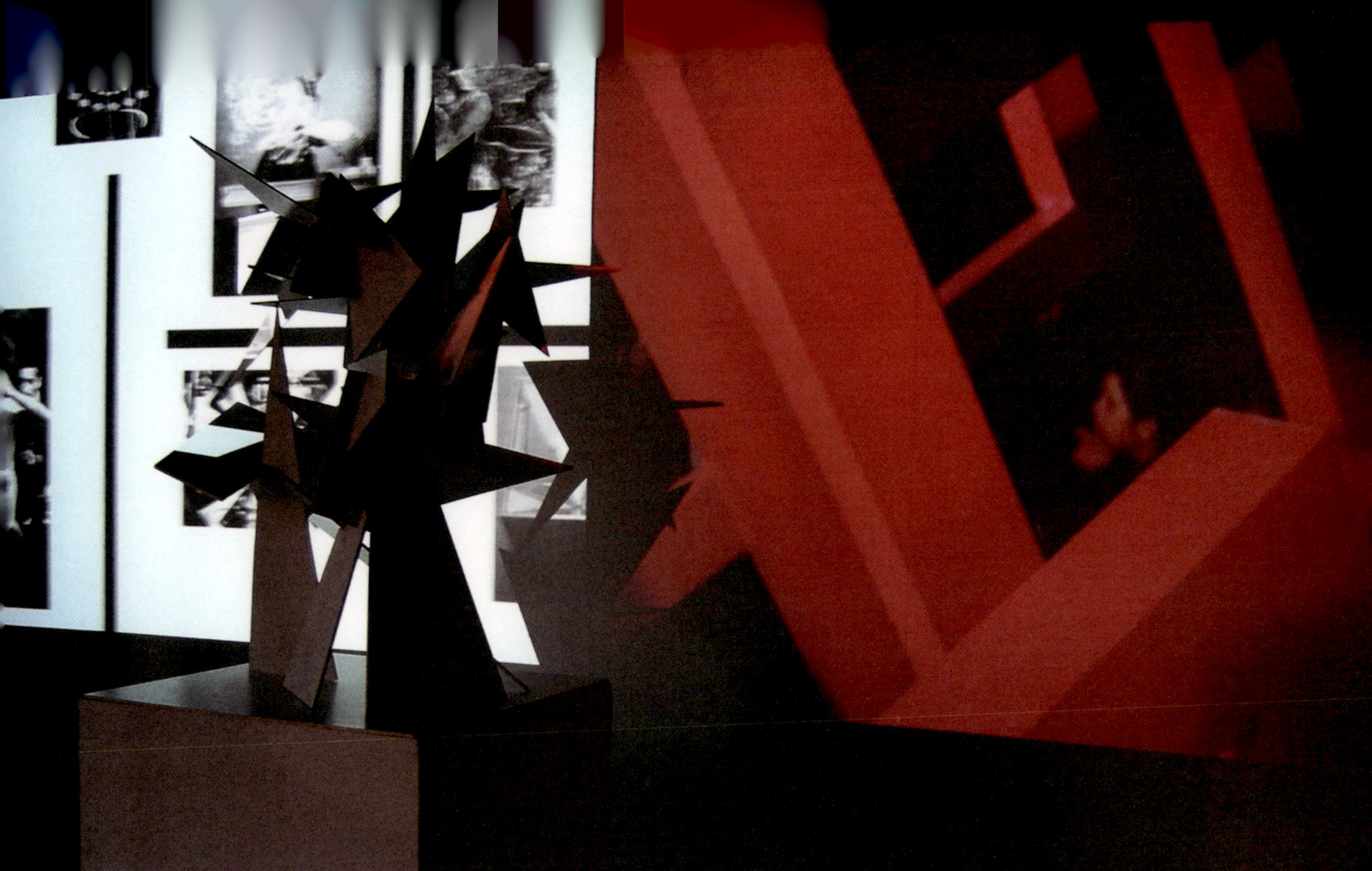

A Sculpture Turning into a Conversation
(Part Zero and Part One), 2006
Video installation

A voice-over reads a text in which a sculpture transmutes into a conversation while a projection on the left (Part Zero) shows a 'camera' panning across a collection of images, diagrams and notes and a projection on the right (Part One) displays a series of photographs.

There's a line of description going through the text. The text starts with the description of an artificial centralised existence, namely a sculpture — not even a real sculpture but one that is described in order to be turned into a conversation.

Description, which serves as the method of construction of the situation, covers the space from the sculpture to the conversation. The situation has an internal time that is part of the method of construction and one of the formal elements of the event. What is actually constructed — the transformation — is both a form and a moment, it is both a transformation of the form and a shift in time-space. In the construction through perception and description, this creates a space that begins, as Max Bill once wrote, on one side and ends in a completely different condition on the other.

So the text starts with the description of an abstract sculpture. The sculpture is described and slowly dissolves into a conversation. The description is set up with the immanent transformation in mind and the need to incorporate, already in the sculpture, the possibilities of this transformation and to create the possibility to move from the formalism of the sculpture to the content of the conversation.

The description is broken up in pieces. The 'descriptive components' are built up individually, relative to each other and sometimes overlapping (although the appearances differ in their description). Shapes are perceived and constructed at the same time, providing a structure of images that potentially forms a unity: the perception fragments, which are obtained through the intentional visualization of possible perceptions and compiled to activate the physical properties of the object's shape. Consisting of imagined fractional views of the object, with deliberate attention directed towards something that lies beyond the formal surface of the sculpture, they form propositional images that point to the potential of the sculpture. FP

Excerpt from the manuscript *A Sculpture Turning into a Conversation (Part One)*.

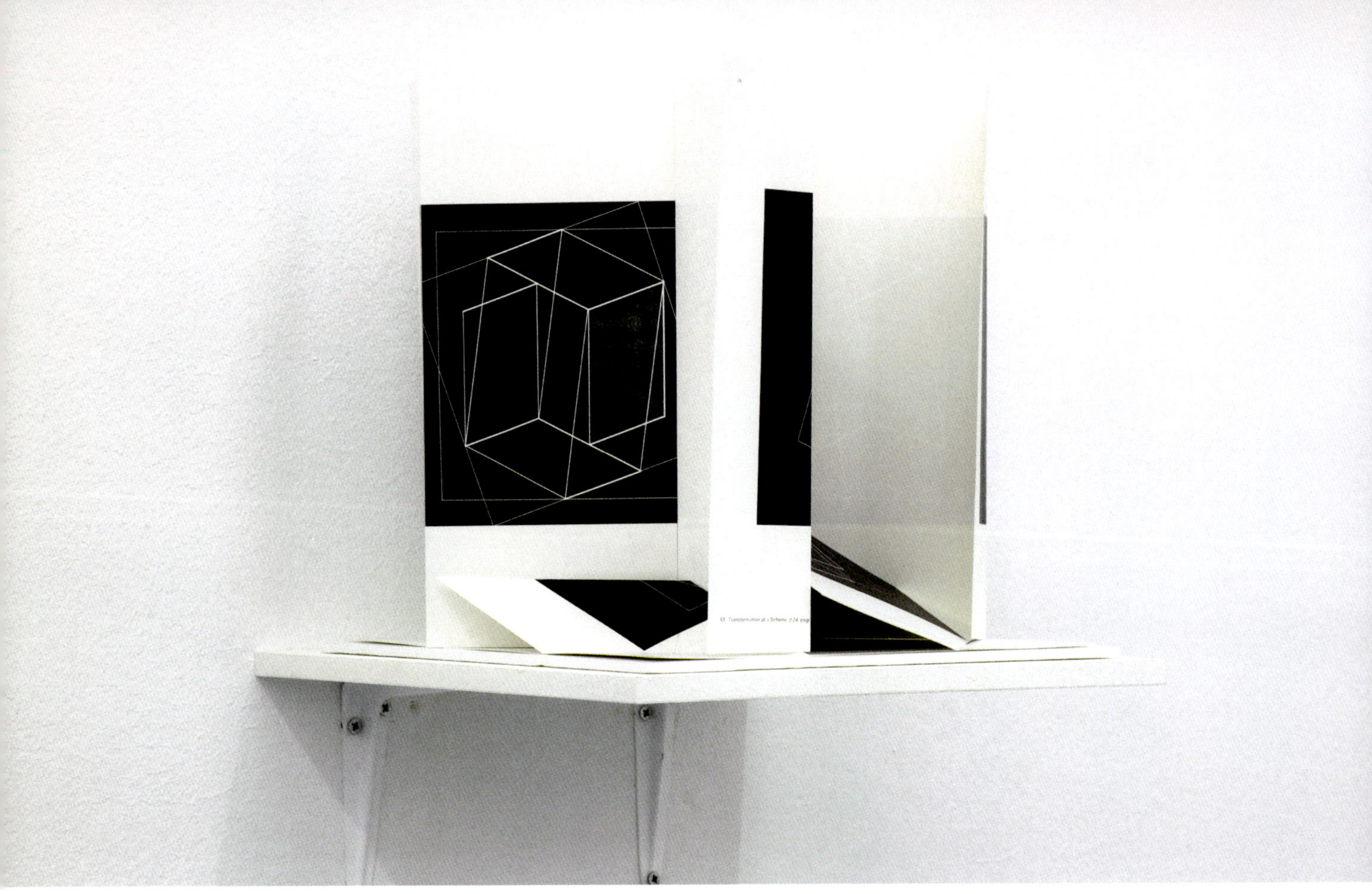

Object of Transformation 1, 2007
Sculpture

The specific subject-object relations of modernist abstraction in the field of art existed in determined contexts, in the Russian Revolution or the social utopias of the Bauhaus for instance. The attempt of these avant-gardes was to reorganise these subject-object relations in terms of the potentiality of aesthetic experience. In contrast, I find it difficult to determine the context in which I work. Therefore the overlap between inquiry, execution and reorganisation of the subject-object relations is addressed within my practice. Taking as a starting point an affectively charged construction of autonomy, transparent construction and positioning of the author subject, this exchange forms the basis for a reconsideration of a performative potential and its ties to the construction of the (modernist) subject. □

Object of Transformation 1, 2007
Sculpture

This is a sculpture based on Josef Albers' works entitled *Structural Constellation, Transformation of a Scheme*. Constructed while trying to follow Albers' logic in his two-dimensional representations of possible three-dimensional transformations — and thus activating the proposed transformations while at the same time fixating them in an object — this sculpture brings together *Structural Constellation, Transformation of a Scheme no. 24* and *no. 30* through the proposed logic of *Structural Constellation, Transformation of a Scheme no. 23.*

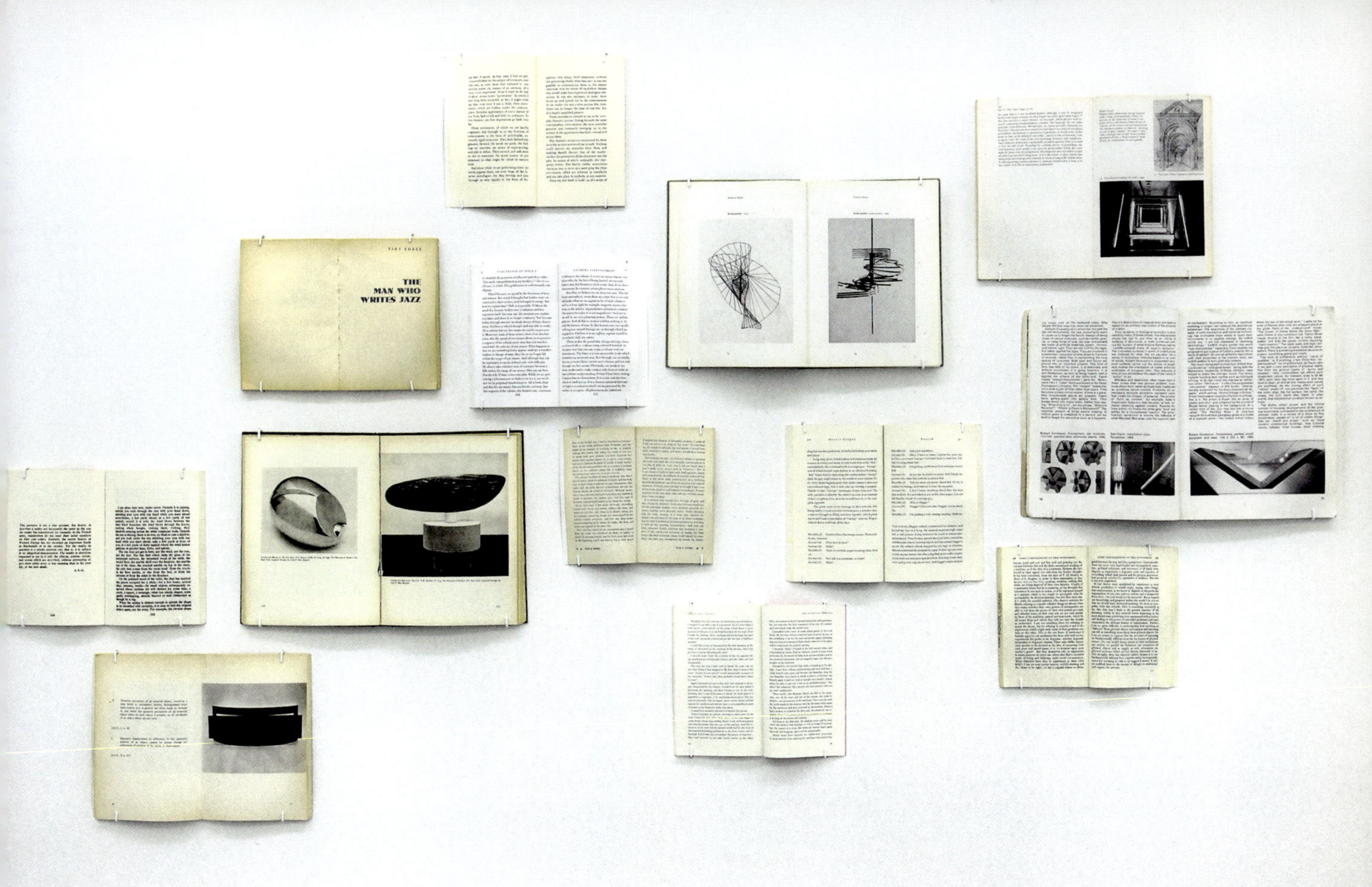

Object Construction 1: Reflective Abstraction (Mishima), 2007
Installation with 13 books

Inverting Italo Calvino's mention in *Six Memos for the Next Millennium of De Rerum Natura* by Lucretius as 'the first great work of poetry in which knowledge of the world tends to dissolve the solidity of the world, leading to the perception of all that is infinitely minute, light and mobile', the aim was to extract from books fragments pointing towards qualities, attributes and forms of possible objects, while the fragments combined to define one specific object and so reconstruct a potential material origin of the knowledge contained in the writings.

Part of the installation is a little publication containing the elements reconstructing the object in thirteen notes/quotations. The first describes the object:

'An object, able to traverse different realities; able to move from the linguistic structure it is created in to the structure of concrete reality to attain stability and a consistency that is not defined by any particular condition but that is part of several at once; able to be expression and subject simultaneously.' SB

Based on and compiled from the artist's manuscripts.

Mathias Poledna

On a basic level this new, yet untitled film work could be described as a portrait of a group of objects. Its subject is a series of crystal glasses produced by the Viennese manufacturer L. & J. Lobmeyr since the late 1920s based on a design by the architect Adolf Loos (1870–1933). The 'bar-set' consists of twelve items: finger bowl, champagne flute, beer glass, wine decanter, water pitcher, water glass, whisky glass double old-fashioned, red wine glass, white wine glass, dessert wine glass, sherry glass and liqueur glass. Unlike traditional glass services from this period, in which individual pieces are distinctively shaped based on their respective function, each item of the group is derived from a single basic shape: a circular body with the walls set at a right-angle to the flat base. Each component of the set can thus be viewed as a variation of this motif, differing only in the relationship between height and diameter of the glass, in accordance with its function. Its vocabulary reflects a complex and contradictory aesthetic program whose historical modernity is rooted in a specific and multiple, fractured understanding of culture. This lineage however is not the focus of the filmic portrait here; on the contrary, it appears replaced by a spatial narrative of movement, repetition, transparency, and absence and movement. The interaction of typological classification, close-up fragmentary encounters and a shifting dramaturgy aims for a kind of choreography of objects that traces the outlines of, and transitions between, typology, historicity, abstraction, historical documentation and an aesthetic of commerce.

Mathias Poledna

Untitled, 2009
Film installation
Production photograph

pp. 183–84
Untitled, 2009
Installation (details)
2 display cases, with each 6 record sleeves
on acrylic glass stands

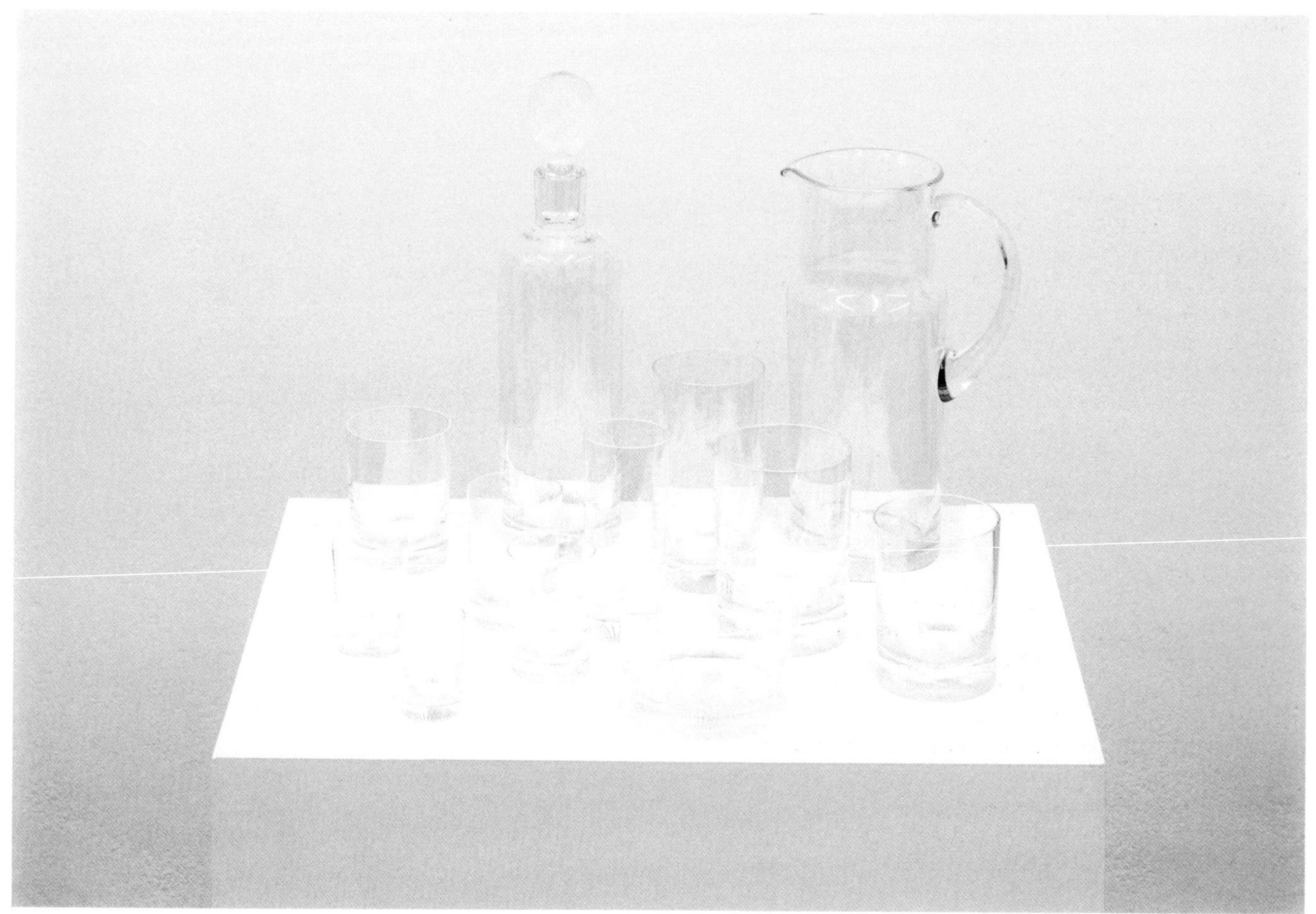

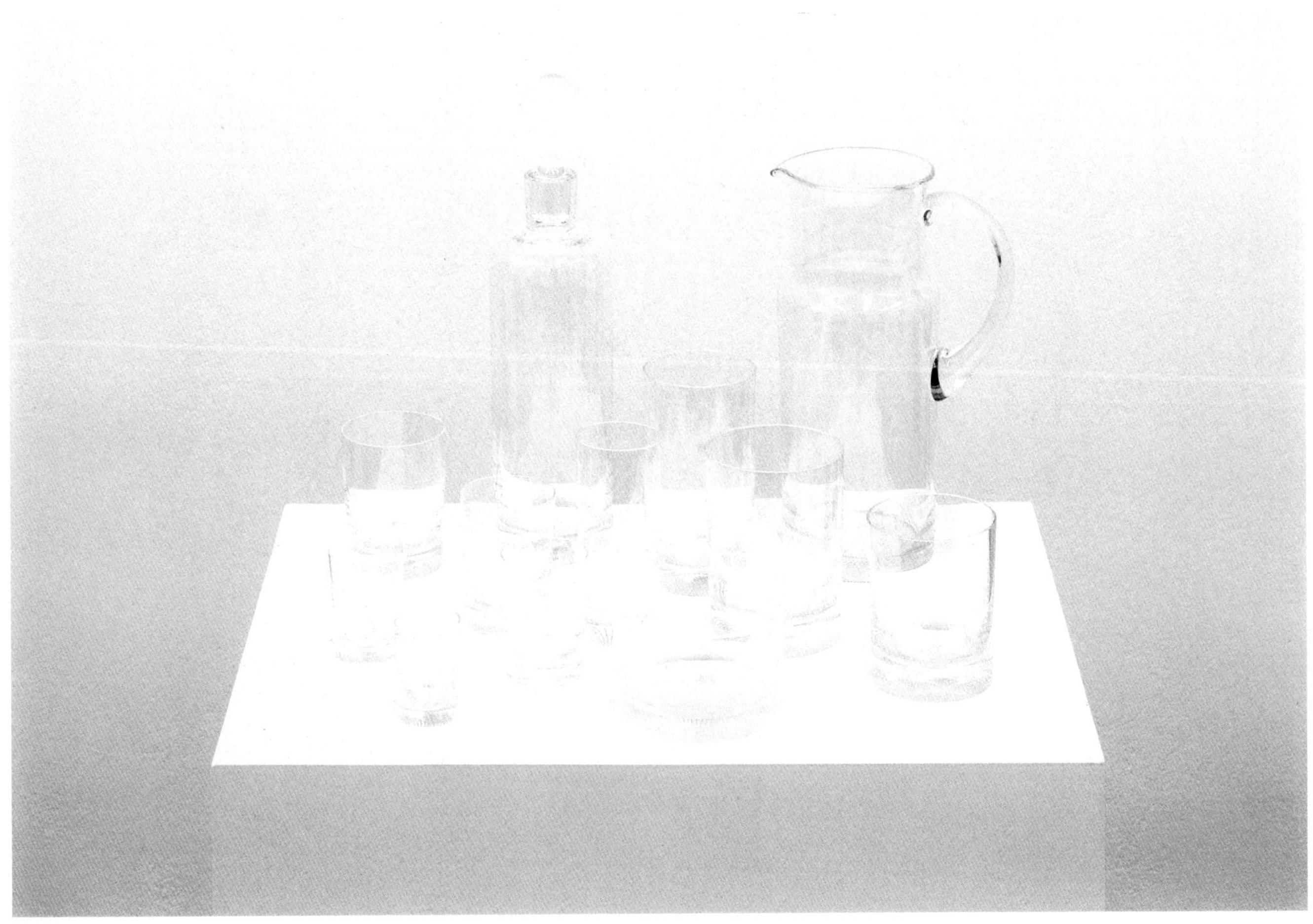

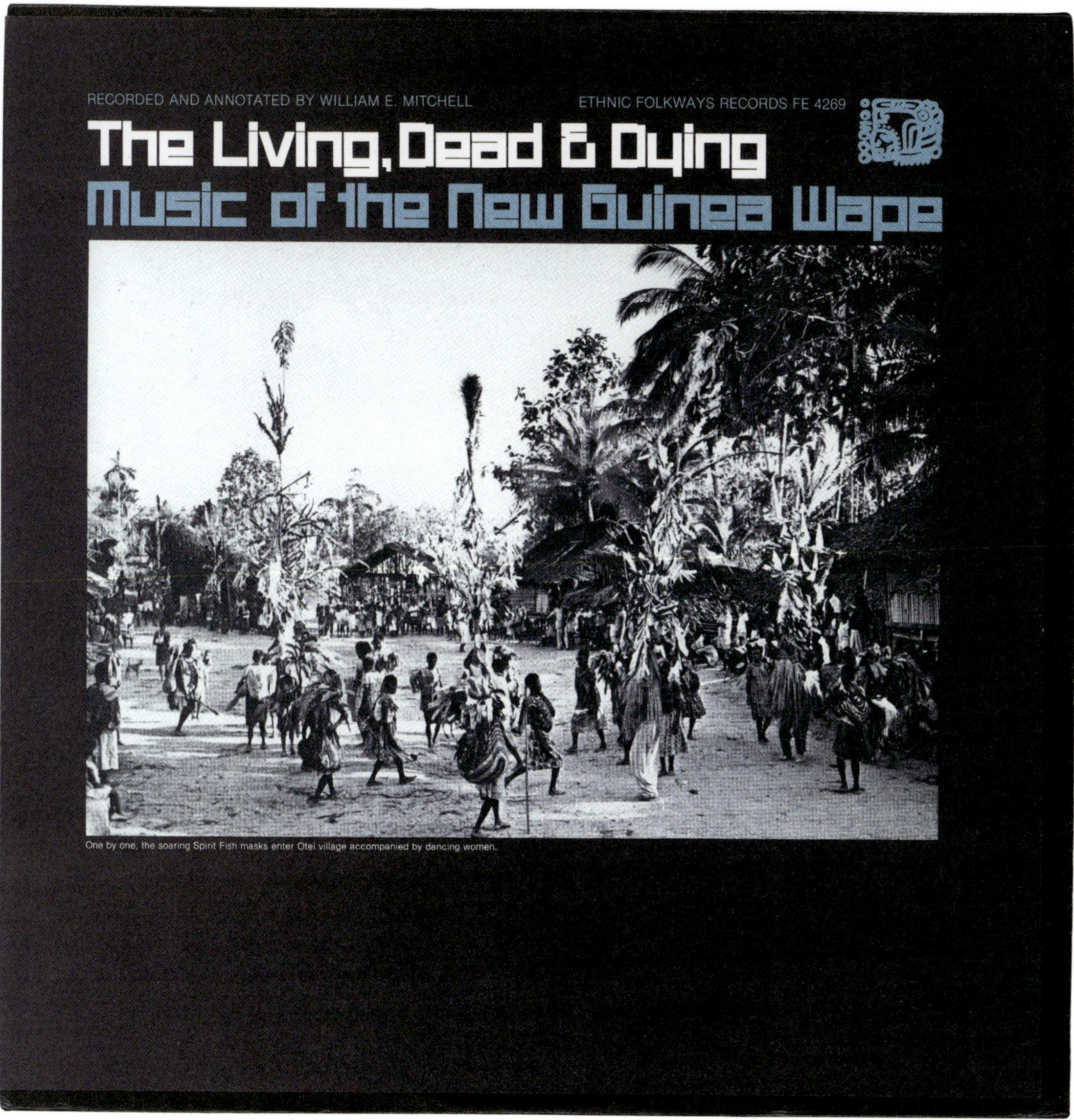
RECORDED AND ANNOTATED BY WILLIAM E. MITCHELL
ETHNIC FOLKWAYS RECORDS FE 4269
The Living, Dead & Dying
Music of the New Guinea Wape
One by one, the soaring Spirit Fish masks enter Otei village accompanied by dancing women.

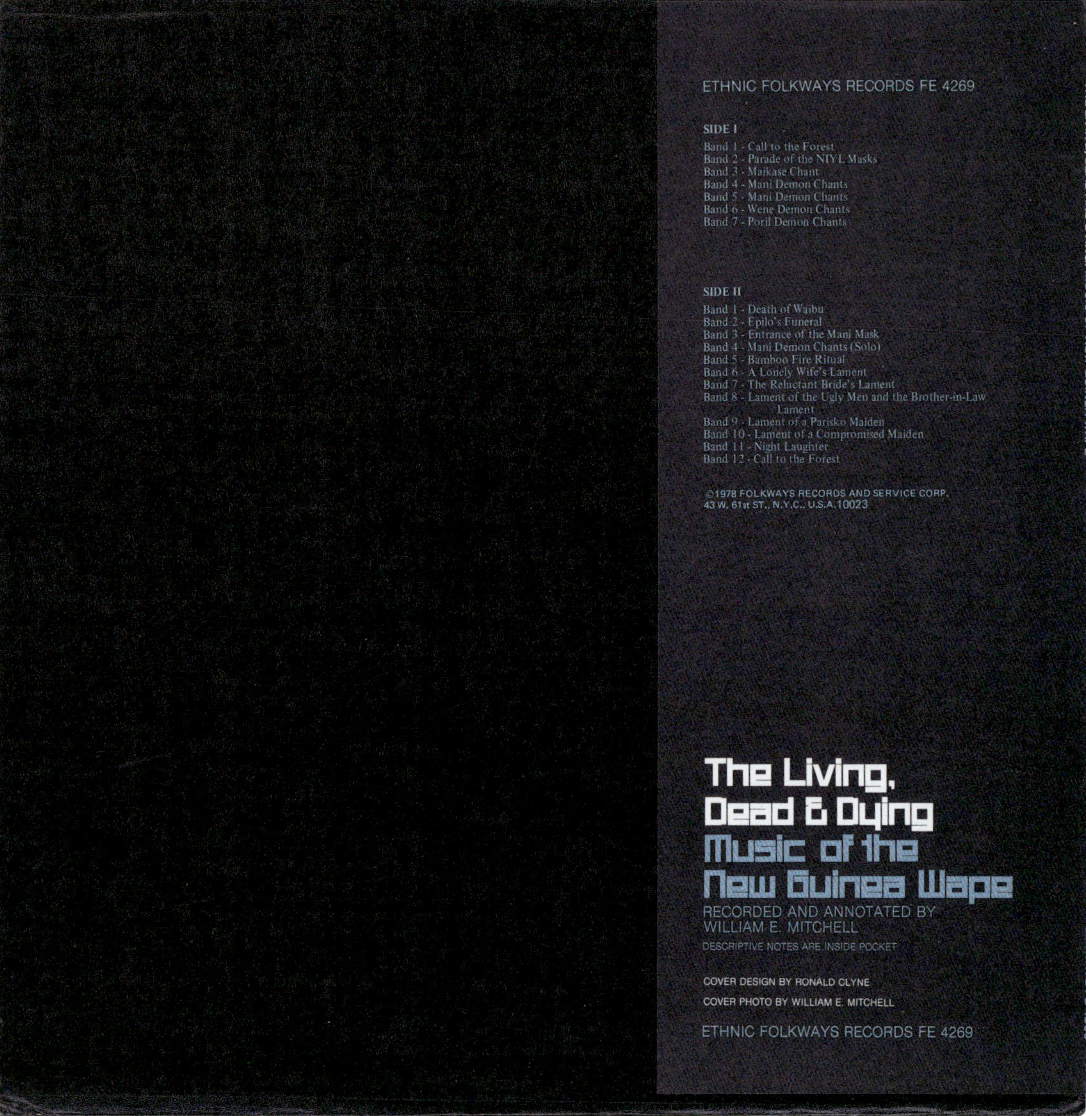
ETHNIC FOLKWAYS RECORDS FE 4269

SIDE I
Band 1 - Call to the Forest
Band 2 - Parade of the NIYL Masks
Band 3 - Maikase Chant
Band 4 - Mani Demon Chants
Band 5 - Mani Demon Chants
Band 6 - Wene Demon Chants
Band 7 - Poril Demon Chants

SIDE II
Band 1 - Death of Waibu
Band 2 - Epilo's Funeral
Band 3 - Entrance of the Mani Mask
Band 4 - Mani Demon Chants (Solo)
Band 5 - Bamboo Fire Ritual
Band 6 - A Lonely Wife's Lament
Band 7 - The Reluctant Bride's Lament
Band 8 - Lament of the Ugly Men and the Brother-in-Law
Lament
Band 9 - Lament of a Parisko Maiden
Band 10 - Lament of a Compromised Maiden
Band 11 - Night Laughter
Band 12 - Call to the Forest

©1978 FOLKWAYS RECORDS AND SERVICE CORP.
43 W. 61st ST., N.Y.C., U.S.A.10023

The Living,
Dead & Dying
Music of the
New Guinea Wape
RECORDED AND ANNOTATED BY
WILLIAM E. MITCHELL
DESCRIPTIVE NOTES ARE INSIDE POCKET

COVER DESIGN BY RONALD CLYNE
COVER PHOTO BY WILLIAM E. MITCHELL

ETHNIC FOLKWAYS RECORDS FE 4269

Folkways was founded in 1948 with the aim of documenting
'the entire world of sound'. Over 2,000 titles — music and
speech records, as well as documentary recordings of individuals, communities and events — were issued by Folkways; since
1987 the Folkways holdings have been part of the Smithsonian
Centre for Folklife and Cultural Heritage, which runs programmes
dedicated to the preservation of cultural diversity and also to
mediating communication between peoples....

With the selection from the Folkways programme,
Poledna highlights the nonsensical, disconnected and still-to-
be connected nature of an archive that has set itself the task
of documenting 'the entire world of sound', as the Smithsonian
Institution's website states. But precisely in doing so, in exhibiting fragments of this archive as riddles he raises the question
of the archive's meaning and promise. But this question is not
raised here as a question that concerns the past as if it were
something that the archive has *already* placed at our disposal,
but as something that involves our future, our responsibility
for tomorrow.[1] In the future however (which always begins
immediately) the meaning of the archive will depend on what
we mean by the 'entire world'.

When the question of its interpretation is raised, the archive
necessarily loses its objectivity and in its place there manifests
itself a capacity to absorb the knowledge that viewers contribute
as they contemplate its objects and to expand as it does so
— though the body of the archive, now swollen and pregnant with
meaning, can never be objecitified as such; it remains open to the
future and is therefore in its substance intangible, like a ghost.[2]

Juliane Rebentisch

1   See Jacques Derrida, *Archive Fever: A Freudian Impression*,
    Chicago and London: The University of Chicago Press, 1996, p. 36.
2   Ibid., p. 68.

Deconfigurations of Community: Mathias Poledna's Version,
Cologne: Galerie Daniel Buchholz (ed.), forthcoming.

Florian Pumhösl

Modernology (Triangular Atelier), 2007
Installation
Partition walls upholstered with black buckram fabric,
joined with partition hinges, reverse glass paintings, display case

Abstract Characters?
Reference and Formalism in the Works of Florian Pumhösl
Modernology — the title quotes an eponymous project by
Japanese architect Kon Wajirō — seemed designed to establish
not so much a decidedly political legibility of its historical references as an aesthetically stringent actualisation of the form
of presentation implicit in this actualisation. An actualisation,
however, that sought to manifest itself not in an assertion of a
here and now, as would have been compatible with the demands
of event culture, but instead in a contrastive presentation of
historical constellations with a view to the capacity for aesthetic
and political articulation inherent in formal abstraction under the
conditions of a globalised exhibition business: as Pumhösl made
references to the 'Triangular Studio' built by the artist and designer
Murayama Tomoyoshi in 1926, to the black walls used in the
Sturm exhibition shown in Tokyo in 1914 and to the reverse glass
paintings by the Jena artist Walter Dexel, who was loosely associated with the Bauhaus, *Modernology* brought to light the processes of exchange — complex and extending beyond Western
Europe — between aesthetic strategies and languages, as well as
their fragilities.

The installation thus registered its objections against the incessant attempts to promote uniformity in accordance with market
demands, attempts that are being made not least in the name of
postmodernity and globalisation. *Modernology* thus raised the
question as to the criteria of distinction that separate Pumhösl's
work from those postmodernist revisions of geometric abstraction
that transposed Lyotard's Kantian credo of the 'aesthetic sublime'
to their 'modernisms': to Mondrian, Malevich, Rodchenko, Rothko
and Newman. The difference is vast, no doubt; it resides — at first
glance — primarily in the rejection of monumental form and visual
opulence, of, for example, a re-auratisation of space and colour.

Pumhösl's preferred techniques thus include the photogram
as well as reverse lacquer glass painting, formal languages, that
is, that play a marginal role in modernism and are marked by
a decidedly graphical presentational quality. As such, they imply
inter-connections between painting, photography and film of the
kind that were characteristic of the international scene between
Dutch 'De Stijl', Russian Constructivism and German Bauhaus
— a scene that developed great ambitions regarding the invention
(and patenting) of new, hybrid techniques and media, drawing
on pre-photographic and pre-cinematographic techniques as
well as ultra-modern painting. For instance, Dexel's 'camera-less
photography' can be related back to photogenic drawings; the flat
geometric vocabulary of his reverse glass paintings; similarly, to
abstract painting and to the abstract films of, for example, Hans

Richter. This effect of scintillation between the handmade unique
exemplar and the reproducible projected image here corresponds
to that between the various uses — artistic, scientific and
technical — to which they can be put. This is precisely where the
movement towards abstraction that is generally regarded as an
accomplishment of modernist 'high art' took place.

In the context of documenta 12, as the epitome of the contemporary art exhibition, Pumhösl's decision to restage historical
moments of the mutual superimposition of heterogeneous
formal languages, media and exhibition displays didn't look like
a 'grand appearance', but rather like a temporary arrangement of
materials that would remain unintelligible from a purely contemporary perspective. By marking claims to historical evidence as
the results of an interpretive (or self-interpreting) and hence inevitably distorting artistic process of translation, *Modernology* enacted
— besides the ambition, presumably directed against the pertinent
historiography, of relating (avant-gardist) functionalism and
(modernist) aesthetics — a close dovetailing of 'functional' and
'autonomous' object languages. For instance, the exhibition design,
loosely based on avant-gardist prints and studio architecture,
was formally reduced to such an extent that one could not emphati-
cally call it either functional or autonomous.
Sabeth Buchmann

Excerpt from *Florian Pumhösl*, Cologne: Galerie Buchholz, 2008
(first published in *Texte zur Kunst*, no. 69, March 2008).

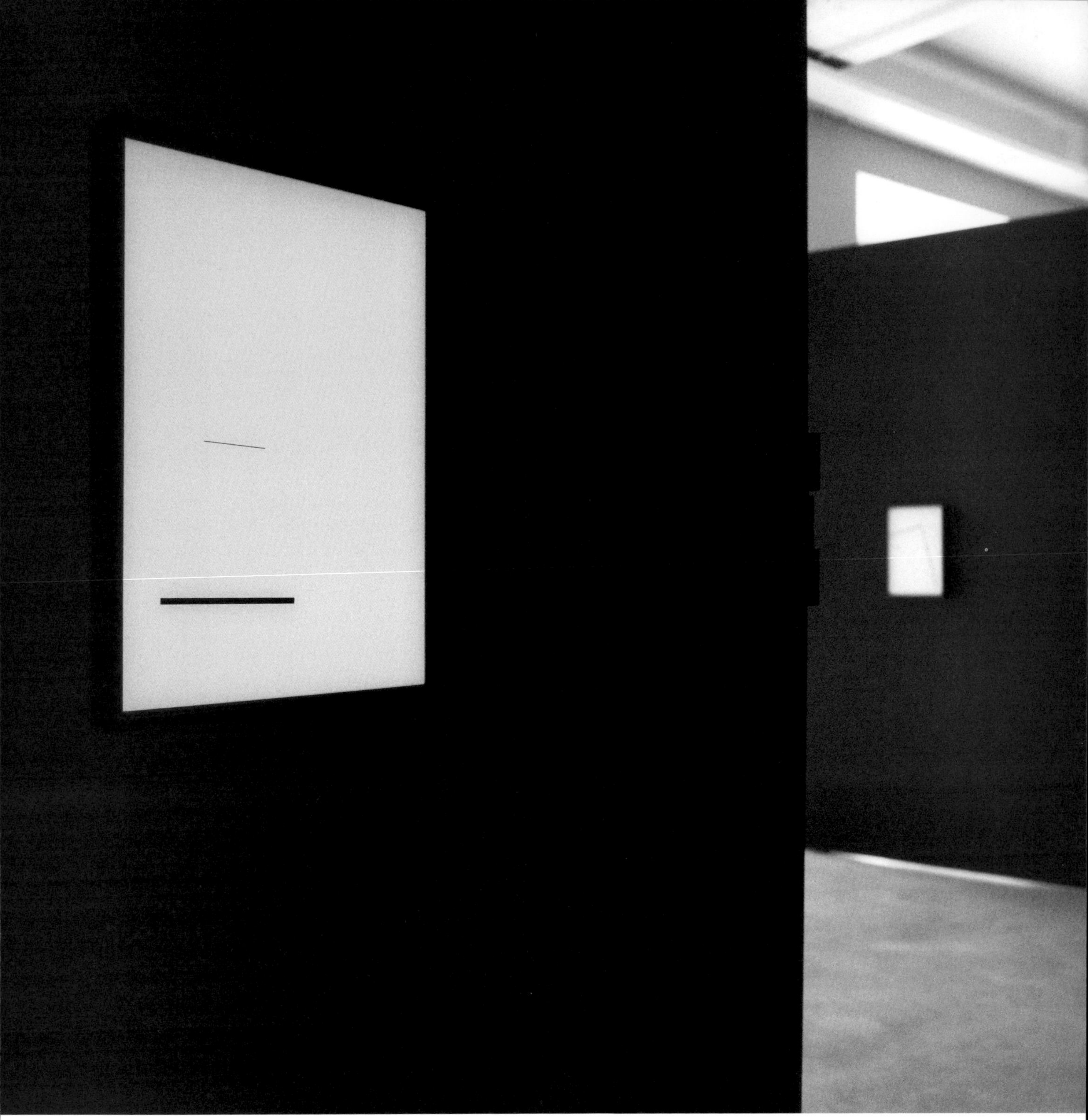

Modernology (Triangular Atelier)
Installation view
documenta 12, Kassel, 2007

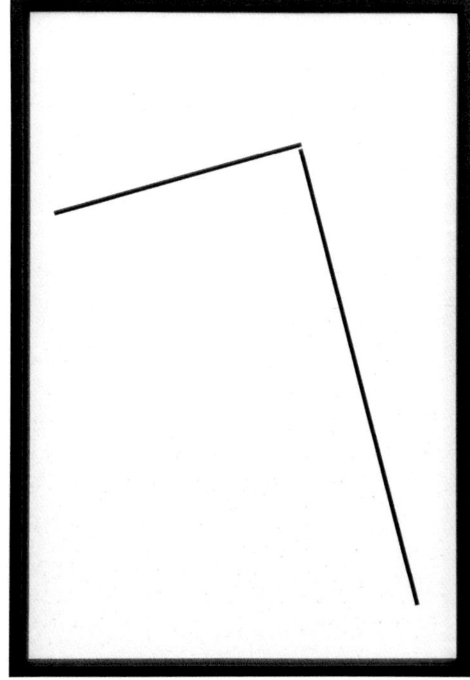

Modernology 26, 2007
Synthetic resin lacquer on reverse of sheet glass

Artistic engagement with modernism and modernity has increased over the past fifteen to twenty years. I believe, however, that it formed a sub-history throughout twentieth-century art, despite interruptions. In his 'modernology' project of the 1930s the Japanese architect Kon Wajirō occupied a position in the cultural tradition of social reform. In my work I aim to create a 'modernology' situation distinguished by distance from historical figures, which represents an extreme contrast to the social reform approach. My space is about aesthetic articulation.

I view 'modernolgy' as an open-ended alternative to 'museology'. This encompasses the fact that artistic appropriation, how works of art are displayed and the incorporation of historical material have themselves become conventions of the 'exhibition business', the substrata of a commercially orientated culture. What interests me about the work of Onchi Koshiro and Murayama Tomoyoshi, to which my reliefs refer, is that cultural transmission, translation and assimilation formed a constitutive part of their artistic practice from the very beginning. ▷

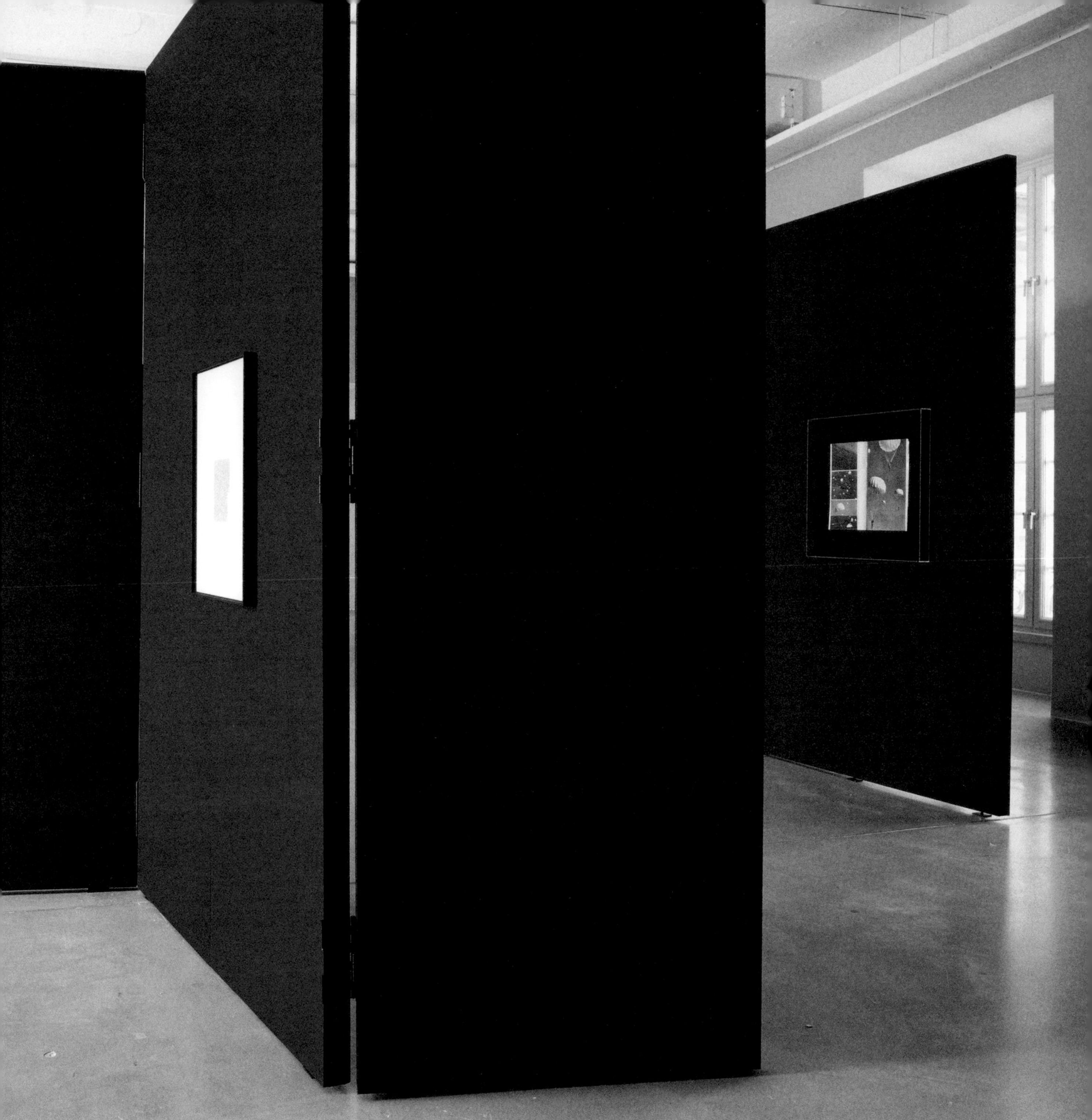

Modernology (Triangular Atelier)
Installation view
documenta 12, Kassel, 2007

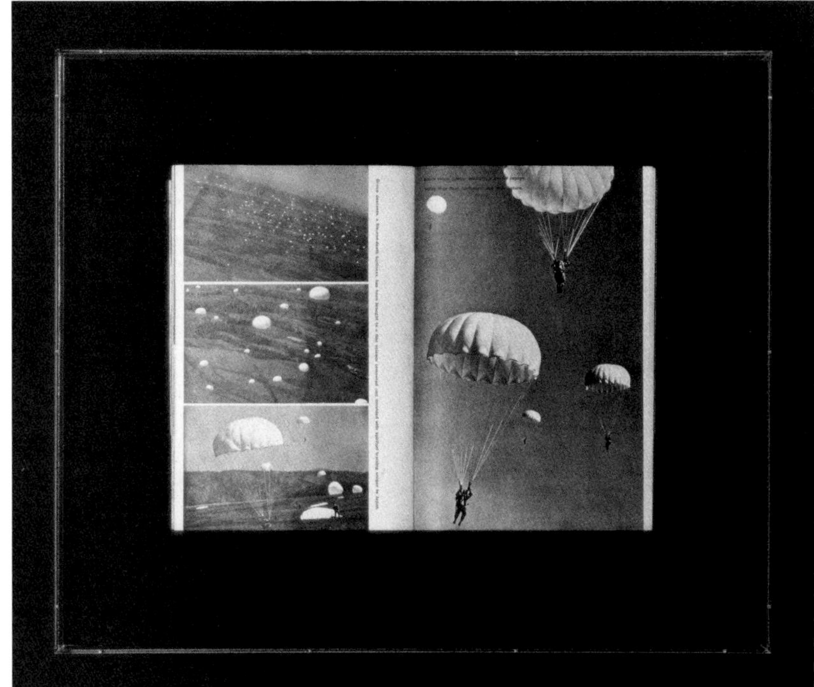

Modernology 14, 2007
Perspex wall-mounted display case containing
a copy of *Front* magazine, 'Parachuting' issue,
no. 7, 1943

A few years ago I reached a point where it no longer
seemed to make sense to engage with the themes and
events of modernism outside the Western canon without
addressing the origins and the 'grammar' of modern art.
I felt that the referential approach, which made sense in
the 1990s as part of a critical reconstruction, had ceased
to be of use to me. I wanted to get down to the basics:
abstraction, autonomy, presence and implementation. □

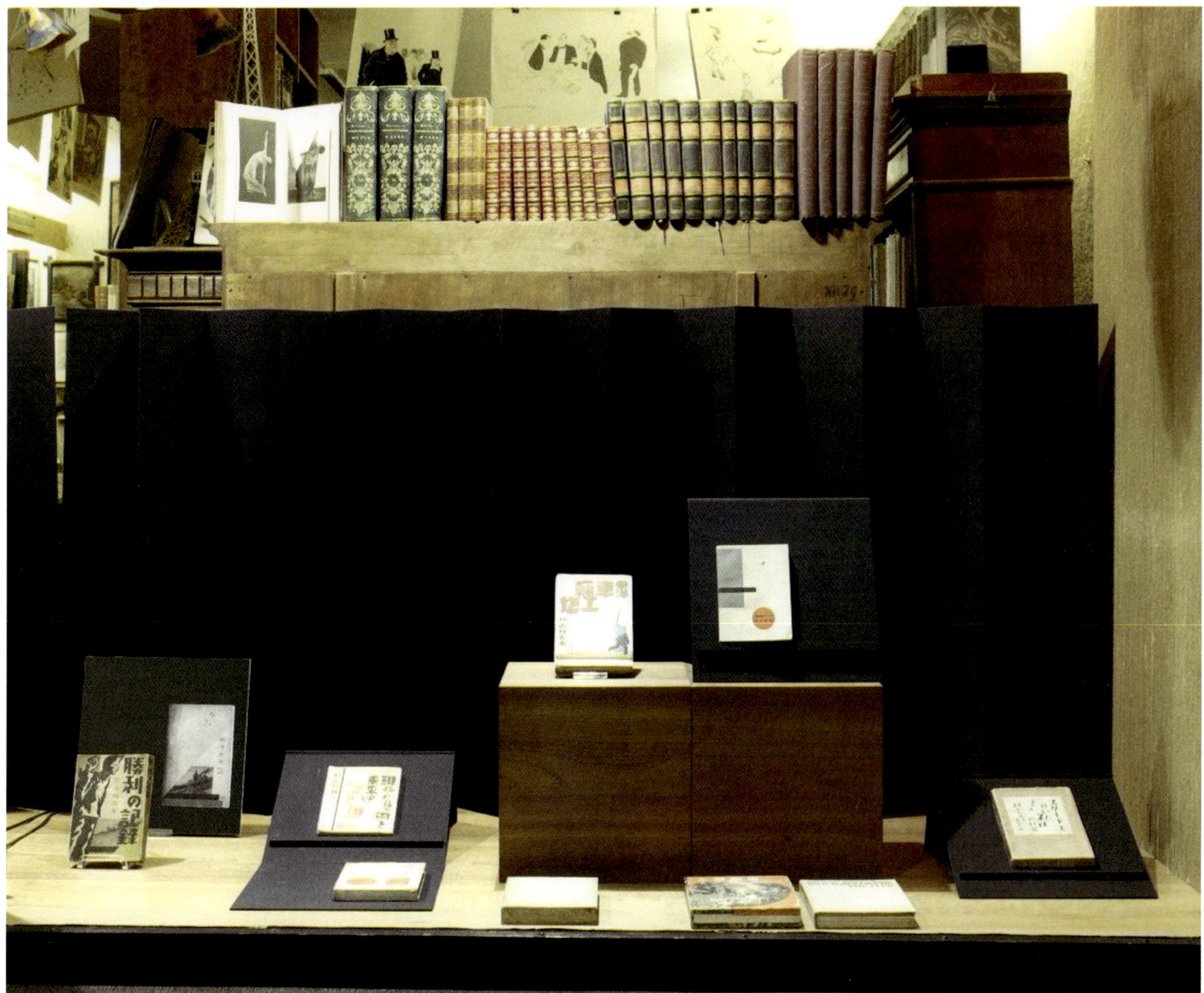

Murayama Tomoyoshi: Book Designs, Translations, Illustrated Books
Shop window selected and designed by Florian Pumhösl
Installation view
Antiquariat Buchholz, Cologne, 2008

This selection of books by Murayama Tomoyoshi (1901–1977) published between 1922 and 1939 was first made for the window of the Buchholz second-hand bookshop in Cologne. It has now been transferred to a moveable glass case intended for wall-mounting. The books include such seminal documents of the Japanese avant-garde as *The Art of the Present and the Future* (1923) and *Study of Constructivism* (1925). Tomoyoshi played a formative role in Japan's avant-garde. On a study trip to Berlin in the early twenties he became acquainted with the latest European avant-garde movements. On his return to Japan in 1923, he founded the Mavo group with Kadowaki Shinro, Ôura Shûzô, Ogata Kamenosuke and Yanase Masamu. The legendary periodical *Mavo* first appeared in July 1924, running to a further six issues by the end of the following year. In addition to organising exhibitions, lectures, theatrical performances and concerts, the artists set up a Mavo friends association and, in the words of Ogata Kamenosuke, offered to 'design posters, window displays, books, stage sets, all kinds of decoration, buildings, etc.'.
Florian Pumhösl

Excerpt from the text of the exhibition at the Galerie Daniel Buchholz, Cologne, 2008.

Martha Rosler

Flower Fields (Color Field Painting), c. 1975
Video, transferred from Super 8 mm film

Martha Rosler filmed broad fields of flowers from a moving car on Interstate 5 Highway near San Diego, in the vicinity where she was living at the time. Flowers are one of the area's few non-military industries. At first the fields of flowers, planted in colourful stripes, can be admired from a distance. A zoom reveals who is producing this abstract coloured painting: Mexican workers bending over and kneeling. Glimpses of passing cars and lorries and a quick shot of the immigration police checkpoint on the way north fade into a romantic view of the scene at night, with pictures of palm trees and the Pacific Ocean beyond concluding this road movie. SB

In *Flower Fields (Color Field Painting)* we see an effort on the part of Southern California commercial growers to produce a pleasant, modernist, minimalist design of colour stripes for drivers on the interstate highway. Labour is made to vanish by means of a broad-brush abstraction. The camera, however, zooms in on the stoop labour in the fields, and as the film continues it passes through the immigration-control station about fifty kilometres further north and on to a stereotypical Southern California sunset.

The anodyne of simple, broad stripes on a vast hillside canvas could not have made sense, of course, before modernism had become the reigning paradigm of art and design. The apparent disappearance of labour in favour of a kind of naturalised machine self-production is likely a consequence of the automated industries of the twentieth century, the mythology of which subsumed not only the individual worker but the work force, even as a concept, in favour of management. ▷

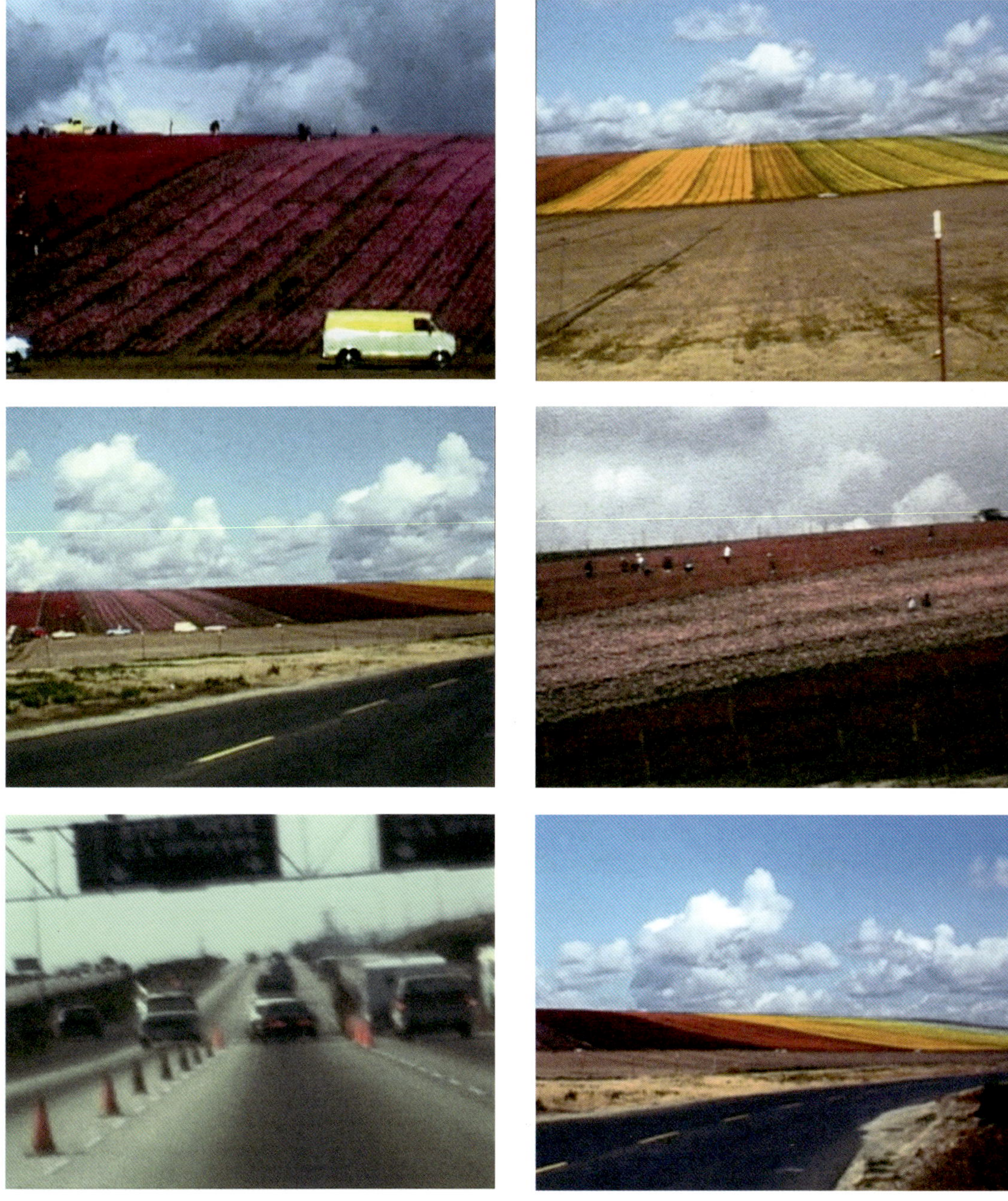

How Do We Know What Home Looks Like?
The Unité d'Habitation *of Le Corbusier at Firminy, France*, 1993
Video

This video was made for the group exhibition *Unité project* (1993) at the *Unité d'Habitation*, one of Le Corbusier's largest social housing projects, at Firminy-Vert, in south central France, finished after the architect's death in the late 1960s. More than thirty artists, groups, designers and architects were invited to present their personal view of the project in some of the empty apartments on the seventh floor of a block that had been closed for ten years. Some see the building complex as a monument to the failure of utopian theory and social practice, but it is staunchly defended by many of its residents and by people working in the fields of architecture and urban planning. In her film Rosler traces the history of the project and indicates how the residents live here now. In her exhibition at the *Unité* she showed the video alongside statistics about the residents mounted on the walls of the apartment.

'I'm happy for everyone to take photos', declares one of Rosler's interviewees. 'Though I prefer architects who come here and draw. Yes, because they render things better in drawings, you know…. And it's true. When you see photos of the Le Corbusier building and you live in it, you say to yourself: "That's not right!" No, even when you see photos of your own flat, you say to yourself: "It's not like that." Nothing at all like that! The volumes of the Le Corbusier building can't be taken in photos.'

The work opens with snapshots of the housing development and its long-since abandoned interiors. Sweeping across the exterior, the camera eventually focuses on the block of empty flats, looking for traces of the former inhabitants. After walking through some of the abandoned apartments and peering at the drawings, stickers, murals and, especially, the lively, if tattered 1960s wallpaper that adorns the once-pristine walls, Rosler lets the inhabitants of the *Unité* speak for themselves. She films children playing outside and in the hallways, which Corbusier had intended as interior streets. She chats with the curators about the architect's decorative and design preferences. And she interviews a tenant representative, a female resident, a group of women sitting on the grass with their children, women working at the radio station and an architecture student and his wife, a teacher, in their apartment. (The North African residents were reticent to be interviewed.) She asks in particular what alterations the tenants have made to the building and how they have adapted to it. After the exhibition curator, Yves Aupetitallot, has decried the tenants' fondness for wallpaper — a typically French taste — Rosler playfully stalks through the empty flats holding a roll of wallpaper. A female resident, a town official living alone, is asked if she chose the furniture in her apartment. She answers: 'Some people say that the Le Corbusier building is a terrorist, [that] it can't be furnished. The Le Corbusier building can't be furnished. The Le Corbusier building, it stops you from mindlessly buying things.'

The privately owned radio station set up in the building in 1981 encourages people 'to take the floor… giving them a degree of assurance'. One tenant explains how neighbours relate to each other. The residents, many of them single and fairly young, get to meet each other through the many associations active in the building. Another occupant tells how his job looking after the terrace on the roof has motivated him 'to get involved politically… to show another side of the left wing'. The architect-teacher couple describes to Rosler how they became fascinated by the building and by the apartments with their fantastic views. They also state that, unlike in their previous home, they have made many acquaintances at 'Le Corbu', as residents call the housing complex. The architect shows some sketches he has made of improvements to the building, shyly proffering a strangely compelling showerhead prototype. The video closes with a view of the garden setting and the building's façade, overlaid with Corbu's spare diagrams and daubed with exuberant children's drawings.

SB and Martha Rosler

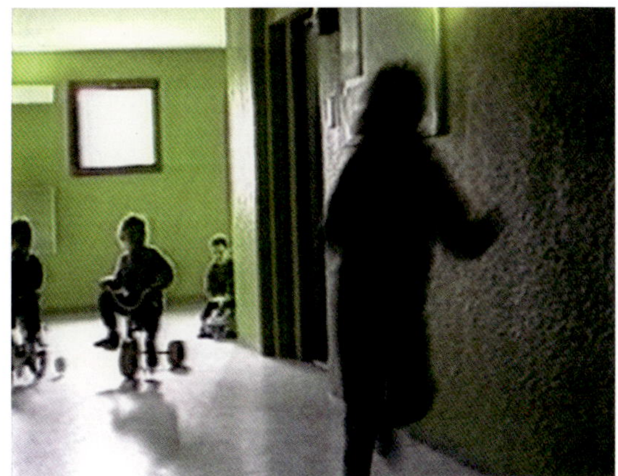
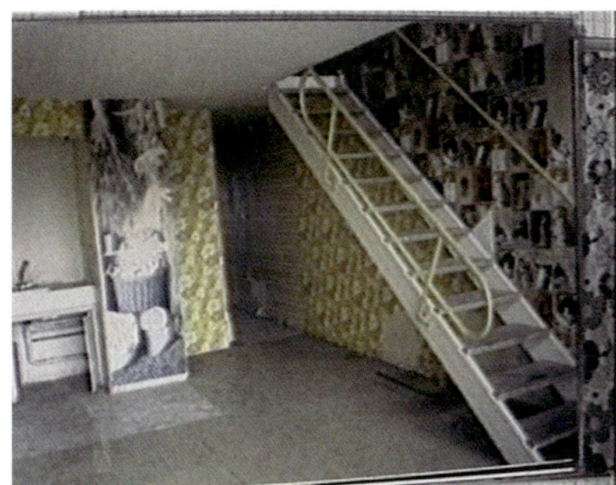
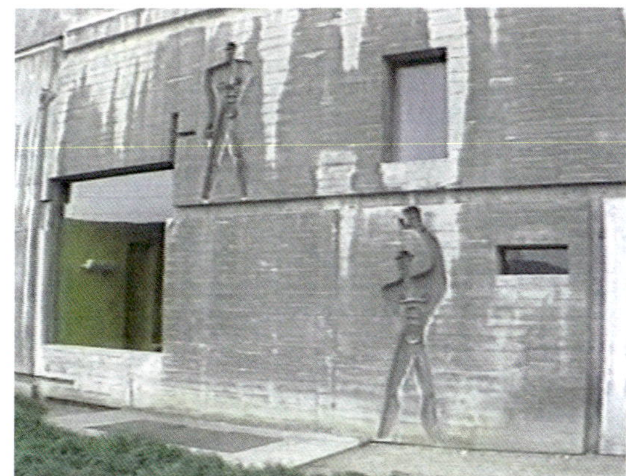
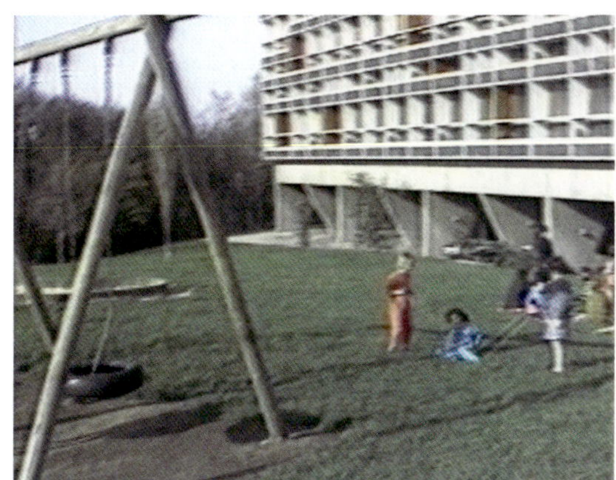
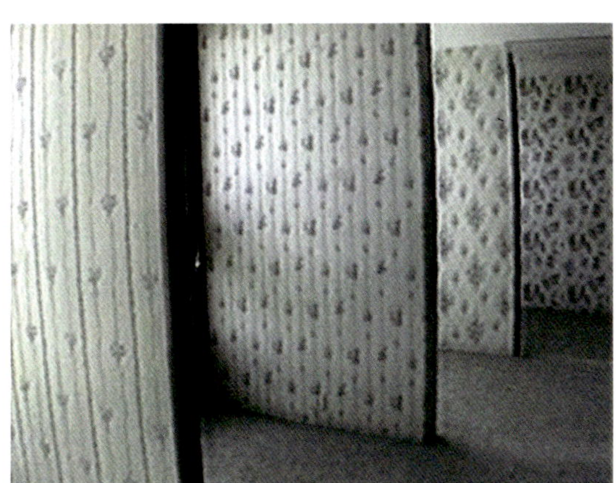
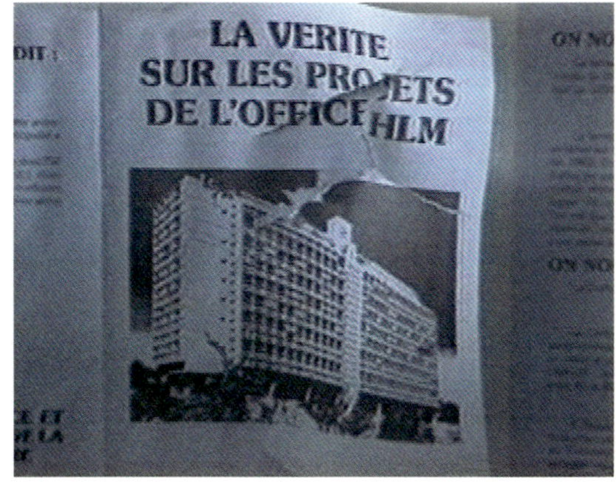
LA VERITE
SUR LES PROJETS
DE L'OFFICE HLM

INTRODUCTION

The *Unité d'Habitation* in the village of Firminy (total population: 23.124) is a very specific building. Actually, when one takes a closer look at its social composition, one notices that it is not at all representative of Firminy, nor of the population that normally lives in H.L.M. (council housing) buildings.

First of all, while the population of Firminy is ageing due to a severe economic decline, the population of the *Unité* still has a low average age. Of the 362 inhabitants 77.4% is younger than 40 years and only 3% older than 60 years, while of the total population of Firminy 49.9% is younger than 40 years and 21.4% older than 60 years.

A significant difference, especially since the average age at the *Unité* is about 29, with a slight increase on the higher floors and especially on the 7th floor, where the majority of inhabitants live since the beginning of the *Unité* (1968). This also explains the significant small number of children on the 6th and 7th floor. On the first two floors, on the contrary, the number of children is relatively high and this makes the average age drop. The 3rd, 4th and 5th floor in their totality account for a small number of children. This can be explained by the types of apartments available for the tenants on these floors. There are mostly F1, F2 and F3 apartments and only some F4, F5 and F6 (even none at the third floor), which causes a disproportionate presence of single persons and childless couples.

Furthermore, the larger households (6 persons and more) live on the first two floors where the bigger apartments are located. These larger households are generally of North african origin, most of them have the French nationality, and have their own culture. However, these do not constitute the totality of larger households at the *Unité*. There are also those originally from the surrounding agricultural regions which have not yet adjusted themselves to urban culture. This type of household is very common in Firminy, those at the *Unité* consider the building as temporary residence. Although some larger households are present at the *Unité*, they are still outnumbered by the single persons, the largest category of inhabitants (39%). Among them is a great group of nurses working at the Hospital in Firminy.

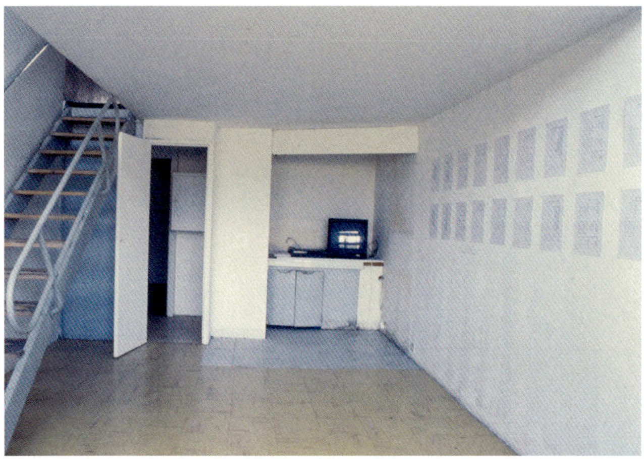

Le Corbusier's housing projects, in contrast, were meant to address the domiciling needs of ordinary people. Yet their insufficiencies led to tenant's demands for improvement. Their response — 'How Do We Know What Home Looks Like?' — was to 'normalise' its interior appearance, with aggressively boisterous 'bourgeois' wallpaper, posters, pictures, children's stickers and even mural paintings. Corbusier believed in the socially transformative role of urban planning and design: modernism — cognisant of humans and nature — and modernity marching hand in hand to 'streamline' historical practices, social structures and ideas. The ability of the bourgeoisie to resist an economically democratic society — and the elevation of possessive individualism so that today it is not at all clear what remains of the public sphere — has so far been able to destroy modernism's promise of modernity as social democracy. □

The *Unité d'Habitation* of Le Corbusier at Firminy, France, 1993
Installation view

The *Unité d'Habitation* of Le Corbusier at Firming, France, 1993
Statistics of inhabitants

I Total population

Firminy

		%
Total	23.124	
Men	11.112	48%
Women	12.012	52%

Specification by age

Age	Total	%	Men	%	Women	%
0 -19	6051	21.1	3199	52.9	2852	47.1
20-39	6205	28.8	3076	49.6	3129	50.4
40-49	2946	12.7	1506	51.1	1440	48.9
50-59	2563	11.0	1219	47.6	1344	52.4
60-74	3311	14.0	1440	43.5	1871	56.5
74- +	2048	7.4	672	32.8	1376	67.2

Unité

		%
Total	362	
Men	186	51.4
Women	176	48.6

Specification by age

Age	Total	%	Men	%	Women	%
0 -19	103	28.5	59	57.2	44	42.7
20-39	177	48.9	85	48.0	92	52.0
40-49	55	15.2	31	56.3	24	43.7
50-59	16	4.4	7	43.75	9	56.25
60-74	10	2.8	3	30.0	7	70.0
75- +	1	0.2	1			

II Average age of population of Unité

	Head of the family (official tenant)	Average of total population
Total building	35	29
Rue 1	35	24
Rue 2	35	27
Rue 3	32	28
Rue 4	32	25
Rue 5	35	27
Rue 6	37	36
Rue 7	40	32

Specification by age

	Rue 1	Rue 2	Rue 3	Rue 4	Rue 5	Rue 6	Rue 7	Total
0 - 5	6	1	1	3	1	0	3	15
5 - 9	12	4	3	7	3	0	4	33
10-19	10	15	6	5	5	4	8	53
20-29	11	34	13	17	17	12	13	117
30-39	16	11	18	18	10	9	8	80
40-49	7	12	6	5	7	2	13	52
50-59	1	4	2	2	0	2	6	17
60- +	2	1	0	1	0	5	3	12
Total	65	82	49	48	43	34	58	379

III Composition of households

Firminy

Household	Total	%	French	%	Other	%
1 person	2.194	25.5	2.115	96.3	79	3.7
2 persons	2.484	28.8	2.376	95.6	108	4.4
3 persons	1.539	17.8	1.449	94.1	90	5.9
4 persons	1.542	19.9	1.455	94.3	87	5.7
5 persons	615	7.2	523	85.0	83	15.0
6 persons and more	236	2.8	114	48.3	122	51.7
Total	8.610		8.032	93.3	576	6.7

Unité

Household	Total	%	French	%	Other	%
1 person	67	41.4	63	94.0	4	6.0
2 persons	36	22.2	35	97.8	1	2.8
3 persons	23	14.2	21	91.3	2	8.7
4 persons	13	8.0	12	92.3	1	7.7
5 persons	13	8.0	10	77.0	3	23.0
6 persons and more	10	6.2	8	80.0	2	20.0
Total	162		149	92.0	13	8.0

Family situation at Unité
(based upon the observation of 154 households)

married	40	26.0 %
cohabitating	34	22.0
single	60	39.0
single with children	10	6.5
widow	3	2.0
divorced	7	4.5

IV Professional status of inhabitants of Unité

1. Men and Women	Total	%
	139	
Salaried	129	92.8
a professional status unknown	0	0.0
b trained or specialized worker	22	17.0
c qualified or highly qualified worker	16	12.4
d shopfloor-management	0	0.0
e technical management	2	1.6
f middle-management: technician, technical designer, salesman etc.	5	3.9
g public administration: teacher, social worker, nurse, etc.	25	19.3
h engineer or administrative management	2	1.6
i public administration: university-lecturer, etc.	20	15.5
j public administration: office worker, maintainance staff, ancilliary worker, etc.	37	28.7
Non-salaried	10	7.2
k free-lancer or employer	7	70.0
l household-help	3	30.0

Specification by age

Profession / Age	a	b	c	d	e	f	g	h	i	j	k	l
15-19	0	0	0	0	0	0	0	0	0	0	0	0
20-24	0	1	2	0	0	1	0	0	1	8	0	1
25-29	0	2	5	0	2	1	7	1	2	16	4	0
30-39	0	9	7	0	0	1	11	0	9	4	2	1
40-49	0	6	2	0	0	2	6	1	6	7	7	1
50-59	0	4	0	0	0	0	0	0	2	2	2	0
60- +	0	0	0	0	0	0	1	0	0	0	0	0

2. Professional status	Total	%
Men	82	59.0
Salaried	77	94.0
a	0	0.0
b	20	25.8
c	15	19.5
d	0	0.0
e	2	2.6
f	5	6.5
g	5	6.5
h	2	2.6
i	10	13.0
j	18	23.3
Non-salaried	5	6.0
k	5	100.0
l	0	0.0

Specification by age

Profession / Age	a	b	c	d	e	f	g	h	i	j	k	l
15-19	0	0	0	0	0	0	0	0	0	0	0	0
20-24	0	0	3	0	0	1	0	0	0	2	0	0
25-29	0	2	5	0	2	1	2	1	1	9	1	0
30-39	0	7	5	0	0	1	2	0	4	1	1	0
40-49	0	6	2	0	0	2	1	1	4	4	2	0
50-59	0	5	0	0	0	0	0	0	1	2	1	0
60- +	0	0	0	0	0	0	0	0	0	0	0	0

3. Professional status	Total	%
Women	57	41.0
Salaried	52	91.2
a	0	0.0
b	2	38.0
c	1	1.9
d	0	0.0
e	0	0.0
f	0	0.0
g	20	38.4
h	0	0.0
i	10	19.2
j	19	36.5
Non-salaried	5	8.8
k	2	40.0
l	3	60.0

Specification by age

Profession / Age	a	b	c	d	e	f	g	h	i	j	k	l
15-19	0	0	0	0	0	0	0	0	0	0	0	0
20-24	0	0	0	0	0	0	0	0	1	5	0	1
25-29	0	0	0	0	0	0	5	0	1	7	0	1
30-39	0	2	1	0	0	0	9	0	5	3	1	0
40-49	0	0	0	0	0	0	5	0	2	2	1	1
50-59	0	0	0	0	0	0	0	0	1	2	0	1
60- +	0	0	0	0	0	0	1	0	0	0	0	0

Salaried women

Firminy	33.42 %
Unité	43.18 %

Specification of other income-groups at Unité

	Total	%	Men	Women
Retired	8	16.8	4	4
Sick-leave	1	2.2	1	0
Child benefit	5	11.0	0	5
Social security	17	37.7	10	7
Student	15	32.3	5	10

V Places where inhabitants of Unité work

	Total	%
Firminy	55	38.0
Saint-Etienne	49	35.0
Region of Loire	21	15.0
Region of Haute-Loire	11	8.0
Lyon	4	2.5
Paris	2	1.0
Other	1	0.5

VI Residential movements in 1982

Firminy

	Population	%	French	%	Other	%
Total	23.124		21.595		1.529	
Same building	12.346	53.3	11.632	53.9	614	40.2
Same village	18.572	80.3	17.386	80.5	1.529	77.6
Other village	4.452	19.3	4.209	19.5	343	22.4

Unité

	Population	%	French	Other
Total	339		297	42
Same apartment	56	16.5	52	4
Same building	116	34.2	96	20
Same village	49	14.5	44	5
Other village (- 30 km)	87	25.7	76	11
Other region	26	7.7	24	2
Abroad	5	1.4	5	0

VII Presence of inhabitants at Unité

Since	Number	Profession	%
1968	3	specialized worker: 2, teacher: 1	1.8
1969	4	civil servant: 1, without profession: 1 teacher: 1, specialized worker: 1	2.4
1970	3	lecturer: 1, civil servant: 1, retired: 1	1.8
1971	1	lecturer: 1	0.6
1972	2	qualified worker: 2	1.2
1973	2	specialized worker: 2	1.2
1974	2	free-lancer: 1, lecturer: 1	1.2
1975	3	teacher: 2, social worker: 1	1.8
1976	1	retired: 1	0.6
1977	2	qualified worker: 1, nurse: 1	1.2
1978	7	civil servant: 1, teacher: 2, lecturer: 1, unemployed: 1, household-help: 2	4.2
1979	2	lecturer: 1, unemployed: 1	1.2
1980	1	qualified worker: 1	0.6
1981	2	specialized worker: 1, household-help: 1	1.2
1982	3	free-lancer: 1, teacher: 1 qualified worker: 1	1.8
1983	8	invalid: 1, worker: 1, doctor: 1, specialized worker: 1, lecturer: 1, qualified worker: 2, nurse: 1	
1984	5	specialized worker: 1, teacher: 1, civil servant: 1, lecturer: 1, youth worker: 1	3.0
1985	8	specialized worker: 1, nurse: 1, without profession: 1, teacher: 2, psychologist: 1, unemployed: 1, household-help: 1	4.8
1986	3	household-help: 1, lecturer: 1, technical designer: 1	1.8

Armando Andrade Tudela

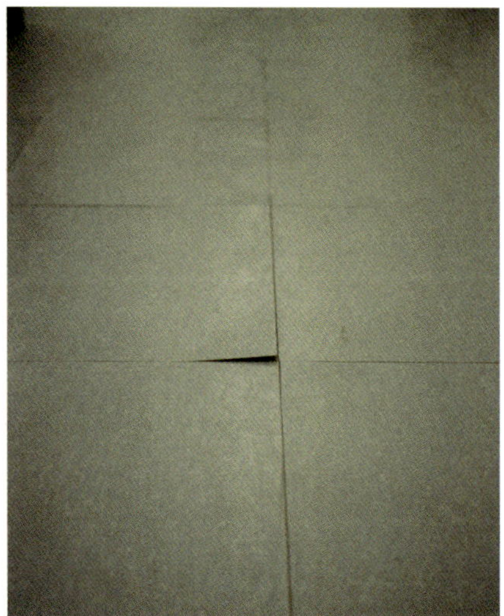

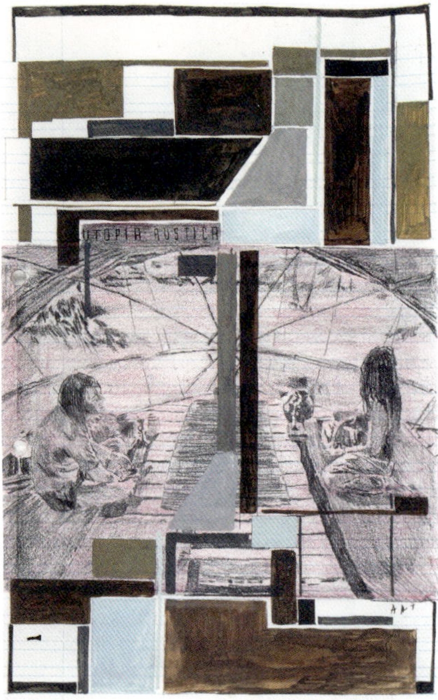

In my practice, I have been developing the idea of 'units of information' — surfaces or modules of information that flow through different aspects of culture: history, architecture, vernacular paraphernalia, etc. Within this process, these surfaces become fields of contact or grounds in which several discourses are forced to migrate or move in acts of ever increasing replacements or displacements. In tracing such moves I pretend, first, to decentralise the conditions by which signs and symbols become fixed and static, and, second, to reinforce the idea that through the reconfiguration or the interruption of values, meanings and processes, one can create imaginary solutions to comprehend more clearly our immediate landscape and historical background.

In my research, I have been focusing on several ways in which aspects of modernity and contemporary culture have been assimilated and understood in Peru. Both processes have been overshadowed by an increasing need to transform external information into concrete and ordinary actions and, at the same time, to reconsider our own historical background in the face of constant calls for adaptation. Hence, these actions not only function as strategies to replace and displace unfamiliar information for applicable, 'real' data, but also as alternative ways of keeping all information in transit and in motion. By the same token, these transformations become a flexible and extendible platform of dialogue and exchange, both of which are not only vital premises within my artwork, but also permanent metaphors of subversion, mobility and change.

Armando Andrade Tudela

Application to the Jan van Eyck Academie as Fine Art Researcher, 2003. http://www.janvaneyck.nl (4.2.2009 – amended)

Open Tile, 2005
Photograph

Utopía Rústica, 2004
Drawing

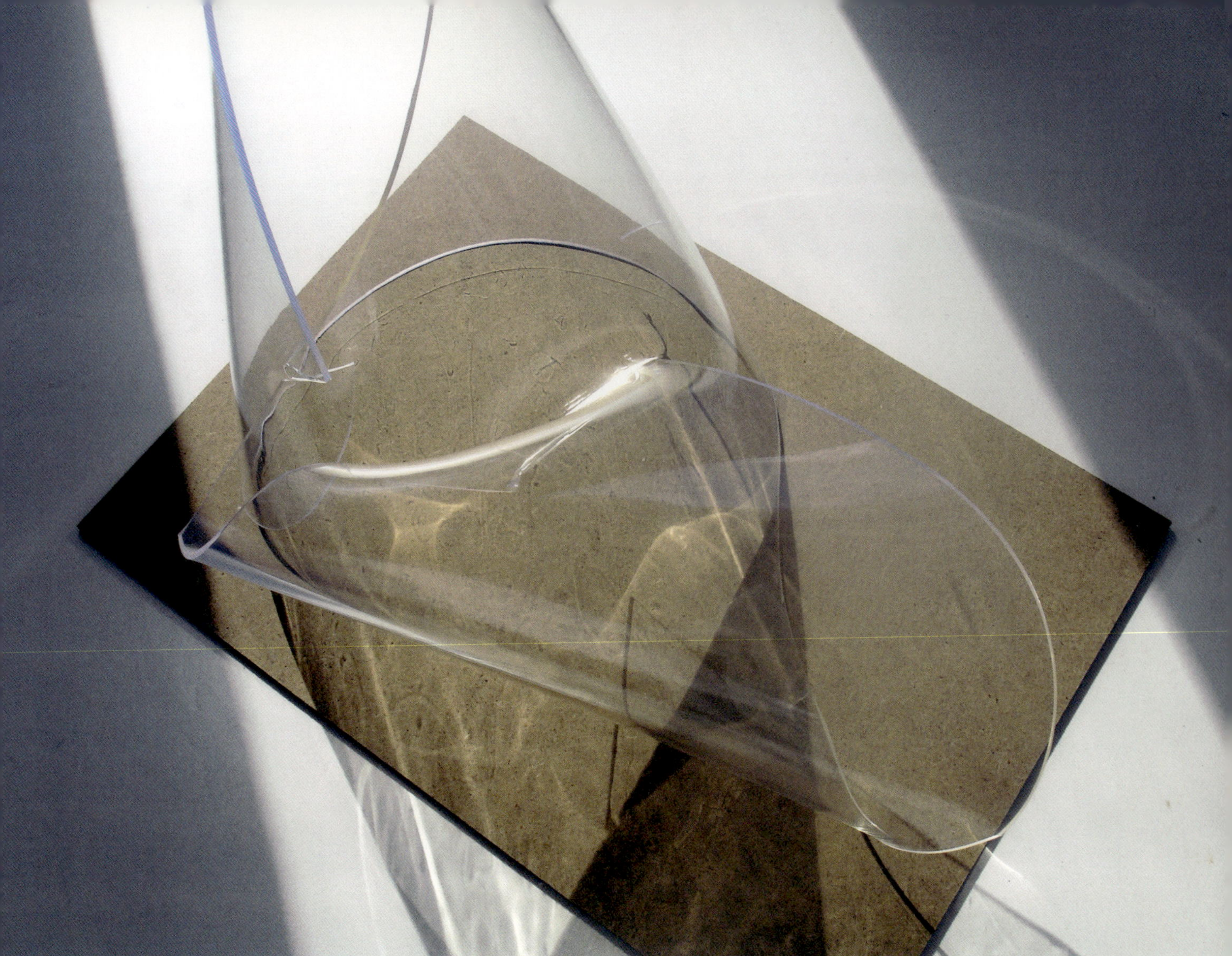

Testing polycarbonate, 2009
Artist's studio

I am interested in the development of a 'Peruvian modernity'. The term is as polymorphous as it is ambulatory, due mainly to a historically ambivalent relationship to popular art, a consistent political manipulation regarding issues of race, class and nationalism and what I see as a cyclical mistrust in geometry and technology as imperative components in the development of abstract and later Minimal and post-Minimal art. Consequently, the official status of modernity in Peru is limited to say the least. My interest then is to focus on these 'latitudes of absence' and consider them as spaces under permanent construction. ▷

Armando Andrade Tudela

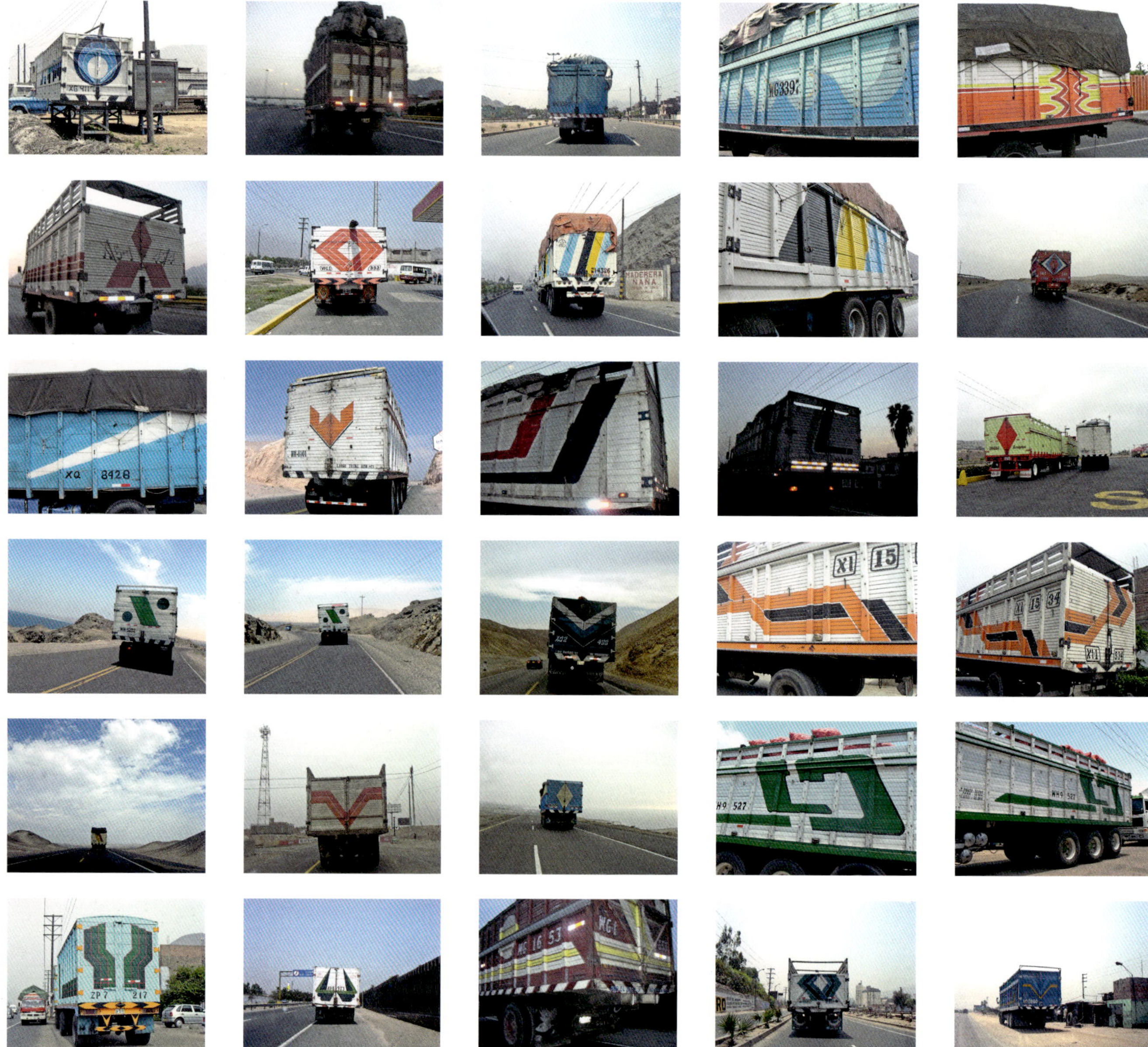

Camión, 2003
Slide projection
60 images, 35 mm slides
Taken by the artist between October and December 2003
at the Carretera Central, Panamericana Sur,
Panamericana Norte and Lima Metropolitana, Peru

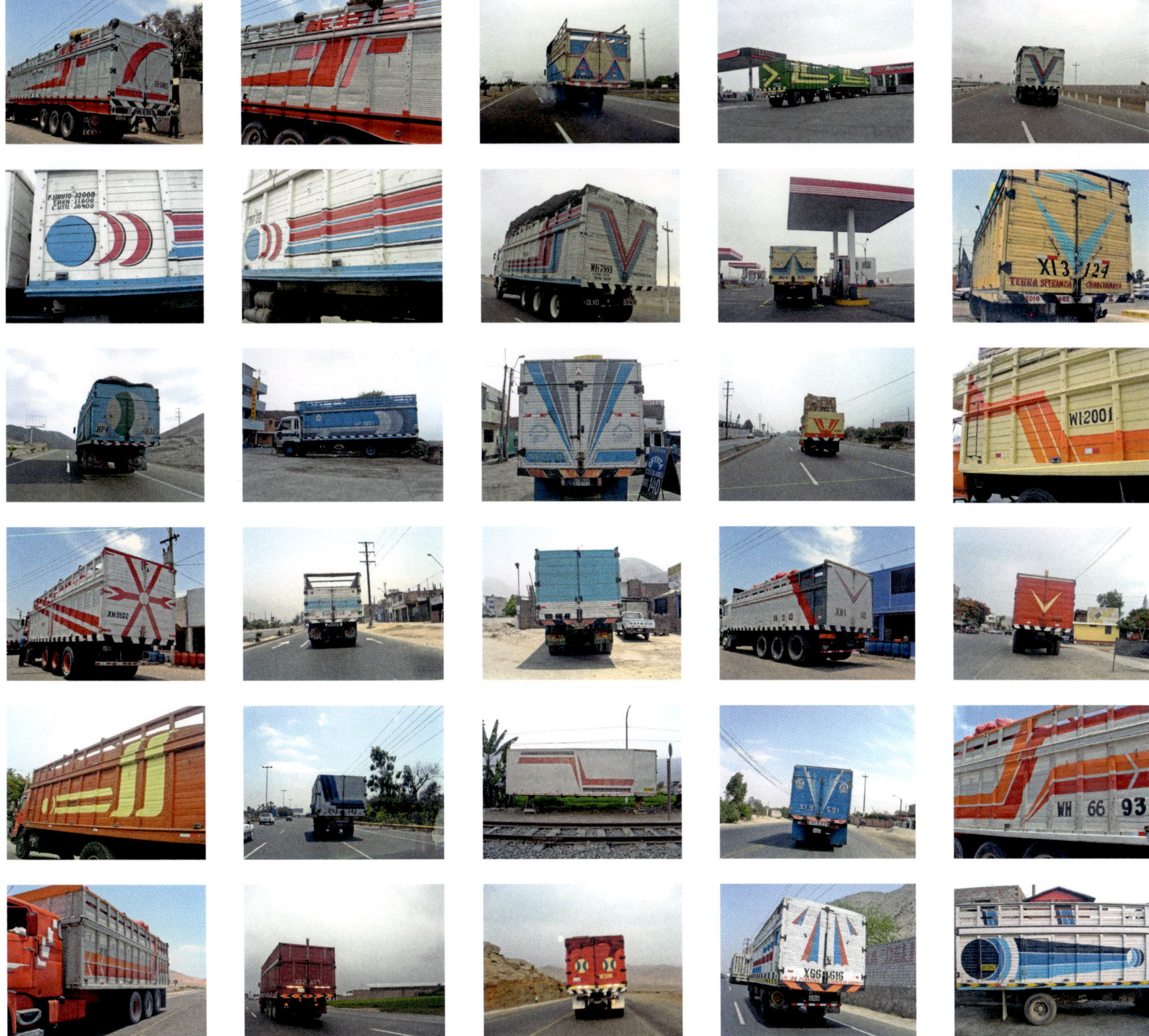

Take for instance the book and slide projection *Camión*, a series of photographs taken mostly on the highway of trucks depicting hardedge geometrical forms. This work came into being as a way of self-questioning the position of geometry in the structuring of abstract languages in Peru. In my perspective, geometric languages could never claim any real discursive and practical space in the development of Peruvian modernity. Yet the use of geometry was indeed found to be alive and active in the social sphere, not in those spaces affiliated with art. The logos painted on the trucks were even in closer affiliation to what Greenberg decoded as 'homeless abstraction' than to any other model of abstraction I had identified in Peru before. ▷

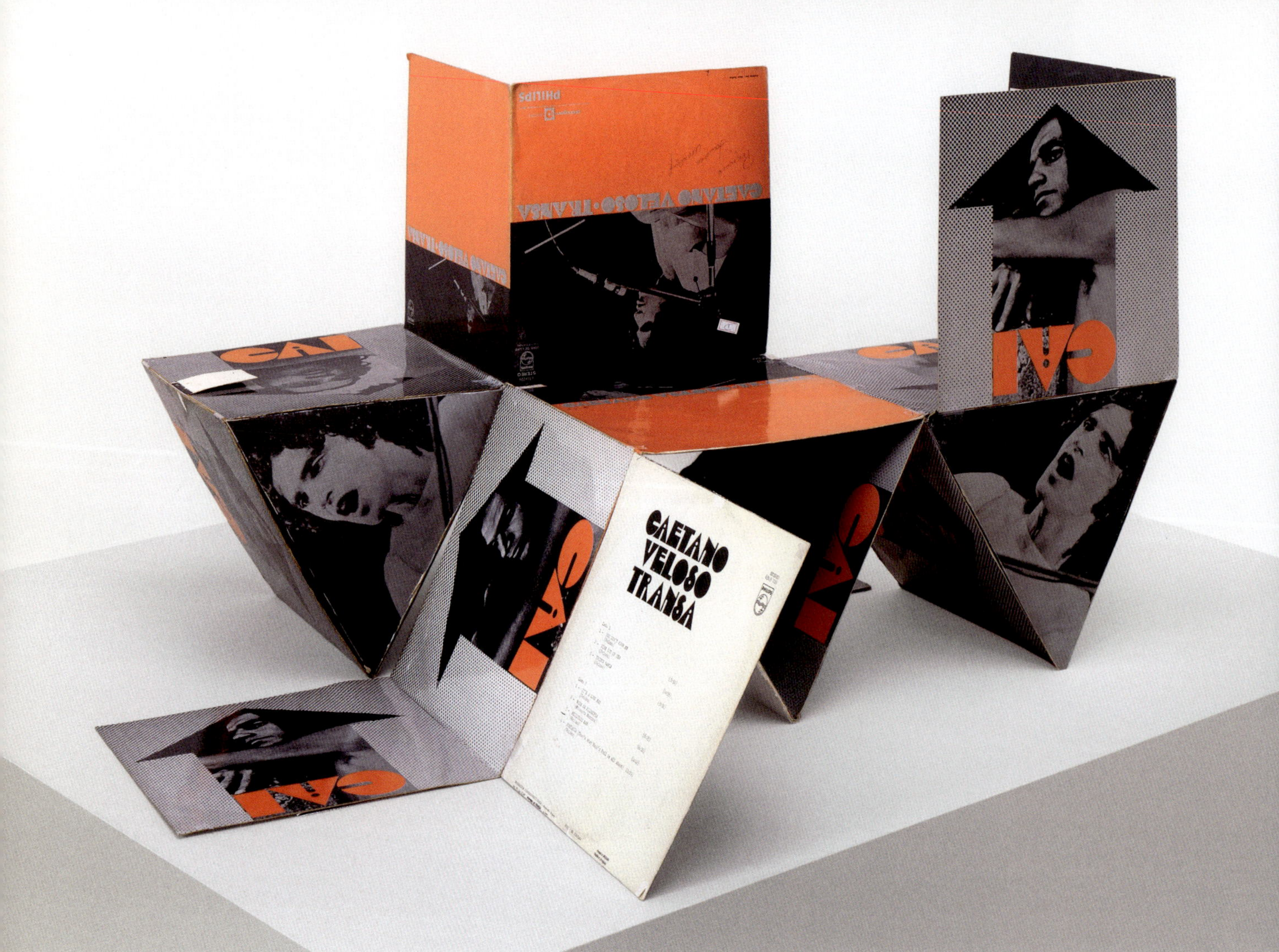

Critically and tactically I found that inside today's frenetic
network of cross-referencing and exhausted media, our
relation to the legacy of modernism has to be considered
from the perspective of an absent link and not an over-
looked process. Similarly, the possibility and impossibility
of words like legacy, affiliation and disruption have
to be practiced not according to linear sequences, but
refractively. □

Transa, 2005
Sculpture

Untitled, 2009
Sculpture
Polycarbonate film, magazine page

pp. 204–05
Untitled (no. 4), 2007–08
Sculpture
Asphalt

Untitled (no. 1), 2008
Sculpture
Wire, rattan

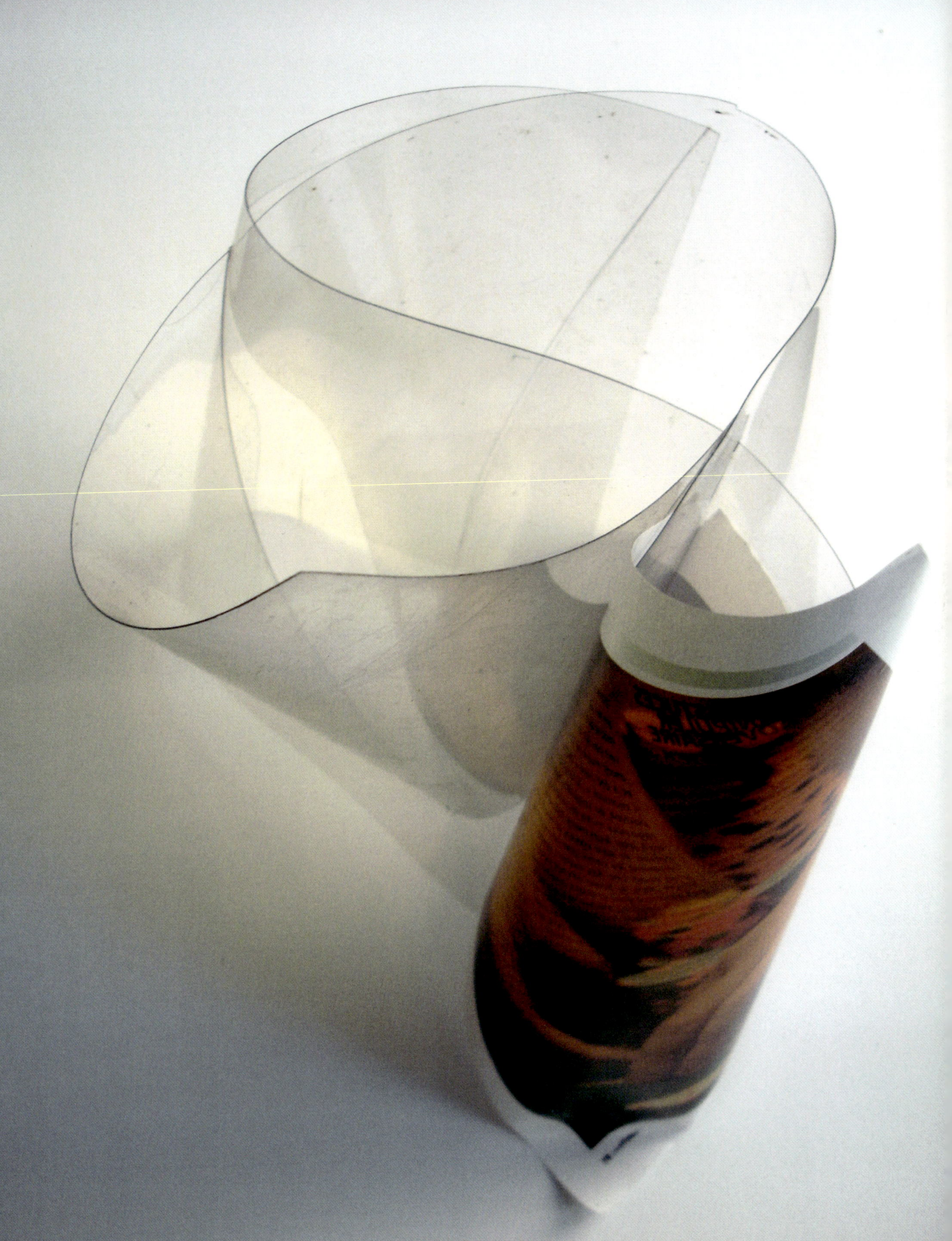

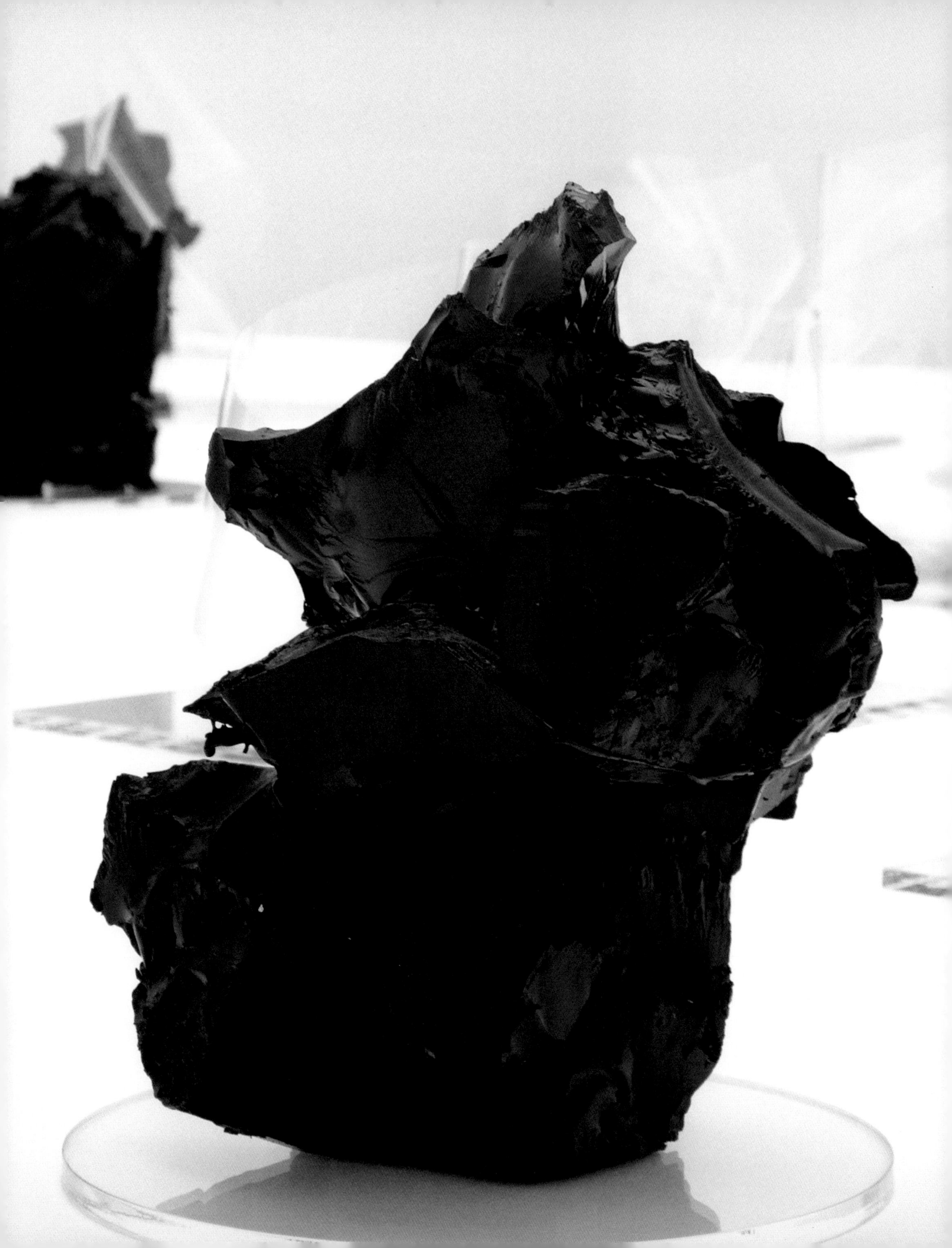

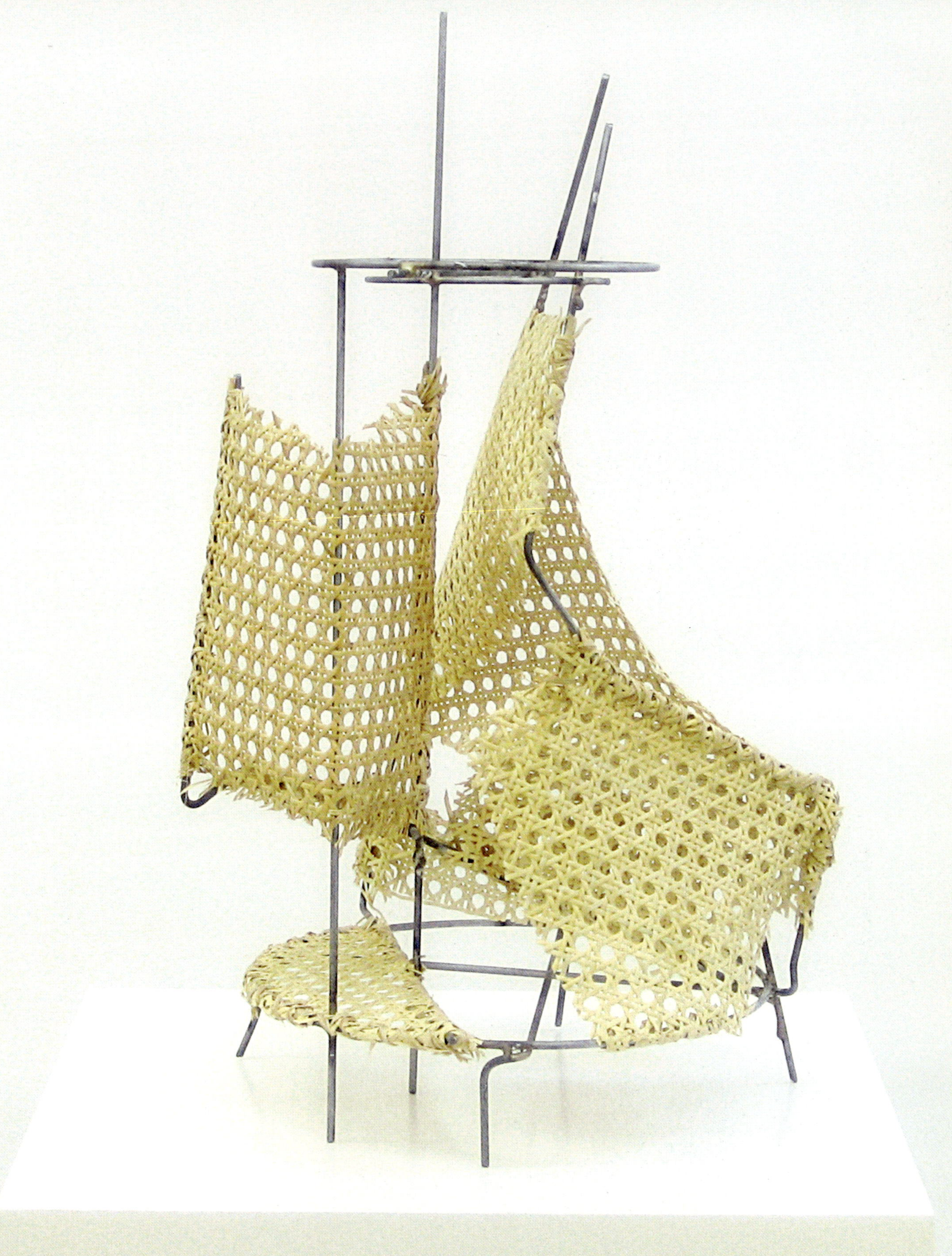

Marion von Osten

In the Desert of Modernity.
Colonial Planning and After, 2008–09
Display set

Installation views
House of World Cultures, Berlin, 2008

'In the Desert of Modernity. Colonial Planning and After' is a research project
and a travelling exhibition initiated by Marion von Osten in collaboration with
the architects, artists, activists and theorists Mogniss Abdallah, An Architektur,
Kader Attia, Tom Avermaete, Wafae Belarbi, Madeleine Bernstorff, Casamémoire,
Jesko Fezer, Hassan Darsi, Kanak Attak, Serhat Karakayali, Brigitta Kuster, Labor
k3000, Andreas Müller, Remember Resistance, Elsa de Seynes, Peter Spillmann,
Anna Voswinckel and Daniel Weiss.

'We regard these buildings in Morocco as the greatest achievement since Le Corbusier's *Unité d'Habitation* at Marseilles.
Whereas the *Unité* was the summation of a technique of thinking
about 'habitat' that started forty years ago, the importance of
the Moroccan buildings is that they are presented as ideas; but
it is their realisation in built form that convinces us that here
is a new universal'[1]

Under colonial rule North Africa served as a laboratory for
European modernisation projects and projections. Cities like
Algier, Oran, Casablanca, Tunis and many others were testing
grounds for several modernisation strategies during and after
the Second World War. Some of these were subsequently implemented in postwar Europe: the management of the migrating
rural population and its urbanisation in new housing projects and,
related to this, educating this population to accept new forms of
industrial production and mass consumption, as well as new
modes of dwelling. Hence, colonial modernisation was not only
directed at and against the colonised, but it also played a major
role within the modernisation projects in Europe's metropolises.

The role of postwar urban planning and architecture in North
Africa, particularly in Casablanca in Morocco, and its influence
on the revision of modern architecture and urbanism in the West
are the subjects of the exhibition and public events of *In the Desert
of Modernity*, held in Berlin in 2008 and in Casablanca and Tel Aviv
in 2009. The project reflects a central paradigm shift in the mass
housing and urban planning discourses and practices of postwar
modernism: from the acknowledgement of the pre-modern
through its translation into modern forms, to the recognition of
everyday practices as the basis of planning methodologies. This
shift in the architectural discourse of high modernism from a
morphological perspective to a focus on local actors and everyday
practices took place in the spaces and at the time of anti-colonial
struggles, during incipient liberation. The project thus shows
how transformations in architectural discourse resonate both with
the colonial and the anti-colonial project and were promoted by
migration.

In the Desert of Modernity offers a shift in perspective, focusing
not on the colonial conditions of modernity and their foundation
in traditional distinctions between civilised/uncivilised, powerful/
powerless, specialist/layman, but on the historical conjunction of
internal critiques of modernity with the collapse of colonial empires
and the emergence of anti-colonial liberation movements on
the stage of history. It tries to understand the heterogeneity of
colonialism and modernism as a constant flux of domination and
resistance sited in simultaneity and dependency and/or in the
chrono-topes of transnational migrations of people, thoughts and
practices. In this way *In the Desert of Modernity* highlights transnational relationships between colonialism and anti-colonialism,
modernity and postmodernity and its crisis.

Marion von Osten

1   Alison and Peter Smithson, 'Collective Housing in Morocco',
    Architectural Design, January 1955, p. 2.

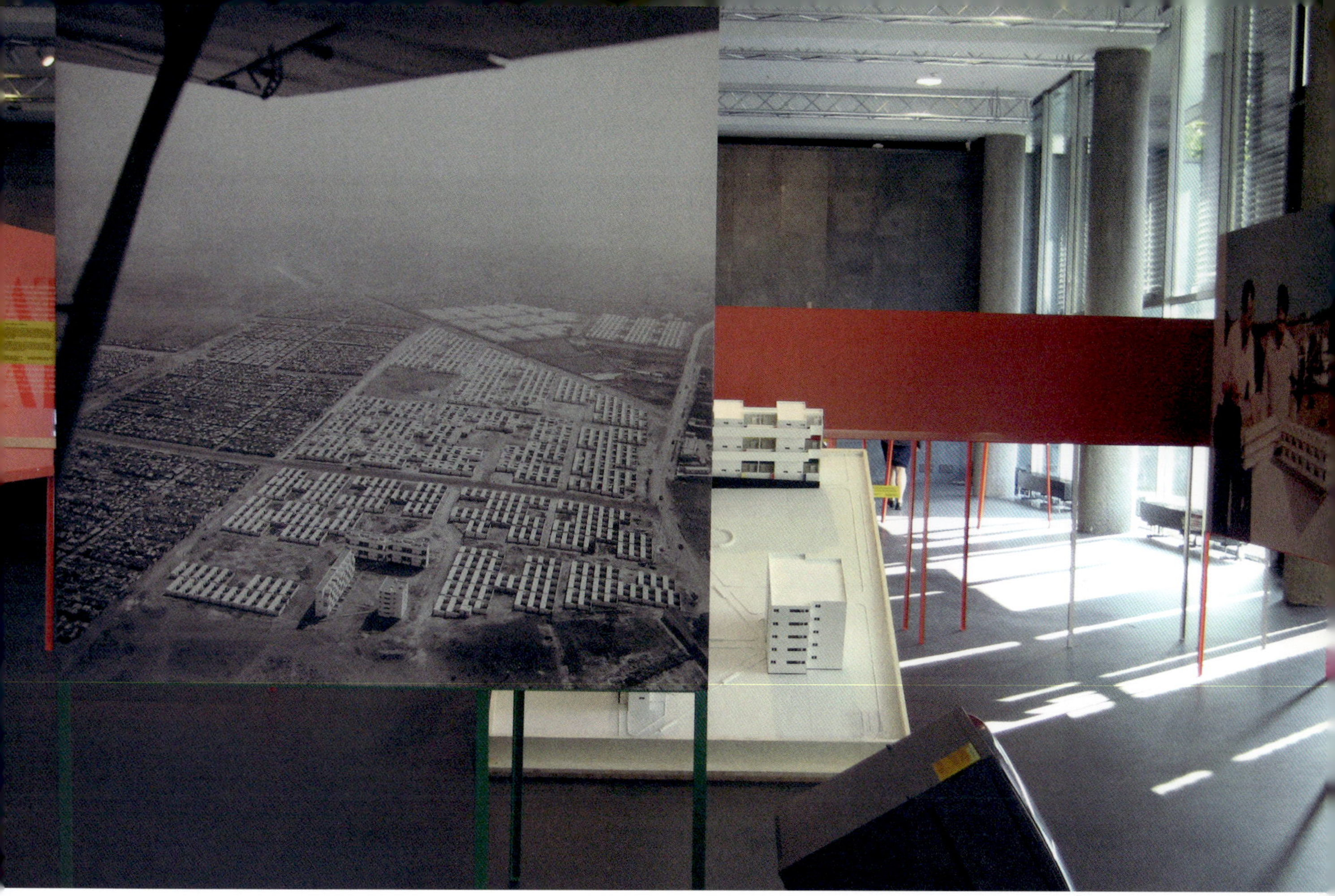

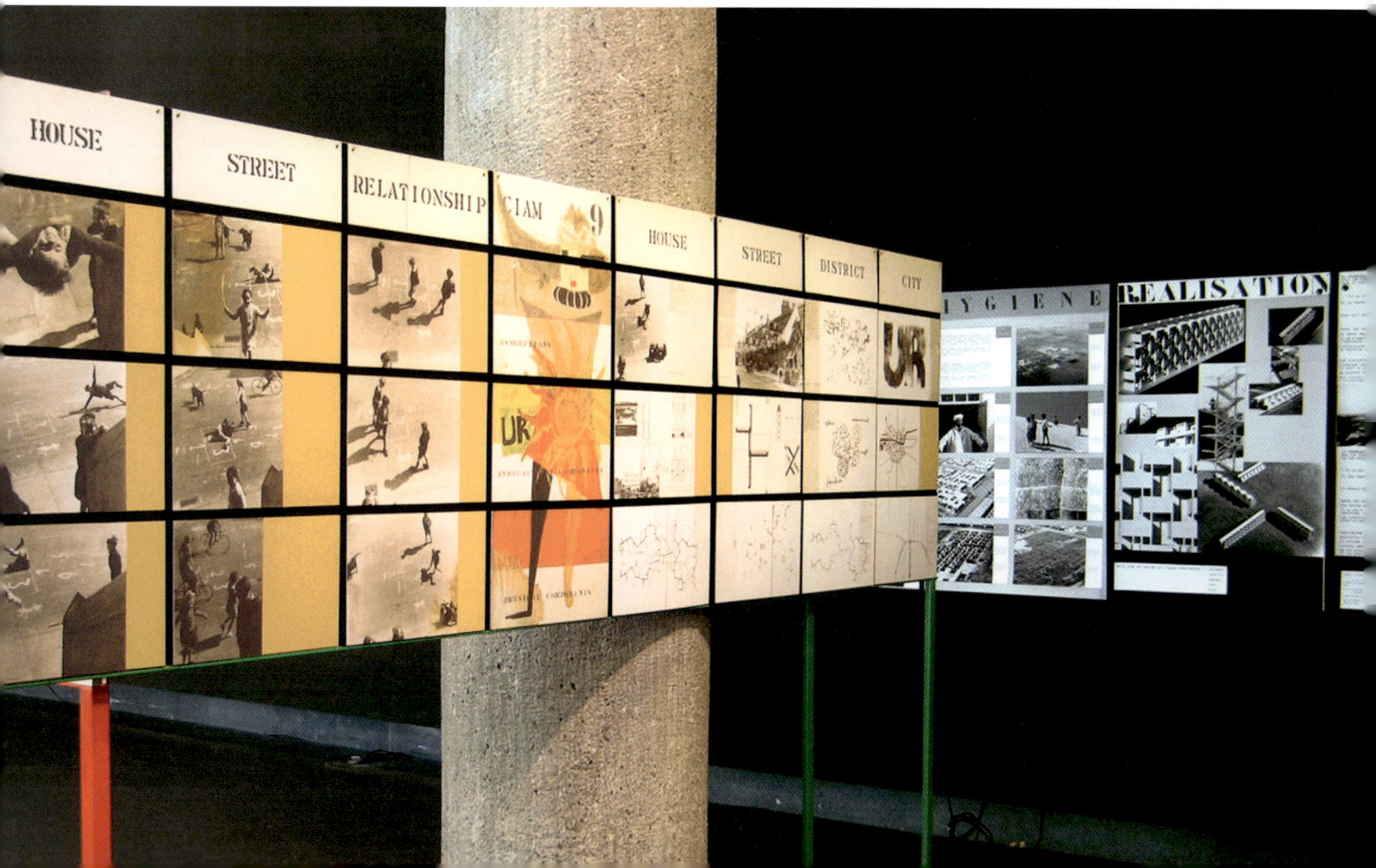

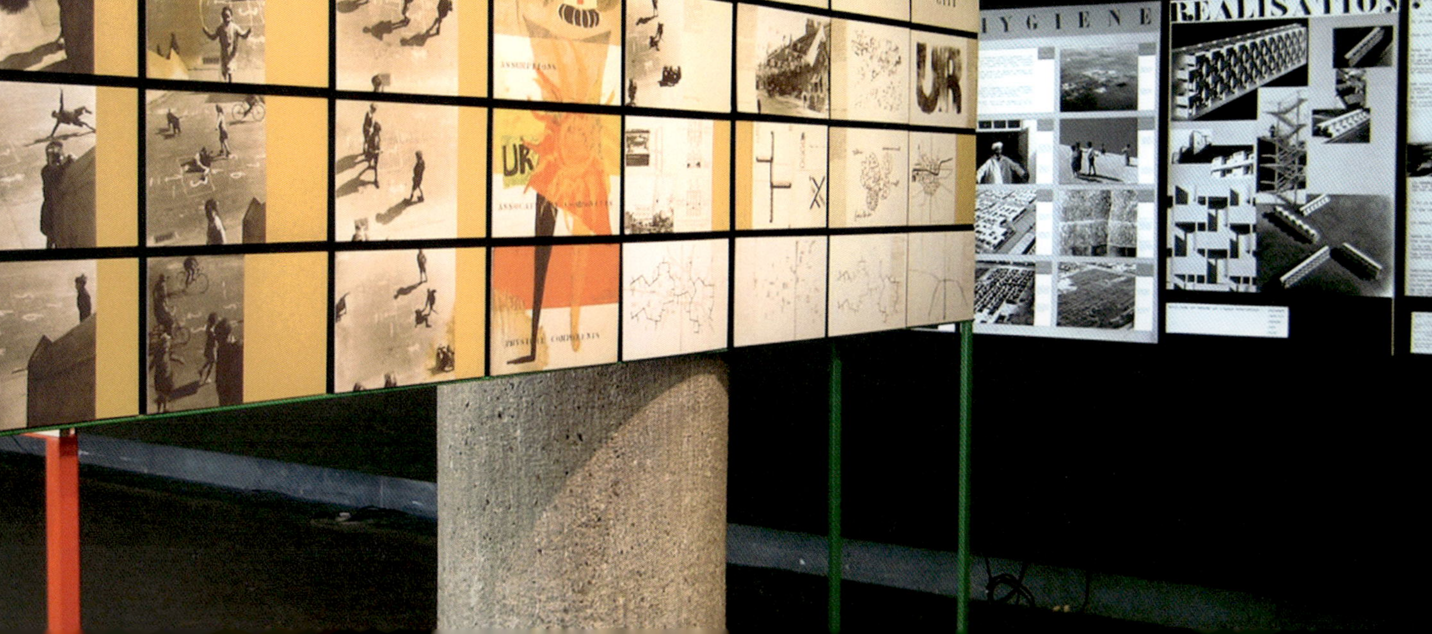
HOUSE
STREET
RELATIONSHIP CIAM 9
HOUSE
STREET
DISTRICT
CITY
HYGIENE
REALISATION
UR

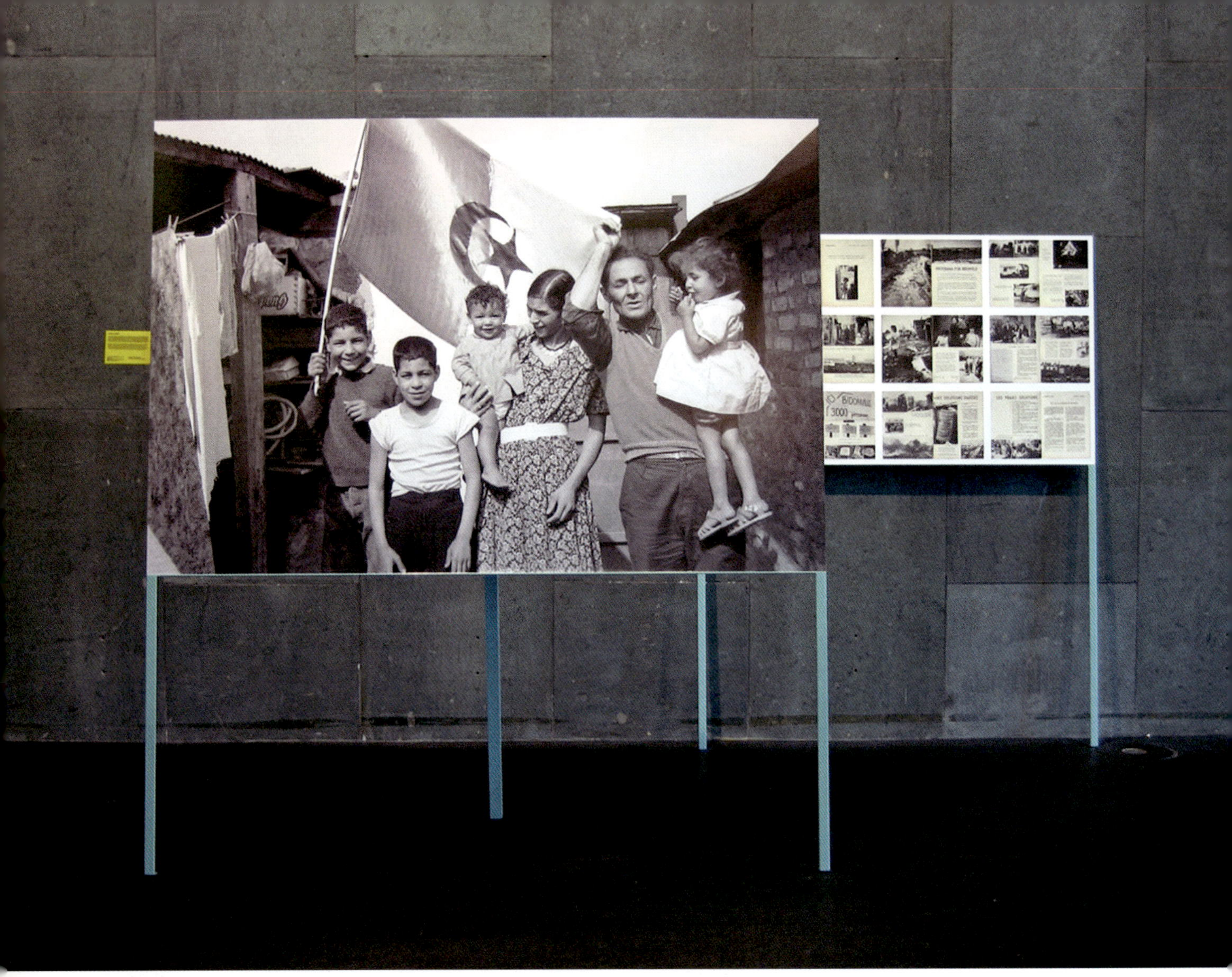

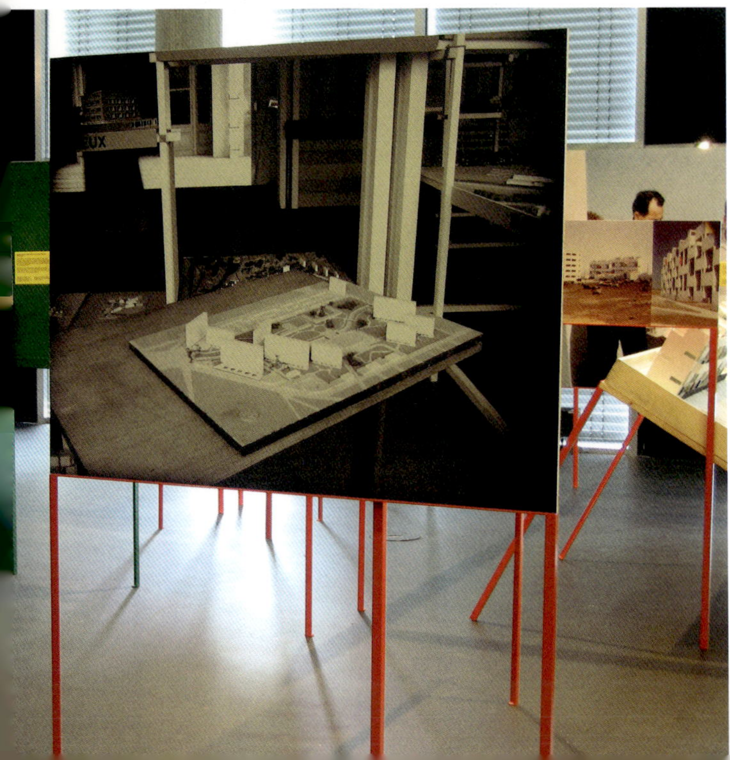
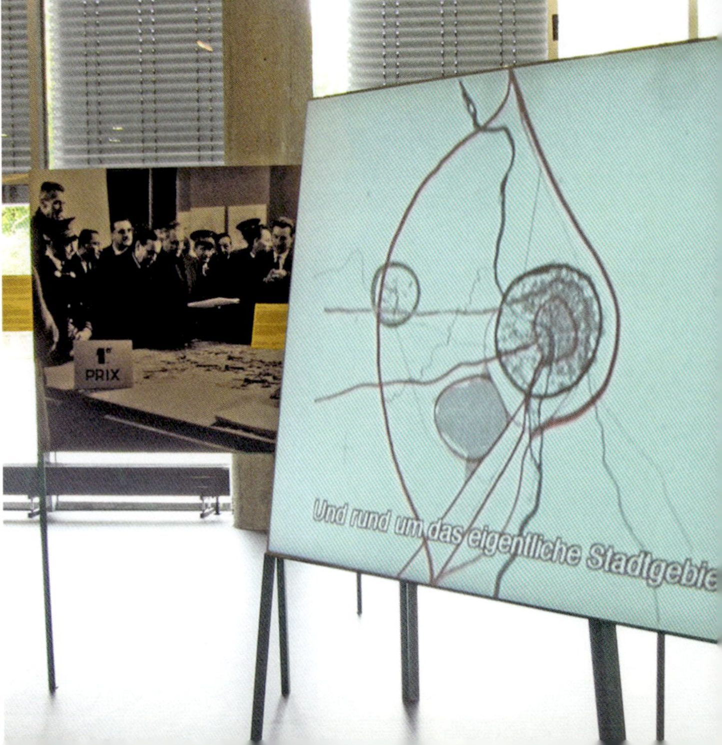
1er PRIX
Und rund um das eigentliche Stadtgebiet

Visit of the Resident General of the French protectorate, Francis
Lacoste, to the *bidonville* Carrières Centrales, Casablanca, 1954
Archives of the Ministry for Foreign Affairs, Nantes

Stephen Willats

Compartmentalised Cliff, June–July 1977
2 panels

The work was made with the active involvement of residents
living in a new tower block situated in a suburb of Paris, in
a modernist environment that was not at that time stigmatised
as most of the buildings of that period and style became later
in the 1980s. Willats also undertook other projects in the same
neighbourhood such as *Les Problèmes de la Nouvelle Réalité*
in 1977, and is currently starting to work on a new project there.
The two panels of this work are the first coloured photographs
used by the artist. SB

Conceptual Living

I am constantly looking for symbols of modern living that I can
embody in my work as recognisable catalysts. One such territory
of symbolism that I am often drawn towards centres on the projected idealisations that appear to show us a future way of life,
a future that is to be emulated, and hence lays out a possible
normality for us all. It does not matter that you have had a direct
experience of the actuality surrounding the idealisation, for
you still know all about them by their cultural projections. One
such symbol that I have constantly used is the residential tower
block; another is the office computer. For, whether you live in
a tower block or not, or use a computer or not, it is not a pre-
condition for having strong associations about them, for knowing
their controversial status in modern life.

The concrete buildings of modernism radiate, by their sheer
physical mass and their grey forms and surfaces, a powerful
message about the nature of modern life. While the planned
environment of modernism projects the idealisations of an
institutional culture that is ultimately highly reductive and deterministic, people's fundamental desire to express their identity
and their innate creativity has resulted in another layer of
meaning surreptitiously spread across the anonymous concrete.
The results are sign systems that denote human presence and
reflect the relativity in the economic, social and psychological
relationship people have with the private, encapsulated environment of their flat and the planned public spaces outside.

I see modernist housing developments as monumental
symbols of planned, modern social thinking, which are filled
with a casual mosaic of objects and signs that exist in random
displacement with each other, and sometimes even in overt
alienation. This random mosaic of information, bombarding the
senses, is psychologically and perceptually ordered into systems,
and sub-systems, that are linked to different states of social
consciousness and behaviour. Moreover, even when elements
from quite alienated sub-systems are positioned next to each
other, accidentally or purposefully occupying the same space,
they are made to co-exist, so as to transform psychologically the
meaning of that space. Thus signs and objects that denoted
authority or order are found to co-exist with those that represented
confrontation, escape, anarchy. Collections of displayed personal
objects co-exist with the consumed and so on, the whole tangen-
tial relationship between the casual displacement of things,
their media, their meaning and context being psychologically
ordered into an overall model of reality.

Stephem Willats (1988)

Conceptual Living. London: Victoria Miro Gallery, 1991 (exh. cat.)

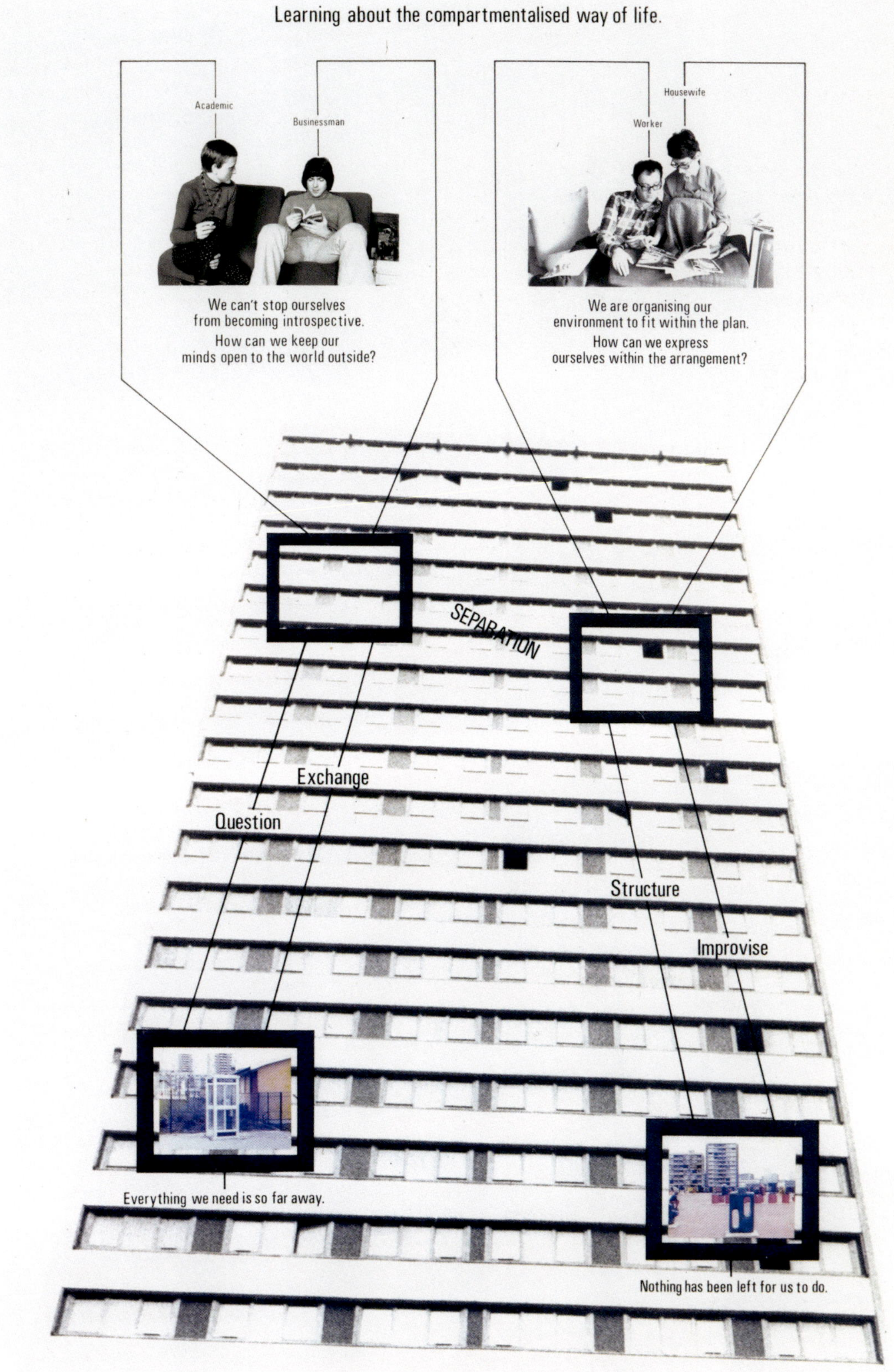
Learning about the compartmentalised way of life.
Academic
Businessman
Worker
Housewife
We can't stop ourselves
from becoming introspective.
How can we keep our
minds open to the world outside?
We are organising our
environment to fit within the plan.
How can we express
ourselves within the arrangement?
SEPARATION
Exchange
Question
Structure
Improvise
Everything we need is so far away.
Nothing has been left for us to do.

Living at a regulated distance from each other.

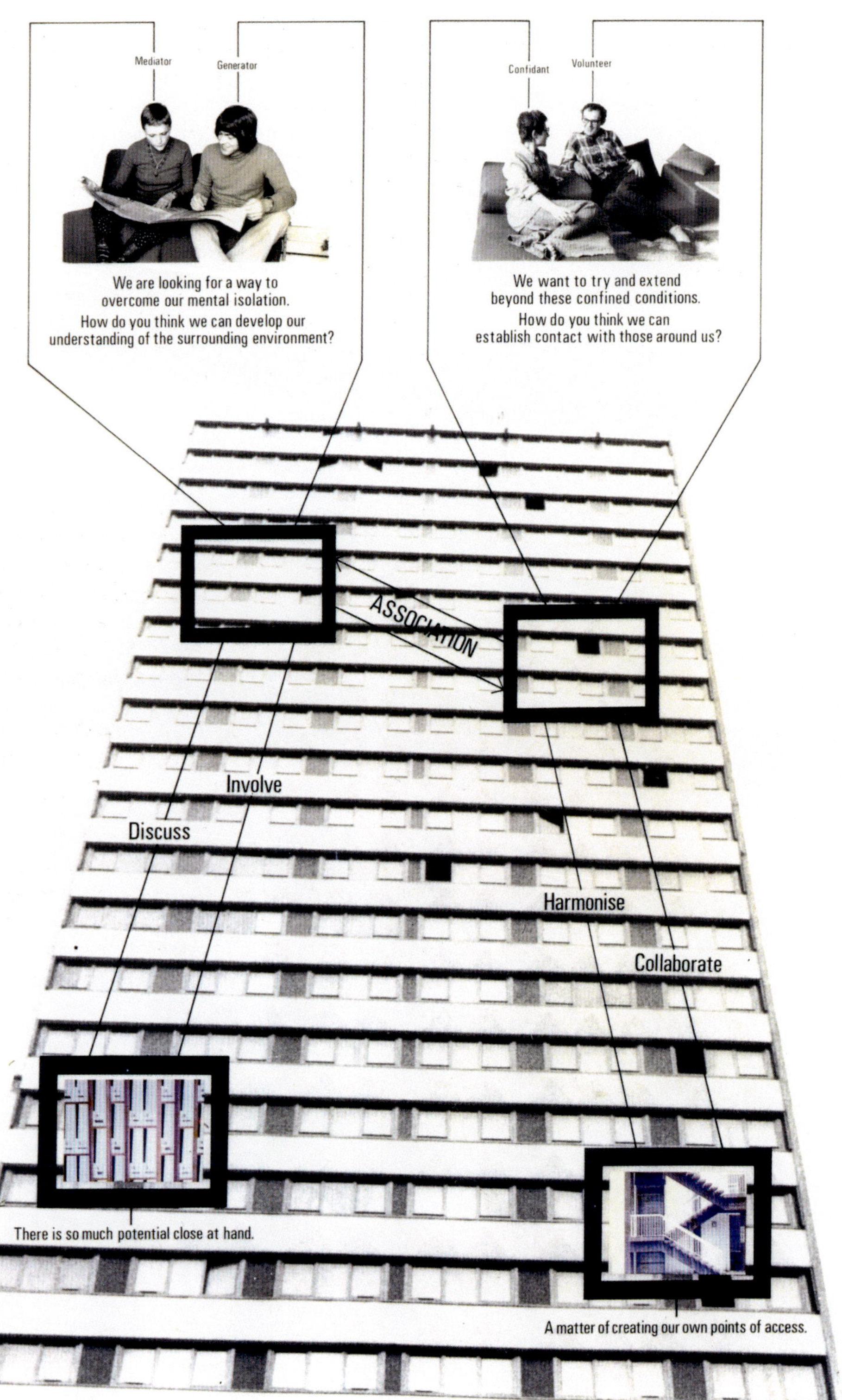

The Symbolism of the Tower Block
Throughout our culture the tower block has come to symbolise
the conflicts of modern living. Whether or not a person actually
lives in a tower block is not crucial to the power this symbol exerts.
Proliferating in the optimistic and paternalistic 1960s, the tower
block was to express externally a monumentality: a vertical icon.
In contrast the internal physicality of the block exerts enormous
pressure on residents, moulding their psychology of themselves,
their relationship to other residents and to society, and consequently it represents the social consciousness of those authoritative institutions that were its creators. Passivity, segmentation,
isolation, distancing from external reality are some of the reductive
forces working against those caught living inside the tower
block. SW

'Brentford Towers', *Society Through Art*, The Hague: Haags Centrum
voor Actuele Kunst (HCAK), 1990.

Concrete Window, November 1990 – July 1991
3 panels

On the left bank of the river dividing Antwerp there is another city,
a satellite seemingly hidden from the visitor to the historic centre
of the main city. This satellite city is a dormitory of apartments
situated in vast slabs of concrete, dotted around like monuments
in a highly ordered, landscaped park. I invited three women,
who were resident in separate parts of an apartment block at Ernest
Claesstraat 12, to participate in making a work centred on the
environment of their living space, photographically documenting
objects they identified as significant under their supervision before
making a tape-recorded discussion as to the personal meanings
they attached to them. The result of each documentation then
formed the context of the 'symbolic world' presented in the work,
founded on the actuality of each woman's unique experience of
a common structure that, unwittingly, links them. SW

Antwerp: Galerie Montevideo, 1991 (exh. cat.)

The housing environment represented in the work was built on
the North bank of the River Schelde dividing Antwerp. The
building plans were originally proposed by Le Corbusier, the city
had bought the plans, and the buildings were then executed by
their own architects. The women represented in the work actively
participated with the artist in developing a picture of their living
environment in which two categories of objects were identified:

1) Objects that represented the determinism of their life in the flat.
2) Objects that symbolised a personal freedom, both psychologically and socially.

The window was of fundamental importance to the women's lives
as a means of perceptual and psychological escape, opening up
to a symbolic world that they could imagine but not touch. Though
the women all looked out onto the same view from the same
housing block, because they lived on different floors this reinforced the relativity of their perceptions and attachments to that
view. SB

There is an inseparable relationship between the physical reality society constructs and its social ideology. For the form of the city, its buildings and spaces, are an externalisation of the social norms and conventions that govern the way we perceive, and relate to, other people. Thus, integral to the production of a society's objects, whether on the scale of public building or personal possession, are the idealisations of that society, which give the object both its physical form and its social meaning.

There is an interplay between the form and function of objects and the social messages they radiate, so that the construction of environments of objects say much more than the practical function of those objects. The organisation of objects in a space can be considered an expressive statement that exhibits a particular sensibility, an ideology that is at variance with the deterministic function society has given to those individual objects.

In my works I represent a polemic: between the determinism of objects and the self-organisational creativity of people, I show a 'symbolic world' that acts as a parallel reality to that of the audience. In the works presented in the exhibition *Concrete Window* at Galerie Montevideo, I have focused on modern apartment blocks for the construction of this 'symbolic world', as I see that they can symbolise this polemic between people and objects. I represent the buildings as monumental objects and icons of society's idealisations that deny the potential variety of the personal realities they contain. The anonymous, concrete, segmented fabric of those apartment blocks totally conceals the mosaic of rich sign systems that are continually being evolved by the occupants in the pursuit of their individual realities. Central to this creation of individual realities is the placement of objects and signs inside people's living spaces, which, while originating from institutional culture, are assigned a new meaning by the position they are given in a network of other objects.

The semiology of these environments is from the creative act of transforming the given determinism of objects into self-expressions of individual identity. This is an act of some subversion, and for my exhibition *Concrete Window* it is the central issue that has acted as a catalyst to the development of the works I made in Antwerp.

So, the vast, modernist apartment blocks that dominate recent housing developments in Antwerp I see as particularly powerful icons of contemporary living, and consequently, two buildings — Jan Denucéstraat III in south Antwerp and Ernest Claesstraat 12 on the left bank — that I was especially drawn towards became the context for three new works discussed here individually. SW

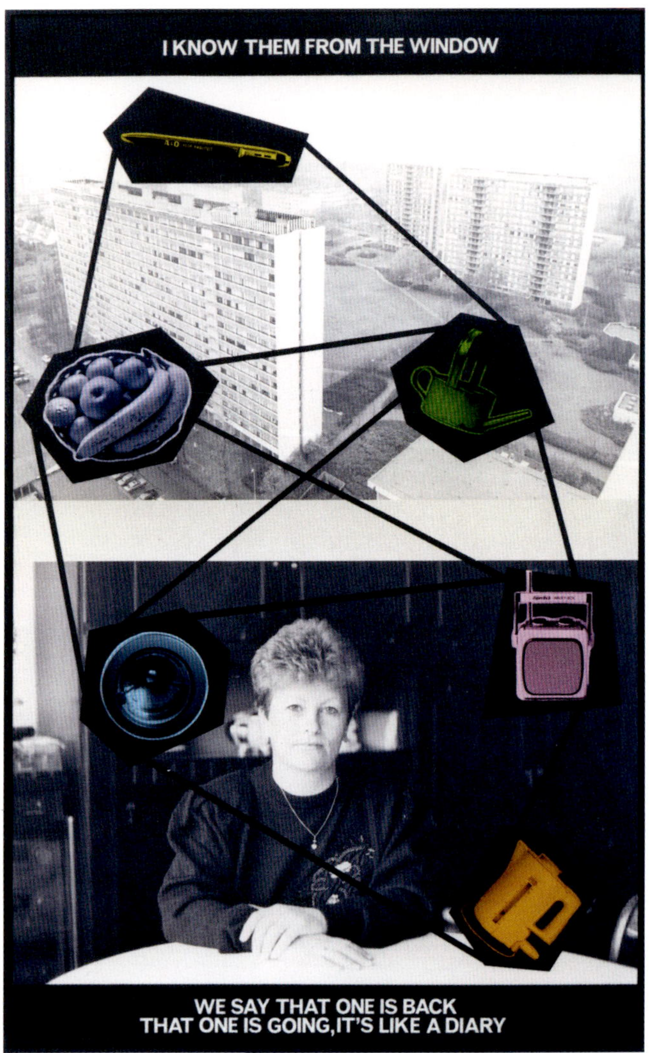

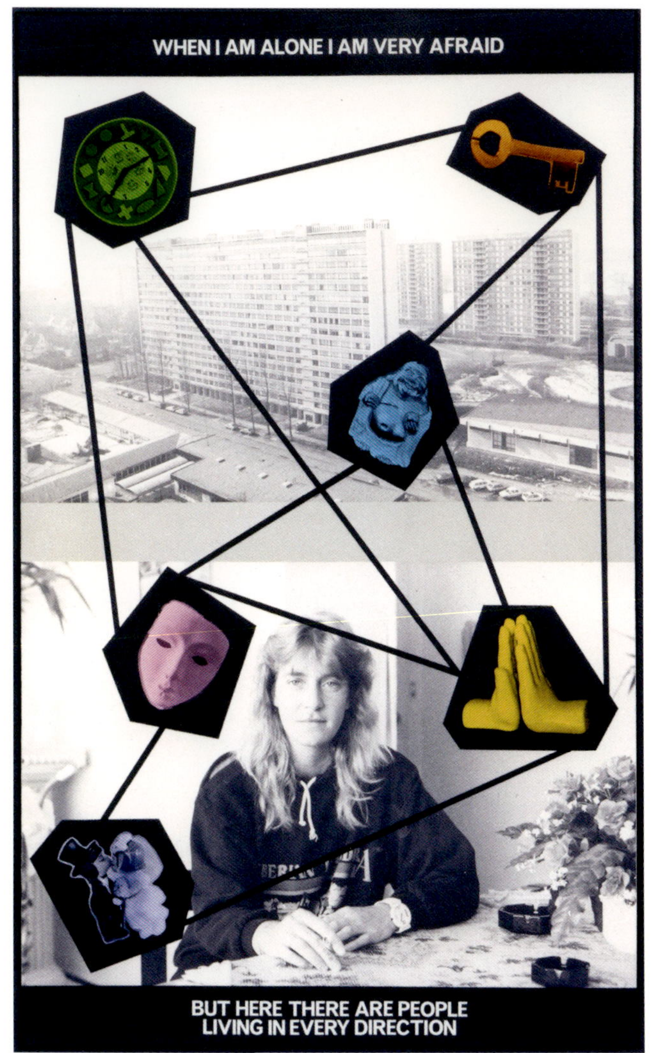
WHEN I AM ALONE I AM VERY AFRAID
BUT HERE THERE ARE PEOPLE
LIVING IN EVERY DIRECTION

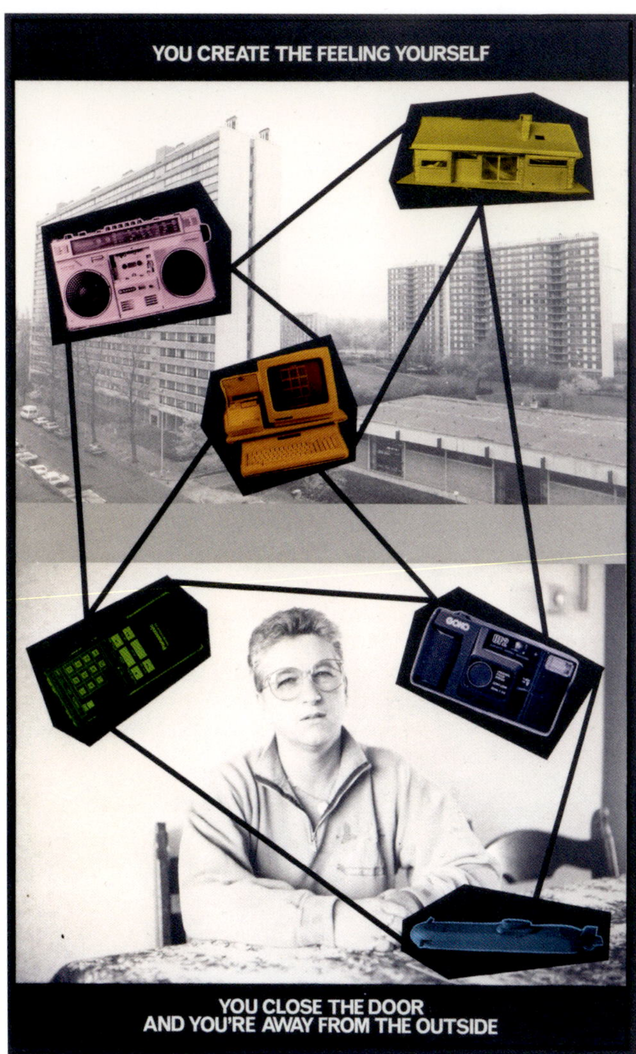
YOU CREATE THE FEELING YOURSELF
YOU CLOSE THE DOOR
AND YOU'RE AWAY FROM THE OUTSIDE

Christopher Williams

**Ablaye Bà, Bira Bà,
Sidath Fall and Aziz Ngom,
La Sénégalaise de L'Imprimerie,
Dakar, Senegal
May 14, 1996 (No. 1, 2)**
1996
2 photographs
Gelatin silver prints

**Modernity as a Modality
The Condition of Photography According to Christoper Williams**

Christopher Williams is not simply a photographer, neither in the professional nor in the purely artistic sense; it is more a case of his artistic work dealing with photography as one of the decisive interfaces in modernity between an autonomous, substantially charged conception of art on the one hand, and the visual processes of industrial production on the other hand, which for their part tend mostly to operate with a more craft-orientated approach to art. Most of the conceptual questions relating to 'art and photography' restrict themselves to the influence of photography on art, especially on painting, but photography as art too restricts its thematic considerations to the specific artistic potential of photography. His roots in the Conceptual art and re-photography of the late 1970s enable Williams to go beyond this and address the challenge that photography as a mode of industrial production and a professional field of activity, as a reproductive medium and as a socio-cultural promise of modernisation represents for every conception of art.

The formulation 'you press the button', along with its one promise, the easy operation of the camera, and the imaginary subject status and appropriation of the world that it confirms, also indicates a further mythical aspect of photography, its speed and instantaneousness, which have always been considered to be the expression of its peculiar truthfulness. Both elements are supposed to produce direct evidential experiences, both for the subject and on the object side of the photographic act. While the mythical ease of operation overlooks the many and various steps, from the grouping of the objects or persons in front of the camera, through the specific camera settings for the shot, and on to the development and printing the photograph and its presentation, the mythical instantaneousness obscures the historicity of the modalities of perception and recording on film. Now both the specific forms of production and the historicity of photography are precisely the central theme around which Christopher Williams's artistic work revolves. These themes are however rarely manifest, but they seem to form one such 'supplementary' subtext, which is formed by the indicators.

Christopher Williams's exhibitions demand considerable input from the viewer in order to connect the modalities involved in his setups — exposure, printing, framing, hanging, installation, poster and catalogue — and furthermore to relate them to the historical horizon of the modalities of modernity, industrial forms of production and political systems of order.▷

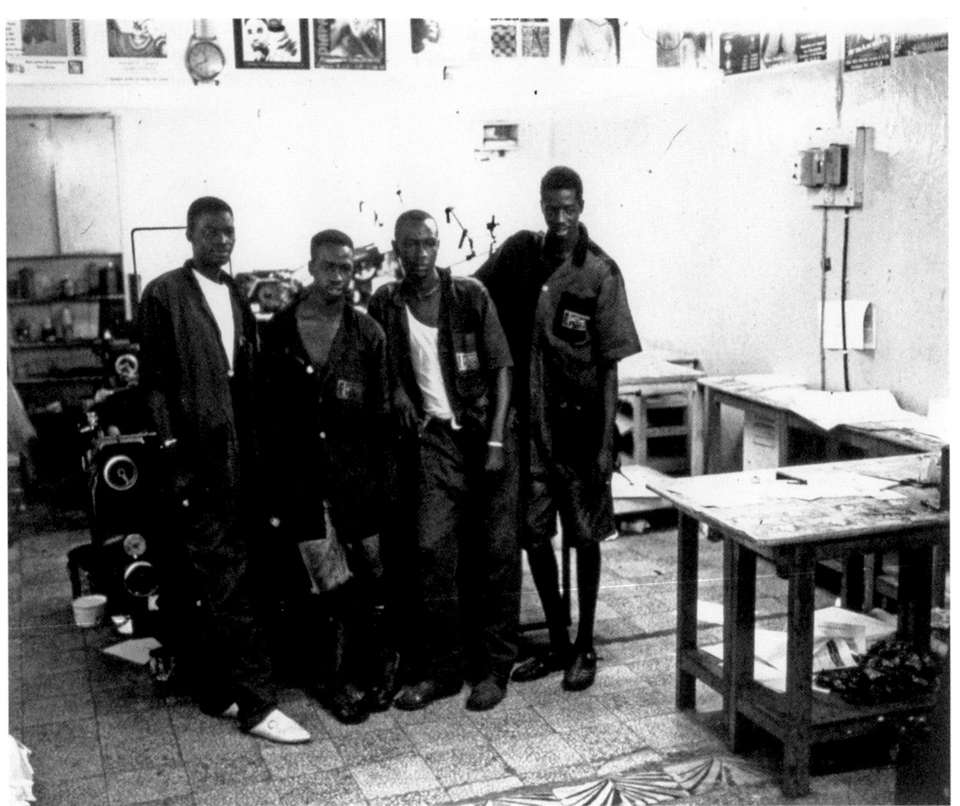

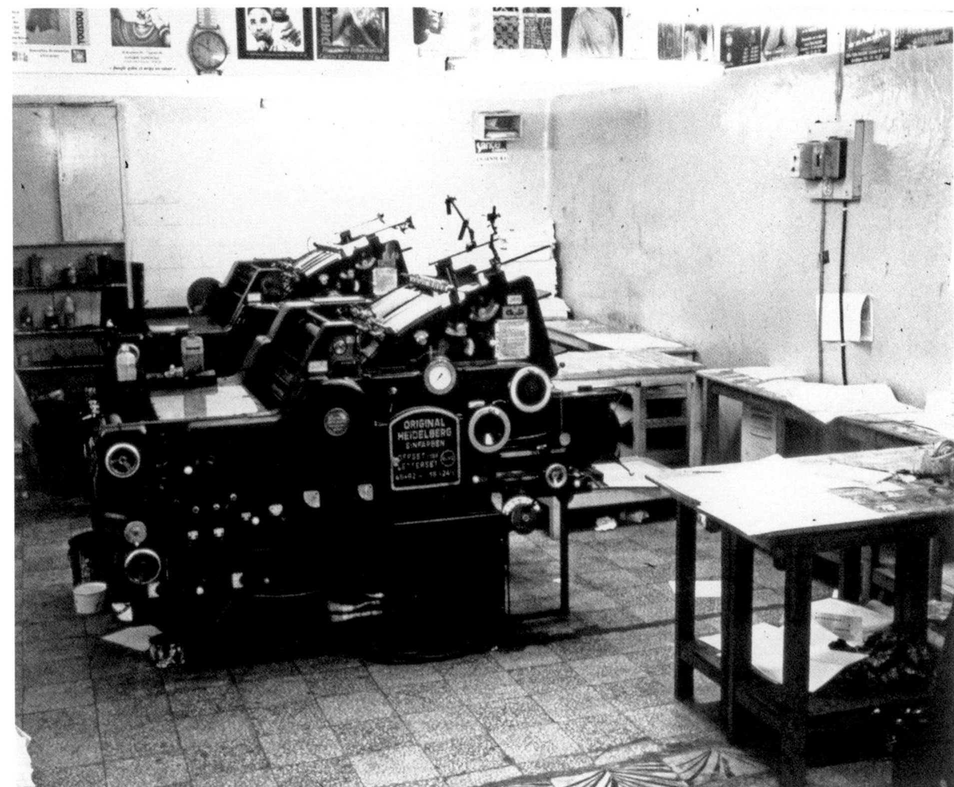

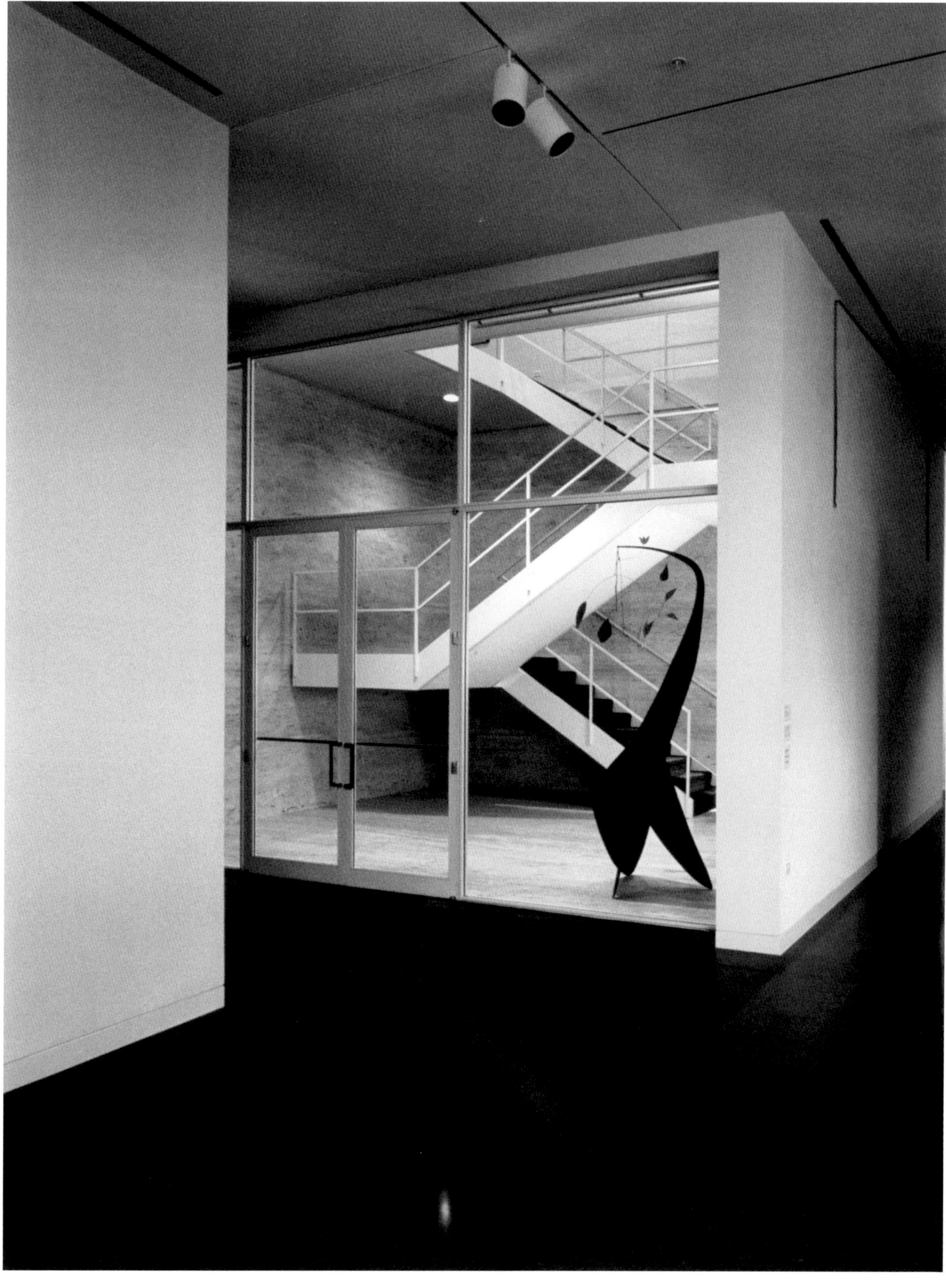

p. 218
**Main Staircase for
the Arts Club of Chicago, 1948–51
Steel, travertine marble
359.4 × 458.8 × 609.3 cm
(141 1/2 × 180 5/8 × 239 7/8")
Arts Club commission 1948–51
Ludwig Mies van der Rohe
109 East Ontario Street
Chicago, Illinois 1951–1995
Repositioned by John Vinci
201 East Ontario Street
Chicago, Illinois
October 1, 1998**
1998
Photograph
Gelatin silver print

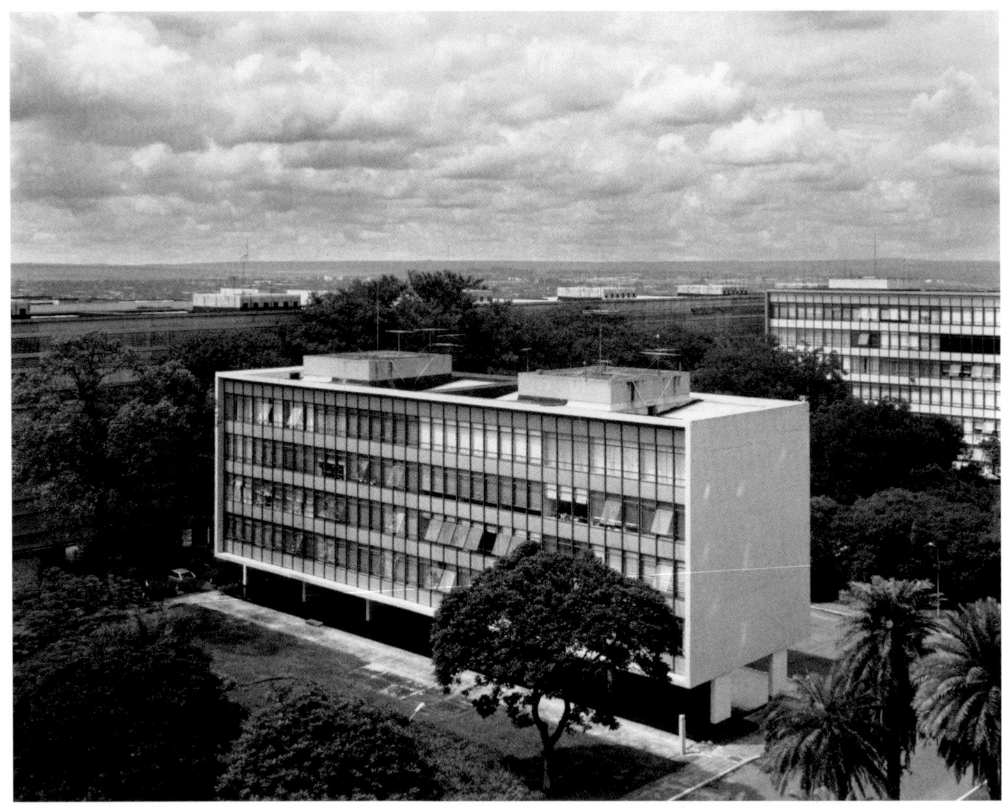

**Super Quadra Sul 308
Bloco 'D' Asa Sul (south wing)
70.355 BRASILIA-DF
Lucio Costa, Oscar Niemeyer, 1960
January 31, 1997 (No. 1, 2)**
1997
2 photographs
Gelatin silver prints

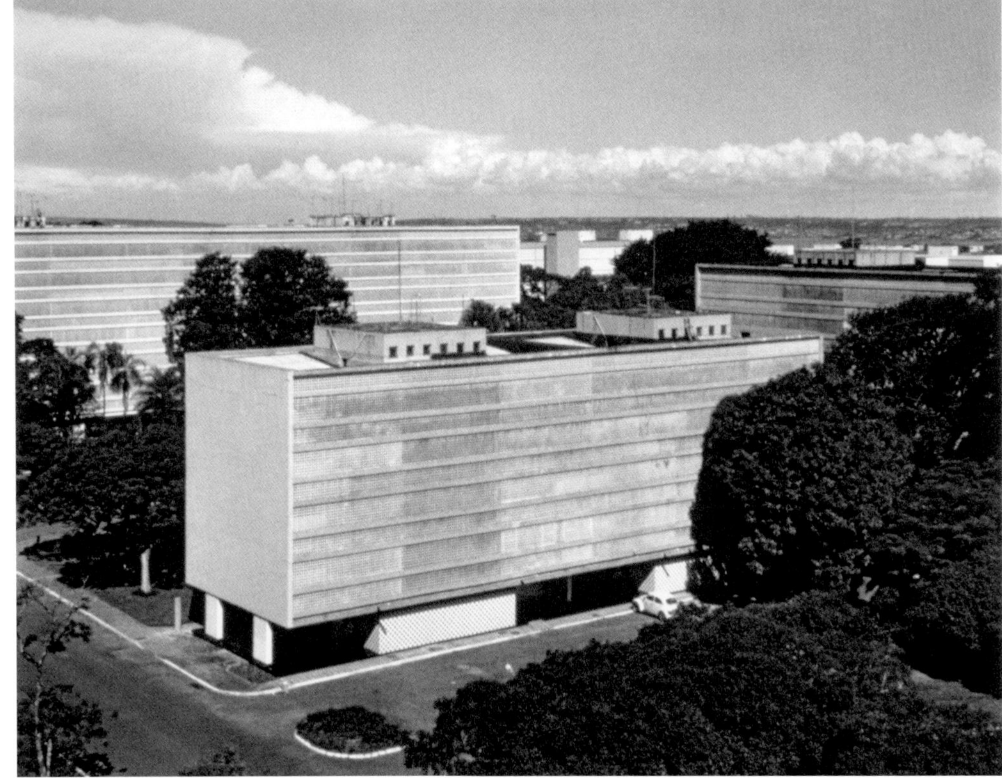

The Code of Reproduction

Instead of placing emphasis on the moments of registration, as modernist theories of photography and film have done,[1] it is the circumstances and conditions of photography that are the issue here. This is shown as a professional production process with its own division of labour within the energy field of the promise of the individual 'snapshot',[2] which can easily be understood as a modernised, democratic variant of the ancient myth of genius and artistic 'creation'. Williams's own artistic production navigates to some extent between production and myth; it activates historical and political systems of reference as well as artistic methods of contextualisation. At first glance the immediacy of the object of course seems to be given, but in most cases there is something that is out of sync. A second glance reveals that there is no longer anything that is direct and immediate — no instant, captured life — rather everything seems artificial in the extreme, constructed and therefore referential. Instead of things that are immediately evident there are referential modalities. They can be read as indicators and thus lead from the literal to the referential. It is not the object that defines the artistic interest of the work, but the code of representation itself. Furthermore, none of these aspects constitutes the correct interpretation of the picture, rather the picture, like most of Christopher Williams's works, generates chains of possible horizons of significance in this manner. Only when one pursues these chains and follows the systematic shifts in meaning, the deceptive beauty of the images, the seemingly straightforward, basic objects, the high production values, the provocative titles of the exhibitions or the meticulous lists of works and tables of reproductions in the catalogues, and finally the proliferating references to which the catalogue texts contribute, can their complex connectedness be understood. The triggers for these multiple disruptions are the 'just-missed-it' principle of delaying the 'right' moment to release the shutter by a fraction of a second in the manner of Japanese fashion photography in the early 1990s, the slight adjustment of the shade of colour..., the 'defacing' of the shampoo pictures and the nuances in their repetition or the disturbing details in a few architectural pictures.[3] By systematically building such provocative moments into his work, Christopher Williams to an extent kick-starts the process of perception and reception, and at least points it in a certain direction. This approach, which oscillates between the work itself and the process of producing it, can now also be related to the genealogy of his own artistic methods, both in relation to and in contradistinction from re-photography and Conceptual art.

Conflicting Modernities

There is no way that the 'programme' Christopher Williams proposes in his exhibition can be taken as a rejection of modernity. We undoubtedly still live in an age of modernity, and in no sense has it become our 'antiquity'.[4] What is being called into question is rather the notion of modernity as a one-dimensional progressive process in science, economics, morality or social emancipation, in which art participated with its visions of a unification of culture in the name of abstraction.[5] For in this sense we actually 'never were modernists'.[6] The term modernity as a

conceptual horizon, however, seems indispensable as a bundle of in many ways contradictory claims, both between the various projects for modernisation, but also within each single one of these projects. Less as a programme that articulates itself in antagonisms between, for example, humanism and fundamentalism, or dogmatism and critical philosophy, but rather as a generative principle of cultural and social change in the face of a scientific, technical, media culture's claims to overall hegemony. Photography in its special way marks the interfaces between these various aspects of modernisation, between production and representation as well as between marketing and actual use. For that reason the modalities of photography that Christopher Williams is addressing in his work always focus on the social conditions themselves, in which the historicity and mediality of photography is present. It is possible, in the specific spaces that these images and installations create, to understand modernity neither as paradigm of reconciliation nor as something that must be ticked off as past history, but it is possible to see the political, economic and cultural forms of modern representation as being 'complex and contradictory',[7] related to one another and part of a pattern of mutual interchange. This offers the chance to reflect on the political implications of modern representation in general and on the concrete situation of its reception in any given case; in other words on the viewer's involvement in the conditions that are the subject of Williams's investigation.

Helmut Draxler

1 Cf. Laura Mulvey, 'Death – 24 Times a Second: the Tensions between Movements and Stillness in the Cinema', *Ojeblikket*, publication for Visual Cultures, special issue vol. 10, no. 2, 2000, pp. 18–47.
2 This promise is repeated in the Internet, but in rather negative form, i.e., away from interactive mobilisation and back to the service-orientated archive, where you click through the negativity.
3 Like the streetlamp in the architectural shot of Lodz that explodes the formal stringency of similar images, as we know it from the former Becher School in Düsseldorf.
4 'Modernity is our Antiquity' is one of the mottos of documenta 12.
5 Christian Kravagna differentiates between various stages in the critique of aesthetic modernism since the 1960s. They range from postmodern radical critique to cautious attempts at reconstruction. Cf. Christian Kravagna 'Kritik und kritische Rekonstruktion: Die Moderne sehen', in Christian Meyer, Mathias Poledna (eds.), *Sharawadgi*, Baden (Vienna), 1998, pp. 241–66.
6 Bruno Latour, *Wir sind nie modern gewesen. Versuch einer symmetrischen Anthropologie*, Frankfurt: Suhrkamp, 1998.
7 In Robert Venturi's case the charge against aesthetic modernism was its lack of complexity and contradiction; here modernity itself appears complex and contradictory. Cf. Robert Venturi, *Complexity and Contradiction in Architecture*, 1966.

Excerpt from *Christopher Williams, Program: For Example, Dix-Huit Leçons Sur la Société Industrielle (Revision I)*, Braunschweig: Kunstverein Braunschweig, 2005. Translated from the German by Hugh Rorrison.

Kiev 88, 4.6 lbs. (2.1 Kg)
Manufacturer:
Zavod Arsenal Factory, Kiev, Ukraine.
Date of production: 1983–87
Douglas M. Parker Studio,
Glendale, California
March 28, 2003 (No. 1, 2, 3)
2003
3 photographs
Dye transfer prints

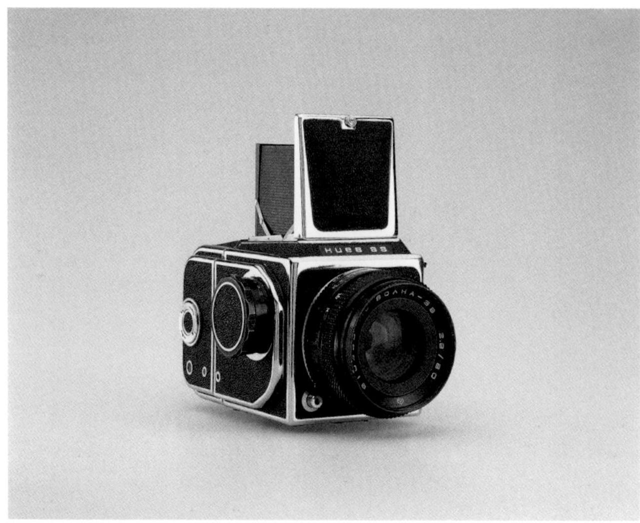

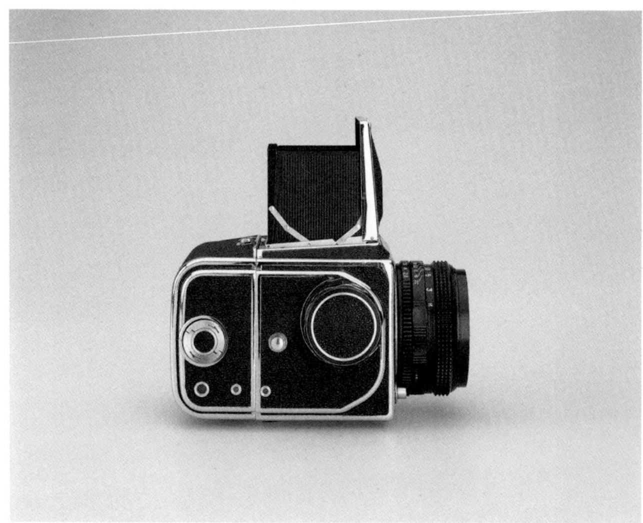

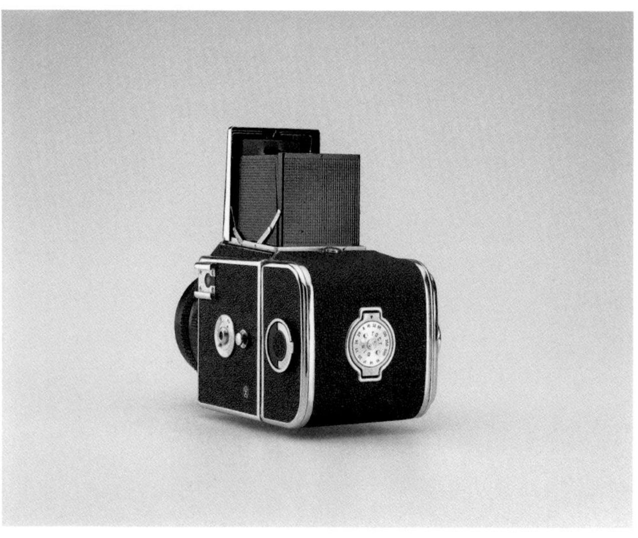

Selected biographies

Anna Artaker (Vienna, 1976)
Lives and works in Vienna

Solo exhibitions
48 Köpfe aus dem Merkurov Museum, Salzburger Kunstverein, Salzburg, 2009;
Untitled (Some Of The Names Of Photoshop), Künstlerhaus, Vienna, 2009;
Did you ever dream of becoming barbarian?, Galerie Public>, Paris (with Meike Schmidt-Gleim), 2003.

Group exhibitions
In Between Document and Fiction, National Centre of Dance, Bucharest, 2009;
Figure/Ground, Galerie Transit, Mechelen, 2009; *Transformation of History or Parallel Histories*, 6th International Gyumri Biennial, Gyumri, 2008; *!Forradalom?*, Mücscarnok, Budapest, 2007/Collegium Hungaricum, Berlin, 2006; *Playlist*, Palais de Tokyo, Paris, 2004.

Publications
'Unbekannte Avantgarde' (picture insert), *Bildpunkt* (Vienna, 2009); '48 Köpfe aus dem Merkurov Museum', *Springerin* (Vienna, 2008); *Are you talking to me?* (Vienna, 2008); *!Forradalom?* (Budapest, 2007); *Long time no see* (Vienna, 2007).

Alice Creischer (Gerolstein, 1960)
and **Andreas Siekmann** (Hamm, 1961)
Both live and work in Berlin

Solo exhibitions
...for the Osmotic Compensation of the Pressure of Wealth. Alice Creischer: Works and Collaborations, MACBA, Barcelona, 2008; *Ex Argentina. La normalidad* (3rd part of the Ex Argentina project), with Andreas Siekmann, Palais de Glace, Buenos Aires; *Apparat zum Osmotischen Druckausgleich von Reichtum bei der Betrachtung von Armut*, Gesellschaft für Aktuelle Kunst, Bremen, 2005; *The Greatest Happiness Principle Party*, Secession, Vienna, 2001.

Group exhibitions
Mach doch heute Lobby, documenta 12, Kassel, 2007; *Occupying Space. Sammlung Generali Foundation* (with Andreas Siekmann), Haus der Kunst, Munich, 2005; *How do We Want To Be Governed?*, Secession, Vienna/Witte de With, Rotterdam, 2005; *Tauchfahrten*, Kunstverein, Hannover, 2004; *Com volem ser governats?*, MACBA, Barcelona, 2004; *The Structure of Survival*, 50th Venice Biennale, 2003.

Publications
Alice Creischer. Apparatus for the Osmotic Compensation ... (Barcelona, 2008); *Alice Creischer. Erpresserbriefe an die Geisteswelt* (Bremen, 2005); *Ex Argentina. Pasos para huir del trabajo al hacer/Schritte zur Flucht von der Arbeit zum Tun* (Buenos Aires/Cologne, 2004); *Die Gewalt ist der Rand aller Dinge* (Vienna, 2002).

Domènec (Mataró, 1962)
Lives and works in Mataró

Solo exhibitions
Real Estate, Espai Zero1, Olot, 2008; *Existenzminimum*, Fundació Espais d'Art Contemporani, Girona, 2002; *Un lloc*, Galeria Antonio de Barnola, Barcelona, 2000; *Bajo cero (como en casa)*, Galeria Fucares, Almagro, 2000; *24 hores de llum artificial*, Sala Montcada, Fundació la Caixa, Barcelona, 1998.

Group exhibitions
Modern Shorts, New Museum of Contemporary Art, New York, 2008; *Moradias Transitorias*, Museu Nacional, Brasilia, 2007; *Passer-by*, Tel Aviv Artists' Studios, Tel Aviv, 2007; *Not Sheep, New Urban Enclosures and Commons*, Artspeak Gallery, Vancouver, 2006; *Mira cómo se mueven*, Fundación Telefónica, Madrid, 2005; *Stand By. Listos para actuar*, Laboratorio Arte Alameda, Mexico City, 2003.

Publications
Domènec, Real Estate (Olot, 2008); *Mira cómo se mueven. See how they move* (Madrid, 2005); *Domènec, Existenzminimum* (Girona, 2002); *Domènec. Domèstic* (Barcelona, 2001); *Domènec. 24 hores de llum artificial* (Barcelona, 1998).

Katja Eydel (Darmstadt, 1969)
Lives and works in Berlin

Solo exhibitions
Model ve Sembol, Kunstverein Göttingen/Kunstverein Salzburg/Neue
Gesellschaft für Bildende Kunst Berlin/Centre d'art Passerelle Brest, 2006/07;
1996–2006, Künstlerhaus Büchsenhausen, Innsbruck, 2006; *Zielscheiben-
Kampagne 99*, Plattform Berlin, 2002.

Group exhibitions
Istanbul traversée, Palais des Beaux-Arts, Lille, 2009; *Migration*, House of World
Cultures, Berlin, 2009; *What if I could be anything?*, Kunstbank Berlin, 2004;
Ökonomien der Zeit, Akademie der Künste, Berlin/Museum Ludwig, Colog-
ne/Migros Museum, Zurich, 2002; *Die Gewalt ist der Rand aller Dinge*, Generali
Foundation, Vienna, 2001.

Publications
Model ve Sembol. Die Erfindung der Türkei (Berlin/New York, 2006); *Teilt mit*
(Berlin, 2006); *Ökonomien der Zeit* (Frankfurt, 2002); *Belgrad Interviews.
Jugoslawien nach Nato-Angriff und 15 Jahren nationalistischem Populismus.
Gespräche, Texte, Fotos* (Berlin, 2000); *Baustop.randstadt zu städtischem
Handeln und politischer Stadttheorie* (Berlin, 1998).

Ângela Ferreira (Maputo, 1958)
Lives and works in Lisbon

Solo exhibitions
Hard Rain Show, Museu Colecção Berardo, Centro Cultural de Belém, Lisbon;
Hard Rain Show, La Criée, Rennes, 2008; *For Mozambique*, Michael Stevenson
Gallery, Cape Town, 2008; *Maison Tropicale*, Portuguese representation in
the 52nd Venice Biennale, 2007; *Random Walk*, Galeria Filomena Soares, Lisbon,
2005.

Group exhibitions
The Great Divide, Art Gallery of New South Wales, Sydney, 2009; *Maputo:
A Tale of One City – Africa in Oslo Festival*, Oslo Museum, IKM, Oslo, 2009;
Front of House, Parasol Unit – Foundation for Contemporary Art, London, 2008;
In Living Contact, 28th Bienal de São Paulo, 2008; *Meridian House*, Frieze
Sculpture Park, London, 2008.

Publications
Ângela Ferreira – Hard Rain Show (Lisbon, 2008); *Ângela Ferreira – Maison
Tropicale* (Lisbon, 2007); *Ângela Ferreira: Em Sítio Algum* (Lisbon, 2003);
Ângela Ferreira – Zip Zap Circus School (Cape Town, 2003); *House Maputo:
an intimate portrait* (Oporto, 1999).

Andrea Fraser (Billings, 1965)
Lives and works in Los Angeles

Solo exhibitions
Projection, Galerie Christian Nagel, Berlin, 2008; *Official Welcome*, The Museum
of Contemporary Art, Los Angeles/Dia: Chelsea, New York/Museum of
Modern Art Foundation Ludwig Vienna, 2005; *Andrea Fraser. Works: 1984 to
2003*, Kunstverein in Hamburg, 2003; *A Project in Two Phases*, EA-Generali
Foundation, Vienna, 1995; *Eine Gesellschaft des Geschmacks (A Society of Taste)*,
Kunstverein München, Munich, 1993; *Museum Highlights: A Gallery Talk*,
Philadelphia Museum of Art, 1989.

Group exhibitions
That was Then... This Is Now, P.S.1 Contemporary Art Center, Museum of Modern
Art Affiliate, New York, 2008; *The World as a Stage*, Tate Modern, London, 2007;
Why Pictures Now, Museum of Modern Art Foundation Ludwig Vienna, 2006;
Big Bang, Centre Pompidou, Paris, 2005; *Body Display*, Secession, Vienna, 2004.

Publications
Museum Highlights: The Writings of Andrea Fraser (Cambridge, MA, 2005);
Exhibition: New Video Work by Andrea Fraser (Vancouver, 2004); *Andrea Fraser.
Works: 1984 to 2003* (Cologne, 2003); *Report* (Vienna, 1995); *Eine Gesellschaft
des Geschmacks* (Munich, 1993).

Isa Genzken (Bad Oldesloe, 1948)
Lives and works in Berlin

Solo exhibitions
Isa Genzken: Open Sesame!, Whitechapel Art Gallery, London/Museum
Ludwig, Cologne, 2009; *Oil*, German Pavilion, 52nd Venice Biennale, 2007;
Isa Genzken, Secession, Vienna, 2006; *Kinder filmen*, Galerie Daniel Buchholz,
Cologne, 2005; *Isa Genzken*, Kunsthalle Zürich, 2003.

Group exhibitions
Birds in a Park, Galerie Daniel Buchholz, Cologne, 2007; *Skulptur Projekte
Münster 07*, Münster, 2007; *Teil 1 Müllberg*, Galerie Daniel Buchholz, Cologne,
2004; *54 Carnegie International*, Carnegie Museum of Art, Pittsburgh, 2004;
50th Venice Biennale, 2003; documenta 11, Kassel, 2002.

Publications
Isa Genzken: Open Sesame! (Cologne/London, 2009); *Oil* (Cologne, 2007);
Isa Genzken, (Cologne, 2006); *Isa Genzken* (London, 2006); *Isa Genzken*
(Cologne, 2003). *Isa Genzken. MetLife* (Vienna, 1996).

Dan Graham (Urbana, 1942)
Lives and works in New York

Solo exhibitions
Dan Graham, Portikus, New Jersey, 2009; *Dan Graham: Beyond*, Whitney
Museum of American Art, New York/The Museum of Contemporary Art,
Los Angeles, 2009; *Dan Graham*, Lisson Gallery, London, 2004; *Dan Graham
Retrospective*, Chiba City Museum of Art, 2003; *Dan Graham Œuvres, 1965–2000*,
Musée d'art moderne de la Ville de Paris/Museu Serralves, Oporto, 2002;
*Children's Day Care Center, CD-Rom, Cartoon, and Computer Screen Library
Project*, Marian Goodman Gallery, New York, 2000.

Group exhibitions
MAN SON 1969. Vom Schrecken der Situation, Hamburger Kunsthalle, Hamburg,
2009; *Stardust*, Park de Oude Warande, Tilburg, 2009; *Color Chart: Reinventing
Color, 1950 to Today*, The Museum of Modern Art, New York, 2008; *Imagine
Action*, Lisson Gallery, London, 2007.

Publications
Dan Graham: Beyond (Cambridge, MA, 2009); *Dan Graham: Works and Collected
Writings* (Barcelona, 2009); *Dan Graham* (Dumont, Cologne, 2008); *Dan Graham:
Half Square Half Crazy* (Barcelona, 2001); *Dan Graham* (Phaidon, New York, 2001).

Tom Holert (Hamburg, 1962)
Lives and works in Berlin and Vienna
Claudia Honecker (Limburg an der Lahn, 1965)
Lives and works in Berlin

Tom Holert and Claudia Honecker exhibited for the first time together
at Manifesta 7, Bolzano, 2008.

Group exhibitions (Tom Holert)
Mimétisme, Extra City – Center for Contemporary Art, Antwerp, 2007;
Un instant... puis la nuit, Dia, Film und Lichtprojekte, Institut im Glaspavillon
der Volksbühne am Rosa-Luxemburg-Platz, Berlin, 2007; *Traurig sicher,
im training*, Grazer Kunstverein, Graz, 2006; *Be Creative. Der kreative Imperativ*,
Museum für Gestaltung, Zurich, 2002.

Publications
Regieren im Bildraum (Berlin, 2008); *Marc Camille Chaimowicz: Celebration?
Realife* (London, 2007); *Kölnbuch* (Berlin, 2007); *Fliehkraft. Gesellschaft
in Bewegung – von Migranten und Touristen* (Cologne, 2006); *Entsichert.
Krieg als Massenkultur im 21. Jahrhundert* (Cologne, 2002).

Marine Hugonnier (Paris, 1969)
Lives and works in London

Solo exhibitions
Konsthall Malmö, 2008; Kunsthalle Bern, 2007; Philadelphia Museum of Art, 2007; Musée d'Art Moderne et Contemporain MAMCO, Geneva, 2007; Stedelijk Museum voor Actuele Kunst, Gent, 2007.

Group exhibitions
Badlands, Mass MoCA, Massachusetts, 2008; *Paraísos indómitos*, MARCO Vigo, 2008; *Pensée Sauvage*, Frankfurter Kunstverein, Frankfurt, 2007; *Cine y casi cine*, Museo Nacional Centro de Arte Reina Sofía, Madrid, 2007; *Think with the Senses – Feel with the Mind. Art in the Present Tense*, 52nd Venice Biennale, 2007.

Publications
The Trilogie: Ariana, The Last Tour, Travelling Amazonia (Torino, 2008).
www.marinehugonnier.com

IRWIN (founded in 1983 in Ljubljana)
Dušan Mandič (Ljubljana, 1954)
Miran Mohar (Novo Mesto, 1958)
Andrej Savski (Ljubljana, 1961)
Roman Uranjek (Trbovlje, 1961)
Borut Vogelnik (Kranj, 1959)

IRWIN is also a cofounder of NSK (Neue Slowenische Kunst) in 1984.

Solo exhibitions
State in Time, Kunsthalle Arhus, 2008; *Like to Like*, Cornerhouse, Manchester, 2004; *Retroprincip*, Kunstlerhaus Bethanien, Berlin, 2003; *IRWIN Live*, Museum of Modern Art, Ljubljana, 2000; *IRWIN*, Städtische Kunsthalle Düsseldorf, 1989.

Group exhibitions
Here Is Every. Four Decades of Contemporary Art, The Museum of Modern Art, New York, 2008/09; *Berlin-Moscow/Moscow-Berlin*, Gropius Bau, Berlin, 2003; *Personal Systems*, 50th Venice Biennale, 2003; *On Life, Beauty, Translations*, Istanbul Biennial, 1997; *Interpol*, Farbfabrik, Institute for Contemporary Art and Architecture, Stockholm, 1996.

Publications
East Art Map (London, 2005); *IRWIN: Retroprincip* (Frankfurt, 2003); *Fiction Reconstructed*, (Vienna, 2000); *NSK Embassy Moscow. How the East sees the East*, (Piran, 1993); *NSK – Neue Slowenische Kunst* (Zagreb/Los Angeles, 1991).

Runa Islam (Dhaka, 1970)
Lives and works in London

Solo exhibitions
Restless Subject, Kunsthaus Zürich/Museum Folkwang, Essen, 2008/09; *Empty the pond to get the fish.*, Museum of Modern Art Foundation Ludwig Vienna, 2008; *Center of Gravity*, Bergen Kunsthall/Nasjonalmuseet, Oslo, 2007; *Out of the Picture*, Camden Arts Centre, London, 2005; *Visages and Voyages*, Dunkers Kulturhus, Helsingborg, 2005.

Group exhibitions
Principle Hope, Manifesta 7, Rovereto, 2008; *The Cinema Effect: Illusion, Reality & The Moving Image, Part II: Realisms*, Hirschhorn/Washington DC, 2008; *Always a Little Further*, Arsenale, 51st Venice Biennale, 2005; *Poetic Justice*, 8th International Istanbul Biennial, Istanbul, 2003; *Squatters*, Museu Serralves, Oporto/Witte de With, Rotterdam, 2001.

Publications
Runa Islam: Restless Subject (Zurich/Essen/London/Heidelberg, 2008); *Empty the pond to get the fish.* (Vienna/London/Cologne, 2009); *Lost Cinema Lost – Runa Islam, Tobias Putrih* (Modena, 2008); *Runa Islam – Visages & Voyages* (Frankfurt, 2005); *Film & Video Works by Runa Islam* (Frankfurt, 2003).

Klub Zwei (founded in 1992)
Simone Bader (Stuttgart, 1964)
Jo Schmeiser (Graz, 1967)
Both live and work in Vienna

Solo exhibitions
Ambivalenzen, Kunst im Kasten, Stuttgart, 2007; *In Zusammenarbeit mit*, Secession, Vienna, 2005; *Noir sur blanc – le revers des images*, Bétonsalon, Paris, 2005; *Things. Places. Years & Arbeit an der Öffentlichkeit* (Klub Zwei/MAIZ), Intervention no. 2, Halle für Kunst e. V., Lüneburg, 2003; *At Home in Vienna*, Austrian Cultural Forum, London, 2001.

Group exhibitions
Talk. Talk. Das Interview als ästhetische Praxis, Galerie der Hochschule für Grafik und Buchkunst, Leipzig/Medienturm Graz/Galerie 5020, Salzburg, 2009; *Recollecting. Raub und Restitution*, MAK – Austrian Museum of Applied Arts/Contemporary Art, Vienna, 2008; *The Greenroom: A Project For CCS Bard*, Center for Curatorial Studies and Hessel Museum of Art, Bard College, New York, 2008; *Data Recovery*, Galleria d'Arte Moderna e Contemporanea, Bergamo, 2008; *Tiefenrausch – Strom des Vergessens*, Offenes Kulturhaus Linz, 2008.

Publications
'Wer fragt? Wer wird gefragt?', *Geschichte/n verwahren (To Store Stories)* (Vienna, 2009); 'Too little, too late', *Recollecting. Raub und Restitution* (Vienna, 2009); 'Who asks the Questions? Who is asked?', *New Feminism. Worlds of Feminism, Queer and Networking Conditions* (Vienna, 2008); *Black and White. The Back of the Images* (Austria, Great Britain, 2007); *Things. Places. Years. Das Wissen Jüdischer Frauen* (Innsbruck, 2005).

John Knight (Los Angeles, 1945)
Lives in Los Angeles and works in situ

Solo exhibitions
Cold Cuts, Espai d'Art Contemporani de Castelló, 2008; Storm King Art Center, Mountainville, New York, 2000; American Fine Arts, Co., New York, 1998; *Bienvenido*, Museum of Contemporary Art San Diego and La Jolla, California, 1990; *Enkele Werken*, Witte de With, Rotterdam, 1990; *Treize Travaux*, Le Nouveau Musée, Villeurbanne, 1989.

Group exhibitions
Los Angeles 1955–1985: Naissance d'une capitale artistique, Centre Pompidou, Paris, 2006; *Treize à la douzaine*, Palais des Beaux-Arts, Brussels, 1991; *Reconsidering the Object of Art*, The Museum of Contemporary Art, Los Angeles, 1995; *De Campagne/The Campaign*, Stroom Den Haag, The Hague, 1993; documenta 7, Kassel, 1982.

Publications
Cold Cuts (Castelló, 2008); Alexandre Alberro, *Meaning at the Margins: The Semiological Inversions of John Knight* (Mountainville, 2001); Anne Rorimer, *New Art in the 60s and 70s: Redefining Reality* (London, 2001); Benjamin H.D. Buchloh, 'Knight's Moves: Situating the Art/Object', *Neo-Avantgarde and Culture Industry: Essays on European and American Art from 1955 to 1975* (London, 2003); Birgit Pelzer, 'The Irresistible Appeal of Utility', *The Campaign* (Brussels, 1996).

Labor k3000

Was founded in 1998 by a group of artists, activists, electronic musicians, graphic and multimedia designers in Zurich. Since then it has served as a platform for several transnational exhibitions, networks and research projects, video and web productions on current social, cultural and political transformations, like *MigMap – Governing Migration* (2005–08), a mapping project about the European border and migration regime directed by Peter Spillmann with the TRANSIT MIGRATON research group (www.transitmigration.org/migmap); *EuroVision2000*, (2000), a transnational video network based in Prague, Bologna and Brussels realised by Peter Spillmann, Susanna Perin, Marion von Osten (www.eurovision2000.net) and *MoneyNations I–II. Constructing the border. Constructing the East* (1998–2000), directed by Marion von Osten and Peter Spillmann (www.moneynations.ch). Since 2008 Labor k3000 has maintained a second base in Berlin. Further information can be found at www.k3000.ch.

Louise Lawler (New York, 1947)
Lives and works in New York

Solo exhibitions
Twice Untitled and Other Pictures (looking back), Wexner Center for the Arts, Columbus, 2006; *A Spot on the Wall*, Kunstverein München, Munich/Neue Galerie, Graz/De Appel, Amsterdam, 1995; *Paperweights, Postcards, Pictures, Cannibalism*, Centre d'Art Contemporain, Geneva, 1994; *Enough, Projects: Louise Lawler*, The Museum of Modern Art, New York, 1987; *Home/Museum – Arranged for Living and Viewing*, Matrix, The Wadsworth Atheneum, Hartford, CT, 1984.

Group exhibitions
The Museum as Muse, The Museum of Modern Art, New York/Museum of Contemporary Art, San Diego, 1999; *Louise Lawler, Cindy Sherman, Laurie Simmons*, Kunsternes Hus, Oslo/Museum of Contemporary Art, Helsinki, 1993; Biennial Exhibition, Whitney Museum of American Art, New York, 1991, 2000, 2008; *Dan Graham, Louise Lawler, Peter Nadin, Lawrence Weiner*, Peter Nadin, New York, 1979; __________, *Louise Lawler, Adrian Piper and Cindy Sherman are participating in an exhibition organized by Janelle Reiring at Artists Space, September 23 to October 28, 1978*. Artists Space, New York, 1978.

Publications
Twice Untitled and Other Pictures (looking back) (Cambridge, MA, 2006); *Louise Lawler and Others* (Ostfildern, 2004); *Louise Lawler: An Arrangement of Pictures* (Paris/New York, 2000); *Spot on the Wall* (Cologne, 1998); *Untitled, Red/Blue & Untitled, Black/White* (New York, 1978). The two books are one publication.

David Maljkovic (Rijeka, 1973)
Lives and works in Zagreb

Solo exhibitions
Museo Nacional Centro de Arte Reina Sofía, Madrid, 2009; *Retired Compositions*, Metro Pictures, New York, 2008; *Parallel Compositions*, Bergen Kunsthall, 2007; *Almost Here*, Kunstverein in Hamburg, 2007; *Scene for New Heritage Trilogy*, Whitechapel Art Gallery, London, 2007.

Group exhibitions
What Keeps Mankind Alive, 11th Istanbul Biennial, Istanbul; Contour, 4th Video Biennial, Mechelen, 2009; *When Things Cast no Shadow*, 5th Berlin Biennial for Contemporary Art, 2008; *Magellanic Cloud*, Centre Pompidou, Paris, 2007; *Kapitaler Glanz*, Kunstverein Düsseldorf, 2007.

Publications
David Maljkovic, Retired Compositions (New York, 2009); *David Maljkovic: Lost Review* (London, 2008); *Almost Here: David Maljkovic* (Cologne, 2007); *Scene for New Heritage* (Belgrade, 2006); *Place with Limited Premeditation* (Amsterdam, 2005).

Dorit Margreiter (Vienna, 1967)
Lives and works in Vienna

Solo exhibitions
Locus Remix. Three Contemporary Positions: Dorit Margreiter, MAK Center for Art and Architecture, Los Angeles, 2009; *Poverty Housing. Americus, Georgia*, MAK – Austrian Museum of Applied Arts/Contemporary Art, Vienna, 2008; *Analog*, Gallery for Contemporary Art, Leipzig, 2006; *10104 Angelo View Drive*, Museum of Modern Art Foundation Ludwig Vienna, 2004; *Short Hills*, Grazer Kunstverein, Graz, 1999.

Group exhibitions
Elke Krystufek, Dorit Margreiter and Lois & Franziska Weinberger, Austrian Pavilion, 53rd Venice Biennale, 2009; *The New Monumentality: Gerard Byrne, Dominique González-Foerster and Dorit Margreiter*, The Henry Moore Institute, Leeds, 2009; *Synchronicity with Roberta Lima and Dorit Margreiter (Austrian contribution)*, 11th International Cairo Biennial, 2008; *Painting the Glass House: Artists Revisit Modern Architecture*, The Aldrich Contemporary Art Museum, Ridgefield, CT, 2008; *Exil des Imaginären. Politik. Ästhetik. Liebe*, Generali Foundation, Vienna, 2007.

Publications
Rebecca Baron, Dorit Margreiter. Poverty Housing. Americus, Georgia (Vienna, 2009); *Anette Baldauf/Dorit Margreiter. The She Zone* (Frankfurt, 2007); *Dorit Margreiter. Analog* (Frankfurt, 2006); *Der Gruen Effekt* (Vienna, 2006); *Dorit Margreiter. 10104 Angelo View Drive* (Cologne, 2004).

Gordon Matta-Clark (New York, 1943–1978)

Solo exhibitions
Gordon Matta-Clark, Palazzo delle Papesse-Centro Arte Contemporanea, Siena, 2008; *Gordon Matta-Clark: You Are The Measure*, Whitney Museum of American Art, New York, 2007–08; *Reorganizing Structure by Drawing Through It: Drawings by Gordon Matta-Clark & Food*, Generali Foundation, Vienna, 1997–2000; *Gordon Matta-Clark Retrospective*, IVAM Centre Julio González, València, 1992–93; *Gordon Matta-Clark: A Retrospective*, Museum of Contemporary Art, Chicago, University Art Museum, California State University/Stedelijk Museum, Amsterdam/Städtisches Museum Abteiberg, Mönchengladbach/Kunsthalle Basel/Le Nouveau Musée, Villeurbanne/Museum Van Hedendaagse Kunst, Antwerp/Pori Taideomuseo/Reina Foundation, Ministry of Culture, Madrid/Carnegie-Mellon University Art Gallery, Pittsburgh/The Brooklyn Museum, Brooklyn, New York/Mackenzie Art Gallery, Regina/University Art Museum, University of California, Berkeley/Musée d'Art Contemporain, Montreal/Herbert F. Johnson Museum, Cornell University, Ithaca, New York, 1985–88.

Group exhibitions
Revolutions 1968, Zacheta National Gallery of Art, Warsaw, 2008; *Open Systems: Rethinking Art c. 1970*, Tate Modern, London, 2005; *L'Informe: mode d'emploi*, Musée national d'art Moderne, Centre Pompidou, Paris, 1996; *Reconsidering the Object of Art 1965–1975*, Museum of Contemporary Art, Los Angeles, 1995; *Jacob's Ladder*, documenta 6, Kassel, 1977.

Publications
Gordon Matta-Clark: You are the Measure (New York, 2007); *Gordon Matta-Clark Works and Collected Writings* (Madrid, 2006); *Gordon Matta-Clark* (London, 2003); *Reorganizing Structure by Drawing Through It: Drawings by Gordon Matta-Clark* (Vienna, 1998); *Gordon Matta-Clark: A Retrospective* (Valencia, 1992).

Gustav Metzger (Nuremberg, 1926)
Lives and works in London

Solo exhibitions
Eichmann and the Angel, Cubitt Gallery, 8 Angel Mews, London, 2005; *Gustav Metzger. Geschichte Geschichte* (retrospective), Generali Foundation, Vienna, 2005; *100,000 Newspapers. A Public-Active Installation*, t1+2 artspace, London, 2003; *Gustav Metzger – Ein Schnitt entlang der Zeit*, Kunsthalle Nürnberg, Nuremberg, 1999; *Gustav Metzger*, Spacex Gallery, Exeter, 1999; *Gustav Metzger*, Museum of Modern Art, Oxford, 1988.

Group exhibitions
Summer of Love. Art of the Psychedelic Era, Tate Liverpool, 2005; *Signatures of the Invisible*, P.S.1, Contemporary Art Center, New York, 2004; *Artists' favourites (act I)*, ICA, London, 2004; *Art and the Sixties – This Was Tomorrow*, Tate Britain, London, 2004; *Independence*, South London Gallery, London, 2004.

Publications
Gustav Metzger. History History (Vienna, 2005); *Gustav Metzger. Ein Schnitt entlang der Zeit* (Nuremberg, 1999); *Gustav Metzger. Retrospectives* (Oxford, 1999); *Gustav Metzger* (Oxford, 1998); *Galerie A. Gustav Metzger. Documents 1959–1992* (Amsterdam, 1992).

Christian Philipp Müller (Biel)

Solo exhibitions
Basics, Museum für Gegenwartskunst, Kunstmuseum Basel, 2007; *Was nahe liegt, ist doch so fern*, Kunstverein Hamburg, 1997; *Forgotten Future*, Kunstverein München, Munich, 1992; *Fixed Values*, Palais des Beaux-Arts, Brussels, 1991; *Porte bonheur*, Maison de la Culture et de la Communication, Saint-Étienne, 1989.

Group exhibitions
Manifesta 7, Rovereto, 2008; *Watershed*, Bard College, New York, 2003;
documenta 10, Kassel, 1997; *Platzwechsel*, Kunsthalle Zürich, 1994;
45th Venice Biennale, Austrian Pavilion (with Andrea Fraser and Gerwald
Rockenschaub), 1993.

Publications
Basics (Ostfildern, 2007); *Portrait of the Museum as a Chair* (Vienna, 2006);
Branding the Campus. Kunst, Architektur, Design, Identitätspolitik (Düsseldorf,
2001); *Platzwechsel* (Zurich, 1995); *Vergessene Zukunft/Forgotten Future*
(Munich, 1992).

Henrik Olesen (Esbjerg, 1967)
Lives and works in Berlin

Solo exhibitions
Kunstverein München at Ludlow 38, New York, 2008; Migros Museum für
Gegenwartskunst, Zurich/Portikus, Frankfurt (with Judith Hopf), 2007; Galerie
Daniel Buchholz, Cologne, 2005; Secession, Vienna, 2004.

Group exhibitions
Konzepte der Liebe, Kölnischer Kunstverein, Cologne/Pinakothek der Moderne,
Munich (with Sergej Jensen), 2008; *Oh Girl, It's a Boy*, Kunstverein
München, Munich, 2007; *Das Achte Feld*, Museum Ludwig, Cologne, 2006;
Und so hat Konzept noch nie Pferd bedeutet, Generali Foundation, Vienna, 2006.

Publications
Some Faggy Gestures (Zurich, 2008); *Türen* (Frankfurt, 2007); *Art After Conceptual
Art* (Vienna, 2006), *Henrik Olesen* (Vienna, 2004); *Henrik Olesen – Anthologie
de l'Amour Sublime* (Hannover, 2003); *Henrik Olesen: What is Authority?*
(Copenhagen, 2002).

Paulina Olowska (Gdansk, 1976)
Lives in Raba Nizna and works in New York

Solo exhibitions
Zofia Stryjeńska, 5th Berlin Biennial for Contemporary Art, 2008; *Attention
à la Peinture*, Galerie Daniel Buchholz, Cologne, 2008; *Salty Water/
What of Salty Water* (with Bonnie Camplin), Portikus, Frankfurt 2007;
Metamorphosis, Museum Abteiberg, Mönchengladbach, Installation,
Sammlung Provinzial Versicherung, 2005; *Metaloplastyka*, Galerie Daniel
Buchholz, Cologne, 2005; *Sie musste die Idee eines Hauses als Metapher
verwerfen*, Kunstverein Braunschweig, 2004.

Group exhibitions
When things cast no shadow, 5th Berlin Biennial for Contemporary Art, 2008;
Noël sur le balcon/Hold the Color, Paulina Olowska/Lucie McKenzie,
Sammlung Goetz, Munich, 2007; *The Subversive Charm of the Bourgeoisie*,
Van Abbemuseum, Eindhoven, 2006; 9th International Istanbul Biennial, 2005;
Clandestine, 50th Venice Biennale, 2003.

Publications
Salty Water/What of Salty Water (Frankfurt, 2007); *Noël sur le balcon/Hold the
Color* (Munich, 2007); *Metamorphosis* (Frankfurt, 2005); *Alphabet* (Cologne,
2005); *Sie musste die Idee eines Hauses als Metapher verwerfen* (Cologne, 2004).

Falke Pisano (Amsterdam, 1978)
Lives and works in Berlin

Solo exhibitions
Figures of Speech (Formation of a Crystal), Hollybush Gardens, London, 2009;
Organon and the wave (with Benoît Maire), Grazer Kunstverein, Graz, 2009;
Organon (and the audience perception) (with Benoît Maire), Croy-Nielsen, Berlin,
2008; Balice Hertling, Paris, 2008; Ellen de Bruijne Projects, Amsterdam, 2007.

Group exhibitions
Making Worlds, 53rd Venice Biennale, 2009; *Time Crevasse*, Yokohama
Triennale, 2008; Manifesta 7, Trento-Alto Adige, 2008; *Word Event*, Kunsthalle
Basel, 2008; *Object, the Undeniable Success of Operations*, SMBA, Amsterdam,
2008.

Publications
Vitamin 3D (London, 2009); *Of this tale, I cannot guarantee a single word*
(London, 2008); 'A Sculpture Turning into a Conversation', *Casco Issues X:
The Great Method* (Amsterdam, 2007); *Into It* (Hildesheim, 2007).

Mathias Poledna (Vienna, 1965)
Lives and works in Los Angeles

Solo exhibitions
New Museum of Contemporary Art, New York, 2009; Bonner Kunstverein
(with Christopher Williams), Bonn, 2009; Galerie Daniel Buchholz, Cologne,
2007; Hammer Museum, Los Angeles, 2007; Witte de With, Rotterdam, 2006;
Richard Telles Fine Art, Los Angeles, 2005; Galerie Meyer Kainer, Vienna, 2004;
Museum of Modern Art Foundation Ludwig Vienna, 2003.

Group exhibitions
Yokohama Triennale, 2008; *Archaeologies of the Future*, Sala Rekalde, Bilbao,
2007; *How Soon is Now*, Fundación Luis Seoane, La Coruña, 2007; *Galerie Daniel
Buchholz*, Cologne, Metro Pictures, New York, 2006; Whitney Biennial, Whitney
Museum of American Art, New York, 2006; Liverpool Biennial, Tate Liverpool,
2004; *20/20 Vision*, Stedelijk Museum, Amsterdam, 2004; 3rd Berlin Biennial
for Contemporary Art, Kunstwerke Berlin, 2004.

Publications
Mathias Poledna. Crystal Palace (Los Angeles/Chicago/New York, 2007);
Mathias Poledna – Western Recording (Vienna, 2006); *Mathias Poledna.
Actualité* (Frankfurt, 2002).

Florian Pumhösl (Vienna, 1971)
Lives and works in Vienna

Solo exhibitions
Florian Pumhösl, Lisson Gallery, London, 2008; *Florian Pumhösl*, Galerie Daniel
Buchholz, Cologne, 2007; *Animated Map*, Neue Kunsthalle Sankt Gallen,
Saint Gallen 2005; *Florian Pumhösl*, Kölnischer Kunstverein, Cologne, 2003;
Florian Pumhösl, Galerie Krobath Wimmer, Vienna, 2001.

Group exhibitions
documenta 12, Kassel, 2007; *Como viver junto*, 27th Bienal de São Paulo, 2006;
Individual Systems, 50th Venice Biennale, 2003; *Designs for the Real World*,
Generali Foundation, Vienna, 2002; Yokohama Triennale, 2001.

Publications
Florian Pumhösl (London/Cologne, 2008); *Animated Map* (Saint Gallen/
Cologne, 2007); *Wachstum und Entwicklung* (Frankfurt, 2003); *Florian Pumhösl*
(Frankfurt, 2003).

Martha Rosler
Lives and works in New York

Solo exhibitions
Martha Rosler: La casa, la calle, la cocina, Centro José Guerrero, Granada, 2009;
Martha Rosler Library (2005–09), e-flux gallery, New York/Frankfurter
Kunstverein, Frankfurt/MuHKA, Antwerp/United Nations Plaza School,
Berlin/INHA, Paris/School of Fine Arts, Liverpool/Stills, Edinburgh; *Location,
location, location*, Portikus, Frankfurt, 2008; *Sur-sous le pavé*, University of
Rennes Art Gallery, 2006; *If Not Now, When?* Sprengel Museum, Hannover,
with the Spectrum International Prize in Photography/NGBK, Haus am
Kleistpark, Berlin, 2005; *Martha Rosler: Positions in the Life World*, Ikon Gallery,
Birmingham/Institut d'Art Contemporain, Villeurbanne/Generali Foundation,
Vienna/MACBA, Barcelona/Netherlands Foto Museum, Rotterdam/
The New Museum of Contemporary Art, New York/International Center
of Photography, New York, 2000–09.

Group exhibitions
WACK! Art and the Feminist Revolution, Geffen Contemporary at Moca,
Los Angeles/National Museum of Women in the Arts and P.S.1, New
York/Vancouver Art Gallery, 2007–09; documenta 12, Kassel, 2007;
Skulptur Projekte Münster, 2007; *Occupying Space*, Sammlung Generali
Foundation, Vienna/Haus der Kunst, Munich/Nederlands Fotomuseum,

TENT and Witte de With, Rotterdam/Zagreb Museum, 2005; *The Last Picture Show: Artists Using Photography*, 1960–82, Walker Art Center, Minneapolis/ Hammer Museum, Los Angeles/MARCO, Vigo/Fotomuseum Winterthur/ Miami Art Central, 2003–05.

Publications
Imágenes públicas: la función política de la imagen (Barcelona, 2007); *Martha Rosler, 3 Works* (Halifax, 2006); *Sur-sous le pavé* (Rennes, 2006); *Passionate Signals* (Ostfildern, 2005); *Decoys and Disruptions: Writings, Selected 1975–2001* (Cambridge, MA, 2004).

Armando Andrade Tudela (Lima, 1975)
Lives and works in Saint Etienne

Solo exhibitions
Torcida, DAAD Gallery, Berlin, 2009, Ikon Gallery, Birmingham, 2009; *Gamblers Die Broke*, Frankfurter Kunstverein/Kunsthalle Basel, 2008; *Les Signaux de l'âme*, Annet Gelink Gallery, Amsterdam, 2007; *Inka Snow*, Carl Freedman Gallery (formerly Counter Gallery), London, 2006; *Camión*, Carl Freedman Gallery, London, 2004.

Group exhibitions
Building, Dwelling, Thinking, Laura Barlett Gallery, London, 2008; *Armando Andrade Tudela*, two-person show with Florian Pumhösl, Galerie Krobath Wimmer, Vienna, 2008; *Neutre Intense*, Carl Freedman Gallery, London, 2008; *Autour de Max Bill*, Swiss Cultural Centre, Paris, 2008; *Open Plan Living*, Helena Rubinstein Pavilion, Tel-Aviv, 2008.

Marion von Osten (Dortmund, 1963)
Lives in Berlin and works in Vienna

Exhibitions
In the Desert of Modernity. Colonial Planning and After, House of World Cultures, Berlin/Abattoirs Casablanca, 2008–09; *reformpause*, Kunstraum der Universität Lüneburg, 2006; *Projekt Migration*, DOMIT e.V., Kölnischer Kunstverein, Cologne; *TRANSIT MIGRATION,* University Frankfurt and the Institute for Theory of Art and Design, Zurich, 2003–05; *Atelier Europa*, Kunstverein München, Munich, 2004; *Be Creative! Der kreative Imperativ*, Museum für Gestaltung, Zurich, 2003.

Publications
Turbulente Ränder. Neue Perspektiven auf Migration an den Grenzen Europas (Bielefeld, 2007); *Projekt Migration* (Cologne, 2005); *Norm der Abweichung*, T:G 04 (Zurich/Vienna/New York, 2003); *Money Nations – Constructing the Border – Constructing East-West* (Vienna, 2003); *Be Creative! The creative imperative!* (Zurich, 2002); *Das Phantom sucht seinen Mörder. Ein Reader zur Kulturalisierung der Ökonomie* (Berlin, 1999).

Stephen Willats (London, 1943)
Lives and works in London

Solo exhibitions
The Ideological Diagram, Galerie Christian Nagel, Cologne, 2009; *In and out the Underworld*, Kunsthalle Köln, Cologne, 2008; *The Architecture of Stephen Willats*, Westfälisches Landesmuseum für Kunst und Kulturgeschichte, Münster, 2008; *Democratic Mosaics and Conceptual Towers*, Galerie Thomas Schulte, Berlin, 2008; *Person to Person/People to People*, Milton Keynes Gallery, Buckinghamshire, 2008.

Group exhibitions
Getting Even – Oppositions + Dialogues in Contemporary Art, Lewis Glucksman Gallery, Cork, 2008; *Soziale Diagramme. Planning Reconsidered*, Künstlerhaus Stuttgart, 2008; Manifesta 7, Rovereto, 2008; *A Town (not a city)*, Kunsthalle Sankt Gallen, Saint Gallen, 2008; *Sammlung/Collection*, Migros Museum für Gegenwartskunst, Zurich, 2008.

Publications
Beyond the Plan (London, 2001); *Art and Social Function* (London/Worcester, 2000); *Between People and Buildings* (London, 1996); *Intervention and Audience* (London, 1986); *City of Concrete* (Birmingham, 1986).

Christopher Williams (Los Angeles, 1956)
Lives in Los Angeles and Cologne

Solo exhibitions
For Example: Dix-Huit Leçons Sur La Société Industrielle (Revision 9), Galerie Gisela Capitain, Cologne, 2009; *For Example: Dix-Huit Leçons Sur La Société Industrielle (Revision 8)*, Capitain Petzel, Berlin, 2009; Bonner Kunstverein, Bonn, 2009 (with Mathias Poledna); *For Example: Dix-Huit Leçons Sur La Société Industrielle (Revision 7)*, David Zwirner, New York, 2008; *For Example: Dix-Huit Leçons Sur La Société Industrielle (Revision 6)*, Kunsthalle Zürich, 2007.

Group exhibitions
Whitney Biennial 2006: Day for Night, Whitney Museum of American Art, New York, 2006; *The Museum as Muse*, The Museum of Modern Art, New York, 1999; Foto Biennale, Rotterdam, 1999; *Jenny Holzer, Stephen Prina, Mark Stahl, Christopher Williams*, Galerie Crousel-Hussenot, Paris/Gewad, Gent/Foundation De Appel, Amsterdam, 1994; *Carnegie International 1991*, The Carnegie Museum of Art, Pittsburgh, 1991.

Publications
*Christopher Williams 97,5 Mhz** (Zurich, 2007); *Christopher Williams. De Rijke/ De Rooij* (Vienna, 2005); *Program. For Example: Dix-Huit Leçons Sur La Société Industrielle (Revision I)* (New York/Berlin, 2005); *Christopher Williams: Couleur européene, couleur soviétique, couleur chinoise* (Krefeld, 2000); *Christopher Williams: For Example: Die Welt ist schön (Final Draft)* (Rotterdam/Basel/ Hamburg, 1997).

Sabine Breitwieser is an independent curator based in Vienna. She is Secretary and Treasurer of CIMAM – International Committee of ICOM for Museums of Modern Art. From 1988–2007 she was Curator and Founding Director of the Generali Foundation in Vienna for which she built the programme and an important collection, both published in *Exhibitions 1989–2007* (2007) and *Occupying Space* (2003). She has curated numerous exhibitions and edited many publications of artists such as Isa Genzken, Dan Graham, Hans Haacke, Theresa Hak Kyung Cha, Andrea Fraser, Mary Kelly, Edward Krasiński, Gordon Matta-Clark, Gustav Metzger, Adrian Piper, Martha Rosler and Allan Sekula. Her most important thematic projects are *Designs for the Real World, double life, RE-PLAY, vivencias/life experience* and *White Cube/Black Box*. Besides *Modernologies*, she is currently curating *Utopia and Monument* in the public space in Graz for the Styrian autumn festival and *Which Life?*, the curators project at the Academy of Fine Arts in Vienna.

Cornelia Klinger is Permanent Fellow of the Institute for Human Sciences in Vienna and Professor of Philosophy at Tübingen University. She has written widely on aesthetic theory, political philosophy and gender issues in philosophy. Among other publications are the following: *Achsen der Ungleichheit. Zum Verhältnis von Klasse, Geschlecht und Ethnizität* (ed. with G.-A. Knapp and B. Sauer); *Das Jahrhundert der Avantgarden* (ed. with W. Müller-Funk); *Continental Philosophy in Feminist Perspective: Re-Reading the Canon in German* (ed. with H. Nagl-Docekal); *Flucht – Trost – Revolte. Die Moderne und ihre ästhetischen Gegenwelten.*

Walter D. Mignolo is William H. Wannamaker Professor of Literature and Romance Studies at Duke University. Among his most significant publications are *The Darker Side of the Renaissance: Literacy, Territoriality and Colonization* (1995) that was awarded the Katherine Singers Kovac Prize, from the Modern Languages Association in 1996; *Local Histories/Global Designs* (2000) and *The Idea of Latin America* (2005), that obtained the Frantz Fanon Award from the Caribbean Philosophical Association. He is director of the Center for Global Studies and the Humanities, Duke University, and has a blog page (waltermignolo.com).

André Rottmann is an art historian and critic based in Berlin. He is the editor of the quarterly journal *Texte zur Kunst* to which he frequently contributes. His writings on contemporary art, particularly focussing on the legacies of conceptualism, site-specificity and institutional critique, have also appeared in *Artforum International* (New York) and *Springerin – Hefte für Gegenwartskunst*, (Vienna) and numerous exhibition catalogues.

Works in the exhibition

Anna Artaker

Unbekannte Avantgarde, 2008
Unknown Avant-garde
Photo installation
10 black-and-white photographs and 10 labels
Photographs, dimensions variable, framed
Wall labels: inkjet print on paper, mounted on polystyrene,
each 21 × 14.8 cm
Edition of 3 plus 1 AP
Courtesy of the artist
pp. 53, 54

мишень / Zielscheibe, Moscow, 1913
The Target Group, Moscow, 1913
10.31 × 14.48 cm, framed 21.8 × 26.1 cm
p. 52

Groupe dada, Paris, 1922
Dada Group, Paris, 1922
17.57 × 30, framed 31 × 43.5 cm
p. 52

Surréalistes, Paris, 1924
Surrealists, Paris, 1924
20 × 27.4 cm, framed 33.5 × 40.5 cm
p. 52

Bauhaus, Dessau, 1926
20 × 28.46 cm, framed 33.5 × 41.5 cm
p. 53

Experimentele Groep, Amsterdam, 1949
Experimental Group, Amsterdam, 1949
6.68 × 10 cm, framed 18.2 × 21.6 cm
p. 54

Cobra, Paris, 1949
20 × 25.66 cm, framed 33.5 × 38.9 cm
p. 54

Abstract Expressionists, New York, 1950
20.28 × 20 cm, framed 33.5 × 33.5 cm
p. 55

Situationist International, London, 1960
25 × 16.54 cm, framed 38 × 30 cm
p. 54

Gruppe Spur, Schwabing, 1961
Spur Group, Schwabing, 1961
18.61 × 30 cm, framed 32 × 43.5 cm
p. 54

Austria Filmmakers Cooperative, Vienna, 1968
20 × 26.62 cm, framed 33.5 × 40 cm
p. 54

48 Köpfe aus dem Merkurov Museum, 2008
48 Heads from the Merkurov Museum
Film installation
16 mm film, black-and-white, silent,
approx. 10 min (looped)
Camera, assistance: Georg Tiller
Courtesy of the artist
p. 57

Alice Creischer/Andreas Siekmann

Atlas (Updating the Arntz and Neurath Atlas), 2003 – work-in-progress
Installation: 18 plates
Digital pigment print, lightfast pigment print on archival paper
17 plates, each 45.9 × 61 cm or 61 × 45.9 cm; 1 plate 61 × 91.8 cm
Updated by professors and students in workshops at the
University of Lüneburg (plates 1 to 3, 6 to 10) and as part of a project run
by the Economics Department of the University of Klagenfurt
(Kunstraum Lakeside, plates 4 and 5)
Edition of 7

Presented on six mobile walls in juxtaposition with 12 pages of the
historical *Atlas Gesellschaft und Wirtschaft – Bildstatistisches Elementarwerk*
(Atlas of Society and Economy – Visual Charts of the Essential Empirical Data
of the World), 1930, by Gerd Arntz and Otto Neurath
pp. 58–65

List of individual plates shown in juxtaposition
with the historical Atlas:

Staaten Bevölkerung 1 und 2, 2003/06
States Population 1 and 2
2 plates (historic maps by Waldseemüller),
each 45.9 × 61 cm
Arntz/Neurath Atlas
Plate 17: *Staaten und Bevölkerung um 1500*
(States and Population around 1500)

Reparationsforderungen (1 bis 6), 2003/06
Demands for Reparations (1 to 6)
6 plates, each 61 × 45.9 cm
Arntz/Neurath Atlas
Plate 18: *1783, 1880, 1930 Britisches Reich: Bevölkerung*
(British Empire: Population)
Plate 19: *1700, 1850, 1930 Französisches Kolonialreich: Bevölkerung*
(French Colonial Empire: Population)
Plate 21: *1783, 1850, 1930 USA: Bevölkerung* (USA: Population)

Minenopfer, minenproduzenten, 2003/06
Land Mine Victims, Mine Producers
2 plates, each 45.9 × 61 cm
Arntz/Neurath Atlas
Plate 28: *Rüstungen vor dem Krieg und jetzt*
(Armaments before the war and now)

Monopolartige Produktionen, 2005/06
Monopolist Production
1 plate, 61 × 45.9 cm
Arntz/Neurath Atlas
Plate 58: *Monopolartige Produktionen europäischer Länder und der U.d.S.S.R.*
(Monopolist Production of European Countries and the USSR)

Der Fall Coltan, 2005/06
The Coltan Case
1 plate, 61 × 91.8 cm
Arntz/Neurath Atlas
Plate 59: *Monopolartige Produktionen außereuropäischer Länder*
(Monopolist Production of Non–European Countries)

Festung Europa (I und II), 2003/06
Fortress Europe (I and II)
2 plates, each 61 × 45.9 cm
Arntz/Neurath Atlas
Plate 75: *Wanderungsfrage am Pazifik*
(Migration Issues in the Pacific)

Gesellschaftsgliederung Lüneburg, 2003/06
Social Structure of Luneburg
1 plate, 61 × 45.9 cm
Arntz/Neurath Atlas
Plate 80: *Gesellschaftsgliederung in Nürnberg*
(Social Structure in Nuremberg)

Streiks, 2003/06
Strikes
1 plate, 45.9 × 61 cm
Arntz/Neurath Atlas
Plate 88: *Streiks und Aussperrungen* (Strikes and Lock Outs)

Ökonomische Ungleichheiten, 2003/06
Economic Disparities
1 plate, 45.9 × 61 cm
Arntz/Neurath Atlas
Plate 90: *Reallöhne 1928* (Real Wages 1928)

Kartographie, 2003/06
Cartography
1 plate, 45.9 × 61 cm
Arntz/Neurath Atlas
Plate 100: *Kartographische Übersicht* (Cartographic Overview)

Generali Foundation Collection, Vienna

Dubai I, 2007
5 plates, laser print on paper
Each 240 × 84 cm
Arntz/Neurath Atlas
Plate 69: *300 AC, 300 PC, 1500, 1930 Damaskus Städtische Entwicklung*
(Damascus Urban Development)
Courtesy of the artists
pp. 62–63

Dubai II, 2007
1 plate, laser print on paper
Each, 120 × 84 cm
Arntz/Neurath Atlas
Plate 69: *300 AC, 300 PC, 1500, 1930 Damaskus Städtische Entwicklung*
(Damascus Urban Development)
Courtesy of the artists

Soja Production, 2009
1 plate, laser print on paper
42 × 59.4 cm (2 DIN A-2)
Arntz/Neurath Atlas
Plate 45: *Entwicklung der Kautschukproduktion seit 1895*
(The Development of Rubber Manufacture since 1895)
Plate 46: *Kautschukwirtschaft der Erde* (The World Rubber Industry)
Courtesy of the artists

Gerhard Arntz/Otto Neurath:
Atlas Gesellschaft und Wirtschaft – Bildstatistisches Elementarwerk, 1930
Atlas of Society and Economy– Visual Charts of the Essential Empirical
Data of the World
Loose-leaf edition of 100 plates, visual charts, and 30 text-plates
8-colour lithographic print on paper
In book linen portfolio
Each 30.5 × 46 cm
Issued by the Gesellschafts-und Wirtschaftsmuseum, Vienna
Published by the Bibliographisches Institut AG, Leipzig, 1930
Generali Foundation Collection, Vienna
pp. 61, 65

Domènec

Existenzminimum, 2002
Existential Minimum
Installation with sculpture, video and leaflet
Sculpture
Medium-density fibreboard, elements for inhabiting the prototype:
sleeping bag, plate, glass, towel, etc.
131 × 100 × 354 cm
Video of installation in public park de la Devesa in Girona
DVD, colour, silent, 7 min. 45 sec
Leaflet, 2009
Offset-print on paper
60 × 80 cm
Courtesy of the artist
pp. 66–69

Katja Eydel

Model ve Sembol. Die Erfindung der Türkei, 2005/06/09
The Invention of Turkey
Photo installation
Wallpaper with a selection of 41 photographs
Each 40 × 32 cm
Digital print
Dimensions variable, approx. 2.50 × 13.50 m
Courtesy of the artist
pp. 70–75

Titles of selected photographs for the catalogue in the artist section (pp. 71–75)

Ângela Ferreira

Maison Tropicale, 2007
Tropical House
2 scale models
Acrylic, expanded PVC
Each 20 × 90 × 20 cm
Fundación ARCO-CGAC Collection, Santiago de Compostela
p. 78

Maison Tropicale, 2007
Tropical House
10 drawings
Graphite on paper
pp. 76, 79, 80, 82

Technical drawing for *Maison Tropicale* sculpture
1 drawing
50 × 70 cm, framed 61 × 81 × 4 cm

Technical drawing for *Maison Tropicale* sculpture
4 drawings, each 70 × 100 cm, framed 81 × 111.2 × 4 cm

Study for Brazzaville site sculpture
Study for *Maison Tropicale* in Fundaco, Venice
Study for *Maison Tropicale* site sculpture,
after Prouvé's buttresses (Brazzaville)
Study for *Maison Tropicale* sculpture

5 drawings, each 21 × 27.5 cm, framed 43.3 × 41.5 × 3 cm
Fundación ARCO-CGAC Collection, Santiago de Compostela

Maison Tropicale (Brazzaville), no. 1, no. 2, no. 3, no. 4, 2007/09
Tropical House (Brazzaville), no. 1, no. 2, no. 3, no. 4
Each 30 × 42 cm
Courtesy of the artist
p. 81

Maison Tropicale (Niamey), no.1, no. 2, no. 3, 2007/09
Tropical House (Niamey)
3 colour photographs
Each 30 × 42 cm
Courtesy of the artist
p. 83

Andrea Fraser

Soldadera **(Scenes from** *Un banquete en Tetlapayac,*
a film by Oliver Debroise), 1998/2001
Video installation
Two-channel video projection, colour, sound, 5 min (looped)
Facsimile letter from Frances Flynn Paine to Mrs Abby Aldrich Rockefeller
Overall dimensions of installation approx. 275 × 730 × 120 cm

Produced with footage shot by Rafael Ortega for the film directed
by Olivier Debroise about Sergei Eisenstein shooting *¡Que viva México!* (1931)
at the Hacienda of Tetlapayac near Mexico City in 1998

Revolutionary peasant/Woman in the audience (Frances Flynn Paine):
Andrea Fraser; revolutionary worker: Cuauhtémoc Medina; revolutionary
intellectual: Lutz Becker; man in the audience (Hunter Kimbrough): James
Oles; man on a horse: Serge Guilbaut; audience: Magalí Arriola, Javier
de la Garza, Silvia Gruner, Alfonso Morales and Enrique Ortiga; director
of photography: Rafael Ortega; film-to-video-transfer: Monica Lombardo;
editing: Andrea Fraser and Peter Norrman; post-production: M.R.G International;
produced by Andrea Fraser and American Fine Arts, Co., New York
Courtesy of the artist
pp. 84–89

Isa Genzken

I Love New York, Crazy City, 1996
3 binders with prints from original portfolios with photomontages
134 laser colour photocopies (exhibition copies)
92 laser colour photocopies
118 laser colour photocopies
(exhibition copies)
Each 42.8 × 32.3 cm, paired in plastic sleeves
In black ring-binder, 44.9 × 37.4 cm
Generali Foundation Collection, Vienna

Oil XI, 2007
Installation
Mixed media
Dimensions variable
pp. 94–96

Oil XI a, 2007
Suitcases, stuffed owls, plastic material, paper, lacquer, metal
Approx. 180 × 600 × 800 cm
pp. 90–91

Oil XI b, 2007
Silkscreen print on laminated fabric, adhesive tape, paper, metal
298 × 157 cm

Oil XI c, 2007
Silkscreen print on laminated fabric, metal
149 × 99.5 cm

Oil XI d, 2007
3 parts, fabric, plastic
Approx. 200 × 60 × 40 cm

Courtesy Goetz Collection, Munich

Isa Genzken and Wilhelm Schnell

Ground Zero, 2007–08
Digital video, colour, silent, 6 min 18 sec (looped)
Courtesy Galerie Daniel Buchholz, Cologne-Berlin and Hauser & Wirth,
Zurich-London
p. 97

Dan Graham and Robin Hurst

Private 'Public' Space: The Corporate Atrium Garden, 1987
6 photomontages
Black-and-white and colour photographs, photographically reproduced
texts mounted on cardboard, total of 6
Each 101.6 × 76.2 cm, framed 104 × 87 cm
Digital exhibition prints from original plates (exhibition copies)
Generali Foundation Collection, Vienna
pp. 98–101

Tom Holert with Claudia Honecker

**Ricostruzione: Disertori / Libera. Towards a Historical Fable about Modernist
Architecture and Psychology**, 2008
Video installation
Photomontage, black-and-white and colour photographs,
127.4 × 220 cm, framed
Video, colour, sound, 19 min 12 sec (looped)
Edit: Adi Wolotzky; voice: Marc Siegel; sound: Moses Schneider,
transporterraum, Berlin; research assistance: Fabrizia Endrizzi,
Katia Anguelova; subtitles: Fabio Paracchini; commissioned
by Manifesta 7 / Italy, 2008, Anselm Franke and Hila Peleg
Courtesy of the artists
pp. 104–05

Marine Hugonnier

The Bedside Book Project

Un Coup De Dés Jamais N'Abolira Le Hasard / L'Espace Social N1, 2007
A throw of the dice will never abolish chance
Stéphane Mallarmé / Marine Hugonnier
Installation
Image clips onto Stéphane Mallarmé's poem *Un coup de dés jamais n'abolira
le hasard*, Éditions Gallimard, 2006
11 double pages, each 31.5 × 49 cm, framed 42 × 59.5 cm
Fundación ARCO-CGAC Collection, Santiago de Compostela
pp. 106–111

Un Coup De Dés Jamais N'Abolira Le Hasard / L'Espace Social N2, 2007
A throw of the dice will never abolish chance
Stéphane Mallarmé / Marine Hugonnier
Installation
Image clips onto Stéphane Mallarmé's poem *Un coup de dés jamais n'abolira
le hasard*, Éditions Gallimard, 2006
11 double pages, each 31.5 × 49 cm, framed each 42 × 59.5 cm
MACBA – Fundació Museu d'Art Contemporani de Barcelona Collection
Fundación Repsol Collection

IRWIN
Dušan Mandić
Miran Mohar
Andrej Savski
Roman Uranjek
Borut Vogelnik

Retroavantgarde, 2000–09
Installation
Digital print on paper
350 × 700 cm
Courtesy of IRWIN and the artists
pp. 112–15

Including a text by theoretician Marina Gržinić
and the artists and works:

Dimitrij Bašičević Mangelos, *Neg.d.p. XX1*, date unknown
Tempera, 25 × 18 cm

Avgust Černigoj, *Construction*, 1924
Photograph (reproduction), 37 × 30 cm

Braco Dimitrijević, *Triptychos Post Historicus*, 1985
Photograph (reproduction), 36.5 × 39 cm

Laibach, *Hammerman*, 1983
Silkscreen print, 103.5 × 73.5 cm

Kasimir Malevich (Belgrade)
Paintings, sculpture, 1985
Suprematism, 1985, 52 × 40 cm
Suprematism, 1985, 29 × 27.5 cm
Suprematism, 1985, 25.5 × 25.5 cm
Sculpture, 1985, height: 32 cm

Gledališče Sester Scipion Nasice
Krst pod Triglavom (Baptism under the Triglav), 1985
Photograph, 30.5 × 40.5 cm

Jossip Seissel, *Balkanite Stand at Attention*, 1922
(reproduction), 29 × 24.5 cm

Mladen Stilinovič, *Exploitation of the Dead*, 1984–90
Objects: 1986, 18.5 × 24.5 cm; 1987, 15 × 14.5 cm; 1990, 9 × 9 cm;
height: 20 cm; 1990, 21.5 × 21.5 cm; 1989, 31.5 × 31.5 cm; 1989, 18 × 20.5 cm;
1989, 20 × 20.5 cm; 1986, 30 × 35 cm; 1988, 12 × 19 cm; 1986, 16.5 × 15 cm.

IRWIN, *Malevich between two wars*, 1984 / 2006, mixed media,
76 × 49 cm

IRWIN, *Cup of Coffee*, 1986, mixed media, 76 × 49 cm

Runa Islam

Empty the pond to get the fish., 2008
Film installation
35 mm film, colour, sound, 12 min 8 sec (looped); produced by Museum of Modern
Art Foundation Ludwig Vienna and White Cube, London

Edition of 5 plus 1 AP
Production: Brains & Pictures, Vienna; project manager: Claudia Dohr; production
assistant: Anna Artaker; Grip / motion control: Gunnar Kaiser; photography:
Thomas Kirschner; gaffer: Thomas Schindler; grip assistant: Alex Brozek;
camera assistant: Oliver Schneider; sound design: Mick Ritchie; sound recordist:
Wolfgang Mohaupt; runner: Clemens Roesch; special thanks to: Matthias
Michalka

Museum of Modern Art Foundation Ludwig Vienna, Donation 2008
pp. 116–21

Klub Zwei
Simone Bader
Jo Schmeiser

Phaidon. Verlage im Exil, 2006/09
Phaidon. Presses in Exile
Video installation
4 videos, colour, sound, 22 min (1 projected, 3 on monitors, looped)
2 benches with inscriptions, wood, each 31 × 295 × 67 cm

German/English language version of three-channel video installation:
Collection of the Department for Cultural affairs of the City of Vienna –
MUSA; version of fourth-channel video with Spanish translation:
produced by MACBA, courtesy of the artists

Interview partners: Elly Miller, art publisher, London; Ursula Seeber,
Austrian Exile Library, Literaturhaus, Vienna; Tamar Wang, writer and editor,
London

Directors: Klub Zwei; camera: Anita Makris (Elly Miller, Katherine Klinger
and Ruth Sands), Daniel Pöhacker (Elly Miller and Tamar Wang), Klub Zwei
(Hannah Fröhlich, Ursula Seeber); translation: Erika Doucette; colour
and sound correction: Friedemann Derschmidt, Volkmar Klien; benches:
Sasha Pirker, Judith Augustinovic, Herbert Stattler
pp. 123–25

Logos Phaidon, 1923 and today, 2009
Installation
2 glass plates, sand blasted
Each 99.2 × 30.3 cm
Courtesy of the artists
p. 122

John Knight

Logotype (project for documenta 7), 1982
Relief
Birch plywood and advertising poster
59.6 × 88.5 × 4 cm
Rüdiger Schöttle Gallery, Munich
pp. 127, 128

Logotype (project for documenta 7), 1982
Relief
Birch plywood and advertising poster
80 × 80 × 4 cm
Ernest and Micheline Delville
pp. 127, 128

Mirror, 1986
Relief
Assembled pine-wood and mirror
196.68 × 106.6 × 1.9 cm
Collection Michèle Lachowsky
pp. 129–31

Mirror, 1986
Relief
Assembled pine-wood and mirror
104 × 104 × 2 cm
Private collection
pp. 129–31

Mirror, 1986
Relief
Assembled pine-wood and mirror
107 × 107 × 2 cm
Private collection, Marseille
pp. 129–31

Mirror, 1986
Relief
Assembled pine-wood and mirror
170 × 170 × 2 cm
Collection Bruno van Lierde, Brussels
pp. 129–31

Labor K3000
Peter Spillmann
Michael Vögeli
Marion von Osten

www.this-was-tomorrow.net
grid one: Von Hochhaus zu Hochhaus, 2008
Installation with website project
Display, Internet, website project
Courtesy of the artists
pp. 132–33

Louise Lawler

Storage, 1986
Installation
Framed Cibachrome print, painted wall in beige, red dot, wall label
139.7 × 198.1 cm
pp. 136–37

Storage, 1986
Cibachrome print
65 × 96.5 cm, framed 88.9 × 120.65 cm
Edition of 5

Stedelijk Museum voor Actuele Kunst (S.M.A.K.) Collection, Gent

Well Being, 1986
Installation
Framed Cibachrome print, painted wall in pink and blue, wall label
183 × 244 cm, dimensions variable
pp. 138–39

La Lecture, 1924, Femme au Livre, 1924, Positioned together,
Tous les Deux, ensemble, New York, 1985
Cibachrome print
67.3 × 97.8 cm, framed 96.5 × 128.3 cm
Edition of 5 (exhibition print)

Museum of Contemporary Art San Diego Collection

David Maljkovic

Retired Form, 2008
Film installation
16 mm, black-and-white, silent, 4 min 33 sec
Camera: Hrvoje Franjic; editing: Sanjin Stanic; production:
David Maljkovic and Metro Pictures, New York
Courtesy of the artist and Metro Pictures
p. 141

Dorit Margreiter

Original Condition (Masters for Sale), 2006
Installation
10 advertisements cut out from newspapers
Various dimensions, each framed 22 × 30 cm
Stampa Galerie, Basel
pp. 146–47

zentrum, 2006
Film installation
16 mm film, black-and-white, silent, 2 min 44 sec (looped)
3 posters, inkjet print on paper, each 112 × 84 cm,
framed each 124.5 × 88.5 cm
Courtesy the artist and Galerie Krobath, Vienna
pp. 142–44

Gordon Matta-Clark

Window Blow-Out, 1976
Document of action, installation
8 black-and-white photographs (exhibition prints)
Each 26.8 × 34 cm, framed 84.5 × 182 cm
Generali Foundation Collection, Vienna
p. 149

Gustav Metzger

Cardboards, Auto-Destructive Monument, 1960
Scale model
Staples, steel, varnished cardboards
24 × 45 × 25 cm
Generali Foundation Collection, Vienna
p. 150

Auto-Destructive Art
London, 4 November 1959 (first manifesto)

Manifesto Auto-Destructive Art
London, 10 March 1960 (second manifesto)
Facsimile of original manifestos
Each 33 × 20.5 cm
p. 151

Five Screens with Computer, 1969
Computer-controlled *Auto-Destructive Monument*
Scale model
Steel
7.2 × 44.4 × 30.9 cm
Generali Foundation Collection, Vienna. Gift by Alan Sutcliffe
p. 153

Five Screens with Computer, 1969
Sketch on graph paper, facsimile
21 × 29.6 cm
Generali Foundation Collection, Vienna
p. 152

Five Screens with Computer, 1969
2 computer drawings, published in *Page Magazine*, facsimile
Each 29.6 × 21 cm
Generali Foundation Collection, Vienna
p. 152

Christian Philipp Müller

Vergessene Zukunft – Forgotten Future, 1992
Installation
Exhibition at the Kunstverein München
from 29 April to 28 June 1992, Munich
pp. 154–59

Box, 57 × 36 × 4 cm
containing 8 numbered black-and-white photographs
(by Joss Bachhofer)
Each 24 × 30 cm in 8 passe-partouts, silkscreen print,
Each 34 × 40 cm
pp. 157–59

The book *Vergessene Zukunft – Forgotten Future:* texts by Helmut Draxler, Manfred Hermes and Wolfgang Theis, silkscreen print, Münchner Kunstverein and Edition Artelier, Munich/Graz, 1992.

1 leaflet, film programme at the Filmmuseum München:
text by Madeleine Bernstorff, 14.8 × 21 cm
Sheet with legend, 34 × 40 cm
p. 155

Edition of 30 plus AP
Artelier Contemporary, Graz

Exhibition poster, 1992
Silkscreen print on paper
118 × 84 cm
Artelier Contemporary, Graz
p. 154

Das dritte Geschlecht, 1992
The Third Sex
Trailer for the exhibition
Video, black-and-white, and colour, sound, 9 min (looped)
Conception and editing: Christian Philipp Müller and Madeleine Bernstorff

Text 1: Advertising copy by Constantin Film AG for *Anders als du und ich* (175) directed by Veit Harlan, 1957

Text 2: Nicolas Schöffer, *Die Kybernetische Stadt*, Munich, 1970
Voice over 1: Comments by Friedrich Joloff a.k.a. Oberst Villa in *Raumpatrouille VII.* ('Invasion')

Voice over 2: A. S. *Paragraph 175 im deutschen Film*, Deutsche Woche, 4 December 1957
Kinetic effects: *Minieffet*, 1970; light organ: Nicolas Schöffer
Edition: Denise René, Paris 218/5000
Clips from: *Das dritte Geschlecht*, 1957, directed by Veit Harlan
FWM-Stiftung, Wiesbaden through the Freiwillige Selbstkontrolle der Filmwirtschaft's (FSK), uncensored version

Courtesy of the artist and Galerie Christian Nagel, Cologne/Berlin

Henrik Olesen

How do I make myself a body?, 2008
Mixed media installation
Collages, various objects and spatial interventions
Dimensions variable
pp. 160–67

Details of individual works:

Schraubenzieher, 2008
Screwdriver
23 × 2.5 × 2.5 cm

1 + 3 Schrauben, 2008
Metal screws
Each 4 × 0.7 cm

Apple (Ghost), 2008
Computer, plastic foil
50 × 40 × 60 cm
p. 163

Imitation/Enigma, 2008
Box, adhesive tape, rope, padding material, blanket
60 × 100 × 30 cm
p. 163

Agent (shoe), 2008
Man's shoe, leather
10 × 27 × 9.5 cm

Some Illustrations to the life of Alan Turing, 2008
16 digital prints
Each 33 × 48 cm
pp. 166–67

Spoon, 2008
Spoon
2 × 14 × 3.5 cm
p. 160

How do I make myself a body, 2008
19 computer collages
Partly worked over with felt pen/ball point pen
Each 29.7 × 21 cm
pp. 164–65

4 Plakate, 2008
4 posters
4 digital prints
Each 48 × 33 cm
Edition of 10 plus 1 AP
p. 162

Portrait d'un imbécile, 2008
Portrait of a fool
Wooden laths, felt pen
385 × 9.5 × 5.5 cm
p. 160

Courtesy of the artist and Galerie Daniel Buchholz, Cologne-Berlin

Paulina Olowska

**Collaged Stryjeńska. Posters, Illustrations, and Paintings
by and about Zofia Stryjeńska**
Exhibition curated by Paulina Olowska
Schinkel Pavilion, 5th Berlin Biennial, 2008
pp. 168–173

3 paintings from a series of a total of 6:

Zofia Stryjeńska, 2008
Painting
Gouache on canvas
230 × 160 cm
Courtesy Goetz Collection, Munich
p. 172

Zofia Stryjeńska, 2008
Painting
Gouache on canvas
230 × 180 cm
Courtesy Goetz Collection, Munich
p. 172

Zofia Stryjeńska, 2008
Painting
Gouache on canvas
230 × 240 cm
Thomas Borgmann, Berlin
p. 172

Poster for Schinkel Pavilion – Zofia Stryjeńska, 2008
3 posters announcing the exhibition
Gouache on paper
Each framed 61 × 83.5 cm
Courtesy Goetz Collection, Munich (couple)
Collection S.A. Weis & Kompanie, Courtesy Galerie Daniel Buchholz,
Cologne-Berlin (boy)
Collection Storch, Cologne (girl)
p. 169

Falke Pisano

Display for videos, posters, booklets of selected lecture performances 2005–2008:

Performance Posters, 2005–08
  Concrete Abstractions, 2005
  A Sculpture Turning into a Conversation (Part Zero and Part One), 2006
  Affecting Abstraction 3 (The Complex Object), 2007
  Object and Disintegration: A Performance in Trialogue Form, 2008
4 digital prints
Each 84.1 × 59.4 cm

Studio Lecture 1, 2006
Lecture, February 2006
Video, DVD, colour, sound, 42 min
p. 176

A Sculpture Turning into a Conversation (Part Zero and Part One), 2006
Two-channel video installation
2 DVDs, colour, sound, each 25 min (looped)
Sculpture
Foam board
60 × 50 × 50 cm
p. 177

Object of Transformation 1, 2007
Sculpture
Paper
30 × 30 × 30 cm
p. 178

Object Construction 1: Reflective Abstraction (Mishima), 2007
Installation with books
Dimensions variable
13 books, various dimensions; booklet, digital print, 16 pages, 29.7 × 21 cm
  Sculpture of the Twentieth Century (Andrew Carnduff Ritchie, pp. 112, 113)
  In the Labyrinth (Alain Robbe-Grillet, pp. 140, 141)
  'Conception of Space' in *F.R, – The 'As yet…' issue* (George Vantongerloo,
  pp. 150, 151)
  Data: Directions in Art, Theory, and Aesthetics (Anthony Hill, ed., pp. 72, 73)
  The World of Jazz (André Hodeir, pp. 140, 141)
  Tropisms (Nathalie Sarraute, foreword)
  Logical Space (James Reineking, pp. 70, 71)
  Sun and Steel (Yukio Mishima, pp. 10, 11)
  The Invention of Morel (Adolfo Bioy Casares, pp. 88, 89)
  Period (Dennis Cooper, pp. 50, 51)
  The Writings of Robert Smithson (Nancy Holt, ed., pp. 10, 11)
  The Nature of Explanation (Kenneth Craik, pp. 98, 99)
  Progress in Art (Suzi Gablik, p. 90)

  Courtesy private collection, Paris
  p. 179

If not mentioned otherwise, all works are courtesy of the artist and Ellen de
Bruijne Projects, Amsterdam; Balice-Hertling, Paris; Hollybush Gardens, London

Mathias Poledna

Untitled, 2009
Installation
Display case, acrylic glass cover, wooden base
170 × 170 × 85 cm
6 record sleeves on acrylic glass stands:
  *Music of the Orient: Japan, China, Bali, Siam, Persia, India, Tunis, Egypt.
  Collected by Dr. E. M. von Hornbostel*
  The Living, Dead and Dying. Music of the New Guinea Wape
  *Music from an Equatorial Microcosm. Fang Bwiti Music with Mbiri Selections
  (Folkways)*
  *Anthology of Brazilian Indian Music. Karajá, Javahé, Kraho, Tukuna, Juruna,
  Suyá, Trumai Shukarramãe*
  Music of Equatorial Africa: Baya, Mboko, Yaswa, Bongili, N'Goundi,

Badouma, Koukouya, Babimga, Okandi, Kouyou
American Banjo – Tunes & Songs in Scruggs Style
pp. 180–85

Untitled, 2009
Installation
Display case, acrylic glass cover, wooden base
170 × 170 × 85 cm
6 record sleeves on acrylic glass stands
   Pre-Columbian Instruments
   Music of the Jos Plateau and other regions of Nigeria
   Mushroom Ceremony of the Mazatec Indians of Mexico
   Songs of the Watusi
   Songs of the Watusi
   Music of the Shakers

Untitled, 2009
Film installation
16 mm film, colour, silent (looped)
Production: Fundació MACBA

All works are courtesy of the artist and Galerie Meyer Kainer, Vienna;
Galerie Daniel Buchholz, Cologne/Berlin; Richard Telles Fine Art,
Los Angeles

Florian Pumhösl

Modernologie (Dreieckiges Atelier), 2007
Modernology (Triangular Atelier)

Installation
Partition walls upholstered with black buckram fabric,
joined with partition hinges, reverse glass paintings,
display case
Dimensions variable

Works displayed on wall system:

Wall 1: segments: 95 × 280 cm, 190 × 280 cm, 285 × 280 cm
pp. 186–191

Modernology 19, 2007
Synthetic resin lacquer on reverse of sheet glass,
36 × 25 cm

Modernology 25, 2007
Synthetic resin lacquer on reverse of sheet glass,
62.9 × 53 cm

Wall 2: segments: 380 × 280 cm, 190 × 280 cm, 285 × 280 cm

Modernology 14, 2007
Perspex wall-mounted display case containing a copy of *Front* magazine,
'Parachuting' issue, no. 7/1943, mounted on panel upholstered in black
buckram fabric
69 × 85 × 8 cm
p. 190

Modernology 20, 2007
Synthetic resin lacquer on reverse of sheet glass,
64 × 46 cm

Modernology 22, 2007
Synthetic resin lacquer on reverse of sheet glass,
65 × 46 cm

Wall 3: segments: 190 × 280 cm, 285 × 280 cm,
475 × 280 cm

Modernology 09, 2007
Synthetic resin lacquer on reverse of sheet glass,
52 × 40.5 cm

Modernology 23, 2007
Synthetic resin lacquer on reverse of sheet glass,
52 × 40.5 cm

Modernology 15, 2007
Synthetic resin lacquer on reverse of sheet glass,
29 × 27 cm

Modernology 26, 2007
Synthetic resin lacquer on reverse of sheet glass,
39 × 27 cm
p. 188

Installation first time produced for documenta 12;
wall system reproduced by MACBA
Courtesy of the artist and Galerie Daniel Buchholz,
Cologne/Berlin

Relief (Study of Constructivism), 2009
Perspex wall-mounted display case, 5 books by Murayama Tomoyoshi,
mounted on panel upholstered in black buckram fabric
160 × 120 × 12 cm

List of books:
   Beast-God, 1937 (Sleeve by Murayama Tomoyoshi)
   The Current Art and Future Art, 1923 (Author: Murayama Tomoyoshi),
   MAVO-publication
   Bokyo, Nostalgia, 1927, Iketanis essay (Design by Murayama Tomoyoshi)
   Sukitowohaita Nero, The Emperor Nero putting on a Skirt, 1926
   (Illustrations by Murayama Tomoyoshi)
   Kouseiha Kenkyo. Study of Constructivism, 1925
   (Author: Murayama Tomoyoshi)

Ulrich Reininghaus, Cologne

Martha Rosler

Flower Fields (Color Field Painting), c. 1975
Video, transferred from Super 8 mm film, colour, silent, 3 min 48 sec (looped)
MACBA Collection. Fons de l'Ajuntament de Barcelona
p. 193

How Do We Know What Home Looks Like?
The *Unité d'Habitation* of Le Corbusier at Firminy, France, 1993
Video, colour, sound, 30 min (looped)
Camera: Martha Rosler; music: Eric Satie; appearances by Mme Bousquet,
la famille Caleyron, Bernadette Celette, Brigitte Marconnet, Jean-Manuel Morilla,
les femmes sur l'herbe, les enfants, Joshua M. R. Neufeld and Yves Aupetitallot
MACBA Collection. Fons de l'Ajuntament de Barcelona
p. 195

The *Unité d'Habitation* of Le Corbusier at Firminy, France, 1993
Facsimiles of statistics of inhabitants
10 pages, US-letter format
Courtesy of the artist
pp. 196–97

Armando Andrade Tudela

Camión, 2003
Slide projection
60 images, 35 mm slides
Taken by the artist between October and December 2003
at the Carretera Central, Panamericana Sur,
Panamericana Norte and Lima Metropolitana, Perú.
Approx. 50 × 65 cm
Edition of 5
Courtesy Carl Freedman Gallery, London
p. 200–01

Utopía Rústica, 2004
Drawing
Mixed media on paper
33 × 21 cm
Private collection
p. 198

Open Tile, 2005
Photograph
C-print
50 × 35 cm
Courtesy Carl Freedman Gallery, London
p. 198

Transa, 2005
Sculpture
Paper and vinyl (9 copies of record sleeves of *Transa* by Caetano Veloso)
59 × 111 × 94.5 cm
Tate Collection: Purchased 2006
p. 202

Untitled (no. 4), 2007–08
Sculpture
Asphalt
20 × 18 × 19 cm
Courtesy of the artist and Carl Freedman Gallery, London
p. 204

Untitled (no. 6), 2007–08
Sculpture
Asphalt
18 × 17 × 22 cm
Courtesy of the artist and Carl Freedman Gallery, London

Untitled (no. 9), 2007–08
Sculpture
Asphalt
21 × 20 × 22 cm
Courtesy of the artist and Carl Freedman Gallery, London

Untitled (no. 1), 2008
Sculpture
Wire, rattan
53.7 × 30.5 × 33.5 cm
MACBA Collection. Fons de l'Ajuntament de Barcelona
p. 205

Untitled (no. 3), 2008
Sculpture
Wire, rattan
51 × 30 × 35 cm
Thomas Dane, London

Untitled (no. 5), 2008
Sculpture
Wire, rattan
55 × 31 × 36 cm
Private Collection, London

Untitled (no.1), 2009
Sculpture
Polycarbonate film
32 × 45 × 33 cm
Courtesy Carl Freedman Gallery, London

Untitled (no. 2), 2009
Sculpture
Polycarbonate film
18 × 43 × 35 cm
Courtesy Carl Freedman Gallery, London

Untitled (no. 3), 2009
Sculpture
Polycarbonate film
31 × 46 × 34 cm
Courtesy Carl Freedman Gallery, London

Marion von Osten

In the Desert of Modernity, 2009
Display set
Steel and wood painted, text
2 slide projections of 80 photographs and drawings by various authors
Reprint of photograph (*Cité verticale housing project*, Casablanca 1952
by George Candilis and Shadrach Woods)
Reprint of magazine, published by the Committee for the Independence
of Morocco in 1953
Various dimensions
pp. 206–09

In the Desert of Modernity. Colonial Planning and After is a research project and
a travelling exhibition initiated by Marion von Osten in collaboration with the
architects, artists, activists and theorists Mogniss Abdallah, An Architektur, Kader
Attia, Tom Avermaete, Wafae Belarbi, Madeleine Bernstorff, Casamémoire, Jesko
Fezer, Hassan Darsi, Kanak Attak, Serhat Karakayali, Brigitta Kuster, Labor k3000,
Andreas Müller, Remember Resistance, Elsa de Seynes, Peter Spillmann, Anna
Voswinckel and Daniel Weiss.
Courtesy of the artist

Stephen Willats

Compartmentalised Cliff, June–July 1977
2 panels
Photographic prints, Letraset text, ink on cardboard, perspex frame
Framed each, 110.3 × 76.3 cm
pp. 210–12

Concrete Window, November 1990 – July 1991
3 panels
Photographic prints, acrylic paint, Letraset text, photographic dye,
on paper and cardboard
perspex frame 121 × 74.5 cm
pp. 213–15

All works: Courtesy of the artist and Galerie Christian Nagel, Cologne

Christopher Williams

**Ablaye Bà, Bira Bà,
Sidath Fall and Aziz Ngom,
La Sénégalaise de L'Imprimerie,
Dakar, Senegal
May 14, 1996 (No. 1, 2)**
1996
2 photographs
Gelatin silver prints
Framed each 64.5 × 74.5 cm
Edition of 12
Museum Boijmans Van Beuningen, Rotterdam
p. 217

**Super Quadra Sul 308
Bloco 'D'Asa Sul (south wing)
70.355 BRASILIA-DF
Lucio Costa, Oscar Niemeyer, 1960
January 31, 1997 (No. 1, 2)**
1997
2 photographs
Gelatin silver prints
Framed each 64.5 × 74.5 cm
Edition of 12
Galerie Gisela Capitain, Cologne
p. 219

**Main Staircase for
the Arts Club of Chicago, 1948–51
Steel, travertine marble
359.4 × 458.8 × 609.3 cm
(141 1/2 × 180 5/8 × 239 7/8")
Arts Club commission 1948–51
Ludwig Mies van der Rohe
109 East Ontario Street
Chicago, Illinois 1951–1995
Repositioned by John Vinci
201 East Ontario Street
Chicago, Illinois
October 1, 1998**
1998
Photograph
Gelatin silver print
Framed each 74.5 × 64.5 cm
Edition of 10
Wendy Gondeln
p. 218

**Kiev 88, 4.6 lbs. (2.1 Kg)
Manufacturer: Zavod Arsenal Factory, Kiev, Ukraine.
Date of production: 1983-87
Douglas M. Parker Studio,
Glendale, California
March 28, 2003 (No. 1, 2, 3)**
2003
3 photographs
Dye transfer prints
Each 40.6 × 50.8 cm, framed each 74 × 81.6 × 3.8 cm
Edition of 10
Haubrok Collection
p. 221

**Activities
in the frame of the exhibition**

Curated by Sabine Breitwieser

Workshop

Workshop on the project *Atlas* with Alice Creischer and Andreas Siekmann, which will undertake the research for the actualization of plates 45 and 46 (The world rubber industry) of the historical 'Atlas of Society and Economy' produced by Otto Neurath and Gerd Arntz (1930)

Panel discussions: Just what is it that makes modernity and modernism for visual artists so different, so appealing today? The politics of artistic research

Introduction by Sabine Breitwieser

The production of space and (de)colonialisation
Ângela Ferreira, Runa Islam and Marion von Osten
Moderator: Chus Martínez

The idea of creating a universal language versus corporate identity and branding
Alice Creischer/Andreas Siekmann, Tom Holert and Florian Pumhösl
Moderator: Miguel López

The politics of display and rewriting the history of modernism
Borut Vogelnik (IRWIN), Christian Philipp Müller and Falke Pisano
Moderator: André Rottmann

Film programme: Modernity and after

Architecture as art, art as architecture

Gordon Matta-Clark
Splitting, 1974
16 mm film, transferred from Super 8 mm film
Black-and-white and colour, silent
10 min 50 sec

Isa Genzken
Chicago Drive, 1992
35 mm film, transferred from 16 mm film, colour, sound
25 min
Courtesy Galerie Daniel Buchholz, Cologne/Berlin

Manthia Diawara
Maison Tropicale, 2008
Tropical House
DVD, colour, sound
58 min

Utopian landscapes and geopolitics

Marine Hugonnier
Ariana, 2003*
Super 16 mm film, transferred to DVD
Colour, sound
18 min 36 sec

The Last Tour, 2004*
Super 16 mm film, transferred to DVD
Colour, sound
14 min 17 sec

Travelling Amazonia, 2006*
Super 16 mm film, transferred to DVD
Colour, sound
23 min 52 sec

Jean Vidal
Salut Casa, 1952
35 mm film, transferred to DVD, black-and-white, sound
33 min
French with English and German subtitles
Courtesy: Archives Françaises du Film/CNC, Bois d'Arcy
France/Claude Vidal-Breton; DVD Production: Labor k3000
Zurich/*In the Desert of Modernity* (2008)

Abstractionism and beyond

David Maljkovic
Images With Their Own Shadows, 2008*
16 mm film, black-and-white and colour, sound
6 min 16 sec

László Moholy-Nagy
Lichtspiel Schwarz-Weiß-Grau, 1930
Lightplay: Black-White-Grey
16 mm film, black-and-white, silent
6 min

Armando Andrade Tudela
Untitled Film no. 2 (Espace Niemeyer and Infra Red Light), 2007*
16 mm film transferred to DVD, colour, silent
9 min 51 sec

Film no. 3 (4 greys and 22 transitions), 2008*
16 mm film transferred to DVD, colour, silent
7 min 36 sec

Oskar Fischinger
Wachsexperimente, 1921–26
Wax Experiments
16 mm film, colour, silent
9 min

Florian Pumhösl
Animated Map, 2005/2006*
16 mm film, colour, silent
4 min 32 sec

*OA 1979-3-5-036; after Take Hiratsugi, Gozen Hiinagata,
(Dress Patterns for noble Ladies), c. 1690*, 2007*
16 mm film, black-and-white, silent
17 min

Percy Smith
Fight for the Dardanelles, 1915
16 mm film, black-and-white, silent
6 min 10 sec

Falke Pisano
Lecture on Abstraction and Evil, 2005/07
DVD, black-and-white and colour, sound
19 min 40 sec

Performing the modern house

Dorit Margreiter
10104 Angelo View Drive, 2004*
16 mm film, colour, silent
6 min

Man Ray
Les Mystères du château du Dé, 1928
The Mysteries of the Château of Dice
16 mm film, black-and-white, silent
partly with music by Eric Satie
25 min

Ursula Mayer
Interiors, 2006*
Super 16 mm film transferred to DVD
colour and black-and-white, sound
3 min 10 sec

Florian Pumhösl
Programm, 2006*
Programme
16 mm film, colour, optical sound
7 min 49 sec

Hans Richter
Die Neue Wohnung, 1930
The New Apartment
16 mm film, black-and-white, silent
28 min

Moira Hille
Chandigarh 1+2, 2008*
DVD, colour, sound
22 min

Modern life and after

Paul Wolff
Neues Bauen in Frankfurt am Main, 1928
A new way of building in Frankfurt
16 mm film, black-and-white, silent with subtitles
34 min

Rebecca Baron and Dorit Margreiter
Poverty Housing. Americus, Georgia, 2008*
35 mm film, colour, sound
13 min 58 sec

Gordon Matta-Clark
Conical Intersect, 1978
16 mm film, colour, silent
18 min 40 sec

Marina Gržinic/Aina Šmid
Postsocialism + Retroavantgarde + IRWIN, 1997
Video, Betacam SP PAL, colour, sound, 22 min 5 sec

* Originally shown in exhibition spaces as loop installation.

Unless otherwise stated, all films included in the *Modernologies*
exhibition are courtesy of the artists.

For further information: www.macba.cat

Acknowledgments

First and foremost I would like sincerely to thank all the artists for making truly invaluable contributions with their artworks, most of which have been especially installed, adapted or even newly produced for this exhibition. I would also like to make special mention of those artists whose works are screened in the film programme, which I consider an important contribution to the exhibition. While working on my essay for this catalogue, all the wonderful conversations, together with the exchange of thoughts and ideas I've had, came back to mind and I would like to emphasise that this is an exhibition strongly shaped through dialogue with the artists. I am deeply grateful to the lenders to the exhibition for providing us with some quite delicate artworks; without them the exhibition would not be what I intended. Additionally, the assistance of the galleries representing the artists was essential to this project.

Cornelia Klinger and Walter D. Mignolo, the authors of the two historiographical and theoretical essays, have made a fundamental contribution to the project of *Modernologies* and I cannot thank them enough for their brilliant reflections on this topic. I am deeply obliged to numerous other authors, namely Inke Arns, Silke Baumann, Benjamin H.D. Buchloh, Sabeth Buchmann, Barbara Clausen, Helmut Draxler, Jordi Font Agulló, Karin Gludovatz, Matthias Michalka, Juliane Rebentisch, Anne Rorimer, Gertrud Sandqvist and Kerstin Stakemeier, who kindly agreed that their key texts on the individual artists be republished in this volume. Some of the artists have also written texts on their works especially for this context and I would like to thank them again, and especially André Rottmann who asked them challenging questions and who has edited the final statements. André was also a great support regarding the project in many aspects.

A project of this kind can only be realised with the help and support of many people, but the first requirement is the invitation to participate in such an undertaking. I was still Director of Generali Foundation in Vienna when Manuel J. Borja-Villel, currently Director of MNCARS in Madrid, asked me to conceive and curate an exhibition on 'another modernity', while he was still Director of the MACBA. Head Curator Bartomeu Marí strongly supported this project from the beginning and has continued to do so since he was appointed Director of the MACBA in 2008. Ainhoa Grandes Massa, Director, Fundació Museu d'Art Contemporani de Barcelona, has made it possible for a new art work to be commissioned and acquired for the MACBA Collection, and in doing so she helped raise our resources in terms of budget and space. Last but not least, I am deeply grateful to the entire MACBA team for their commitment to this extensive project, and especially to Chus Martínez for being so positive about the project and Friedrich Meschede who helped raising funds. Also from the exhibition department, Teresa Grandas and Meritxell Colina; the exhibition architects Isabel Bachs and Núria Guarro; the conservators, technicians and installation crew; the publications department, including Clara Plasencia, Ester Capdevila and Loli Acebal; and those responsible for the activities programme, formerly Jorge Ribalta and currently Marta Garcia. It was a true pleasure to work with them on the entire production.

Modernologies will travel to the new Museum of Modern Art in Warsaw and I would like to thank Joanna Mytkowska and her entire team, especially Magdalena Lispka and Ana Janevski.

Kenneth Pietrobono was of great help assisting Louise Lawler regarding research on two of her early installations and the new print of a photograph. Ewout Vellekoop was wonderful to work with as Runa Islam's assistant, and I would also like to mention Wolfgang Konrad for providing us with the 35 mm film projector and looper, and also for helping us to install Runa's film loop in Barcelona.

I have previously collaborated with Martha Stutteregger on one of the first books I edited for the Generali Foundation and it was great to work again with Martha and her team — Rosina Huth and Johannes Lang — in Vienna and Barcelona on the design of the present catalogue. In Vienna, Agnes Falkner was of invaluable assistance regarding the numerous images she had to collect for the catalogue, also in contacting authors for publishing permissions in what turned out to be a very long list.

Support in relation to research regarding specific artists, related issues and publications was provided by many colleagues, I can only try to remember most of them: Emilio Álvarez, Barcelona; Hildegund Amanshauser, Münster/Salzburg; Tuula Arkio, Helsinki; Christine van Assche and Didier Schulmann/MNAM Centre Pompidou, Paris; Zdenka Badovinac, Ljubljana; Madeleine Bernstorff and Brigitta Kuster, Berlin; Gerd Blum and Johan Frederik Hartle, Münster; Jürgen Bock, Maumaus, Lissabon; Carolyn Christov-Bakargiev, Torino/Kassel; Yilmaz Dziewior, Hamburg/Bregenz; Gabriele Horn, Kunstwerke Berlin; Matthias Michalka, Museum Moderner Kunst Stiftung Ludwig, Vienna; Philippe Pirotte, Kunsthalle, Bern; Andrzeij Przywara, Foksal Gallery Foundation, Warsaw; Britta Schmitz, Hamburger Bahnhof, Berlin; Ralph Wernicke, Berlin; WHW (What, How and for Whom): Ivet Curlin, Ana Devic, Natasha Ilic and Sabina Sabolevic.

As with all my projects of the past years, my partner, Werner Kaligofsky, was *the* strong and sustainable support in all matters.

Financial support for the Austrian artists was generously provided by the Austrian Ministry for Education, Arts and Culture in Vienna, thanks to the Minister Dr Claudia Schmidt, the head of the Art Department Dr Andrea Ecker, the head of the art section Mag. Joseph Secky, succeeded by Dr Bernd Hartmann, as well as Mag. Olga Okunev.

Sabine Breitwieser

Lenders and Collaborators

Gunda Achleitner
Emilio Álvarez
Yaelle Amir
Yves Aupetitallot
Juliana Balestin
Daniele Balice
Jennifer Bailey
Charlie Blightman
Jürgen Bock
Rom Bohez
Thomas Borgmann
Kate Bradbury
Ellen de Bruijne
Daniel Buchholz
Gisela Capitain
Philippe van Cauteren
André Chêdas
Catherine Clement
Caroline Collier
Jane Crawford
Thomas Cullinan
Thomas Dane
Philippe Davet
Hugh M. Davies
Ernest Delville
Andrea Ecker
Berthold Ecker
Isabelle Erben
Sjarel Ex
Lourdes Fernández
Sabine Folie
Carl Freedman
Stephen Friedman
Lars Friedrich
Anna Garcia
Wendy Gondeln
Ingvild Goetz
Ines Grosso
Gabriela Gutmann
Karin Haas
Sophie Haaser
Axel Haubrok
Sabine Heuser-Hauck
Lise Hoshour
Therese James

Ekkehard Kneer
Edelbert Köb
Wolfgang Konrad
Helga Krobath
Peter Krobath
Jutta Kuepper
Michèle Lachowsky
Doris Leutgeb
Bruno van Lierde
Inge Linder-Gallaird
Joris Lindhout
M. Lökermann
Martin McGeown
Mathias Michalka
Manuela Mozo
Andreas Müller
Christopher Müller
Katharina Forero du Mund
Albert Oehlen
Manuel Olveira
Amaya Ortuondo
Roger Pailhas
Marie-Christine Pailhas
Jerôme Pantalacci
Susana Pellicer
Kenneth Pietrobono
Anaëlle Pirat
Jacqueline Rapmund
Ulrich Reininghaus
Isabella Ritter
Michel Samuel-Weis
Odona Sánchez
Joanna Stella Sawicka
Petra Schilcher
Claudia Schmied
Julia Schneider
Rudiger Schöttle
Lourdes Pardo Seoane
Nicole Simöes da Silva
Dorothée Sorge
Susanne Spieler
Gilli Stampa
Claudia and Kurt von Storch
Stephan Urbaschek
Ewout Vellekoop
Maria José Villaluenga
Andrew Wheastley
Irina Witoszynskyj

Artelier Contemporary Graz
Blondeau Fine Arts Services – BFAS
Cabinet London
Carl Freedman Gallery, London
Colección Fundación ARCO – CGAC, Santiago
de Compostela
Collection of the Department for Cultural Affairs
of the City of Vienna - MUSA
Ellen de Bruijne Projects, Amsterdam
Galeria Filomena Soares, Lisbon
Galerie Balice Hertling, Paris
Galerie Christian Nagel, Cologne/Berlin
Galerie Daniel Buchholz, Cologne/Berlin
Galerie Gisela Capitain, Cologne
Galerie Meyer Kainer, Vienna
Galerie Neugerriemschneider, Berlin
Galerie Rüdiger Schöttle, Munich
Generali Foundation, Vienna
Goetz Collection, Munich
Hollybush Gardens, London
IFEMA – Fundación ARCO, Madrid
Krobath, Vienna
Metro Pictures, New York
MUMOK (Museum Moderner Kunst Stiftung Ludwig
Wien), Vienna
Museum Boijmans van Beuningen, Rotterdam
Museum of Contemporary Art San Diego
S.A. Weis & Kompanie, Mulhouse
S.M.A.K. Stedelijk Museum voor Actuele Kunst, Gent
Stampa Galerie, Basel
Stephen Friedman Gallery, London
Tate, London
The Boston Consulting Group, Brussels

The artists and those who have preferred
to remain anonymous.

This exhibition has been possible thanks
to the generous support of the Austrian Ministry
for Education, Arts and Culture.

This catalogue has been published on the occasion of the exhibition *Modernologies. Contemporary Artists Researching Modernity and Modernism* presented by the Museu d'Art Contemporani de Barcelona (23 September 2009 – 17 January 2010), and at the Muzeum Sztuki Nowoczesnej w Warszawie (Museum of Modern Art in Warsaw, February-March 2010).

Director for the Project
Bartomeu Marí

Exhibition

Curator
Sabine Breitwieser

Chief of Production
Anna Borrell

Curator's Assistant
Teresa Grandas

Assistant of Coordination
Meritxell Colina, with the collaboration of Lorena Martín

Registrar
Denis Iriarte

Assistant of Registrar
Patricia Quesada

Conservation
Àlex Castro
Samuel Mestre
Caridad de la Pea Galiano
Xavier Rossell

Architecture
Isabel Bachs
Eva Font
Núria Guarro

Audiovisual Technicians
Miquel Giner
Jordi Martínez
Joan Sureda
Albert Toda

General Services
Miguel Ángel Fernández
Elena Llempén
Alberto Santos

Interns
Victor Conesa
Sabel Gabaldón
Jordi Pedrol
Ana Sena

Publication

Concept and Editor
Sabine Breitwieser

Responsible for the Project
Clara Plasencia

Coordination and Editing
Ester Capdevila

Photo and Text Research Artist's Section
Agnes Falkner

Photo Research
Dolores Acebal
Gemma Planell

Graphic Design
Martha Stutteregger

Translation
Dawn Michelle d'Atri (from German)
Jane Brodie/Wendy Gosselin/e-verba (from Spanish)

Proof-reading
Keith Patrick

Pre-printing
Cousins

Printing
Igol

Publisher
Museu d'Art Contemporani de Barcelona
Plaça dels Àngels, 1
08001 Barcelona (Spain)
t:+ 34 93 412 08 10
f:+ 34 93 412 46 02
www.macba.cat

ISBN: 978-84-92505-13-5
DL: B-36106-2009

Typography: Neutral
Paper: Invercote 300 g, G Print 130 g

Sponsor
bm:uk

Communication Sponsor
LA VANGUARDIA

With the support of
iCat fm